Lecture Notes in Computer Science 3125

Commenced Publication in 1973
Founding and Former Series Editors:
Gerhard Goos, Juris Hartmanis, and Jan van Leeuwen

Dexter Kozen (Ed.)

Mathematics of Program Construction

7th International Conference, MPC 2004
Stirling, Scotland, UK, July 12-14, 2004
Proceedings

 Springer

Volume Editor

Dexter Kozen
Cornell University
Department of Computer Science
Ithaca, NY 14853-7501, USA
E-mail: kozen@cs.cornell.edu

Library of Congress Control Number: 2004108032

CR Subject Classification (1998): F.3, F.4, D.2, F.1, D.3

ISSN 0302-9743
ISBN 3-540-22380-0 Springer-Verlag Berlin Heidelberg New York

Springer-Verlag is a part of Springer Science+Business Media

springeronline.com

© Springer-Verlag Berlin Heidelberg 2004
Printed in Germany

Typesetting: Camera-ready by author, data conversion by Olgun Computergrafik
Printed on acid-free paper   SPIN: 11019305   06/3142   5 4 3 2 1 0

Preface

This volume contains the proceedings of MPC 2004, the Seventh International Conference on the Mathematics of Program Construction. This series of conferences aims to promote the development of mathematical principles and techniques that are demonstrably useful in the process of constructing computer programs, whether implemented in hardware or software. The focus is on techniques that combine precision with conciseness, enabling programs to be constructed by formal calculation. Within this theme, the scope of the series is very diverse, including programming methodology, program specification and transformation, programming paradigms, programming calculi, and programming language semantics.

The quality of the papers submitted to the conference was in general very high, and the number of submissions was comparable to that for the previous conference. Each paper was refereed by at least four, and often more, committee members.

This volume contains 19 papers selected for presentation by the program committee from 37 submissions, as well as the abstract of one invited talk: *Extended Static Checking for Java* by Greg Nelson, Imaging Systems Department, HP Labs, Palo Alto, California.

The conference took place in Stirling, Scotland. The previous six conferences were held in 1989 in Twente, The Netherlands; in 1992 in Oxford, UK; in 1995 in Kloster Irsee, Germany; in 1998 in Marstrand near Göteborg, Sweden; in 2000 in Ponte de Lima, Portugal; and in 2002 in Dagstuhl, Germany. The proceedings of these conferences were published as LNCS 375, 669, 947, 1422, 1837, and 2386, respectively.

Three other international events were co-located with the conference: the Tenth International Conference on Algebraic Methodology And Software Technology (AMAST 2004), the Sixth AMAST Workshop on Real-Time Systems (ARTS 2004), and the Fourth International Workshop on Constructive Methods for Parallel Programming (CMPP 2004). We thank the organizers of these events for their interest in sharing the atmosphere of the conference.

May 2004   Dexter Kozen

Acknowledgments

We are grateful to the members of the program committee and their referees for their care and diligence in reviewing the submitted papers. We are also grateful to the sponsoring institutions and to the FACS Specialist Group. Finally, we would like to extend a special thanks to Kelly Patwell for all her hard work with the organization of the conference.

Program Committee

Roland Backhouse (UK)
Stephen Bloom (USA)
Eerke Boiten (UK)
Jules Desharnais (Canada)
Thorsten Ehm (Germany)
Jeremy Gibbons (UK)
Ian Hayes (Australia)
Eric Hehner (Canada)
Johan Jeuring (The Netherlands)
Dexter Kozen (USA, chair)

K. Rustan M. Leino (USA)
Hans Leiss (Germany)
Christian Lengauer (Germany)
Lambert Meertens (USA)
Bernhard Moeller (Germany)
David Naumann (USA)
Alberto Pardo (Uruguay)
Georg Struth (Germany)
Jerzy Tiuryn (Poland)
Mark Utting (NZ)

Sponsoring Institutions

The generous support of the following institutions is gratefully acknowledged.

Cornell University
University of Stirling
Formal Aspects of Computing Science (FACS) Specialist Group

External Referees

All submitted papers were carefully reviewed by members of the program committee and the following external referees, who produced extensive review reports that were transmitted to the authors. We apologize for any omissions or inaccuracies.

Viviana Bono
Ana Bove
David Carrington
Maximiliano Cristiá
Sharon Curtis
Colin Fidge
Marcelo Frias
Christoph Herrmann

Wim H. Hesselink
Marcin Jurdzinski
Stefan Kahrs
Zhiming Liu
Clare Martin
Diethard Michaelis
Ernst-Rüdiger Olderog
Bruno Oliveira

Steve Reeves
Andreas Schäfer
Luis Sierra
Michael Anthony Smith
Jerzy Tyszkiewicz
Pawel Urzyczyn
Geoffrey Watson
Paolo Zuliani

Best Paper Award

Modelling Nondeterminism
Clare E. Martin, Sharon A. Curtis, and Ingrid Rewitzky

Table of Contents

Extended Static Checking for Java

Greg Nelson

Imaging Systems Department
HP Labs
Mail Stop 1203
1501 Page Mill Road
Palo Alto, CA 94304, USA
gnelson@hp.com

Abstract. The talk provides an overview and demonstration of an Extended Static Checker for the Java programming language, a program checker that finds errors statically but has a much more accurate semantic model than existing static checkers like type checkers and data flow analysers. For example, ESC/Java uses an automatic theorem-prover and reasons about the semantics of assignments and tests in the same way that a program verifier does. But the checker is fully automatic, and feels to the programmer more like a type checker than like a program verifier. A more detailed account of ESC/Java is contained in a recent PLDI paper [1]. The checker described in the talk and in the PLDI paper is a research prototype on which work ceased several years ago, but Joe Kiniry and David Cok have recently produced a more up-to-date checker, ESC/Java 2 [2].

References

1. Cormac Flanagan, K. Rustan M. Leino, Mark Lillibridge, Greg Nelson, James B. Saxe, and Raymie Stata. Extended Static Checking for Java. *Proc. PLDI'02*. ACM. Berlin, Germany, 2002.
2. David Cok and Joe Kiniry. ESC/Java 2 project page. http://www.cs.kun.nl/sos/research/escjava/main.html.

D. Kozen (Ed.): MPC 2004, LNCS 3125, p. 1, 2004.
© Springer-Verlag Berlin Heidelberg 2004

Constructing Polymorphic Programs
with Quotient Types

Michael Abbott[1], Thorsten Altenkirch[2], Neil Ghani[1], and Conor McBride[3]

[1] Department of Mathematics and Computer Science, University of Leicester
michael@araneidae.co.uk, ng13@mcs.le.ac.uk
[2] School of Computer Science and Information Technology, Nottingham University
txa@cs.nott.ac.uk
[3] Department of Computer Science, University of Durham
c.t.mcbride@durham.ac.uk

Abstract. The efficient representation and manipulation of data is one of the fundamental tasks in the construction of large software systems. Parametric polymorphism has been one of the most successful approaches to date but, as of yet, has not been applicable to programming with quotient datatypes such as unordered pairs, cyclic lists, bags etc. This paper provides the basis for writing polymorphic programs over quotient datatypes by extending our recently developed theory of containers.

1 Introduction

The efficient representation and manipulation of data is one of the fundamental tasks in the construction of large software systems. More precisely, one aims to achieve amongst other properties: i) abstraction so as to hide implementation details and thereby facilitate modular programming; ii) expressivity so as to uniformly capture as wide a class of data types as possible; iii) disciplined recursion principles to provide convenient methods for defining generic operations on data structures; and iv) formal semantics to underpin reasoning about the correctness of programs. The most successful approach to date has been Hindley-Milner polymorphism which provides predefined mechanisms for manipulating data structures providing they are *parametric* in the data. Canonical examples of such parametric polymorphic functions are the `map` and `fold` operations which can be used to define a wide variety of programs in a structured and easy to reason about manner.

However, a number of useful data types and associated operations are not expressible in the Hindley-Milner type system and this has lead to many proposed extensions including, amongst others, generic programming, dependent types (Altenkirch and McBride, 2003), higher order types (Fiore et al., 1999), shapely types (Jay, 1995), imaginary types (Fiore and Leinster, 2004) and type classes. However, one area which has received less attention is that of quotient types such as, for example, unordered pairs, cyclic lists and the bag type. This is because the problem is fundamentally rather difficult – on the one hand one wants to allow as wide a theory as possible so as to encompass as many quotient types as possible while, on the other hand, one wants to restrict one's definition to derive a well-behaved meta-theory which provides support

D. Kozen (Ed.): MPC 2004, LNCS 3125, pp. 2–15, 2004.

for key programming paradigms such as polymorphic programming etc. Papers such as Hofmann (1995) have tended to consider quotients of specific types rather than quotients of data structures which are independent of the data stored. As a result, this paper is original in giving a detailed analysis of how to program with quotient data structures in a polymorphic fashion. In particular,

- We provide a syntax for declaring quotient datatypes which encompasses a variety of examples. This syntax is structural which we argue is essential for any theory of polymorphism to be applicable.
- We show how the syntax of such a declaration gives rise to a quotient datatype.
- We provide a syntax for writing polymorphic programs between these quotient datatypes and argue that these programs do indeed deserve to be called polymorphic.
- We show that every polymorphic function between our quotient datatypes is represented uniquely by our syntax. That is, our syntax captures all polymorphic programs in a unique manner.

To execute this program of research we extend our work on container datatypes (Abbott, 2003; Abbott et al., 2003a,b). Container types represent types via a set of shapes and locations in each shape where data may be stored. They are therefore like Jay's shapely types (Jay, 1995) but more general as we discuss later. In previous papers cited above, we have shown how these container types are closed under a wide variety of useful constructions and can also be used as a framework for generic programming, eg they support a generic notion of differentiation (Abbott et al., 2003b) which derives a data structure with a hole from a data structure.

This paper extends containers to cover quotient datatypes by saying that certain labellings of locations with data are equivalent to others. We call these structures quotient containers. As such they correspond to the step from normal functors to analytic functors in Joyal (1986). However, our quotient containers are more general than analytic functors as they allow infinite sets of positions to model coinductive datatypes. In addition, our definition of the morphisms between quotient containers is new as is all of their applications to programming. In addition, while pursuing the above program, we also use a series of running examples to aid the reader. We assume only the most basic definitions from category theory like category, functor and natural transformations. The exception is the use of left Kan extensions for which we supply the reader with the two crucial properties in section 2. Not all category theory books contain information on these constructions, so the reader should use Mac Lane (1971); Borceux (1994) as references.

The paper is structured as follows. In section 2 we recall the basic theory of containers, container morphisms and their application to polymorphic programming. We also discuss the relationship between containers and shapely types. In section 3 we discuss how quotient datatypes can be represented in container theoretic terms while in section 4 we discuss how polymorphic programs between quotient types can be represented uniquely as morphisms between quotient containers. We conclude in section 5 with some conclusions and proposals for further work.

2   A Brief Summary of Containers

Notation: We write $\mathbb{N}$ for the set of natural numbers and if $n \in \mathbb{N}$, we write $\underline{n}$ for the set $\{0,\ldots,n-1\}$. We assume the basic definitions of category theory and if $f : X \to Y$ and $g : Y \to Z$ are morphisms in a category, we write their composite $g \circ f : X \to Z$ as is standard categorical practice. We write K_1 for the constantly 1 valued functor from any category to **Sets**. If A is a set and B is an A indexed family of sets, we write $\sum a{:}A.\ B(a)$ for the set $\{(a,b) \mid a \in A, b \in B(a)\}$. We write ! for the empty map from the empty set to any other set. Injections into the coproduct are written inl and inr.

  This paper uses left Kan extensions to extract a universal property of containers which is not immediately visible. We understand that many readers will not be familiar with these structures so we supply all definitions and refer the reader to Mac Lane (1971) for more details. Their use is limited to a couple of places and hence doesn't make the paper inaccessible to the non-cogniscenti. Given a functor $I : \mathscr{A} \to \mathscr{B}$ and a category $\mathscr{C}$, precomposition with I defines a functor $\_ \circ I : [\mathscr{B},\mathscr{C}] \to [\mathscr{A},\mathscr{C}]$. The problem of left Kan extensions is the problem of finding a left adjoint to $\_ \circ I$. More concretely, given a functor $F : \mathscr{A} \to \mathscr{C}$, the left Kan extension of F along I is written $\text{Lan}_I F$ defined via the natural isomorphism

$$[\mathscr{B},\mathscr{C}](\text{Lan}_I F, H) \cong [\mathscr{A},\mathscr{C}](F, H \circ I) \tag{1}$$

One can use the following coend formula to calculate the action of a left Kan extension when $\mathscr{C} = $ **Sets** and $\mathscr{A}$ is small

$$(\text{Lan}_I F)X \;=\; \int^{A \in \mathscr{A}} \mathscr{B}(IA,X) \times FA \tag{2}$$

What Are Containers? Containers capture the idea that concrete datatypes consist of memory locations where data can be stored. For example, any element of the type of lists $\text{List}(X)$ of X can be uniquely written as a natural number n given by the length of the list, together with a function $\{0,\ldots,n-1\} \to X$ which labels each position within the list with an element from X. Thus we may write

$$\text{List}(X) \;\equiv\; \sum n{:}\mathbb{N}.\ \{0,\ldots.n-1\} \to X \tag{3}$$

We may think of the set $\{0,\ldots,n-1\}$ as n memory locations while the function f attaches to these memory locations, the data to be stored there. Similarly, any binary tree tree can be uniquely described by its underlying shape (which is obtained by deleting the data stored at the leaves) and a function mapping the positions in this shape to the data thus:

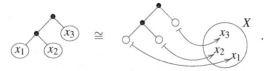

More generally, we are led to consider datatypes which are given by a set of shapes S and, for each $s \in S$, a set of positions $P(s)$ which we think of as locations in memory where data can be stored. This is precisely a container

Definition 2.1 (Container). *A container $(S \triangleright P)$ consists of a set S and, for each $s \in S$, a set of positions $P(s)$.*

Of course, in general we do not want to restrict ourselves to the category of sets since we want our theory to be applicable to domain theoretic models. Rather, we would develop our theory over locally cartesian closed categories (Hofmann, 1994), certain forms of fibrations such as comprehension categories (Jacobs, 1999) or models of Martin-Löf type theory – see our previous work (Abbott, 2003; Abbott et al., 2003a,b) for such a development. However, part of the motivation for this paper was to make containers accessible to the programming community where we believe they provide a flexible platform for supporting generic forms of programming. Consequently, we have deliberately chosen to work over **Sets** so as to enable us to get our ideas across without an overly mathematical presentation.

As suggested above, lists can be presented as a container

Example 2.2 *The list type is given by the container with shapes given by the natural numbers $\mathbb{N}$ and, for $n \in \mathbb{N}$, define the positions $P(n)$ to be the set $\{0, \ldots, n-1\}$.*

To summarise, containers are our presentations of datatypes in the same way that `data` declarations are presentations of datatypes in Haskell. The semantics of a container is an endofunctor on some category which, in this paper, is **Sets**. This is given by

Definition 2.3 (Extension of a Container). *Let $(S \triangleright P)$ be a container. Its semantics, or extension, is the functor $T_{S \triangleright P} : \textbf{Sets} \to \textbf{Sets}$ defined by*

$$T_{S \triangleright P}(X) = \sum s : S. \ (P(s) \to X)$$

An element of $T_{S \triangleright P}(X)$ is thus a pair (s, f) where $s \in S$ is a shape and $f : P(s) \to X$ is a labelling of the positions over s with elements from X. Note that $T_{S \triangleright P}$ really is a functor since its action on a function $g : X \to Y$ sends the element (s, f) to the element $(s, g \circ f)$. Thus for example, the extension of the container for lists is the functor mapping X to

$$\sum n : \mathbb{N}. \ \{0, \ldots, n-1\} \to X \ .$$

As we commented upon in equation 3, this is the list functor.

The theory of containers was developed in a series of recent papers (Abbott, 2003; Abbott et al., 2003a,b) which showed that containers encompass a wide variety of types as they are closed under various type forming operations such as sums, products, constants, fixed exponentiation, (nested) least fixed points and (nested) greatest fixed points. Thus containers encapsulate a large number of datatypes. So far, we have dealt with containers in one variable whose extensions are functors on **Sets**. The extension to n-ary containers, whose extensions are functors $\textbf{Sets}^n \to \textbf{Sets}$, is straightforward. Such containers consist of a set of shapes S, and for each $s \in S$ there are n position sets $P_n(s)$. See the above references for details.

We finish this section with a more abstract presentation of containers which will be used to exhibit the crucial universal property that they satisfy. This universal property underlies the key result about containers. First, note that the data in a container $(S \triangleright P)$

can be presented as a functor $P : S \to \mathbf{Sets}$ where here we regard the set S as a discrete category and P maps each s to $P(s)$. In future, we will switch between these two views of a container at will. The semantic functor $T_{S \triangleright P}$ has a universal property given by the following lemma.

Lemma 2.4. *Let $P : S \to \mathbf{Sets}$ be a container. Then $T_{S \triangleright P}$ is the left Kan extension of K_1 along P*

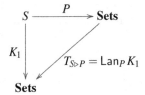

Proof We calculate as follows

$$(\mathsf{Lan}_P K_1)X \;=\; \int^{s:S} \mathbf{Sets}(Ps, X) \times K_1 s \;=\; \sum s:S.\; \mathbf{Sets}(Ps, X) \;=\; T_{S \triangleright P}(X)$$

where the first equality is the classic coend formula for left Kan extensions of equation 2, the second equality holds as S is a discrete category and 1 is the unit for the product, and the last equality is the definition of $T_{S \triangleright P}(X)$. $\qquad \square$

As we shall see, this universal property will be vital to our representation theorem.

2.1   Container Morphisms

Containers are designed for implementation. Thus, we imagine defining lists in a programming language by writing something like

$$data \;\; List = (n : \mathbb{N} \triangleright \underline{n})$$

although the type dependency means we need a dependently typed language. If we were to make such declarations, how should we program? The usual definitions of lists based upon initial algebras or final coalgebras give rise naturally to recursive forms of programming. As an alternative, we show that all polymorphic functions between containers are captured uniquely by *container morphisms*.

Consider first the reverse function applied to a list written in container form (n, g). Its reversal must be a list and hence of the form (n', g'). In addition, n' should only depend upon n since reverse is polymorphic and hence shouldn't depend upon the actual data in the list given by g. Thus there is a function $\mathbb{N} \to \mathbb{N}$. In the case of reverse, the length of the list doesn't change and hence this is the identity. To define g' which associates to each position in the output a piece of data, we should first associate to each position in the output a position in the input and then look up the data using g.

Pictorially we have:

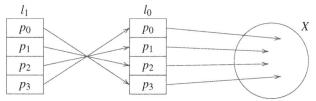

Here we start with a list l_0 which has 4 positions and a labelling function g into X. The result of reversing l_0 is the list l_1 with 4 positions and labelling function given by the above composite. In general, we therefore define

Definition 2.5 (Container Morphisms). *A morphism* $(A \triangleright B) \rightarrow (C \triangleright D)$ *consists of a pair* (u, f) *where* $u : A \rightarrow C$ *and an* A-*indexed family of maps* $f_a : D(ua) \rightarrow B(a)$. *The category of containers and container morphisms is written* **Cont**

Example 2.6 *The reverse program is given by the container morphism* (Id, f) *where the function* $f_n : \{0, \ldots, n-1\} \rightarrow \{0, \ldots, n-1\}$ *is defined by* $f_n(i) = n - i - 1$

We stress that this would be the actual definition of reverse in a programming language based upon containers. The process of translating other, more abstract and higher level, definitions of reverse into the above form indicates the potential use of containers as an optimisation tool. Note also how f_n says that the data stored at the $i'th$ cell after reversing a list is that data stored at the $n - i - 1$'th cell in the input list.

Consider the tail function $\mathsf{tail}:: \mathsf{List}(X) \rightarrow 1 + \mathsf{List}(X)$. The shapes of the datatype $1 + \mathsf{List}(X)$ is $1 + \mathbb{N}$ with the shapes above $\mathsf{inl}(*)$ being empty while the shapes above $\mathsf{inr}(n)$ is the set $\{0, \ldots, n-1\}$. We therefore write this container as $(1 + n : \mathbb{N} \triangleright 0 + \underline{n})$.

Example 2.7 *The tail function* (u, f) *is given by the container morphism* $(n : \mathbb{N} \triangleright \underline{n}) \rightarrow (1 + n : \mathbb{N} \triangleright 0 + \underline{n})$ *defined by*

$$u(0) = \mathsf{inl}(*) \qquad u(n+1) = \mathsf{inr}(n)$$

and with $f_0 =\,!$ *and* $f_{n+1} : \underline{n} \rightarrow \underline{n+1}$ *defined by* $f_{n+1}(i) = i + 1$.

Thus the i'th cell in the output of a nonempty list comes from the $i + 1$'th cell in the input list. Readers may check their understanding at this point by wondering what function is defined by setting $f_{n+1}(i) = i$ in the above example. We finish this section with two final points. First, a categorical re-interpretation of a container morphism analogous to the categorical interpretation of a container $A \triangleright B$ as a presheaf $B : A \rightarrow \mathbf{Sets}$ as in lemma 2.4.

Lemma 2.8. *A morphism of containers* $(u, f) : (A \triangleright B) \rightarrow (C \triangleright D)$ *is given by a functor* $u : A \rightarrow C$ *and a natural transformation* $f : Du \rightarrow B$. *Pictorially, this can be represented:*

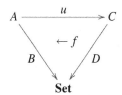

Proof Since A and C are discrete categories, a functor is just a function. Since A is discrete, the natural transformation is just a family of maps of the given form.   □

Finally, containers are more than just a programming tool – they can also simplify reasoning. For example, consider proving that reverse ○ reverse is the identity. Using the usual recursive definition one soon runs into problems and must strengthen the inductive hypothesis to reflect the interaction of reverse and append. Using the container definition, this problem is trivial as we can reason as follows: $(Id, f) \circ (Id, f) = (Id, f \circ f) = (Id, Id)$ since, for each n, the function f_n is clearly idempotent.

2.2   From Container Morphisms to Polymorphic Functions and Back

Given a container morphism $(u, f) : (A \triangleright B) \to (S \triangleright P)$ does (u, f) really define a polymorphic function $T_{A \triangleright B} \to T_{S \triangleright P}$? If so, are all polymorphic functions of this form?. And in a unique manner? To answer these questions we have to describe mathematically what a polymorphic function is. In the theory of program language semantics, covariant datatypes are usually represented as functors while polymorphic functions between covariant datatypes are represented by natural transformations (Bainbridge et al., 1990). Other representations of polymorphic functions are as terms in various polymorphic lambda calculi and via the theory of logical relations. Various theoretical results show that these are equivalent so in the following we take a polymorphic function to be a natural transformation.

Our key theorem is the following which ensures that our syntax for defining polymorphic functions as container morphisms is flexible enough to cover all polymorphic functions.

Theorem 2.9. *Container morphisms* $(A \triangleright B) \to (C \triangleright D)$ *are in bijection with natural transformations* $T_{A \triangleright B} \to T_{C \triangleright D}$. *Formally,* $T : \mathbf{Cont} \to [\mathbf{Sets}, \mathbf{Sets}]$ *is full and faithful.*

Proof The proof is a special case of Theorem 4.3. Alternatively, see Abbott et al. (2003a); Abbott (2003)   □

Containers vs Shapely Types: In Jay and Cockett (1994) and Jay (1995) *shapely types* (in one parameter) in **Sets** are pullback preserving functors $F : \mathbf{Sets} \to \mathbf{Sets}$ equipped with a cartesian natural transformation to the list functor. This means there are natural maps $FX \to \mathrm{List}(X)$ which extract the data from an element of FX and place it in a list thereby obtaining a decomposition of data into shapes and positions similar to what occurs in containers.

Note however that the positions in a list have a notion of order and hence a shapely type is also equipped with an order on positions. Typically, when we declare a datatype we do not want to declare such an ordering over it and, indeed, in the course of programming we may wish to traverse a data structure with different orders. At a more theoretical level, by reducing datatypes to lists, a classification theorem such as Theorem 2.9 would reduce polymorphic functions to polymorphic functions between lists but would not be able to classify what these are. Containers do not impose such an order and instead reduce datatypes to the more primitive idea of a family of positions indexed by shapes.

3   Containers and Quotient Types

The purpose of this paper is to extend our previous results on containers to cover quotient datatypes and polymorphic functions between them. In particular we want to

- Generalise the notion of container to cover as many quotient datatypes as possible and thereby derive a syntax for declaring quotient datatypes.
- Define a notion of morphism between such generalised containers and thereby derive a syntax for polymorphic programming with quotient types.
- Prove the representation theorem for these polymorphic programs thereby proving that the quotient container morphisms really are polymorphic functions and that all such polymorphic functions are captured by quotient container morphisms.

3.1   Unordered Pairs and Cyclic Lists

We begin with an example of unordered pairs. Note first that the type $X \times X$ is given by the container $(1 \triangleright 2)$. These are ordered pairs of elements of X. The type of unordered pairs of X is written as $X \otimes X$ and is defined as $X \times X / \sim$ where $\sim$ is the equivalence relation defined by

$$\langle x, y \rangle \sim \langle y, x \rangle$$

Recall our analysis of the pair type was as one shape, containing two positions $(1 \triangleright 2)$. Lets call these positions p_1 and p_2. An element of the pair type then consists of a labelling for these positions, ie a function $f : \{p_1, p_2\} \to X$ for a set X. To move from ordered pairs to unordered pairs is exactly to note that the labelling f should be regarded the same as the labelling $f \circ \mathsf{swap}$ where $\mathsf{swap} : \{p_1, p_2\} \to \{p_1, p_2\}$ is the function sending p_1 to p_2 and p_2 to p_1. Thus

Example 3.1 *The type of unordered pairs of elements of X is given by*

$$(\{p_1, p_2\} \to X) / \sim$$

where $\sim$ is the equivalence relation on $\{p_1, p_2\} \to X$ obtained by setting $f \circ \mathsf{swap} \sim f$.

Let's cement our intuitions by doing another example. A cyclic list is a list with no starting or ending point. Here is a cyclic list of length 5

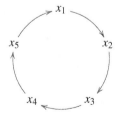

Can we represent cyclic lists in the same style as we used for unordered pairs? Recall from equation 3 that lists were given by $\mathsf{List}(X) \equiv \sum n : \mathbb{N}. \{0, \ldots, n-1\} \to X$. Now, in a cyclic list of length n, a labelling $f : \{0, \ldots, n-1\} \to X$ should be equivalent to the labelling $f \circ \lambda i. (i + k) \bmod n$ where $k \in \{0, \ldots, n-1\}$. Thus we may define

Example 3.2 *The type of cyclic lists of elements of X is given by*

$$\mathsf{CList}(X) \equiv \sum n : \mathbb{N}. \ (\{0, \ldots n-1\} \to X) / \sim_n$$

where $\sim_n$ is the equivalence relation on $\{0, \ldots n-1\} \to X$ obtained by setting $f \sim_n f \circ \lambda i.(i+k) \bmod n$ where $k \in \{0, \ldots, n-1\}$.

The observant reader will have spotted that, in example 3.2, there is actually an equivalence relation for each shape. Examples 3.1 and 3.2 exemplify the kind of structures we wish to compute with, ie the structures for which we want to find a clean syntax supporting program construction and reasoning. In general they consist of a container as defined before with an equivalence relation on labellings of positions. To ensure the equivalence relation is structural, ie independent of data as one would expect in a polymorphic setting, the equivalence relation is defined by identifying a labelling $f : P(s) \to X$ with the labelling $f \circ \alpha$ where α is one of a given set of isomorphisms on $P(s)$. Hence we define

Definition 3.3 (Quotient Containers). *A quotient container $(S \triangleright P/G)$ is given by a container $(S \triangleright P)$ and, for each shape $s \in S$, a set $G(s)$ of isomorphisms of $P(s)$ closed under composition, inverses and containing the identity.*

Thus a quotient container has an underlying container and, every container as in Definition 2.1 is a quotient container with, for each shape s, the set $G(s)$ containing only the identity isomorphism on $P(s)$. Another way of describing the isomorphisms in a quotient container $(S \triangleright P/G)$ is to say that for each $s \in S$, $G(s)$ is a subgroup of the automorphism, or permutation, group on $P(s)$.

Often we present a quotient container $(S \triangleright P/G)$ by defining, for each shape $s \in S$, the group $G(s)$ to be the smallest group containing a given set. However, the advantage of requiring $G(s)$ to be a group is that if we define $f \sim_G f'$ iff there is a $g \in G(s)$ such that $f = f' \circ g$, then $\sim_G$ is automatically an equivalence relation and so we don't have to consider its closure. A more categorical presentation of quotient containers reflecting the presentation of containers used in lemma 2.4 is the following.

Lemma 3.4. *A quotient container is exactly a functor $P : S \to \mathbf{Sets}$ where every morphism of S is both an endomorphism and an isomorphism.*

Proof Given a quotient container $(S \triangleright P/G)$, we think of S as the category with objects elements $s \in S$ and, as endomorphisms of s, the set $G(s)$. The functor P is the obvious functor mapping s to $P(s)$. □

Given a quotient container, $(S \triangleright P/G)$, of course we want to calculate the associated datatype or functor $T_{S \triangleright P/G} : \mathbf{Sets} \to \mathbf{Sets}$. As with the presentation of containers we do this concretely and then more abstractly to uncover a hidden universal property.

Definition 3.5 (Extension of a Quotient Container). *Given a quotient container, say $(S \triangleright P/G)$, its extension is the functor $T_{S \triangleright P/G} : \mathbf{Sets} \to \mathbf{Sets}$ defined by*

$$T_{S \triangleright P/G}(X) = \sum s : S. \ (P(s) \to X) / \sim_s$$

where $\sim_s$ is the equivalence relation on the set of functions $P(s) \to X$ defined by $f \sim_s f'$ if there is a $g \in G(s)$ such that $f' = f \circ g$.

So a quotient container is like a container except that in the datatype it gives rise to, a labelling f of positions with data is defined to be the same as the labelling $f \circ g$ obtained by bijectively renaming the positions using $g \in G(s)$ and then performing the labelling f. The more abstract formulation is given by the next lemma which uses lemma 3.4 to regard a quotient container $(S \rhd P/G)$ as a presheaf $P : S \to \mathbf{Sets}$.

Lemma 3.6. *Let $P : S \to \mathbf{Sets}$ be a quotient container. Then $T_{S \rhd P/G}$ is the left Kan extension of K_1 along P*

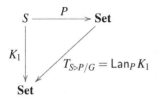

Proof We can calculate the left Kan extension as follows

$$(\mathsf{Lan}_P K_1)X \cong \int^{s:S} \mathbf{Sets}(Ps, X) \times K_1 s$$
$$\cong \sum s : S. \ \mathbf{Sets}(Ps, X)/\sim_s$$
$$= T_{S \rhd P/G}(X)$$

where by first equality the classic coend formula of equation 2, the second is the reduction of coends to colimits and the third is the definition of $T_{S \rhd P/G}$. This is because, the equivalence relation $\sim_s$ in the coend has $f \sim_s f'$ iff there is a $g : s \to s$ such that $f' = f \circ P(g)$ where $f, f' : P(s) \to X$. This is exactly the definition of the extension of a quotient container. $\qquad\square$

The theory of containers thus generalises naturally to quotient containers as the same formula of left Kan extension calculates both the semantics of a container and that of a quotient container.

We finish this section on the presentation of quotient types with the example of finite bags (also called multisets) as promised. Bags of other sizes are of course a straightforward generalisation. Given this remark, we henceforth refer to finite bags as simply bags. The key intuition is that a bag is like a set but elements may have multiple occurrences - one may thus define a bag as $\mathsf{Bag}(X) = X \to \mathbb{N}$. By putting all the elements of a bag in a list we get a representation of the bag but of course there are many such representations since there is no order of elements in the bag but there is in a list. Thus we get a bijection between bags and lists quotiented out by all rearrangements of positions. Hence

Example 3.7 *The bag type is the quotient container $(S \rhd P/G)$ where $(S \rhd P)$ is the container for lists and, for $n : \mathbb{N}$, we take $G(n)$ to be the set of all isomorphisms on the set $\{0, \ldots, n-1\}$.*

4 Programming with Quotient types

We have identified a class of quotient data structures and axiomatised them as quotient containers. These quotient containers can be seen as datatype declarations in a programming language and so we now ask how we program polymorphically with these quotient containers.

Recall a container morphism $(S \triangleright P) \to (Q \triangleright R)$ consisted of a translation of shapes $u : S \to Q$ and, for each $s \in S$, a map $f_s : R(us) \to P(s)$ sending positions in the output to positions in the input. If we now ask what is a map of quotient containers $(S \triangleright P/G) \to (Q \triangleright R/H)$ its reasonable to require a map $(u, f) : (S \triangleright P) \to (Q \triangleright R)$ of the underlying containers which takes into account the respective quotients. There are two issues:

- Since the maps $f_s : R(us) \to P(s)$ are labellings, the quotient given by H says that a quotient container morphism (u, f) is the same as another quotient container morphism (u, f') if for each $s \in S$, there is an $h_s \in H(us)$ such that $f_s = f'_s \circ h_s$.
- Given a map $f_s : R(us) \to P(s)$ and a $g \in G(s)$ then the labellings f and $g \circ f$ should be regarded as equal as labellings of $R(us)$. Hence there should be an $h_g \in H(us)$ such that $f \circ h_g = g \circ f$.

Hence we define

Definition 4.1 (Quotient Container Morphism). *A pre-morphism of quotient containers $(S \triangleright P/G) \to (Q \triangleright R/H)$ is a morphism of the underlying containers $(u, f) : (S \triangleright P) \to (Q \triangleright R)$ such that for each $s \in S$ and each $g \in G(s)$, there is an $h_g \in H(us)$ such that*

$$
\begin{array}{ccc}
R(us) & \xrightarrow{\ f_s\ } & P(s) \\
{\scriptstyle h_g}\downarrow & & \downarrow{\scriptstyle g} \\
R(us) & \xrightarrow[\ f_s\ ]{} & P(s)
\end{array}
$$

The morphisms $(S \triangleright P/G) \to (Q \triangleright R/H)$ are the premorphisms quotiented by the equivalence relation

$$(u, f) \sim (u, f') \text{ iff for all } s \in S, \text{ there exists } h_s \in H(us) \text{ such that } f_s = f'_s \circ h_s$$

Intuitively, the first condition is precisely the naturality of the quotient container morphism while the second reflects the fact that labellings are defined upto quotient. Is this a good definition of a polymorphic program between quotient containers? We answer this in two ways. On a theoretical level we show that all polymorphic programs can be uniquely captured by such quotient container morphisms while on a practical level we demonstrate a number of examples.

Lemma 4.2. *The quotient container morphisms $(S \triangleright P/G) \to (Q \triangleright R/H)$ are in one-to-one bijection with natural transformations $K_1 \to T_{Q \triangleright R/H} P$ where in the latter we regard $P : S \to \textbf{Sets}$ as a presheaf as described in lemma 2.4.*

Proof Such natural transformations are exactly S-indexed maps $K_1(s) \to T_{Q \triangleright R/H} P(s)$ which are natural in S. Thus we have, for each $s \in S$, maps

$$1 \; \to \; \textstyle\sum q : Q. \; (R(q) \to P(s)) / \sim_q$$

which are natural in S. Such a family of S-indexed maps is exactly a map $u : S \to Q$ and an S-indexed family of elements of $(R(us) \to P(s)) / \sim_{us}$ natural in S. An element of $(R(us) \to P(s)) / \sim_{us}$ is clearly an equivalence class of functions while the naturality corresponds to the commuting diagram above. $\qquad \square$

Theorem 4.3. *Quotient container morphisms are in one-to-one bijection with natural transformations between their extensions. Hence there is a full and faithful embedding $T : \mathbf{QCont} \to [\mathbf{Sets}, \mathbf{Sets}]$.*

Proof Natural transformations $T_{S \triangleright P/G} \to T_{Q \triangleright R/H}$ are by lemma 3.6 exactly natural transformations $\mathsf{Lan}_P K_1 \to \mathsf{Lan}_R K_1$. By the universal property of Kan extensions given in equation 1, these are in one-to-one bijection with natural transformations $K_1 \to T_{Q \triangleright R/H} P$ which by lemma 4.2 are in one-to-one bijection with quotient container morphisms $(S \triangleright P/G) \to (Q \triangleright R/H)$. $\qquad \square$

Notice the key role of the left Kan extension here. It identifies a universal property of the extension of a quotient container which is exactly what is required to prove Theorem 4.3. Also note that Theorem 2.9 is a corollary as there is clearly a full and faithful embedding of **Cont** into **QCont**.

We now finish with some examples. Firstly, if $(S \triangleright P/G)$ is a container and for each $s \in S$ the group $G(s)$ is a subgroup of $H(s)$, then there is a morphism of quotient containers $(S \triangleright P/G) \to (S \triangleright P/H)$. Thus

Example 4.4 *The canonical maps* $\mathsf{List}(X) \to \mathsf{CList}(X) \to \mathsf{Bag}(X)$ *are polymorphic as, for a given $n \in \mathbb{N}$, they arise as container morphisms from the inclusions of the singleton group into the group of functions $\{\lambda i. i + k \bmod n \mid k \in \{0, \ldots, n-1\}\}$ and of this group into the group of all isomorphisms on $\{0, \ldots, n-1\}$.*

Example 4.5 *Every datatype given by a quotient container $(S \triangleright P/G)$ has a* map *operation which is given by the action of functor $T_{S \triangleright P/G}$ on morphisms.*

Example 4.6 *We can extend the operation of reversing a list to a reverse on cyclic lists. One simply needs to check the commutation condition that for each size n and $k \in \{0, \ldots, n-1\}$, there is a k' such that*

$$\lambda i. (i + k) \bmod n \; \circ \; \lambda i. n - i - 1 \; = \; \lambda i. n - i - 1 \; \circ \; \lambda i. (i + k') \bmod n$$

Of course we simply take $k' = n - k - 1$.

In general this shows how simple our theory is to apply in practice. We simply have one condition to check!

5   Conclusions and Further Work

We have provided a synthesis of polymorphism with quotient datatypes in such a way as to facilitate programming and reasoning with such quotient structures. This work is based upon an extension of our previous work on containers which, going further than shapely types, present datatypes via a collection of shapes and, for each shape, a collection of positions where data may be stored. The treatment of quotient datatypes is structural in that the quotient is determined by a collection of isomorphisms on these position sets which induce a quotient on the labellings of positions with data. On top of this presentation of datatypes, we have provided a means for programming with such structures by defining morphisms of quotient containers. These are essentially morphisms of the underlying containers which respect the relevant quotients. This simple axiomatisation is proven correct in that we show that these morphisms determine exactly the polymorphic programs between these quotient data structures.

As for further work, we believe containers are an excellent platform for generic program and we wish to develop this application of containers. With specific relationship to these quotient containers, we have begun investigating their application to programming in the Theory of Species which was Joyal's motivation for developing analytic functors. From a more practical perspective, we would like to increase the examples of programs covered by both containers and quotient containers to include, for example, searching and sorting algorithms. Note such programs are not strictly polymorphic as their result depends upon inspection of the data. Of course this can already be done concretely by accessing the data in a container via the labellings. However, a greater challenge is to describe the degree to which such algorithms are polymorphic. In Haskell, one uses type classes so we would be looking for a container-theoretic approach to type classes.

Bibliography

M. Abbott. *Categories of Containers*. PhD thesis, University of Leicester, 2003.

M. Abbott, T. Altenkirch, and N. Ghani. Categories of containers. In A. Gordon, editor, *Proceedings of FOSSACS 2003*, number 2620 in Lecture Notes in Computer Science, pages 23–38. Springer-Verlag, 2003a.

M. Abbott, T. Altenkirch, N. Ghani, and C. McBride. Derivatives of containers. In *Typed Lambda Calculi and Applications, TLCA 2003*, number 2701 in Lecture notes in Computer Science, pages 16–30. Springer, 2003b.

T. Altenkirch and C. McBride. Generic programming within dependently typed programming. In *Generic Programming*, 2003. Proceedings of the IFIP TC2 Working Conference on Generic Programming.

E. S. Bainbridge, P. J. Freyd, A. Scedrov, and P. J. Scott. Functorial polymorphism, preliminary report. In G. Huet, editor, *Logical Foundations of Functional Programming*, chapter 14, pages 315–327. Addison-Wesley, 1990.

F. Borceux. *Handbook of Categorical Algebra*. Encyclopedia of Mathematics. CUP, 1994.

M. Fiore, G. Plotkin, and D. Turi. Abstract syntax and variable binding (extended abstract). In *Proc. 14th LICS Conf.*, pages 193–202. IEEE, Computer Society Press, 1999.

M. P. Fiore and T. Leinster. Objects of categories as complex numbers. *Advances in Mathematics.*, 2004. To appear.

M. Hofmann. On the interpretation of type theory in locally cartesian closed categories. In *CSL*, pages 427–441, 1994.

M. Hofmann. A simple model of quotient types. volume 902 of *Lecture Notes in Computer Science*, pages 216–234. Springer, 1995.

B. Jacobs. *Categorical Logic and Type Theory*. Number 141. Elsevier, 1999.

C. B. Jay. A semantics for shape. *Science of Computer Programming*, 25:251–283, 1995.

C. B. Jay and J. R. B. Cockett. Shapely types and shape polymorphism. In *Proceedings of ESOP'94*, Lecture Notes in Computer Science, pages 302–316. Springer, 1994.

A. Joyal. Foncteurs analytiques et espéces de structures. In *Combinatoire énumérative*, number 1234 in LNM, pages 126 – 159. 1986.

S. Mac Lane. *Categories for the Working Mathematician*. Number 5 in Graduate Texts in Mathematics. Springer-Verlag, 1971.

Optimizing Generic Functions

Artem Alimarine and Sjaak Smetsers

Computing Science Institute
University of Nijmegen
Toernooiveld 1, 6525 ED Nijmegen, The Netherlands
{alimarin,sjakie}@cs.kun.nl

Abstract. Generic functions are defined by induction on the structural representation of types. As a consequence, by defining just a single generic operation, one acquires this operation over any particular type. An instance on a specific type is generated by interpretation of the type's structure. A direct translation leads to extremely inefficient code that involves many conversions between types and their structural representations. In this paper we present an optimization technique based on compile-time symbolic evaluation. We prove that the optimization removes the overhead of the generated code for a considerable class of generic functions. The proof uses typing to identify intermediate data structures that should be eliminated. In essence, the output after optimization is similar to hand-written code.

1 Introduction

The role of generic programming in the development of functional programs is steadily becoming more important. The key point is that a single definition of a generic function is used to automatically generate instances of that function for arbitrarily many types. These generic functions are defined by induction on a structural representation of types. Adding or changing a type does not require modifications in a generic function; the appropriate code will be generated automatically. This eradicates the burden of writing similar instances of one particular function for numerous different data types, significantly facilitating the task of programming. Typical examples include generic equality, mapping, pretty-printing, and parsing.

Current implementations of generic programming [AP01,CHJ+02,HP01], generate code which is strikingly slow because generic functions work with structural representations rather than directly with data types. The resulting code requires numerous conversions between representations and data types. Without optimization automatically generated generic code runs nearly 10 times slower than its hand-written counterpart.

In this paper we prove that compile-time (*symbolic*) evaluation is capable of reducing the overhead introduced by generic specialization. The proof uses typing to predict the structure of the result of a symbolic computation. More specifically, we show that if an expression has a certain type, say σ, then its symbolic normal form will contain no other data-constructors than those belonging to σ.

D. Kozen (Ed.): MPC 2004, LNCS 3125, pp. 16–31, 2004.
© Springer-Verlag Berlin Heidelberg 2004

It appears that general program transformation techniques used in current implementations of functional languages are not able to remove the generic overhead. It is even difficult to predict what the result of applying such transformations on generic functions will be, not to mention a formal proof of completeness of these techniques.

In the present paper we are looking at generic programming based on the approach of kind-indexed types of Hinze [Hin00a], used as a basis for the implementation of generic classes of Glasgow Haskell Compiler (GHC) [HP01], Generic Haskell [CHJ+02] and Generic Clean [AP01]. The main sources of inefficiency in the generated code are due to heavy use of higher-order functions, and conversions between data structures and their structural representation. For a large class of generic functions, our optimization removes both of them, resulting in code containing neither parts of the structural representation (binary sums and products) nor higher-order functions introduced by the generic specialization algorithm.

The rest of the paper is organized as follows. In section 2 we give motivation for our work by presenting the code produced by the generic specialization procedure. The next two sections are preliminary; they introduce a simple functional language and the typing rules. In section 5, we extend the semantics of our language to evaluation of open expressions, and establish some properties of this so-called symbolic evaluation. In section 6 we discuss termination issues of symbolic evaluation of the generated code. Section 7 discusses related work. Section 8 reiterates our conclusions.

2   Generics

In this section we informally present the generated code using as an example the generic mapping specialized to lists. The structural representation of types is made up of just the unit type, the binary product type and the binary sum type [Hin99]:

$$\textbf{data } \mathbb{1} \quad = \mathbb{1}$$
$$\textbf{data } \alpha \times \beta = (\alpha, \beta)$$
$$\textbf{data } \alpha + \beta = \mathsf{Inl} \; \alpha \mid \mathsf{Inr} \; \beta$$

For instance, the data types

$$\textbf{data List } \alpha \quad = \mathsf{Nil} \mid \mathsf{Cons} \; \alpha \; (\mathsf{List} \; \alpha)$$
$$\textbf{data Tree } \alpha \; \beta = \mathsf{Tip} \; \alpha \mid \mathsf{Bin} \; \beta \; (\mathsf{Tree} \; \alpha \; \beta) \; (\mathsf{Tree} \; \alpha \; \beta)$$

are represented as

$$\textbf{type List}^{\circ} \; \alpha \quad = \mathbb{1} + \alpha \times (\mathsf{List} \; \alpha)$$
$$\textbf{type Tree}^{\circ} \; \alpha \; \beta = \alpha + \beta \times \mathsf{Tree} \; \alpha \; \beta \times \mathsf{Tree} \; \alpha \; \beta$$

Note that the representation of a recursive type is not recursive.

The structural representation of a data type is isomorphic to that data type. The conversion functions establish the isomorphism:

$$
\begin{aligned}
&\text{to}_{\text{List}} \quad : \text{List } \alpha \to \text{List}^\circ \ \alpha \\
&\text{to}_{\text{List}} \quad = \lambda l.\text{case } l \text{ of} \\
&\qquad\qquad\qquad \text{Nil} \ \to \ \text{Inl } \mathbb{1} \\
&\qquad\qquad\qquad \text{Cons } x \ xs \ \to \ \text{Inr } (x, xs) \\
&\text{from}_{\text{List}} : \text{List}^\circ \ \alpha \to \text{List } \alpha \\
&\text{from}_{\text{List}} = \lambda l.\text{case } l \text{ of} \\
&\qquad\qquad\qquad \text{Inl } u \ \to \ \text{case } u \text{ of } \mathbb{1} \ \to \ \text{Nil} \\
&\qquad\qquad\qquad \text{Inr } p \ \to \ \text{case } p \text{ of } (x, xs) \ \to \ \text{Cons } x \ xs
\end{aligned}
$$

The generic specializer automatically generates the type synonyms for structural representations and the conversion functions.

Data types may contain the arrow type. To handle such types the conversion functions are packed into *embedding-projection pairs* [HP01]

$$\textbf{data } \alpha \rightleftarrows \beta = \text{EP } (\alpha \to \beta) \ (\beta \to \alpha)$$

The projections, the inversion and the (infix) composition of embedding-projections are defined as follows:

$$
\begin{aligned}
&\text{to} \quad : (\alpha \rightleftarrows \beta) \to (\alpha \to \beta) \\
&\text{to} \quad = \lambda x.\text{case } x \text{ of EP } t \ f \ \to \ t \\
&\text{from} : (\alpha \rightleftarrows \beta) \to (\beta \to \alpha) \\
&\text{from} = \lambda x.\text{case } x \text{ of EP } t \ f \ \to \ f \\
&\text{inv} \quad : (\alpha \rightleftarrows \beta) \to (\beta \rightleftarrows \alpha) \\
&\text{inv} \quad = \lambda x.\text{EP } (\text{from } x) \ (\text{to } x) \\
&\bullet \quad : (\beta \rightleftarrows \gamma) \to (\alpha \rightleftarrows \beta) \to (\alpha \rightleftarrows \gamma) \\
&\bullet \quad = \lambda a.\lambda b.\text{EP } (\text{to } a \ \circ \ \text{to } b) \ (\text{from } b \ \circ \ \text{from } a)
\end{aligned}
$$

For instance, the generic specializer generates the following embedding-projection pair for lists:

$$
\begin{aligned}
&\text{conv}_{\text{List}} : \text{List } \alpha \rightleftarrows \text{List}^\circ \ \alpha \\
&\text{conv}_{\text{List}} = \text{EP } \text{to}_{\text{List}} \ \text{from}_{\text{List}}
\end{aligned}
$$

To define a generic (*polytypic*) function the programmer provides the basic *poly-kinded type* [Hin00b] and the instances on the base types. For example, the generic mapping is given by the type

$$\textbf{type } \text{Map } \alpha \ \beta = \alpha \to \beta$$

and the base cases

$$
\begin{aligned}
&\text{map}_{\mathbb{1}} \ : \mathbb{1} \to \mathbb{1} \\
&\text{map}_{\mathbb{1}} = \lambda x.\text{case } x \text{ of } \mathbb{1} \ \to \ \mathbb{1} \\
&\text{map}_\times : \forall \alpha_1 \alpha_2 \beta_1 \beta_2.(\alpha_1 \to \beta_1) \to (\alpha_2 \to \beta_2) \to (\alpha_1 \times \alpha_2 \to \beta_1 \times \beta_2) \\
&\text{map}_\times = \lambda f.\lambda g.\lambda p.\text{case } p \text{ of } (x, y) \ \to \ (f \ x, g \ y) \\
&\text{map}_+ : \forall \alpha_1 \alpha_2 \beta_1 \beta_2.(\alpha_1 \to \beta_1) \to (\alpha_2 \to \beta_2) \to (\alpha_1 + \alpha_2 \to \beta_1 + \beta_2) \\
&\text{map}_+ = \lambda f.\lambda g.\lambda e.\text{case } e \text{ of} \\
&\qquad\qquad\qquad \text{Inl } x \ \to \ \text{Inl } (f \ x) \\
&\qquad\qquad\qquad \text{Inr } y \ \to \ \text{Inr } (g \ y)
\end{aligned}
$$

The generic specializer generates the code for the structural representation T° of a data type T by interpreting the structure of T°. For instance,

$$\mathsf{map}_{\mathsf{List}^\circ} : (\alpha \to \beta) \to \mathsf{List}^\circ \ \alpha \to \mathsf{List}^\circ \ \beta$$
$$\mathsf{map}_{\mathsf{List}^\circ} = \lambda f.\mathsf{map}_+ \ \mathsf{map}_\mathbb{1} \ (\mathsf{map}_\times \ f \ (\mathsf{map}_{\mathsf{List}} \ f))$$

Note that the structure of $\mathsf{map}_{\mathsf{List}^\circ}$ reflects the structure of List°.

The way the arguments and the result of a generic function are converted from and to the structural representation depends on the base type of the generic function. Embedding-projections are used to devise the automatic conversion. Actually, embedding-projections form a predefined generic function that is used for conversions in all other generic functions (e.g. map) [Hin00a]. The type of this generic function is $\alpha \rightleftarrows \beta$ and the base cases are

$$
\begin{aligned}
\mathsf{ep}_\mathbb{1} &: \mathbb{1} \rightleftarrows \mathbb{1} \\
\mathsf{ep}_\mathbb{1} &= \mathsf{EP} \ \mathsf{map}_\mathbb{1} \ \mathsf{map}_\mathbb{1} \\
\mathsf{ep}_+ &: (\alpha_1 \rightleftarrows \alpha_2) \to (\beta_1 \rightleftarrows \beta_2) \to (\alpha_1 + \beta_1 \rightleftarrows \alpha_2 + \beta_2) \\
\mathsf{ep}_+ &= \lambda a.\lambda b.\mathsf{EP} \ (\mathsf{map}_+ \ (\mathsf{to} \ a) \ (\mathsf{to} \ b)) \ (\mathsf{map}_+ \ (\mathsf{from} \ a) \ (\mathsf{from} \ b)) \\
\mathsf{ep}_\times &: (\alpha_1 \rightleftarrows \alpha_2) \to (\beta_1 \rightleftarrows \beta_2) \to (\alpha_1 \times \beta_1 \rightleftarrows \alpha_2 \times \beta_2) \\
\mathsf{ep}_\times &= \lambda a.\lambda b.\mathsf{EP} \ (\mathsf{map}_\times \ (\mathsf{to} \ a) \ (\mathsf{to} \ b)) \ (\mathsf{map}_\times \ (\mathsf{from} \ a) \ (\mathsf{from} \ b)) \\
\mathsf{ep}_\to &: (\alpha_1 \rightleftarrows \alpha_2) \to (\beta_1 \rightleftarrows \beta_2) \to ((\alpha_1 \to \beta_1) \rightleftarrows (\alpha_2 \to \beta_2)) \\
\mathsf{ep}_\to &= \lambda a.\lambda b.\mathsf{EP} \ (\lambda f.\mathsf{to} \ b \ \circ \ f \ \circ \ \mathsf{from} \ a) \ (\lambda f.\mathsf{from} \ b \ \circ \ f \ \circ \ \mathsf{to} \ a) \\
\mathsf{ep}_\rightleftarrows &: (\alpha_1 \rightleftarrows \alpha_2) \to (\beta_1 \rightleftarrows \beta_2) \to ((\alpha_1 \rightleftarrows \beta_1) \rightleftarrows (\alpha_2 \rightleftarrows \beta_2)) \\
\mathsf{ep}_\rightleftarrows &= \lambda a.\lambda b.\mathsf{EP} \ (\lambda e.b \ \bullet \ e \ \bullet \ \mathsf{inv} \ a) \ (\lambda e.\mathsf{inv} \ b \ \bullet \ e \ \bullet \ a)
\end{aligned}
$$

The generic specializer generates the instance of ep specific to a generic function. The generation is performed by interpreting the base (kind-indexed) type of the function. For mapping (with the base type $\mathsf{Map} \ \alpha \ \beta$) we have:

$$\mathsf{ep}_{\mathsf{Map}} : (\alpha_1 \rightleftarrows \alpha_2) \to (\beta_1 \rightleftarrows \beta_2) \to ((\alpha_1 \to \beta_1) \rightleftarrows (\alpha_2 \to \beta_2))$$
$$\mathsf{ep}_{\mathsf{Map}} = \lambda a.\lambda b.\mathsf{ep}_\to \ a \ b$$

Now there are all the necessary components to generate the code for a generic function specialized to any data type. In particular, for mapping on lists the generic specializer generates

$$\mathsf{map}_{\mathsf{List}} : (\alpha \to \beta) \to \mathsf{List} \ \alpha \to \mathsf{List} \ \beta$$
$$\mathsf{map}_{\mathsf{List}} = \mathsf{from} \ (\mathsf{ep}_{\mathsf{Map}} \ \mathsf{conv}_{\mathsf{List}} \ \mathsf{conv}_{\mathsf{List}}) \circ \mathsf{map}_{\mathsf{List}^\circ}$$

This function is much more complicated than its hand-coded counterpart

$$
\begin{aligned}
\mathsf{map}_{\mathsf{List}} = \lambda f.\lambda l.&\mathsf{case} \ l \ \mathsf{of} \\
&\mathsf{Nil} \ \to \ \mathsf{Nil} \\
&\mathsf{Cons} \ x \ xs \ \to \ \mathsf{Cons} \ (f \ x) \ (\mathsf{map}_{\mathsf{List}} \ f \ xs)
\end{aligned}
$$

The reasons for inefficiency are the intermediate data structures for the structural representation and extensive usage of higher-order functions. In the rest of the paper we show that symbolic evaluation guarantees that the intermediate data structures are not created by the resulting code. The resulting code is comparable to the hand-written code.

3   Language

In the following section we present the syntax and operational semantics of a core functional language. Our language supports essential aspects of functional programming such as pattern matching and higher-order functions.

3.1   Syntax

Definition 1 (Expressions and Functions)

a) *The set of expressions is defined by the following syntax. In the definition, x ranges over variables, $\mathbf{C}$ over constructors and $\mathbf{F}$ over function symbols. Below the notation $\vec{a}$ stands for $(a_1, \ldots, a_k)$.*

$$E ::= x \mid \mathbf{C}\vec{E} \mid \mathbf{F} \mid \lambda x.E \mid E\ E' \mid \text{case } E \text{ of } P_1 \to E_1 \cdots P_n \to E_n$$
$$P ::= \mathbf{C}\vec{x}$$

b) *A function definition is an expression of the form $\mathbf{F} = E_{\mathbf{F}}$ with $\mathrm{FV}(E_{\mathbf{F}}) = \emptyset$. With $\mathrm{FV}(E)$ we denote the set of free variables occurring in E.*

The distinction between *applications* (expressions) and *specifications* (functions) is reflected by our language definition. *Expressions* are composed from applications of function symbols and constructors. Constructors have a fixed arity, indicating the number of arguments to which they are applied. Partially applied constructors can be expressed by λ-expressions. A function expression is applied to an argument expression by an (invisible, binary) application operator. Finally, there is a case-construction to indicate pattern matching. *Functions* are simply named expressions (with no free variables).

3.2   Semantics

We will describe the evaluation of expressions in the style of *natural operational semantics*, e.g. see [NN92]. The underlying idea is to specify the result of a computation in a compositional, syntax-driven manner.

In this section we focus on evaluation to *normal form* (i.e. expressions being built up from constructors and λ-expressions only). In section 5, we extend this standard evaluation to so-called *symbolic evaluation*: evaluation of expressions containing free variables.

Definition 2 (Standard Evaluation)
Let E, N be expressions. Then E is said to evaluate to N (notation $E \Downarrow N$) if $E \Downarrow N$ can be produced in the following derivation system.

$$\lambda x.E \Downarrow \lambda x.E \quad (E\text{-}\lambda) \qquad \frac{\vec{E} \Downarrow \vec{N}}{\mathbf{C}\vec{E} \Downarrow \mathbf{C}\vec{N}} \ (E\text{-cons}) \qquad \frac{\mathbf{F} = E_{\mathbf{F}} \quad E_{\mathbf{F}} \Downarrow N}{\mathbf{F} \Downarrow N} \ (E\text{-fun})$$

$$\frac{E \Downarrow \mathbf{C}_i \vec{E} \quad D_i[\vec{x} := \vec{E}] \Downarrow N}{\text{case } E \text{ of } \ldots \mathbf{C}_i\vec{x} \to D_i \ldots \Downarrow N} \ (E\text{-case}) \qquad \frac{E \Downarrow \lambda x.E'' \quad E''[x := E'] \Downarrow N}{E\ E' \Downarrow N} \ (E\text{-app})$$

Here $E[x := E']$ denotes the term that is obtained when x in E is substituted by E'.

Observe that our evaluation does not lead to standard normal forms (expressions without redexes): if such an expression contains λs, there may still be redexes below these λs.

4 Typing

Typing systems in functional languages are used to ensure consistency of function applications: the type of each function argument should match some specific input type. In generic programming types also serve as a basis for specialization. Additionally, we will use typing to predict the constructors that appear in the result of a symbolic computation.

Syntax of Types

Types are defined as usual. We use $\forall$-types to express polymorphism.

Definition 3 (Types)
The set of types is given by the following syntax. Below, α ranges over type variables, and T *over type constructors.*

$$\sigma, \tau ::= \alpha \mid \mathrm{T} \mid \sigma {\rightarrow} \tau \mid \sigma\ \tau \mid \forall \alpha.\sigma$$

We will sometimes use $\vec{\sigma} {\rightarrow} \tau$ as a shorthand for $\sigma_1 {\rightarrow} \ldots {\rightarrow} \sigma_k {\rightarrow} \tau$. The set of free type variables of σ is denoted by $\mathrm{FV}(\sigma)$.

The main mechanism for defining new data types in functional languages is via algebraic types.

Definition 4 (Type environments)
a) *Let $\mathcal{A}$ be an algebraic type system, i.e. a collection of algebraic type definitions. The type specifications in $\mathcal{A}$ give the types of the algebraic data constructors. Let*

$$\mathrm{T}\ \vec{\alpha} = \cdots \mid \mathbf{C}_i\ \vec{\sigma_i} \mid \cdots$$

be the specification of T *in $\mathcal{A}$. Then we write*

$$\mathcal{A} \vdash \mathbf{C}_i : \forall \vec{\alpha}.\vec{\sigma_i} {\rightarrow} \mathrm{T}\ \vec{\alpha}.$$

b) *The function symbols are supplied with a type by a function type environment $\mathcal{F}$, containing declarations of the form $\mathbf{F} : \sigma$.*

For the sequel, fix a function type environment $\mathcal{F}$, and an algebraic type system $\mathcal{A}$.

Type Derivation

Definition 5 (Type Derivation)

a) *The type system deals with typing statements of the form*

$$B \vdash E : \sigma,$$

where B is a type basis (i.e a finite set of declarations of the form $x : \tau$). Such a statement is valid if it can be produced using the following derivation rules.

$$
\begin{array}{ccc}
B, x : \sigma \vdash x : \sigma \quad (\sigma\text{-var}) & \dfrac{\mathbf{F} : \sigma \in \mathcal{F}}{B \vdash \mathbf{F} : \sigma} (\sigma\text{-}\mathcal{F}) & \dfrac{\mathcal{A} \vdash \mathbf{C} : \sigma}{B \vdash \mathbf{C} : \sigma} (\sigma\text{-}\mathcal{A})
\end{array}
$$

$$
\dfrac{B \vdash \mathbf{C} : \vec{\tau} \to \sigma \quad B \vdash \vec{E} : \vec{\tau}}{B \vdash \mathbf{C}\vec{E} : \sigma} (\sigma\text{-cons})
$$

$$
\dfrac{B \vdash E : \tau \quad B \vdash \mathbf{C}_i : \vec{\rho_i} \to \tau \quad B, \vec{x_i} : \vec{\rho_i} \vdash E_i : \sigma}{B \vdash \text{ case } E \text{ of } \cdots \mathbf{C}_i \vec{x_i} \to E_i \cdots : \sigma} (\sigma\text{-case})
$$

$$
\begin{array}{cc}
\dfrac{B \vdash E : \tau \to \sigma \quad B \vdash E' : \tau}{B \vdash E \, E' : \sigma} (\sigma\text{-app}) & \dfrac{B, x : \tau \vdash E : \sigma}{B \vdash \lambda x.E : \tau \to \sigma} (\sigma\text{-}\lambda)
\end{array}
$$

$$
\begin{array}{cc}
\dfrac{B \vdash E : \sigma \quad \alpha \notin \mathrm{FV}(B)}{B \vdash E : \forall \alpha.\sigma} (\sigma\text{-}\forall\text{-intro}) & \dfrac{B \vdash E : \forall \alpha.\sigma}{B \vdash E : \sigma[\alpha := \tau]} (\sigma\text{-}\forall\text{-elim})
\end{array}
$$

b) *The function type environment $\mathcal{F}$ is type correct if each function definition is type correct, i.e. for $\mathbf{F}$ with type σ and definition $\mathbf{F} = E_{\mathbf{F}}$ one has $\emptyset \vdash E_{\mathbf{F}} : \sigma$.*

5 Symbolic Evaluation

The purpose of symbolic evaluation is to reduce expressions at compile-time, for instance to simplify the generated mapping function for lists (see section 2).

If we want to evaluate expressions containing free variables, evaluation cannot proceed if the value of such a variable is needed. This happens, for instance, if a pattern match on such a free variable takes place. In that case the corresponding case-expression cannot be evaluated fully. The most we can do is to evaluate all alternatives of such a case-expression. Since none of the pattern variables will be bound, the evaluation of these alternatives is likely to get stuck on the occurrences of variables again.

Symbolic evaluation gives rise to a new (extended) notion of normal form, where in addition to constructors and λ-expressions, also variables, cases and higher-order applications can occur. This explains the large number of rules required to define the semantics.

Definition 6 (Symbolic Evaluation) *We adjust definition 2 of evaluation by replacing the E-λ rule, and by adding rules for dealing with new combinations of expressions.*

$$x \Downarrow x \quad \text{(E-var)} \qquad \frac{E \Downarrow N}{\lambda x.E \Downarrow \lambda x.N} \text{ (E-}\lambda\text{)}$$

$$\frac{E \Downarrow \text{case } D \text{ of } \cdots P_i \rightarrow D_i \cdots \qquad \text{case } D_i \text{ of } \cdots Q_j \rightarrow E_j \cdots \Downarrow N_i}{\text{case } E \text{ of } \cdots Q_j \rightarrow E_j \cdots \Downarrow \text{case } D \text{ of } \cdots P_i \rightarrow N_i} \text{ (E-case-case)}$$

$$\frac{E \Downarrow x \qquad E_i \Downarrow N_i}{\text{case } E \text{ of } \cdots P_i \rightarrow E_i \cdots \Downarrow \text{case } x \text{ of } \cdots P_i \rightarrow N_i \cdots} \text{ (E-case-var)}$$

$$\frac{E \Downarrow E' \ E'' \qquad E_i \Downarrow N_i}{\text{case } E \text{ of } \cdots P_i \rightarrow E_i \cdots \Downarrow \text{case } E' \ E'' \text{ of } \cdots P_i \rightarrow N_i \cdots} \text{ (E-case-app)}$$

$$\frac{E \Downarrow \text{case } D \text{ of } \cdots P_i \rightarrow D_i \cdots \qquad D_i \ E' \Downarrow N_i}{E \ E' \Downarrow \text{case } D \text{ of } \cdots P_i \rightarrow N_i \cdots} \text{ (E-app-case)}$$

$$\frac{E \Downarrow x \qquad E' \Downarrow N}{E \ E' \Downarrow x \ N} \text{ (E-app-var)} \qquad \frac{E \Downarrow D \ D' \qquad E' \Downarrow N}{E \ E' \Downarrow D \ D' \ N} \text{ (E-app-app)}$$

Note that the rules (*E*-case) and (*E*-app) from definition 2 are responsible for removing constructor-destructor pairs and applications of the lambda-terms. These two correspond to the two sources of inefficiency in the generated programs: intermediate data structures and higher-order functions. The rules (*E*-case-case) and (*E*-app-case) above are called code-motion rules [DMP96]: their purpose is to move code to facilitate further transformations. For instance, the (*E*-case-case) rule pushes the outer case in the alternatives of the inner case in hope that an alternative is a constructor. If so, the (*E*-case) rule is applicable and the intermediate data are removed. Similarly, (*E*-app-case) pushes the application arguments in the case alternatives hoping that an alternative is a lambda-term. In this case (*E*-app) becomes applicable.

Example 7 (Symbolic Evaluation) Part of the derivation tree for the evaluation of the expression $\text{map}_\times \ f_1 \ g_1 \ (\text{map}_\times \ f_2 \ g_2 \ p)$ is given below. The function $\text{map}_\times$ is defined in section 2.

$$\frac{\text{map}_\times \Downarrow \atop \begin{array}{l}\lambda f.\lambda g.\lambda p.\text{case } p \text{ of} \\ (x,y) \rightarrow (f \ x, g \ y)\end{array} \qquad \frac{\text{map}_\times \ f_2 \ g_2 \ p \Downarrow \atop \begin{array}{l}\text{case } p \text{ of} \\ (x',y') \rightarrow (f_2 \ x', g_2 \ y')\end{array} \qquad \begin{array}{l}\text{case } (f_2 \ x', g_2 \ y') \text{ of} \\ (x,y) \rightarrow (f_1 \ x, g_1 \ y) \Downarrow \\ (f_1 \ (f_2 \ x'), g_1 \ (g_2 \ y'))\end{array}}{\begin{array}{l}\text{case map}_\times \ f_2 \ g_2 \ p \text{ of} \\ (x,y) \rightarrow (f_1 \ x, g_1 \ y) \Downarrow \\ \text{case } p \text{ of} (x',y') \rightarrow (f_1 \ (f_2 \ x'), g_1 \ (g_2 \ y'))\end{array}}}{\text{map}_\times \ f_1 \ g_1 \ (\text{map}_\times \ f_2 \ g_2 \ p) \Downarrow \text{case } p \text{ of} (x',y') \rightarrow (f_1 \ (f_2 \ x'), g_1 \ (g_2 \ y'))}$$

The following definition characterizes the results of symbolic evaluation.

Definition 8 (Symbolic Normal Forms) *The set of symbolic normal forms (indicated by N_s) is defined by the following syntax.*

$$N_s ::= \mathbf{C}\vec{N_s} \mid \lambda x.N_s \mid N_h \mid \text{case } N_h \text{ of } \cdots P_i \rightarrow N_s \cdots$$
$$N_h ::= x \mid N_h \ N_s$$

Proposition 9 (Correctness of Symbolic Normal Form)

$$E \Downarrow N \Rightarrow N \in N_s$$

Proof: By induction on the derivation of $E \Downarrow N$. □

5.1   Symbolic Evaluation and Typing

In this subsection we will show that the type of an expression (or the type of a function) can be used to determine the constructors that appear (or will appear after reduction) in the symbolic normal form of that expression. Note that this is not trivial because an expression in symbolic normal form might still contain potential redexes that can only be determined and reduced during actual evaluation. Recall that one of the reasons for introducing symbolic evaluation is the elimination of auxiliary data structures introduced by the generic specialization procedure.

The connection between evaluation and typing is usually given by the so-called *subject reduction property* indicating that typing is preserved during reduction.

Proposition 10 (Subject Reduction Property)

$$B \vdash E : \sigma, E \Downarrow N \Rightarrow B \vdash N : \sigma$$

Proof: By induction on the derivation of $E \Downarrow N$. □

There are two ways to determine constructors that can be created during the evaluation of an expression, namely, (1, directly) by analyzing the expression itself or (2, indirectly) by examining the type of that expression.

In the remainder of this section we will show that (2) includes all the constructors of (1), provided that (1) is determined after the expression is evaluated symbolically. The following definition makes the distinction between the different ways of indicating constructors precise.

Definition 11 (Constructors of normal forms and types)
- Let N be an expression in symbolic normal form. The set of constructors appearing in N (denoted as $C_N(N)$) is inductively defined as follows.

$$
\begin{array}{ll}
C_N(\mathbf{C}\vec{N}) & = \{\mathbf{C}\} \cup C_N(\vec{N}) \\
C_N(\lambda x.N) & = C_N(N) \\
C_N(x) & = \emptyset \\
C_N(N \ N') & = C_N(N) \cup C_N(N') \\
C_N(\text{case } N \text{ of } \cdots P_i \rightarrow N_i \cdots) & = C_N(N) \cup (\cup_i C_N(N_i))
\end{array}
$$

Here $C_N(\vec{N})$ should be read as $\cup_i C_N(N_i)$.

- Let σ be a type. The set of constructors in σ (denoted as $C_T(\sigma)$) is inductively defined as follows.

$$
\begin{aligned}
C_T(\alpha) \quad &= \emptyset \\
C_T(\mathrm{T}) \quad &= \cup_i[\{\mathbf{C}_i\} \cup C_T(\vec{\sigma_i})], \qquad \text{where } \mathrm{T} = \cdots \mid \mathbf{C}_i\vec{\sigma_i} \mid \cdots \\
C_T(\tau{\rightarrow}\sigma) &= C_T(\tau) \cup C_T(\sigma) \\
C_T(\tau \; \sigma) \quad &= C_T(\tau) \cup C_T(\sigma) \\
C_T(\forall\alpha.\sigma) &= C_T(\sigma)
\end{aligned}
$$

- Let B be a basis. By $C_T(B)$ we denote the set $\cup C_T(\sigma)$ for each $x : \sigma \in B$.

Example 12 For the List type from section 2 and for the Rose tree

$$\textbf{data } \mathsf{Rose}\ \alpha = \mathsf{Node}\ \alpha\ (\mathsf{List}\ (\mathsf{Rose}\ \alpha))$$

we have $C_T(\mathsf{List}) = \{\mathsf{Nil}, \mathsf{Cons}\}$ and $C_T(\mathsf{Rose}) = \{\mathsf{Node}, \mathsf{Nil}, \mathsf{Cons}\}$.

As a first step towards a proof of the main result of this section we concentrate on expressions that are already in symbolic normal form. Then their typings give a safe approximation of the constructors that are possibly generated by those expressions. This is stated by the following property. In fact, this result is an extension of the *Canonical Normal Forms Lemma*, e.g. see [Pie02].

Proposition 13 *Let $N \in N_s$. Then*

$$B \vdash N : \sigma \;\Rightarrow\; C_N(N) \subseteq C_T(B) \cup C_T(\sigma).$$

Proof: By induction on the structure of N_s. $\square$

The main result of this section shows that symbolic evaluation is adequate to remove constructors that are not contained in the typing statement of an expression. For traditional reasons we call this the *deforestation property*.

Proposition 14 (Deforestation Property)

$$B \vdash E : \sigma, E \Downarrow N \;\Rightarrow\; C_N(N) \subseteq C_T(B) \cup C_T(\sigma)$$

Proof: By proposition 9, 13, and 10. $\square$

5.2   Optimising Generics

Here we show that, by using symbolic evaluation, one can implement a compiler that for a generic operation yields code as efficient as a dedicated hand coded version of this operation.

The code generated by the generic specialization procedure is type correct [Hin00a]. We use this fact to establish the link between the base type of the generic function and the type of a specialized instance of that generic function.

Proposition 15 *Let g be a generic function of type σ, T a data-type, and let g_T be the instance of g on T. Then g_T is typeable. Moreover, there are no other type constructors in the type of g_T than T itself or those appearing in σ.*

Proof: See [AS03]. □

Now we combine typing of generic functions with the deforestation property leading to the following.

Proposition 16 *Let g be a generic function of type σ, T a data-type, and let g_T be the instance of g on T. Suppose $g_T \Downarrow N$. Then for any data type S one has*

$$\text{S} \notin \sigma, \text{T} \;\Rightarrow\; C_T(\text{S}) \cap C_N(N) = \emptyset.$$

Proof: By proposition 14, 10, and 15. □

Recall from section 2 that the intermediate data introduced by the generic specializer are built from the structural representation base types $\{\times, +, \mathbb{1}, \rightleftarrows\}$. It immediately follows from the proposition above that, if neither σ nor T contains a structural representation base type S, then the constructors of S are not a part of the evaluated right-hand side of the instance g_T.

6   Implementation Aspects: Termination of Symbolic Evaluation

Until now we have avoided the termination problem of the symbolic evaluation. In general, this termination problem is undecidable, so precautions have to be taken if we want to use the symbolic evaluator at compile-time. It should be clear that non-termination can only occur if some of the involved functions are recursive. In this case such a function might be unfolded infinitely many times (by applying the rule (E-fun)). The property below follows directly form proposition 16.

Corollary 17 (Efficiency of generics) *Non-recursive generic functions can be implemented efficiently. More precisely, symbolic evaluation removes intermediate data structures and functions concerning the structural representation base types.*

The problem arises when we deal with generic instances on recursive data types. Specialization of a generic function to such a type will lead to a recursive function. For instance, the specialization of map to List contains a call to $\text{map}_{\text{List}}{}^\circ$ which, in turn, calls recursively map_{List}. We can circumvent this problem by breaking up the definition into a non-recursive part and to reintroduce recursion via the standard fixed point combinator $Y = \lambda f.f(Yf)$. Then we can apply symbolic evaluation to the non-recursive part to obtain an optimized version of our generic function. The standard way to remove recursion is to add an extra parameter to a recursive function, and to replace the call to the function itself by a call to that parameter.

Example 18 (Non-recursive specialization) The specialization of map to List without recursion:

$$\text{map}'_{\text{List}} = \lambda m.\text{from } (\text{ep}_\rightarrow \text{ conv}_{\text{List}} \text{ conv}_{\text{List}}) \circ$$
$$(\lambda f.\text{map}_+ \text{ map}_\mathbb{1} \text{ }(\text{map}_\times \text{ } f \text{ }(m \text{ } f)))$$
$$\text{map}_{\text{List}} = Y \text{map}'_{\text{List}}$$

After evaluating $\text{map}'_{\text{List}}$ symbolically we get

$$
\begin{array}{ll}
\text{map}'_{\text{List}} = \lambda m.\lambda f.\lambda x. \text{ case } x \text{ of} \\
\quad\quad\quad \text{Nil} & \rightarrow \text{Nil} \\
\quad\quad\quad \text{Cons } y \text{ } ys & \rightarrow \text{Cons } (f \text{ } y) \text{ } (m \text{ } f \text{ } ys)
\end{array}
$$

showing that all intermediate data structures are eliminated.

Suppose the generic instance has type τ. Then the non-recursive variant (with the extra recursion parameter) will have type $\tau \rightarrow \tau$, which obviously has the same set of type constructors as τ.

However, this way of handling recursion will not work for generic functions whose base type contains a recursive data type. Consider for example the monadic mapping function for the list monad mapl with the base type

$$\textbf{type} \quad \text{Mapl } \alpha \text{ } \beta = \alpha \rightarrow \text{List } \beta$$

and the base cases

$$
\begin{array}{l}
\text{mapl}_\mathbb{1} \text{ } : \text{ } \mathbb{1} \rightarrow \text{List } \mathbb{1} \\
\text{mapl}_\mathbb{1} = \text{return } \mathbb{1} \\
\text{mapl}_\times \text{ } : \text{ } \forall \alpha_1 \alpha_2 \beta_1 \beta_2.(\alpha_1 \rightarrow \text{List } \beta_1) \rightarrow (\alpha_2 \rightarrow \text{List } \beta_2) \rightarrow \alpha_1 \times \alpha_2 \\
\quad\quad\quad \rightarrow \text{List } (\beta_1 \times \beta_2) \\
\text{mapl}_\times = \lambda f.\lambda g.\lambda p.\text{case } p \text{ of } (x, y) \rightarrow f \text{ } x \gg= \lambda x'.g \text{ } y \gg= \lambda y'.\text{return } (x', y') \\
\text{mapl}_+ \text{ } : \text{ } \forall \alpha_1 \alpha_2 \beta_1 \beta_2.(\alpha_1 \rightarrow \text{List } \beta_1) \rightarrow (\alpha_2 \rightarrow \text{List } \beta_2) \rightarrow \alpha_1 + \alpha_2 \\
\quad\quad\quad \rightarrow \text{List } (\beta_1 + \beta_2) \\
\text{mapl}_+ = \lambda f.\lambda g.\lambda e.\text{case } e \text{ of} \\
\quad\quad\quad \text{Inl } x \rightarrow f \text{ } x \gg= \lambda x'.\text{return } (\text{Inl } x') \\
\quad\quad\quad \text{Inr } y \rightarrow g \text{ } y \gg= \lambda y'.\text{return } (\text{Inr } y')
\end{array}
$$

where

$$
\begin{array}{l}
\text{return} = \lambda x.\text{Cons } x \text{ Nil} \\
(\gg=) = \lambda l.\lambda f.\text{flatten } (\text{map } f \text{ } l)
\end{array}
$$

are the monadic return and (infix) bind for the list monad. The specialization of mapl to any data type, e.g. Tree, uses the embedding-projection specialized to Mapl (see section 2).

$$
\begin{array}{l}
\text{mapl}_{\text{Tree}} \text{ } : \text{ } (\alpha \rightarrow \text{List } \beta) \rightarrow \text{Tree } \alpha \rightarrow \text{List } (\text{Tree } \beta) \\
\text{mapl}_{\text{Tree}} = \text{from } (\text{ep}_{\text{Mapl}} \text{ conv}_{\text{Tree}} \text{ conv}_{\text{Tree}}) \circ \text{mapl}_{\text{Tree}}\circ
\end{array}
$$

The embedding-projection $\mathsf{ep_{Mapl}}$

$$\mathsf{ep_{Mapl}} \; : \; (\alpha_1 \rightleftarrows \alpha_2) \rightarrow (\beta_1 \rightleftarrows \beta_2) \rightarrow ((\alpha_1 \rightarrow \mathsf{List}\ \beta_1) \rightleftarrows (\alpha_2 \rightarrow \mathsf{List}\ \beta_2))$$
$$\mathsf{ep_{Mapl}} = \lambda a.\lambda b.\mathsf{ep_\rightarrow}\ a\ (\mathsf{ep_{List}}\ b)$$

contains a call to the (recursive) embedding-projection for lists $\mathsf{ep_{List}}$

$$\mathsf{ep_{List}} \quad : \; (\alpha \rightleftarrows \beta) \rightarrow (\mathsf{List}\ \alpha \rightleftarrows \mathsf{List}\ \beta)$$
$$\mathsf{ep_{List}} \; = \mathsf{from}\ (\mathsf{ep_\rightleftarrows}\ \mathsf{conv_{List}}\ \mathsf{conv_{List}}) \circ \mathsf{ep_{List}^\circ}$$
$$\mathsf{ep_{List}^\circ} \; : \; (\alpha \rightleftarrows \beta) \rightarrow (\mathsf{List}^\circ\ \alpha \rightleftarrows \mathsf{List}^\circ\ \beta)$$
$$\mathsf{ep_{List}^\circ} = \lambda f.\mathsf{ep_+}\ \mathsf{ep_\mathbb{1}}\ (\mathsf{ep_\times}\ f\ (\mathsf{ep_{List}}\ f))$$

We cannot get rid of this recursion (using the Y-combinator) because it is not possible to replace the call to $\mathsf{ep_{List}}$ in $\mathsf{ep_{mapl}}$ by a call to a non-recursive variant of $\mathsf{ep_{List}}$ and to reintroduce recursion afterwards.

Online Non-termination Detection

A way to solve the problem of non-termination is to extend symbolic evaluation with a mechanism for so-called *online non-termination detection*. A promising method is based on the notion of *homeomorphic embedding* (*HE*) [Leu98]: a (partial) ordering on expressions used to identify 'infinitely growing expressions' leading to non-terminating evaluation sequences. Clearly, in order to be safe, this technique will sometimes indicate unjustly expressions as dangerous. We have done some experiments with a prototype implementation of a symbolic evaluator extended with termination detection based on HEs. It appeared that in many cases we get the best possible results. However, guaranteeing success when transforming arbitrary generics seems to be difficult. The technique requires careful fine-tuning in order not to pass the border between termination and non-termination. This will be a subject to further research.

In practice, our approach will handle many generic functions as most of them do not contain recursive types in their base type specifications, and hence, do not require recursive embedding-projections. For instance, all generic functions in the generic Clean library (except the monadic mapping) fulfill this requirement.

7   Related Work

The generic programming scheme that we use in the present paper is based on the approach by Hinze[Hin00a]. Derivable type classes of GHC [HP01], Generic Haskell [CHJ+02] and Generic Clean [AP01] are based on this specialization scheme. We believe symbolic evaluation can also be used to improve the code generated by PolyP [JJ97]. The authors of [HP01] show by example that inlining and standard transformation techniques can get rid of the overhead of conversions between the types and their representations. The example presented does not involve embedding-projections and only treats non-recursive conversions from a data type to its generic representation. In contrast, our paper gives a formal treatment of optimization of generics. Moreover, we have run GHC 6.0.1 with the maximum level of optimization (-O2) on derived instances of the generic equality function: the result code was by far not free from the structural representation overhead.

Initially, we have tried to optimize generics by using *deforestation* [Wad88] and *fusion* [Chi94,AGS03]. Deforestation is not very successful because of its demand that functions have to be in *treeless form*. Too many generic functions do not meet this requirement. But even with a more liberal classification of functions we did not reach an optimal result. We have extended the original fusion algorithm with so-called *depth analysis* [CK96], but this does not work because of the *producer classification*: recursive embedding-projections are no proper producers. We also have experimented with alternative producer classifications but without success. Moreover, from a theoretical point of view, the adequacy of these methods is hard to prove. [Wad88] shows that with deforestation a composition of functions can be transformed to a single function without loss of efficiency. But the result we are aiming at is much stronger, namely, all overhead due to the generic conversion should be eliminated.

Our approach based on symbolic evaluation resembles the work that has been done on the field of compiler generation by partial evaluation. E.g., both [ST96] and [Jø92] start with an interpreter for a functional language and use partial evaluation to transform this interpreter into a more or less efficient compiler or optimizer. This appears to be a much more general goal. In our case, we are very specific about the kind of results we want to achieve.

Partial evaluation in combination with typing is used in [DMP96,Fil99,AJ01]. They use a two-level grammar to distinguish static terms from dynamic terms. Static terms are evaluated at compile time, whereas evaluation of dynamic terms is postponed to run time. Simple type systems are used to guide the optimization by classifying terms into static and dynamic. In contrast, in the present work we do not make explicit distinction between static and dynamic terms. Our semantics and type system are more elaborate: they support arbitrary algebraic data types. The type system is used to reason about the result of the optimization rather than to guide the optimization.

8   Conclusions and Future Work

The main contributions of the present paper are the following:

- We have introduced a symbolic evaluation algorithm and proved that the result of the symbolic evaluation of an expression will not contain data constructors not belonging to the type of that expression.
- We have shown that for a large class of generic functions symbolic evaluation can be used to remove the overhead of generic specialization. This class includes generic functions that do not contain recursive types in their base type.

Problems arise when involved generic function types contain recursive type constructors. These type constructors give rise to recursive embedding projections which can lead to non-termination of symbolic evaluation. We could use fusion to deal with this situation but then we have to be satisfied with a method that sometimes produces less optimal code. It seems to be more promising to extend symbolic evaluation with online termination analysis, most likely based on the homeomorphic embedding [Leu98]. We already did some research in this area but this has not yet led to the desired results.

We plan to study other optimization techniques in application to generic programming, such as program transformation in computational form [TM95]. Generic specialization has to be adopted to generate code in computational form, i.e. it has to yield *hylomorphisms* for recursive types.

Generics are implemented in Clean 2.0. Currently, the fusion algorithm of the Clean compiler is used to optimize the generated instances. As stated above, for many generic functions this algorithm does not yield efficient code. For this reason we plan to use the described technique extended with termination analysis to improve performance of generics.

References

[AGS03] Diederik van Arkel, John van Groningen, and Sjaak Smetsers. Fusion in practice. In Ricardo Peña and Thomas Arts, editors, *The 14th International Workshop on the Implementation of Functional Languages, IFL'02, Selected Papers*, volume 2670 of *LNCS*, pages 51–67. Departamento de Sistemas Informáticos y Programación, Universidad Complutense de Madrid, Springer, 2003.

[AJ01]   Klaus Aehlig and Felix Joachimski. Operational aspects of normalization by evaluation. Submitted to MSCS. Available from http://www.mathematik.uni-muenchen.de/~joachski, 2001.

[AP01]   Artem Alimarine and Rinus Plasmijer. A generic programming extension for Clean. In Thomas Arts and Markus Mohnen, editors, *Proceedings of the 13th International Workshop on Implementation of Functional Languages, IFL 2001*, pages 257–278, Stockholm, Sweden, September 2001. Ericsson Computer Science Laboratory.

[AS03]   Artem Alimarine and Sjaak Smetsers. Efficient generic functional programming. Technical report, Nijmegen Institute for Computing and Information Sciences, University of Nijmegen, The Netherlands, 2003. to appear.

[Chi94] Wei-Ngan Chin. Safe fusion of functional expressions II: further improvements. *Journal of Functional Programming*, 4(4):515–555, October 1994.

[CHJ⁺ 02] Dave Clarke, Ralf Hinze, Johan Jeuring, Andres Löh, and Jan de Wit. The generic haskell user's guide. Technical report, uu-cs-2002-047, Utrecht University, 2002.

[CK96]   Wei-Ngan Chin and Siau-Cheng Khoo. Better consumers for program specializations. *Journal of Functional and Logic Programming*, 1996(4), November 1996.

[DMP96] Olivier Danvy, Karoline Malmkjær, and Jens Palsberg. Eta-expansion does the trick. *ACM Transactions on Programming Languages and Systems*, 18(6):730–751, 1996.

[Fil99] Andrzej Filinski. A semantic account of type-directed partial evaluation. In *Principles and Practice of Declarative Programming*, pages 378–395, 1999.

[Hin99]   Ralf Hinze. A generic programming extension for Haskell. In Erik Meijer, editor, *Proceedings of the 3rd Haskell Workshop*. Paris, France, September 1999. The proceedings appeared as a technical report of Universiteit Utrecht, UU-CS-1999-28.

[Hin00a]   Ralf Hinze. Generic programs and proofs. Habilitationsschrift, Universität Bonn, October 2000.

[Hin00b]   Ralf Hinze. Polytypic values possess polykinded types. In Roland Backhouse and J.N. Oliveira, editors, *Proceedings of the Fifth International Conference on Mathematics of Program Construction (MPC 2000)*, volume 1837, pages 2–27, July 2000.

[HP01]   Ralf Hinze and Simon Peyton Jones. Derivable type classes. In Graham Hutton, editor, *Proceedings of the 2000 ACM SIGPLAN Haskell Workshop*, volume 41.1 of Electronic Notes in Theoretical Computer Science. Elsevier Science, August 2001. The preliminary proceedings appeared as a University of Nottingham technical report.

[JJ97]   P. Jansson and J. Jeuring. Polyp - a polytypic programming language extension. In *The 24th ACM Symposium on Principles of Programming Languages, POPL '97*, pages 470–482. ACM Press, 1997.

[Jø92]   Jesper Jørgensen. Generating a compiler for a lazy language by partial evaluation, popl '92. In *The 19th ACM Symposium on Principles of Programming Languages*, pages 258–268. Albuquerque, New Mexico, ACM Press, January 1992.

[Leu98]   Michael Leuschel. Homeomorphic embedding for online termination. Technical Report DSSE-TR-98-11, Department of Electronics and Computer Science, University of Southampton, UK, October 1998.

[NN92]   Hanne Riis Nielson and Flemming Nielson. *Semantics with Applications: A Formal Introduction*. Wiley Professional Computing, 1992. ISBN 0 471 92980 8.

[Pie02]   Benjamin C. Pierce. *Types and Programming Languages*. The MIT Press, 2002. ISBN 0–262–16209–1.

[ST96]   Michael Sperber and Peter Thiemann. Realistic compilation by partial evaluation. In *Proceedings of the ACM SIGPLAN '96 Conference on Programming Language Design and Implementation*, pages 206–214, May 1996.

[TM95]   Akihiko Takano and Erik Meijer. Shortcut deforestation in calculational form. In *Conf. Record 7th ACM SIGPLAN/SIGARCH Int. Conf. on Functional Programming Languages and Computer Architecture, FPCA'95*, pages 306–313, New York, June 1995. La Jolla, San Diego, CA, USA, ACM Press.

[Wad88]   Phil Wadler. Deforestation: transforming programs to eliminate trees. In *Proceedings of the European Symposium on Programming*, number 300 in LNCS, pages 344–358, Berlin, Germany, March 1988. Springer-Verlag.

Inferring Type Isomorphisms Generically

Frank Atanassow and Johan Jeuring

Institute of Information & Computing Sciences
Utrecht University
The Netherlands
{franka,johanj}@cs.uu.nl

Abstract. Datatypes which differ inessentially in their names and structure are said to be isomorphic; for example, a ternary product is isomorphic to a nested pair of binary products. In some canonical cases, the conversion function is uniquely determined solely by the two types involved. In this article we describe and implement a program in Generic Haskell which automatically infers this function by normalizing types w.r.t. an algebraic theory of canonical isomorphisms. A simple generalization of this technique also allows to infer some non-invertible coercions such as projections, injections and *ad hoc* coercions between base types. We explain how this technique has been used to drastically improve the usability of a Haskell–XML Schema data binding, and suggest how it might be applied to improve other type-safe language embeddings.

1 Introduction

Typed functional languages like Haskell [27] and ML [16, 25] typically support the declaration of user-defined, polymorphic algebraic datatypes. In Haskell, for example, we might define a datatype representing dates in a number of ways. The most straightforward and conventional definition is probably the one given by Date below,

data Date = *Date* Int Int Int

but a more conscientious Dutch programmer might prefer Date_NL:

data Date_NL = *Date_NL* Day Month Year
data Day = *Day* Int
data Month = *Month* Int
data Year = *Year* Int .

An American programmer, on the other hand, might opt for Date_US, which follows the US date format:

data Date_US = *Date_US* Month Day Year .

If the programmer has access to an existing library which can compute with dates given as Int-triples, though, he or she may prefer Date2,

data Date2 = *Date2* (Int, Int, Int) ,

D. Kozen (Ed.): MPC 2004, LNCS 3125, pp. 32–53, 2004.

for the sake of simplifying data conversion between his application and the library. In some cases, for example when the datatype declarations are machine-generated, a programmer might even have to deal with more unusual declarations such as:

data Date3 = *Date3* (Int, (Int, Int))
data Date4 = *Date4* ((Int, Int), Int)
data Date5 = *Date5* (Int, (Int, (Int, ()))) .

Though these types all represent the same abstract data structure[1], they represent it differently; they are certainly all unequal, firstly because they have different names, but more fundamentally because they exhibit different surface structures. Consequently, programs which use two or more of these types together must be peppered with applications of conversion functions. In this case, the amount of code required to define such a conversion function is not so large, but if the declarations are machine-generated, or the number of representations to be simultaneously supported is large, then the size of the conversion code might become unmanageable. In this paper we show how to infer such conversions automatically.

1.1   Isomorphisms

The fact that all these types represent the same abstract type is captured by the notion of *isomorphism*: two types are isomorphic if there exists an invertible function between them, our desired conversion function. Besides invertibility, two basic facts about isomorphisms (isos for short) are: the identity function is an iso, so every type is isomorphic to itself; and, the composition of two isos is an iso. Considered as a relation, then, isomorphism is an equivalence on types.

Other familiar isos are a consequence of the semantics of base types. For example, the conversion between meters and miles is a non-identity iso between the floating point type Double and itself; (if we preserve the origin), the conversion between cartesian and polar coordinates is another example. Finally, some polymorphic isos arise from the structure of types themselves; for example, one often hears that products are associative "up to isomorphism".

It is the last sort, often called *canonical* or *coherence* (iso)morphisms, which are of chief interest to us. Canonical isos are special because they are uniquely determined by the types involved, that is, there is at most one canonical iso between two polymorphic type schemes.

Monoidal Isos. A few canonical isos of Haskell are summarized by the syntactic theory below[2].

---

[1] We will assume all datatypes are strict; otherwise, Haskell's non-strict semantics typically entails that some transformations like nesting add a new value $\perp$ which renders this claim false.

[2] We use the type syntax familiar from the Generic Haskell literature, i.e., Unit and :*: are respectively nullary and binary product, and Zero and :+: are respectively nullary and binary sum constructors.

$$a :*: \text{Unit} \cong a \qquad \text{Unit} :*: a \cong a \qquad (a :*: b) :*: c \cong a :*: (b :*: c)$$
$$a :+: \text{Zero} \cong a \qquad \text{Zero} :+: a \cong a \qquad (a :+: b) :+: c \cong a :+: (b :+: c)$$

The isomorphisms which witness these identities are the evident ones. The first two identities in each row express the fact that Unit (resp. Zero) is a right and left unit for :*: (resp. :+:); the last says that :*: (resp. :+:) is associative. We call these isos collectively the *monoidal isos*.

This list is not exhaustive. For example, binary product and sum are also canonically commutative:

$$a :*: b \cong b :*: a \qquad\qquad\qquad a :+: b \cong b :+: a$$

and the currying and the distributivity isos are also canonical:

$$(a :*: b) \to c \cong a \to (b \to c) \qquad a :*: (b :+: c) \cong (a :*: b) :+: (a :*: c)$$

There is a subtle but important difference between the monoidal isos and the other isos mentioned above. Although all are canonical, and so possess unique polymorphic witnesses determined by the *type schemes* involved, only in the case of the monoidal isos does the uniqueness property transfer unconditionally to the setting of *types*.

To see this, consider instantiating the product-commutativity iso scheme to obtain:

$$\text{Int} :*: \text{Int} \cong \text{Int} :*: \text{Int} .$$

This identity has two witnesses: one is the intended twist map, but the other is the identity function.

This distinction is in part attributable to the form of the identities involved; the monoidal isos are all *strongly regular*, that is:

1. each variable that occurs on the left-hand side of an identity occurs exactly once on the right-hand side, and *vice versa*, and
2. they occur in the same order on both sides.

The strong regularity condition is adapted from work on generalized multicategories [15, 14, 10]. We claim, but have not yet proved, that strong regularity is a sufficient – but not necessary – condition to ensure that a pair of types determines a unique canonical iso witness.

Thanks to the canonicality and strong regularity properties, given two types we can determine if a unique iso between them exists, and if so can generate it automatically. Thus our program infers all the monoidal isos, but not the commutativity or distributivity isos; we have not yet attempted to treat the currying iso.

Datatype Isos. In Generic Haskell each datatype declaration effectively induces a canonical iso between the datatype and its underlying "structure type". For example, the declaration

data List a   =   *Nil* | *Cons* a (List a)

induces the canonical iso

List a $\cong$ Unit :+: (a :*: List a) .

We call such isos *datatype isos*.

Note that datatype isos are *not* strongly regular in general; for example the List identity mentions a twice on the right-hand side. Intuitively, though, there is only one witness to a datatype iso: the constructor(s). Again, we claim, and hope in the future to prove, that isos of this sort uniquely determine a canonical witness. Largely as a side effect of the way Generic Haskell works, our inference mechanism *does* infer datatype isos.

1.2 Outline

The remainder of this article is organized as follows. In section 2 we give an informal description of the user interface to our inference mechanism. Section 3 discusses a significant application of iso inference, a way of automatically customizing a Haskell–XML Schema data binding. In section 4 we examine the Generic Haskell implementation of our iso inferencer. Finally, in section 5 we summarize our results, and discuss related work and possibilities for future work in this area.

2 Inferring Isomorphisms

From a Generic Haskell user's point of view, iso inference is a simple matter based on two generic functions,

$$
\begin{array}{lll}
reduce\{\!|t|\!\} & :: & \text{t} \rightarrow \text{Univ} \\
expand\{\!|t'|\!\} & :: & \text{Univ} \rightarrow \text{t}' \; .
\end{array}
$$

$reduce\{\!|t|\!\}$ takes a value of any type and converts it into a universal, normalized representation denoted by the type Univ; $expand\{\!|t'|\!\}$, its dual, converts such a universal value back to a 'regular' value, if possible. The iso which converts from t to t' is thus expressed as:

$expand\{\!|t'|\!\} \circ reduce\{\!|t|\!\}$.

If $t = t'$, then $expand\{\!|t'|\!\}$ and $reduce\{\!|t|\!\}$ are mutual inverses. If t and t' are merely isomorphic, then expansion *may* fail; it always succeeds if the two types are *canonically* isomorphic, $t \cong t'$, according to the monoidal and datatype iso theories.

As an example, consider the expression

$(expand\{\!|(\text{Bool}, \text{Bool} :+: (\text{Int} :+: \text{String}))|\!\} \circ$
    $reduce\{\!|(\text{Bool}, ((), (\text{Bool} :+: \text{Int}) :+: \text{String}))|\!\})$
        $(\mathit{True}, ((), \mathit{Inl} \; (\mathit{Inr} \; 7)))$,

which evaluates to

$(\mathit{True}, \mathit{Inr} \; (\mathit{Inl} \; 7))$.

Function *reduce*⦃t⦄ picks a type in each isomorphism class which serves as a normal form, and uses the canonical witness to convert values of t to that form. Normalized values are represented in a special way in the abstract type Univ; a typical user need not understand the internals of Univ unless *expand*⦃t′⦄ fails. If t and t′ are 'essentially' the same, yet structurally substantially different then this automatic conversion can save the user a substantial amount of typing, time and effort.

Our functions also infer two coercions which are not invertible:

$$a :\!*\!: b \leqslant a \qquad\qquad a \leqslant a :\!+\!: b$$

The canonical witnesses here are the first projection of a product and the left injection of a sum. Thanks to these reductions, the expression

$$(expand⦃\mathsf{Either\ Bool\ Int}⦄ \circ reduce⦃(\mathsf{Bool},\mathsf{Int})⦄)\ (True, 4)$$

evaluates to *Left True*; note that it cannot evaluate to *Right* 4 because such a reduction would involve projecting a suffix and injecting into the right whereas we infer only prefix projections and left injections. Of course, we would prefer our theory to include the dual pair of coercions as well, but doing so would break the property that each pair of types determines a unique canonical witness. Nevertheless, we will see in section 3.4 how these coercions, when used with a cleverly laid out datatype, can be used to simulate single inheritance.

Now let us look at some examples which fail.

1. The conversion

$$expand⦃(\mathsf{Bool},\mathsf{Int})⦄ \circ reduce⦃(\mathsf{Int},\mathsf{Bool})⦄$$

   fails because our theory does not include commutativity of :*:.
2. The conversion

$$expand⦃\mathsf{Bool}⦄ \circ reduce⦃\mathsf{Int}⦄$$

   fails because the types are neither isomorphic nor coercible.
3. The conversion

$$expand⦃\mathsf{Bool}⦄ \circ reduce⦃\mathsf{Either}\ ()\ ()⦄$$

   fails because we chose to represent certain base types like Bool as abstract: they are not destructured when reducing.

Currently, because our implementation depends on the "universal" type Univ, failure occurs at run-time and a message helpful for pinpointing the error's source is printed. In section 5, we discuss some possible future work which may provide static error detection.

3   Improving a Haskell–XML Schema Data Binding

A program that processes XML documents can be implemented using an *XML data binding*. An XML data binding [23] translates an XML document to a value of some programming language. Such bindings have been defined for a number of programming languages including Java [21, 24], Python [26], Prolog [7] and Haskell [35, 37, 1]. The default translation scheme of a data binding may produce unwieldy, convoluted and redundant types and values. Our own Haskell–XML Schema binding, called UUXML [1], suffers from this problem.

In this section we use UUXML as a case study, to show how iso inference can be used to address a practical problem, the problem of overwhelmingly complex data representation which tends to accompany type-safe language embeddings. We outline the problem, explain how the design criteria gave rise to it, and finally show how to attack it.

In essence, our strategy will be to define a customized datatype, one chosen by the client programmer especially for the application. We use our mechanism to automatically infer the functions which convert to and from the customized representation by bracketing the core of the program with $reduce\{|\mathbf{t}|\}$ and $expand\{|\mathbf{t}|\}$. Generic Haskell does the rest, and the programmer is largely relieved from the burden imposed by the UUXML data representation.

The same technique might be used in other situations, for example, compilers and similar language processors which are designed to exploit type-safe data representations.

3.1   The Problem with UUXML

We do not have the space here to describe UUXML in detail, but let us briefly give the reader a sense of the magnitude of the problem.

Consider the following XML schema, which describes a simple bibliographic record doc including a sequence of authors, a title and an optional publication date, which is a year followed by a month.

```
<element name="doc" type="docType"/>
<complexType name="docType">
  <sequence>
    <element ref="author" minOccurs="0" maxOccurs="unbounded"/>
    <element ref="title"/>
    <element ref="pubDate" minOccurs="0"/>
  </sequence>
  <attribute name="key" type="string"/>
</complexType>
<element name="author" type="string"/>
<element name="title"  type="string"/>
<complexType name="pubDateType">
  <sequence>
    <element ref="year"/>
    <element ref="month"/>
  </sequence>
</complexType>
<element name="pubDate" type="pubDateType"/>
<element name="year"  type="int"/>
<element name="month" type="int"/>
```

An example document which validates against this schema is:

```
<doc key="homer-iliad">
  <author>Homer</author>
  <title>The Iliad</title>
</doc>
```

Our binding tool translates each of the types doc and docType into a pair of types (explained in the next section),

$$
\begin{aligned}
\textbf{data } \textsf{E\_doc u} &= \textit{E\_doc} \; (\textsf{Elem LE\_E\_doc LE\_T\_docType u}) \\
\textbf{data } \textsf{LE\_E\_doc u} &= \textit{EQ\_E\_doc} \; (\textsf{E\_doc u}) \\
\textbf{data } \textsf{T\_docType u} &= \textit{T\_docType} \; (\textsf{Seq A\_key (Seq (Rep LE\_E\_author ZI)} \\
&\qquad \textsf{(Seq LE\_E\_title (Rep LE\_E\_pubDate} \\
&\qquad \textsf{(ZS ZZ)))) u)} \\
\textbf{data } \textsf{LE\_T\_docType u} &= \textit{EQ\_E\_docType} \; (\textsf{T\_docType u}) \\
&\mid \;\; \textit{LE\_T\_publicationType} \; (\textsf{LE\_T\_publicationType u})
\end{aligned}
$$

and the example document above into:

EQ_E_doc (E_doc (Elem () (EQ_T_docType (T_docType (Seq (A_key (Attr (EQ_T_string (T_string "homer-iliad"*))))(Seq (Rep (ZI [EQ_E_author (E_author (Elem () (EQ_T_string (T_string* "Homer"*))))])) (Seq (EQ_E_title (E_title (Elem () (EQ_T_string (T_string* "The Iliad"*)))))(Rep (ZS Nothing (Rep ZZ)))))))))))*

Even without knowing the details of the encoding or definitions of the unfamiliar datatypes, one can see the problem here; if a user wants to, say, retrieve the content of the author field, he or she must pattern-match against no less than ten constructors before reaching "homer-iliad". For larger, more complex documents or document types, the problem can be even worse.

3.2 Conflicting Issues in UUXML

UUXML's usability issues are a side effect of its design goals. We discuss these here in some depth, and close by suggesting why similar issues may plague other applications which process typed languages.

First, UUXML is type-safe and preserves as much static type information as possible to eliminate the possibility of constructing invalid documents. In contrast, Java–XML bindings tend to ignore a great deal of type information, such as the types of repeated elements (only partly because of the limitations of Java collections).

Second, UUXML translates (a sublanguage of) XML Schema types rather than the less expressive DTDs. This entails additional complexity compared with bindings such as HaXML [37] that merely target DTDs. For example, XML Schema supports not just one but two distinct notions of subtyping and a more general treatment of mixed content[3] than DTDs.

---

[3] "Mixed content" refers to character data interspersed with elements. For example, in XHTML a p element can contain both character data and other elements like **em**.

Third, the UUXML translation closely follows the Model Schema Language (MSL) formal semantics [4], even going so far as to replicate that formalism's abstract syntax as closely as Haskell's type syntax allows. This has advantages: we have been able to prove the soundness of the translation, that is, that valid documents translate to typeable values, and the translator is relatively easy to correctly implement and maintain. However, our strict adherence to MSL has introduced a number of 'dummy constructors' and 'wrappers' which could otherwise be eliminated.

Fourth, since Haskell does not directly support subtyping and XML Schema does, our binding tool emits a *pair* of Haskell datatypes for each schema type t: an 'equational' variant which represents documents which validate *exactly* against t, and a 'down-closed' variant, which represents all documents which validate against all subtypes of t[4]. Our expectation was that a typical Haskell user would read a document into the down-closed variant, pattern-match against it to determine which exact/equational type was used, and do the bulk of their computation using that.

Finally, UUXML was intended, first and foremost, to support the development of 'schema-aware' XML applications using Generic Haskell. This moniker describes programs, such as our XML compressor XComprez [1], which operate on documents of any schema, but not necessarily parametrically. XComprez, for example, exploits the type information of a schema to improve compression ratios.

Because Generic Haskell works by traversing the structure of datatypes, we could not employ methods, such as those in WASH [35], which encode schema information in non-structural channels such as Haskell's type class system. Such information is instead necessarily expressed in the structure of UUXML's types, and makes them more complex.

For schema-aware applications this complexity is not such an issue, since generic functions typically need not pattern-match deeply into a datatype. But if we aim to use UUXML for more conventional applications, as we have demonstrated, it can become an overwhelming problem.

In closing, we emphasize that many similar issues are likely to arise, not only with other data bindings and machine-generated programs, but also with any type-safe representation of a typed object language in a metalanguage such as Haskell. Preserving the type information necessarily complicates the representation. If the overall 'style' of the object language is to be preserved, as was our desire in staying close to MSL, then the representation is further complicated. If subtyping is involved, yet more. If the representation is intended to support generic programming, then one is obliged to express as much information as possible structurally, and this too entails some complexity.

For reasons such as these, one might be tempted to eschew type-safe embeddings entirely, but then what is the point of programming in a statically typed

---

[4] To help illustrate this in the example schema translation, we posited that docType had a hypothetical subtype publicationType. It appears as the body of the second constructor of LE_T_docType in section 3.1.

language if not to exploit the type system? Arguably, the complexity problem arises not from static typing itself, but rather the insistence on using only a *single* data representation. In the next section, we show how iso inference drastically simplifies dealing with *multiple* data representations.

3.3   Exploiting Isomorphisms

Datatypes produced by UUXML are unquestionably complicated. Let us consider instead what our ideal translation target might look like. Here is an obvious, very conventional, Haskell-style translation image of doc:

> **module** *Doc* **where**
> **data** Doc   =   *Doc*{ *key* :: String,
>   *authors* :: [String],
>   *title* :: String,
>   *pubDate* :: Maybe PubDate }
> **data** PubDate =   *PubDate*{ *year* :: Integer,
>   *month* :: Integer }

Observe in particular that:

- the target types Doc and PubDate have conventional, Haskellish names which do not look machine-generated;
- the fields are typed by conventional Haskell datatypes like String, lists and Maybe;
- the attribute *key* is treated just like other elements; and
- intermediate 'wrapper' elements like *title* and *year* have been elided and do not generate new types;
- the positional information encoded in wrappers is available in the field projection names;
- the field name *authors* has been changed from the element name *author*, which is natural since *authors* projects a list whereas each *author* tag wraps a single author.

Achieving an analogous result in Java with a data binding like JAXB would require annotating (editing) the source schema directly, or writing a 'binding customization file' which is substantially longer than the two datatype declarations above. Both methods also require learning another XML vocabulary and some details of the translation process, and the latter uses XPath syntax to denote the parts which require customization – a maintenance hazard since the schema structure may change.

With our iso inference system, provided that the document is known to be exactly of type doc and not a proper subtype, all that is required is the above Haskell declaration plus the following modest incantation:

> *expand*{|Doc|} ∘ *reduce*{|E_doc|}

This expression denotes a function of type E_doc → Doc which converts the unwieldy UUXML representation of doc into the idealized form above.

For example, the following is a complete Generic Haskell program that reads in a doc-conforming document from standard input, deletes all authors named "De Sade", and writes the result to standard output.

```
module Censor where
import UUXML     -- our framework
import XDoc      -- automatically translated XML Schema
import Doc       -- the two datatype declarations above
main      =  interact work
work      =  toE_doc ∘ censor ∘ toDoc
censor d  =  d{ authors = filter (≢ "De Sade") (authors d)}
toE_doc   =  unparse⦇E_doc⦈ ∘ expand⦇E_doc⦈ ∘ reduce⦇Doc⦈
toDoc     =  expand⦇Doc⦈ ∘ reduce⦇E_doc⦈ ∘ parse⦇E_doc⦈
```

3.4   The Role of Coercions

Recall that our system infers two non-invertible coercions:

$$a :*: b \leqslant a \qquad\qquad\qquad a \leqslant a :+: b$$

Of course, this is only half of the story we would like to hear! Though we could easily implement the dual pair of coercions, we cannot implement them both together except in an *ad hoc* fashion (and hence refrain from doing so). This is only partly because, in reducing to a universal type, we have thrown away the type information. Even if we knew the types involved, it is not clear, for example, whether the coercion a → a :+: a should determine the left or the right injection.

Fortunately, even this 'biased' form of subtyping proves quite useful. In particular, XML Schema's so-called 'extension' subtyping exactly matches the form of the first projection coercion, as it only allows documents validating against a type t to be used in contexts of type s if s matches a prefix of t: so t is an extension of s.

Schema's other form of subtyping, called 'restriction', allows documents validating against type t to be used in contexts of type s if every document validating against t also validates against s: so t is a restriction of s. This can only happen if s, regarded as a grammar, can be reformulated as a disjunction of productions, one of which is t, so it appears our left injection coercion can capture part of this subtyping relation as well.

Actually, due to a combination of circumstances, the situation is better than might be expected. First, subtyping in Schema is *manifest* or *nominal*, rather than purely *structural*: consequently, restriction only holds between types assigned a name in the schema. Second, our translation models subtyping by generating a Haskell datatype declaration for the down-closure of each named schema type. For example, the 'colored point' example familiar from the object-oriented literature would be expressed thus:

```
data Point      =   Point...
data CPoint     =   CPoint...
data LE_Point   =   EQ_Point Point
                |   LE_CPoint LE_CPoint
data LE_CPoint  =   EQ_CPoint CPoint
                |   ...
```

Third, we have arranged our translator so that the $EQ_-...$ constructors always appear in the leftmost summand. This means that the injection from the 'equational' variant of a translated type to its down-closed variant is always the leftmost injection, and consequently picked out by our expansion mechanism.

$$EQ\_Point \quad :: \quad \text{Point} \to \text{LE\_Point}$$
$$EQ\_CPoint \quad :: \quad \text{CPoint} \to \text{LE\_CPoint}$$

Since Haskell is, in itself, not so well-equipped at dealing subtyping, when *reading* an XML document we would rather have the coercion the other way around, that is, we should like to read an LE_Point into a Point, but of course this is unsafe. However, when *writing* a value to a document these coercions save us some work inserting constructors.

Of course, since, unlike Schema itself, our coercion mechanism is structural, we can employ this capability in other ways. For instance, when writing a value to a document, we can use the fact that *Nothing* is the leftmost injection into the Maybe a type to omit optional elements.

3.5   Conclusion

Let us summarize the main points of this case study.

We demonstrated first by example that UUXML-translated datatypes are overwhelmingly complex and redundant. To address complaints that this problem stems merely from a bad choice of representation, we enumerated some of UUXML's design criteria, and explained why they necessitate that representation. We also suggested why other translations and type-safe embeddings might succumb to the same problem. Finally, we described how to exploit our iso inference mechanism to address this problem, and how coercion inference can also be used to simplify the treatment of object language features such as subtyping and optional values which the metalanguage does not inherently support.

4   Generic Isomorphisms

In this section, we describe how to automatically generate isomorphisms between pairs of datatypes. Our implementation platform is Generic Haskell, and in particular we use dependency-style GH [17]. This section assumes a basic familiarity with Generic Haskell, but the definitions are all remarkably simple.

We address the problem in four parts, treating first the product and sum isos in isolation, then showing how to merge those implementations. Finally, we describe a simple modification of the resulting program which implements the non-invertible coercions.

In each case, we build the requisite morphism by reducing a value $v :: \mathsf{t}$ to a value of a universal data type $u = reduce\{\!|\mathsf{t}|\!\}\ v :: \mathsf{Univ}$. The type Univ plays the role of a normal form from which we can then expand to a value $expand\{\!|\mathsf{t}'|\!\}\ u :: \mathsf{t}'$ of the desired type, where $\mathsf{t} \leqslant \mathsf{t}'$ canonically, or $\mathsf{t} \cong \mathsf{t}'$ for the isos.

4.1 Handling Products

We define the functions $reduce\{\!|\mathsf{t}|\!\}$ and $expand\{\!|\mathsf{t}|\!\}$ which infer the isomorphisms expressing associativity and identities of binary products:

$$\mathsf{a} :\!*\!: \mathsf{Unit} \cong \mathsf{a} \qquad \mathsf{Unit} :\!*\!: \mathsf{a} \cong \mathsf{a} \qquad (\mathsf{a} :\!*\!: \mathsf{b}) :\!*\!: \mathsf{c} \cong \mathsf{a} :\!*\!: (\mathsf{b} :\!*\!: \mathsf{c})$$

We assume a set of base types, which may include integers, booleans, strings and so on. For brevity's sake, we mention only integers in our code.

data $\mathsf{UBase} = UInt\ \mathsf{Int} \mid UBool\ \mathsf{Bool} \mid UString\ \mathsf{String} \mid \cdots$

The following two functions merely serve to convert back and forth between the larger world and our little universe of base types.

type $\mathsf{ReduceBase}\{\!\![\star]\!\!\}\ \mathsf{t}$	$=$		$\mathsf{t} \to \mathsf{UBase}$
$reducebase\{\!|\mathsf{t} :: \kappa|\!\}$	$::$		$\mathsf{ReduceBase}\{\!\![\kappa]\!\!\}\ \mathsf{t}$
$reducebase\{\!|\mathsf{Int}|\!\}\ i$	$=$		$UInt\ i$
type $\mathsf{ExpandBase}\{\!\![\star]\!\!\}\ \mathsf{t}$	$=$		$\mathsf{UBase} \to \mathsf{t}$
$expandbase\{\!|\mathsf{t} :: \kappa|\!\}$	$::$		$\mathsf{ExpandBase}\{\!\![\kappa]\!\!\}\ \mathsf{t}$
$expandbase\{\!|\mathsf{Int}|\!\}\ (UInt\ i)$	$=$		i

Now, as Schemers well know, if we ignore the types and remove all occurrences of Unit, a right-associated tuple is simply a cons-list, hence our representation, Univ is defined:

type $\mathsf{Univ} = [\mathsf{UBase}]$.

Our implementation of $reduce\{\!|\mathsf{t}|\!\}$ depends on an auxiliary function $red\{\!|\mathsf{t}|\!\}$, which accepts a value of t along with an accumulating argument of type Univ; it returns the normal form of the t-value with respect to the laws above. The role of $reduce\{\!|\mathsf{t}|\!\}$ is just to prime $red\{\!|\mathsf{t}|\!\}$ with an empty list.

type $\mathsf{Red}\{\!\![\star]\!\!\}\ \mathsf{t}$	$=$	$\mathsf{t} \to \mathsf{Univ} \to \mathsf{Univ}$
$red\{\!|\mathsf{t} :: \kappa|\!\}$	$::$	$\mathsf{Red}\{\!\![\kappa]\!\!\}\ \mathsf{t}$
$red\{\!|\mathsf{Int}|\!\}\ i\ u$	$=$	$reducebase\{\!|\mathsf{Int}|\!\}\ i : u$
$red\{\!|\mathsf{Unit}|\!\}\ ()$	$=$	id
$red\{\!|\mathsf{a} :\!*\!: \mathsf{b}|\!\}\ (a :\!*\!: b)$	$=$	$red\{\!|\mathsf{a}|\!\}\ a \circ red\{\!|\mathsf{b}|\!\}\ b$
$reduce\{\!|\mathsf{t} :: \star|\!\}$	$::$	$\mathsf{t} \to \mathsf{Univ}$
$reduce\{\!|\mathsf{t}|\!\}\ x$	$=$	$red\{\!|\mathsf{t}|\!\}\ x\ [\,]$

Here is an example of $reduce\{\!|t|\!\}$ in action:

$$reduce\{\!|((\mathsf{Int},(\mathsf{Int},\mathsf{Int})),())|\!\}\ ((2,(3,4)),()) = [\,UInt\ 2,\ UInt\ 3,\ UInt\ 4\,]\ .$$

Function $expand\{\!|t|\!\}$ takes a value of the universal data type, and returns a value of type t. It depends on the generic function $len\{\!|t|\!\}$, which computes the length of a product, that is, the number of components of a tuple:

$$
\begin{aligned}
\textbf{type Len}\{\!|\star|\!\}\ \mathsf{t} &= \mathsf{Int} \\
len\{\!|\mathsf{t} :: \kappa|\!\} &:: \mathsf{Len}\{\!|\kappa|\!\}\ \mathsf{t} \\
len\{\!|\mathsf{Int}|\!\} &= 1 \\
len\{\!|\mathsf{Unit}|\!\} &= 0 \\
len\{\!|\mathsf{a} :\!*\!: \mathsf{b}|\!\} &= len\{\!|\mathsf{a}|\!\} + len\{\!|\mathsf{b}|\!\}\ .
\end{aligned}
$$

Observe that Unit is assigned length zero.

Now we can write $expand\{\!|t|\!\}$; like $reduce\{\!|t|\!\}$, it is defined in terms of a helper function $exp\{\!|t|\!\}$, this time in a dual fashion with the 'unparsed' remainder appearing as output.

$$
\begin{aligned}
\textbf{type Exp}\{\!|\star|\!\}\ \mathsf{t} &= \mathsf{Univ} \rightarrow (\mathsf{t}, \mathsf{Univ}) \\
exp\{\!|\mathsf{t} :: \kappa|\!\} &:: \mathsf{Exp}\{\!|\kappa|\!\}\ \mathsf{t} \\
exp\{\!|\mathsf{Int}|\!\}\ (u : us) &= (expandbase\{\!|\mathsf{Int}|\!\}\ u, us) \\
exp\{\!|\mathsf{Int}|\!\}\ [\,] &= error\ \texttt{"exp"} \\
exp\{\!|\mathsf{Unit}|\!\}\ us &= (\mathsf{Unit}, us) \\
exp\{\!|\mathsf{a} :\!*\!: \mathsf{b}|\!\}\ us &= \textbf{let}\ (u, us') = exp\{\!|\mathsf{a}|\!\}\ us \\
&\qquad\quad (v, us'') = exp\{\!|\mathsf{b}|\!\}\ us' \\
&\quad\textbf{in}\ (u :\!*\!: v, us'') \\[4pt]
\textbf{type Expand}\{\!|\star|\!\}\ \mathsf{t} &= \mathsf{Univ} \rightarrow \mathsf{t} \\
expand\{\!|\mathsf{t} :: \kappa|\!\} &:: \mathsf{Expand}\{\!|\kappa|\!\}\ \mathsf{t} \\
expand\{\!|\mathsf{t}|\!\}\ u &= \textbf{case}\ exp\{\!|\mathsf{t}|\!\}\ u\ \textbf{of} \\
&\qquad (v, [\,]) \rightarrow v \\
&\qquad (v, \_) \rightarrow error\ \texttt{"expand"}
\end{aligned}
$$

In the last case, we compute the lengths of each factor of the product to determine how many values to project there – remember that a need not be a base type. This information tells us how to split the list between recursive calls.

Here is an example of $expand\{\!|t|\!\}$ in action:

$$expand\{\!|((\mathsf{Int},(\mathsf{Int},\mathsf{Int})),())|\!\}\ [\,UInt\ 2,\ UInt\ 3,\ UInt\ 4\,] = ((2,(3,4)),())$$

4.2   Handling Sums

We now turn to the treatment of associativity and identity laws for sums:

$$\mathsf{a} :\!+\!: \mathsf{Zero} \cong \mathsf{a} \qquad \mathsf{Zero} :\!+\!: \mathsf{a} \cong \mathsf{a} \qquad (\mathsf{a} :\!+\!: \mathsf{b}) :\!+\!: \mathsf{c} \cong \mathsf{a} :\!+\!: (\mathsf{b} :\!+\!: \mathsf{c})\ .$$

We can implement **Zero** as an abstract type with no (visible) constructors:

data Zero .

As we will be handling sums alone in this section, we redefine the universal type as a right-associated sum of values:

data Univ = $UInl$ UBase | $UInr$ Univ .

Note that this datatype Univ is isomorphic to:

data Univ = UIn Int UBase .

We prefer the latter as it simplifies some definitions. We also add a second integer field:

data Univ = UIn Int Int UBase .

If $u = UIn\ r\ a\ b$ then we shall call a the *arity* of u – it remembers the "width" of the sum value we reduced; we call r the *rank* of u – it denotes a zero-indexed position within the arity, the choice which was made. We guarantee, then, that $0 \leqslant r < a$. Of course, unlike Unit, Zero has no observable values so there is no representation for it in Univ.

UBase, $reducebase\{\!|t|\!\}$ and $expandbase\{\!|t|\!\}$ are defined as before.

This time around, function $reduce\{\!|t|\!\}$ represents values by ignoring choices against Zero and right-associating sums. The examples below show some example inputs and how they are reduced (we write I for Int and u for $UInt\ i$):

i	:: I	$\mapsto$	$UIn\ 0\ 1\ u$
$Inl\ i$	:: I :+: Zero	$\mapsto$	$UIn\ 0\ 1\ u$
$Inr\ i$	:: Zero :+: I	$\mapsto$	$UIn\ 0\ 1\ u$
$Inl\ i$	:: I :+: I	$\mapsto$	$UIn\ 0\ 2\ u$
$Inr\ i$	:: I :+: I	$\mapsto$	$UIn\ 1\ 2\ u$
$Inl\ (Inl\ i)$	:: (I :+: I) :+: I	$\mapsto$	$UIn\ 0\ 3\ u$
$Inl\ (Inr\ i)$	:: (I :+: I) :+: I	$\mapsto$	$UIn\ 1\ 3\ u$
$Inr\ i$	:: (I :+: I) :+: I	$\mapsto$	$UIn\ 2\ 3\ u$

Function $reduce\{\!|t|\!\}$ depends on the generic value $arity\{\!|t|\!\}$, which counts the number of choices in a sum.

type Arity$\{\!|\star|\!\}$ t	=	Int
$arity\{\!|t :: \kappa|\!\}$	::	Arity$\{\!|\kappa|\!\}$ t
$arity\{\!|\text{Int}|\!\}$	=	1
$arity\{\!|\text{Zero}|\!\}$	=	0
$arity\{\!|a :+: b|\!\}$	=	$arity\{\!|a|\!\} + arity\{\!|b|\!\}$

Now we can define $reduce\{|t|\}$:

$$
\begin{array}{lll}
\textbf{type } \mathsf{Reduce}\{|\star|\}\ t & = & t \to \mathsf{Univ} \\
reduce\{|t :: \kappa|\} & :: & \mathsf{Reduce}\{|\kappa|\}\ t \\
reduce\{|\mathsf{Int}|\}\ i & = & UIn\ 0\ 1\ (reducebase\{|\mathsf{Int}|\}\ i) \\
reduce\{|\mathsf{Zero}|\}\ \_ & = & \bot \\
reduce\{|a :+: b|\}\ (Inl\ x) & = & UIn\ r\ (a + arity\{|b|\})\ u \\
\quad \textbf{where } UIn\ r\ a\ u & = & reduce\{|a|\}\ x \\
reduce\{|a :+: b|\}\ (Inr\ x) & = & UIn\ (r + arity\{|a|\})\ (arity\{|a|\} + a)\ u \\
\quad \textbf{where } UIn\ r\ a\ u & = & reduce\{|b|\}\ x\ .
\end{array}
$$

This treats base types as unary sums, and computes the rank of a value by examining the arities of each summand, effectively 'flattening' the sum.

The function $expand\{|t|\}$ is defined as follows:

$$
\begin{array}{lll}
\textbf{type } \mathsf{Expand}\{|\star|\}\ t & = & \mathsf{Univ} \to t \\
expand\{|t :: \kappa|\} & :: & \mathsf{Expand}\{|\kappa|\}\ t \\
expand\{|\mathsf{Int}|\}\ (UIn\ 0\ 1\ u) & = & expandbase\{|\mathsf{Int}|\}\ i \\
expand\{|\mathsf{Zero}|\}\ \_ & = & error\ \texttt{"expand"} \\
expand\{|a :+: b|\}\ (UIn\ r\ a\ u) & & \\
\quad |\ a \equiv aa + ab \wedge r < aa & = & Inl\ (expand\{|a|\}\ (UIn\ r\ (a - ab)\ u)) \\
\quad |\ a \equiv aa + ab & = & Inr\ (expand\{|b|\}\ (UIn\ (r - aa)\ (a - aa)\ u)) \\
\quad |\ otherwise & = & error\ \texttt{"expand"} \\
\quad \textbf{where } (aa, ab) & = & (arity\{|a|\}, arity\{|b|\})\ .
\end{array}
$$

The logic in the last case checks that the universal value 'fits' in the sum type a :+: b, and injects it into the appropriate summand by comparing the value's rank with the arity of a, being sure to adjust the rank and arity on recursive calls.

4.3   Sums and Products Together

It may seem that a difficulty in handling sums and products simultaneously arises in designing the type Univ, as a naïve amalgamation of the sum Univ (call it UnivS) and the product Univ (call it UnivP) permits multiple representations of values identified by the canonical isomorphism relation. However, since the rules of our isomorphism theory do not interact – in particular, we do not account for any sort of distributivity – , a simpler solution exists: we can nest our two representations and add the top layer as a new base type. For example, we can use UnivP in place of UBase in UnivS and add a new constructor to UBase to encapsulate sums.

$$
\begin{array}{lll}
\textbf{data } \mathsf{UnivS} & = & UIn\ \mathsf{Integer}\ \mathsf{UnivP} \\
\textbf{data } \mathsf{UnivP} & = & UNil\ |\ UCons\ \mathsf{UBase}\ \mathsf{UnivP} \\
\textbf{data } \mathsf{UBase} & = & UInt\ \mathsf{Int}\ |\ USum\ \mathsf{UnivS}
\end{array}
$$

We omit the details, as the changes to our code examples are straightforward.

4.4 Handling Coercions

The reader may already have noticed that our expansion functions impose some unnecessary limitations. In particular:

- when we expand to a product, we require that the length of our universal value equals the number computed by $len\{t\}$, and
- when we expand to a sum, we require that the arity of our universal value equals the number computed by $arity\{t\}$.

If we lift these restrictions, replacing equality by inequality, we can project a prefix of a universal value onto a tuple of smaller length, and inject a universal value into a choice of larger arity. The modified definitions are shown below for products:

$$expand\{t\}\ u\ \ =\ \ \textbf{case}\ exp\{t\}\ u\ \textbf{of}$$
$$(v, \_) \rightarrow v$$

and for sums:

$$
\begin{aligned}
&expand\{\text{a} :+: \text{b}\}\ (UIn\ r\ a\ u)\\
&\quad \mid a \leqslant aa + ab \land r < aa &=\ &Inl\ (expand\{\text{a}\}\ (UIn\ r\ (a - ab)\ u))\\
&\quad \mid a \leqslant aa + ab &=\ &Inr\ (expand\{\text{b}\}\ (UIn\ (r - aa)\ (a - aa)\ u))\\
&\quad \mid otherwise &=\ &error\ \texttt{"expand"}\\
&\quad \textbf{where}\ (aa, ab) &=\ &(arity\{\text{a}\}, arity\{\text{b}\})\ .
\end{aligned}
$$

These changes implement our canonical coercions, the first projection of a product and left injection of a sum:

$$\text{a} :*: \text{b} \leqslant \text{a} \qquad\qquad\qquad \text{a} \leqslant \text{a} :+: \text{b}$$

***Ad Hoc* Coercions.** Schema (and most other conventional languages) also defines a subtyping relation between primitive types. For example, `int` is a subtype of `integer` which is a subtype of `decimal`. We can easily model this by (adding some more base types and) modifying the functions which convert base types.

$$
\begin{aligned}
expandbase\{\text{Decimal}\}\ (UDecimal\ x) &=\ x\\
expandbase\{\text{Decimal}\}\ (UInteger\ x) &=\ integer2dec\ x\\
expandbase\{\text{Decimal}\}\ (UInt\ x) &=\ int2dec\ x\\
expandbase\{\text{Integer}\}\ (UInteger\ x) &=\ x\\
expandbase\{\text{Integer}\}\ (UInt\ x) &=\ int2integer\ x\\
expandbase\{\text{Int}\}\ (UInt\ x) &=\ x
\end{aligned}
$$

Such primitive coercions are easy to handle, but without due care are likely to break the coherence properties of inference, so that the inferred coercion depends on operational details of the inference algorithm.

5   Conclusions

In this paper, we have described a simple, powerful and general mechanism for automatically inferring a well-behaved class of isomorphisms, and demonstrated how it addresses some usability problems stemming from the complexity of our Haskell-XML Schema data binding, UUXML. Our mechanism leverages the power of an existing tool, Generic Haskell, and the established and growing theory of type isomorphisms.

We believe that both the general idea of exploiting isomorphisms and our implementation technique have application beyond UUXML. For example, when libraries written by distinct developers are used in the same application, they often include different representations of what amounts to the same datatype. When passing data from one library to the other the data must be converted to conform to each library's internal conventions. Our technique could be used to simplify this conversion task; to make this sort of application practical, though, iso inference should probably be integrated with type inference, and the class of isos inferred should be enlarged. We discuss such possibilities for future work below.

5.1   Related Work

Besides UUXML, we have already mentioned the HaXML [37] and WASH [35] XML data bindings for Haskell. The Model Schema Language semantics [4] is now superseded by newer work [32]; we are investigating how to adapt our encoding to the more recent treatment. Special-purpose languages, such as XSLT [36], XDuce [12], Yatl [6], XMλ [22, 31], SXSLT [13] and Xtatic [9], take a different approach to XML problems.

In computer science, the use of type isomorphisms seem to have been popularized first by Rittri who demonstrated their value in software retrieval tasks, such as searching a software library for functions matching a query type [29]. Since then the area has ballooned; good places to start on the theory of type isomorphisms is Di Cosmo's book [8] and the paper by Bruce et al. [5]. More recent work has focused on linear type isomorphisms [2, 33, 30, 20].

In category theory, Mac Lane initiated the study of coherence in a seminal paper [18]; his book [19] treats the case for monoidal categories. Beylin and Dybjer's use [3] of Mac Lane's coherence theorem influenced our technique here. The strong regularity condition is sufficient for ensuring that an algebraic theory is *cartesian*; cartesian monads have been used by Leinster [15, 14] and Hermida [10] to formalize the notion of generalized multicategory, which generalizes a usual category by imposing an algebraic theory on the objects, and letting the domain of an arrow be a term of that theory.

5.2   Future Work

Schema Matching. In areas like database management and electronic commerce, the plethora of data representation standards – formally, 'schemas' – used to transmit and store data can hinder reuse and data exchange. To deal with this growing problem, 'schema matching', the problem of how to construct a mapping between elements of two schemas, has become an active research area. Because the size, complexity and number of schemas is only increasing, finding ways to accurately and efficiently automate this task has become more and more important; see Rahm and Bernstein [28] for a survey of approaches.

We believe that our approach, which exploits not only the syntax but semantics of types, could provide new insights into schema matching. In particular, the notion of canonical (iso)morphism could help clarify when a mapping's semantics is forced entirely by structural considerations, and when additional information (linguistic, descriptive, *etc.*) is provably required to disambiguate a mapping.

Implicit Coercions. Thatte introduced a declaration construct for introducing user-defined, *implicit* conversions between types [34], using, like us, an equational theory on types. Thatte also presents a principal type inference algorithm for his language, which requires that the equational theory is *unitary*, that is, every unifiable pair of types has a unique most general unifier. To ensure theories be unitary, Thatte demands they be *finite* and *acyclic*, and uses a syntactic condition related to, but different from, strong regularity to ensure finiteness. In Thatte's system, coherence seems to hold if and only if the user-supplied conversions are true inverses.

The relationship between Thatte's system and ours requires further investigation. In some ways Thatte's system is more liberal, allowing for example distributive theories. On the other hand, the unitariness requirement rules out associative theories, which are infinitary. The acyclicity condition also rules out commutative theories, which are not strongly regular, but also the currying iso, which is. Another difference between Thatte's system and ours is that his catches errors at compile-time, while the implementation we presented here does so at run-time. A final difference is that, although the finite acyclicity condition is decidable, the requirement that conversions be invertible is not; consequently, users may introduce declarations which break the coherence property (produce ambiguous programs). In our system, any user-defined conversions are obtained structurally, as datatype isos from datatype declarations, which cannot fail to be canonical; hence it is not possible to break coherence.

The Generic Haskell Implementation. We see several ways to improve our current implementation of iso inference.

- We would like to detect inference errors statically rather than dynamically (see below).
- Inferring more isomorphisms (such as the linear currying isos) and more powerful kinds of isomorphisms (such as commutativity of products and sums, and distributivity of one over the other) is also attractive.
- Currently, adding new *ad hoc* coercions requires editing the source code; since such coercions typically depend on the domain of application, a better approach would be to somehow parametrize the code by them.

– We could exploit the fact that Generic Haskell allows to define type cases on the → type constructor: instead of providing two generic functions $reduce\{|t|\}$ and $expand\{|t|\}$, we would provide only a single generic function:

$$coerce\{|t \rightarrow t'|\} = expand\{|t'|\} \circ reduce\{|t|\} \; .$$

– The fact that the unique witness property does not readily transfer from type schemes to types might be circumvented by inferring first-class polymorphic functions which can then be instantiated at suitable types. Generic Haskell does not currently allow to do so, but if we could write expressions like $coerce\{|\forall a\; b\, . \, (a, b) \rightarrow (b, a)|\}$ we could infer all canonical isos, without restriction, and perhaps handle examples like Date_NL and Date_US from section 1.

Inference Failure. Because our implementation depends on the "universal" type Univ, failure occurs dynamically and a message helpful for pinpointing the error's source is printed. This situation is unsatisfactory, though, since every invocation of the expand and reduce functions together mentions the types involved; in principle, we could detect failures statically, thus increasing program reliability.

Such early detection could also enable new optimizations. For example, if the types involved are not only isomorphic but equal, then the conversion is the identity and a compiler could omit it altogether. But even if the types are only isomorphic, the reduction might not unreasonably be done at compile-time, as our isos are all known to be terminating; this just amounts to adjusting the data representation 'at one end' or the other to match exactly.

We have investigated, but not tested, an approach for static failure detection based on an extension of Generic Haskell's *type-indexed datatypes* [11]. The idea is to introduce a type-indexed datatype NF$\{|t|\}$ which denotes the normal form of type t w.r.t. to the iso theory, and then reformulate our functions so that they are assigned types:

$$
\begin{array}{lcl}
reduce\{|t|\} & :: & t \rightarrow \mathsf{NF}\{|t|\} \\
expand\{|t|\} & :: & \mathsf{NF}\{|t|\} \rightarrow t \; .
\end{array}
$$

For example, considering only products, the type NF$\{|t|\}$ could be defined as follows:

$$
\begin{array}{lcl}
\textbf{type NF}\{|t|\} & = & \mathsf{Norm}\{|t|\}\; \mathsf{Unit} \\
\textbf{data Norm}\{|\mathsf{Unit}|\}\; t & = & NUnit\; t \\
\textbf{data Norm}\{|a :*: b|\}\; t & = & NProd\; (a :*: (b :*: t)) \\
\textbf{data Norm}\{|\mathsf{Int}|\}\; t & = & NBase\; (\mathsf{Int} :*: t) \; .
\end{array}
$$

This would give the GH compiler enough information to reject bad conversion at compile-time.

Unfortunately, the semantics of GH's type-indexed datatypes is too "generative" for this approach to work. The problem is apparent if we try to compile the expression:

$expand\{|Int|\} \circ reduce\{|(Int, ())|\}$.

GH flags this as a type error, because it treats $NF\{|Int|\}$ and $NF\{|(Int, ())|\}$ as distinct (unequal), though structurally identical, datatypes.

A possible solution to this issue may be a recently considered GH extension called *type-indexed types* (as opposed to *type-indexed datatypes*). If $NF\{|t|\}$ is implemented as a type-indexed type, then, like Haskell's type synonyms, structurally identical instances like the ones above will actually be forced to be equal, and the expression above should compile. However, type-indexed types – as currently envisioned – also share the limitations of Haskell's type synonyms w.r.t. recursion; a type-indexed type like $NF\{|List Int|\}$ is likely to cause the compiler to loop as it tries to expand recursive occurrences while traversing the datatype body. Nevertheless, of the several approaches we have considered to addressing the problem of static error detection, type-indexed types seems the most promising.

Acknowledgements

The authors thank Dave Clarke, Bastiaan Heeren and Andres Löh for their comments on this paper, and Eelco Dolstra and Fermin Reig for comments on an earlier version. Tom Leinster kindly clarified some of our questions about cartesian monads and the strong regularity condition. Wouter Swierstra helped investigate approaches to static detection of inference failure.

References

1. Frank Atanassow, Dave Clarke, and Johan Jeuring. Scripting XML with Generic Haskell. In *Proc. 7th Brazilian Symposium on Programming Languages*, 2003. See also Utrecht University technical report UU-CS-2003.
2. Vincent Balat and Roberto Di Cosmo. A linear logical view of linear type isomorphisms. In *CSL*, pages 250–265, 1999.
3. Ilya Beylin and Peter Dybjer. Extracting a proof of coherence for monoidal categories from a proof of normalization for monoids. In *TYPES*, pages 47–61, 1995.
4. Allen Brown, Matthew Fuchs, Jonathan Robie, and Philip Wadler. MSL: A model for W3C XML Schema. In *Proc. WWW10*, May 2001.
5. Kim B. Bruce, Roberto Di Cosmo, and Giuseppe Longo. Provable isomorphisms of types. *Mathematical Structures in Computer Science*, 2(2):231–247, 1992.
6. Sophie Cluet and Jérôme Siméon. YATL: a functional and declarative language for XML, 2000.
7. Jorge Coelho and Mário Florido. Type-based XML processing in logic programming. In *PADL 2003*, pages 273–285, 2003.
8. Roberto Di Cosmo. *Isomorphisms of Types: From lambda-calculus to Information Retrieval and Language Design*. Birkhäuser, 1995.

9. Vladimir Gapeyev and Benjamin C. Pierce. Regular object types. In *European Conference on Object-oriented Programming (ECOOP 2003)*, 2003.
10. C. Hermida. Representable multicategories. *Advances in Mathematics*, 151:164–225, 2000.
11. Ralf Hinze, Johan Jeuring, and Andres Löh. Type-indexed data types. In *Proceedings of the 6th Mathematics of Program Construction Conference, MPC'02*, volume 2386 of *LNCS*, pages 148–174, 2002.
12. Haruo Hosoya and Benjamin C. Pierce. XDuce: A typed XML processing language. In *Third International Workshop on the Web and Databases (WebDB), volume 1997 of Lecture Notes in Computer Science*, pages 226–244, 2000.
13. Oleg Kiselyov and Shriram Krishnamurti. SXSLT: manipulation language for XML. In *PADL 2003*, pages 226–272, 2003.
14. Thomas S.H. Leinster. *Operads in Higher-Dimensional Category Theory*. PhD thesis, Trinity College and St John's College, Cambridge, 2000.
15. Tom Leinster. *Higher Operads, Higher Categories*. Cambridge University Press, 2003.
16. Xavier Leroy et al. *The Objective Caml system release 3.07, Documentation and user's manual*, December 2003. Available from `http://caml.inria.fr/ocaml/htmlman/`.
17. Andres Löh, Dave Clarke, and Johan Jeuring. Dependency-style Generic Haskell. In *Proceedings of the International Conference on Functional Programming (ICFP '03)*, August 2003.
18. Saunders Mac Lane. Natural associativity and commutativity. *Rice University Studies*, 49:28–46, 1963.
19. Saunders Mac Lane. *Categories for the Working Mathematician*, volume 5 of *Graduate Texts in Mathematics*. Springer-Verlag, New York, 2nd edition, 1997. (1st ed., 1971).
20. Bruce McAdam. How to repair type errors automatically. In *Trends in Functional Programming (Proc. Scottish Functional Programming Workshop)*, volume 3, 2001.
21. Brett McLaughlin. *Java & XML data binding*. O'Reilly, 2003.
22. Erik Meijer and Mark Shields. XMLambda: A functional language for constructing and manipulating XML documents. Available from `http://www.cse.ogi.edu/~mbs/`, 1999.
23. Eldon Metz and Allen Brookes. XML data binding. *Dr. Dobb's Journal*, pages 26–36, March 2003.
24. Sun Microsystems. Java Architecture for XML Binding (JAXB). `http://java.sun.com/xml/jaxb/`, 2003.
25. Robin Milner, Mads Tofte, Robert Harper, and David MacQueen. *The Definition of Standard ML (Revised)*. MIT Press, May 1997.
26. Uche Ogbuji. Xml data bindings in python, parts 1 & 2. *xml.com*, 2003. `http://www.xml.com/pub/a/2003/06/11/py-xml.html`.
27. Simon Peyton Jones, John Hughes, et al. Haskell 98 – A non-strict, purely functional language. Available from `http://haskell.org`, February 1999.
28. Erhard Rahm and Philip A. Bernstein. A survey of approaches to automatic schema matching. *VLDB Journal: Very Large Data Bases*, 10(4):334–350, 2001.
29. Mikael Rittri. Retrieving library identifiers via equational matching of types. In *Conference on Automated Deduction*, pages 603–617, 1990.
30. Mikael Rittri. Retrieving library functions by unifying types modulo linear isomorphism. *Informatique Theorique et Applications*, 27(6):523–540, 1993.

31. Mark Shields and Erik Meijer. Type-indexed rows. In *The 28th Annual ACM SIG-PLAN - SIGACT Symposium on Principles of Programming Languages*, pages 261–275, 2001. Also available from http://www.cse.ogi.edu/~mbs/.
32. Jérôme Siméon and Philip Wadler. The essence of XML. In *Proc. POPL 2003*, 2003.
33. Sergei Soloviev. A complete axiom system for isomorphism of types in closed categories. In A. Voronkov, editor, *Proceedings 4th Int. Conf. on Logic Programming and Automated Reasoning, LPAR'93, St. Petersburg, Russia, 13–20 July 1993*, volume 698, pages 360–371. Springer-Verlag, Berlin, 1993.
34. Satish R. Thatte. Coercive type isomorphism. In *Proceedings of the 5th ACM conference on Functional programming languages and computer architecture*, volume 523 of *LNCS*, pages 29–49. Springer-Verlag New York, Inc., 1991.
35. Peter Thiemann. A typed representation for HTML and XML documents in Haskell. *Journal of Functional Programming*, 12(4&5):435–468, July 2002.
36. W3C. XSL Transformations 1.0. http://www.w3.org/TR/xslt, 1999.
37. Malcolm Wallace and Colin Runciman. Haskell and XML: Generic combinators or type-based translation? In *International Conference on Functional Programming*, pages 148–159, 1999.

Friends Need a Bit More:
Maintaining Invariants Over Shared State

Mike Barnett [1] and David A. Naumann [2, *]

[1] Microsoft Research
mbarnett@microsoft.com
[2] Stevens Institute of Technology
naumann@cs.stevens-tech.edu

Abstract. In the context of a formal programming methodology and verification system for ownership-based invariants in object-oriented programs, a *friendship* system is defined. Friendship is a flexible protocol that allows invariants expressed over shared state. Such invariants are more expressive than those allowed in exisiting ownership type systems because they link objects that are not in the same ownership domain. Friendship permits the modular verification of cooperating classes. This paper defines friendship, sketches a soundness proof, and provides several realistic examples.

1 Introduction

Whether they are implicit or explicit, object invariants are an important part of object-oriented programming. An object's invariant is, in general, a *healthiness* guarantee that the object is in a "good" state, i.e., a valid state for calling methods on it.

For example, in a base class library for collection types, certain method calls may be made on an enumerator only if the underlying collection has not been modified since the enumerator was created. Other examples are that a graph remains acyclic or that an array stays sorted.

Various proposals have been made on how object invariants can be formally expressed and on different mechanisms for either guaranteeing that such invariants hold [LN02, LG86, Mül02] or at least dynamically recognizing moments in execution where they fail to hold [BS03, CL02, Mey97]. For the most part, these systems require some kind of partitioning of heap objects so that an object's invariant depends only on those objects over which it has direct control. This is intuitive, since it is risky for one data structure to depend on another over which it has no control. However, systems such as *ownership types* [CNP01, Cla01, BLS03, Mül02] are inflexible in that they demand object graphs to be hierarchically partitionable so that the dependencies induced by object invariants do not cross ownership boundaries. There are many situations where an object depends on another object but cannot reasonably own it.

We relax these restrictions with a new methodology; we define a protocol by which a *granting class* can give privileges to another *friend class* that allows the invariant

* Partially supported by the National Science Foundation under grants CCR-0208984 and CCR-ITR-0326540, the Office of Naval Research under grant N00014-01-1-0837, and Microsoft Research, Redmond, WA.

D. Kozen (Ed.): MPC 2004, LNCS 3125, pp. 54–84, 2004.

in the friend class to depend on fields in the granting class. As in real life, friendship demands the active cooperation of both parties. A friend class can publish restrictions on field updates of the granting class. The granting class must be willing to operate within these restrictions. In return, each instance of the friend class must register itself with the instance of the granting class that it is dependent on. And as in real life, the quality of the friendship depends on how onerous its burdens are. We believe our system imposes a minimal set of constraints on the participating parties.

Our method builds on ownership-based invariants [BDF$^+$03a], formalized using an auxiliary field *owner* [LM04]. We refer to the combination of [BDF$^+$03a] and [LM04] as the *Boogie methodology*. An on-going project at Microsoft Research named "Boogie" is building a tool based on that methodology. To make this paper self-contained, we review the relevant features of the object invariant system from that work in Section 2.

Section 3 presents a representative example of an instance of a granting class performing a field update that could violate the invariant of an instance of a friend class. We describe the required proof obligations for the granting object to perform the field update without violating the invariants of its friends or the object invariant system. In Section 3.1, we describe how a granting class declares which classes are its friends and how granting objects track friends that are dependent upon it. Section 3.2 describes how a granting object sees an abstraction of the invariants of its friends, rather than the full details. In Section 3.3, we define the obligations incumbent upon the friend class for notifying granting objects of the dependence. Section 3.4 summarizes all of the features of our method.

Section 4 provides a sketch of a soundness argument. Section 5 describes two extensions. The first, in Section 5.1, presents a convenient methodology that shows how reasoning about dependents can be linked to the code of the granting class. In Section 5.2, we describe a syntactic means for transmitting information after a field update back to the granting object from a friend object. We give several challenging examples in Section 6. Section 7 reviews related work and Section 8 summarizes our contribution and points out future work.

We assume some familiarity with the principles of object-oriented programming and the basics of assertions (pre- and post-conditions, modifies clause, and invariants) as well as their use in the static modular verification of sequential object-oriented programs. However, we do not presuppose any particular verification technology.

For simplicity, we omit any description of subtyping. The full treatment is described in a forthcoming technical report; it follows the same pattern as the Boogie work [BDF$^+$03a]. A companion paper [NB04] gives a rigorous proof of soundness in a semantic model. The concrete syntax that we use is not definitive and illustrates one particular encoding.

2   Using Auxiliary Fields for Ownership-Based Invariants: A Review

Using the contrived example code in Figure 1 we review the Boogie approach to invariants and ownership. In our illustrative object-oriented language, class types are implicitly reference types; we use the term "object" to mean object reference.

```
class Set {                              class Node {
    fst : Node := null;                      val : int
    insert(x : int)´                         next : Node
    {                                        Node(x : int)
        t : Node := new Node(x);             {val := x; next := null}
        "code to insert t"               }
    }                                    class Fun {
    remove(x : int)                          apply(x : int) : int
    {"delete first node with val x" }        { return x mod 7; }
    map(g : Fun)                         }
    {"apply g to all elements; remove duplicates"}
}
```

Fig. 1. A set of integers is represented by a linked list, without duplicate values, rooted at fst. Method $insert$ adds an element if not already present. Method $map(g)$ updates the set to be its image through $g.apply$. Class $Node$ has only a constructor; nodes are manipulated in Set.

An instance of class Set maintains an integer set represented by a sequence without duplicates, so that $remove(x)$ can be implemented using a linear search that terminates as soon as x is found. The specification of class Set could include invariant

Inv_{Set} : fst is the root of an acyclic sequence without duplicate values.

We denote the invariant for a class T by Inv_T. Note that since the invariant mentions instance fields, it is parameterized by an instance of type T. We write $Inv_T(o)$ where o is an object of type T when we want to make explicit the value of an invariant for a particular instance.

An object invariant is typically conceived as a pre- and post-condition for every method of the class. For example, if $remove(x)$ is invoked in a state where there are duplicates, it may fail to establish the intended postcondition that x is not in the set. Constructors establish invariants.

The method map takes the function supplied as an argument and, abstractly, maps the function over the set to yield an updated set. Suppose it is implemented by first updating all of the values in place and only after that removing duplicates to re-establish the invariant. One difficulty in maintaining object invariants is the possibility of reentrant calls: If an object g has access to the instance s on which $s.map(g)$ is invoked, then within the resulting call to $g.apply$ there could be an invocation of $s.remove$. But s at that point is in an inconsistent state – i.e., a state in which $Inv_{Set}(s)$ does not hold. It is true that by considering the body of $apply$ as given in Figure 1 we can rule out this possibility. But for modular reasoning about Set we would only have a specification for $apply$ – quite likely an incomplete one. (Also, Fun could have been written as an interface; or $apply$ can be overridden in a subclass of Fun.)

A sound way to prevent the problem of re-entrance is for the invariant to be an *explicit* precondition and postcondition for every method: $apply$ would be required to establish $Inv_{Set}(s)$ before invoking $s.remove$, and it cannot do so in our scenario. But this solution violates the principle of information hiding: Using *Node* and maintaining Inv_{Set} are both decisions that might be changed in a revision of *Set* (or in a subclass). Indeed, we might want the field *fst* to be private to *Set* whereas the precondition of a public method should mention only visible fields.

It is possible to maintain proper encapsulation by making it the responsibility of *Set* to ensure that its invariant hold at *every* "observable state", not only at the beginning and end of every method but also before any "out" call is made from within a method. In the example, *Set* would have to establish $Inv_{Set}(s)$ within *map* before each call to *apply*. Though frequently proposed, this solution is overly restrictive. For instance, it would disallow the sketched implementation of *map* in which removal of duplicates is performed only after all the calls to *apply*. In a well structured program with hierarchical abstractions there are many calls "out" from an encapsulation unit, most of which do not lead to reentrant callbacks.

Programmers often guard against reentrant calls using a "call in progress" field; this field can be explicitly mentioned in method specifications. In some respects this is similar to a lock bit for mutual exclusion in a concurrent setting. Disallowing a call to *remove* while a call to *map* is in progress can be seen as a protocol and it can be useful to specify allowed sequences of method invocations [DF01, DF03].

We wish to allow reentrant calls. They are useful, for example, in the ubiquitous Subject-View pattern where a reentrant callback is used by a View to inspect the state of its Subject. On the other hand, general machinery for call protocols seems onerous for dealing with object invariants in sequential programs. Moreover this is complicated by subclassing: a method added in a subclass has no superclass specification to be held to.

Boogie associates a boolean field *inv* with the object invariant. This association is realized in the following *program invariant*, a condition that holds in *every* state. (That is, at every control point in the program text.)

$$(\forall o \bullet o.inv \ \Rightarrow \ Inv_T(o) \quad \text{where } T = \textbf{type}(o) \ ) \tag{1}$$

Here and throughout the paper, quantification ranges over objects allocated in the current state. The dynamic (allocated) class of o is written $\textbf{type}(o)$. Also, logical connectives (such as conjunction) should not be assumed to be commutative since we often write expressions such as $o \neq \textbf{null} \ \wedge \ o.f = \ldots$ where the right-hand conjunct has a meaning only if the left-hand side is true.

As part of the methodology to ensure that (1) is in fact a program invariant, we stipulate that the auxiliary field *inv* may only be used in specifications and in special statements **pack** and **unpack**. If the methods of *Set* all require *inv* as precondition, then *apply* is prevented from invoking *s.remove* as in the first solution above – but without exposing Inv_{Set} in a public precondition. Nevertheless, the body of *remove* can be verified under precondition Inv_{Set} owing to precondition *inv* and program invariant (1).

The special statements **pack** and **unpack** enforce a discipline to ensure that (1) holds in every state. Packing an object sets *inv* to **true**; it requires that the object's invariant holds. Unpacking an object sets *inv* to **false**. Since an update to some field *o.f* could falsify the invariant of o, we require that each update be preceded by **assert** $\neg o.inv$.

The details are deferred so we can turn attention to another issue raised by the example, namely representation exposure. The nodes reached from $Set.fst$ are intended to comprise an encapsulated data structure, but even if fst is declared private there is a risk that node references are *leaked*: e.g., some client of a set s could change the value in a node and thereby falsify the invariant. Representation exposure due to shared objects has received considerable attention [LN02, BN02a], including ownership type systems [Mül02, CD02, BLS03] and Separation Logic [OYR04]. In large part these works are motivated by a notion of *ownership*: the $Nodes$ reached from $s.fst$, on which $Inv_{Set}(s)$ depends, are owned by that instance s and should not be accessed except by s. This ensures that the invariant of s is maintained so long as methods of Set maintain it.

With the exception of Separation Logic, which does not yet deal with object-oriented programs, the cited works suffer from inflexibility due to the conservatism necessary for static enforcement of alias confinement. For example, type systems have difficulty with transferring ownership. However, transfer is necessary in many real-world examples and state encapsulation does not necessarily entail a fixed ownership relation. (This is emphasized in [OYR04, BN03].)

A more flexible representation of ownership can be achieved using auxiliary fields $owner$ and $comm$ in the way proposed by Barnett *et al.*[BDF[+]03a] and refined by Leino and Müller [LM04]. The field $owner$, of type $Object$, designates the owner, or **null** if there is no owner. The boolean field $comm$ designates whether the object is currently *committed to* its owner: if it is true, then its invariant holds and its owner is depending on having sole access for modifying it. The latter is true whenever the owner, o, sets its own inv bit, $o.inv$. Since o's invariant may depend on the objects that it owns, it cannot guarantee its invariant unless no other object can update any object p where $p.owner = o$, or where p is a transitively owned object. There are two associated program invariants. The first is that $o.inv$ implies that every object p owned by o is committed.

$$(\forall o \bullet o.inv \Rightarrow (\forall p \bullet p.owner = o \Rightarrow p.comm)) \tag{2}$$

The second ties commitment to invariants:

$$(\forall o \bullet o.comm \Rightarrow o.inv) \tag{3}$$

The special fields $inv, comm, owner$ are allowed in pre- and post-conditions; only $owner$ is allowed to occur in object invariants. A consequence is that in a state where o transitively owns p, we have $o.inv \Rightarrow p.comm$.

The point of ownership is to constrain the dependence of invariants and to encapsulate the objects on which an invariant Inv_T depends so that it cannot be falsified except by methods of T.

Definition 1 (admissible object invariant). *An* admissible object invariant $Inv_T(o)$ *is one such that in any state, if* $Inv_T(o)$ *depends on some object field* $p.f$ *in the sense that update of* $p.f$ *can falsify* $Inv_T(o)$, *then either*

- $p = o$ *(this means that* **this**.f *is in the formula for* Inv_T *); or*
- p *is transitively owned by* o.

Moreover, Inv_T is not falsifiable by creation of new objects.

Transitive ownership is inductively defined to mean that either $p.owner = o$ or that $p.owner$ is transitively owned by o.

Creation of a new object can falsify a predicate by extending the range of a quantification. For example, the predicate $(\forall p \bullet p = o)$ asserts that o is the only object and is falsifiable by creation of new objects. It would be difficult to maintain (1) for this predicate without impractical restrictions on **new**. A quantification ranging over owned objects, i.e., of the form

$$(\forall p \mid p.owner = o \bullet \ldots)$$

is not falsifiable by creation of new objects, because the *owner* field of a new object is **null** [1].

Remarkably, f in the Definition is allowed to be public, though for information hiding it is often best for it to be private or protected. The ownership discipline makes it impossible for an object to update a public field of another object in a way that violates invariants. But no restriction is imposed on reading.

Aside 1 *The methodology handles situations where an object owns others that it does not directly reference, e.g., nodes in a linked list. But a common situation is direct reference like field fst. To cater for this, it is possible to introduce a syntactic marker* **rep** *on a field, to designate that its value is owned. It is not difficult to devise annotation rules to maintain the associated program invariant*

$$(\forall o \bullet o.inv \wedge o.f \neq \textbf{null} \Rightarrow o.f.owner = o)$$

for every **rep** *field f. On the other hand, one can simply include "***this**.f = **null** $\vee$ **this**.f.owner = o *" as a conjunct of the invariant, so in this paper we omit this feature. A similar feature is to mark a field f as* **peer***, to maintain the invariant* **this**.f = **null** $\vee$ **this**.f.owner = **this**.owner *[LM04]. Again, it is useful but does not solve the problems addressed in this paper and is subsumed under our proposal.*

The program invariants hold in every state – loosely put, "at every semicolon" – provided that field updates to the field f, with expressions E and D, are annotated as

$$\textbf{assert } \neg E.inv; \qquad (4)$$
$$E.f := D;$$

and the special fields inv, $comm$, and $owner$ are updated only by the special statements defined below. Most important are the special statements for inv and $comm$ [2].

---

[1] Leino and Müller [LM04] intended, but omitted to say in their definition of admissibility, that quantifications over objects must have this form. We prefer a semantic formulation, for calculational flexibility and because it highlights what is needed in the soundness proof for the case of **new**.

[2] Note that the "**foreach**" statement in **unpack** updates the auxiliary field $comm$ of an unbounded number of objects. An equivalent expression, more in the flavor of a specification statement in which the field $comm$ is viewed as an array indexed by objects, is this: **change** $comm$ **such that** $(\forall p \bullet p.comm \equiv (old(p.comm) \wedge p.owner \neq E))$.

The statement **unpack** E makes object E susceptible to update; **pack** E does the reverse, re-asserting the invariant for E.

unpack E	$\equiv$	**assert** $E \neq$ **null** $\wedge\ E.inv \wedge \neg E.comm$;
		$E.inv :=$ **false**;
		foreach p **such that** $p.owner = E$ **do** $p.comm :=$ **false**;
pack E	$\equiv$	**assert** $E \neq$ **null** $\wedge\ \neg E.inv \wedge Inv_T(E)$
		$\wedge\ (\forall p \bullet\ p.owner = E \Rightarrow \neg p.comm \wedge p.inv\ )$;
		foreach p **such that** $p.owner = E$ **do** $p.comm :=$ **true**;
		$E.inv :=$ **true**;

Proofs that **pack** and **unpack** maintain the program invariants (1), (2), and (3) can be found in [BDF$^+$03a] and [NB04]. Let us consider how (4) maintains (1). An admissible invariant for an object o depends only on objects owned by o and thus can only be falsified by update of the field of such an object. But an update of $p.f$ is only allowed if $\neg p.inv$. If p is owned by o then $\neg p.inv$ can only be achieved by unpacking p, which can only be done if p is not committed. But to un-commit p requires unpacking o – and then, since $\neg o.inv$, there is no requirement for $Inv_T(o)$ to hold.

The special statements **pack** and **unpack** effectively impose a hierarchical discipline of ownership, consistent with the dependence of invariants on transitively owned objects. Because the discipline is imposed in terms of auxiliary state and verification conditions rather than as an invariant enforced by a static typing system [Mül02, Cla01, BLS03, BN02a], the temporary violations permitted by **pack** and **unpack** offer great flexibility.

Every constructor begins implicitly with initialization

$$inv, comm, owner := \textbf{false}, \textbf{false}, \textbf{null}.$$

which means that constructors do not need to unpack before assigning to fields.

The last of the special statements is used to update *owner*.

set-owner E **to** D	$\equiv$	**assert** $E \neq$ **null** $\wedge\ \neg E.inv \wedge (D =$ **null** $\vee \neg D.inv)$;
		$E.owner := D$;

At first glance it might appear that the precondition $E.owner =$ **null** $\vee \neg E.owner.inv$ is needed as well, but for non-null $E.owner$, we get $\neg E.owner.inv$ from $\neg E.inv$ by the program invariants.

A cycle of ownership can be made using **set-owner**, but the precondition for **pack** cannot be established for an object in such a cycle.

One of the strengths of this approach to ownership is that **set-owner** can be used to transfer ownership as well as to initialize it (see the example in Section 6.3). Another strength is the way invariants may be declared at every level of an inheritance chain; we have simplified those few parts of the methodology which are concerned with subclassing. The reader may refer to the previous papers [BDF$^+$03a, LM04] for more discussion.

3   The Problem: Objects without Borders

The Boogie methodology is adequate for the maintenance of ownership-based invariants. Such invariants are over objects within a single domain, i.e., encapsulated by the ownership boundary. Our contribution in this paper, summarized in Section 3.4, is to go beyond ownership to cooperating objects, ones whose invariants "cross the border".

We use the code in Fig. 2 as our running example. It uses standard specification constructs for method pre-conditions and post-conditions and class invariants. The in-

```
class Master {                          class Clock {
    time : int;                             t : int;
    invariant 0 ≤ time;                     m : Master;
    Master()                                invariant m ≠ null ∧ 0 ≤ t ≤ m.time;
        ensures inv ∧ ¬comm;                Clock(mast : Master)
    { time := 0; pack this; }                   requires mast ≠ null ∧ mast.inv;
    Tick(n : int)                               ensures inv ∧ ¬comm;
        requires inv ∧ ¬comm ∧ 0 ≤ n;       { m := mast; t := 0; pack this; }
        modifies time;                      Sync()
        ensures time ≥ old(time);               requires inv ∧ ¬comm;
    {                                           modifies t;
        unpack this;                            ensures t = m.time;
        time := time + n;                   { unpack this; t := m.time; pack this; }
        pack this;                          }
    }
}
```

Fig. 2. A simple system for clocks synchronized with a master clock. $Inv_{Clock}(\mathbf{this})$ depends on $\mathbf{this}.m.time$ but does not own $\mathbf{this}.m$.

variant $0 \leq time$ in class $Master$ abbreviates $0 \leq \mathbf{this}.time$. Thus, by our notational convention, $Inv_{Master}(o)$ denotes $0 \leq o.time$. According to the rules for admissible invariants in Section 2, Inv_{Master} is allowed.

The constructor for $Master$ exemplifies the usual pattern for constructors: it first initializes the fields in order to establish the invariant and then uses **pack** to set the inv bit. Methods that update state typically first execute **unpack** to turn off the inv bit and then are free to modify field values. Before they return, they use **pack** once their invariant has been reestablished.

The predicate Inv_{Clock} is not an admissible invariant: it depends on $m.time$, but a clock does not own its master. Otherwise a master could not be associated with more than one clock. While it might be reasonable to let the master own the clocks that point to it, we wish to address situations where this ownership relation would not be suitable. More to the point, such a solution would only allow Inv_{Master} to depend on the clocks whereas we want Inv_{Clock} to depend on the master.

Although Inv_{Clock} is not admissible according to Definition 1, the update of $time$ in $Tick$ increases the value of $time$, which cannot falsify Inv_{Clock}. The problem that our methodology solves is to allow non-ownership dependence in a situation like this, i.e., to support modular reasoning about the cooperative relationship wherein $Tick$ does not violate Inv_{Clock}.

However, while $Tick$ is a safe method in relation to Inv_{Clock}, we want to preclude the class $Master$ from defining a method $Reset$:

$$Reset()$$
$$\textbf{requires } inv;$$
$$\textbf{modifies } time;$$
$$\{\ \textbf{unpack this};\ time := 0;\ \textbf{pack this};\ \}$$

This is easily shown correct in terms of Inv_{Master}, but $o.Reset$ can falsify the invariant of any clock c with $c.m = o$. If we allow Inv_{Clock} to depend on $m.time$ and yet prevent this error, a precondition stronger than that in (4) must be used for field update.

In Section 5.1, we show how $Reset$ can be correctly programmed without violating the invariant of $Clock$. For now, we continue to focus on the assignment to $time$ as motivation for a methodology that justifies the code in Figure 2.

Leino and Müller's discipline [LM04], strengthens (4) to yield the following annotation:

$$\textbf{assert } \neg\textbf{this}.inv \land (\forall p \mid \textbf{type}(p) = Clock \bullet \neg p.inv\ );$$
$$\textbf{this}.time := 0;$$

Unfortunately, this does not seem to be a very practical solution. How can modular specifications and reasoning about an arbitrary instance of $Master$ hope to establish a predicate concerning all clocks whatsoever, even in the unlikely event that the predicate is true? Given the ownership system, it is also unlikely that an instance of $Master$ would be able to **unpack** any clock that refers to it via its m field and whose inv field was true.

Consider taking what appears to be a step backwards, concerning the Boogie methodology. We could weaken the annotation in the preceding paragraph to allow the master to perform the field update to $time$ as long as it does not invalidate the invariants of any clocks that could possibly be referring to it.

$$\textbf{assert } \neg\textbf{this}.inv \land$$
$$(\forall p \mid \textbf{type}(p) = Clock \bullet \neg p.inv \lor (Inv_{Clock}(p))_0^{\textbf{this}.time}\ );$$
$$\textbf{this}.time := 0;$$

The substitution expression P_E^x represents the expression P with all unbound occurrences of x replaced by E, with renaming as necessary to prevent name capture. We use substitution to express the weakest precondition and assume that aliasing is handled correctly[3]. But the revised precondition does not appear to provide any benefit: while $\neg\textbf{this}.inv$ is established by the preceding **unpack** in $Reset$, there is still no clear

---

[3] Substitution for updates of object fields can be formalized in a number of ways and the technical details are not germane in this paper [AO97, FLL⁺ 02, PdB03]. In general, object update has a global effect, and our aim is to achieve sound localized reasoning about such updates.

way to establish either of the disjuncts for arbitrary instances p of $Clock$. In addition, as stated, this proposal has the flaw that it exposes Inv_{Clock} outside of class $Clock$.

We solve both of these problems. Given the following general scheme:

$$\textbf{assert } \neg E.inv \wedge (\forall p, T \mid \ldots \bullet \neg p.inv \vee (Inv_T(p))_D^{E.f}); \tag{5}$$
$$E.f := D;$$

where the missing condition "$\ldots$" somehow expresses that $\textbf{type}(p) = T$ and $Inv_T(p)$ depends on E, our methodology provides a way to manage the range of p and a way to abstract from $(Inv_T(p))_D^{E.f}$.

In the following three subsections we first deal with restricting the range of p in (5). Then we show how to abstract from $(Inv_T(p))_D^{E.f}$ in (5) to achieve class-oriented information hiding. Finally we complete the story about the range of p and redefine admissible invariants.

3.1   Representing Dependence

The first problem is to determine which objects p have $Inv_{Clock}(p)$ dependent on a given instance of $Master$. (In general, there could be other classes with invariants that depend on instances of $Master$, further extending the range of p needed for soundness.) To allow for intentional cooperation, we introduce an explicit *friend declaration*

$$\textbf{friend } Clock \textbf{ reads } time;$$

in class $Master$ [4]. For a friend declaration appearing in class T':

$$\textbf{friend } T \textbf{ reads } f;$$

we say T' is the *granting* class and T the *friend*. Field f is visible in code and specifications in class T. (Read access is sufficient.) There are some technical restrictions on f listed in Section 3.4. When $Inv_T(p)$ depends on $o.f$ for some granting object o, then o is reachable from p. For simplicity in this paper, we confine attention to paths of length one, so $o = p.g$ for some field g which we call a *pivot field*. (We also allow $p.g.f.h$ in $Inv_T(p)$, where h is an immutable field of f, e.g., the length of an array.)

One of the benefits of our methodology is to facilitate the decentralized formulation of invariants which lessens the need for paths in invariants. An example is the condition linking adjacent nodes in a doubly-linked list: reachability is needed if this is an invariant of the list header, but we can maintain the invariant by imposing a local invariant on each node that refers only to its successor node; see the example in Section 6.3.

To further restrict the range of p in (5) to relevant friends, we could explore more complicated syntactic conditions, but with predictable limitations due to static analysis. We choose instead to use auxiliary state to track which friend instances are susceptible to having their invariants falsified by update of fields of a granting object.

We introduce an auxiliary field $deps$ of type "set of object". We will arrange that for any o in any state, $o.deps$ contains all p such that $p.g = o$ for some pivot field g

---

[4] Similar features are found in languages including C++ and C#, and in the Leino-Müller work.

by which $Inv(p)$ depends as friend on some field of o. As with $owner$, this facilitates making explicit the relevant program invariants. Both $owner$ and $deps$ function as "back pointers" in the opposite direction of a dependence.

The associated program invariant is roughly this:

$$(\forall o : T' \bullet (\forall p : T \mid p.inv \wedge \text{"}Inv_T(p) \text{ depends on } o.f\text{"} \bullet p \in o.deps)) \quad (6)$$

for every T, T' such that T is a friend of T' reading f. It should become clear later, when we define admissibility for invariants, that dependence happens via a pivot field.

It is not necessary for $o.deps$ to contain $only$ the objects p such that $Inv_T(p)$ depends on $o.f$.

We have reached the penultimate version of the rule for update of a field with friend dependents:

$$\textbf{assert } \neg E.inv \wedge (\forall p \mid p \in E.deps \bullet \neg p.inv \vee (Inv_{\textbf{type}(p)}(p))_D^{E.f}); \quad (7)$$
$$E.f := D;$$

A friend declaration could trigger a requirement that field updates in the granting class be guarded as in (7) and one could argue that in return for visibility of f in T, Inv_T should simply be visible in T'. This is essentially to say that the two classes are in a single module. Our methodology facilitates more hiding of information than that, while allowing cooperation and dealing with the problem of the range of p in (7). In the next subsection we eliminate the exposure of Inv in this rule, and then in the following subsection we deal with reasoning about $deps$.

3.2   Abstracting from the Friend's Invariant

Our solution is to abstract from $(Inv_T)_D^{E.f}$ not as an auxiliary field but as a predicate U (for $update\ guard$). The predicate U is declared in class T, and there it gives rise to a proof obligation, roughly this: if both the friend object's invariant holds and the update guard holds, then the assignment statement will not violate the friend object's invariant. This predicate plays a role in the interface specification of class T, describing not an operation provided by T but rather the effect on T of operations elsewhere. There is a resemblance to behavioral assumptions in Rely-Guarantee reasoning for concurrent programs [Jon83, dRdBH+01].

In the friend class T it is the pivot field g and the friend field f that are visible, not the expressions E and D in an update that occurs in the code of the granting class T'. So, in order to define the update guard we introduce a special variable, $\textbf{val}$, to represent the value the field is being assigned:

$$\textbf{guard } g.f := \textbf{val by } U(\textbf{this}, g, \textbf{val});$$

This construct appears in the friend class and must be expressed in terms that are visible to the granting class (thus allowing the friend class to hide its private information). We write $U(friend, granter, val)$ to make the parameters explicit. That is, U is defined in the context of T using vocabulary $(\textbf{this}, g, \textbf{val})$ but instantiated by the triple

(p, E, D) at the update site in a granter method (see (7) and below). For example, the update guard declared in the friend class *Clock* is:

$$\textbf{guard } m.time := \textbf{val by } m.time \leq \textbf{val};$$

Thus $U_{Clock}(\textbf{this}, m, \textbf{val}) \equiv (m.time \leq \textbf{val})$. Notice that **this** does not appear in this particular update guard. That is because, as stated earlier, it does not depend on the state of the instance of *Clock*.

Like a method declaration, an update guard declaration imposes a proof obligation. The obligations on the friend class T are:

$$Inv_T(\textbf{this}) \wedge U(\textbf{this}, g, \textbf{val}) \Rightarrow (Inv_T(\textbf{this}))_{\textbf{val}}^{g.f} \tag{8}$$

for each pivot g of type T' and friend field f. A suitable default is to take U to be **false** so that the proof obligation is vacuous. Then the update rule is equivalent to that in [LM04]. At the other extreme, if, despite the declarations, *Inv* does not in fact depend on the pivot then U can be taken to be **true**.

We have now reached the final version of the rule for update of a friend field:

$$\begin{aligned} &\textbf{assert } \neg E.inv \wedge (\forall p \mid p \in E.deps \bullet \neg p.inv \vee U(p, E, D));\\ &E.f := D; \end{aligned} \tag{9}$$

We are now in a position that a field update may be performed without violating the invariants of an object's friends by establishing the precondition

$$(\forall p \mid p \in E.deps \bullet \neg p.inv \vee U(p, E, D))$$

where U was written by the author of the class T in such a way that the class T' is able to (at least potentially) satisfy it. That is, it is an expression containing values and variables that are accessible in the context of T' and need not involve the private implementation details of T.

In the design of class T, some state variables may be introduced and made visible to T' precisely in order to express U, without revealing too much of the internal representation of T. We pursue this further in Section 5.2.

For the clock example, $U_{Clock}(p, \textbf{this}, time + n) = (time \leq time + n)$ which follows easily from precondition $0 \leq n$ of method *Tick*; thus the update precondition can be established independent from any reasoning about *deps*. On the other hand, within the method *Reset*, $U_{Clock}(p, \textbf{this}, 0) = (time \leq 0)$ which does not follow from $p \in \textbf{this}.deps$ and the precondition given for *Reset*.

Reset should only be allowed if no clocks depend on this master, which would follow from $deps = \emptyset$ according to program invariant (6). We show our discipline for reasoning about *deps* in the next subsection.

3.3 Notification of Dependence

To maintain program invariant (6) we force each friend object to register itself with the granting object in order to include itself in the granting object's *deps* field. Definition 2 of admissibility in Section 3.4 requires that Inv_T satisfies the following, for each pivot field g:

$$Inv_T(\textbf{this}) \;\Rightarrow\; g = \textbf{null} \;\vee\; \textbf{this} \in g.deps \qquad\qquad (10)$$

One way to satisfy (10) is to add $g = \textbf{null} \vee \textbf{this} \in g.deps$ as a conjunct of Inv_T.

We allow the field $deps$ to be updated only by the special statements **attach** and **detach** which add and remove an object from $\textbf{this}.deps$.

$$
\begin{aligned}
\textbf{attach } E \;&\equiv\; \textbf{assert } E \neq \textbf{null} \wedge \neg inv; \\
& deps := deps \cup \{E\}; \\[2mm]
\textbf{detach } E \;&\equiv\; \textbf{assert } E \neq \textbf{null} \wedge \neg E.inv \wedge \neg inv; \\
& deps := deps - \{E\};
\end{aligned}
$$

The attach and detach statements are allowed only in the code of the class T' where T' declares T to be a friend; their effect is to update $\textbf{this}.deps$. It is in code of T' that we need to reason about $deps$ and thus to use **attach**. This means that it is incumbent upon a friend to call some method in the granter when setting a pivot field to refer to the granter. This gives the granter a chance to either record the identity of the dependent (see the Subject/View example in Section 6.1) or to change some other data structure to reflect the fact that the dependent has registered itself (as in the Clock example, completed in Section 3.4).

Aside 2 *One could imagine that attachment is triggered automatically by the assignment in a dependent to its pivot field. It is possible to work out such a system but it has the flaw that the granter is not given a chance to establish and maintain invariants about* deps*. Also, the conjunct* $\neg E.inv$ *in the precondition to* **detach** *is stronger than necessary. The alternative is to require either that* E *is unpacked or that it no longer has its pivot field referring to* **this**, *but that would require the granter to know more about the pivot fields in its friends than we would like. In [NB04], we formulate the detach statement with the weaker pre-condition.*

3.4 Summary

To summarize the required annotations and program invariants, we begin with our original example from Figure 2 and rewrite it as shown in Figure 3. The two invariant declarations in $Clock$ are conjoined to be the invariant for the class. In the constructor for $Clock$, t must be initialized to zero and the call to $m.Connect$ must occur in order to satisfy the class invariant before calling **pack**. Note that Inv_{Clock} now satisfies (10) owing to the conjunct $\textbf{this} \in m.deps$. This conjunct is established in the constructor by the invocation $m.Connect(\textbf{this})$. In this case, $Connect$ is needed only for reasoning. In most friendship situations the granter needs some method for registering friends in order to maintain more information about them. For example, only when the $Master$ class maintains concrete program state about each object in its $deps$ field is it possible to introduce the $Reset$ method, see Section 5.1. All of the examples shown in Section 6 also show this pattern.

```
class Master {                          class Clock {
    time : int;                             t : int;
    invariant 0 ≤ time;                     m : Master;
    friend Clock reads time;                invariant m ≠ null ∧ 0 ≤ t ≤ m.time;
    Master()                                invariant this ∈ m.deps;
        ensures inv ∧ ¬comm;                guard m.time := val by m.time ≤ val;
    { time := 0; pack this; }               Clock(mast : Master)
    Tick(n : int)                               requires mast ≠ null ∧ mast.inv;
        requires inv ∧ ¬comm ∧ 0 ≤ n;           ensures inv ∧ ¬comm;
        modifies time;                      {
        ensures time ≥ old(time);               m := mast;
    {                                           t := 0;
        unpack this;                            m.Connect(this);
        time := time + n;                       pack this;
        pack this;                          }
    }                                       Sync()
    Connect(c : Clock)                          requires inv ∧ ¬comm;
        requires inv;                           modifies t;
        ensures c ∈ this.deps;                  ensures t = m.time;
    {                                       { unpack this; t := m.time; pack this; }
        unpack this;
        attach c;                           }
        pack this;
    }
}
```

Fig. 3. Clocks synchronized with a master clock. $Inv_{Clock}(\textbf{this})$ depends on $\textbf{this}.m.time$ but a clock does not own $\textbf{this}.m$.

To summarize our methodology, we first recall the rule for annotation of field update, (9). A separate guard U_f is declared for each field f on which a friend depends, so the rule is as follows.

$$\textbf{assert}\ \neg E.inv \land (\,\forall p \mid p \in E.deps \bullet \neg p.inv \lor U_f(p, E, D)\,);$$
$$E.f := D;$$

It is straightforward to adapt this rule to cater for there being more than one friend class, or more than one pivot field of the same granter type but we omit the details (see [NB04]). Here, for simplicity, we disallow multiple pivots of the same type.

A friend may declare more than one update guard for a given f. Each update guard

$$\textbf{guard}\ g.f := \textbf{val by}\ U(\textbf{this}, g, val);$$

gives rise to a proof obligation to be discharged in the context of the friend class:

$$Inv_T(\textbf{this}) \land U(\textbf{this}, g, \textbf{val}) \Rightarrow (Inv_T(\textbf{this}))^{g.f}_{\textbf{val}}$$

For the precondition of a particular update of f in the granter, the reasoner may choose any of the update guards given for f.

The four auxiliary fields $inv, comm, owner, deps$ may all appear in method specifications and assertions, but they are updated only by special statements.

We refrain from repeating the definitions of **pack** and **unpack**, which remain unchanged from Section 2. The **set-owner** statement needs to be revised: a friend may be granted access to $owner$, in which case there needs to be an update guard for $owner$ just like for ordinary fields:

$$\textbf{set-owner } E \textbf{ to } D \equiv$$
$$\textbf{assert } E \neq \textbf{null} \wedge \neg E.inv \wedge (D = \textbf{null} \vee \neg D.inv);$$
$$\textbf{assert } (\forall p \mid p \in E.deps \bullet \neg p.inv \vee U_{owner}(p, E, D));$$
$$E.owner := D;$$

Note that if D is an object, it must be unpacked as its invariant is at risk when E becomes owned.

Definition 2 (admissible invariant). *An invariant* $Inv_T(o)$ *is* admissible *just if for every* $X.f$ *on which it depends,* $f \not\equiv inv$, $f \not\equiv comm$, *and either*

- X *is* o *(in the formula that means* X *is* **this***);*
- X *is transitively owned by* o *and* $f \not\equiv deps$; *or*
- X *is* $o.g$ *where field* g *(called a* pivot*) has some type* T' *that declares "friend* T *reads* f *".*

Moreover, the implication

$$Inv_T(o) \Rightarrow g = \textbf{null} \vee o \in g.deps \tag{11}$$

must be valid. Finally, $Inv_T(o)$ *is not falsifiable by creation of new objects.*

We write $\equiv$ for syntactic equality, not logical equivalence.

There are easy syntactic checks for the ownership condition, e.g., it holds if X has the form $g.h.\ldots.j$ where each is a **rep** field, or if X is variable bound by $(\forall X \mid X.owner = o \bullet \ldots)$. Requirement (11) is met by including either the condition **this** $\in g.deps$ or the condition $g = \textbf{null} \vee \textbf{this} \in g.deps$ as a conjunct of the declared invariant. (A fine point is that an admissible invariant should *only* depend on $deps$ in this way; see [NB04].) Although we do not use it in this paper, it is possible to have a **pivot** tag that marks the fields in the friend class that appear in the friend's invariant. Then there would be an easy syntactic process for imposing the requirement and allowing no other dependence on $deps$.

We extend the three *program invariants* (1–3) with a fourth invariant. Taken together, they ensure the following, for all o, T, f with $\textbf{type}(o) = T$.

$$o.inv \Rightarrow Inv_T(o) \tag{12}$$
$$o.inv \Rightarrow (\forall p \mid p.owner = o \bullet p.comm) \tag{13}$$
$$o.comm \Rightarrow o.inv \tag{14}$$
$$\text{For every } T', g, p \text{ such that } \textbf{type}(p) = T' \text{ and } Inv_{T'} \text{ depends on pivot } g \tag{15}$$
$$p.g = o \wedge p.inv \Rightarrow p \in o.deps$$

It is the first invariant that is the key to the entire methodology. It abstracts an object's invariant, preserving data encapsulation and allowing flexibility for reentrancy. The other invariants are all mechanisms needed in order to maintain (12) in the presence of inter-object dependence. The second and third work within ownership domains while our contribution adds cooperating objects.

4 Soundness

Consider any program annotated with invariants, friend declarations, and update guards satisfying the stated restrictions. We confine attention to the core methodology summarized in Section 3.4. Suppose that the obligations are met: the invariants are admissible and the update guard obligations are satisfied. Suppose also that every field update is preceded by the stipulated assertion, or one that implies it. We claim that (12–15) are program invariants, that is, true in every state. We refrain from formalizing precisely what that means, to avoid commitment to a particular verification system or logic.

A detailed formal proof of soundness for the full methodology is given in a companion paper [NB04]. An informal argument has been given for the features already present in the previous Boogie papers [BDF$^+$03a, LM04]; we have augmented the preconditions used in those papers. We consider highlights for the new features.

Consider first the new invariant (15), and the statements which could falsify it.

- **pack** sets $p.inv$, but under the precondition $Inv(p)$, and by admissibility this implies $p \in o.deps$ for any o on which p has a friend dependence.
- **new** initializes $deps = \emptyset$ but also $inv = \textbf{false}$. By freshness, no existing object has an owner or friend dependency on the new object.
- A field update $E.f := D$ can falsify it only if f is a pivot of E, but this is done under precondition $\neg E.inv$.
- **detach** removes an element from **this**.$deps$ but under precondition $\neg$**this**.inv.

Invariants (13) and (14) do not merit much attention as they do not involve the new fields and the new commands **attach** and **detach** do not involve inv or $comm$.

For (12), we must reconsider field update, $E.f := E'$, because $Inv_T(o)$ can have friend dependencies. By invariant (15), if o is a friend dependent on E, either $\neg o.inv$ or $o \in E.deps$. In the latter case, the precondition for update requires $U_f(o, E, E')$. The proof obligation for this update guard yields that $Inv_T(o)$ is not falsified by the update.

Both **attach** and **detach** have the potential to falsify (12) insofar as object invariants are allowed to depend on $deps$ fields. A local dependence on **this**.$deps$ is no problem, owing to precondition $\neg$**this**.inv. An admissible invariant is not allowed to depend on the $deps$ field of an owned object. What about friends? An admissible invariant is *required* to depend on $g.deps$ for each pivot g, but in a specific way that cannot be falsified by **attach** and that cannot be falsified by **detach** under its precondition. Finally, the **detach** E statement has the potential to falsify the consequent in (15), and this too is prevented by its precondition that either $\neg E.inv$ or E has no pivots referring to **this**. The intricacy of this interdependence is one motivation for carrying out a rigorous semantic proof of soundness.

5   Extensions

In this section, we present two extensions. The first is a methodology for creating an invariant that eases the burden of reasoning about the *deps* field in the granting class. The second is a syntactic extension to the update guard that provides extra information to the granting class after it performs a field update.

5.1   Tracking Dependencies in Invariants

We look again at the *Reset* method in *Clock*. In order to set *time* to zero, an instance of *Master* must know either that each of the clocks referring to it have their value of *t* also as zero or that there are no clocks referring to it. By program invariant (15), the latter case is true when *deps* is empty. For this example, it suffices for the master clock to maintain a reference count, *clocks*, of the clocks that are referring to it via their field *m*, incrementing it each time **attach** is executed and decrementing it upon each **detach**. That is, variable *clocks* maintains the invariant $clocks = size(deps)$. Given that invariant, the precondition for the update to *time* in *Reset* can be that *clocks* is equal to zero.

In general, we refer to the invariant that the granting class maintains about its *deps* variable as *Dep*. The invariant must be strong enough to derive enough information about *all* objects $p \in deps$ to establish the precondition in (9). Thus we formulate *Dep* as a predicate on an element of *deps* and introduce the following invariant as a proof obligation in the granting class.

$$(\forall p \mid p \in deps \bullet Dep(\textbf{this}, p)) \tag{16}$$

As with U, we make **this** an explicit parameter in the declaration.

We extend the *friend* syntax in the granting class to define *Dep*:

$$\textbf{friend } x : T \textbf{ reads } f \textbf{ keeping } Dep(\textbf{this}, x)$$

It binds x in predicate *Dep* which may also depend on state visible in the granting class. The default is $Dep(\textbf{this}, x) = \textbf{true}$, easing the obligation but providing no help in reasoning about *deps*. Like any invariant, *Dep* cannot depend on *inv* or *comm*. In terms of the verification of the granting class, the effect is to conjoin (16) to any declared invariant.

Figure 4 shows a version of *Master* with *Reset*. Note that in the constructor, the value of *clocks* must be set to zero in order to establish the "keeping" predicate, since initially *deps* is empty. The preconditions for *Connect* and *Disconnect* restrict the value of *deps* in order to keep an accurate count of the number of clocks referring to the master clock. Class *Clock* need not be revised from Figure 3.

In this example, *Dep* is independent of the individual identities of the friend objects. The Subject/View example (Section 6.1) shows a more typical use of *Dep*.

5.2   Getting Results from Friendship

In contrast to the fixed pack/unpack/ *inv* protocol which abstracts $Inv(p)$ to a boolean field, we have formulated the friend-invariant rule in terms of a shared state predicate.

```
class Master {
    time : int;
    clocks : int;
    invariant 0 ≤ time;
    friend c : Clock reads time keeping clocks = size(deps);
    Master()
        ensures inv ∧ ¬comm;
        { time := 0; clocks := 0; pack this; }
    Tick(n : int)
        requires inv ∧ ¬comm ∧ 0 ≤ n;
        modifies time;
        ensures time ≥ old(time);
        { unpack this; time := time + n; pack this; }
    Reset()
        requires inv ∧ clocks = 0;
        modifies time;
        { unpack this; time = 0; pack this; }
    Connect(c : Clock)
        requires inv ∧ c ∉ deps;
        modifies clocks;
        ensures c ∈ deps;
        { unpack this; clocks := clocks + 1; attach c; pack this; }
    Disconnect(c : Clock)
        requires inv ∧ c ∈ deps;
        modifies clocks;
        ensures c ∉ deps;
        { unpack this; clocks := clocks - 1; detach c; pack this; }
}
```

Fig. 4. Master clock with reset.

The associated methodology is to introduce public (or module-scoped) state variables with which to express U. Minimizing the state space on which U depends could facilitate fast protocol checking as in Fugue [DF01, DF03].

Whereas invariants are invariant, states get changed. The proposal so far is that the public interface of the dependent class T should reveal information about changes relevant to T. Given that T publishes the condition under which shared state may be changed, why not also publish the effect of such changes?

We extend the update guard declaration to include predicate Y for the result state:

guard $g.f := $ **val by** $U(\textbf{this}, g, \textbf{val})$ **yielding** $Y(\textbf{this}, g, \textbf{val})$;

The proof obligation on the friend class becomes

$$Inv_T(\textbf{this}) \ \wedge\ U(\textbf{this}, g, \textbf{val}) \ \Rightarrow\ (Inv_T(\textbf{this}) \ \wedge\ Y(\textbf{this}, g, \textbf{val}))^{g.f}_{\textbf{val}}$$

Note the resemblance to a pre/post specification in which the invariant is explicit.

At a field update site in the granting class, the yielding predicate can be depended on after the update:

> **assert** $\neg E.inv$;
> **assert** $(\forall p \mid p \in E.deps \bullet \neg p.inv \lor U(p, E, D))$
> $E.f := D$
> **assume** $(\forall p \mid p \in E.deps \bullet \neg p.inv \lor Y(p, E, D))$

The predicates U and Y are likely to be useful in specifications of methods of T. Together with method specifications, the **guard/yielding** statements of a class give the protocol by which it may be used.

6 Examples

In this section, we present several examples with some, but not all, of the details of their verification. The Subject/View example 6.1 demonstrates the enforcement a behavioral protocol. In Section 6.2, the cooperation involves the use of a shared data structure. Finally, Section 6.3 illustrates how the *peer* concept[LM04] mentioned in Aside 1 can be easily encoded as a friendship relation.

6.1 Subject/View

In Figure 5, the class *Subject* represents an object that maintains a collection of objects of type *View* that depend on it. We refer to the object of type *Subject* as the subject and each object that it holds a reference to in its collection *vs* as a view. In particular,

```
class Subject {
    val : int;
    version : int;
    rep vs : Collection⟨View⟩;
    friend v : View reads version, val keeping v ∈ this.vs

    Update(n : int)
        requires inv ∧ ¬comm ∧ (∀ v ∈ vs • v.inv ∧ ¬v.comm ∧ Sync(v, this)); )
        modifies val, version;
        ensures val = n ∧ version = old(version) + 1 ∧ (∀ v ∈ vs • Sync(v, this) );
    {
        unpack this;
        version := version + 1;
        val := n;
        pack this;
        foreach v ∈ vs do v.notify();
    }
}
```

Fig. 5. The class *Subject*.

each view depends on the fact that whenever the state of the subject, represented by the *val* field (which could be a much more elaborate data structure), is changed in the method *Update*, then it will receive a call to its *Notify* method. As part of its *Notify* method, a view will make callbacks to its subject to retrieve whatever parts of the updated state it is interested in. We do not show these state-querying methods (also known as *observers*).

To express the synchronization, the subject maintains a field *version* which indicates the number of times that *Update* has been called. A view also keeps track of a version number, *vsn* ; a view is up to date if its version matches that of its subject.

In this example, the method *Update* requires that the views be uncommitted so that they can be re-synchronized using their *Notify* method. This is much easier to establish than the requirement that they be unpacked. For example, it is sufficient for the views to be peers of the subject, i.e., that they have the same owner.

Note that the subject packs itself before calling *Notify* for all of its views. The views are then free to make state-observing calls on the subject, all of which presumably have a precondition that *inv* holds for the subject. Yet it is very important to realize that *Update* is safe from re-entrant calls while it is in the middle of notifying all of the views, because a view would not be able to establish the pre-condition that all of the views are in sync with the subject. It is only *after* the method *Update* has terminated that a view can be sure all of the views have been notified, and if it makes a re-entrant call, then that would come before *Update* terminates.

The exception to this is if a view somehow knew that it was the only view for the subject. But in that case, a re-entrant call to *Update* does not cause any problems with the synchronization property. It still can lead to non-termination, but that is outside of the scope of our specification.

In Figure 6, the class *View* publishes an update guard and update result for updates by the subject to its *version* field, and an update guard without an update result for modifications to the subject's *val* field. The guards given are not the weakest possible, but rather are chosen to avoid exposing internal state. We define *Sync* and *Out* as:

$$Sync(x : View, y : Subject) \quad \equiv \quad x.vsn = y.version$$
$$Out(x : View, y : Subject) \quad \equiv \quad x.vsn + 1 = y.version$$

Even though the class *Subject* uses *View*'s field *vsn* in the precondition and postcondition of *Update*, *View* does not have to declare it as a friend class. However, the field must be accessible in the scope of the class *Subject* , e.g., by being public. To keep control of it, the class *View* could define a read-only property [Gun00] and make the field itself private. We leave such details out of our examples. The invariant for the class is the conjunction of the two separately declared invariants.

The formal definitions for the update guards are:

$$U_{version}(x, y, z) = Sync(x, y) \land z = x.vsn + 1$$
$$U_{val}(x, y, z) = \neg Sync(x, y)$$

Note that because of the implication in Inv_{View}, the update guard for *s.val* is written so as to falsify the antecedent; the guard is independent of z, which represents the

```
class View {
   private s : Subject;
   vsn : int;
   private cache : int;
   invariant s.version − 1 ≤ vsn ≤ s.version ∧ (Sync(this, s) ⇒ cache = s.val);
   invariant s = null ∨ this ∈ s.deps;
   guard s.version := val by Sync(this, s) ∧ val = vsn + 1 yielding Out(this, s);
   guard s.val := val by ¬Sync(this, s);
   Notify()
      requires ¬comm ∧ inv ∧ s.inv ∧ Out(this, s);
      ensures Sync(this, s);
      modifies vsn;
   {
      unpack this;
      vsn := vsn + 1;
      "read state from s, update cache" ; // This is why s.inv was required.
      pack this;
   }
}
```

Fig. 6. The class *View*.

value assigned to the field. This enforces a restriction on the order in which the *Subject* can update the fields, even though the reverse order has equivalent effect. The *Subject* must first update its *version* field to make the implication vacuously true, and only then update its *val* field.

Allowing the *View* to impose this requirement on *Subject* seems unfortunate, especially since the *Subject* has unpacked itself at the beginning of *Update* and so it would seem it should be able to update its fields in any order as long as it can re-establish its invariant before it tries to pack itself again. The example illustrates the price to be paid for the Boogie approach. Having the program invariants hold at "every semicolon" is conceptually simple and technically robust, but like any programming discipline this one disallows some programs that are arguably correct and well designed. If an inconsequential ordering of two assignments is the only annoyance then we are doing very well indeed.

We demonstrate the verification of the proof obligations imposed by our methodology. In the granting class *Subject*, the assert before each of the two field updates in *Update* must be satisfied (see (9)). We also have to show that the *Dep* predicate holds for every member of *deps* (see (16)); i.e., we have to show that the following condition is invariant:

$$(\forall p \mid p \in deps \bullet p \in vs) \tag{17}$$

To verify the assignment to *version* in *Subject.Update*, the corresponding update guard from *View* must be satisfied.

$(\forall p \mid p \in \mathbf{this}.deps \bullet \neg p.inv \vee U_{version}(p, \mathbf{this}, \mathbf{this}.version + 1))$
≡ {Definition of guard $U_{version}$}
$(\forall p \mid p \in deps \bullet \neg p.inv \vee (Sync(p, \mathbf{this}) \wedge \mathbf{this}.version + 1 = p.vsn + 1))$
⇐ {Strengthening}

$$(\forall p \mid p \in deps \bullet Sync(p, \textbf{this}) \wedge \textbf{this}.version + 1 = p.vsn + 1)$$
$$\Leftarrow \{(17)\}$$
$$(\forall p \mid p \in vs \bullet Sync(p, \textbf{this}) \wedge \textbf{this}.version + 1 = p.vsn + 1)$$
$$\Leftarrow \{\text{pre-cond. of } Update: Sync(p, \textbf{this}), \text{ which implies } p.vsn = \textbf{this}.version\}$$
$$(\forall p \mid p \in vs \bullet \textbf{this}.version + 1 = \textbf{this}.version + 1)$$
$$\Leftarrow \textbf{true}$$

This fulfills the proof obligation (9).

To verify the assignment to *val* in *Subject.Update*, we use the update guard in *View* for *val*.

$$(\forall p \mid p \in \textbf{this}.deps \bullet \neg p.inv \vee U_{val}(p, \textbf{this}, n))$$
$$\equiv \{\text{Definition of guard } U_{val}\}$$
$$(\forall p \mid p \in \textbf{this}.deps \bullet \neg p.inv \vee \neg Sync(p, \textbf{this}))$$
$$\Leftarrow \{(17)\}$$
$$(\forall p \mid p \in vs \bullet \neg p.inv \vee \neg Sync(p, \textbf{this}))$$
$$\Leftarrow \{\text{By definition, } Out(x, y) \Rightarrow \neg Sync(x, y)\}$$
$$(\forall p \mid p \in vs \bullet \neg p.inv \vee Out(p, \textbf{this}))$$

The last line is a precondition for the update of *val*, owing to the **yielding** clause in the update guard for *version* (see Section 5.2). This fulfills the proof obligation (9).

In order to maintain invariance of (17), while allowing dependent views, *Subject* can provide a method with an **attach** statement:

```
Register(v : View)
    requires ¬comm ∧ inv ∧ v ∉ vs;
    ensures v ∈ vs;
    modifies vs;
{
    unpack this;
    vs := vs + {v};
    attach v;
    pack this;
}
```

Clearly, this makes (17) an invariant, since there are no other occurrences of **attach** that could modify the value of *deps*. In Figures 5 and 6 we omit constructors; the constructor of *View* would call *Register*.

The obligations on the friend class *View* are that its advertised update guards maintain its invariant (see (8)) and that it is in the *deps* field of the subject upon which it is dependent (see (10)). The condition required by (10) is a declared conjunct of the invariant of *View*.

Each update guard in *View* must be shown to fulfill the obligation of (8), that its invariant will not be violated as long as the guard holds. Here we show only the update guard for *version*, the one for *val* is even easier.

$(Inv_{View} \wedge Sync(\mathbf{this}, s) \wedge \mathbf{val} = \mathbf{this}.vsn + 1) \Rightarrow (Inv_{View})_{\mathbf{val}}^{s.version}$
$\equiv \{\text{Simplifying } Sync(\mathbf{this}, s) \wedge Inv_{View}\}$
$(\mathbf{this}.vsn = s.version \wedge \mathbf{val} = \mathbf{this}.vsn + 1) \Rightarrow (Inv_{View})_{\mathbf{val}}^{s.version}$
$\equiv \{\text{Substitution}\}$
$(vsn = s.version \wedge \mathbf{val} = vsn + 1) \Rightarrow$
$\qquad \mathbf{val} - 1 \leq vsn \leq \mathbf{val} \wedge (vsn = \mathbf{val} \Rightarrow cache = s.val)$
$\Leftarrow \{\text{Simplification}\}$
true

6.2   Producer/Consumer

In this example, we show two objects that share a common cyclic buffer. There are two classes, *Producer* and *Consumer*. Their definitions are shown in Figure 7 and Figure 8, respectively.

```
class Producer {
    buf : int[ ];  n : int;  con : Consumer;
    invariant 0 ≤ n < buf.length;
    friend o : Consumer reads con, n, buf keeping o = con;

    Producer(b : int[ ])
        requires b ≠ null ∧ b.length > 1;
        ensures deps = ∅ ∧ inv ∧ ¬comm ∧ n = 0;
    { buf := b;  n := 0;  pack this; }
    SetCon(c : Consumer)
        requires inv ∧ ¬comm ∧ c ≠ null ∧ deps = ∅;
        modifies con;
        ensures deps = {c} ∧ con = c;
    { unpack this;  attach c;  con := c;  pack this; }
    Produce(x : int)
        requires inv ∧ ¬comm ∧ con ≠ null ∧ con.n ≠ n;  // con.n = n ≡ buffer full
        modifies n, buf;
        ensures n ∈ [old(n)..old(con.n)];
    { unpack this;  buf[n % buf.length] := x;  n := (n + 1) % buf.length;  pack this; }
}
```

Fig. 7. The class *Producer* .

We call instances of the former *producers* and instances of the latter *consumers*. A producer places elements into a circular buffer while consumers read them. Each object maintains a cursor into the common buffer; the producer can place more elements into the buffer as long as it does not overrun the consumer. Likewise, the consumer can only read elements from the buffer as long as its cursor does not overrun the producer's cursor. The buffer is empty when the producer's cursor is one element ahead (modulo the buffer length) of the consumer's cursor. When the cursors are equal, then the buffer

```
class Consumer {
    buf : int[ ];  n : int;  pro : Producer;
    invariant pro.con = this ∧ buf ≠ null;
    invariant 0 ≤ n < buf.length;

    guard pro.buf := val by false;
    guard pro.con := val by val = this;
    guard pro.n := val by val ∈ [pro.n..n);

    Consumer(p : Producer)
        requires p.inv ∧ ¬p.comm ∧ p.con = null;
        modifies p.con;
        ensures inv
    { buf := p.buf;  pro := p;  n := buf.length − 1;  pro.SetCon(this);  pack this; }
    Consume() : int
        requires inv ∧ ¬comm ∧ (n + 1) % buf.length < pro.n;
        modifies n;
        ensures n ∈ [old(n)..old(pro.n));
    { unpack this;  n := (n + 1) % buf.length;  pack this;  return(buf[n]); }
}
```

Fig. 8. The class *Consumer*.

is full. Because of this encoding, the buffer's length must be greater than one and its capacity is one less than its length. In the specifications we use the notation $[i..j)$ for the open interval between i and j, allowing for possible "wraparound" due to the modular arithmetic, i.e., if n is 5, then $[3..1)$ is $[3, 4, 0]$. Similarly, $[i..j]$ stands for the closed interval.

It is important to note that this is not a full specification of the functional behavior of the two classes. The specification is only of the synchronization between the two, just as was done for the Subject/View example. For schematic patterns this is especially useful; the specification can be combined with a particular usage of the pattern to fill out the details.

The class *Consumer* is given friend access to *buf*, *con*, and *n*. Being given access to *buf* does not give the consumer the right to depend on the contents of *buf* in its invariant. Such a dependence would be a dependence path of length two: one step to *buf* and then to some index i. We do not allow this; we allow only direct dependence on a pivot field.

The friend access for *buf* is given to the consumer because it needs to make sure the producer does not update the field to a new, different buffer. This is expressed by the update guard for *pro.buf* being **false**. It is possible to allow the producer to change its buffer, either by requiring that the buffer is empty, or even to allow the consumer to continue reading from the old buffer as long as the producer no longer is using it. We leave these variations as an exercise for the reader.

The update guard for *con* is slightly different: it allows the producer to modify the field, but only to assign the consumer to it. The update guard for the producer's cursor, n, allows the producer to fill as many slots as are available, even though in this particular implementation, the producer fills only one slot at a time.

We do not show the proofs for the field updates in *Producer*; all of the proofs are immediate.

6.3   Doubly-Linked List with Transfer

For our last example, we consider a doubly-linked list. The class *List* with its *Insert* and *Push* methods is shown in Figure 9. Each *List* object has a reference to an object

```
class List {
    head : Node;
    invariant head = null ∨ (head.prev = null ∧ head.owner = this);
    Insert(x : int)
        requires x > 0 ∧ inv ∧ ¬comm;
        modifies ;
        ensures ;
    { n : Node; n := new Node(x); this.Push(n); }
    Push(n : Node)
        requires inv ∧ ¬comm;
        requires n ≠ null ∧ n.prev = null ∧ n.next = null;
        requires n.inv ∧ ¬n.comm ∧ n.owner = null;
        modifies head, n.comm, n.owner;
        ensures n.comm ∧ n.owner = this;
    {
        unpack this;
        set-owner n to this;
        if (head = null) head := n;  else  head := head.Insert(n);
        pack this;
    }
}
```

Fig. 9. The class *List*. The design caters for a method that transfers ownership of a node, to be added in Figure 12.

of type *Node*; the nodes have forward and backward references to other *Node* objects. In [LM04], this example serves to explain the concept of *peers*: objects who share a common owner. Remember by Definition 2 that an object's invariant is allowed to depend on its peers. The class *Node* is shown in Figure 10. Because each of the nodes that are linked into a particular list share the same owner, if a node is able to pack and unpack itself, then it is also able to do that for any other node in the list. In terms of our methodology, this means no update guards are needed. Instead, the recursive friend access is needed so that a node's invariant can depend on the node to which its *next* field points. The **keeping** clause maintains that a node keeps a reference to its friend in its *prev* field. Thus the quantification in the precondition for field update can be simplified by

```
class Node {
  val : int;
  prev : Node;
  next : Node; // pivot field
  friend n : Node reads prev, owner keeping n = prev
  invariant 0 < val ∧ prev ≠ this ∧
    (next = null ∨ (next.owner = owner ∧ next.prev = this));
  Node(x : int)
    requires 0 < x;
    ensures val = x ∧ inv ∧ prev = null ∧ next = null;
  { val := x; prev := null; next := null; pack this; }
  ...
}
```

Fig. 10. Part of the class *Node*. Other methods are in subsequent Figures.

the one-point rule. Notice that within the outer "else" clause of *Insert* (Figure 11), we unpack the argument n so that we can assign to its pivot field *next* without worrying about violating $Inv_{Node}(n)$. All of the conditions required before packing it back up are met through a combination of the (rather elaborate) pre-conditions on the method and the assignments that take place in the body of the method. We do not show the details; all of the required conditions are immediately present.

The *Insert* method, in Figure 11, returns a value; the post-condition refers to the return value as **result**. The modifies clause uses a simple path notation to indicate that *Insert* may modify the fields *next* and *prev* on nodes that are reached by following a path of accesses along the *next* field. In the former case, the path may be of zero length, while in the latter case the path must be of positive length.

To add realistic complications to the code, the list is maintained in ascending order and if desired this could be expressed using node invariants, again avoiding reachability expressions.

Figure 12 shows an example of transferring ownership. In this case, the first node in one list is moved to another list, s. It is important to see that it transfers the actual object of type *Node*, as well as the contents of the node. The helper function, *Disconnect*, removes a node from the entanglements of the pointers in its list and maintains *deps*.

7 Related Work

The most closely related work is that of Leino and Müller [LM04] which uses an explicit *owner* field that holds a pair (o, T) of the owner together with the type T at which o has a relevant invariant. The paper by Müller et al. [MPHL03] lucidly explains both the challenges of modular reasoning about object invariants and the solution using owner-ship. They prove soundness for a system using types to formulate ownership, based on Müller's dissertation [Mül02] which deals with significant design patterns in a realistic object-oriented language. They also discuss the problem of dependence on non-owned objects and describe how the problem can be addressed soundly by ensuring that an

```
Insert(n : Node) : Node
  requires inv ∧ ¬comm;
  requires n ≠ null ∧ n.val > 0 ∧ n.next = null ∧ n.prev = null;
  requires n.inv ∧ ¬n.comm;
  requires prev = null ∨ prev.val ≤ n.val;
  requires owner = n.owner;
  modifies next*.next, next⁺.prev;
  ensures result ≠ null ∧ result.prev = old(this.prev);
{
  result : Node;
  unpack this;
  if (n.val ≥ val) {// insert after self
    if (next = null) {// this is the last node
      next := n;
    } else {// pass it down the line
      next := next.Insert(n);
    }
    unpack next;
    next.Attach(this);
    pack next;
    result := this;
  } else {// insert before self
    unpack n;
    n.next := this;
    this.Attach(n);
    pack n;
    result := n;
  }
  pack this;
  return result;
}
Attach(n : Node)
  requires ¬inv ∧ n ≠ null;
  ensures prev = n ∧ n ∈ deps;
  modifies deps, prev;
{ attach n; prev := n; }
Detach(n : Node)
  requires ¬inv ∧ n ≠ null ∧ ¬n.inv;
  ensures prev = null ∧ n ∉ deps;
  modifies deps, prev;
{ detach n; prev := null; }
```

Fig. 11. The methods *Insert*, *Attach*, and *Detach* in class *Node*.

object's invariant is visible where it may be violated; thus sound proof obligations can be imposed, as is developed further in [LM04]. Section 2 has reviewed [LM04] and the other Boogie paper [BDF⁺03a] at length and we encourage the reader to consult them for further comparisons.

$Disconnect()$
  requires $inv \land prev = \textbf{null} \land \neg comm \land next \neq \textbf{null} \land next.inv$;
  ensures $next = \textbf{null} \land \textbf{old}(next).prev = \textbf{null}$;
  modifies $next, next.prev, next.deps$;
{
  unpack this;
  unpack $next$;
  $next.Detach(\textbf{this})$;
  pack $next$;
  $next := \textbf{null}$;
  pack this;
}
$TransferHeadTo(s : List)$
  requires $s \neq \textbf{this} \land head \neq \textbf{null} \land \neg comm \land inv \land \neg s.comm \land s.inv$;
{
  unpack this;
  $n : Node;\ n := head;\ head := head.next$;
  if $(n.next \neq \textbf{null})\ n.Disconnect()$;
  set-owner n **to null**;
  pack this;
  $s.Push(n)$;
}

Fig. 12. Methods $TransferHeadTo$ and $Disconnect$ in class $List$.

Object invariants are treated in the Extended Static Checking project, especially ESC/Modula-3 [DLNS98, LN02, FLL [+] 02], by what Müller [Mül02] calls the visibility approach which requires invariants to be visible, and thus liable for checking, wherever they may be violated. This can significantly increase the number of proof obligations for a given verification unit and the focus of the work is on mitigation by abstraction. An idiom is used for expressing invariants as implications $valid \Rightarrow \ldots$ where $valid$ is an ordinary boolean field, serving like inv.

Liskov, Wing, and Guttag [LG86, LW94] treat object invariants but in a way that is not sound for invariants that depend on more than one object. There has been a lot of work on alias control to circumscribe dependency. Ownership type systems [CNP01, Cla01] explicitly address the problem of encapsulating representation objects on which an invariant may sensibly depend. Much of this line of work struggles to reconcile efficient static checking with the challenges of practical design patterns. Boyapati, Liskov and Shrira [BLS03] argue that their variation on ownership types achieves encapsulation sufficient for sound modular reasoning but they do not formalize reasoning. They exploit the semantics of inner objects in Java which provides a form of $owner$ field but suffers from semantic intricacies and precludes ownership transfer.

Banerjee and Naumann [BN02a] use a semantic formulation of ownership in terms of heap separation and show that it ensures preservation of object invariants. They focus on two-state invariants, i.e., simulation relations, to obtain a representation independence result. For this purpose, read access by clients is restricted. The ownership property is enforced by a static analysis that does not impose the annotation burden of ownership types but like ownership types it requires the ownership invariant to hold in every state. A version has been developed that includes transfer of ownership, but it depends on a static analysis for uniqueness and the proof of soundness was difficult [BN03]. The representation-independence theorem states that the invariant of a class T is preserved by clients *if* it is preserved by methods of T. The theorem allows invocation of state-mutating methods on pointers outgoing from encapsulated representation objects, including reentrancy. Unlike work such as [MPHL03], the problem of verifying methods of T is not addressed.

Separation logic [Rey02] uses new logical connectives to express very directly that a predicate depends only on some subset of the objects in the heap. It has successfully treated modular reasoning about an object invariant in the case of a single class with a single instance [OYR04]. Some of the attractive features are achieved in part by a restriction to a low-level language without object-oriented features, e.g., the atomic points-to predicate describes the complete state of an object. This is an exciting and active line of research and it will be interesting to see how it scales to specifications and programs like those in Section 6.

8   Conclusions

Formal systems for programming must always cope with the conflict between the flexibility real programs display and the restrictions formal analysis demands. Our work extends Boogie's system for object invariants to cope with a real-world situation: dependence across ownership boundaries. We have constructed a protocol that imposes minimal obligations upon the participating classes; it is inevitable that there are some extra verification conditions. In addition, we have tried to maintain Boogie's mantra: hiding private implementation details while providing explicit knowledge about the state of an object's invariant. Our contribution is a workable system for specifying and verifying cooperating classes.

While one approach would be to allow, or even to insist, for cooperating classes to be knowledgeable about each other's private implementation state, we believe that is important to provide for as much abstraction as possible. The protocols could all be expressed in terms of more abstract properties instead of concrete fields allowing a class implementation to change without disturbing its friend classes.

Our presentation has left out all mention of sub-classing, but the actual definitions have all been made taking it into account.

There are many ways in which we plan to extend our work. For instance, our methodology could be presented independently from ownership. Currently, we think it best to use ownership where possible and thus it is important that friendship fits well with ownership. We also need to explore the use of static analysis for alias control in common cases.

Our update guards are related to *constraints* [LW94]; it would be interesting to formulate them as constraints, thus shifting more of the burden to the granting class instead of the friend class.

We will continue to explore different design decisions to weaken the obligations. The tradeoffs are between being able to easily verify the specifications and code against allowing the most flexibility for the programmer.

We are implementing our scheme as part of the Boogie project. Empirical evaluation will doubtless point out many problems and opportunities for improvement.

Acknowledgements

We would like to thank Rustan Leino for all of his comments and help. Wolfram Schulte made many helpful suggestions, especially pointing out the connection between update guards and constraints. Anindya Banerjee and Rob DeLine made helpful expository suggestions. Cees Pierik pointed out that admissible invariants should not be falsifiable by object construction. The anonymous referees also made many helpful suggestions.

References

[AO97]   K.R. Apt and E.-R. Olderog. *Verification of Sequential and Concurrent Programs*. Springer, 2 edition, 1997.

[BDF⁺03a]   M. Barnett, R. DeLine, M. Fähndrich, K.R.M. Leino, and W. Schulte. Verification of object-oriented programs with invariants. In S. Eisenbach, G.T. Leavens, P. Müller, A. Poetzsch-Heffter, and E. Poll, editors, *Formal Techniques for Java-like Programs 2003*, July 2003. Available as Technical Report 408, Department of Computer Science, ETH Zurich. A newer version of this paper is [BDF⁺03b].

[BDF⁺03b]   M. Barnett, R. DeLine, M. Fähndrich, K.R.M. Leino, and W. Schulte. Verification of object-oriented programs with invariants. Manuscript KRML 122b, December 2003. Available from http://research.microsoft.com/˜leino/papers.html.

[BLS03]   C. Boyapati, B. Liskov, and L. Shrira. Ownership types for object encapsulation. In *POPL*, pages 213–223, 2003.

[BN02a]   A. Banerjee and D.A. Naumann. Ownership confinement ensures representation independence for object-oriented programs. Extended version of [BN02b]. Available from http://www.cs.stevens-tech.edu/˜naumann/oceri.ps, 2002.

[BN02b]   A. Banerjee and D.A. Naumann. Representation independence, confinement and access control. In *POPL*, pages 166–177, 2002.

[BN03]   A. Banerjee and D.A. Naumann. Ownership transfer and abstraction. Technical Report TR 2004-1, Computing and Information Sciences, Kansas State University, 2003.

[BS03]   M. Barnett and W. Schulte. Runtime verification of .NET contracts. *The Journal of Systems and Software*, 65(3):199–208, 2003.

[CD02]   D. Clarke and S. Drossopoulou. Ownership, encapsulation and the disjointness of type and effect. In *OOPSLA*, November 2002.

[CL02]   Y.Cheon and G.T. Leavens. A runtime assertion checker for the Java Modeling Language (JML). In H.R. Arabnia and Y. Mun, editors, *Proceedings of the International Conference on Software Engineering Research and Practice (SERP '02), Las Vegas, Nevada, USA, June 24-27, 2002*, pages 322–328. CSREA Press, June 2002.

[Cla01]   D. Clarke. Object ownership and containment. Dissertation, Computer Science and Engineering, University of New South Wales, Australia, 2001.

[CNP01]   D.G. Clarke, J. Noble, and J.M. Potter. Simple ownership types for object containment. In *ECOOP*, 2001.

[DF01]   R. DeLine and M. Fähndrich. Enforcing high-level protocols in low-level software. In *PLDI*, pages 59–69, 2001.

[DF03]   R. DeLine and M. Fähndrich. The Fugue protocol checker: Is your software baroque? Available from http://research.microsoft.com/~maf/papers.html, 2003.

[DLNS98]   D.L. Detlefs, K.R.M. Leino, G. Nelson, and J.B. Saxe. Extended static checking. Research Report 159, Compaq Systems Research Center, December 1998.

[dRdBH⁺ 01] W.-P. de Roever, F. de Boer, U. Hannemann, J. Hooman, Y. Lakhnech, M. Poel, and J. Zwiers. *Concurrency Verification: Introduction to Compositional and Noncompositional Methods*. Cambridge University, 2001.

[FLL⁺ 02]   C. Flanagan, K.R.M. Leino, M. Lillibridge, G. Nelson, J.B. Saxe, and R. Stata. Extended static checking for Java. In *PLDI*, pages 234–245, 2002.

[Gun00]   E. Gunnerson. *A Programmer's Introduction to C#*. Apress, Berkeley, CA, 2000.

[Jon83]   C.B. Jones. Tentative steps towards a development method for interfering programs. *ACM Transactions on Programming Languages and Systems*, 5(4):596–619, 1983.

[LG86]   B. Liskov and J. Guttag. *Abstraction and Specification in Program Development*. MIT Press, 1986.

[LM04]   K.R.M. Leino and P. Müller. Object invariants in dynamic contexts. In *ECOOP*, 2004. To appear.

[LN02]   K.R.M. Leino and G. Nelson. Data abstraction and information hiding. *ACM Transactions on Programming Languages and Systems*, 24(5):491–553, 2002.

[LW94]   B.H. Liskov and J.M. Wing. A behavioral notion of subtyping. *ACM Transactions on Programming Languages and Systems*, 16(6), 1994.

[Mey97]   B. Meyer. *Object-oriented Software Construction*. Prentice Hall, New York, second edition, 1997.

[MPHL03]   P. Müller, A. Poetzsch-Heffter, and G.T. Leavens. Modular invariants for object structures. Technical Report 424, ETH Zürich, Chair of Software Engineering, October 2003.

[Mül02]   P. Müller. *Modular Specification and Verification of Object-Oriented Programs*. Number 2262 in LNCS. Springer, 2002.

[NB04]   D.A. Naumann and M. Barnett. Towards imperative modules: Reasoning about invariants and sharing of mutable state (extended abstract). In *LICS*, 2004. To appear.

[OYR04]   P.W. O'Hearn, H. Yang, and J.C. Reynolds. Separation and information hiding. In *POPL*, pages 268–280, 2004.

[PdB03]   C. Pierik and F.S. de Boer. A syntax-directed Hoare logic for object-oriented programming concepts. In *FMOODS*, pages 64–78, 2003.

[Rey02]   J.C. Reynolds. Separation logic: a logic for shared mutable data structures. In *LICS*, pages 55–74, 2002.

Chasing Bottoms

A Case Study in Program Verification in the Presence of Partial and Infinite Values

Nils Anders Danielsson and Patrik Jansson[*]

Computing Science, Chalmers University of Technology, Gothenburg, Sweden

Abstract. This work is a case study in program verification: We have written a simple parser and a corresponding pretty-printer in a non-strict functional programming language with lifted pairs and functions (Haskell). A natural aim is to prove that the programs are, in some sense, each other's inverses. The presence of partial and infinite values in the domains makes this exercise interesting, and having lifted types adds an extra spice to the task. We have tackled the problem in different ways, and this is a report on the merits of those approaches. More specifically, we first describe a method for testing properties of programs in the presence of partial and infinite values. By testing before proving we avoid wasting time trying to prove statements that are not valid. Then we prove that the programs we have written are in fact (more or less) inverses using first fixpoint induction and then the approximation lemma.

1 Introduction

Infinite values are commonly used in (non-strict) functional programs, often to improve modularity [5]. Partial values are seldom used explicitly, but they are still present in all non-trivial Haskell programs because of non-termination, pattern match failures, calls to the *error* function etc. Unfortunately, proofs about functional programs often ignore details related to partial and infinite values.

This text is a case study where we explore how one can go about testing and proving properties even in the presence of partial and infinite values. We use random testing (Sect. 5) and two proof methods, fixpoint induction (Sect. 7) and the approximation lemma (Sect. 8), both described in Gibbons' and Hutton's tutorial [4].

The programs that our case study revolves around are a simple pretty-printer and a corresponding parser. Jansson and Jeuring define several more complex (polytypic) pretty-printers and parsers and prove them correct for total, finite input [7]. The case study in this paper uses cut down versions of those programs (see Sect. 2) but proves a stronger statement. On some occasions we have been

---

[*] This work is partially funded by the Swedish Foundation for Strategic Research as part of the research programme "Cover – Combining Verification Methods in Software Development".

D. Kozen (Ed.): MPC 2004, LNCS 3125, pp. 85–109, 2004.

tempted to change the definitions of the programs to be able to formulate our proofs in a different way. We have not done that, since one part of our goal is to explore what it is like to prove properties about programs that have not been written with a proof in mind. We have transformed our programs into equivalent variants, though; note that this carries a proof obligation.

Before starting to prove something it is often useful to test the properties. That way one can avoid spending time trying to prove something which is not true anyway. However, testing partial and infinite values can be tricky. In Sect. 5 we describe two techniques for doing that. Infinite values can be tested with the aid of the approximation lemma, and for partial values we make use of a Haskell extension, implemented in several Haskell environments. (The first technique is a generalisation of another one, and the last technique is previously known.)

As indicated above the programming language used for all programs and properties is Haskell [12], a non-strict, pure functional language where all types are lifted. Since we are careful with all details there will necessarily be some Haskell-specific discussions below, but the main ideas should carry over to other similar languages. Some knowledge of Haskell is assumed of the reader, though.

We begin in Sect. 2 by defining the two programs that this case study focuses on. Section 3 discusses the computational model and in Sect. 4 we give idealised versions of the main properties that we want to prove. By implementing and testing the properties (in Sect. 5) we identify a flaw in one of the them and we give a new, refined version in Sect. 6. The proofs presented in Sects. 7 and 8 are discussed in the concluding Sect. 9.

2   Programs

The programs under consideration parse and pretty-print a simple binary tree data type T without any information in the nodes:

data $T = L \mid B\ T\ T$

The pretty-printer is really simple. It performs a preorder traversal of the tree, emitting a 'B' for each branching point and an 'L' for each leaf:

$pretty' :: T \rightarrow String$
$pretty'\ L \qquad = \texttt{"L"}$
$pretty'\ (B\ l\ r) = \texttt{"B"} \mathbin{+\!\!+} pretty'\ l \mathbin{+\!\!+} pretty'\ r$

The parser reconstructs a tree given a string of the kind produced by $pretty'$. Any remaining input is returned together with the tree:

$parse :: String \rightarrow (T, String)$
$parse\ (\texttt{'L'} : cs) = (L, cs)$
$parse\ (\texttt{'B'} : cs) = (B\ l\ r, cs'')$
$\quad \textbf{where}\ (l, cs')\ = parse\ cs$
$\qquad \qquad (r, cs'') = parse\ cs'$

We wrap up *pretty'* so that the printer and the parser get symmetric types:

$$pretty :: (T, String) \rightarrow String$$
$$pretty\ (t, cs) = pretty'\ t \mathbin{+\!\!+} cs$$

These programs are obviously written in a very naive way. A real pretty-printer would not use a quadratic algorithm for printing trees and a real parser would use a proper mechanism for reporting parse failures. However, the programs have the right level of detail for our application; they are very straightforward without being trivial. The tree structure makes the recursion "nonlinear", and that is what makes these programs interesting.

3   Computational Model

Before we begin reasoning about the programs we should specify what our underlying computational model is. We use Haskell 98 [12], and it is common to reason about Haskell programs by using equational reasoning, assuming that a simple denotational semantics for the language exists. This is risky, though, since this method has not been formally verified to work; there is not even a formal semantics for the language to verify it against. (We should mention that some work has been done on the static semantics [3].)

Nevertheless we will follow this approach, taking some caveats into account (see below). Although our aim is to explore what a proof would look like when all issues related to partial and infinite values are considered, it may be that we have missed some subtle aspect of the Haskell semantics. We have experimented with different levels of detail and believe that the resolution of such issues most likely will not change the overall structure of the proofs, though. Even if we would reject the idea of a clean denotational semantics for Haskell and instead use Sands' improvement theory [13] based on an operational model, we still believe that the proof steps would be essentially the same.

Now on to the caveats. All types in Haskell are (by default) pointed and lifted; each type is a complete partial order with a distinct least element $\perp$ (bottom), and data constructors are not strict. For pairs this means that $\perp \neq (\perp, \perp)$, so we do not have surjective pairing. It is possible to use strictness annotations to construct types that are not lifted, e.g. the smash product of two types, for which $\perp = (\perp, \perp)$ but we still do not have surjective pairing. There is however no way to construct the ordinary cartesian product of two types.

One has to be careful when using pattern matching in conjunction with lifted types. The expression **let** $(a, b) = x$ **in** $g\ (a, b)$ is equivalent to $g\ x$ iff $x \neq \perp$ or $g\ (\perp, \perp) = g\ \perp$. The reason is that, if $x = \perp$, then in the first case g will still be applied to $(\perp, \perp)$, whereas in the second case g will be applied to $\perp$. Note here that the pattern matching in a **let** clause is not performed until the variables bound in the pattern are actually used. Hence **let** $(a, b) = \perp$ **in** (a, b) is equivalent to $(\perp, \perp)$, whereas $(\lambda(a, b) \rightarrow (a, b)) \perp = \perp$.

The function type is also lifted; we can actually distinguish between $\perp :: a \rightarrow a$ and $\lambda x \rightarrow \perp :: a \rightarrow a$ by using *seq*, a function with the following semantics [12]:

$$seq :: a \rightarrow b \rightarrow b$$
$$seq \perp b = \perp$$
$$seq\ a\ \ b = b$$

(Here a is any value except for $\perp$.) In other words η-conversion is not valid for Haskell functions, so to verify that two functions are equal it is not enough to verify that they produce identical output when applied to identical input; we also have to verify that none (or both) of the functions are $\perp$. A consequence of the lack of η-conversion is that one of the monadic identity laws fails to hold for some standard *Monad* instances in Haskell, such as the state "monad". The existence of a polymorphic *seq* also weakens Haskell's parametricity properties [8], but that does not directly affect us because our functions are not polymorphic.

Another caveat, also related to *seq*, is that $f = \lambda \, True \; x \rightarrow x$ is not identical to $f' = \lambda \, True \rightarrow \lambda x \rightarrow x$. By careful inspection of Haskell's pattern matching semantics [12] we can see that $f \; False = \lambda x \rightarrow \perp$ while $f' \; False = \perp$, since the function f is interpreted as

$$\lambda a \rightarrow \lambda b \rightarrow \textbf{case } (a, b) \textbf{ of}$$
$$(True, x) \rightarrow x$$

whereas the function f' is interpreted as

$$\lambda a \rightarrow \textbf{case } a \textbf{ of}$$
$$True \rightarrow \lambda x \rightarrow x \; .$$

This also applies if f and f' are defined by $f \; True \; x = x$ and $f' \; True = \lambda x \rightarrow x$. We do not get any problems if the first pattern is a simple variable, though. We will avoid problems related to this issue by never pattern matching on anything but the last variable in a multiple parameter function definition.

4   Properties: First Try

The programs in Sect. 2 are simple enough. Are they correct? That depends on what we demand of them. Let us say that we want them to form an embedding-projection pair, i.e.

$$parse \circ pretty = id :: (T, String) \rightarrow (T, String) \tag{1}$$

and

$$pretty \circ parse \sqsubseteq id :: String \rightarrow String. \tag{2}$$

The operator $\sqsubseteq$ denotes the ordering of the semantical domain, and $=$ is semantical equality.

More concretely (1) means that for all pairs $p :: (T, String)$ we must have $parse \, (pretty \; p) = p$. (Note that η-conversion is valid since none of the functions involved are equal to $\perp$; they both expect at least one argument.) The quantification is over all pairs of the proper type, including infinite and partial values.

If we can prove this equality, then we are free to exchange the left and right hand sides in any well-typed context. This means that we can use the result very easily, but we have to pay a price in the complexity of the proof. In this section we "cheat" by only quantifying over finite, total trees so that we can use simple structural induction. We return to the full quantification in later sections.

Parse after Pretty. Let us prove (1) for finite, total trees and arbitrary strings, just to illustrate what this kind of proof usually looks like. First we observe that both sides are distinct from $\bot$, and then we continue using structural induction. The inductive hypothesis used is

$$\forall cs :: String . \ (parse \circ pretty) \ (t, cs) = id \ (t, cs),$$

where $t :: T$ is any immediate subtree of the tree treated in the current case. We have two cases, for the two constructors of T. The first case is easy (for an arbitrary $cs :: String$):

$$(parse \circ pretty) \ (L, cs)$$
$$= \{\circ\}$$
$$parse \ (pretty \ (L, cs))$$
$$= \{pretty\}$$
$$parse \ (pretty' \ L + cs)$$
$$= \{pretty'\}$$
$$parse \ (\texttt{"L"} + cs)$$
$$= \{+\}$$
$$parse \ (\texttt{'L'} : cs)$$
$$= \{parse\}$$
$$(L, cs)$$

The second case requires somewhat more work, but is still straightforward. (The use of **where** here is not syntactically correct, but is used for stylistic reasons. Just think of it as a postfix **let**.)

$$(parse \circ pretty) \ (B \ l \ r, cs)$$
$$= \{\circ, pretty\}$$
$$parse \ (pretty' \ (B \ l \ r) + cs)$$
$$= \{pretty', + associative, +\}$$
$$parse \ (\texttt{'B'} : pretty' \ l + pretty' \ r + cs)$$
$$= \{parse\}$$
$$(B \ l' \ r', cs'')$$
$$\quad \textbf{where} \ (l', cs') = parse \ (pretty' \ l + pretty' \ r + cs)$$
$$\qquad\qquad (r', cs'') = parse \ cs'$$
$$= \{pretty, \circ\}$$
$$(B \ l' \ r', cs'')$$
$$\quad \textbf{where} \ (l', cs') = (parse \circ pretty) \ (l, pretty' \ r + cs)$$
$$\qquad\qquad (r', cs'') = parse \ cs'$$
$$= \{\text{Inductive hypothesis}\}$$

$$(B\ l'\ r',\ cs'')$$
$$\quad \textbf{where}\ (l',\ cs') = id\ (l,\ pretty'\ r \mathbin{+\!\!+} cs)$$
$$\qquad\qquad (r',\ cs'') = parse\ cs'$$
$$= \{id,\ \textbf{where}\}$$
$$(B\ l\ r',\ cs'')$$
$$\quad \textbf{where}\ (r',\ cs'') = parse\ (pretty'\ r \mathbin{+\!\!+} cs)$$
$$= \{pretty,\ \circ\}$$
$$(B\ l\ r',\ cs'')$$
$$\quad \textbf{where}\ (r',\ cs'') = (parse \circ pretty)\ (r,\ cs)$$
$$= \{\text{Inductive hypothesis}\}$$
$$(B\ l\ r',\ cs'')$$
$$\quad \textbf{where}\ (r',\ cs'') = id\ (r,\ cs)$$
$$= \{id,\ \textbf{where}\}$$
$$(B\ l\ r,\ cs)$$

Hence we have proved using structural induction that $(parse \circ pretty)\ (t,\ cs)$ $= (t,\ cs)$ for all finite, total $t :: T$ and for all $cs :: String$. Thus we can draw the conclusion that (1) is satisfied for that kind of input.

Pretty after Parse. We can show that (2) is satisfied in a similar way, using the fact that all Haskell functions are continuous and hence monotone with respect to $\sqsubseteq$. In fact, the proof works for arbitrary partial, finite input. We show the case for $cs :: String$, $head\ cs = \text{'B'}$, i.e. $cs = \text{'B'} : cs_1$ for some (partial and finite) $cs_1 :: String$:

$$(pretty \circ parse)\ (\text{'B'} : cs_1)$$
$$= \{\circ,\ parse\}$$
$$pretty\ (B\ l\ r,\ cs''_1)$$
$$\quad \textbf{where}\ (l,\ cs'_1) = parse\ cs_1$$
$$\qquad\qquad (r,\ cs''_1) = parse\ cs'_1$$
$$= \{pretty,\ pretty',\ \mathbin{+\!\!+}\ \text{associative}\}$$
$$\text{"B"} \mathbin{+\!\!+} pretty'\ l \mathbin{+\!\!+} pretty'\ r \mathbin{+\!\!+} cs''_1$$
$$\quad \textbf{where}\ (l,\ cs'_1) = parse\ cs_1$$
$$\qquad\qquad (r,\ cs''_1) = parse\ cs'_1$$
$$= \{pretty\}$$
$$\text{"B"} \mathbin{+\!\!+} pretty'\ l \mathbin{+\!\!+} pretty\ (r,\ cs''_1)$$
$$\quad \textbf{where}\ (l,\ cs'_1) = parse\ cs_1$$
$$\qquad\qquad (r,\ cs''_1) = parse\ cs'_1$$
$$= \{\textbf{where},\ pretty\ \bot = pretty\ (\bot, \bot),\ \circ\}$$
$$\text{"B"} \mathbin{+\!\!+} pretty'\ l \mathbin{+\!\!+} (pretty \circ parse)\ cs'_1$$
$$\quad \textbf{where}\ (l,\ cs'_1) = parse\ cs_1$$
$$\sqsubseteq \{\text{Inductive hypothesis, monotonicity}\}$$
$$\text{"B"} \mathbin{+\!\!+} pretty'\ l \mathbin{+\!\!+} id\ cs'_1$$
$$\quad \textbf{where}\ (l,\ cs'_1) = parse\ cs_1$$
$$= \{id,\ pretty,\ \textbf{where},\ pretty\ \bot = pretty\ (\bot, \bot),\ \circ\}$$
$$\text{"B"} \mathbin{+\!\!+} (pretty \circ parse)\ cs_1$$
$$\sqsubseteq \{\text{Inductive hypothesis, monotonicity}\}$$
$$\text{"B"} \mathbin{+\!\!+} id\ cs_1$$
$$= \{id,\ \mathbin{+\!\!+}\}$$
$$\text{'B'} : cs_1$$

The other cases ($head\ cs \notin \{\text{'L'},\text{'B'}\}$ and $head\ cs = \text{'L'}$) are both straightforward.

Parse after Pretty, Revisited. If we try to allow partial input in (1) instead of only total input, then we run into problems, as this counterexample shows:

$(parse \circ pretty) (\bot, cs)$
$= \{\circ,\ pretty\}$
$\quad parse\ (pretty'\ \bot + cs)$
$= \{pretty',\ +\}$
$\quad parse\ \bot$
$= \{parse\}$
$\quad \bot :: (T, String)$
$\neq \{(,)\ \text{is not strict}\}$
$\quad (\bot, cs) :: (T, String)$

We summarise our results so far in a table; we have proved (2) for finite, partial input and (1) for finite, total input. We have also disproved (1) in the case of partial input. The case marked with ? is treated in Sect. 5 below.

	Total	Partial
Finite	(2), (1)	(2), $\neg$ (1)
Infinite	?	$\neg$ (1)

Hence the programs are not correct if we take (1) and (2) plus the type signatures of *pretty* and *parse* as our specification. Instead of refining the programs to meet this specification we will try to refine the specification. This approach is in line with our goal from Sect. 1: To prove properties of programs, without changing them.

5   Tests

As seen above we have to refine our properties, at least (1). To aid us in finding properties which are valid for partial and infinite input we will test the properties before we try to prove them.

How do we test infinite input in finite time? An approach which seems to work fine is to use the approximation lemma [6]. For T the function *approx* is defined as follows (*Nat* is a data type for natural numbers):

data $Nat = Zero \mid Succ\ Nat$
$approx :: Nat \to T \to T$
$approx\ (Succ\ n) = \lambda t \to \textbf{case}\ t\ \textbf{of}$
$\quad L\quad \to L$
$\quad B\ l\ r \to B\ (approx\ n\ l)\ (approx\ n\ r)$

Note that *approx Zero* is undefined, i.e. $\bot$. Hence *approx* $n\ t$ traverses n levels down into the tree t and replaces everything there by $\bot$.

For the special case of trees the approximation lemma states that, for any $t_1, t_2 :: T$,

$$t_1 = t_2 \quad \text{iff} \quad \forall n \in Nat_{\text{fin}}.\ approx\ n\ t_1 = approx\ n\ t_2. \tag{3}$$

Here Nat_{fin} stands for the total and finite values of type Nat, i.e. Nat_{fin} corresponds directly to $\mathbb{N}$. If we want to test that two expressions yielding possibly infinite trees are equal then we can use the right hand side of this equivalence. Of course we cannot test the equality for all n, but if it is not valid then running the test for small values of n should often be enough to find a counterexample.

Testing equality between lists using $take :: Int \rightarrow [a] \rightarrow [a]$ and the take lemma, an analogue to the approximation lemma, is relatively common. However, the former does not generalise as easily to other data types as the latter does. The approximation lemma generalises to any type which can be defined as the least fixpoint of a locally continuous functor [6]. This includes not only all polynomial types, but also much more, like nested and exponential types.

Using the approximation lemma we have now reduced testing of infinite values to testing of partial values. Thus even if we were dealing with total values only, we would still need to include $\bot$ in our tests. Generating the value $\bot$ is easily accomplished:

$$\bot :: a$$
$$\bot = error \text{ "}_-\text{|}_-\text{"}$$

(Note that the same notation is used for the expression that generates a $\bot$ as for the value itself.)

The tricky part is testing for equality. If we do not want to use a separate tool then we necessarily have to use some impure extension, e.g. exception handling [11]. Furthermore it would be nice if we could perform these tests in pure code, such as QuickCheck [2] properties (see below). This can only be accomplished by using the decidedly unsafe function $unsafePerformIO :: IO\ a \rightarrow a$ [1, 11]. The resulting function $isBottom :: a \rightarrow Bool$[1] has to be used with care; it only detects a $\bot$ that results in an exception. However, that is enough for our purposes, since pattern match failures, $error$ "..." and $undefined$ all raise exceptions. If $isBottom\ x$ terminates properly, then we can be certain that the answer produced ($True$ or $False$) is correct.

Using $isBottom$ we define a function that compares two arbitrary finite trees for equality:

$$(\hat{=}) :: T \rightarrow T \rightarrow Bool$$
$$t_1 \hat{=} t_2 = \textbf{case}\ (isBottom\ t_1, isBottom\ t_2)\ \textbf{of}$$
$$\quad (True,\ True) \rightarrow True$$
$$\quad (False,\ False) \rightarrow \textbf{case}\ (t_1, t_2)\ \textbf{of}$$
$$\qquad (L, L) \qquad\quad \rightarrow True$$
$$\qquad (B\ l\ r, B\ l'\ r') \rightarrow l \hat{=} l' \wedge r \hat{=} r'$$
$$\qquad \_ \qquad\qquad\ \rightarrow False$$
$$\quad \_ \rightarrow False$$

---

[1] The function $isBottom$ used here is a slight variation on the version implemented by Andy Gill in the libraries shipped with the GHC Haskell compiler. We have to take care not to catch e.g. stack overflow exceptions, as these may or may not correspond to bottoms.

Similarly we can define a function $(\hat{\sqsubseteq}) :: T \to T \to \mathit{Bool}$ which implements an approximation of the semantical domain ordering $(\sqsubseteq)$. The functions approx, $(\hat{=})$ and $(\hat{\sqsubseteq})$ are prime candidates for generalisation. We have implemented them using type classes; instances are generated automatically using the "Scrap Your Boilerplate" approach to generic programming [9].

QuickCheck is a library for defining and testing properties of Haskell functions [2]. By using the framework developed above we can now give QuickCheck implementations of properties (1) and (2):

$$\mathit{prop}_1\ n = \mathit{forAll}\ \mathit{pair}\ (\lambda p \to$$
$$\quad \mathit{approxPair}\ n\ ((\mathit{parse} \circ \mathit{pretty})\ p) \mathbin{\hat{=}} \mathit{approxPair}\ n\ (\mathit{id}\ p))$$
$$\mathit{prop}_2\ n = \mathit{forAll}\ \mathit{string}\ (\lambda cs \to$$
$$\quad \mathit{approx}\ n\ ((\mathit{pretty} \circ \mathit{parse})\ cs) \mathbin{\hat{\sqsubseteq}} \mathit{approx}\ n\ (\mathit{id}\ cs))$$
$$\mathit{approxPair}\ n\ (t, cs) = (\mathit{approx}\ n\ t, \mathit{approx}\ (2\,\hat{}\ n)\ cs)$$

These properties can be read more or less as ordinary set theoretic predicates, e.g. for prop_1 "for all pairs p the equality ... holds". The generators pair and string (defined in Appendix A) ensure that many different finite and infinite partial values are used for p and cs in the tests. Some values are never generated, though; see the end of this section.

If we run these tests then we see that prop_1 fails almost immediately, whereas prop_2 succeeds all the time. In other words (1) is not satisfied (which we already knew, see Sect. 4), but on the other hand we can be relatively certain that (2) is valid.

You might be interested in knowing whether (1) holds for *total* infinite input, a case which we have neglected above. We can easily write a test for such a case:

$$\mathit{infiniteTree} = B\ \mathit{infiniteTree}\ L$$
$$\mathit{propInfiniteTotal}\ n =$$
$$\quad \mathit{approxPair}\ n\ ((\mathit{parse} \circ \mathit{pretty})\ p) \mathbin{\hat{=}} \mathit{approxPair}\ n\ (\mathit{id}\ p)$$
$$\qquad \textbf{where}\ p = (\mathit{infiniteTree}, \texttt{""})$$

(The value $\mathit{infiniteTree}$ is a left-infinite tree.) When executing this test we run into trouble, though; the test does not terminate for any $n \in \mathit{Nat}_{\mathrm{fin}}$. The reason is that the left-hand side does not terminate, and no part of the second component of the output pair is ever created (i.e. it is $\bot$). This can be seen by unfolding the expression a few steps:

$$\mathit{approxPair}\ n\ ((\mathit{parse} \circ \mathit{pretty})\ (\mathit{infiniteTree}, \texttt{""}))$$
$$= \{\text{Unfold, rearrange slightly}\}$$
$$(\mathit{approx}\ n\ (B\ l\ r), \mathit{approx}\ (2\,\hat{}\ n)\ cs'')$$
$$\qquad \textbf{where}\ (l, cs') = (\mathit{parse} \circ \mathit{pretty})\ (\mathit{infiniteTree}, \texttt{"L"})$$
$$\qquad\qquad (r, cs'') = \mathit{parse}\ cs'$$

One of the subexpressions is $(\mathit{parse} \circ \mathit{pretty})\ (\mathit{infiniteTree}, \texttt{"L"})$, which is essentially the same expression as the one that we started out with, and cs'' will not be generated until that subexpression has produced any output in its second

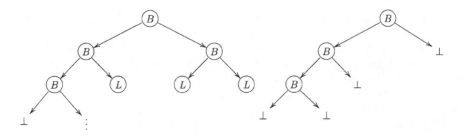

Fig. 1. With the left tree called t, the right tree is $t' = (fst \circ parse \circ pretty')\ t$.

component. The right-hand side does terminate, though, so (1) is not valid for total, infinite input.

Since $prop_1$ does not terminate for total, infinite trees we have designed our QuickCheck generators so that they do not generate such values. This is of course a slight drawback.

6   Properties: Second Try

As noted above (1) is not valid in general. If we inspect what happens when $fst \circ parse \circ pretty'$ is applied to a partial tree, then we see that as soon as a $\perp$ is encountered all nodes encountered later in a preorder traversal of the tree are replaced by $\perp$ (see Fig. 1).

We can easily verify that the example in the figure is correct (assuming that the part represented by the vertical dots is a left-infinite total tree):

$$t = B\ (B\ (B \perp infiniteTree)\ L)\ (B\ L\ L)$$
$$t' = B\ (B\ (B \perp \perp \qquad\quad)\perp)\perp$$
$$propFigure = t' \mathrel{\hat{=}} (fst \circ parse \circ pretty')\ t$$

Evaluating $propFigure$ yields $True$, as expected.

Given this background it is not hard to see that $(snd \circ parse \circ pretty)\ (t, cs) = \perp$ whenever the tree t is not total. Furthermore $(parse \circ pretty)\ (t, cs) = \perp$ iff $t = \perp$. Using the preceding results we can write a replacement $strictify$ for id that makes

$$parse \circ pretty = strictify :: (T, String) \rightarrow (T, String) \tag{1'}$$

a valid refinement of (1) (as we will see below):

$$strictify :: (T, a) \rightarrow (T, a)$$
$$strictify\ (t, a) = t\ `seq`\ (t', tTotal\ `seq`\ a)$$
$$\textbf{where}\ (t', tTotal) = strictify'\ t$$

If $t = \bot$ then $\bot$ should be returned, hence the first *seq*. The helper function *strictify'*, which does the main trunk of the work, returns the strictified tree in its first component. The second component, which is threaded bottom-up through the computation, is () whenever the input tree is total, and $\bot$ otherwise; hence the second *seq*. In effect we use the Haskell type () as a boolean type with $\bot$ as falsity and () as truth. It is the threading of this "boolean", in conjunction with the sequential nature of *seq*, which enforces the preorder traversal and strictification indicated in the figure above:

$$strictify' :: T \rightarrow (T, ())$$
$$strictify'\ L \qquad = (L, ())$$
$$strictify'\ (B\ l\ r) = (B\ l'\ (lTotal\ `seq`\ r'), lTotal\ `seq`\ rTotal)$$
$$\textbf{where}\ (l', lTotal) = strictify'\ l$$
$$\qquad\qquad (r', rTotal) = strictify'\ r$$

Note that if the left subtree l is not total, then the right subtree r should be replaced by $\bot$; hence the use of *lTotal `seq` r'* above. The second component should be () iff both subtrees are total, so we use *seq* as logical and between *lTotal* and *rTotal*; $a\ `seq`\ b = ()$ iff $a = ()$ and $b = ()$ for $a, b :: ()$.

Before we go on to prove (1'), let us test it:

$$prop_1'\ n = forAll\ pair\ (\lambda p \rightarrow$$
$$approxPair\ n\ ((parse \circ pretty)\ p) \triangleq approxPair\ n\ (strictify\ p))$$

This test seems to succeed all the time – a good indication that we are on the right track.

7   Proofs Using Fixpoint Induction

Now we will prove (1') and (2) using two different methods, fixpoint induction (in this section) and the approximation lemma (in Sect. 8). All details will not be presented, since that would take up too much space.

In this section let ψ, ψ_i etc. stand for arbitrary types.

To be able to use fixpoint induction [4, 14] all recursive functions have to be defined using *fix*, which is defined by

$$fix\ f = \bigsqcup_{i=0}^{\infty} f^i \bot \tag{4}$$

for any continuous function $f :: \psi \rightarrow \psi$. (The notation f^i stands for f composed with itself i times.) It is easy to implement *fix* in Haskell, but proving that the two definitions are equivalent would take up too much space, and is omitted:

$$fix :: (a \rightarrow a) \rightarrow a$$
$$fix\ f = f\ (fix\ f)$$

Let P be a chain-complete predicate, i.e. a predicate which is true for the least upper bound of a chain whenever it is true for all the elements in the chain. In other words, if $P(f^i \bot)$ is true for all $i \in \mathbb{N}$ and some $f :: \psi \to \psi$, then we know that $P(\mathit{fix}\ f)$ is true (we only consider ω-chains). Generalising we get the following inference rule from ordinary induction over natural numbers (and some simple domain theory):

$$\frac{P(\bot, \bot, \ldots, \bot) \qquad \begin{array}{c} \forall n \in \mathbb{N}.\ (P(f_1^n \bot, f_2^n \bot, \ldots, f_m^n \bot) \Rightarrow \\ P(f_1^{n+1} \bot, f_2^{n+1} \bot, \ldots, f_m^{n+1} \bot)) \end{array}}{P(\mathit{fix}\ f_1, \mathit{fix}\ f_2, \ldots, \mathit{fix}\ f_m)} \qquad (5)$$

Here $m \in \mathbb{N}$ and the f_i are continuous functions $f_i :: \psi_i \to \psi_i$. We also have the following useful variant which follows immediately from the previous one, assuming that the ψ_i are function types, $\psi_i = \psi_i' \to \psi_i''$, and that all f_i are strictness-preserving, i.e. if g_i is strict then $f_i\ g_i$ should be strict as well.

$$\frac{P(\bot, \bot, \ldots, \bot) \qquad \begin{array}{c} \forall\ \text{strict}\ g_1 :: \psi_1, g_2 :: \psi_2, \ldots, g_m :: \psi_m.\ \\ P(g_1, g_2, \ldots, g_m) \Rightarrow P(f_1\ g_1, f_2\ g_2, \ldots, f_m\ g_m) \end{array}}{P(\mathit{fix}\ f_1, \mathit{fix}\ f_2, \ldots, \mathit{fix}\ f_m)} \qquad (6)$$

That is all the theory that we need for now; on to the proofs. Let us begin by defining variants of our recursive functions using fix:

$$
\begin{aligned}
&\mathit{pretty}'_{\mathit{fix}} :: T \to \mathit{String} \\
&\mathit{pretty}'_{\mathit{fix}} = \mathit{fix}\ \mathit{pretty}_{\mathit{step}} \\
&\mathit{pretty}_{\mathit{step}} :: (T \to \mathit{String}) \to T \to \mathit{String} \\
&\mathit{pretty}_{\mathit{step}}\ p\ L \qquad\ = \texttt{"L"} \\
&\mathit{pretty}_{\mathit{step}}\ p\ (B\ l\ r) = \texttt{"B"} \mathbin{+\!\!+} p\ l \mathbin{+\!\!+} p\ r
\end{aligned}
$$

$$
\begin{aligned}
&\mathit{parse}_{\mathit{fix}} :: \mathit{String} \to (T, \mathit{String}) \\
&\mathit{parse}_{\mathit{fix}} = \mathit{fix}\ \mathit{parse}_{\mathit{step}} \\
&\mathit{parse}_{\mathit{step}} :: (\mathit{String} \to (T, \mathit{String})) \to \mathit{String} \to (T, \mathit{String}) \\
&\mathit{parse}_{\mathit{step}}\ p'\ (\texttt{'L'} : cs) = (L, cs) \\
&\mathit{parse}_{\mathit{step}}\ p'\ (\texttt{'B'} : cs) = (B\ l\ r, cs'') \\
&\quad \textbf{where}\ (l,\ cs')\ = p'\ cs \\
&\qquad\qquad\ (r, cs'') = p'\ cs'
\end{aligned}
$$

$$
\begin{aligned}
&\mathit{strictify}'_{\mathit{fix}} :: T \to (T, ()) \\
&\mathit{strictify}'_{\mathit{fix}} = \mathit{fix}\ \mathit{strictify}_{\mathit{step}} \\
&\mathit{strictify}_{\mathit{step}} :: (T \to (T, ())) \to T \to (T, ()) \\
&\mathit{strictify}_{\mathit{step}}\ s\ L \qquad\ = (L, ()) \\
&\mathit{strictify}_{\mathit{step}}\ s\ (B\ l\ r) = (B\ l'\ (lTotal\ `seq`\ r'), lTotal\ `seq`\ rTotal) \\
&\quad \textbf{where}\ (l', lTotal) = s\ l \\
&\qquad\qquad\ (r', rTotal) = s\ r
\end{aligned}
$$

Of course using these definitions instead of the original ones implies a proof obligation; we have to show that the two sets of definitions are equivalent to each other. In a standard domain theoretic setting this would follow immediately from the interpretation of a recursively defined function. In the case of Haskell this requires some work, though. The proofs are certainly possible to perform, but they would lead us too far astray, so we omit them here.

The properties have to be unrolled to fit the requirements of the inference rules. To make the properties more readable we define new versions of some other functions as well:

$$pretty_{fix} :: (T \rightarrow String) \rightarrow (T, String) \rightarrow String$$
$$pretty_{fix}\ p\ (t, cs) = p\ t \mathbin{+\!\!+} cs$$
$$strictify_{fix} :: (T \rightarrow (T, ())) \rightarrow (T, a) \rightarrow (T, a)$$
$$strictify_{fix}\ s\ (t, a) = t\ `seq`\ (t', tTotal\ `seq`\ a)$$
$$\textbf{where}\ (t', tTotal) = s\ t$$

We end up with

$$P_1(p, p', s) = \tag{7}$$
$$p' \circ pretty_{fix}\ p = strictify_{fix}\ s$$

and

$$P_2(p, p') = \tag{8}$$
$$pretty_{fix}\ p \circ p' \sqsubseteq id.$$

However, we cannot use P_1 as it stands since $P_1(\bot, \bot, \bot)$ is not true. To see this, pick an arbitrary $cs :: String$ and a $t :: T$ satisfying $t \neq \bot$:

$$(\bot \circ pretty_{fix}\ \bot)\ (t, cs)$$
$$= \{\circ, \bot\}$$
$$\bot :: (T, String)$$
$$\neq \{seq,\ t \neq \bot, (,)\ \text{is not strict}\}$$
$$t\ `seq`\ (\bot, \bot) :: (T, String)$$
$$= \{seq\}$$
$$t\ `seq`\ (\bot, \bot\ `seq`\ cs) :: (T, String)$$
$$= \{\textbf{where},\ \text{pattern matching}\}$$
$$t\ `seq`\ (t', tTotal\ `seq`\ cs) :: (T, String)$$
$$\quad \textbf{where}\ (t', tTotal) = \bot$$
$$= \{\bot\}$$
$$t\ `seq`\ (t', tTotal\ `seq`\ cs) :: (T, String)$$
$$\quad \textbf{where}\ (t', tTotal) = \bot\ t$$
$$= \{strictify_{fix}\}$$
$$strictify_{fix}\ \bot\ (t, cs)$$

We can still go on by noticing that we are only interested in the property in the limit and redefining it as

$$P_1'(p, p', s) = P_1(pretty_{step}\ p, parse_{step}\ p', strictify_{step}\ s), \tag{7'}$$

i.e. $P_1'(p, p', s)$ is equivalent to

$$parse_{step}\ p' \circ pretty_{fix}\ (pretty_{step}\ p) = strictify_{fix}\ (strictify_{step}\ s). \tag{9}$$

With P_1' we avoid the troublesome base case since $P_1'(\bot, \bot, \bot)$ is equivalent to $P_1(pretty_{step}\ \bot, parse_{step}\ \bot, strictify_{step}\ \bot)$.

Now it is straightforward to verify that $P_1'(\bot, \bot, \bot)$ and $P_2(\bot, \bot)$ are valid (P_1' requires a tedious but straightforward case analysis). It is also easy to verify that the predicates are chain-complete using general results from domain theory [14]. As we have already stated above, verifying formally that $P_1'(fix\ pretty_{step},\ fix\ parse_{step},\ fix\ strictify_{step})$ is equivalent to (1') and similarly that $P_2(fix\ pretty_{step},\ fix\ parse_{step})$ is equivalent to (2) requires more work and is omitted.

Pretty after Parse. Now on to the main work. Let us begin with P_2. Since we do not need the tighter inductive hypothesis of inference rule (5) we will use inference rule (6); it is easy to verify that $pretty_{step}$ and $parse_{step}$ are strictness-preserving. Assume now that $P_2(p, p')$ is valid for strict $p :: T \rightarrow String$ and $p' :: String \rightarrow (T, String)$. We have to show that $P_2(pretty_{step}\ p, parse_{step}\ p')$ is valid. After noting that both sides of the inequality are distinct from $\bot$, take an arbitrary element $cs :: String$. The proof is a case analysis on $head\ cs$.

First case, $head\ cs \notin \{\text{'L'}, \text{'B'}\}$:

> $(pretty_{fix}\ (pretty_{step}\ p) \circ (parse_{step}\ p'))\ cs$
> $= \{\circ,\ parse_{step},\ head\ cs \notin \{\text{'L'}, \text{'B'}\}\}$
> $pretty_{fix}\ (pretty_{step}\ p)\ \bot$
> $= \{pretty_{fix}\}$
> $\bot :: String$
> $\sqsubseteq \{\bot$ is the least element in the domain$\}$
> $id\ cs$

Second case, $head\ cs = \text{'L'}$, i.e. $cs = \text{'L'} : cs_1$ for some $cs_1 :: String$:

> $(pretty_{fix}\ (pretty_{step}\ p) \circ (parse_{step}\ p'))\ cs$
> $= \{\circ,\ parse_{step},\ cs = \text{'L'} : cs_1\}$
> $pretty_{fix}\ (pretty_{step}\ p)\ (L, cs_1)$
> $= \{pretty_{fix}\}$
> $pretty_{step}\ p\ L \mathbin{+\!\!+} cs_1$
> $= \{pretty_{step},\ +\!\!+,\ id\}$
> $id\ cs$

Last case, $head\ cs = \text{'B'}$, i.e. $cs = \text{'B'} : cs_1$ for some $cs_1 :: String$:

> $(pretty_{fix}\ (pretty_{step}\ p) \circ (parse_{step}\ p'))\ cs$
> $= \{\circ,\ parse_{step},\ cs = \text{'B'} : cs_1\}$
> $pretty_{fix}\ (pretty_{step}\ p)\ (B\ l\ r, cs_1'')$
> $\quad$ **where** $(l, cs_1') = p'\ cs_1$
> $\quad\quad\quad\quad (r, cs_1'') = p'\ cs_1'$

$$= \{pretty_{fix}, pretty_{step}, +\!\!\!+ \text{ associative}\}$$
"B" $+\!\!\!+$ p l $+\!\!\!+$ $(p$ r $+\!\!\!+$ $cs_1'')$
    where $(l, cs_1') = p'$ cs_1
            $(r, cs_1'') = p'$ cs_1'
$$= \{pretty_{fix}\}$$
"B" $+\!\!\!+$ p l $+\!\!\!+$ $pretty_{fix}$ p (r, cs_1'')
    where $(l, cs_1') = p'$ cs_1
            $(r, cs_1'') = p'$ cs_1'
$$= \{\text{where}, p \text{ strict implies that } pretty_{fix} \ p \perp = pretty_{fix} \ p \ (\perp, \perp), \circ\}$$
"B" $+\!\!\!+$ p l $+\!\!\!+$ $(pretty_{fix}$ $p \circ p')$ cs_1'
    where $(l, cs_1') = p'$ cs_1
$\sqsubseteq$ {Inductive hypothesis, monotonicity}
"B" $+\!\!\!+$ p l $+\!\!\!+$ id cs_1'
    where $(l, cs_1') = p'$ cs_1
$$= \{id, pretty_{fix}, \text{where}, p \text{ strict}, \circ\}$$
"B" $+\!\!\!+$ $(pretty_{fix}$ $p \circ p')$ cs_1
$\sqsubseteq$ {Inductive hypothesis, monotonicity}
"B" $+\!\!\!+$ id cs_1
$$= \{id, +\!\!\!+, id\}$$
id cs

This concludes the proof for P_2.

Parse after Pretty. For P_1' we will also use inference rule (6); in addition to $pretty_{step}$ and $parse_{step}$ it is easy to verify that $strictify_{step}$ is strictness-preserving. Assume that $P_1'(p_0, p_0', s_0)$ is valid, where p_0, p_0' and s_0 are all strict. We have to prove that $P_1'(pretty_{step} \ p_0, parse_{step} \ p_0', strictify_{step} \ s_0)$ is valid. This is equivalent to proving $P_1(pretty_{step} \ p, parse_{step} \ p', strictify_{step} \ s)$, where $p = pretty_{step} \ p_0$, $p' = parse_{step} \ p_0'$ and $s = strictify_{step} \ s_0$. The first step of this proof is to note that both sides of the equality in P_1' are distinct from $\perp$. The rest of the proof is, as before, performed using case analysis, this time on $pair$, an arbitrary element in (T, cs). The cases $pair = \perp$, $pair = (\perp, cs)$ and $pair = (L, cs)$ for an arbitrary $cs :: String$ are straightforward and omitted.

Last case, $pair = (B \ l \ r, cs)$ for arbitrary subtrees $l, r :: T$ and an arbitrary $cs :: String$:

$(parse_{step} \ p' \circ pretty_{fix} \ (pretty_{step} \ p)) \ (B \ l \ r, cs)$
$= \{\circ, pretty_{fix}\}$
    $parse_{step} \ p' \ (pretty_{step} \ p \ (B \ l \ r) +\!\!\!+ cs)$
$= \{pretty_{step}, +\!\!\!+, +\!\!\!+ \text{ associative}\}$
    $parse_{step} \ p' \ ('B' : p \ l +\!\!\!+ (p \ r +\!\!\!+ cs))$
$= \{parse_{step}\}$
    $(B \ l' \ r', cs'')$
        where $(l', cs') = p' \ (p \ l +\!\!\!+ (p \ r +\!\!\!+ cs))$
                $(r', cs'') = p' \ cs'$
$= \{pretty_{fix}, \circ\}$

$$(B\ l'\ r',\ cs'')$$
$$\textbf{where}\ (l',\ cs') = (p' \circ \mathit{pretty}_{\mathit{fix}}\ p)\ (l, p\ r \mathbin{+\!\!+} cs)$$
$$\qquad\qquad (r',\ cs'') = p'\ cs'$$
$$= \{\text{Inductive hypothesis}\}$$
$$(B\ l'\ r',\ cs'')$$
$$\textbf{where}\ (l',\ cs') = \mathit{strictify}_{\mathit{fix}}\ s\ (l, p\ r \mathbin{+\!\!+} cs)$$
$$\qquad\qquad (r',\ cs'') = p'\ cs'$$
$$= \{\mathit{strictify}_{\mathit{fix}}\}$$
$$(B\ l'\ r',\ cs'')$$
$$\textbf{where}\ (l',\ cs') \quad = l\ \grave{}seq\grave{}\ (t', tTotal\ \grave{}seq\grave{}\ p\ r \mathbin{+\!\!+} cs)$$
$$\qquad\qquad (t', tTotal) = s\ l$$
$$\qquad\qquad (r',\ cs'') \quad = p'\ cs'$$
$$= \{\text{Simple case analysis on } l\ (\bot \text{ or not } \bot), \text{pattern matching}\}$$
$$(B\ l'\ r',\ cs'')$$
$$\textbf{where}\ (l',\ cs') \quad = (l\ \grave{}seq\grave{}\ t', l\ \grave{}seq\grave{}\ tTotal\ \grave{}seq\grave{}\ p\ r \mathbin{+\!\!+} cs)$$
$$\qquad\qquad (t', tTotal) = s\ l$$
$$\qquad\qquad (r',\ cs'') \quad = p'\ cs'$$
$$= \{seq, \text{ if } l = \bot \text{ then } t' = tTotal = \bot \text{ since } s \text{ is strict}\}$$
$$(B\ l'\ r',\ cs'')$$
$$\textbf{where}\ (l',\ cs') \quad = (t', tTotal\ \grave{}seq\grave{}\ p\ r \mathbin{+\!\!+} cs)$$
$$\qquad\qquad (t', tTotal) = s\ l$$
$$\qquad\qquad (r',\ cs'') \quad = p'\ cs'$$
$$= \{\textbf{where}\}$$
$$(B\ t'\ r',\ cs'')$$
$$\textbf{where}\ (t', tTotal) = s\ l$$
$$\qquad\qquad (r',\ cs'') \quad = p'\ (tTotal\ \grave{}seq\grave{}\ p\ r \mathbin{+\!\!+} cs)$$
$$= \{\text{Rename variables}\}$$
$$(B\ l'\ r',\ cs'')$$
$$\textbf{where}\ (l', lTotal) = s\ l$$
$$\qquad\qquad (r',\ cs'') \quad = p'\ (lTotal\ \grave{}seq\grave{}\ p\ r \mathbin{+\!\!+} cs)$$

The rest of the proof is straightforward. Using case analysis on $lTotal$ we prove that

$$(B\ l'\ r',\ cs'')$$
$$\textbf{where}\ (r',\ cs'') = p'\ (lTotal\ \grave{}seq\grave{}\ p\ r \mathbin{+\!\!+} cs)$$
$$=$$
$$(B\ l'\ (lTotal\ \grave{}seq\grave{}\ r'), lTotal\ \grave{}seq\grave{}\ rTotal\ \grave{}seq\grave{}\ cs)$$
$$\textbf{where}\ (r', rTotal) = s\ r$$

is valid. In one branch one can observe that p' is strict. In the other the inductive hypothesis can be applied, followed by reasoning analogous to the one for $l\ \grave{}seq\grave{}$ above. Given this equality the rest of the proof is easy. Hence we can draw the conclusion that $P_1(\mathit{pretty}_{\mathit{step}}\ p, \mathit{parse}_{\mathit{step}}\ p', \mathit{strictify}_{\mathit{step}}\ s)$ is valid, which means that we have finished the proof.

8   Proofs Using the Approximation Lemma

Let us now turn to the approximation lemma. This lemma was presented above in Sect. 5, but we still have a little work to do before we can go to the proofs.

Pretty after Parse. Any naive attempt to prove (2) using the obvious inductive hypothesis fails. Using the following less obvious reformulated property does the trick, though:

$$\forall m \in \mathbb{N}. \ pp_m \sqsubseteq id :: String \rightarrow String. \tag{10}$$

Here we use a family of helper functions pp_m $(m \in \mathbb{N})$:

$$pp_m \ cs = pretty' \ t_1 +\!\!+ pretty' \ t_2 +\!\!+ \ldots +\!\!+ pretty' \ t_m +\!\!+ cs_m$$
$$\textbf{where} \ (t_1, \ cs_1) \ = parse \ cs$$
$$(t_2, \ cs_2) \ = parse \ cs_1$$
$$\vdots$$
$$(t_m, cs_m) = parse \ cs_{m-1}$$

(We interpret pp_0 as id.) It is straightforward to verify that this property is equivalent to (2).

Note that we cannot use the approximation lemma directly as it stands, since the lemma deals with equalities, not inequalities. However, replacing each $=$ with $\sqsubseteq$ in the proof of the approximation lemma in Gibbons' and Hutton's article [4, Sect. 4] is enough to verify this variant. We get that, for all $m \in \mathbb{N}$ and $cs :: String$,

$$pp_m \ cs \sqsubseteq id \ cs \quad \text{iff}$$
$$\forall n \in Nat_{\text{fin}}. \ approx \ n \ (pp_m \ cs) \sqsubseteq approx \ n \ (id \ cs). \tag{11}$$

Hence all that we need to do is to prove the last statement above (after noticing that both pp_m and id are distinct from $\bot$, for all $m \in \mathbb{N}$). We do that by induction over n, after observing that we can change the order of the universal quantifiers so that we get

$$\forall n \in Nat_{\text{fin}}. \ \forall m \in \mathbb{N}. \ \forall cs :: String.$$
$$approx \ n \ (pp_m \ cs) \sqsubseteq approx \ n \ (id \ cs), \tag{12}$$

which is equivalent to the inequalities above.

For lists we have the following variant of *approx*:

$$approx :: Nat \rightarrow [a] \rightarrow [a]$$
$$approx \ (Succ \ n) = \lambda(x : xs) \rightarrow x : approx \ n \ xs$$

Since *approx Zero* is undefined the statement (12) is trivially true for $n = Zero$. Assume now that $\forall m \in \mathbb{N}$. $\forall cs :: String$. $approx\ n\ (pp_m\ cs) \sqsubseteq approx\ n\ (id\ cs)$ is true for some $n \in Nat_{\text{fin}}$. Take an arbitrary $m \in \mathbb{N}$. Note that the property that we want to prove is trivially true for $m = 0$, so assume that $m \geq 1$. We proceed by case analysis on *head cs*.

First case, *head cs* $\notin \{\text{'L'}, \text{'B'}\}$:

$$approx\ (Succ\ n)\ (pp_m\ cs)$$
$$= \{parse, \textbf{where}, pretty', +\!\!+\}$$
$$approx\ (Succ\ n)\ \bot$$
$$\sqsubseteq \{\bot \text{ is the least element, monotonicity}\}$$
$$approx\ (Succ\ n)\ (id\ cs)$$

Second case, *head cs* $= \text{'L'}$, i.e. $cs = \text{'L'} : cs'$ for some $cs' :: String$:

$$approx\ (Succ\ n)\ (pp_m\ (\text{'L'} : cs'))$$
$$= \{pp_m, m \geq 1\}$$
$$approx\ (Succ\ n)\ (pretty'\ t_1 +\!\!+ pretty'\ t_2 +\!\!+ \ldots +\!\!+ pretty'\ t_m +\!\!+ cs_m)$$
$$\quad \textbf{where}\ (t_1,\ cs_1)\ = parse\ (\text{'L'} : cs')$$
$$\quad\quad\quad\quad (t_2,\ cs_2)\ = parse\ cs_1$$

$$\vdots$$

$$\quad\quad\quad\quad (t_m, cs_m) = parse\ cs_{m-1}$$
$$= \{parse, \textbf{where}, \text{note that if } m = 1 \text{ then } cs_m = cs'\}$$
$$approx\ (Succ\ n)\ (pretty'\ L +\!\!+ pretty'\ t_2 +\!\!+ \ldots +\!\!+ pretty'\ t_m +\!\!+ cs_m)$$
$$\quad \textbf{where}\ (t_2,\ cs_2)\ = parse\ cs'$$

$$\vdots$$

$$\quad\quad\quad\quad (t_m, cs_m) = parse\ cs_{m-1}$$
$$= \{pretty', +\!\!+\}$$
$$approx\ (Succ\ n)\ (\text{'L'} : pretty'\ t_2 +\!\!+ \ldots +\!\!+ pretty'\ t_m +\!\!+ cs_m)$$
$$\quad \textbf{where}\ (t_2,\ cs_2)\ = parse\ cs'$$

$$\vdots$$

$$\quad\quad\quad\quad (t_m, cs_m) = parse\ cs_{m-1}$$
$$= \{approx\}$$
$$\text{'L'} : approx\ n\ (pretty'\ t_2 +\!\!+ \ldots +\!\!+ pretty'\ t_m +\!\!+ cs_m)$$
$$\quad \textbf{where}\ (t_2,\ cs_2)\ = parse\ cs'$$

$$\vdots$$

$$\quad\quad\quad\quad (t_m, cs_m) = parse\ cs_{m-1}$$
$$= \{pp_{m-1}, m \geq 1\}$$
$$\text{'L'} : approx\ n\ (pp_{m-1}\ cs')$$
$$\sqsubseteq \{\text{Inductive hypothesis, monotonicity}\}$$
$$\text{'L'} : approx\ n\ (id\ cs')$$
$$= \{id, approx\}$$
$$approx\ (Succ\ n)\ (\text{'L'} : cs')$$

Last case, $head\ cs = \text{'B'}$, i.e. $cs = \text{'B'} : cs'$ for some $cs' :: String$:

$approx\ (Succ\ n)\ (pp_m\ (\text{'B'} : cs'))$
$= \{pp_m,\ m \geq 1\}$
$\quad approx\ (Succ\ n)\ (pretty'\ t_1 \mathbin{+\!\!+} pretty'\ t_2 \mathbin{+\!\!+} \ldots \mathbin{+\!\!+} pretty'\ t_m \mathbin{+\!\!+} cs_m)$
$\qquad \mathbf{where}\ (t_1,\ cs_1)\ = parse\ (\text{'B'} : cs')$
$\qquad\qquad\ (t_2,\ cs_2)\ = parse\ cs_1$
$\qquad\qquad\qquad \vdots$
$\qquad\qquad\ (t_m, cs_m) = parse\ cs_{m-1}$
$= \{parse,\ \mathbf{where}\}$
$\quad approx\ (Succ\ n)\ (pretty'\ (B\ l\ r) \mathbin{+\!\!+} pretty'\ t_2 \mathbin{+\!\!+} \ldots \mathbin{+\!\!+} pretty'\ t_m \mathbin{+\!\!+} cs_m)$
$\qquad \mathbf{where}\ (l,\ \ ls)\ \ = parse\ cs'$
$\qquad\qquad\ (r,\ \ rs)\ \ = parse\ ls$
$\qquad\qquad\ (t_2,\ cs_2)\ = parse\ rs$
$\qquad\qquad\qquad \vdots$
$\qquad\qquad\ (t_m, cs_m) = parse\ cs_{m-1}$
$= \{pretty',\ \mathbin{+\!\!+},\ \mathbin{+\!\!+}\ \text{associative}\}$
$\quad approx\ (Succ\ n)$
$\qquad (\text{'B'} : pretty'\ l \mathbin{+\!\!+} pretty'\ r \mathbin{+\!\!+} pretty'\ t_2 \mathbin{+\!\!+} \ldots \mathbin{+\!\!+} pretty'\ t_m \mathbin{+\!\!+} cs_m)$
$\qquad \mathbf{where}\ (l,\ \ ls)\ \ = parse\ cs'$
$\qquad\qquad\ (r,\ \ rs)\ \ = parse\ ls$
$\qquad\qquad\ (t_2,\ cs_2)\ = parse\ rs$
$\qquad\qquad\qquad \vdots$
$\qquad\qquad\ (t_m, cs_m) = parse\ cs_{m-1}$
$= \{approx\}$
$\quad \text{'B'} : approx\ n\ (pretty'\ l \mathbin{+\!\!+} pretty'\ r \mathbin{+\!\!+} pretty'\ t_2 \mathbin{+\!\!+} \ldots \mathbin{+\!\!+} pretty'\ t_m \mathbin{+\!\!+} cs_m)$
$\qquad \mathbf{where}\ (l,\ \ ls)\ \ = parse\ cs'$
$\qquad\qquad\ (r,\ \ rs)\ \ = parse\ ls$
$\qquad\qquad\ (t_2,\ cs_2)\ = parse\ rs$
$\qquad\qquad\qquad \vdots$
$\qquad\qquad\ (t_m, cs_m) = parse\ cs_{m-1}$
$= \{pp_{m+1}\}$
$\quad \text{'B'} : approx\ n\ (pp_{m+1}\ cs')$
$\sqsubseteq \{\text{Inductive hypothesis, monotonicity}\}$
$\quad \text{'B'} : approx\ n\ (id\ cs')$
$= \{id,\ approx\}$
$\quad approx\ (Succ\ n)\ (\text{'B'} : cs')$

Hence we have yet again proved (2), this time using the approximation lemma.

Parse after Pretty. Let us now turn to (1'). We want to verify that $parse \circ pretty = strictify :: (T, String) \to (T, String)$ holds. This can be done using the approximation lemma as given in equivalence (3). To ease the presentation we will use the following helper function:

$$approxP :: Nat \rightarrow (T, a) \rightarrow (T, a)$$
$$approxP \; n \; (t, a) = (approx \; n \; t, a)$$

Using this function we can formulate the approximation lemma as

$$p1 = p2 \quad \text{iff} \quad \forall n \in Nat_{\text{fin}} . \; approxP \; n \; p1 = approxP \; n \; p2 \qquad (13)$$

for arbitrary pairs $p1, p2 :: (T, \psi)$, where ψ is an arbitrary type. In our case $\psi = String$, $p1 = (parse \circ pretty) \; p$ and $p2 = strictify \; p$ for an arbitrary pair $p :: (T, String)$.

The proof proceeds by induction over n as usual; and as usual we first have to observe that $parse \circ pretty$ and $strictify$ are both distinct from $\bot$. The case $n = Zero$ is trivial. Now assume that we have proved $approxP \; n \; ((parse \circ pretty) \; p) = approxP \; n \; (strictify \; p)$ for some $n \in Nat_{\text{fin}}$ and all $p :: (T, String)$. (All p since we can change the order of the universal quantifiers like we did to arrive at inequality (12).) We prove the corresponding statement for $Succ \; n$ by case analysis on p. All cases except for the one where $p = (B \; l \; r, cs)$ for arbitrary subtrees $l, r :: T$ and an arbitrary $cs :: String$ are straightforward and omitted, so we go directly to the last case:

$$approxP \; (Succ \; n) \; ((parse \circ pretty) \; (B \; l \; r, cs))$$
$= \{\circ, pretty, pretty', +\!\!+, +\!\!+ \text{ associative}\}$
$\quad approxP \; (Succ \; n) \; (parse \; ('B' : pretty' \; l +\!\!+ pretty' \; r +\!\!+ cs))$
$= \{parse, pretty, \circ\}$
$\quad approxP \; (Succ \; n) \; (B \; l' \; r', cs'')$
$\qquad \textbf{where } (l', cs') = (parse \circ pretty) \; (l, pretty' \; r +\!\!+ cs)$
$\qquad \qquad \quad (r', cs'') = parse \; cs'$
$= \{approxP, approx\}$
$\quad (B \; (approx \; n \; l') \; (approx \; n \; r'), cs'')$
$\qquad \textbf{where } (l', cs') = (parse \circ pretty) \; (l, pretty' \; r +\!\!+ cs)$
$\qquad \qquad \quad (r', cs'') = parse \; cs'$
$= \{\text{Push } approx \; n \text{ through the pairs, turning it into } approxP \; n\}$
$\quad (B \; l' \; r', cs'')$
$\qquad \textbf{where } (l', cs') = approxP \; n \; ((parse \circ pretty) \; (l, pretty' \; r +\!\!+ cs))$
$\qquad \qquad \quad (r', cs'') = approxP \; n \; (parse \; cs')$
$= \{\text{Inductive hypothesis}\}$
$\quad (B \; l' \; r', cs'')$
$\qquad \textbf{where } (l', cs') = approxP \; n \; (strictify \; (l, pretty' \; r +\!\!+ cs))$
$\qquad \qquad \quad (r', cs'') = approxP \; n \; (parse \; cs')$
$= \{strictify\}$
$\quad (B \; l' \; r', cs'')$
$\qquad \textbf{where } (l', cs') = \quad approxP \; n \; (l \; `seq` \; (t', tTotal \; `seq` \; pretty' \; r +\!\!+ cs))$
$\qquad \qquad \quad (t', tTotal) = strictify' \; l$
$\qquad \qquad \quad (r', cs'') = \quad approxP \; n \; (parse \; cs')$

The proof proceeds by case analysis on l. We omit the cases $l = \bot$ and $l = L$ and go to the last case, $l = B \; l_1 \; r_1$ for arbitrary subtrees $l_1, r_1 :: T$:

$(B \ l' \ r', cs'')$
    where
    $(l', cs') \quad = approxP \ n \ (B \ l_1 \ r_1 \ `seq` \ (t', tTotal \ `seq` \ pretty' \ r + cs))$
    $(t', tTotal) = strictify' \ (B \ l_1 \ r_1)$
    $(r', cs'') \quad = approxP \ n \ (parse \ cs')$
$= \{seq, strictify', \textbf{where}\}$
 $(B \ l' \ r', cs'')$
    where
    $(l', cs') \quad = approxP \ n \ (B \ l'_1 \ (lTotal \ `seq` \ r'_1),$
    $\qquad\qquad\qquad\qquad\qquad (lTotal \ `seq` \ rTotal) \ `seq` \ pretty' \ r + cs)$
    $(l'_1, lTotal) = strictify' \ l_1$
    $(r'_1, rTotal) = strictify' \ r_1$
    $(r', cs'') \quad = approxP \ n \ (parse \ cs')$
$= \{approxP, \textbf{where}\}$
 $(B \ (approx \ n \ (B \ l'_1 \ (lTotal \ `seq` \ r'_1))) \ r', cs'')$
    where
    $(l'_1, lTotal) = strictify' \ l_1$
    $(r'_1, rTotal) = strictify' \ r_1$
    $(r', cs'') \quad = approxP \ n \ (parse \ ((lTotal \ `seq` \ rTotal) \ `seq` \ pretty' \ r + cs))$

Now we have two cases, depending on whether $lTotal \ `seq` \ rTotal$, i.e. snd $(strictify' \ l_1) \ `seq` \ snd \ (strictify' \ r_1)$, equals $\bot$ or not. We omit the case where the equality holds and concentrate on the case where $lTotal `seq` rTotal = () \neq \bot$:

 $(B \ (approx \ n \ (B \ l'_1 \ (lTotal \ `seq` \ r'_1))) \ r', cs'')$
    where $(l'_1, lTotal) = strictify' \ l_1$
    $\qquad\quad (r'_1, rTotal) = strictify' \ r_1$
    $\qquad\quad (r', cs'') \quad = approxP \ n \ (parse \ (() \ `seq` \ pretty' \ r + cs))$
$= \{seq, pretty, \circ\}$
 $(B \ (approx \ n \ (B \ l'_1 \ (lTotal \ `seq` \ r'_1))) \ r', cs'')$
    where $(l'_1, lTotal) = strictify' \ l_1$
    $\qquad\quad (r'_1, rTotal) = strictify' \ r_1$
    $\qquad\quad (r', cs'') \quad = approxP \ n \ ((parse \circ pretty) \ (r, cs))$
$= \{\text{Inductive hypothesis}\}$
 $(B \ (approx \ n \ (B \ l'_1 \ (lTotal \ `seq` \ r'_1))) \ r', cs'')$
    where $(l'_1, lTotal) = strictify' \ l_1$
    $\qquad\quad (r'_1, rTotal) = strictify' \ r_1$
    $\qquad\quad (r', cs'') \quad = approxP \ n \ (strictify \ (r, cs))$
$= \{\text{Push } approxP \ n \text{ through the pair, turning it into } approx \ n\}$
 $(B \ (approx \ n \ (B \ l'_1 \ (lTotal \ `seq` \ r'_1))) \ (approx \ n \ r'), cs'')$
    where $(l'_1, lTotal) = strictify' \ l_1$
    $\qquad\quad (r'_1, rTotal) = strictify' \ r_1$
    $\qquad\quad (r', cs'') \quad = strictify \ (r, cs)$
$= \{approx, approxP\}$
 $approxP \ (Succ \ n) \ (B \ (B \ l'_1 \ (lTotal \ `seq` \ r'_1)) \ r', cs'')$
    where $(l'_1, lTotal) = strictify' \ l_1$
    $\qquad\quad (r'_1, rTotal) = strictify' \ r_1$
    $\qquad\quad (r', cs'') \quad = strictify \ (r, cs)$

The rest of the proof consists of transforming the expression above to *approxP* (*Succ n*) (*strictify* (*B* (*B* l_1 r_1) *r, cs*)). This is relatively straightforward and omitted. Thus we have, yet again, proved (1').

9   Discussion and Future Work

In this paper we have investigated how different verification methods can handle partial and infinite values in a simple case study about data conversion. We have used random testing, fixpoint induction and the approximation lemma.

Using *isBottom* and *approx* for testing in the presence of partial and infinite values is not fool proof but works well in practice. The approach is not that original; testing using *isBottom* and *take* is (indirectly) mentioned already in the original QuickCheck paper [2]. However, testing using *approx* has probably not been done before. Furthermore, the functionality of $\hat{=}$ and $\hat{\sqsubseteq}$ has not been provided by any (widespread) library.

The two methods used for proving the properties (1') and (2) have different qualities. Fixpoint induction required us to rewrite both the functions and the properties. Furthermore one property did not hold for the base case, so it had to be rewritten (7'), and proving the base case required some tedious but straightforward work. On the other hand, once the initial work had been completed the "actual proofs" were comparatively short. The corresponding "actual proofs" were longer when using the approximation lemma. The reason for this is probably that the approximation lemma requires that the function *approx* is "pushed" inside the expressions to make it possible to apply the inductive hypothesis. For fixpoint induction that is not necessary. For instance, when proving (1') using the approximation lemma we had to go one level further down in the tree when performing case analysis, than in the corresponding proof using fixpoint induction. This was in order to be able to use the inductive hypothesis.

Nevertheless, the "actual proofs" are not really what is important. They mostly consist of performing a case analysis, evaluating both sides of the (in-) equality being proved as far as possible and then, if the proof is not finished yet, choosing a new expression to perform case analysis on. The most important part is really finding the right inductive hypothesis. (Choosing the right expression for case analysis is also important, but easier.) Finding the right inductive hypothesis was easier when using fixpoint induction than when using the approximation lemma. Take the proofs of (2), for instance. When using fixpoint induction almost no thought was needed to come up with the inductive hypothesis, whereas when using the approximation lemma we had to come up with the complex hypothesis based on property (10), the one involving pp_m. The reason was the same as above; *approx* has to be in the right position. It is of course possible that easier proofs exist.

It is also possible that there are other proof methods which work better than the ones used here. Coinduction and fusion, two other methods mentioned in Gibbons' and Hutton's tutorial [4], might belong to that category. We have made some attempts at using unfold fusion. Due to the nature of the programs the standard fusion method seems inapplicable, though; a monadic variant is a better fit. The programs can be transformed into monadic variants (which of course carries extra proof obligations). We have not yet figured out where to go from there, though. For instance, the monadic anamorphism fusion law [10, Equation (17)] only applies to a restrictive class of monads, and our "monad" does not even satisfy all the monad laws (compare Sect. 3).

Above we have compared different proof techniques in the case where we allow infinite and partial input. Let us now reflect on whether one should consider anything but finite, total values. The proofs of (1') and (2) valid for all inputs were considerably longer than the ones for (1) and (2) limited to finite (and in one case total) input, especially if one takes into account all work involved in rewriting the properties and programs. It is not hard to see why people often ignore partial and infinite input; handling it does seem to require nontrivial amounts of extra work.

However, as argued in Sect. 1 we often need to reason about infinite values. Furthermore, in reality, bottoms do occur; *error* is used, cases are left out from case expressions, and sometimes functions do not reach a weak head normal form even if they are applied to total input (for instance we have *reverse* $[1..] = \bot$). Another reason for including partial values is that in our setting of equational reasoning it is easier to use a known identity if the identity is valid without a precondition stating that the input has to be total. Of course, proving the identity without this precondition is only meaningful if the extra work involved is less than the accumulated work needed to verify the precondition each time the identity is used. This extra work may not amount to very much, though. Even if we were to ignore bottoms, we would still sometimes need to handle infinite values, so we would have to use methods like those used in this text. In this case the marginal cost for also including bottoms would be small.

Another approach is to settle for approximate results by e.g. assuming that $\lambda x \rightarrow \bot$ is $\bot$ when reasoning about programs. These results would be practically useful; we might get some overly conservative results if we happened to evaluate *seq* $(\lambda x \rightarrow \bot)$, but nothing worse would happen. On the other hand, many of the caveats mentioned in Sect. 3 would vanish. Furthermore most people tend to ignore these issues when doing ordinary programming, so in a sense an approximate semantics is already in use. The details of an approximate semantics for Haskell still need to be worked out, though. We believe that an approach like this will make it easier to scale up the methods used in this text to larger programs.

Acknowledgements

We would like to thank Andreas Abel, Ulf Norell and the anonymous referees for some helpful comments and/or discussions.

References

1. Manuel Chakravarty et al. *The Haskell 98 Foreign Function Interface 1.0, An Addendum to the Haskell 98 Report*, 2003. Available online at http://www.haskell.org/definition/.

2. Koen Claessen and John Hughes. QuickCheck: A lightweight tool for random testing of Haskell programs. In *Proceedings of the Fifth ACM SIGPLAN International Conference on Functional Programming*, pages 268–279. ACM Press, 2000.
3. Karl-Filip Faxén. A static semantics for Haskell. *Journal of Functional Programming*, 12(4&5):295–357, July 2002.
4. Jeremy Gibbons and Graham Hutton. Proof methods for corecursive programs. Submitted to Fundamenta Informaticae Special Issue on Program Transformation. Available online at http://www.cs.nott.ac.uk/~gmh/bib.html, March 2004.
5. John Hughes. Why functional programming matters. *Computer Journal*, 32(2):98–107, 1989.
6. Graham Hutton and Jeremy Gibbons. The generic approximation lemma. *Information Processing Letters*, 79(4):197–201, August 2001.
7. Patrik Jansson and Johan Jeuring. Polytypic data conversion programs. *Science of Computer Programming*, 43(1):35–75, 2002.
8. Patricia Johann and Janis Voigtländer. Free theorems in the presence of *seq*. In *Proceedings of the 31st ACM SIGPLAN-SIGACT Symposium on Principles of Programming Languages*, pages 99–110. ACM Press, 2004.
9. Ralf Lämmel and Simon Peyton Jones. Scrap your boilerplate: A practical design pattern for generic programming. *ACM SIGPLAN Notices*, 38(3):26–37, March 2003.
10. Alberto Pardo. Monadic corecursion – definition, fusion laws, and applications –. In Bart Jacobs, Larry Moss, Horst Reichel, and Jan Rutten, editors, *Electronic Notes in Theoretical Computer Science*, volume 11. Elsevier, 2000.
11. Simon Peyton Jones. *Engineering Theories of Software Construction*, volume 180 of *NATO Science Series: Computer & Systems Sciences*, chapter Tackling the Awkward Squad: monadic input/output, concurrency, exceptions, and foreign-language calls in Haskell, pages 47–96. IOS Press, 2001. Updated version available online at http://research.microsoft.com/~simonpj/.
12. Simon Peyton Jones, editor. *Haskell 98 Language and Libraries, The Revised Report*. Cambridge University Press, 2003.
13. D. Sands. Total correctness by local improvement in the transformation of functional programs. *ACM Transactions on Programming Languages and Systems (TOPLAS)*, 18(2):175–234, March 1996.
14. David A. Schmidt. *Denotational Semantics: A Methodology for Language Development*. W.C. Brown, Dubuque, Iowa, 1988.

A   QuickCheck Generators

The QuickCheck generators used in this text are defined as follows:

```
tree :: Gen T
tree = frequency [(6, liftM2 B tree tree),
                  (2, return L),
                  (1, return ⊥)]

string :: Gen String
string = frequency [(1, bottomString),
                    (1, finiteString),
                    (1, infiniteString),
                    (3, treeString)]
```

where

$$
\begin{aligned}
bottomString &= liftM2 \; approx & arbitrary \; & infiniteString \\
finiteString &= liftM2 \; (take \circ abs) & arbitrary \; & infiniteString \\
infiniteString &= liftM2 \; (:) & char \quad & infiniteString \\
treeString &= tree \ggg return \circ pretty'
\end{aligned}
$$

$char :: Gen \; Char$
$char = frequency \; [(10, return \; \text{'B'}),$
$\qquad\qquad\qquad\quad (10, return \; \text{'L'}),$
$\qquad\qquad\qquad\quad (1, \quad return \; \text{'?'}),$
$\qquad\qquad\qquad\quad (1, \quad return \; \bot)]$

$pair :: Gen \; (T, String)$
$pair = frequency \; [(50, liftM2 \; (,) \; tree \; string),$
$\qquad\qquad\qquad\quad (1, \quad return \; \bot)]$

A straightforward *Arbitrary* instance for *Nat* (yielding only total, finite values) is also required.

The generator *tree* is defined so that the generated trees have a probability of $\frac{1}{2}$ of being finite, and the finite trees have an expected depth of 2 [2]. We do not generate any total, infinite trees. The reason is that some of the tests above do not terminate for such trees, as shown in Sect. 5.

To get a good mix of finite and infinite partial strings the *string* generator is split up into four cases. The last case ensures that some strings that actually represent trees are also included. It would not be a problem to include total, infinite strings, but we do not want to complicate the definitions above too much, so they are also omitted.

Finally the *pair* generator constructs pairs using *tree* and *string*, forcing some pairs to be $\bot$.

By using *collect* we have observed that the actual distributions of generated values correspond to our expectations.

---

[2] Assuming that QuickCheck uses a random number generator that yields independent values from a uniform distribution.

Describing Gen/Kill Static Analysis Techniques with Kleene Algebra*

Therrezinha Fernandes and Jules Desharnais

Département d'informatique et de génie logiciel
Université Laval, Québec, QC, G1K 7P4 Canada
{Therrezinha.Fernandes,Jules.Desharnais}@ift.ulaval.ca

Abstract. Static program analysis consists of compile-time techniques for determining properties of programs without actually running them. Using Kleene algebra, we formalize four instances of a static data flow analysis technique known as gen/kill analysis. This formalization clearly reveals the dualities between the four instances; although these dualities are known, the standard formalization does not reveal them in such a clear and concise manner. We provide two equivalent sets of equations characterizing the four analyses for two representations of programs, one in which the statements label the nodes of a control flow graph and one in which the statements label the transitions.

1 Introduction

Static program analysis consists of compile-time techniques for determining properties of programs without actually running them. Information gathered by these techniques is traditionally used by compilers for optimizing the object code [1] and by CASE tools for software engineering and reengineering [2, 3]. Among the more recent applications is the detection of malicious code or code that might be maliciously exploited [4, 5]. Due to ongoing research in this area [5], the latter application is the main motivation for developing the algebraic approach to static analysis described in this paper (but we will not discuss applications to security here). Our goal is the development of an algebraic framework based on Kleene algebra (KA) [6–11], in which the relevant properties can be expressed in a compact and readable way.

In this paper, we examine four instances of a static data flow analysis technique known as gen/kill analysis [1, 12, 13]. The standard description of the four instances is given in Sect. 2. The necessary concepts of Kleene algebra are then presented in Sect. 3. The four gen/kill analyses are formalized with KA in Sect. 4. This formalization clearly reveals the dualities between the four kinds of analysis; although these dualities are known, the standard formalization does not reveal them in such a clear and concise manner. We provide two equivalent sets of equations characterizing the four analyses for two representations of programs, one in which the statements label the nodes of a control flow graph and one in

---

* This research is supported by NSERC (Natural Sciences and Engineering Research Council of Canada).

D. Kozen (Ed.): MPC 2004, LNCS 3125, pp. 110–128, 2004.

which the statements label the transitions. In the conclusion, we make additional comments on the approach and on directions for future research.

2   Four Different Gen/Kill Analyses

The programming language we will use is the standard while language, with atomic statements skip and $x := E$ (assignment), and compound statements $S_1; S_2$ (sequence), if b then S_1 else S_2 (conditional) and while b do S (while loop). In data flow analysis, it is common to use an abstract graph representation of a program from which one can extract useful information. Traditionally [1, 12, 13], this representation is a *control flow graph* (CFG), which is a directed graph where each node corresponds to a statement and the edges describe how control might flow from one statement to another. *Labeled Transition Systems* (LTSs) can also be used. With LTSs, edges (arcs, arrows) are labeled by the statements of the program and nodes are points from which and toward which control leaves and returns. Figure 1 shows CFGs and LTSs for the compound statements, and the corresponding matrix representations; the CFG for an atomic statement consists of a single node while its LTS consists of two nodes linked by an arrow labeled with the statement. The numbers at the left of the nodes for the CFGs and inside the nodes for the LTSs are labels that also correspond to the lines/columns in the matrix representations. Note that the two arrows leaving node 1 in the LTSs of the conditional and while loop are both labelled b, i.e., the cases where b holds and does not hold are not distinguished. This distinction will not be needed here (and it is not present in the CFGs either). For both representations, the nodes of the graphs will usually be called *program points*, or *points* for short.

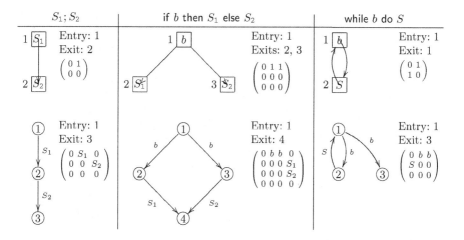

Fig. 1. CFGs and LTSs for compound statements

The four instances of gen/kill analysis that we will consider are *Reaching Definitions Analysis* (RD), *Live Variables Analysis* (LV), *Available Expressions Analysis* (AE) and *Very Busy Expressions Analysis* (VBE). An informal description, extracted from [13], follows.

RD Reaching definitions analysis determines, for each program point, which assignments *may* have been made and not overwritten when program execution reaches this point along *some* path.

A main application of RD is in the construction of direct links between statements that produce values and statements that use them.

LV A variable is *live* at the exit from a program point if *there exists a path*, from that point to a use of the variable, that does not redefine the variable. Live variables analysis determines, for each program point, which variables are live at the exit from this point.

This analysis might be used as the basis for *dead code elimination*. If a variable is not live at the exit from a statement, then, if the statement is an assignment to the variable, the statement can be eliminated.

AE Available expressions analysis determines, for each program point, which expressions have already been computed, and not later modified, on *all paths* to the program point.

This information can be used to avoid the recomputation of an expression.

VBE An expression is *very busy* at the exit from a program point if, *no matter which path* is taken from that point, the expression is always evaluated before any of the variables occurring in it are redefined. Very busy expressions analysis determines, for each program point, which expressions are very busy at the exit from the point.

A possible optimization based on this information is to evaluate the expression and store its value for later use.

Each of the four analyses uses a universal dataset D whose type of elements depends on the analysis. This set D contains information about the program under consideration, and possibly also information about the environment of the program if it appears inside a larger program. Statements *generate* and *kill* elements from D. Statements are viewed either as producing a subset out $\subseteq D$ from a subset in $\subseteq D$, or as producing in $\subseteq D$ from out $\subseteq D$, depending on the direction of the analysis. Calculating in from out (or the converse) is the main goal of the analysis. Each analysis is either *forward* or *backward*, and is said to be either a *may* or *must* analysis. This is detailed in the following description.

RD The set D is a set of *definitions*. A definition is a pair (x, l), where l is the label of an assignment $x := E$. The assignment $x := E$ at label l generates the definition (x, l) and kills all other definitions of x. From the above definition of RD, it can be seen that, for each program point, the analysis looks at paths between the entry point of the program and that program point; thus, the analysis is a forward one. Also, it is a may analysis, since the existence of a path with the desired property suffices.

LV The set D is a set of variables. The analysis looks for the existence of a path with a specific property between program points and the exit of the program. It is thus a backward may analysis.

AE The set D is a set of expressions or subexpressions. The paths considered are those between the entry point of the program and the program points (forward analysis). Since all paths to a program point must have the desired property, it is a must analysis.

VBE The set D is a set of expressions or subexpressions. The paths considered are those between the program points and the exit point of the program (backward analysis). Since all paths from a program point must have the desired property, it is a must analysis.

Table 1. Gen/kill values for atomic statements and tests. The symbol l denotes a label and the symbol b a test

	$l : x := E$		skip		b	
	gen	kill	gen	kill	gen	kill
RD	$\{(x,l)\}$	$\{(x,l') \in D \mid l' \neq l\}$	$\emptyset$	$\emptyset$	$\emptyset$	$\emptyset$
LV	$\mathrm{Var}(E)$	$\{x\} - \mathrm{Var}(E)$	$\emptyset$	$\emptyset$	$\mathrm{Var}(b)$	$\emptyset$
AE	$\{E' \in \mathrm{Exp}(E) \mid x \notin \mathrm{Var}(E')\}$	$\{E' \in D \mid x \in \mathrm{Var}(E')\}$	$\emptyset$	$\emptyset$	$\mathrm{Exp}(b)$	$\emptyset$
VBE	$\mathrm{Exp}(E)$	$\{E' \in D \mid x \in \mathrm{Var}(E')\} - \mathrm{Exp}(E)$	$\emptyset$	$\emptyset$	$\mathrm{Exp}(b)$	$\emptyset$

Table 1 gives the definitions of **gen** and **kill** for the atomic statements and tests for the four analyses. Note that for each statement S, $\mathbf{gen}(S) \subseteq \overline{\mathbf{kill}(S)}$ (the complement of $\mathbf{kill}(S)$) for the four analyses. This is a natural property, meaning that if something is generated, then it is not killed. In this table, $\mathsf{Var}(E)$ denotes the set of variables of expression E and $\mathsf{Exp}(E)$ denotes the set of its subexpressions. These definitions can be extended recursively to the case of compound statements (Table 2). The forward/backward duality is apparent when comparing the values of $\mathbf{gen}(S_1; S_2)$ and $\mathbf{kill}(S_1; S_2)$ for RD and AE with those for LV and VBE. The may/must duality between RD, LV and AE, VBE is most visible for the conditional (uses of $\cup$ vs $\cap$ in the expressions for **gen**).

Finally, Table 3 shows how $\mathbf{out}(S)$ and $\mathbf{in}(S)$ can be recursively calculated. Here too, the dualities forward/backward and may/must are easily seen.

We now illustrate RD analysis with the program given in Fig. 2. We will use this program all along the paper. The numbers at the left of the program are labels. These labels are the same in the given CFG representation.

The set of definitions that appear in the program is $\{(x,1), (x,3), (y,4)\}$. Assume that this program is embedded in a larger program that contains the definitions $(x,5)$ and $(y,6)\}$ (they may appear before label 1, even if they have a larger number as label) and that these definitions reach the entry point of the example program. Using Table 1 for RD, we get the following gen/kill values for the atomic statements, where S_l denotes the atomic statement at label l:

Table 2. Gen/kill expressions for compound statements

	$S_1; S_2$	
	gen	kill
RD, AE	$\text{gen}(S_2) \cup (\text{gen}(S_1) - \text{kill}(S_2))$	$\text{kill}(S_2) \cup (\text{kill}(S_1) - \text{gen}(S_2))$
LV, VBE	$\text{gen}(S_1) \cup (\text{gen}(S_2) - \text{kill}(S_1))$	$\text{kill}(S_1) \cup (\text{kill}(S_2) - \text{gen}(S_1))$

	if b then S_1 else S_2	
	gen	kill
RD	$\text{gen}(S_1) \cup \text{gen}(S_2)$	$\text{kill}(S_1) \cap \text{kill}(S_2)$
LV	$\text{gen}(b) \cup \text{gen}(S_1) \cup \text{gen}(S_2)$	$(\text{kill}(S_1) \cap \text{kill}(S_2)) - \text{gen}(b)$
AE	$(\text{gen}(S_1) \cap \text{gen}(S_2)) \cup (\text{gen}(b) - (\text{kill}(S_1) \cup \text{kill}(S_2)))$	$\text{kill}(S_1) \cup \text{kill}(S_2)$
VBE	$\text{gen}(b) \cup (\text{gen}(S_1) \cap \text{gen}(S_2))$	$(\text{kill}(S_1) \cup \text{kill}(S_2)) - \text{gen}(b)$

	while b do S_1	
	gen	kill
RD	$\text{gen}(S_1)$	$\emptyset$
LV	$\text{gen}(b) \cup \text{gen}(S_1)$	$\emptyset$
AE, VBE	$\text{gen}(b)$	$\text{kill}(S_1) - \text{gen}(b)$

Table 3. Linking in and out ("imm." abbreviates "immediately")

	$\text{in}(S)$	$\text{out}(S)$
RD	$\bigcup(S' \mid S' \text{ imm. precedes } S : \text{out}(S'))$	$\text{gen}(S) \cup (\text{in}(S) - \text{kill}(S))$
LV	$\text{gen}(S) \cup (\text{out}(S) - \text{kill}(S))$	$\bigcup(S' \mid S' \text{ imm. follows } S : \text{in}(S'))$
AE	$\bigcap(S' \mid S' \text{ imm. precedes } S : \text{out}(S'))$	$\text{gen}(S) \cup (\text{in}(S) - \text{kill}(S))$
VBE	$\text{gen}(S) \cup (\text{out}(S) - \text{kill}(S))$	$\bigcap(S' \mid S' \text{ imm. follows } S : \text{in}(S'))$

$$
\begin{aligned}
\text{gen}(S_1) &= \{(x,1)\}, & \text{kill}(S_1) &= \{(x,3),(x,5)\}, \\
\text{gen}(S_2) &= \emptyset, & \text{kill}(S_2) &= \emptyset, \\
\text{gen}(S_3) &= \{(x,3)\}, & \text{kill}(S_3) &= \{(x,1),(x,5)\}, \\
\text{gen}(S_4) &= \{(y,4)\}, & \text{kill}(S_4) &= \{(y,6)\}.
\end{aligned}
\tag{1}
$$

Using Table 2 for RD, we get

$$
\begin{aligned}
\text{gen}(S_1; \text{if } S_2 \text{ then } S_3 \text{ else } S_4) &= \{(x,3),(y,4)\} \cup (\{(x,1)\} - \emptyset) \\
&= \{(x,1),(x,3),(y,4)\}, \\
\text{kill}(S_1; \text{if } S_2 \text{ then } S_3 \text{ else } S_4) &= \emptyset \cup (\{(x,3),(x,5)\} - \{(x,3),(y,4)\}) \\
&= \{(x,5)\}.
\end{aligned}
$$

Finally, Table 3 for RD yields

$$
\begin{aligned}
\text{in}(S_1; \text{if } S_2 \text{ then } S_3 \text{ else } S_4) &= \{(x,5),(y,6)\}, \\
\text{out}(S_1; \text{if } S_2 \text{ then } S_3 \text{ else } S_4) &= \{(x,1),(x,3),(y,4)\} \cup \\
&\quad (\{(x,5),(y,6)\} - \{(x,5)\}) \\
&= \{(x,1),(x,3),(y,4),(y,6)\}.
\end{aligned}
$$

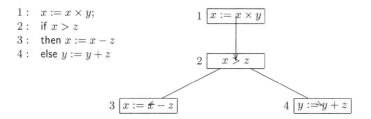

```
1 :   x := x × y;
2 :   if x > z
3 :   then x := x − z
4 :   else y := y + z
```

Fig. 2. CFG for running example

3   Kleene Algebra with Tests

In this section, we first introduce Kleene algebra [6, 9] and a specialization of it, namely Kleene algebra with tests [10]. Then, we recall the notion of matrices over a Kleene algebra and discuss how we will use them for our application.

Definition 1. *A* Kleene algebra *(KA) [9] is a structure* $\mathcal{K} = (K, +, \cdot, ^*, 0, 1)$ *such that* $(K, +, 0)$ *is a commutative monoid,* $(K, \cdot, 1)$ *is a monoid, and the following laws hold:*

$$
\begin{array}{ll}
a + a = a, & a \cdot (a + b) = a \cdot a + a \cdot b, \\
a \cdot 0 = 0 \cdot a = 0, & (a + b) \cdot c = a \cdot c + b \cdot c, \\
1 + a \cdot a^* = a^*, & b + a \cdot c \leq c \Rightarrow a^* \cdot b \leq c, \\
1 + a^* \cdot a = a^*, & b + c \cdot a \leq c \Rightarrow b \cdot a^* \leq c,
\end{array}
$$

where $\leq$ *is the partial order induced by* $+$, *that is,*

$$
a \leq b \Leftrightarrow a + b = b .
$$

   A Kleene algebra with tests *[10] is a two-sorted algebra* $(K, T, +, \cdot, ^*, 0, 1, \neg)$ *such that* $(K, +, \cdot, ^*, 0, 1)$ *is a Kleene algebra and* $(T, +, \cdot, \neg, 0, 1)$ *is a Boolean algebra, where* $T \subseteq K$ *and* $\neg$ *is a unary operator defined only on* T.
   Operator precedence, from lowest to highest, is $+, \cdot, (^*, \neg)$.

   It is immediate from the definition that $t \leq 1$ for any test $t \in T$. The meet of two tests $t, u \in T$ is their product $t \cdot u$. Every KA can be made into a KA with tests, by taking $\{0, 1\}$ as the set of tests.
   Models of KA with tests include algebras of languages over an alphabet, algebras of path sets in a directed graph [14], algebras of relations over a set and abstract relation algebras with transitive closure [15, 16].
   A very simple model of KA with tests is obtained by taking K to be the powerset of some set D and defining, for every $a, b \subseteq D$,

$$
0 \stackrel{\mathrm{def}}{=} \emptyset, \quad 1 \stackrel{\mathrm{def}}{=} D, \quad a^* \stackrel{\mathrm{def}}{=} D, \quad \neg a \stackrel{\mathrm{def}}{=} \bar{a}, \quad a + b \stackrel{\mathrm{def}}{=} a \cup b, \quad a \cdot b \stackrel{\mathrm{def}}{=} a \cap b. \quad (2)
$$

   The set of matrices of size $n \times n$ over a KA with tests can itself be turned into a KA with tests by defining the following operations. The notation $\mathbf{A}[i, j]$ refers to the entry in row i and column j of $\mathbf{A}$.

1. **0**: matrix whose entries are all 0, i.e., $\mathbf{0}[i,j] = 0$,
2. **1**: identity matrix (square), i.e., $\mathbf{1}[i,j] = \begin{cases} 1 & \text{if } i = j \\ 0 & \text{if } i \neq j, \end{cases}$
3. $(\mathbf{A} + \mathbf{B})[i,j] \overset{\text{def}}{=} \mathbf{A}[i,j] + \mathbf{B}[i,j]$,
4. $(\mathbf{A} \cdot \mathbf{B})[i,j] \overset{\text{def}}{=} \sum(k \mid : \mathbf{A}[i,k] \cdot \mathbf{B}[k,j])$,
5. The Kleene star of a square matrix is defined recursively [9]. If $\mathbf{A} = (\,a\,)$, for some $a \in K$, then $\mathbf{A}^* \overset{\text{def}}{=} (\,a^*\,)$. If

$$\mathbf{A} = \begin{pmatrix} a & b \\ c & d \end{pmatrix} \qquad \text{(with graphic representation} \quad$$

$$),$$

for some $a, b, c, d \in K$, then

$$\mathbf{A}^* \overset{\text{def}}{=} \begin{pmatrix} f^* & f^* \cdot b \cdot d^* \\ d^* \cdot c \cdot f^* & d^* + d^* \cdot c \cdot f^* \cdot b \cdot d^* \end{pmatrix}, \tag{3}$$

where $f = a + b \cdot d^* \cdot c$; the automaton corresponding to $\mathbf{A}$ helps understand that f^* corresponds to paths from state 1 to state 1. If $\mathbf{A}$ is a larger matrix, it is decomposed as a 2×2 matrix of submatrices: $\mathbf{A} = \begin{pmatrix} \mathbf{B} & \mathbf{C} \\ \mathbf{D} & \mathbf{E} \end{pmatrix}$, where $\mathbf{B}$ and $\mathbf{E}$ are square and nonempty. Then $\mathbf{A}^*$ is calculated recursively using (3). For our simple application below, $\mathbf{A}^* = \sum(n \mid n \geq 0 : \mathbf{A}^n)$, where $\mathbf{A}^0 = \mathbf{1}$ and $\mathbf{A}^{n+1} = \mathbf{A} \cdot \mathbf{A}^n$.

By setting up an appropriate type discipline, one can define *heterogeneous Kleene algebras* as is done for heterogeneous relation algebras [17–19]. One can get a heterogeneous KA by considering matrices with different sizes over a KA; matrices can be joined or composed only if they satisfy appropriate size constraints.

In Sect. 4, we will only use matrices whose entries are all tests. Such matrices are relations [20]; indeed, a top relation can be defined as the matrix filled with 1. However, this is not completely convenient for our purpose. Rather, we will use a matrix $\mathbf{S}$ to represent the structure of programs and consider only matrices below the reflexive transitive closure $\mathbf{S}^*$ of $\mathbf{S}$. Complementation can then be defined as complementation relative to $\mathbf{S}^*$:

$$(\overline{\mathbf{A}})[i,j] \overset{\text{def}}{=} \neg(\mathbf{A}[i,j]) \cdot \mathbf{S}^*[i,j] .$$

It is easily checked that applying all the above operations to matrices below $\mathbf{S}^*$ results in a matrix below $\mathbf{S}^*$. This means that the KA we will use is Boolean, with a top element $\top$ satisfying $1 \leq \top$ (reflexivity) and $\top \cdot \top \leq \top$ (transitivity).

As a final remark in this section, we point out that a (square) matrix $\mathbf{T}$ is a test iff it is a diagonal matrix whose diagonal contains tests (this implies $\mathbf{T} \leq 1$). For instance, if t_1, t_2 and t_3 are tests,

$$\begin{pmatrix} t_1 & 0 & 0 \\ 0 & t_2 & 0 \\ 0 & 0 & t_3 \end{pmatrix} \text{ is a test and } \neg \begin{pmatrix} t_1 & 0 & 0 \\ 0 & t_2 & 0 \\ 0 & 0 & t_3 \end{pmatrix} = \begin{pmatrix} \neg t_1 & 0 & 0 \\ 0 & \neg t_2 & 0 \\ 0 & 0 & \neg t_3 \end{pmatrix}.$$

4   Gen/Kill Analysis with KA

In order to illustrate the approach, we present in Sect. 4.1 the equations describing RD analysis and apply them to the same example as in Sect. 2. The equations for the other analyses are presented in Sect. 4.2.

4.1   RD Analysis

We first explain how the data and programs to analyze are modelled. Then we show how to carry out RD analysis, first by using a CFG-related matrix representation and then an LTS-related matrix representation.

Recall that the set of definitions for the whole program is

$$D \stackrel{\text{def}}{=} \{(x,1),(x,3),(y,4),(x,5),(y,6)\} \ . \tag{4}$$

We consider the powerset of D as a Kleene algebra, as explained in Sect. 3 (see (2)).

The input to the analysis consists of three matrices $\mathbf{S}, \mathbf{g}$ and $\mathbf{k}$ representing respectively the structure of the program, what is generated and what is killed at each label. Here is an abstract definition of these matrices, where $g_i \subseteq D$ and $k_i \subseteq D$, for $i = 1, \ldots, 4$.

$$\mathbf{S} = \begin{pmatrix} 0 & 1 & 0 & 0 \\ 0 & 0 & 1 & 1 \\ 0 & 0 & 0 & 0 \\ 0 & 0 & 0 & 0 \end{pmatrix} \quad \mathbf{g} = \begin{pmatrix} g_1 & 0 & 0 & 0 \\ 0 & g_2 & 0 & 0 \\ 0 & 0 & g_3 & 0 \\ 0 & 0 & 0 & g_4 \end{pmatrix} \quad \mathbf{k} = \begin{pmatrix} k_1 & 0 & 0 & 0 \\ 0 & k_2 & 0 & 0 \\ 0 & 0 & k_3 & 0 \\ 0 & 0 & 0 & k_4 \end{pmatrix}$$

Recall that $1 = D$ (see (2)). Using the values already found in (1), we get the following as concrete instantiations for the example program (with g_i for $\mathsf{gen}(S_i)$ and k_i for $\mathsf{kill}(S_i)$):

$$\begin{array}{llll} g_1 \stackrel{\text{def}}{=} \{(x,1)\}, & g_2 \stackrel{\text{def}}{=} \emptyset, & g_3 \stackrel{\text{def}}{=} \{(x,3)\}, & g_4 \stackrel{\text{def}}{=} \{(y,4)\}, \\ k_1 \stackrel{\text{def}}{=} \{(x,3),(x,5)\}, & k_2 \stackrel{\text{def}}{=} \emptyset, & k_3 \stackrel{\text{def}}{=} \{(x,1),(x,5)\}, & k_4 \stackrel{\text{def}}{=} \{(y,6)\}. \end{array} \tag{5}$$

Note that $\mathbf{g}$ and $\mathbf{k}$ are tests. The entries in their diagonal represent what is generated or killed by the atomic instruction at each node. Table 1 imposes the condition $\mathsf{gen}(S) \subseteq \overline{\mathsf{kill}(S)}$ for any atomic statement S; this translates to $\mathbf{g} \leq \neg\mathbf{k}$ for the matrices given above.

Table 4 contains the equations that describe how to carry out RD analysis. This table has a simple and natural reading:

1. G: To generate something, move on a path from an entry point (S^*), generate that something (g), then move to an exit point while not killing what was generated ($(S \cdot \neg k)^*$).
2. $\overline{K}$: To not kill something, do not kill it on the first step and move along the program while not killing it, or generate it.

Table 4. RD existential ("may") gen/kill parameters for CFGs. Complementation is relative to S^*

	RD
G	$S^* \cdot g \cdot (S \cdot \neg k)^*$
$\overline{K}$	$\neg k \cdot (S \cdot \neg k)^* + G$
O	$G + i \cdot \overline{K}$

3. O: To output something, generate it or, if it comes from the environment (the test i), do not kill it. Note how the expression for O is close to that for out given in Table 3, namely $\mathsf{gen}(S) \cup (\mathsf{in}(S) - \mathsf{kill}(S))$.

We use the table to calculate $\mathbf{G}$ and $\overline{\mathbf{K}}$ for RD [1]. It is a simple task to verify the following result (one has to use $\mathbf{g} \leq \neg\mathbf{k}$, i.e., $g_i \leq \neg k_i$, for $i = 1, \ldots, 4$). We give the result for the abstract matrices, because it is more instructive.

$$\mathbf{G} = \begin{pmatrix} g_1 & g_2 + g_1 \cdot \neg k_2 & g_3 + g_2 \cdot \neg k_3 + g_1 \cdot \neg k_2 \cdot \neg k_3 & g_4 + g_2 \cdot \neg k_4 + g_1 \cdot \neg k_2 \cdot \neg k_4 \\ 0 & g_2 & g_3 + g_2 \cdot \neg k_3 & g_4 + g_2 \cdot \neg k_4 \\ 0 & 0 & g_3 & 0 \\ 0 & 0 & 0 & g_4 \end{pmatrix}$$

$$\overline{\mathbf{K}} = \begin{pmatrix} \neg k_1 & g_2 + \neg k_1 \cdot \neg k_2 & g_3 + g_2 \cdot \neg k_3 + \neg k_1 \cdot \neg k_2 \cdot \neg k_3 & g_4 + g_2 \cdot \neg k_4 + \neg k_1 \cdot \neg k_2 \cdot \neg k_4 \\ 0 & \neg k_2 & g_3 + \neg k_2 \cdot \neg k_3 & g_4 + \neg k_2 \cdot \neg k_4 \\ 0 & 0 & \neg k_3 & 0 \\ 0 & 0 & 0 & \neg k_4 \end{pmatrix}$$

Consider the entry $\mathbf{G}[1,3]$, for instance. This entry shows that what is generated when executing all paths from label 1 to label 3 – here, since there is a single path, this means executing statements at labels 1, 2 and 3 – is what is generated at label 3, plus what is generated at label 2 and not killed at label 3, plus what is generated at label 1 and not killed at labels 2 and 3. Similarly, $\overline{\mathbf{K}}[1, 2]$ shows that what is not killed on the path from label 1 to label 2 is either what is generated at label 2 or what is not killed at either of labels 1 and 2.

To compare these results with those of the classical approach of Sect. 2, it suffices to collect from $\mathbf{G}$ the data generated and from $\overline{\mathbf{K}}$ the data not killed between the entry point of the program (label 1) and its exit points (labels 3 and 4). This can always be done by means of a row vector $\mathbf{s}$ selecting the entry points and a column vector $\mathbf{t}$ selecting the exit points. For our program,

$$\mathbf{s} \stackrel{\text{def}}{=} (1 \quad 0 \quad 0 \quad 0) \qquad \text{and} \qquad \mathbf{t} \stackrel{\text{def}}{=} \begin{pmatrix} 0 \\ 0 \\ 1 \\ 1 \end{pmatrix},$$

so that

$$\mathsf{gen} = \mathbf{s} \cdot \mathbf{G} \cdot \mathbf{t} = g_3 + g_4 + (g_2 + g_1 \cdot \neg k_2) \cdot (\neg k_3 + \neg k_4) \tag{6}$$

---

[1] We use bold letters for matrices. Because the concepts of Table 4 may apply to other kinds of KAs, the variables in the table are typeset in the usual mathematical font.

and

$$\neg\mathsf{kill} = \mathbf{s}\cdot\overline{\mathbf{K}}\cdot\mathbf{t} = g_3 + g_4 + (g_2 + \neg k_1\cdot\neg k_2)\cdot(\neg k_3 + \neg k_4) \ .$$

Negating yields

$$\mathsf{kill} = k_3\cdot k_4 + k_2\cdot\neg g_3\cdot\neg g_4 + k_1\cdot\neg g_2\cdot\neg g_3\cdot\neg g_4 \ .$$

This is easily read and understood by looking at the CFG. Using the concrete values in (4) and (5) provides $\mathsf{gen} = \{(x,1),(x,3),(y,4)\}$ and $\mathsf{kill} = \{(x,5)\}$, just like in Sect. 2.

One can get $\mathbf{K}$ from the above matrix $\overline{\mathbf{K}}$ by complementing, but complementation must be done relatively to $\mathbf{S}^*$; the reason is that anything that gets killed is killed along a program path, and unconstrained complementation incorrectly introduces nonzero values outside program paths. The result is

$$\mathbf{K} = \begin{pmatrix} k_1 & k_2 + k_1\cdot\neg g_2 & k_3 + k_2\cdot\neg g_3 + k_1\cdot\neg g_2\cdot\neg g_3 & k_4 + k_2\cdot\neg g_4 + k_1\cdot\neg g_2\cdot\neg g_4 \\ 0 & k_2 & k_3 + k_2\cdot\neg g_3 & k_4 + k_2\cdot\neg g_4 \\ 0 & 0 & k_3 & 0 \\ 0 & 0 & 0 & k_4 \end{pmatrix}$$

One might think that $\mathsf{kill} = \mathbf{s}\cdot\mathbf{K}\cdot\mathbf{t}$, but this is not the case. It is easy to see that $\mathbf{s}\cdot\mathbf{K}\cdot\mathbf{t} = \mathbf{K}[1,3] + \mathbf{K}[1,4]$, whereas the value of kill that we obtained above is $\neg(\overline{\mathbf{K}}[1,3] + \overline{\mathbf{K}}[1,4]) = \mathbf{K}[1,3]\cdot\mathbf{K}[1,4]$, and the latter is the right value. The reason for this behavior is that for RD, *not killing*, like *generating*, is existential, in the sense that results from converging paths are joined ("may" analysis). In the case of *killing*, these results should be intersected. But the effect of $\mathbf{s}\cdot\mathbf{K}\cdot\mathbf{t}$ is to join all entries of the form $\mathbf{K}[\text{entry point, exit point}]$ ($\mathbf{K}[1,3] + \mathbf{K}[1,4]$ for the example). Note that if the program has only one entry and one exit point, one may use either $\mathbf{s}\cdot\mathbf{K}\cdot\mathbf{t}$ or $\neg(\mathbf{s}\cdot\overline{\mathbf{K}}\cdot\mathbf{t})$; the equivalence follows from the fact that $\mathbf{s}$ is then a total function, while $\mathbf{t}$ is injective and surjective.

There remains one value to find for our example, that of $\mathbf{O}$. In Table 4, the equation for $\mathbf{O}$ is $O = G + i\cdot\overline{K}$. The symbol i denotes a test that characterizes the data that come from the environment of the program (a larger program containing it). For our example, i has the form

$$\mathbf{i} = \begin{pmatrix} i_1 & 0 & 0 & 0 \\ 0 & i_2 & 0 & 0 \\ 0 & 0 & i_3 & 0 \\ 0 & 0 & 0 & i_4 \end{pmatrix} \ .$$

Using the same $\mathbf{s}$ and $\mathbf{t}$ as above, we calculate $\mathbf{s}\cdot\mathbf{O}\cdot\mathbf{t}$, which is the information that gets out at the exit points as a function of what gets in at the entry point. We get

$$\begin{aligned}
\mathbf{s}\cdot\mathbf{O}\cdot\mathbf{t} = \mathbf{s}\cdot(\mathbf{G}+\mathbf{i}\cdot\overline{\mathbf{K}})\cdot\mathbf{t} = \ & g_3 + g_4 + \\
& g_2\cdot(\neg k_3 + \neg k_4) + \\
& g_1\cdot\neg k_2\cdot(\neg k_3 + \neg k_4) + \\
& i_1\cdot\neg k_1\cdot\neg k_2\cdot(\neg k_3 + \neg k_4) \ .
\end{aligned}$$

Thus, what gets out at exit labels 3 and 4 is what is generated at labels 3 and 4, plus what is generated at labels 1 and 2 and not killed after, plus what comes from the environment at label 1 and is not killed after. With the instantiations given in (4) and (5),

$$\mathbf{s} \cdot \mathbf{O} \cdot \mathbf{t} \ = \ \{(x,1),(x,3),(y,4)\} + i_1 \cdot \{(x,1),(y,4),(y,6)\} \ .$$

If – as in Sect. 2 – we assume that the data coming from the environment at label 1 is $i_1 \stackrel{\text{def}}{=} \{(x,5),(y,6)\}$, then $\mathbf{s} \cdot \mathbf{O} \cdot \mathbf{t} = \{(x,1),(x,3),(y,4),(y,6)\}$ – as in Sect. 2.

We now turn to the LTS representation of programs, which is often more natural. For instance, it is used for the representation of automata, or for giving relational descriptions of programs [19]. Our example program and its LTS graph are given in Fig. 3. As mentioned in Sect. 2, we do not distinguish the two possible run-time results of the test $x > z$, since this does not change any of the four analyses.

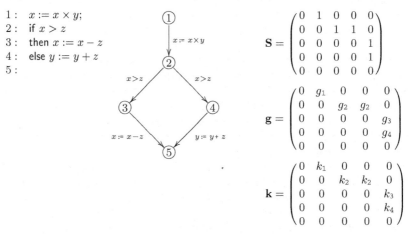

Fig. 3. LTS for running example

The matrices $\mathbf{S}$, $\mathbf{g}$ and $\mathbf{k}$ again respectively represent the structure of the program, what is generated and what is killed by atomic statements. Note that $\mathbf{g}$ and $\mathbf{k}$ are not tests as for the CFG representation. Rather, entries g_i and k_i label arrows and in a way can be viewed as an abstraction of the effect of the corresponding statements. The concrete instantiations (4) and (5) still apply.

Table 5 can then be used in the same manner as Table 4 to derive G, K and O. In this table, as usual, a^+ denotes $a \cdot a^*$. The variable i still denotes a test. The operator $\tilde{\ }$ denotes complementation with respect to S^+, so that $K = \widetilde{\overline{K}} \sqcap S^+$. For CFGs, complementation is done with respect to S^*, because the instructions are on the nodes. For LTSs, the instructions are on the arcs, so that no killing or generation can occur at a node, unless it occurs via a nonnull circular path; this explains why complementation is done with respect to S^+.

Table 5. RD existential ("may") gen/kill parameters for LTSs. The operator ˜ is complementation relative to S^+

	RD
G	$S^* \cdot g \cdot (\overline{k} \sqcap S)^*$
$\tilde{K}$	$(\overline{k} \sqcap S)^+ + G$
O	$G + i \cdot \tilde{K}$

The calculation of **G** gives

$$
\mathbf{G} = \begin{pmatrix}
0 & g_1 & g_2 + g_1 \cdot \neg k_2 & g_2 + g_1 \cdot \neg k_2 & g_3 + g_4 + (g_2 + g_1 \cdot \neg k_2) \cdot (\neg k_3 + \neg k_4) \\
0 & 0 & g_2 & g_2 & g_3 + g_4 + g_2 \cdot (\neg k_3 + \neg k_4) \\
0 & 0 & 0 & 0 & g_3 \\
0 & 0 & 0 & 0 & g_4 \\
0 & 0 & 0 & 0 & 0
\end{pmatrix}.
$$

Using

$$
\mathbf{s} \stackrel{\text{def}}{=} (1 \ \ 0 \ \ 0 \ \ 0 \ \ 0) \qquad \text{and} \qquad \mathbf{t} \stackrel{\text{def}}{=} \begin{pmatrix} 0 \\ 0 \\ 0 \\ 0 \\ 1 \end{pmatrix},
$$

we obtain for $\mathbf{gen} = \mathbf{s} \cdot \mathbf{G} \cdot \mathbf{t}$ the same result as for the CFG (see (6)).

4.2   Gen/Kill Analysis for the Four Analyses

In this section, we present the equations for all four analyses. We begin with the CFG representation (Table 6). The following remarks are in order.

1. Reading the expressions is mostly done as for RD. For LV and VBE, it is better to read the expressions backward, because they are backward analyses. The reading is then the same as for RD, except that o is used instead of i to denote what comes from the environment and I is used instead of O for the result. This was done simply to have a more exact correspondence with Table 3. Although o is input data, the letter o is used because the data is provided at the exit points; similarly, the letter I is used for the output data because it is associated with the entry points.
2. For all atomic and compound statements and all equations of Table 6, one can do the same kind of abstract comparison with the results given by Tables 1 and 2 as we have done for the example in Sect. 4.1. The results are the same.
3. The forward/backward and may/must dualities are apparent in the tables of Sect. 2, but they are much more visible and clear here.
   (a) The forward/backward correspondences RD ↔ LV and AE ↔ VBE are obtained by reading the expressions in the reverse direction and by switching in and out: $i ↔ o$ and $O ↔ I$. One can also use the relational converse operator ˘; then, for LV, $G = (\neg k \cdot S)^* \cdot g \cdot S^* =$

Table 6. Existential ("may") gen/kill parameters for CFGs. Complementation is relative to S^*

	RD	LV	AE	VBE
G	$S^* \cdot g \cdot (S \cdot \neg k)^*$	$(\neg k \cdot S)^* \cdot g \cdot S^*$		
$\overline{G}$			$\neg g \cdot (S \cdot \neg g)^* + K$	$(\neg g \cdot S)^* \cdot \neg g + K$
K			$S^* \cdot k \cdot (S \cdot \neg g)^*$	$(\neg g \cdot S)^* \cdot k \cdot S^*$
$\overline{K}$	$\neg k \cdot (S \cdot \neg k)^* + G$	$(\neg k \cdot S)^* \cdot \neg k + G$		
O	$G + i \cdot \overline{K}$			
I		$G + \overline{K} \cdot o$		
$\overline{O}$			$K + \neg i \cdot \overline{G}$	
$\overline{I}$				$K + \overline{G} \cdot \neg o$

$(S^{\smile *} \cdot g^{\smile} \cdot (S^{\smile} \cdot \neg k^{\smile})^*)^{\smile}$. The same can be done for $\overline{K}$ and I. Thus, to make an LV analysis, one can switch i, o, reverse the program, do the calculations of an RD analysis, reverse the result and switch I, O (of course, g and k are those for LV, not for RD). The same can be said about AE and VBE.

(b) The may/must duality between RD and AE is first revealed by the fact that $G, \overline{K}$ and O are existential for RD, whereas $\overline{G}, K$ and $\overline{O}$ are existential for AE (similar comment for LV and VBE). But the correspondences RD $\leftrightarrow$ AE and LV $\leftrightarrow$ VBE are much deeper and can in fact be obtained simply by switching gen and kill, and complementing in and out: $g \leftrightarrow k$, $G \leftrightarrow K$, $i \leftrightarrow \neg i$, $o \leftrightarrow \neg o$, $I \leftrightarrow \overline{I}$, $O \leftrightarrow \overline{O}$.

These dualities mean that only one kind of analysis is really necessary, since the other three can be obtained by simple substitutions and simple additional operations (converse and complementation).

4. All nonempty entries in Table 6 correspond to existential cases; collecting data with entry and exit vectors as we have done in Sect. 4.1 should be done with the parameters as given in Table 6 and not on their negation (unless there is only one entry and one exit point).

5. Table 6 can be applied to programs with goto statements to fixed labels without any additional machinery.

The equations for LTSs are given in Table 7. Similar comments can be made about this table as for Table 6.

The formulae in Tables 6 and 7 are obviously related, but it is interesting to see how the connection can be described formally and this is what we now do. We will also show the following: If P denotes any of the parameters in the left column of either Table 6 or Table 7 and if s and t denote the entry and exit vectors appropriate for the representation (CFG or LTS), then the value of $s \cdot P \cdot t$ is the same for both approaches, provided only the existential equations given in the tables are used (no complementation before merging the data with s and t). Note that the main goal of the analyses is to calculate $s \cdot O \cdot t$ or $s \cdot I \cdot t$.

Table 7. Existential ("may") gen/kill parameters for LTSs. The operator ˜ is complementation relative to S^+

	RD	LV	AE	VBE
G	$S^* \cdot g \cdot (\overline{k} \sqcap S)^*$	$(\overline{k} \sqcap S)^* \cdot g \cdot S^*$		
$\tilde{G}$			$(\overline{g} \sqcap S)^+ + K$	$(\overline{g} \sqcap S)^+ + K$
K			$S^* \cdot k \cdot (\overline{g} \sqcap S)^*$	$(\overline{g} \sqcap S)^* \cdot k \cdot S^*$
$\tilde{K}$	$(\overline{k} \sqcap S)^+ + G$	$(\overline{k} \sqcap S)^+ + G$		
O	$G + i \cdot \tilde{K}$			
I		$G + \tilde{K} \cdot o$		
$\tilde{O}$			$K + \neg i \cdot \tilde{G}$	
$\tilde{I}$				$K + \tilde{G} \cdot \neg o$

The basic idea is best explained in terms of graphs. To go from a CFG to an LTS, it suffices to add a new node and to add arrows from the exit nodes of the CFG to the new node – which becomes the new and only exit node – and then to "push" the information associated to nodes of the CFG to the appropriate arrows of the LTS.

Let us see how this is done with matrices. For these explanations, we append a subscript $_L$ to the matrices related to a LTS. The following matrices $\mathbf{S}$ and $\mathbf{S}_L$ represent the structure of the CFG of Fig. 2 and that of the LTS of Fig. 3, respectively.

$$\mathbf{S} = \begin{pmatrix} 0 & 1 & 0 & 0 \\ 0 & 0 & 1 & 1 \\ 0 & 0 & 0 & 0 \\ 0 & 0 & 0 & 0 \end{pmatrix} \qquad \mathbf{S}_L = \begin{pmatrix} 0 & 1 & 0 & 0 & 0 \\ 0 & 0 & 1 & 1 & 0 \\ 0 & 0 & 0 & 0 & 1 \\ 0 & 0 & 0 & 0 & 1 \\ 0 & 0 & 0 & 0 & 0 \end{pmatrix} = \begin{pmatrix} \mathbf{S} & \mathbf{t} \\ \mathbf{0} & \mathbf{0} \end{pmatrix}$$

The matrix $\mathbf{S}_L$ is structured as a matrix of four submatrices, one of which is the CFG matrix $\mathbf{S}$ and another is the column vector $\mathbf{t}$ that was used in (6) to select the exit nodes of the CFG. The rôle of this vector in $\mathbf{S}_L$ is to add links from the exit nodes of the CFG to the new node corresponding to column 5.

Now consider the matrices of Sect. 4.1. The CFG matrix $\mathbf{g}$ can be converted to the LTS matrix $\mathbf{g}$, here called $\mathbf{g}_L$, as follows.

$$\mathbf{g}_L = \begin{pmatrix} \mathbf{g} \cdot \mathbf{S} & \mathbf{g} \cdot \mathbf{t} \\ \mathbf{0} & \mathbf{0} \end{pmatrix} = \begin{pmatrix} \mathbf{g} & \mathbf{x} \\ \mathbf{0} & \mathbf{y} \end{pmatrix} \cdot \begin{pmatrix} \mathbf{S} & \mathbf{t} \\ \mathbf{0} & \mathbf{0} \end{pmatrix} = \begin{pmatrix} \mathbf{g} & \mathbf{x} \\ \mathbf{0} & \mathbf{y} \end{pmatrix} \cdot \mathbf{S}_L$$

The value of the submatrices $\mathbf{x}$ and $\mathbf{y}$ does not matter, since these disappear in the result of the composition. One can use the concrete values given in Sect. 4.1 and check that indeed in that case $\mathbf{g}_L = \begin{pmatrix} \mathbf{g} \cdot \mathbf{S} & \mathbf{g} \cdot \mathbf{t} \\ \mathbf{0} & \mathbf{0} \end{pmatrix}$. The same holds for $\mathbf{G}$ and

$\overline{\mathbf{K}}$. The matrix $\begin{pmatrix} \mathbf{g} & \mathbf{x} \\ \mathbf{0} & \mathbf{y} \end{pmatrix}$ is an embedding of the CFG $\mathbf{g}$ in a larger graph with an additional node. Composition with $\mathbf{S}_L$ "pushes" the information provided by $\mathbf{g}$ on the appropriate arrows of $\mathbf{g}_L$.

We now abstract from the matrix context. We assume an heterogeneous Boolean KA such that, given correctly typed elements a, b, c, d, it is possible to form matrices like $\begin{pmatrix} a & b \\ c & d \end{pmatrix}$. To distinguish expressions related to CFGs and LTSs, we add a subscript $_L$ to variables in the latter expressions.

We will show that the RD CFG expressions given in Table 6 can be transformed into the corresponding LTS expressions given in Table 7. An analogous treatment can be done for the other analyses.

We begin with G, whose expression is $S^* \cdot g \cdot (S \cdot \neg k)^*$, and show that it transforms to $S_L^* \cdot g_L \cdot (\overline{k_L} \sqcap S_L)^*$. We first note the following two properties:

$$\begin{pmatrix} a & ? \\ 0 & ? \end{pmatrix} \cdot \begin{pmatrix} b & ? \\ 0 & ? \end{pmatrix} = \begin{pmatrix} a \cdot b & ? \\ 0 & ? \end{pmatrix} \quad \text{and} \quad \begin{pmatrix} a & ? \\ 0 & ? \end{pmatrix}^* = \begin{pmatrix} a^* & ? \\ 0 & ? \end{pmatrix}, \quad (7)$$

where "?" means that the exact value is not important for our purpose (we use the same convention below). Now let $f(a) \overset{\text{def}}{=} \begin{pmatrix} a & t \\ 0 & 0 \end{pmatrix}$. We will use the assumptions $S_L = f(S)$, $g_L = f(g) \cdot f(S)$, $k_L = f(k) \cdot f(S)$ and $G_L = \begin{pmatrix} G \cdot S & G \cdot t \\ 0 & 0 \end{pmatrix}$, which hold for matrices, as noted above. Before giving the main derivation, we prove the auxiliary result

$$f(\neg k) \cdot f(S) = \overline{k_L} \sqcap S_L . \quad (8)$$

$\qquad f(\neg k) \cdot f(S)$

$=\qquad \langle$ Definition of f $\rangle$

$\qquad \begin{pmatrix} \neg k & t \\ 0 & 0 \end{pmatrix} \cdot \begin{pmatrix} S & t \\ 0 & 0 \end{pmatrix}$

$=\qquad \langle$ Matrix composition $\rangle$

$\qquad \begin{pmatrix} \neg k & 0 \\ 0 & 0 \end{pmatrix} \cdot \begin{pmatrix} S & t \\ 0 & 0 \end{pmatrix}$

$=\qquad \langle$ The left matrix is a test $\rangle$

$\qquad \neg \begin{pmatrix} k & 0 \\ 0 & 0 \end{pmatrix} \cdot \begin{pmatrix} S & t \\ 0 & 0 \end{pmatrix}$

$=\qquad \langle$ In a Boolean KA, for any a and test p, $\neg p \cdot a = \overline{p \cdot a} \sqcap a$ $\rangle$

$\qquad \overline{\begin{pmatrix} k & 0 \\ 0 & 0 \end{pmatrix} \cdot \begin{pmatrix} S & t \\ 0 & 0 \end{pmatrix}} \sqcap \begin{pmatrix} S & t \\ 0 & 0 \end{pmatrix}$

$=\qquad \langle$ Matrix composition $\rangle$

$\qquad \overline{\begin{pmatrix} k & t \\ 0 & 0 \end{pmatrix} \cdot \begin{pmatrix} S & t \\ 0 & 0 \end{pmatrix}} \sqcap \begin{pmatrix} S & t \\ 0 & 0 \end{pmatrix}$

$=\qquad \langle$ Definition of f $\rangle$

$\qquad \overline{f(k) \cdot f(S)} \sqcap f(S)$

$$= \overline{k_L} \sqcap S_L$$
$\langle$ Assumptions $\rangle$

An now comes the proof that $G_L = S_L^* \cdot g_L \cdot (\overline{k_L} \sqcap S_L)^*$.

G_L

$=$ $\quad\langle$ Assumption $\rangle$

$$\begin{pmatrix} G \cdot S & G \cdot t \\ 0 & 0 \end{pmatrix}$$

$=$ $\quad\langle$ Matrix composition $\rangle$

$$\begin{pmatrix} G & ? \\ 0 & ? \end{pmatrix} \cdot \begin{pmatrix} S & t \\ 0 & 0 \end{pmatrix}$$

$=$ $\quad\langle$ Expression for G and definition of f $\rangle$

$$\begin{pmatrix} S^* \cdot g \cdot (S \cdot \neg k)^* & ? \\ 0 & ? \end{pmatrix} \cdot f(S)$$

$=$ $\quad\langle$ Definition of f and induction using (7) $\rangle$

$$(f(S))^* \cdot f(g) \cdot (f(S) \cdot f(\neg k))^* \cdot f(S)$$

$=$ $\quad\langle$ KA sliding rule: $(a \cdot b)^* \cdot a = a \cdot (b \cdot a)^*$ $\rangle$

$$(f(S))^* \cdot f(g) \cdot f(S) \cdot (f(\neg k) \cdot f(S))^*$$

$=$ $\quad\langle$ Assumptions and (8) $\rangle$

$$S_L^* \cdot g_L \cdot (\overline{k_L} \sqcap S_L)^*$$

The transformation of the CFG subexpression $\neg k \cdot (S \cdot \neg k)^*$ (appearing in the definition of $\overline{K}$ in Table 6) is done in a similar fashion, except that the last steps are

$$f(\neg k) \cdot (f(S) \cdot f(\neg k))^* \cdot f(S)$$

$=$ $\quad\langle$ KA sliding rule: $(a \cdot b)^* \cdot a = a \cdot (b \cdot a)^*$ $\rangle$

$$f(\neg k) \cdot f(S) \cdot (f(\neg k) \cdot f(S))^*$$

$=$ $\quad\langle$ $a \cdot a^* = a^+$ and (8) $\rangle$

$$(\overline{k_L} \sqcap S_L)^+$$

What remains to establish is the correspondence between i for CFGs and i_L for LTSs. Since we want i_L to be a test just like i, we cannot take $i_L = f(i) \cdot f(S)$ like for the other matrices. It turns out that $i_L \overset{\text{def}}{=} \begin{pmatrix} i & 0 \\ 0 & 0 \end{pmatrix}$ is convenient and is indeed what we would choose using intuition, because it does not make sense to feed information to the additional exit node, since it is past all the instructions. One then has

$$O_L = \begin{pmatrix} (G + i \cdot \overline{K}) \cdot S & (G + i \cdot \overline{K}) \cdot t \\ 0 & 0 \end{pmatrix} = G_L + \begin{pmatrix} i & 0 \\ 0 & 0 \end{pmatrix} \cdot (\overline{K})_L = G_L + i_L \cdot \tilde{K}_L \ .$$

Finally, we show that the calculation of the information along paths between entry and exit nodes gives the same result for CFGs and LTSs. For CFGs, this information is obtained by calculating $s \cdot P \cdot t$, where s is the vector of entry nodes, t is the vector of exit nodes and P is any of the existential parameters $(G, \overline{K}, O, \ldots)$, depending on the analysis. For LTSs, the corresponding expression is $s_L \cdot P_L \cdot t_L$. As above, we assume $P_L = \begin{pmatrix} P \cdot S & P \cdot t \\ 0 & 0 \end{pmatrix}$, and $s_L = \begin{pmatrix} s & 0 \end{pmatrix}$ and $t_L = \begin{pmatrix} 0 \\ 1 \end{pmatrix}$, meaning essentially that the additional node cannot be an entry point and must be the only exit point. We then have

$$s_L \cdot P_L \cdot t_L = \begin{pmatrix} s & 0 \end{pmatrix} \cdot \begin{pmatrix} P \cdot S & P \cdot t \\ 0 & 0 \end{pmatrix} \cdot \begin{pmatrix} 0 \\ 1 \end{pmatrix} = \begin{pmatrix} s & 0 \end{pmatrix} \cdot \begin{pmatrix} P \cdot t \\ 0 \end{pmatrix} = s \cdot P \cdot t \; ,$$

so that using either a CFG or an LTS gives the same result.

Note that no property of s or t has been used in the explanation of the transformation from CFGs to LTSs.

5   Conclusion

We have shown how four instances of gen/kill analysis can be described using Kleene algebra. This has been done for a CFG-like and an LTS-like representation of programs (using matrices). The result of this exercise is a very concise and very readable set of equations characterizing the four analyses. This has revealed the symmetries between the analyses much more clearly than the classical approach.

We have in fact used relations for the formalization, so that the framework of relation algebra with transitive closure [15, 16] could have been used instead of that of Kleene algebra. Note however that converse has been used only to explain the forward/backward dualities, but is used nowhere in the calculations. We prefer Kleene algebra or Boolean Kleene algebra because the results have wider applicability. It is reasonable to expect to find examples where the equations of Tables 6 and 7 could be used for something else than relations. Also, we hope to connect the Kleene formulation of the gen/kill analyses with representations of programs where Kleene algebra is already used. For instance, Kleene algebra is already employed to analyze sequences of abstract program actions for security properties [11]. Instead of keeping only the name of an action (instruction), it would be possible to construct a triple (name, gen, kill) giving information about the name assigned to the instruction and what it generates and kills. Such triples can be elements of a KA by applying KA operations componentwise. Is it then possible to prove stronger security properties in the framework of KA, given that more information is available?

We plan to investigate other types of program analysis to see if the techniques presented in this paper could apply to them. We would also like to describe the analyses of this paper using a KA-based deductive approach in the style of that used in [21]. Another intriguing question is whether the set-based program analysis framework of [22] is related to our approach.

Acknowledgements

The authors thank Bernhard Möller and the MPC referees for thoughtful comments and additional pointers to the literature.

References

1. Aho, A.V., Sethi, R., Ullman, J.D.: Compilers: Principles, Techniques and Tools. Addison-Wesley (1989)
2. Overstreet, C.M., Cherinka, R., Sparks, R.: Using bidirectional data flow analysis to support software reuse. Technical Report TR-94-09, Old Dominion University, Computer Science Department (1994)
3. Moonen, L.: Data flow analysis for reverse engineering. Master's thesis, Programming Research Group, University of Amsterdam (1996)
4. Lo, R.W., Levitt, K.N., Olsson, R.A.: MCF: A malicious code filter. Computers and Security **14** (1995) 541–566
5. Bergeron, J., Debbabi, M., Desharnais, J., Erhioui, M.M., Lavoie, Y., Tawbi, N.: Static detection of malicious code in executable programs. In: 1st Symposium on Requirements Engineering for Information Security, Indianapolis, IN (2001)
6. Conway, J.H.: Regular Algebra and Finite Machines. Chapman and Hall, London (1971)
7. Desharnais, J., Möller, B., Struth, G.: Kleene algebra with domain. Technical Report 2003-7, Institut für Informatik, Universität Augsburg, D-86135 Augsburg (2003)
8. Desharnais, J., Möller, B., Struth, G.: Modal Kleene algebra and applications – A survey. Technical Report DIUL-RR-0401, Département d'informatique et de génie logiciel, Université Laval, D-86135 Augsburg (2004)
9. Kozen, D.: A completeness theorem for Kleene algebras and the algebra of regular events. Information and Computation **110** (1994) 366–390
10. Kozen, D.: Kleene algebra with tests. ACM Transactions on Programming Languages and Systems **19** (1997) 427–443
11. Kozen, D.: Kleene algebra with tests and the static analysis of programs. Technical Report 2003-1915, Department of Computer Science, Cornell University (2003)
12. Fischer, C.N., LeBlanc, Jr., R.J.: Crafting a Compiler. Benjamin/Cummings Publishing Company, Menlo Park, CA (1988)
13. Nielson, F., Nielson, H.R., Hankin, C.: Principles of Program Analysis. Springer (1999)
14. Möller, B.: Derivation of graph and pointer algorithms. In Möller, B., Partsch, H.A., Schuman, S.A., eds.: Formal Program Development. Volume 755 of Lecture Notes in Computer Science. Springer, Berlin (1993) 123–160
15. Ng, K.C.: Relation algebras with transitive closure. PhD thesis, University of California, Berkeley (1984)
16. Ng, K.C., Tarski, A.: Relation algebras with transitive closure. Notices of the American Mathematical Society **24** (1977) A29–A30
17. Kozen, D.: Typed Kleene algebra. Technical Report 98-1669, Computer Science Department, Cornell University (1998)
18. Schmidt, G., Hattensperger, C., Winter, M.: Heterogeneous relation algebra. In Brink, C., Kahl, W., Schmidt, G., eds.: Relational Methods in Computer Science. Springer (1997)

19. Schmidt, G., Ströhlein, T.: Relations and Graphs. EATCS Monographs in Computer Science. Springer, Berlin (1993)
20. Desharnais, J.: Kleene algebra with relations. In Berghammer, R., Möller, B., Struth, G., eds.: Relational and Kleene-Algebraic Methods. Volume 3051 of Lecture Notes in Computer Science., Springer (2004) 8–20
21. Kozen, D., Patron, M.C.: Certification of compiler optimizations using Kleene algebra with tests. In Lloyd, J., Dahl, V., Furbach, U., Kerber, M., Lau, K.K., Palamidessi, C., Pereira, L.M., Sagiv, Y., Stuckey, P.J., eds.: Proc. 1st Int. Conf. on Computational Logic (CL2000), London. Volume 1861 of Lecture Notes in Artificial Intelligence., London, Springer (2000) 568–582
22. Heintze, N.: Set Based Program Analysis. PhD thesis, School of Computer Science, Computer Science Division, Carnegie Mellon University, Pittsburgh, PA (1992) CMU-CS-92-201.

A Free Construction of Kleene Algebras with Tests

Hitoshi Furusawa[*]

Research Center for Verification and Semantics, AIST,
3-11-46 Nakoji, Amagasaki, Hyogo, 661-0974, Japan
hitoshi.furusawa@aist.go.jp

Abstract. In this paper we define Kleene algebra with tests in a slightly more general way than Kozen's definition. Then we give an explicit construction of the free Kleene algebra with tests generated by a pair of sets. We also show that the category **KAT** of Kleene algebras with tests and the category **KAT**$^\subseteq$ of Kozen's Kleene algebras with tests are related by an adjunction. This fact shows that an infinitely-generated free Kleene algebra with tests in the sense of Kozen can be obtained as the image of our free algebra under the left adjoint from **KAT** to **KAT**$^\subseteq$; moreover, the image is isomorphic to itself. Therefore, our free Kleene algebra with tests is isomorphic to Kozen and Smith's free Kleene algebra with tests if their construction available. Finally, we show that Kozen and Smith's free Kleene algebra with tests can be presented as a coproduct of Kleene algebras. This is induced from our free construction.

1 Introduction

Kozen [6] defined a Kleene algebra with tests to be a Kleene algebra with an embedded Boolean algebra. The starting point of this paper is the observation that the important point of this notion is not the subset property, but the fact that their underlying idempotent semiring structure is shared. Due to this observation, we define a Kleene algebra with tests as a triple consisting of a Boolean algebra, a Kleene algebra, and a function from the carrier set of the Boolean algebra to the carrier of the Kleene algebra which is a homomorphism between their underlying idempotent semiring. So the category **KAT** of our Kleene algebras with tests is the comma category (U_{BI}, U_{KI}) of the functor U_{BI} from the category **Bool** of Boolean algebras to the category **ISR** of idempotent semirings and the functor U_{KI} from the category **Kleene** of Kleene algebra to **ISR**.

Kozen and Smith [7] showed that the Kleene algebra with tests consisting of the set of regular sets of guarded strings is the free Kleene algebra with tests generated by a pair of finite sets. [3, 4] showed the existence of the free algebra generated by a pair of sets using the technique of finite limit sketches instead of

·[*] Part of this work is done during the author is visiting at McMaster University by Japan Society for the Promotion of Science (JSPS) Bilateral Programs for Science Exchanges.

D. Kozen (Ed.): MPC 2004, LNCS 3125, pp. 129–141, 2004.

showing an explicit construction. Though these two results were established on slightly different definitions, we did not analyse the difference of these two.

In this paper, we give an explicit construction of the free Kleene algebra with tests generated by a pair of sets using adjunctions between **Kleene** and the categories of related algebraic structures, and coproducts in **Kleene**. Though Kozen and Smith's construction requires finiteness of generators, our construction never requires this. We also show that the category **KAT** of our Kleene algebras with tests and the category **KAT**$^\subseteq$ of Kozen's Kleene algebras with tests are related by an adjunction. The image of our free algebra under the left adjoint from **KAT** to **KAT**$^\subseteq$ is isomorphic to itself. So, our free algebra and Kozen and Smith's are isomorphic whenever Kozen and Smith's construction is available, that is, a generator of the Boolean algebra is finite. Finally, we show that Kozen and Smith's free algebra can be presented as a coproduct in **Kleene** since our free algebra is also given as a coproduct. Our explicit free construction makes clear such an algebraic characterisation of Kozen and Smith's free algebras.

2   Kleene Algebras

In this section we recall some basics of Kleene algebras [5] and related algebraic structures. [2] contains several examples of Kleene algebras. For basic notions of category theory we refer to [1, 8].

Definition 1 (Kleene algebra). A *Kleene algebra* is a set K equipped with nullary operators 0, 1 and binary operators $+$, $\cdot$, and a unary operator *, where the tuple $(K, +, \cdot, 0, 1)$ is an idempotent semiring and these data satisfy the following:

$$1 + (p \cdot p^*) = p^*$$
$$1 + (p^* \cdot p) = p^*$$
$$p \cdot r \leq r \implies p^* \cdot r \leq r$$
$$r \cdot p \leq r \implies r \cdot p^* \leq r$$

where $\leq$ refers to the natural partial order

$$p \leq q \overset{\text{def}}{\iff} p + q = q \quad .$$

A Kleene algebra will be called *trivial* if $0 = 1$, otherwise, called *non-trivial*. The category of Kleene algebras and homomorphisms between them will be denoted by **Kleene**.

Remark 1. **Kleene** has binary coproducts.

For two Kleene algebras $\mathbf{K}_1$ and $\mathbf{K}_2$, $\mathbf{K}_1 + \mathbf{K}_2$ denotes a coproduct of $\mathbf{K}_1$ and $\mathbf{K}_2$. For two Kleene algebra homomorphisms $f \colon \mathbf{K}_1 \to \mathbf{K}_2$ and $g \colon \mathbf{K}_1' \to \mathbf{K}_2'$, $f + g$ denotes the unique Kleene algebra homomorphism such that the following two diagrams commutes.

$$\mathbf{K}_1 \xrightarrow{\quad i \quad} \mathbf{K}_1 + \mathbf{K}_2 \xleftarrow{\quad j \quad} \mathbf{K}_2$$

$$\left. f \downarrow \qquad\qquad f + g \downarrow \qquad\qquad g \downarrow \right.$$

$$\mathbf{K}'_1 \xrightarrow[\quad i' \quad]{} \mathbf{K}'_1 + \mathbf{K}'_2 \xleftarrow[\quad j' \quad]{} \mathbf{K}'_2$$

where i and j are the coproduct injections of $\mathbf{K}_1 + \mathbf{K}_2$, and i' and j' of $\mathbf{K}'_1 + \mathbf{K}'_2$.

The coproduct injections in **Kleene** are not always one-to-one. Trivial Kleene algebras have only one element since, for each a,

$$a = a \cdot 1 = a \cdot 0 = 0 \ .$$

For each Kleene algebra K, there exists a unique Kleene algebra homomorphism from K to each trivial one. From a trivial Kleene algebra, there exists a Kleene algebra homomorphism if the target is also trivial. So, the coproduct of a trivial Kleene algebra and a non-trivial one is trivial again. Then, we have an injection which is not one-to-one. This example is due to Wolfram Kahl.

A Kleene algebra $\mathbf{K}$ is called *integral* if it has no zero divisors, that is,

$$a \neq 0 \ \wedge \ b \neq 0 \implies a \cdot b \neq 0$$

holds for all $a, b \in K$. This notion is introduced in [2].

Proposition 1. *Let* $\mathbf{J} = (J, +_J, \cdot_J, {}^{*_J}, 0_J, 1_J)$ *and* $\mathbf{K} = (K, +_K, \cdot_K, {}^{*_K}, 0_K, 1_K)$ *be non-trivial Kleene algebras. If* $\mathbf{K}$ *is integral, then the following holds.*

(i) The mapping $f\colon K \to J$ *defined to be* $f(a) = 0_J$ *if* $a = 0_K$, *and otherwise* $f(a) = 1_J$, *is a Kleene algebra homomorphism.*

(ii) The first injection $j\colon \mathbf{J} \to \mathbf{J} + \mathbf{K}$ *is one-to-one.*

Proof. Since $\mathbf{K}$ is non-trivial, we possibly have a Kleene algebra homomorphism from $\mathbf{K}$ to a non-trivial one. For each $a, b \in K$, if $a \neq 0_K$ and $b \neq 0_K$, $a +_K b \neq 0_K$ and $a \cdot_K b \neq 0_K$ since $\mathbf{K}$ is integral. So, *(i)* follows from

$$\begin{aligned}
f(a) +_J f(b) &= 1_J +_J 1_J = 1_J = f(a +_K b) \\
f(a) \cdot_J f(b) &= 1_J \cdot_J 1_J = 1_J = f(a \cdot_K b) \\
f(a)^{*_J} &= 1_J^{*_J} = 1_J = f(a^{*_K}) \ .
\end{aligned}$$

(ii) will be proved using the f given in *(i)*. Take $\mathrm{id}_{\mathbf{J}}$ and f, then a unique intermediating arrow $h\colon \mathbf{J} + \mathbf{K} \to \mathbf{J}$ with respect to them exists. By the definition of coproducts, h satisfies $\mathrm{id}_{\mathbf{J}} = h \circ j$. Thus j is one-to-one.

Let **Set**, **ISR**, and **Bool** denote the categories of sets and functions, idempotent semirings and their homomorphisms, and Boolean algebras and their homomorphisms, respectively. $U_K\colon$ **Kleene** $\to$ **Set** denotes the forgetful functor which takes a Kleene algebra to its carrier set. The functor U_K can be decomposed into functors $U_{KI}\colon$ **Kleene** $\to$ **ISR** and $U_I\colon$ **ISR** $\to$ **Set**, where $U_{KI}(\mathbf{K})$ is an idempotent semiring obtained by forgetting the * operator and U_I takes an idempotent semiring to its carrier set. These two functors U_{KI} and U_I have left adjoints F_{IK} and F_I respectively. $F_K \overset{\text{def}}{=} F_{IK} \circ F_I$ is a left adjoint to U_K.

*Remark 2 (**Reg**(Σ) [5]).* For a set Σ, $\textbf{Reg}(\Sigma)$ denotes the Kleene algebra consisting of the set of regular sets over Σ together with the standard operations on regular sets. Clearly, $\textbf{Reg}(\Sigma)$ is integral. Moreover, it is known that $\textbf{Reg}(\Sigma) \cong F_K(\Sigma)$.

Since we consider Kleene algebras with tests in this paper, Boolean algebras are also important. We denote the forgetful functor which takes a Boolean algebra to its carrier set by $U_B \colon \textbf{Bool} \to \textbf{Set}$. U_B satisfies similar properties to U_K together with U_I. We denote the forgetful functor from $\textbf{Bool}$ to $\textbf{ISR}$ and its left adjoint by U_{BI} and F_{IB} respectively. $F_B \overset{\text{def}}{=} F_{IB} \circ F_I$ is a left adjoint to U_B.

The situation we state above is as follows:

$$\textbf{Bool} \underset{U_{BI}}{\overset{F_{IB}}{\underset{\longrightarrow}{\overset{\longleftarrow}{\perp}}}} \textbf{ISR} \underset{U_{KI}}{\overset{F_{IK}}{\underset{\longleftarrow}{\overset{\longrightarrow}{\perp}}}} \textbf{Kleene}$$

$$U_I \vdash F_I$$

$$\textbf{Set}$$

$$F_B \overset{\text{def}}{=} F_{IB} \circ F_I \quad F_K \overset{\text{def}}{=} F_{IK} \circ F_I$$
$$U_B = U_I \circ U_{BI} \quad U_K = U_I \circ U_{KI}$$

Let us now explicitly state some of the facts constituting the adjunction $F_{IK} \dashv U_{KI}$. For each idempotent semiring $\textbf{S}$ and Kleene algebra $\textbf{K}$, the bijection from $\textbf{Kleene}(F_{IK}(\textbf{S}), \textbf{K})$ to $\textbf{ISR}(\textbf{S}, U_{KI}(\textbf{K}))$ is denoted by $\varphi_{\textbf{S},\textbf{K}}$. Indeed, for each arrow $f \colon \textbf{S}' \to \textbf{S}$ in $\textbf{ISR}$ and $g \colon \textbf{K} \to \textbf{K}'$ in $\textbf{Kleene}$, the following diagram in $\textbf{Set}$ commutes:

$$
\begin{array}{ccc}
\textbf{Kleene}(F_{IK}(\textbf{S}), \textbf{K}) & \overset{\varphi_{\textbf{S},\textbf{K}}}{\longrightarrow} & \textbf{ISR}(\textbf{S}, U_{KI}(\textbf{K})) \\
{\scriptstyle \textbf{Kleene}(F_{IK}(f), g)} \big\downarrow & & \big\downarrow {\scriptstyle \textbf{ISR}(f, U_{KI}(g))} \\
\textbf{Kleene}(F_{IK}(\textbf{S}'), \textbf{K}') & \underset{\varphi_{\textbf{S}',\textbf{K}'}}{\longrightarrow} & \textbf{ISR}(\textbf{S}', U_{KI}(\textbf{K}'))
\end{array}
$$

where $\textbf{Kleene}(F_{IK}(f), g)$ maps

$$\textbf{Kleene}(F_{IK}(\textbf{S}), \textbf{K}) \ni h \mapsto g \circ h \circ F_{IK}(f) \in \textbf{Kleene}(F_{IK}(\textbf{S}'), \textbf{K}')$$

and $\textbf{ISR}(f, U_{KI}(g))$ does

$$\textbf{ISR}(\textbf{S}, U_{KI}(\textbf{K})) \ni k \mapsto U_{KI}(g) \circ k \circ f \in \textbf{ISR}(\textbf{S}', U_{KI}(\textbf{K}')) \ .$$

This property is called *naturality* of φ. The subscript $\textbf{S}, \textbf{K}$ will be omitted unless confusions occur.

The next property follows from the naturality.

Lemma 1. *Diagram* (1) *commutes if and only if diagram* (2) *commutes.*

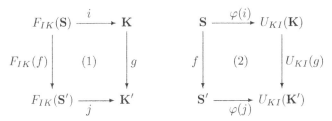

Proof. Assume that (1) commutes. j is taken to $\varphi(j \circ F_{IK}(f))$ and $\varphi(j) \circ f$ by $\varphi \circ \mathbf{Kleene}(F_{IK}(f), \mathrm{id}_{\mathbf{K}'})$ and $\mathbf{ISR}(f, U_{KI}(\mathrm{id}_{\mathbf{K}'})) \circ \varphi$, respectively. By the naturality of φ, we have $\varphi(j \circ F_{IK}(f)) = \varphi(j) \circ f$. Similarly, considering $\mathbf{Kleene}(F_{IK}(\mathrm{id}_{\mathbf{S}}), g)$ and $\mathbf{ISR}(\mathrm{id}_{\mathbf{S}}, U_{KI}(g))$, we obtain $\varphi(g \circ i) = U_{KI}(g) \circ \varphi(i)$. By the assumption, we have $\varphi(j) \circ f = U_{KI}(g) \circ \varphi(i)$. The opposite direction is proved similarly using bijectivity in addition to naturality.

For each idempotent semiring $\mathbf{S}$, the idempotent-semiring homomorphism $\varphi(\mathrm{id}_{F_{IK}(\mathbf{S})}) \colon \mathbf{S} \to U_{KI}(F_{IK}(\mathbf{S}))$ is called a component of the *unit* of the adjunction $F_{IK} \dashv U_{KI}$ with respect to $\mathbf{S}$. By Lemma 1, $\varphi(\mathrm{id}_{F_{IK}(\mathbf{S})})$ satisfies $f = U_{KI}(\varphi^{-1}(f)) \circ \varphi(\mathrm{id}_{F_{IK}(\mathbf{S})})$ for each Kleene algebra $\mathbf{K}$ and each idempotent-semiring homomorphism $f \colon \mathbf{S} \to U_{KI}(\mathbf{K})$ since the following diagram commutes.

$$
\begin{array}{ccc}
F_{IK}(\mathbf{S}) & \xrightarrow{\ \mathrm{id}_{F_{IK}(\mathbf{S})}\ } & F_{IK}(\mathbf{S}) \\[2pt]
{\scriptstyle F_{IK}(\mathrm{id}_{\mathbf{S}})}\Big\downarrow & & \Big\downarrow{\scriptstyle \varphi^{-1}(f)} \\[2pt]
F_{IK}(\mathbf{S}) & \xrightarrow[\ \varphi^{-1}(f)\ ]{} & \mathbf{K}
\end{array}
$$

Proposition 2. *Let* $\mathbf{S} = (S, +, \cdot, 0, 1)$ *be an idempotent semiring such that, for each* $s \in S$, $s \le 1$. *Then,* $F_{IK}(S) \cong (S, +, \cdot, {}^{*}, 0, 1)$, *where* * *maps each* $s \in S$ *to* 1.

Proof. Set $\mathbf{S}' = (S, +, \cdot, {}^{*}, 0, 1)$. For each Kleene algebra $\mathbf{K}$, an idempotent-semiring homomorphism $h \colon \mathbf{S} \to U_{KI}(\mathbf{K})$ is also a Kleene algebra homomorphism from $\mathbf{S}'$ to $\mathbf{K}$ by the definition of $\mathbf{S}'$ and the assumption on $\mathbf{S}$. Take $\varphi(\mathrm{id}_{F_{IK}(\mathbf{S})}) \colon \mathbf{S} \to U_{KI}(F_{IK}(\mathbf{S}))$, then the following diagram commutes.

$$
\begin{array}{ccc}
\mathbf{S} & \xrightarrow{\ \mathrm{id}_{\mathbf{S}}\ } & U_{KI}(\mathbf{S}')\ (= \mathbf{S}\,) \\[2pt]
{\scriptstyle \mathrm{id}_{\mathbf{S}}}\Big\downarrow & & \Big\downarrow{\scriptstyle U_{KI}(\varphi(\mathrm{id}_{F_{IK}(\mathbf{S})}))\ (= \varphi(\mathrm{id}_{F_{IK}(\mathbf{S})}))} \\[2pt]
\mathbf{S} & \xrightarrow[\ \varphi(\mathrm{id}_{F_{IK}(\mathbf{S})})\ ]{} & U_{KI}(F_{IK}(\mathbf{S}))
\end{array}
$$

By Lemma 1, the following diagram commutes.

$$
\begin{array}{ccc}
F_{IK}(\mathbf{S}) & \xrightarrow{\varphi^{-1}(\mathrm{id}_{\mathbf{S}})} & \mathbf{S}' \\
{\scriptstyle F_{IK}(\mathrm{id}_{\mathbf{S}})} \downarrow & & \downarrow {\scriptstyle \varphi(\mathrm{id}_{F_{IK}(\mathbf{S})})} \\
F_{IK}(\mathbf{S}) & \xrightarrow[\mathrm{id}_{F_{IK}(\mathbf{S})}]{} & F_{IK}(\mathbf{S})
\end{array}
$$

So, we have $\mathrm{id}_{F_{IK}(\mathbf{S})} = \varphi(\mathrm{id}_{F_{IK}(\mathbf{S})}) \circ \varphi^{-1}(\mathrm{id}_{\mathbf{S}})$. Since $\varphi(\mathrm{id}_{F_{IK}(\mathbf{S})})$ is a component of the unit of $F_{IK} \dashv U_{KI}$ with respect to $\mathbf{S}$, and $\mathbf{S} = U_{KI}(\mathbf{S}')$, we have $\mathrm{id}_{\mathbf{S}} = U_{KI}(\varphi^{-1}(\mathrm{id}_{\mathbf{S}})) \circ \varphi(\mathrm{id}_{F_{IK}(\mathbf{S})})$. Here, $U_{KI}(\varphi^{-1}(\mathrm{id}_{\mathbf{S}}))$ is $\varphi^{-1}(\mathrm{id}_{\mathbf{S}})$ itself. Thus we have $\mathrm{id}_{\mathbf{S}} = \varphi^{-1}(\mathrm{id}_{\mathbf{S}}) \circ \varphi(\mathrm{id}_{F_{IK}(\mathbf{S})})$.

Proposition 3. *Let* $\mathbf{B} = (B, +, \cdot, ^{-}, 0, 1)$ *and* $\mathbf{S} = (S, +, \cdot, 0, 1)$ *be a Boolean algebra and an idempotent semiring, respectively. The image* $\mathrm{im}(f)$ *of B under the idempotent-semiring homomorphism* $f \colon U_{BI}(\mathbf{B}) \to \mathbf{S}$ *forms a Boolean algebra.*

Proof. The set $\mathrm{im}(f)$ is closed under $+$ and $\cdot$. Also, $\mathrm{im}(f)$ is a distributive lattice together with $+$, $\cdot$, 0, and 1. For each $x \in \mathrm{im}(f)$, define $\neg x \overset{\mathrm{def}}{=} f(\bar{a})$ for some $a \in B$ such that $x = f(a)$. $\neg x$ is well defined since, if $f(a) = f(b)$,

$$
\begin{aligned}
f(\bar{a}) &= f(\bar{a}) \cdot 1 = f(\bar{a}) \cdot (f(\bar{b}) + f(b)) = f(\bar{a}) \cdot (f(\bar{b}) + f(a)) = f(\bar{a}) \cdot f(\bar{b}) \\
&= (f(b) \cdot f(\bar{b})) + (f(\bar{a}) \cdot f(\bar{b})) = (f(a) + f(\bar{a})) \cdot f(\bar{b}) = 1 \cdot f(\bar{b}) = f(\bar{b}) \ .
\end{aligned}
$$

Then, $(\mathrm{im}(f), +, \cdot, \neg, 0, 1)$ is a Boolean algebra.

For idempotent-semiring homomorphism $f \colon U_{BI}(\mathbf{B}) \to \mathbf{S}$, the Boolean algebra $(\mathrm{im}(f), +, \cdot, \neg, 0, 1)$ will be denoted by $f[\mathbf{B}]$.

3   Kleene Algebras with Tests

We provide a definition of Kleene algebras with tests. The definition is slightly more general than Kozen's.

Definition 2 (Kleene algebra with tests). A Kleene algebra with tests is a triple $\langle \mathbf{B}, \mathbf{K}, i \rangle$ where

- **B** is a Boolean algebra,
- **K** is a Kleene algebra, and
- i is an idempotent-semiring homomorphism from $U_{BI}(\mathbf{B})$ to $U_{KI}(\mathbf{K})$.

The category of Kleene algebras with tests and their homomorphisms, which is denoted by **KAT**, is the comma category (U_{BI}, U_{KI}), that is, an arrow $\langle f, g \rangle$

from $\langle \mathbf{B}, \mathbf{K}, i \rangle$ to $\langle \mathbf{B}', \mathbf{K}', i' \rangle$ in $\mathbf{KAT}$ is a pair of a Boolean algebra homomorphism $f\colon \mathbf{B} \to \mathbf{B}'$ and a one of Kleene algebra $g\colon \mathbf{K} \to \mathbf{K}'$ such that the following diagram commutes.

$$
\begin{array}{ccc}
U_{BI}(\mathbf{B}) & \xrightarrow{\ i\ } & U_{KI}(\mathbf{K}) \\[2pt]
\Big\downarrow U_{BI}(f) & & \Big\downarrow U_{KI}(g) \\[2pt]
U_{BI}(\mathbf{B}') & \xrightarrow[\ i'\ ]{} & U_{KI}(\mathbf{K}')
\end{array}
$$

For details of comma categories, see [8].

A Kleene algebra with tests in the sense of Kozen [6] is a special case where i is an inclusion. $\mathbf{KAT}^{\subseteq}$ denotes the category of Kleene algebras with tests in the sense of Kozen.

Example 1. The triple

$$\langle (\{0, 1, a, \overline{a}\}, \vee, \wedge, ^{-}, 0, 1), (\{0, 1\}, +, \cdot, ^{*}, 0, 1), \{0 \mapsto 0, 1 \mapsto 1, a \mapsto 1, \overline{a} \mapsto 0\} \rangle$$

is an object in $\mathbf{KAT}$ but not an object in $\mathbf{KAT}^{\subseteq}$.

The following property is immediate from Proposition 3.

Proposition 4. *For each object* $\langle \mathbf{B}, \mathbf{K}, i \rangle$ *in* $\mathbf{KAT}$, $\langle i[\mathbf{B}], \mathbf{K}, \subseteq \rangle$ *is an object in* $\mathbf{KAT}^{\subseteq}$, *where* $i[\mathbf{B}]$ *is the Boolean algebra consisting of* $\mathrm{im}(i)$. *Moreover, if* i *is one-to-one,* $\langle \mathbf{B}, \mathbf{K}, i \rangle \cong \langle i[\mathbf{B}], \mathbf{K}, \subseteq \rangle$.

Definition 3 (free Kleene algebra with tests). A *free Kleene algebra with tests* generated by a pair (T, Σ) of sets T and Σ is defined to be a Kleene algebra with tests $\langle \mathbf{B}, \mathbf{K}, i \rangle$ and a pair (η_T, η_Σ) of maps $\eta_T\colon T \to B$ from T to the carrier set B of $\mathbf{B}$ and $\eta_\Sigma\colon \Sigma \to K$ from Σ to the carrier set K of $\mathbf{K}$ which satisfy the following universal property:

for each Kleene algebra with tests $\langle \mathbf{B}', \mathbf{K}', i' \rangle$ and each pair (f, g) of maps $f\colon T \to B'$ from T to the carrier set B' of $\mathbf{B}'$ and $g\colon \Sigma \to K'$ from Σ to the carrier set K' of $\mathbf{K}'$, there is a unique arrow $\langle \hat{f}, \hat{g} \rangle\colon \langle \mathbf{B}, \mathbf{K}, i \rangle \to \langle \mathbf{B}', \mathbf{K}', i' \rangle$ in $\mathbf{KAT}$ such that

$$f = \hat{f} \circ \eta_T \quad \text{and} \quad g = \hat{g} \circ \eta_\Sigma \ .$$

Kozen and Smith [7] gave a construction of the free Kleene algebra with tests generated by a pair of finite sets of atomic tests and atomic actions through a construction of the set of languages of guarded strings. Though Kozen and Smith require the finiteness of the two sets, it is not necessary that the set of atomic actions is finite. Since their result is based on Kozen's definition, i and i' in definition 3 are required to be inclusions. After giving our construction of free Kleene algebra with tests (in Section 4), we compare Kozen-Smith's and ours (in Section 5).

4   Free Construction of Kleene Algebra with Tests

In [3, 4], the existence of the free Kleene algebra with tests generated by a pair of (possibly infinite) sets was shown using the technique of finite limit sketches. With this technique, an explicit construction is not necessary for the proof, so none was given. This section provides an explicit construction using adjunctions and coproducts in **Kleene**. This construction does not require the finiteness of generators.

If the forgetful functor $U \colon \mathbf{KAT} \to \mathbf{Set} \times \mathbf{Set}$ which takes an object $\langle \mathbf{B}, \mathbf{K}, f \rangle$ to a pair (B, K) of their carrier sets and an arrow $\langle h, k \rangle$ to a pair (h, k) of functions has a left adjoint, the image of the pair (T, Σ) of sets under the left adjoint together with the unit of the adjunction is the free Kleene algebra with tests generated by (T, Σ).

Since we already have the adjunctions $F_B \dashv U_B$ and $F_K \dashv U_K$, the functor $F_B \times F_K \colon \mathbf{Set} \times \mathbf{Set} \to \mathbf{Bool} \times \mathbf{Kleene}$ is a left adjoint to the functor $U_B \times U_K \colon \mathbf{Bool} \times \mathbf{Kleene} \to \mathbf{Set} \times \mathbf{Set}$.

Define Ψ to be the functor from $\mathbf{KAT}$ to $\mathbf{Bool} \times \mathbf{Kleene}$ which takes an object $\langle \mathbf{B}, \mathbf{K}, f \rangle$ to the pair $(\mathbf{B}, \mathbf{K})$ of algebras and an arrow $\langle h, k \rangle$ to the pair (h, k) of homomorphisms. Then it holds that $U = (U_B \times U_K) \circ \Psi$. So, if Ψ has a left adjoint, we obtain a left adjoint to U. Thus we may have the free Kleene algebra with tests generated by a pair of sets.

For a pair of a Boolean algebra $\mathbf{B}$ and a Kleene algebra $\mathbf{K}$, we have a Kleene algebra with tests

$$\langle \mathbf{B}, F_{IK}(U_{BI}(\mathbf{B})) + \mathbf{K}, \varphi(i) \rangle$$

where i is the first injection of the coproduct

$$F_{IK}(U_{BI}(\mathbf{B})) \xrightarrow{i} F_{IK}(U_{BI}(\mathbf{B})) + \mathbf{K} \xleftarrow{j} \mathbf{K}$$

And for a pair of a Boolean algebra homomorphism $f \colon \mathbf{B} \to \mathbf{B}'$ and a Kleene algebra homomorphism $g \colon \mathbf{K} \to \mathbf{K}'$ we have two idempotent-semiring homomorphisms $U_{BI}(f)$ and $U_{KI}(F_{IK}(U_{BI}(f)) + g)$. Then these two satisfy the following.

Proposition 5. $\varphi(i') \circ U_{BI}(f) = U_{KI}(F_{IK}(U_{BI}(f)) + g) \circ \varphi(i)$ where i and i' are the first injections of the coproducts $F_{IK}(U_{BI}(\mathbf{B})) + \mathbf{K}$ and $F_{IK}(U_{BI}(\mathbf{B}')) + \mathbf{K}'$, respectively.

Proof. By the definition of $F_{IK}(U_{BI}(f)) + g$ the diagram

$$
\begin{array}{ccc}
F_{IK}(U_{BI}(\mathbf{B})) & \xrightarrow{\ i\ } & F_{IK}(U_{BI}(\mathbf{B})) + \mathbf{K} \\
{\scriptstyle F_{IK}(U_{BI}(f))} \downarrow & & \downarrow {\scriptstyle F_{IK}(U_{BI}(f)) + g} \\
F_{IK}(U_{BI}(\mathbf{B}')) & \xrightarrow[\ i'\ ]{} & F_{IK}(U_{BI}(\mathbf{B}')) + \mathbf{K}'
\end{array}
$$

commutes. So the diagram

$$
\begin{array}{ccc}
U_{BI}(\mathbf{B}) & \xrightarrow{\;\varphi(i)\;} & U_{KI}(F_{IK}(U_{BI}(\mathbf{B})) + \mathbf{K}) \\
{\scriptstyle U_{BI}(f)}\Big\downarrow & \;\cdot\; & \Big\downarrow{\scriptstyle U_{KI}(F_{IK}(U_{BI}(f)) + g)} \\
U_{BI}(\mathbf{B}') & \xrightarrow[\;\varphi(i')\;]{} & U_{KI}(F_{IK}(U_{BI}(\mathbf{B}')) + \mathbf{K}')
\end{array}
$$

commutes by Lemma 1.

Therefore, $\langle f, F_{IK}(U_{BI}(f)) + g \rangle$ is an arrow from $\langle \mathbf{B}, F_{IK}(U_{BI}(\mathbf{B})) + \mathbf{K}, \varphi(i) \rangle$ to $\langle \mathbf{B}', F_{IK}(U_{BI}(\mathbf{B}')) + \mathbf{K}', \varphi(i') \rangle$ in **KAT**.

Define Φ to be the functor from **Bool** $\times$ **Kleene** to **KAT** which takes an object $(\mathbf{B}, \mathbf{K})$ to the object $\langle \mathbf{B}, F_{IK}(U_{BI}(\mathbf{B})) + \mathbf{K}, \varphi(i) \rangle$ and an arrow (f, g) to the arrow $\langle f, F_{IK}(U_{BI}(f)) + g \rangle$. Then the following holds.

Theorem 1. Φ *is a left adjoint to* Ψ.

Proof. Define the mapping $\xi_{(\mathbf{B},\mathbf{K}),\langle \mathbf{B}',\mathbf{K}',i' \rangle}$ from $\mathbf{KAT}(\Phi(\mathbf{B},\mathbf{K}), \langle \mathbf{B}', \mathbf{K}', i' \rangle)$ to $\mathbf{Bool} \times \mathbf{Kleene}((\mathbf{B}, \mathbf{K}), \Psi(\langle \mathbf{B}', \mathbf{K}', i' \rangle))$ for each object $(\mathbf{B}, \mathbf{K})$ in $\mathbf{Bool} \times \mathbf{Kleene}$ and $\langle \mathbf{B}', \mathbf{K}', i' \rangle$ in **KAT** as follows:

$$
\left\langle
\begin{array}{cc}
\mathbf{B} & F_{IK}(U_{BI}(\mathbf{B})) + \mathbf{K} \\
{\scriptstyle f}\Big\downarrow & \Big\downarrow{\scriptstyle g} \\
\mathbf{B}' & \mathbf{K}'
\end{array}
\right\rangle
\;\longmapsto\;
\left(
\begin{array}{cc}
\mathbf{B} & \mathbf{K} \\
{\scriptstyle f}\Big\downarrow & \Big\downarrow{\scriptstyle g \circ j} \\
\mathbf{B}' & \mathbf{K}'
\end{array}
\right)
$$

where j is the second injection of $F_{IK}(U_{BI}(\mathbf{B})) + \mathbf{K}$. In the sequel, ξ means $\xi_{(\mathbf{B},\mathbf{K}),\langle \mathbf{B}',\mathbf{K}',i' \rangle}$. It is sufficient to show that ξ is bijective. Assume that $\xi(\langle f, g \rangle) = \xi(\langle f', g' \rangle)$, that is, $f = f'$ and $g \circ j = g' \circ j$. Since $\langle f, g \rangle$ and $\langle f', g' \rangle$ are arrows in **KAT**, the following diagram commutes both for $y = g$ and for $y = g'$.

$$
\begin{array}{ccc}
U_{BI}(\mathbf{B}) & \xrightarrow{\;\varphi(i)\;} & U_{KI}(F_{IK}(U_{BI}(\mathbf{B})) + \mathbf{K}) \\
{\scriptstyle U_{BI}(f)}\Big\downarrow & & \Big\downarrow{\scriptstyle U_{KI}(y)} \quad (y = g \text{ or } g') \\
U_{BI}(\mathbf{B}') & \xrightarrow[\;i'\;]{} & U_{KI}(\mathbf{K}')
\end{array}
$$

So, by Lemma 1, the diagram

$$F_{IK}(U_{BI}(\mathbf{B})) \xrightarrow{\quad i \quad} F_{IK}(U_{BI}(\mathbf{B})) + \mathbf{K}$$

with left vertical arrow $F_{IK}(U_{BI}(f))$, right vertical arrow y $(y = g \text{ or } g')$, and bottom

$$F_{IK}(U_{BI}(\mathbf{B}')) \xrightarrow[\varphi^{-1}(i')]{} \mathbf{K}'$$

commutes again. Since $g \circ j = g' \circ j$ is assumed, it holds that $g = g'$ by the uniqueness of the intermediating arrow of $F_{IK}(U_{BI}(\mathbf{B})) + \mathbf{K}$ with respect to $\varphi^{-1}(i') \circ F_{IK}(U_{BI}(f))$ and $g' \circ j$. Therefore, ξ is one-to-one. Given an arrow $(h,k) \colon (\mathbf{B},\mathbf{K}) \to \Psi(\langle \mathbf{B}',\mathbf{K}',i'\rangle)$ in **Bool** × **Kleene**, we obtain two arrows $U_{BI}(h)$ and $U_{KI}(m)$ in **ISR**, where m is the unique intermediating arrow of $F_{IK}(U_{BI}(\mathbf{B})) + \mathbf{K}$ with respect to $\varphi^{-1}(i') \circ F_{IK}(U_{BI}(h))$ and k. By the definition of m, the diagram

$$F_{IK}(U_{BI}(\mathbf{B})) \xrightarrow{\quad i \quad} F_{IK}(U_{BI}(\mathbf{B})) + \mathbf{K}$$

with left vertical arrow $F_{IK}(U_{BI}(h))$, right vertical arrow m, and bottom

$$F_{IK}(U_{BI}(\mathbf{B}')) \xrightarrow[\varphi^{-1}(i')]{} \mathbf{K}'$$

commutes. So, by Lemma 1, the following diagram commutes, too.

$$U_{BI}(\mathbf{B}) \xrightarrow{\varphi(i)} U_{KI}(F_{IK}(U_{BI}(\mathbf{B})) + \mathbf{K})$$

with left vertical arrow $U_{BI}(h)$, right vertical arrow $U_{KI}(m)$, and bottom

$$U_{BI}(\mathbf{B}') \xrightarrow[\quad i' \quad]{} U_{KI}(\mathbf{K}')$$

So, $\langle h,m \rangle$ is an arrow from $\Phi(\mathbf{B},\mathbf{K})$ to $\langle \mathbf{B}',\mathbf{K}',i'\rangle$ in **KAT**. Moreover, since $\xi(\langle h,m\rangle) = (h, m \circ j)$ and $m \circ j = k$, $\xi(\langle h,m\rangle) = (h,k)$. Therefore, ξ is onto.

Corollary 1. *A component of the unit of $\Phi \dashv \Psi$ with respect to an object $(\mathbf{B},\mathbf{K})$ in* **Bool** × **Kleene** *is* $(\mathrm{id}_\mathbf{B}, j)$, *where j is the second injection of the coproduct $F_{IK}(U_{BI}(\mathbf{B})) + \mathbf{K}$.*

Proof. It is immediate from $\xi(\mathrm{id}_{\Phi(\mathbf{B},\mathbf{K})}) = (\mathrm{id}_\mathbf{B}, j)$.

Corollary 2. $\Phi \circ (F_B \times F_K)$ *is a left adjoint to U.*

Corollary 3. $\langle F_B(T), F_{IK}(U_{BI}(F_B(T))) + F_K(\Sigma), \varphi(i)\rangle$ *together with the pair $(\eta'_T, U_K(j) \circ \eta''_\Sigma)$ of maps η'_T and $U_K(j) \circ \eta''_\Sigma$ is the free Kleene algebra with tests* *generated by the pair (T, Σ) of (possibly infinite) sets, where i and j are the coproduct injections of $F_{IK}(U_{BI}(F_B(T))) + F_K(\Sigma)$, η' and η'' are the units of $F_B \dashv U_B$ and $F_K \dashv U_K$.*

5   Comparison

In this section Kozen-Smith's free Kleene algebra with tests and ours are compared.

We begin to compare **KAT** and $\mathbf{KAT}^{\subseteq}$. The category $\mathbf{KAT}^{\subseteq}$ is a full subcategory of **KAT**. The forgetful functor from $\mathbf{KAT}^{\subseteq}$ to **KAT** is denoted by G. Conversely, Proposition 4 provides the mapping from the set of objects in **KAT** to the set of objects in $\mathbf{KAT}^{\subseteq}$, that is, $\langle \mathbf{B}, \mathbf{K}, i \rangle \mapsto \langle i[\mathbf{B}], \mathbf{K}, \subseteq \rangle$, where $i[\mathbf{B}]$ is a Boolean algebra consisting of $\mathsf{im}(i)$. This mapping determines a functor F from **KAT** to $\mathbf{KAT}^{\subseteq}$. For an arrow $\langle f, g \rangle$ from $\langle \mathbf{B}, \mathbf{K}, i \rangle$ to $\langle \mathbf{B}', \mathbf{K}', i' \rangle$ in **KAT**, $F(\langle f, g \rangle) = \langle g|_{\mathsf{im}(i)}, g \rangle$, where $g|_{\mathsf{im}(i)}$ is a restriction of g with respect to the set $\mathsf{im}(i)$.

Theorem 2. *The functor F is a left adjoint to G.*

Proof. For each object $\langle \mathbf{B}, \mathbf{K}, i \rangle$ in **KAT** and $\langle \mathbf{B}', \mathbf{K}', \subseteq \rangle$ in $\mathbf{KAT}^{\subseteq}$, define the mapping $\phi_{\langle \mathbf{B}, \mathbf{K}, i \rangle, \langle \mathbf{B}', \mathbf{K}', \subseteq \rangle}$ from the homset $\mathbf{KAT}^{\subseteq}(F(\langle \mathbf{B}, \mathbf{K}, i \rangle), \langle \mathbf{B}', \mathbf{K}', \subseteq \rangle)$ to the homset $\mathbf{KAT}(\langle \mathbf{B}, \mathbf{K}, i \rangle, U(\langle \mathbf{B}', \mathbf{K}', \subseteq \rangle))$ as follows:

In the sequel, ϕ means $\phi_{\langle \mathbf{B}, \mathbf{K}, i \rangle, \langle \mathbf{B}', \mathbf{K}', \subseteq \rangle}$. For each arrow $\langle h, k \rangle$ form $\langle \mathbf{B}, \mathbf{K}, i \rangle$ to $\langle \mathbf{B}', \mathbf{K}', \subseteq \rangle$ in **KAT**, there exists an arrow $\langle k|_{\mathsf{im}(i)}, k \rangle$ from $\langle i[\mathbf{B}], \mathbf{K}, \subseteq \rangle$ to $\langle \mathbf{B}', \mathbf{K}', \subseteq \rangle$ in $\mathbf{KAT}^{\subseteq}$, and satisfies $\phi(\langle k|_{\mathsf{im}(i)}, k \rangle) = \langle h, k \rangle$ since $k|_{\mathsf{im}(i)} \circ i = k \circ i = h$. Thus, ϕ is onto. If $\phi(\langle f, g \rangle) = \phi(\langle f', g' \rangle)$, it is immediate that $g = g'$, then we have $f = f'$ since f and f' are determined by g as a restriction. So, ϕ is one-to-one. Therefore, ϕ is an isomorphism.

We now have the following sequence of adjunctions:

$$\mathbf{Set} \times \mathbf{Set} \underset{U_B \times U_K}{\overset{F_B \times F_K}{\rightleftarrows}} \bot \; \mathbf{Bool} \times \mathbf{Kleene} \underset{\Psi}{\overset{\Phi}{\rightleftarrows}} \bot \; \mathbf{KAT} \underset{G}{\overset{F}{\rightleftarrows}} \bot \; \mathbf{KAT}^{\subseteq}$$

The completeness theorem in [7] provides the property that the Kleene algebra with tests $\langle \mathbf{B}_T, \mathbf{K}_{T,\Sigma}, \subseteq \rangle$ given by Kozen-Smith's construction is isomorphic to $F(\Phi((F_B \times F_K)(T, \Sigma)))$ for a finite set T and (possibly infinite) set Σ, where $\mathbf{B}_T$ is a Boolean algebra consisting of the powerset $\wp(\mathcal{A}_{F_B(T)})$ of the set of atoms of the Boolean algebra $F_B(T)$, $\mathbf{K}_{T,\Sigma}$ is a Kleene algebra consisting of the set of regular sets of guarded strings over T and Σ. Note that, since T is finite, $F_B(T)$ is atomic and $F_B(T) \cong \mathbf{B}_T$.

The second half of Proposition 4 suggests that if the third component $\varphi(i)$ of the free Kleene algebra with tests $\langle F_B(T), F_{IK}(U_{BI}(F_B(T))) + F_K(\Sigma), \varphi(i)\rangle$ is one-to-one, this is isomorphic to $F(\Phi((F_B \times F_K)(T, \Sigma)))$ for each sets T and Σ. However, Example 1 shows that the third component of our Kleene algebra with tests is not always one-to-one. Also, the injections of a coproduct of Kleene algebras are not always one-to-one.

For a (possibly infinite) set T, the greatest element and the least element of $F_B(T)$ are not equal. So, by Proposition 2, $F_{IK}(U_{BI}(F_B(T)))$ is non-trivial. Also, by Remark 2, $F_K(\Sigma)$ is integral. Thus we have the following property.

Theorem 3. *The third component $\varphi(i)$ of the• free Kleene algebra with tests $\langle F_B(T), F_{IK}(U_{BI}(F_B(T))) + F_K(\Sigma), \varphi(i)\rangle$ is one-to-one for each pair (T, Σ) of sets.*

Proof. Take the free Kleene algebra $\langle F_B(T), F_{IK}(U_{BI}(F_B(T))) + F_K(\Sigma), \varphi(i)\rangle$. $U_{KI}(i)$ is one-to-one since, by Proposition 1, i is one-to-one and $U_{KI}(i)$ is i itself. Replace $\mathbf{S}$ with $U_{BI}(F_B(T))$ in the proof of Proposition 2. Then, $\varphi(i) = U_{KI}(i) \circ \varphi(\mathrm{id}_{F_{IK}(U_{BI}(F_B(T)))})$ since $\varphi(\mathrm{id}_{F_{IK}(U_{BI}(F_B(T)))})$ is a component of the unit of $F_{IK} \dashv U_{KI}$ with respect to $U_{BI}(F_B(T))$. As in the proof of Proposition 2, $\varphi(\mathrm{id}_{F_{IK}(U_{BI}(F_B(T)))})$ is an isomorphism from $U_{BI}(F_B(T))'$ to $F_{IK}(U_{BI}(F_B(T)))$ in **Kleene**. Thus, $\varphi(\mathrm{id}_{F_{IK}(U_{BI}(F_B(T)))})$ is one-to-one. Therefore, $\varphi(i)$ is one-to-one.

Corollary 4. *Our free algebra $\langle F_B(T), F_{IK}(U_{BI}(F_B(T))) + F_K(\Sigma), \varphi(i)\rangle$ is isomorphic to $F(\Phi((F_B \times F_K)(T, \Sigma)))$.*

Corollary 5. *If T is a finite set, $\langle F_B(T), F_{IK}(U_{BI}(F_B(T))) + F_K(\Sigma), \varphi(i)\rangle$ is isomorphic to the Kleene algebra with tests $\langle \mathbf{B}_T, \mathbf{K}_{T,\Sigma}, \subseteq\rangle$ given by Kozen-Smith's construction.*

In [3, 4] it was shown that the unital quantale $\mathbf{Q}_{T,\Sigma}$ consisting of the set of languages of guarded strings over T and Σ can be presented as a coproduct of unital quantales [9]:

> Unital quantales are monoids with arbitrary join in which left and right multiplications are universally additive. Left adjoints to the forgetful functors from the category of unital quantales to **Set** and to **ISR** exist, which are denoted by F_Q and F_{IQ}, respectively. Then $\mathbf{Q}_{T,\Sigma}$ is a coproduct of $F_{IQ}(U_{BI}(F_B(T)))$ and $F_{IQ}(\Sigma)$.

By Corollary 5, analogously, $\mathbf{K}_{T,\Sigma}$ is presented as a coproduct of Kleene algebras.

Proposition 6. *The Kleene algebra $\mathbf{K}_{T,\Sigma}$ is a coproduct of $F_{IK}(U_{BI}(F_B(T)))$ and $F_K(\Sigma)$ in **Kleene**.*

6   Conclusion

Starting from a definition of Kleene algebras with tests that is slightly more general than Kozen's definition, we have provided a free construction of Kleene algebras with tests. Though the starting point is different from Kozen and Smith, the results of both constructions are isomorphic to each other. Since our construction has been given as a combination of basic notions such as adjunctions between **Kleene** and the categories of related algebraic structures, and coproducts in **Kleene**, the free algebras are generated quite systematically. Especially, the bijective correspondence φ provided by the adjunction $F_{IK} \dashv U_{KI}$ and the notion of coproduct in **Kleene** played an important rôle for our free construction. This systematic manner allowed us to construct free Kleene algebras with tests generated by infinitely many generators without extra effort. The fact that the Kleene algebras consisting of regular sets of guarded strings are presented as coproducts in **Kleene** may be helpful for more mathematical investigation of these Kleene algebras.

Acknowledgement

The author would like to thank Millie Rhoss de Guzman, Jules Desharnais, Wolfram Kahl, Ridha Khedri, Michael Winter, and the anonymous referees for discussions and helpful comments.

References

1. M. Barr and C. Wells. Category Theory for Computing Science, Third Edition, Les Publications CRM, (1999).
2. J. Desharnais, B. Möller, and G. Struth. Kleene Algebra with Domain, *Technical Report 2003-07, Institut für Informatik, Universität Augsburg* (2003).
3. H. Furusawa and Y. Kinoshita. Essentially Algebraic Structure for Kleene Algebra with Tests and Its Application to Semantics of **While** Programs, *IPSJ Transactions on Programming*, Vol. 44, No. SIG 4 (PRO 17), pp. 47–53 (2003).
4. Y. Kinoshita and H. Furusawa. Essentially Algebraic Structure for Kleene Algebra with Tests, *Computer Software*, Vol. 20, No. 2, pp. 47–53 (2003). In Japanese.
5. Dexter Kozen. A Completeness Theorem for Kleene Algebras and the Algebra of Regular Events. *Information and Computation*, 110:366–390 (1994).
6. Dexter Kozen. Kleene Algebra with Tests. *ACM Transactions on Programming Languages and Systems*, Vol. 19, No. 3, pp. 427–443 (1997).
7. D. Kozen and F. Smith. Kleene algebra with tests: Completeness and decidability. *Proc 10th Int. Workshop Computer Science Logic (CSL'96)* (D. van Delen and M. Bezem (eds.)), volume 1258 of *Springer Lecture Notes in Computer Science*, pp. 244–259 (1996).
8. Saunders Mac Lane. Categories for Working Mathematician, Second Edition, Springer, (1998).
9. C. Mulvey and J. Pelletier. A Quantisation of the Calculus of Relations, *Proc. of Category Theory 1991*, CMS Conference Proceedings, No. 13, Amer. Math. Soc., pp. 345–360 (1992).

Streaming Representation-Changers

Jeremy Gibbons

Computing Laboratory, University of Oxford
jeremy.gibbons@comlab.ox.ac.uk
www.comlab.ox.ac.uk/oucl/work/jeremy.gibbons

Abstract. *Unfolds* generate data structures, and *folds* consume them. A *hylomorphism* is a fold after an unfold, generating then consuming a *virtual data structure*. A *metamorphism* is the opposite composition, an unfold after a fold; typically, it will convert from one data representation to another. In general, metamorphisms are less interesting than hylomorphisms: there is no automatic *fusion* to *deforest* the intermediate virtual data structure. However, under certain conditions fusion is possible: some of the work of the unfold can be done before all of the work of the fold is complete. This permits *streaming metamorphisms*, and among other things allows conversion of *infinite data representations*. We present a theory of metamorphisms and outline some examples.

1 Introduction

Folds and *unfolds* in functional programming [18, 28, 3] are well-known tools in the programmer's toolbox. Many programs that consume a data structure follow the pattern of a fold; and dually, many that produce a data structure do so as an unfold. In both cases, the structure of the program is determined by the structure of the data it processes.

It is natural to consider also compositions of these operations. Meijer [30] coined the term *hylomorphism* for the composition of a fold after an unfold. The *virtual data structure* [35] produced by the unfold is subsequently consumed by the fold; the structure of that data determines the structure of both its producer and its consumer. Under certain rather weak conditions, the intermediate data structure may be eliminated or *deforested* [39], and the two phases fused into one slightly more efficient one.

In this paper, we consider the opposite composition, of an unfold after a fold. Programs of this form consume an input data structure using a fold, constructing some intermediate (possibly unstructured) data, and from this intermediary produce an output data structure using an unfold. Note that the two data structures may now be of different shapes, since they do not meet. Indeed, such programs may often be thought of as *representation changers*, converting from one structured representation of some abstract data to a different structured representation. Despite the risk of putting the reader off with yet another neologism of Greek origin, we cannot resist coining the term *metamorphism* for such compositions, because they typically metamorphose representations.

D. Kozen (Ed.): MPC 2004, LNCS 3125, pp. 142–168, 2004.
© Springer-Verlag Berlin Heidelberg 2004

In general, metamorphisms are perhaps less interesting than hylomorphisms, because there is no nearly-automatic deforestation. Nevertheless, sometimes fusion is possible; under certain conditions, some of the unfolding may be performed before all of the folding is complete. This kind of fusion can be helpful for controlling the size of the intermediate data. Perhaps more importantly, it can allow conversions between infinite data representations. For this reason, we call such fused metamorphisms *streaming algorithms*; they are the main subject of this paper. We encountered them fortuitously while trying to describe some data compression algorithms [4], but have since realized that they are an interesting construction in their own right.

The remainder of this paper is organized as follows. Section 2 summarizes the theory of folds and unfolds. Section 3 introduces metamorphisms, which are unfolds after folds. Section 4 presents a theory of streaming, which is the main topic of the paper. Section 5 provides an extended application of streaming, and Section 6 outlines two other applications described in more detail elsewhere. Finally, Section 7 discusses some ideas for generalizing the currently rather list-oriented theory, and describes related work.

2   Origami Programming

We are interested in capturing and studying *recurring patterns of computation*, such as folds and unfolds. As has been strongly argued by the recently popular *design patterns* movement [8], identifying and exploring such patterns has many benefits: reuse of abstractions, rendering 'folk knowledge' in a more accessible format, providing a common vocabulary of discourse, and so on. What distinguishes patterns in functional programming from patterns in object-oriented and other programming paradigms is that the better 'glue' available in the former [20] allows the patterns to be expressed as *abstractions within the language*, rather than having to resort to informal prose and diagrams.

We use the notation of Haskell [25], the de facto standard lazy functional programming language, except that we take the liberty to use some typographic effects in formatting, and to elide some awkwardnesses (such as type coercions and qualifications) that are necessary for programming but that obscure the points we are trying to make.

Most of this paper involves the datatype of lists:

data $[\alpha] = [\,] \mid \alpha : [\alpha]$

That is, the datatype $[\alpha]$ of lists with elements of type α consists of the empty list $[\,]$, and non-empty lists of the form $a : x$ with head $a :: \alpha$ and tail $x :: [\alpha]$.

The primary patterns of computation over such lists are the *fold*, which consumes a list and produces some value:

$$
\begin{array}{ll}
\mathsf{foldr} & :: (\alpha \to \beta \to \beta) \to \beta \to [\alpha] \to \beta \\
\mathsf{foldr}\ f\ b\ [\,] & \triangleq b \\
\mathsf{foldr}\ f\ b\ (a : x) & \triangleq f\ a\ (\mathsf{foldr}\ f\ b\ x)
\end{array}
$$

and the *unfold* [16], which produces a list from some seed:

$$\text{unfoldr} \quad :: (\beta \to \text{Maybe}\,(\alpha, \beta)) \to \beta \to [\alpha]$$
$$\text{unfoldr}\,f\,b \mathrel{\widehat{=}} \textbf{case}\,f\,b\,\textbf{of}$$
$$\qquad\qquad \text{Just}\,(a, b') \to a : \text{unfoldr}\,f\,b'$$
$$\qquad\qquad \text{Nothing} \quad \to []$$

Here, the datatype Maybe augments a type α with an additional value Nothing:

data Maybe $\alpha = $ Nothing $|$ Just α

The foldr pattern consumes list elements from right to left (following the way lists are constructed); as a variation on this, there is another fold which consumes elements from left to right:

$$\text{foldl} \qquad\quad :: (\beta \to \alpha \to \beta) \to \beta \to [\alpha] \to \beta$$
$$\text{foldl}\,f\,b\,[] \qquad \mathrel{\widehat{=}} b$$
$$\text{foldl}\,f\,b\,(a : x) \mathrel{\widehat{=}} \text{foldl}\,f\,(f\,b\,a)\,x$$

We also use the operator scanl, which is like foldl but which returns all partial results instead of just the final one:

$$\text{scanl} \qquad\quad :: (\beta \to \alpha \to \beta) \to \beta \to [\alpha] \to [\beta]$$
$$\text{scanl}\,f\,b\,[] \qquad \mathrel{\widehat{=}} [b]$$
$$\text{scanl}\,f\,b\,(a : x) \mathrel{\widehat{=}} b : \text{scanl}\,f\,(f\,b\,a)\,x$$

We introduce also a datatype of internally-labelled binary trees:

data Tree $\alpha = $ Node (Maybe $(\alpha, \text{Tree}\,\alpha, \text{Tree}\,\alpha)$)

with fold operator

$$\text{foldt} \qquad\qquad\qquad :: (\text{Maybe}\,(\alpha, \beta, \beta) \to \beta) \to \text{Tree}\,\alpha \to \beta$$
$$\text{foldt}\,f\,(\text{Node Nothing}) \qquad \mathrel{\widehat{=}} f\,\text{Nothing}$$
$$\text{foldt}\,f\,(\text{Node}\,(\text{Just}\,(a, t, u))) \mathrel{\widehat{=}} f\,(\text{Just}\,(a, \text{foldt}\,f\,t, \text{foldt}\,f\,u))$$

and unfold operator

$$\text{unfoldt} \quad :: (\beta \to \text{Maybe}\,(\alpha, \beta, \beta)) \to \beta \to \text{Tree}\,\alpha$$
$$\text{unfoldt}\,f\,b \mathrel{\widehat{=}} \textbf{case}\,f\,b\,\textbf{of}$$
$$\qquad\qquad \text{Nothing} \qquad\quad \to \text{Node Nothing}$$
$$\qquad\qquad \text{Just}\,(a, b_1, b_2) \to \text{Node}\,(\text{Just}\,(a, \text{unfoldt}\,f\,b_1, \text{unfoldt}\,f\,b_2))$$

(It would be more elegant to define lists and their recursion patterns in the same style, but for consistency with the Haskell standard prelude we adopt its definitions. We could also condense the above code by using various higher-order combinators, but for accessibility we refrain from doing so.)

The remaining notation will be introduced as it is encountered. For more examples of the use of these and related patterns in functional programming, see [13], and for the theory behind this approach to programming, see [12]; for a slightly different view of both, see [3].

3   Metamorphisms

In this section we present three simple examples of metamorphisms, or representation changers in the form of unfolds after folds. These three represent the entire spectrum of possibilities: it turns out that the first permits streaming automatically (assuming lazy evaluation), the second does so with some work, and the third does not permit it at all.

3.1   Reformatting Lines

The classic application of metamorphisms is for dealing with *structure clashes* [22]: data is presented in a format that is inconvenient for a particular kind of processing, so it needs to be rearranged into a more convenient format. For example, a piece of text might be presented in 70-character lines, but required for processing in 60-character lines. Rather than complicate the processing by having to keep track of where in a given 70-character line a virtual 60-character line starts, good practice would be to separate the concerns of rearranging the data and of processing it. A *control-oriented* or *imperative* view of this task can be expressed in terms of coroutines: one coroutine, the processor, repeatedly requests the other, the rearranger, for the next 60-character line. A *data-oriented* or *declarative* view of the same task consists of describing the intermediate data structure, a list of 60-character lines. With lazy evaluation, the two often turn out to be equivalent; but the data-oriented view may be simpler, and is certainly the more natural presentation in functional programming.

We define the following Haskell functions.

$$
\begin{aligned}
&reformat && :: Integer \to [[\alpha]] \to [[\alpha]] \\
&reformat\ n && \mathrel{\widehat{=}} writeLines\ n \cdot readLines \\[4pt]
&readLines && :: [[\alpha]] \to [\alpha] \\
&readLines && \mathrel{\widehat{=}} \mathsf{foldr}\ (\mathbin{+\!\!+})\ [\,] \\
&writeLines && :: Integer \to [\alpha] \to [[\alpha]] \\
&writeLines\ n && \mathrel{\widehat{=}} \mathsf{unfoldr}\ (split\ n) \quad \textbf{where}\ split\ n\ [\,] \mathrel{\widehat{=}} \mathsf{Nothing} \\
& && \qquad\qquad\qquad\qquad\qquad\ split\ n\ x \mathrel{\widehat{=}} \mathsf{Just}\ (splitAt\ n\ x)
\end{aligned}
$$

The function *readLines* is just what is called *concat* in the Haskell standard prelude; we have written it explicitly as a fold here to emphasize the program structure. The function *writeLines* n partitions a list into segments of length n, the last segment possibly being short. (The operator '·' denotes function composition, and '++' is list concatenation.)

The function *reformat* fits our definition of a metamorphism, since it consists of an unfold after a fold. Because ++ is non-strict in its right-hand argument, *reformat* is automatically streaming when lazily evaluated: the first lines of output can be produced before all the input has been consumed. Thus, we need not maintain the whole concatenated list (the result of *readLines*) in memory at once, and we can even reformat infinite lists of lines.

3.2   Radix Conversion

Converting fractions from one radix to another is a change of representation. We define functions *radixConvert*, *fromBase* and *toBase* as follows:

$$radixConvert \qquad :: (Integer, Integer) \to [Integer] \to [Integer]$$
$$radixConvert\ (b, b') \cong toBase\ b' \cdot fromBase\ b$$

$$fromBase \qquad :: Integer \to [Integer] \to Rational$$
$$fromBase\ b \qquad \cong \mathsf{foldr}\ step_b\ 0$$

$$toBase \qquad :: Integer \to Rational \to [Integer]$$
$$toBase\ b \qquad \cong \mathsf{unfoldr}\ next_b$$

where

$$step_b\ n\ x \cong (x + n) \div b$$
$$next_b\ 0 \quad \cong \mathsf{Nothing}$$
$$next_b\ x \quad \cong \mathsf{Just}\ (\lfloor y \rfloor, y - \lfloor y \rfloor) \quad \textbf{where}\ y \cong b \times x$$

Thus, *fromBase b* takes a (finite) list of digits and converts it into a fraction; provided the digits are all at least zero and less than b, the resulting fraction will be at least zero and less than one. For example,

$$fromBase\ 10\ [2, 5] = step_{10}\ 2\ (step_{10}\ 5\ 0) = {}^1\!/_4$$

Then *toBase b* takes a fraction between zero and one, and converts it into a (possibly infinite) list of digits in base b. For example,

$$toBase\ 2\ ({}^1\!/_4) = 0 : \mathsf{unfoldr}\ next_2\ ({}^1\!/_2) = 0 : 1 : \mathsf{unfoldr}\ next_2\ 0 = [0, 1]$$

Composing *fromBase* for one base with *toBase* for another effects a change of base.

At first blush, this looks very similar in structure to the reformatting example of Section 3.1. However, now the fold operator $step_b$ is strict in its right-hand argument. Therefore, *fromBase b* must consume its whole input before it generates any output — so these conversions will not work for infinite fractions, and even for finite fractions the entire input must be read before any output is generated.

Intuitively, one might expect to be able to do better than this. For example, consider converting the decimal fraction $[2, 5]$ to the binary fraction $[0, 1]$. The initial 2 alone is sufficient to justify the production of the first bit 0 of the output: whatever follows (provided that the input really does consist of decimal digits), the fraction lies between $^2/_{10}$ and $^3/_{10}$, and so its binary representation must start with a zero. We make this intuition precise in Section 4; it involves, among other steps, inverting the structure of the traversal of the input by replacing the foldr with a foldl.

Of course, digit sequences like this are not a good representation for fractions: many useful operations turn out to be uncomputable. In Section 5, we look at a better representation. It still turns out to leave some operations uncomputable (as any non-redundant representation must), but there are fewer of them.

3.3   Heapsort

As a third introductory example, we consider tree-based sorting algorithms. One such sorting algorithm is a variation on Hoare's Quicksort [19]. What makes Quicksort particularly quick is that it is in-place, needing only logarithmic extra space for the control stack; but it is difficult to treat in-place algorithms functionally, so we ignore that aspect. Structurally, Quicksort turns out to be a hylomorphism: it unfolds the input list by repeated partitioning to produce a binary search tree, then folds this tree to yield the output list.

We use the datatype of binary trees from Section 2. We also suppose functions

$$partition :: [\alpha] \rightarrow \mathsf{Maybe}\ (\alpha, [\alpha], [\alpha])$$
$$join \qquad :: \mathsf{Maybe}\ (\alpha, [\alpha], [\alpha]) \rightarrow [\alpha]$$

The first partitions a non-empty list into a pivot and the smaller and larger elements (or returns Nothing given an empty list); the second concatenates a pair of lists with a given element in between (or returns the empty list given Nothing); we omit the definitions for brevity. Given these auxiliary functions, we have

$$quicksort \mathrel{\widehat{=}} \mathsf{foldt}\ join \cdot \mathsf{unfoldt}\ partition$$

as a hylomorphism.

One can sort also as a tree metamorphism: the same type of tree is an intermediate data structure, but this time it is a *minheap* rather than a binary search tree: the element stored at each node is no greater than any element in either child of that node. Moreover, this time the tree producer is a *list fold* and the tree consumer is a *list unfold*.

We suppose functions

$$insert \quad :: \alpha \rightarrow \mathsf{Tree}\ \alpha \rightarrow \mathsf{Tree}\ \alpha$$
$$splitMin :: \mathsf{Tree}\ \alpha \rightarrow \mathsf{Maybe}\ (\alpha, \mathsf{Tree}\ \alpha)$$

The first inserts an element into a heap; the second splits a heap into its least element and the remainder (or returns Nothing, given the empty heap). Given these auxilliary functions, we have

$$heapsort \mathrel{\widehat{=}} \mathsf{unfoldr}\ splitMin \cdot \mathsf{foldr}\ insert\ (\mathsf{Node}\ \mathsf{Nothing})$$

as a metamorphism. (Contrast this description of heapsort with the one given by Augusteijn [1] in terms of hylomorphisms, driving the computation by the shape of the intermediate tree rather than the two lists.)

Here, unlike in the reformatting and radix conversion examples, there is no hope for streaming: the second phase cannot possibly make any progress until the entire input is read, because the first element of the sorted output (which is the least element of the list) might be the last element of the input. Sorting is inherently a memory-intensive process, and cannot be performed on infinite lists.

4   Streaming

Of the three examples in Section 3, one automatically permits streaming and one can never do; only one, namely radix conversion, warrants further investigation in this regard. As suggested in Section 3.2, it ought to be possible to produce some of the output before all of the input is consumed. In this section, we see how this can be done, developing some general results along the way.

4.1   The Streaming Theorem

The second phase of the metamorphism involves producing the output, maintaining some state in the process; that state is initialized to the result of folding the entire input, and evolves as the output is unfolded. Streaming must involve starting to unfold from an earlier state, the result of folding only some initial part of the input. Therefore, it is natural to consider metamorphisms in which the folding phase is an instance of foldl:

   unfoldr f · foldl g c

Essentially the problem is a matter of finding some kind of *invariant* of this state that determines the initial behaviour of the unfold. This idea is captured by the following definition.

Definition 1. *The* streaming condition *for f and g is:*

$$f\ c = \mathsf{Just}\ (b, c') \;\Rightarrow\; f\ (g\ c\ a) = \mathsf{Just}\ (b, g\ c'\ a)$$

for all a, b, c and c'.

Informally, the streaming condition states the following: if c is a state from which the unfold would produce some output element (rather than merely the empty list), then so is the modified state $g\,c\,a$ for any a; moreover, the element b output from c is the same as that output from $g\,c\,a$, and the residual states c' and $g\,c'\,a$ stand in the same relation as the starting states c and $g\,c\,a$. In other words, 'the next output produced' is invariant under consuming another input.

   This invariant property is sufficient for the unfold and the fold to be fused into a single process, which alternates (not necessarily strictly) between consuming inputs and producing outputs. We define:

$$\begin{array}{ll}
stream & :: (\gamma \to \mathsf{Maybe}\ (\beta, \gamma)) \to (\gamma \to \alpha \to \gamma) \to \gamma \to [\alpha] \to [\beta] \\
stream\ f\ g\ c\ x \ \widehat{=}\ \mathbf{case}\ f\ c\ \mathbf{of} \\
\qquad\qquad\quad \mathsf{Just}\ (b, c') \to b : stream\ f\ g\ c'\ x \\
\qquad\qquad\quad \mathsf{Nothing}\quad \to \mathbf{case}\ x\ \mathbf{of} \\
\qquad\qquad\qquad\qquad\qquad\qquad a : x' \to stream\ f\ g\ (g\ c\ a)\ x' \\
\qquad\qquad\qquad\qquad\qquad\qquad [\,] \quad\ \to [\,]
\end{array}$$

Informally, $stream\ f\ g :: \gamma \to [\alpha] \to [\beta]$ involves a producer f and a consumer g; maintaining a state c, it consumes an input list x and produces an output list y. If f can produce an output element b from the state c, this output is delivered and the state revised accordingly. If f cannot, but there is an input a left, this input is consumed and the state revised accordingly. When the state is 'wrung dry' and the input is exhausted, the process terminates.

Formally, the relationship between the metamorphism and the streaming algorithm is given by the following theorem.

Theorem 2 (Streaming Theorem [4]). *If the streaming condition holds for f and g, then*

$$stream\ f\ g\ c\ x = \mathsf{unfoldr}\ f\ (\mathsf{foldl}\ g\ c\ x)$$

on finite lists x.

Proof. The proof is given in [4]. We prove a stronger theorem (Theorem 4) later.

Note that the result relates behaviours on finite lists only: on infinite lists, the foldl never yields a result, so the metamorphism may not either, whereas the streaming process can be productive — indeed, that is the main point of introducing streaming in the first place.

As a simple example, consider the functions *unCons* and *snoc*, defined as follows:

$$
\begin{aligned}
unCons\ [] &\;\widehat{=}\; \mathsf{Nothing} \\
unCons\ (a:x) &\;\widehat{=}\; \mathsf{Just}\ (a,x) \\[4pt]
snoc\ x\ a &\;\widehat{=}\; x + [a]
\end{aligned}
$$

The streaming condition holds for *unCons* and *snoc*: $unCons\ x = \mathsf{Just}\ (b, x')$ implies $unCons\ (snoc\ x\ a) = \mathsf{Just}\ (b, snoc\ x'\ a)$. Therefore, Theorem 2 applies, and

$$\mathsf{unfoldr}\ unCons \cdot \mathsf{foldl}\ snoc\ [] = stream\ unCons\ snoc\ []$$

on finite lists (but not infinite ones!). The left-hand side is a two-stage copying process with an unbounded intermediate buffer, and the right-hand side a one-stage copying queue with a one-place buffer.

4.2   Reversing the Order of Evaluation

In order to make a streaming version of radix conversion, we need to rewrite *fromBase b* as an instance of foldl rather than of foldr. Fortunately, there is a standard technique for doing this:

$$\mathsf{foldr}\ f\ b = applyto\ b \cdot \mathsf{foldr}\ (\cdot)\ \mathsf{id} \cdot \mathsf{map}\ f$$

where $applyto\ b\ f \;\widehat{=}\; f\ b$. Because composition is associative with unit id, the foldr on the right-hand side can — by the First Duality Theorem [6] — be replaced by a foldl.

Although valid, this is not always very helpful. In particular, it can be quite inefficient — the fold now constructs a long composition of little functions of the form $f\ a$, and this composition typically cannot be simplified until it is eventually applied to b. However, it is often possible that we can find some *representation* of those little functions that admits composition and application in constant time. Reynolds [34] calls this transformation *defunctionalization*.

Theorem 3. *Given fold arguments $f :: \alpha \to \beta \to \beta$ and $b :: \beta$, suppose there is a type ρ of representations of functions of the form $f\ a$ and their compositions, with the following operations:*

- *a representation function rep $:: \alpha \to \rho$ (so that rep a is the representation of $f\ a$);*
- *an abstraction function abs $:: \rho \to \beta \to \beta$, such that abs (rep a) $= f\ a$;*
- *an analogue $\odot :: \rho \to \rho \to \rho$ of function composition, such that abs $(r \odot s) =$ abs $r \cdot$ abs s;*
- *an analogue ident $:: \rho$ of the identity function, such that abs ident $=$ id;*
- *an analogue $app_b :: \rho \to \beta$ of application to b, such that $app_b\ r =$ abs $r\ b$.*

Then

$$\text{foldr } f\ b = app_b \cdot \text{foldl } (\odot)\ ident \cdot \text{map } rep$$

The foldl and the map can be fused:

$$\text{foldr } f\ b = app_b \cdot \text{foldl } (\circledast)\ ident$$

where $r \circledast a \mathrel{\widehat{=}} r \odot rep\ a$.

(Note that the abstraction function *abs* is used above only for stating the correctness conditions; it is not applied anywhere.)

For example, let us return to radix conversion, as introduced in Section 3.2. The 'little functions' here are of the form $step_b\ n$, or equivalently, $(\div b) \cdot (+n)$. This class of functions is closed under composition:

$$
\begin{aligned}
&(step_c\ n \cdot step_b\ m)\ x \\
={}& \{\text{composition}\} \\
&step_c\ n\ (step_b\ m\ x) \\
={}& \{step\} \\
&((x + m) \div b + n) \div c \\
={}& \{\text{arithmetic}\} \\
&(x + m + b \times n) \div (b \times c) \\
={}& \{\text{composition}\} \\
&((\div(b \times c)) \cdot (+m + b \times n))\ x
\end{aligned}
$$

We therefore defunctionalize $step_b\ n$ to the pair (n, b), and define:

$$
\begin{aligned}
rep_b\ n &\mathrel{\widehat{=}} (n, b) \\
abs\ (n, b)\ x &\mathrel{\widehat{=}} (x + n) \div b \\
(n, c) \odot (m, b) &\mathrel{\widehat{=}} (m + b \times n, b \times c) \\
(n, c) \circledast_b m &\mathrel{\widehat{=}} (n, c) \odot rep_b\ m \mathrel{\widehat{=}} (m + b \times n, b \times c) \\
ident &\mathrel{\widehat{=}} (0, 1) \\
app\ (n, b) &\mathrel{\widehat{=}} abs\ (n, b)\ 0 \mathrel{\widehat{=}} n \div b
\end{aligned}
$$

Theorem 3 then tells us that

$$fromBase\ b = app \cdot \text{foldl } (\circledast_b)\ ident$$

4.3   Checking the Streaming Condition

We cannot quite apply Theorem 2 yet, because the composition of $toBase\ b'$
and the revised $fromBase\ b$ has the abstraction function app between the unfold
and the fold. Fortunately, that app fuses with the unfold. For brevity below, we
define

$$mapl\ f\ \mathsf{Nothing}\qquad \widehat{=}\ \mathsf{Nothing}$$
$$mapl\ f\ (\mathsf{Just}\ (a,b))\ \widehat{=}\ \mathsf{Just}\ (a,f\ b)$$

(that is, $mapl$ is the map operation of the base functor for the list datatype);
then

$$\mathsf{unfoldr}\ next_c \cdot app = \mathsf{unfoldr}\ nextapp_c$$
$$\Leftarrow\quad \{\text{unfold fusion}\}$$
$$next_c \cdot app = mapl\ app \cdot nextapp_c$$

and

$$next_c\ (app\ (n,r))$$
$$=\quad \{app,\ next_c;\ \text{let}\ u\ \widehat{=}\ \lfloor n \times c \div r \rfloor\}$$
$$\quad \textbf{if}\ n\texttt{==}0\ \textbf{then}\ \mathsf{Nothing}\ \textbf{else}\ \mathsf{Just}\ (u, n{\times}c{\div}r - u)$$
$$=\quad \{app;\ \text{there is some leeway here (see below)}\}$$
$$\quad \textbf{if}\ n\texttt{==}0\ \textbf{then}\ \mathsf{Nothing}\ \textbf{else}\ \mathsf{Just}\ (u, app\ (n - u{\times}r{\div}c, r{\div}c))$$
$$=\quad \{mapl\}$$
$$\quad mapl\ app\ (\textbf{if}\ n\texttt{==}0\ \textbf{then}\ \mathsf{Nothing}\ \textbf{else}\ \mathsf{Just}\ (u, (n - u{\times}r{\div}c, r{\div}c)))$$

Therefore we try defining

$$nextapp_c\ (n,r)\ \widehat{=}\ \textbf{if}\ n\texttt{==}0\ \textbf{then}\ \mathsf{Nothing}\ \textbf{else}\ \mathsf{Just}\ (u, (n - u{\times}r{\div}c, r{\div}c))$$
$$\textbf{where}\ u\ \widehat{=}\ \lfloor n \times c \div r \rfloor$$

Note that there was some leeway here: we had to partition the rational $n{\times}c{\div}r - u$
into a numerator and denominator, and we chose $(n - u{\times}r{\div}c, r{\div}c)$ out of the
many ways of doing this. One might perhaps have expected $(n{\times}c - u{\times}r, r)$
instead; however, this leads to a dead-end, as we show later. Note that our
choice involves generalizing from integer to rational components.

Having now massaged our radix conversion program into the correct format:

$$radixConvert\ (b,c) = \mathsf{unfoldr}\ nextapp_c \cdot \mathsf{foldl}\ (\circledast_b)\ ident$$

we may consider whether the streaming condition holds for $nextapp_c$ and $\circledast_b$;
that is, whether

$$nextapp_c\ (n,r) = \mathsf{Just}\ (u,(n',r'))$$
$$\Rightarrow$$
$$nextapp_c\ ((n,r) \circledast_b m) = \mathsf{Just}\ (u,(n',r') \circledast_b m)$$

An element u is produced from a state (n,r) iff $n \neq 0$, in which case $u = \lfloor n \times c \div r \rfloor$. The modified state $(n,r) \circledast_b m$ evaluates to $(m + b \times n, b \times r)$. Since
$n,b > 0$ and $m \geq 0$, this necessarily yields an element; this element v equals

$\lfloor (m + b \times n) \times c \div (b \times r) \rfloor$. We have to check that u and v are equal. Sadly, in general they are not: since $0 \leq m < b$, it follows that v lies between u and $\lfloor (n+1) \times c \div r \rfloor$, but these two bounds need not meet.

Intuitively, this can happen when the state has not completely determined the next output, and further inputs are needed in order to make a commitment to that output. For example, consider having consumed the first digit 6 while converting the sequence $[6, 7]$ in decimal (representing 0.67_{10}) to ternary. The fraction 0.6_{10} is about 0.1210_3; nevertheless, it is not safe to commit to producing the digit 1, because the true result is greater than 0.2_3, and there is not enough information to decide whether to output a 1 or a 2 until the 7 has been consumed as well.

This is a common situation with streaming algorithms: the producer function (*nextapp* above) needs to be more cautious when interleaved with consumption steps than it does when all the input has been consumed. In the latter situation, there are no further inputs to invalidate a commitment made to an output; but in the former, a subsequent input might invalidate whatever output has been produced. The solution to this problem is to introduce a more sophisticated version of streaming, which proceeds more cautiously while input remains, but switches to the normal more aggressive mode if and when the input is exhausted. That is the subject of the next section.

4.4   Flushing Streams

The typical approach is to introduce a 'restriction'

$$snextapp = \mathsf{guard}\ safe\ nextapp$$

of *nextapp* for some predicate *safe*, where

$$\mathsf{guard}\ p\ f\ x \mathrel{\hat{=}} \mathbf{if}\ p\ x\ \mathbf{then}\ f\ x\ \mathbf{else}\ \mathsf{Nothing}$$

and to use *snextapp* as the producer for the streaming process. In the case of radix conversion, the predicate $safe_c$ (dependent on the output base c) could be defined

$$safe_c\ (n, r) \mathrel{\hat{=}} (\lfloor n \times c \div r \rfloor == \lfloor (n+1) \times c \div r \rfloor)$$

That is, the state (n, r) is safe for the output base c if these lower and upper bounds on the next digit meet; with this proviso, the streaming condition holds, as we checked above. (In fact, we need to check not only that the same elements are produced from the unmodified and the modified state, but also that the two residual states are related in the same way as the two original states. With the definition of $nextapp_c$ that we chose above, this second condition does hold; with the more obvious definition involving $(n \times c - u \times r, r)$ that we rejected, it does not.)

However, with this restricted producer the streaming process no longer has the same behaviour on finite lists as does the plain metamorphism: when the input is exhausted, the more cautious *snextapp* may have left some outputs still to be produced that the more aggressive *nextapp* would have emitted. The streaming process should therefore switch into a final 'flushing' phase when all the input has been consumed.

This insight is formalized in the following generalization of *stream*:

$$fstream :: (\gamma \rightarrow \mathsf{Maybe}\ (\gamma, \beta)) \rightarrow (\gamma \rightarrow \alpha \rightarrow \gamma) \rightarrow (\gamma \rightarrow [\beta]) \rightarrow \gamma \rightarrow [\alpha] \rightarrow [\beta]$$

$$
\begin{array}{l}
fstream\ f\ g\ h\ c\ x \mathrel{\widehat{=}} \mathbf{case}\ f\ c\ \mathbf{of} \\
\qquad\qquad\qquad \mathsf{Just}\ (b, c') \rightarrow b : fstream\ f\ g\ h\ c'\ x \\
\qquad\qquad\qquad \mathsf{Nothing}\quad \rightarrow \mathbf{case}\ x\ \mathbf{of} \\
\qquad\qquad\qquad\qquad\qquad\qquad a : x' \rightarrow fstream\ f\ g\ h\ (g\ c\ a)\ x' \\
\qquad\qquad\qquad\qquad\qquad\qquad [\,]\quad\ \rightarrow h\ c
\end{array}
$$

The difference between *fstream* and *stream* is that the former has an extra argument, h, a 'flusher'; when the state is wrung as dry as it can be and the input is exhausted, the flusher is applied to the state to squeeze the last few elements out. This is a generalization, because supplying the trivial flusher that always returns the empty list reduces *fstream* to *stream*.

The relationship of metamorphisms to flushing streams is a little more complicated than that to ordinary streams. One way of expressing the relationship is via a generalization of unfoldr, whose final action is to generate a whole tail of the resulting list rather than the empty list. This is an instance of *primitive corecursion* (called an *apomorphism* by Vene and Uustalu [37]), which is the categorical dual of *primitive recursion* (called a *paramorphism* by Meertens [29]).

$$
\begin{array}{l}
\mathsf{apol} \qquad :: (\beta \rightarrow \mathsf{Maybe}\ (\alpha, \beta)) \rightarrow (\beta \rightarrow [\alpha]) \rightarrow \beta \rightarrow [\alpha] \\
\mathsf{apol}\ f\ h\ b \mathrel{\widehat{=}} \mathbf{case}\ f\ b\ \mathbf{of} \\
\qquad\qquad\quad\ \mathsf{Just}\ (a, b') \rightarrow a : \mathsf{apol}\ f\ h\ b' \\
\qquad\qquad\quad\ \mathsf{Nothing}\quad \rightarrow h\ b
\end{array}
$$

Informally, apol$f\ h\ b = $ unfoldr$f\ b \mathbin{+\!\!+} h\ b'$, where b' is the final state of the unfold (if there is one — and if there is not, the value of $h\ b'$ is irrelevant), and unfoldr$f = $ apol$f$ (const $[\,]$). On finite inputs, provided that the streaming condition holds, a flushing stream process yields the same result as the ordinary streaming process, but with the results of flushing the final state (if any) appended.

Theorem 4 (Flushing Stream Theorem). *If the streaming condition holds for f and g, then*

$$fstream\ f\ g\ h\ c\ x = \mathsf{apol}\ f\ h\ (\mathsf{foldl}\ g\ c\ x)$$

on finite lists x.

The proof uses the following lemma [4], which lifts the streaming condition from single inputs to finite lists of inputs.

Lemma 5. *If the streaming condition holds for f and g, then*

$$f\ c = \mathsf{Just}\ (b, c') \Rightarrow f\ (\mathsf{foldl}\ g\ c\ x) = \mathsf{Just}\ (b, \mathsf{foldl}\ g\ c'\ x)$$

for all b, c, c' and finite lists x.

It also uses the *approximation lemma* [5, 15].

Lemma 6 (Approximation Lemma). *For finite, infinite or partial lists* x *and* y,

$$x = y \equiv \forall n.\ approx\ n\ x = approx\ n\ y$$

where

$$approx \qquad\qquad :: Int \to [\alpha] \to [\alpha]$$
$$approx\ (n+1)\ [] \quad = []$$
$$approx\ (n+1)\ (a:x) = a : approx\ n\ x$$

(Note that $approx\ 0\ x = \bot$ *for any* x, *by case exhaustion.)*

Proof (of Theorem 4). By Lemma 6, it suffices to show, for fixed f, g, h and for all n and finite x, that

$$\forall c.\ approx\ n\ (fstream\ f\ g\ h\ c\ x) = approx\ n\ (\text{apol}\ f\ h\ (\text{foldl}\ g\ c\ x))$$

under the assumption that the streaming condition holds for f and g. We use a 'double induction' simultaneously over n and the length $\#x$ of x. The inductive hypothesis is that

$$\forall c.\ approx\ m\ (fstream\ f\ g\ h\ c\ y) = approx\ m\ (\text{apol}\ f\ h\ (\text{foldl}\ g\ c\ y))$$

for any m, y such that $m < n \wedge \#y \leq \#x$ or $m \leq n \wedge \#y < \#x$. We then proceed by case analysis to complete the inductive step.

Case $f\ c = \mathsf{Just}\ (b, d)$. In this case, we make a subsidiary case analysis on n.

> **Subcase** $n = 0$. Then the result holds trivially.
> **Subcase** $n = n' + 1$. Then we have:
>
> $$approx\ (n'+1)\ (\text{apol}\ f\ h\ (\text{foldl}\ g\ c\ x))$$
> $$= \quad \{\text{Lemma 5: } f\ (\text{foldl}\ g\ c\ x) = \mathsf{Just}\ (b, \text{foldl}\ g\ d\ x)\}$$
> $$approx\ (n'+1)\ (b : \text{apol}\ f\ h\ (\text{foldl}\ g\ d\ x))$$
> $$= \quad \{approx\}$$
> $$b : approx\ n'\ (\text{apol}\ f\ h\ (\text{foldl}\ g\ d\ x))$$
> $$= \quad \{\text{induction: } n' < n\}$$
> $$b : approx\ n'\ (fstream\ f\ g\ h\ d\ x)$$
> $$= \quad \{approx\}$$
> $$approx\ (n'+1)\ (b : fstream\ f\ g\ h\ d\ x)$$
> $$= \quad \{fstream; \text{ case assumption}\}$$
> $$approx\ (n'+1)\ (fstream\ f\ g\ h\ c\ x)$$

Case $f\ c = \mathsf{Nothing}$. In this case, we make a subsidiary case analysis on x.

> **Subcase** $x = a : x'$. Then
>
> $$\text{apol}\ f\ h\ (\text{foldl}\ g\ c\ (a : x'))$$
> $$= \quad \{\text{foldl}\}$$
> $$\text{apol}\ f\ h\ (\text{foldl}\ g\ (g\ c\ a)\ x'))$$
> $$= \quad \{\text{induction: } \#x' < \#x\}$$
> $$fstream\ f\ g\ h\ (g\ c\ a)\ x'$$
> $$= \quad \{fstream; \text{ case assumption}\}$$
> $$fstream\ f\ g\ h\ c\ (a : x')$$

Subcase $x = [\,]$. Then

$$
\begin{aligned}
&\mathsf{apol}\ f\ h\ (\mathsf{foldl}\ g\ c\ [\,]) \\
=\quad &\{\mathsf{foldl}\} \\
&\mathsf{apol}\ f\ h\ c \\
=\quad &\{\text{case assumption}\} \\
&h\ c \\
=\quad &\{\textit{fstream};\ \text{case assumption}\} \\
&\textit{fstream}\ f\ g\ h\ c\ [\,]
\end{aligned}
$$

4.5   Invoking the Flushing Stream Theorem

Theorem 4 gives conditions under which an apomorphism applied to the result of a foldl may be streamed. This seems of limited use, since such scenarios are not commonly found. However, they can be constructed from more common scenarios in which the apomorphism is replaced with a simpler unfold. One way is to introduce the trivial apomorphism, whose flusher always returns the empty list. A more interesting, and the most typical, way is via the observation that

$$\mathsf{apol}\ (\mathsf{guard}\ p\ f)\ (\mathsf{unfoldr}\ f) = \mathsf{unfoldr}\ f$$

for any predicate p. Informally, the work of an unfold can be partitioned into 'cautious' production, using the more restricted producer **guard** $p\ f$, followed by more 'aggressive' production using simply f when the more cautious producer blocks.

4.6   Radix Conversion as a Flushing Stream

Returning for a final time to radix conversion, we define

$$snextapp_c\ (n, r) \mathrel{\widehat=} \mathsf{guard}\ safe_c\ nextapp_c$$

We verified in Sections 4.3 and 4.4 that the streaming condition holds for $snextapp_c$ and $\circledast_b$. Theorem 4 then tells us that we can convert from base b to base c using

$$radixConvert\ (b, c) = fstream\ snextapp_c\ (\circledast_b)\ (\mathsf{unfoldr}\ nextapp_c)\ (0, 1)$$

This program works for finite or infinite inputs, and is always productive. (It does, however, always produce an infinite result, even when a finite result would be correct. For example, it will correctly convert $\frac{1}{3}$ from base 10 to base 2, but in converting from base 10 to base 3 it will produce an infinite tail of zeroes. One cannot really hope to do better, as returning a finite output depending on the entire infinite input is uncomputable.)

5   Continued Fractions

Continued fractions are finite or infinite constructions of the form

$$b_0 + \cfrac{a_0}{b_1 + \cfrac{a_1}{b_2 + \cfrac{a_2}{b_3 + \cdots}}}$$

in which all the coefficients are integers. They provide an elegant representation of numbers, both rational and irrational. They have therefore been proposed by various authors [2, 17, 24, 38, 26, 27] as a good format in which to carry out *exact real arithmetic*. Some of the algorithms for simple arithmetic operations on continued fractions can be seen as metamorphisms, and as we shall show here, they can typically be streamed.

We consider algorithms on *regular* continued fractions: ones in which all the a_i coefficients are 1, and all the b_i coefficients (except perhaps b_0) are at least 1. We denote regular continued fractions more concisely in the form $\langle b_0, b_1, b_2, \ldots \rangle$. For example, the continued fraction for π starts $\langle 3, 7, 15, 1, 292, \ldots \rangle$. Finite continued fractions correspond to rationals; infinite continued fractions represent irrational numbers.

5.1   Converting Continued Fractions

We consider first conversions between rationals and finite regular continued fractions. To complete the isomorphism between these two sets, we need to augment the rationals with $^1\!/_0 = \infty$, corresponding to the empty continued fraction. We therefore introduce a type *ExtRat* of rationals extended with ∞.

Conversion from rationals to continued fractions is straightforward. Infinity, by definition, is represented by the empty fraction. A finite rational $^a\!/_b$ has a first term given by $a \, \underline{div} \, b$, the integer obtained by rounding the fraction down; this leaves a remainder of $(a \bmod b)/b$, whose reciprocal is the rational from which to generate the remainder of the continued fraction. Note that as a consequence of rounding the fraction down to get the first term, the remainder is between zero and one, and its reciprocal is at least one; therefore the next term (and by induction, all subsequent terms) will be at least one, yielding a regular continued fraction as claimed.

```
type CF = [Integer]

toCF    :: ExtRat → CF
toCF    ≘ unfoldr get
             where get x ≘ if    x == ∞
                           then Nothing
                           else  Just (⌊x⌋, 1/(x−⌊x⌋))
```

Converting in the opposite direction is more difficult: of course, not all continued fractions correspond to rationals. However, finite ones do, and for these we can compute the rational using a fold — it suffices to fold with the inverse of *get* (or at least, what would have been the inverse of *get*, if foldr had been defined to take an argument of type Maybe $(\alpha, \beta) \rightarrow \beta$, dualizing unfoldr).

$$fromCF \; :: \; CF \rightarrow ExtRat$$
$$fromCF \mathrel{\hat{=}} \mathsf{foldr} \; put \; \infty \quad \textbf{where} \; put \; n \; y \mathrel{\hat{=}} n + {}^{1}\!/_{y}$$

Thus, $fromCF \cdot toCF$ is the identity on extended rationals, and $toCF \cdot fromCF$ is the identity on finite continued fractions. On infinite continued fractions, $fromCF$ yields no result: put is strict, so the whole list of coefficients is required. One could compute an infinite sequence of rational approximations to the irrational value represented by an infinite continued fraction, by converting to a rational each of the convergents. But this is awkward, because the fold starts at the right, and successive approximations will have no common subexpressions — it does not constitute a scan. It would be preferable if we could write $fromCF$ as an instance of foldl; then the sequence of approximations would be given as the corresponding scanl.

Fortunately, Theorem 3 comes to the rescue again. This requires defunctionalizations of functions of the form $put \; n$ and their compositions. For proper rationals, we reason:

$$put \; n \; (put \; m \; {}^{a}\!/_{b})$$
$$= \quad \{put\}$$
$$put \; n \; (m + {}^{b}\!/_{a})$$
$$= \quad \{\text{arithmetic}\}$$
$$put \; n \; ({}^{m \times a + b}\!/_{a})$$
$$= \quad \{put\}$$
$$n + {}^{a}\!/_{m \times a + b}$$
$$= \quad \{\text{arithmetic}\}$$
$$(n \times (m \times a + b) + a)/(m \times a + b)$$
$$= \quad \{\text{collecting terms; dividing through by } b\}$$
$$((n \times m + 1) \times {}^{a}\!/_{b} + n)/(m \times {}^{a}\!/_{b} + 1)$$

This is a ratio of integer-coefficient linear functions of ${}^{a}\!/_{b}$, sometimes known as a *rational function* or *linear fractional transformation* of ${}^{a}\!/_{b}$. The general form of such a function takes x to $(q\,x + r)/(s\,x + t)$ (denoting multiplication by juxtaposition for brevity), and can be represented by the four integers q, r, s, t.

For the improper rational ∞, we reason:

$$put \; n \; (put \; m \; \infty)$$
$$= \quad \{put\}$$
$$put \; n \; (m + {}^{1}\!/_{\infty})$$
$$= \quad \{{}^{1}\!/_{\infty} = 0\}$$
$$put \; n \; m$$
$$= \quad \{put\}$$
$$n + {}^{1}\!/_{m}$$
$$= \quad \{\text{arithmetic}\}$$
$$(n \times m + 1)/m$$

which agrees with the result for proper rationals, provided we take the reasonable interpretation that $(q \times a/b + r)/(s \times a/b + t) = {}^{q \times a + r \times b}/_{s \times a + t \times b}$ when $b = 0$.

Following Theorem 3, then, we choose four-tuples of integers as our representation; for reasons that will become clear, we write these four-tuples in the form $\left(\begin{smallmatrix} q & r \\ s & t \end{smallmatrix}\right)$. The abstraction function abs applies the rational function:

$$abs \left(\begin{smallmatrix} q & r \\ s & t \end{smallmatrix}\right) x \;\hat{=}\; {}^{q\,x + r}/_{s\,x + t}$$

and the representation function rep injects the integer n into the representation of $put\ n$:

$$rep\ n \;\hat{=}\; \left(\begin{smallmatrix} n & 1 \\ 1 & 0 \end{smallmatrix}\right)$$

The identity function is represented by $ident$:

$$ident \;\hat{=}\; \left(\begin{smallmatrix} 1 & 0 \\ 0 & 1 \end{smallmatrix}\right)$$

We verify that rational functions are indeed closed under composition, by constructing the representation of function composition:

$$
\begin{aligned}
& abs \left(\left(\begin{smallmatrix} q & r \\ s & t \end{smallmatrix}\right) \odot \left(\begin{smallmatrix} q' & r' \\ s' & t' \end{smallmatrix}\right)\right) x \\
=\; & \{\text{requirement}\} \\
& abs \left(\begin{smallmatrix} q & r \\ s & t \end{smallmatrix}\right) \left(abs \left(\begin{smallmatrix} q' & r' \\ s' & t' \end{smallmatrix}\right) x\right) \\
=\; & \{abs\} \\
& abs \left(\begin{smallmatrix} q & r \\ s & t \end{smallmatrix}\right) ((q'\,x + r')/(s'\,x + t')) \\
=\; & \{abs\ \text{again}\} \\
& (q\,(q'\,x+r') + r\,(s'\,x+t'))/(s\,(q'\,x+r') + t\,(s'\,x+t')) \\
=\; & \{\text{collecting terms}\} \\
& ((q\,q'+r\,s')\,x + (q\,r'+r\,t'))/((s\,q'+t\,s')\,x + (s\,r'+t\,t')) \\
=\; & \{abs\} \\
& abs \left(\begin{smallmatrix} q\,q'+r\,s' & q\,r'+r\,t' \\ s\,q'+t\,s' & s\,r'+t\,t' \end{smallmatrix}\right) x
\end{aligned}
$$

We therefore define

$$\left(\begin{smallmatrix} q & r \\ s & t \end{smallmatrix}\right) \odot \left(\begin{smallmatrix} q' & r' \\ s' & t' \end{smallmatrix}\right) \;\hat{=}\; \left(\begin{smallmatrix} q\,q'+r\,s' & q\,r'+r\,t' \\ s\,q'+t\,s' & s\,r'+t\,t' \end{smallmatrix}\right)$$

Finally, we define an extraction function

$$
\begin{aligned}
app \left(\begin{smallmatrix} q & r \\ s & t \end{smallmatrix}\right) &\;\hat{=}\; abs \left(\begin{smallmatrix} q & r \\ s & t \end{smallmatrix}\right) \infty \\
&= q/s
\end{aligned}
$$

(Notice that $\odot$ turns out to be matrix multiplication, and $ident$ the unit matrix, which explains the choice of notation. These matrices are sometimes called *homographies*, and the rational functions they represent *homographic functions* or *Möbius transformations*. They can be generalized from continued fractions to many other interesting exact representations of real numbers [32], including redundant ones. In fact, the same framework also encompasses radix conversions, as explored in Section 3.2.)

By Theorem 3 we then have

$$fromCF = app \cdot \mathsf{foldl}\,(\circledast)\ ident \quad \textbf{where } \left(\begin{smallmatrix} q & r \\ s & t \end{smallmatrix}\right) \circledast n \;\hat{=}\; \left(\begin{smallmatrix} n\,q+r & q \\ n\,s+t & s \end{smallmatrix}\right)$$

Of course, this still will not work for infinite continued fractions; however, we can now define

$$fromCFi :: CF \to [ExtRat]$$
$$fromCFi \triangleq \text{map } app \cdot \text{scanl } (\circledast) \ ident$$

yielding the (infinite) sequence of finite convergents of an (infinite) continued fraction.

5.2   Rational Unary Functions of Continued Fractions

In Section 5.1, we derived the program

$$fromCF = app \cdot \text{foldl } (\circledast) \left(\begin{smallmatrix} 1 & 0 \\ 0 & 1 \end{smallmatrix}\right)$$

for converting a finite continued fraction to an extended rational. In fact, we can compute an arbitrary rational function of a continued fraction, by starting this process with an arbitrary homography in place of the identity $\left(\begin{smallmatrix} 1 & 0 \\ 0 & 1 \end{smallmatrix}\right)$. This is because composition $\odot$ fuses with the fold:

$$abs \ h \ (fromCF \ ns)$$
$$= \quad \{fromCF\}$$
$$abs \ h \ (app \ (\text{foldl } (\circledast) \ ident \ ns))$$
$$= \quad \{\text{specification of } app\}$$
$$abs \ h \ (abs \ (\text{foldl } (\circledast) \ ident \ ns) \ \infty)$$
$$= \quad \{\text{requirement on } abs \text{ and } \odot\}$$
$$abs \ (h \odot \text{foldl } (\circledast) \ ident \ ns) \ \infty$$
$$= \quad \{\text{fold fusion: } \odot \text{ is associative, and } ident \text{ its unit}\}$$
$$abs \ (\text{foldl } (\circledast) \ h \ ns) \ \infty$$
$$= \quad \{\text{specification of } app \text{ again}\}$$
$$app \ (\text{foldl } (\circledast) \ h \ ns)$$

For example, suppose we want to compute the rational $2/_{x-3}$, where x is the rational represented by a particular (finite) continued fraction ns. We could convert ns to the rational x, then perform the appropriate rational arithmetic. Alternatively, we could convert ns to a rational as above, starting with the homography $\left(\begin{smallmatrix} 0 & 2 \\ 1 & -3 \end{smallmatrix}\right)$ instead of $\left(\begin{smallmatrix} 1 & 0 \\ 0 & 1 \end{smallmatrix}\right)$, and get the answer directly. If we want the result as a continued fraction again rather than a rational, we simply post-apply $toCF$.

Of course, this will not work to compute rational functions of *infinite* continued fractions, as the folding will never yield a result. Fortunately, it is possible to applying streaming, so that terms of the output are produced before the whole input is consumed. This is the focus of the remainder of this section. The derivation follows essentially the same steps as were involved in radix conversion.

The streaming process maintains a state in the form of a homography, which represents the mapping from what is yet to be consumed to what is yet to be produced. The production steps of the streaming process choose a term to output, and compute a reduced homography for the remainder of the computation.

Given a current homography $\left(\begin{smallmatrix} q & r \\ s & t \end{smallmatrix}\right)$, and a chosen term n, the reduced homography $\left(\begin{smallmatrix} q' & r' \\ s' & t' \end{smallmatrix}\right)$ is determined as follows:

$$(q\,x + r)/(s\,x + t) = n + 1/((q'\,x + r')/(s'\,x + t'))$$
$\equiv$ {reciprocal}
$$(q\,x + r)/(s\,x + t) = n + (s'\,x + t')/(q'\,x + r')$$
$\equiv$ {rearrange}
$$(s'\,x + t')/(q'\,x + r') = (q\,x + r)/(s\,x + t) - n$$
$\equiv$ {incorporate n into fraction}
$$(s'\,x + t')/(q'\,x + r') = (q\,x + r - n\,(s\,x + t))/(s\,x + t)$$
$\equiv$ {collect x and non-x terms}
$$(s'\,x + t')/(q'\,x + r') = ((q - n\,s)\,x + r - n\,t)/(s\,x + t)$$
$\Leftarrow$ {equating terms}
$$q' = s, r' = t, s' = q - n\,s, t' = r - n\,t$$

That is,

$$\left(\begin{smallmatrix} q' & r' \\ s' & t' \end{smallmatrix}\right) = \left(\begin{smallmatrix} 0 & 1 \\ 1 & -n \end{smallmatrix}\right) \odot \left(\begin{smallmatrix} q & r \\ s & t \end{smallmatrix}\right)$$

We therefore define

$$emit \left(\begin{smallmatrix} q & r \\ s & t \end{smallmatrix}\right) n \mathrel{\widehat{=}} \left(\begin{smallmatrix} 0 & 1 \\ 1 & -n \end{smallmatrix}\right) \odot \left(\begin{smallmatrix} q & r \\ s & t \end{smallmatrix}\right)$$
$$= \left(\begin{smallmatrix} s & t \\ q-n\,s & r-n\,t \end{smallmatrix}\right)$$

Making It a Metamorphism. In most of what follows, we assume that we have a *completely regular* continued fraction, namely one in which every coefficient including the first is at least one. This implies that the value represented by the continued fraction is between one and infinity. We see at the end of the section what to do about the first coefficient, in case it is less than one.

Given the representation of a rational function in the form of a homography h, we introduce the function *rfc* ('*r*ational *f*unction of a *c*ompletely regular continued fraction') to apply it as follows:

$$rfc\ h \mathrel{\widehat{=}} toCF \cdot app \cdot foldl\ (\circledast)\ h$$

This is almost a metamorphism: $toCF$ is indeed an unfold, but we must get rid of the projection function app in the middle. Fortunately, it fuses with the unfold:

$$\mathsf{unfoldr}\ get \cdot app = \mathsf{unfoldr}\ geth$$

where $geth$ (for 'get on homographies') is defined by

$$geth \left(\begin{smallmatrix} q & r \\ s & t \end{smallmatrix}\right) \mathrel{\widehat{=}} \mathbf{if}\ s \mathrel{==} 0\ \mathbf{then}\ \mathsf{Nothing}\ \mathbf{else}\ \mathsf{Just}\ (n, emit \left(\begin{smallmatrix} q & r \\ s & t \end{smallmatrix}\right) n)$$
$$\mathbf{where}\ n \mathrel{\widehat{=}} q\ \underline{div}\ s$$

as can easily be verified.

This yields a metamorphism:

$$rfc\ h = \mathsf{unfoldr}\ geth \cdot foldl\ (\circledast)\ h$$

Checking the Streaming Condition. Now we must check that the streaming condition holds for *geth* and ⊛. We require that when

$$geth\ h = \mathsf{Just}\ (n, h')$$

then, for any subsequent term m (which we can assume to be at least 1, this being a completely regular continued fraction),

$$geth\ (h \circledast m) = \mathsf{Just}\ (n, h' \circledast m)$$

Unpacking this, when $h = \left(\begin{smallmatrix} q & r \\ s & t \end{smallmatrix}\right)$ and $h' = \left(\begin{smallmatrix} q' & r' \\ s' & t' \end{smallmatrix}\right)$, we have $s \neq 0$, $n = q\ \underline{div}\ s$, $q' = s$, and $s' = q\ \underline{mod}\ s$; moreover, $\left(\begin{smallmatrix} q & r \\ s & t \end{smallmatrix}\right) \circledast m = \left(\begin{smallmatrix} m\,q+r & q \\ m\,s+t & s \end{smallmatrix}\right)$. We require among other things that $m\,s + t \neq 0$ and $(m\,q + r)\ \underline{div}\ (m\,s + t) = q\ \underline{div}\ s$. Sadly, this does not hold; for example, if $m = 1$ and s, t are positive,

$$^{q+r}/_{s+t} < 1 + {}^q/_s \equiv s\,(q+r) < (q+s)\,(q+t) \equiv r\,s < q\,t + s\,t + s^2$$

which fails if r is sufficiently large.

Cautious Progress. As with the radix conversion algorithm in Section 4.3, the function that produces the next term of the output must be more cautious when it is interleaved with consumption steps that it may be after all the input has been consumed. The above discussion suggests that we should commit to an output only when it is safe from being invalidated by a later input; in symbols, only when $(m\,q + r)\ \underline{div}\ (m\,s + t) = q\ \underline{div}\ s$ for any $m \geq 1$. This follows if s and t are non-zero and have the same sign, and if $(q + r)\ \underline{div}\ (s + t) = q\ \underline{div}\ s$, as a little calculation will verify.

(Another way of looking at this is to observe that the value represented by a completely regular continued fraction ranges between 1 and ∞, so the result of transforming it under a homography $\left(\begin{smallmatrix} q & r \\ s & t \end{smallmatrix}\right)$ ranges between

$$abs\ \left(\begin{smallmatrix} q & r \\ s & t \end{smallmatrix}\right) 1 = {}^{q+r}/_{s+t}$$

and

$$abs\ \left(\begin{smallmatrix} q & r \\ s & t \end{smallmatrix}\right) \infty = {}^q/_s$$

if $s \neq 0$. If the two denominators have the same sign, the result ranges between these two; if they have different signs, it ranges outside them. Therefore, the first coefficient of the output is determined if the denominators have the same sign (which follows if s and t are non-zero and of the same sign) and the two fractions have the same integer parts.)

We therefore define *gets* (for 'safe *get*') by

$$gets\ \left(\begin{smallmatrix} q & r \\ s & t \end{smallmatrix}\right) \mathrel{\widehat{=}} \mathbf{let}\ n \mathrel{\widehat{=}} q\ \underline{div}\ s\ \mathbf{in}$$
$$\qquad \mathbf{if} \quad s\,t > 0 \wedge (q + r)\ \underline{div}\ (s + t) == n$$
$$\qquad \mathbf{then}\ \mathsf{Just}\ (n, emit\ \left(\begin{smallmatrix} q & r \\ s & t \end{smallmatrix}\right) n)$$
$$\qquad \mathbf{else}\ \ \mathsf{Nothing}$$

Note that whenever *gets* produces a value, *geth* produces the same value; but sometimes *gets* produces nothing when *geth* produces something. The streaming condition *does* hold for *gets* and ⊛, as the reader may now verify.

Flushing Streams. It is not the case that unfoldr *get* · *app* = unfoldr *gets*, of course, because the latter is too cautious. However, it does follow that

$$\text{unfoldr } get \cdot app = apol\ gets\ (\text{unfoldr } geth)$$

This cautiously produces elements while it it safe to do so, then throws caution to the winds and produces elements anyway when it ceases to be safe. Moreover, Theorem 4 applies to the cautious part, and so

$$\begin{aligned}
rfc\ h &= \text{unfoldr } get \cdot app \cdot \text{foldl } (\circledast)\ h \\
&= fstream\ gets\ (\circledast)\ (\text{unfoldr } geth)\ h
\end{aligned}$$

This streaming algorithm can compute a rational function of a finite or infinite completely regular continued fraction, yielding a finite or infinite regular continued fraction as a result.

Handling the First Term. A regular but not completely regular continued fraction may have a first term of 1 or less, invalidating the reasoning above. However, this is easy to handle, simply by consuming the first term immediately. We introduce a wrapper function *rf*:

$$\begin{aligned}
rf\ h\ [\,] &\ \widehat{=}\ rfc\ h\ [\,] \\
rf\ h\ (n:x) &\ \widehat{=}\ rfc\ (h \circledast n)\ x
\end{aligned}$$

This streaming algorithm can compute any rational function of a finite or infinite regular continued fraction, completely regular or not.

5.3   Rational Binary Functions of Continued Fractions

The streaming process described in Section 5.2 allows us to compute a unary rational function $(a\,x+b)/(c\,x+d)$ of a single continued fraction x. The technique can be adapted to allow a binary rational function $(a\,x\,y+b\,x+c\,y+d)/(e\,x\,y+f\,x+g\,y+h)$ of continued fractions x and y. This does not fit into our framework of metamorphisms and streaming algorithms, because it combines two arguments into one result; nevertheless, much of the same reasoning can be applied. We intend to elaborate on this in a companion paper.

6   Two Other Applications

In this section, we briefly outline two other applications of streaming; we have described both in more detail elsewhere, and we refer the reader to those sources for the details.

6.1   Digits of π

In [14] we present an *unbounded spigot algorithm* for computing the digits of π. This work was inspired by Rabinowitz and Wagon [33], who coined the term *spigot algorithm* for an algorithm that yields output elements incrementally and does not reuse them after they have been output — so the digits drip out one by one, as if from a leaky tap. (In contrast, most algorithms for computing approximations to π, including the best currently known, work inscrutably until they deliver a complete response at the end of the computation.) Although incremental, Rabinowitz and Wagon's algorithm is *bounded*, since one needs to decide at the outset how many digits are to be computed, whereas our algorithm yields digits indefinitely. (This is nothing to do with evaluation order: Rabinowitz and Wagon's algorithm is just as bounded in a lazy language.)

The algorithm is based on the following expansion:

$$\pi = \sum_{i=0}^{\infty} \frac{(i!)^2 2^{i+1}}{(2i+1)!}$$

$$= \left(2 + \frac{1}{3} \times\right)\left(2 + \frac{2}{5} \times\right)\left(2 + \frac{3}{7} \times\right) \cdots \left(2 + \frac{i}{2i+1} \times\right) \cdots$$

A streaming algorithm can convert this infinite sequence of linear fractional transformations (represented as homographies) into an infinite sequence of decimal digits. The consumption operator is matrix multiplication, written $\odot$ in Section 5.1. When a digit n is produced, the state h should be transformed into

$$\begin{pmatrix} 10 & -10n \\ 0 & 1 \end{pmatrix} \odot h$$

Any tail of the input sequence represents a value between 3 and 4, so homography h determines the next digit when

$$\lfloor abs\ h\ 3 \rfloor \mathrel{\hat{=}} \lfloor abs\ h\ 4 \rfloor$$

(in which case, the digit is the common value of these two expressions). This reasoning gives us the following program:

$$pi \mathrel{\hat{=}} stream\ prod\ (\odot)\ ident\ lfts$$

where

$$lfts \quad \mathrel{\hat{=}} \left[\begin{pmatrix} k & 4k+2 \\ 0 & 2k+1 \end{pmatrix} \mid k \leftarrow [1..]\right]$$

$$prod\ h \mathrel{\hat{=}} \textbf{if}\ \lfloor abs\ h\ 4 \rfloor == n\ \textbf{then}\ \textsf{Just}\ (n, \begin{pmatrix} 10 & -10n \\ 0 & 1 \end{pmatrix} \odot h)\ \textbf{else}\ \textsf{Nothing}$$
$$\textbf{where}\ n \mathrel{\hat{=}} \lfloor abs\ h\ 3 \rfloor$$

6.2   Arithmetic Coding

Arithmetic coding [40] is a method for data compression. It can be more *effective* than rival schemes such as Huffman coding, while still being as *efficient*. Moreover, it is well suited to *adaptive* encoding, in which the coding scheme evolves to match the text being encoded.

The basic idea of arithmetic encoding is simple. The message to be encoded is broken into *symbols*, such as characters, and each symbol of the message is associated with a semi-open *subinterval* of the unit interval $[0 .. 1)$. Encoding starts with the unit interval, and *narrows* it according to the intervals associated with each symbol of the message in turn. The encoded message is the binary representation of some *fraction* chosen from the final 'target' interval.

In [4] we present a detailed derivation of arithmetic encoding and decoding. We merely outline the development of encoding here, to show where streaming fits in. Decoding follows a similar process to encoding, starting with the unit interval and homing in on the binary fraction, reconstructing the plaintext in the process; but we will not discuss it here.

The encoding process can be captured as follows. The type *Interval* represents intervals of the real line, usually *subunits* (subintervals of the unit interval):

$$unit :: Interval$$
$$unit \stackrel{\frown}{=} [0 .. 1)$$

Narrowing an interval *lr* by a subunit *pq* yields a subinterval of *lr*, which stands in the same relation to *lr* as *pq* does to *unit*.

$$narrow :: Interval \to Interval \to Interval$$
$$narrow [l .. r) [p .. q) \stackrel{\frown}{=} [l + (r-l) \times p .. l + (r-l) \times q)$$

We consider only non-adaptive encoding here for simplicity: adaptivity turns out to be orthogonal to streaming. We therefore represent each symbol by a fixed interval.

Encoding is a two-stage process: narrowing intervals to a target interval, and generating the binary representation of a fraction within that interval (missing its final 1).

$$encode :: [Interval] \to [Bool]$$
$$encode \stackrel{\frown}{=} \mathsf{unfoldr}\ nextBit \cdot \mathsf{foldl}\ narrow\ unit$$

where

$$nextBit\ (l, r)$$
$$\mid r \leq \tfrac{1}{2} \quad \stackrel{\frown}{=} \mathsf{Just}\ (False, narrow\ (0, 2)\ (l, r))$$
$$\mid \tfrac{1}{2} \leq l \quad \stackrel{\frown}{=} \mathsf{Just}\ (True, narrow\ (-1, 1)\ (l, r))$$
$$\mid l < \tfrac{1}{2} < r \stackrel{\frown}{=} \mathsf{Nothing}$$

This is a metamorphism.

As described, this is not a very efficient encoding method: the entire message has to be digested into a target interval before any of the fraction can be generated. However, the streaming condition holds, and bits of the fraction can be produced before all of the message is consumed:

$$encode \quad :: [Interval] \to [Bool]$$
$$encode\ m = stream\ nextBit\ narrow\ unit$$

7   Future and Related Work

The notion of metamorphisms in general and of streaming algorithms in particular arose out of our work on arithmetic coding [4]. Since then, we have seen the same principles cropping up in other areas, most notably in the context of various kinds of numeric representations: the radix conversion problem from Section 3.2, continued fractions as described in Section 5, and computations with infinite compositions of homographies as used in Section 6.1. Indeed, one might even see arithmetic coding as a kind of numeric representation problem.

7.1   Generic Streaming

Our theory of metamorphisms could easily be generalized to other datatypes: there is nothing to prevent consideration of folds consuming and unfolds producing datatypes other than lists. However, we do not currently have any convincing examples.

Perhaps related to the lack of convincing examples for other datatypes, it is not clear what a generic theory of streaming algorithms would look like. List-oriented streaming relies essentially on foldl, which does not generalize in any straightforward way to other datatypes. (We have in the past attempted to show how to generalize scanl to arbitrary datatypes [9–11], and Pardo [31] has improved on these attempts; but we do not see yet how to apply those constructions here.)

However, the unfold side of streaming algorithms does generalize easily, to certain kinds of datatype if not obviously all of them. Consider producing a data structure of the type

data $Generic\ \tau\ \alpha = Gen\ (\mathsf{Maybe}\ (\alpha, \tau\ (Generic\ \tau\ \alpha)))$

for some instance τ of the type class *Functor*. (Lists essentially match this pattern, with τ the identity functor. The type Tree of internally-labelled binary trees introduced in Section 2 matches too, with τ being the pairing functor. In general, datatypes of this form have an empty structure, and all non-empty structures consist of a root element and an τ-shaped collection of children.) It is straightforward to generalize the streaming condition to such types:

$$f\ c = \mathsf{Just}\ (b, c') \Rightarrow f\ (g\ c\ a) = \mathsf{Just}\ (b, fmap\ (\lambda u \rightarrow g\ u\ a)\ c')$$

(This has been called an 'τ-invariant' or 'mongruence' [23] elsewhere.) Still, we do not have any useful applications of an unfold to a *Generic* type after a foldl.

7.2   Related Work: Back to Basics

Some of the ideas presented here appeared much earlier in work of Hutton and Meijer [21]. They studied *representation changers*, consisting of a function followed by the converse of a function. Their representation changers are analogous to our metamorphisms, with the function corresponding to the fold and the converse of a function to the unfold: in a relational setting, an unfold is just the converse of a fold, and so our metamorphisms could be seen as a special case of representation changers in which both functions are folds. We feel that restricting attention to the special case of folds and unfolds is worthwhile, because we can capitalize on their universal properties; without this restriction, one has to resort to reasoning from first principles.

Hutton and Meijer illustrate with two examples: carry-save incrementing and radix conversion. The carry-save representation of numbers is redundant, using the redundancy to avoid rippling carries. Although incrementing such a number can be seen as a change of representation, it is a rather special one, as the point of the exercise is to copy as much of the input as possible straight to the output; it isn't immediately clear how to fit that constraint into our pattern of folding to an abstract value and independently unfolding to a different representation. Their radix conversion is similar to ours, but their resulting algorithm is not streaming: all of the input must be read before any of the output is produced.

Acknowledgements

The material on arithmetic coding in Section 6.2, and indeed the idea of streaming algorithms in the first place, came out of joint work with Richard Bird [4] and Barney Stratford. The principles behind reversing the order of evaluation and defunctionalization presented in Section 4.2 have been known for a long time [7, 34], but the presentation used here is due to Geraint Jones.

We are grateful to members of the *Algebra of Programming* research group at Oxford and of *IFIP Working Group 2.1*, the participants in the *Datatype-Generic Programming* project, and the anonymous *Mathematics of Program Construction* referees for their helpful suggestions regarding this work.

References

1. Lex Augusteijn. Sorting morphisms. In S. D. Swierstra, P. R. Henriques, and J. N. Oliveira, editors, *Advanced Functional Programming*, volume 1608 of *Lecture Notes in Computer Science*, pages 1–27, 1998.
2. M. Beeler, R. W. Gosper, and R. Schroeppel. Hakmem. AIM 239, MIT, February 1972.
3. Richard Bird and Oege de Moor. *The Algebra of Programming*. Prentice-Hall, 1996.
4. Richard Bird and Jeremy Gibbons. Arithmetic coding with folds and unfolds. In Johan Jeuring and Simon Peyton Jones, editors, *Advanced Functional Programming 4*, volume 2638 of *Lecture Notes in Computer Science*. Springer-Verlag, 2003.
5. Richard S. Bird. *Introduction to Functional Programming Using Haskell*. Prentice-Hall, 1998.
6. Richard S. Bird and Philip L. Wadler. *An Introduction to Functional Programming*. Prentice-Hall, 1988.
7. Eerke Boiten. The many disguises of accumulation. Technical Report 91-26, Department of Informatics, University of Nijmegen, December 1991.
8. Erich Gamma, Richard Helm, Ralph Johnson, and John Vlissides. *Design Patterns: Elements of Reusable Object-Oriented Software*. Addison-Wesley, 1995.
9. Jeremy Gibbons. *Algebras for Tree Algorithms*. D. Phil. thesis, Programming Research Group, Oxford University, 1991. Available as Technical Monograph PRG-94. ISBN 0-902928-72-4.

10. Jeremy Gibbons. Polytypic downwards accumulations. In Johan Jeuring, editor, *Proceedings of Mathematics of Program Construction*, volume 1422 of *Lecture Notes in Computer Science*, Marstrand, Sweden, June 1998. Springer-Verlag.

11. Jeremy Gibbons. Generic downwards accumulations. *Science of Computer Programming*, 37:37–65, 2000.

12. Jeremy Gibbons. Calculating functional programs. In Roland Backhouse, Roy Crole, and Jeremy Gibbons, editors, *Algebraic and Coalgebraic Methods in the Mathematics of Program Construction*, volume 2297 of *Lecture Notes in Computer Science*, pages 148–203. Springer-Verlag, 2002.

13. Jeremy Gibbons. Origami programming. In Jeremy Gibbons and Oege de Moor, editors, *The Fun of Programming*, Cornerstones in Computing. Palgrave, 2003.

14. Jeremy Gibbons. An unbounded spigot algorithm for the digits of π. Draft, November 2003.

15. Jeremy Gibbons and Graham Hutton. Proof methods for corecursive programs. Submitted for publication, March 2004.

16. Jeremy Gibbons and Geraint Jones. The under-appreciated unfold. In *Proceedings of the Third ACM SIGPLAN International Conference on Functional Programming*, pages 273–279, Baltimore, Maryland, September 1998.

17. Bill Gosper. Continued fraction arithmetic. Unpublished manuscript, 1981.

18. Tatsuya Hagino. A typed lambda calculus with categorical type constructors. In D. H. Pitt, A. Poigné, and D. E. Rydeheard, editors, *Category Theory and Computer Science*, volume 283 of *Lecture Notes in Computer Science*, pages 140–157. Springer-Verlag, September 1987.

19. C. A. R. Hoare. Quicksort. *Computer Journal*, 5:10–15, 1962.

20. John Hughes. Why functional programming matters. *Computer Journal*, 32(2):98–107, April 1989. Also in [36].

21. Graham Hutton and Erik Meijer. Back to basics: Deriving representation changers functionally. *Journal of Functional Programming*, 6(1):181–188, 1996.

22. M. A. Jackson. *Principles of Program Design*. Academic Press, 1975.

23. Bart Jacobs. Mongruences and cofree coalgebras. In *Algebraic Methodology and Software Technology*, volume 936 of *Lecture Notes in Computer Science*, 1995.

24. Simon Peyton Jones. Arbitrary precision arithmetic using continued fractions. INDRA Working Paper 1530, Dept of CS, University College, London, January 1984.

25. Simon Peyton Jones. *The Haskell 98 Language and Libraries: The Revised Report*. Cambridge University Press, 2003.

26. David Lester. Vuillemin's exact real arithmetic. In Rogardt Heldal, Carsten Kehler Holst, and Philip Wadler, editors, *Glasgow Functional Programming Workshop*, pages 225–238, 1991.

27. David Lester. Effective continued fractions. In *Proceedings of the Fifteenth IEEE Arithmetic Conference*, 2001.

28. Grant Malcolm. Data structures and program transformation. *Science of Computer Programming*, 14:255–279, 1990.

29. Lambert Meertens. Paramorphisms. *Formal Aspects of Computing*, 4(5):413–424, 1992.

30. Erik Meijer, Maarten Fokkinga, and Ross Paterson. Functional programming with bananas, lenses, envelopes and barbed wire. In John Hughes, editor, *Functional Programming Languages and Computer Architecture*, volume 523 of *Lecture Notes in Computer Science*, pages 124–144. Springer-Verlag, 1991.

31. Alberto Pardo. Generic accumulations. In Jeremy Gibbons and Johan Jeuring, editors, *Generic Programming*, pages 49–78. Kluwer Academic Publishers, 2003. Proceedings of the IFIP TC2 Working Conference on Generic Programming, Schloß Dagstuhl, July 2002. ISBN 1-4020-7374-7.

32. Peter John Potts. *Exact Real Arithmetic using Möbius Transformations*. PhD thesis, Imperial College, London, July 1998.

33. Stanley Rabinowitz and Stan Wagon. A spigot algorithm for the digits of π. *American Mathematical Monthly*, 102(3):195–203, 1995.

34. John C. Reynolds. Definitional interpreters for higher-order programming languages. *Higher Order and Symbolic Computing*, 11(4):363–397, 1998. Reprinted from the Proceedings of the 25th ACM National Conference, 1972.

35. Doaitse Swierstra and Oege de Moor. Virtual data structures. In Bernhard Möller, Helmut Partsch, and Steve Schumann, editors, *IFIP TC2/WG2.1 State-of-the-Art Report on Formal Program Development*, volume 755 of *Lecture Notes in Computer Science*, pages 355–371. Springer-Verlag, 1993.

36. David A. Turner, editor. *Research Topics in Functional Programming*. University of Texas at Austin, Addison-Wesley, 1990.

37. Varmo Vene and Tarmo Uustalu. Functional programming with apomorphisms (corecursion). *Proceedings of the Estonian Academy of Sciences: Physics, Mathematics*, 47(3):147–161, 1998. 9th Nordic Workshop on Programming Theory.

38. Jean Vuillemin. Exact real arithmetic with continued fractions. *IEEE Transactions on Computers*, 39(8):1087–1105, August 1990.

39. Philip Wadler. Deforestation: Transforming programs to eliminate trees. *Theoretical Computer Science*, 73:231–248, 1990.

40. I. H. Witten, R. M. Neal, and J. G. Cleary. Arithmetic coding for data compression. *Communications of the ACM*, 30(6):520–540, June 1987.

Probabilistic Predicative Programming

Eric C.R. Hehner

Department of Computer Science, University of Toronto, Toronto ON, M5S 2E4, Canada
hehner@cs.utoronto.ca

Abstract. This paper shows how probabilistic reasoning can be applied to the predicative style of programming.

0 Introduction

Probabilistic programming refers to programming in which the probabilities of the values of variables are of interest. For example, if we know the probability distribution from which the inputs are drawn, we may calculate the probability distribution of the outputs. We may introduce a programming notation whose result is known only probabilistically. A formalism for probabilistic programming was introduced by Kozen [3], and further developed by Morgan, McIver, Seidel and Sanders [4]. Their work is based on the predicate transformer semantics of programs; it generalizes the idea of predicate transformer from a function that produces a boolean result to a function that produces a probability result. The work of Morgan et al. is particularly concerned with the interaction between probabilistic choice and nondeterministic choice, which is required for refinement.

The term "predicative programming" [0,2] describes programming according to a first-order semantics, or relational semantics. The purpose of this paper is to show how probabilistic reasoning can be applied to the predicative style of programming.

1 Predicative Programming

Predicative programming is a way of writing programs so that each programming step is proven as it is made. We first decide what quantities are of interest, and introduce a variable for each such quantity. A specification is then a boolean expression whose variables represent the quantities of interest. The term "boolean expression" means an expression of type boolean, and is not meant to restrict the types of variables and subexpressions, nor the operators, within a specification. Quantifiers, functions, terms from the application domain, and terms invented for one particular specification are all welcome.

In a specification, some variables may represent inputs, and some may represent outputs. A specification is implemented on a computer when, for any values of the input variables, the computer generates (computes) values of the output variables to satisfy the specification. In other words, we have an implementation when the specification is true of every computation. (Note that we are specifying computations, not programs.) A specification S is implementable if

$$\forall \sigma \cdot \exists \sigma' \cdot S$$

where $\sigma = x, y, \ldots$ are the inputs and $\sigma' = x', y', \ldots$ are the outputs. In addition, specification S is deterministic if, for each input, the satisfactory output is unique. A program is a specification that has been implemented, so that a computer can execute it.

Suppose we are given specification S. If S is a program, a computer can execute it. If not, we have some programming to do. That means building a program P such that

D. Kozen (Ed.): MPC 2004, LNCS 3125, pp. 169–185, 2004.
© Springer-Verlag Berlin Heidelberg 2004

$S \Leftarrow P$ is a theorem; this is called refinement. Since S is implied by P, all computer behavior satisfying P also satisfies S. We might refine in steps, finding specifications R, Q, ... such that $S \Leftarrow R \Leftarrow Q \Leftarrow ... \Leftarrow P$.

2   Notation

Here are all the notations used in this paper, arranged by precedence level.

0.	$\top \perp$ 0 1 2 ∞ x y ( )	booleans, numbers, variables, bracketed expressions
1.	f x	function application
2.	x^y →	exponentiation, function space
3.	× /	multiplication, division
4.	+ – ⊕	addition, subtraction, modular addition
5.	,...	from (including) to (excluding)
6.	= ⧧ < > ≤ ≥ :	comparisons, inclusion
7.	¬	negation
8.	∧	conjunction
9.	∨	disjunction
10.	⇒ ⇐	implications
11.	:= **if then else**	assignment, conditional composition
12.	∀· ∃· Σ· ;	quantifiers, sequential composition
13.	$=$ $\Rightarrow$ $\Leftarrow$ $\geq$	equality, implications, comparison

Exponentiation serves to bracket all operations within the exponent. The infix operators / – associate from left to right. The infix operators × + ⊕ ∧ ∨ ; are associative (they associate in both directions). On levels 6, 10, and 13 the operators are continuing; for example, $a=b=c$ neither associates to the left nor associates to the right, but means $a=b \land b=c$. On any one of these levels, a mixture of continuing operators can be used. For example, $a \leq b < c$ means $a \leq b \land b < c$. The operators $=$ $\Rightarrow$ $\Leftarrow$ $\geq$ are identical to = ⇒ ⇐ ≥ except for precedence.

   We use unprimed and primed identifiers (for example, x and x') for the initial and final values of a variable. We use ok to specify that all variables are unchanged.

$$ok \quad = \quad x'=x \land y'=y \land ...$$

The assignment notation $x:= e$ specifies that x is assigned the value e and that all other variables are unchanged.

$$x:= e \quad = \quad x'=e \land y'=y \land ...$$

Conditional composition is defined as follows:

$$\textbf{if } b \textbf{ then } P \textbf{ else } Q \quad = \quad (b \Rightarrow P) \land (\neg b \Rightarrow Q)$$
$$= \quad b \land P \lor \neg b \land Q$$

Sequential composition is defined as follows:

$$P;Q \quad = \quad \exists \sigma''· \text{ (substitute } \sigma'' \text{ for } \sigma' \text{ in } P \text{)} \land \text{ (substitute } \sigma'' \text{ for } \sigma \text{ in } Q \text{)}$$

where $\sigma = x, y, ...$ are the initial values, $\sigma'' = x'', y'', ...$ are the intermediate values, and $\sigma' = x', y', ...$ are the final values of the variables. There are many laws that can be proven from these definitions; one of the most useful is the Substitution Law:

$$x:= e; P \quad = \quad \text{(for } x \text{ substitute } e \text{ in } P \text{)}$$

where P is a specification not employing the assignment or sequential composition operators. To account for execution time, we use a time variable; we use t for the time at which execution starts, and t' for the time at which execution ends. In the case of nontermination, $t'=\infty$.

3 Example of Predicative Programming

As an example of predicative programming, we write a program that cubes using only addition, subtraction, and test for zero. Let x and y be natural (non-negative integer valued) variables, and let n be a natural constant. Then $x'=n^3$ specifies that the final value of variable x is n^3. One way to refine (or implement) this specification is as follows:

$$x'=n^3 \quad \Longleftarrow \quad x:= n; \ x'=x\times n; \ x'=x\times n$$

An initial assignment of n to x followed by two multiplications implies $x'=n^3$. Now we need to refine $x'=x\times n$.

$$x'=x\times n \quad \Longleftarrow \quad y:= x; \ x:= 0; \ x' = x + y\times n$$

This one is proven by two applications of the Substitution Law: in the specification at the right end $x' = x + y\times n$, first replace x by 0 and then replace y by x; after simplification, the right side is now identical to the left side, and so the implication is proven. Now we have to refine $x' = x + y\times n$.

$$x' = x + y\times n \quad \Longleftarrow \quad \textbf{if } y=0 \textbf{ then } ok \textbf{ else } (x:= x+n; \ y:= y-1; \ x' = x + y\times n)$$

To prove it, let's start with the right side.

$$
\begin{aligned}
&\quad \textbf{if } y=0 \textbf{ then } ok \textbf{ else } (x:= x+n; \ y:= y-1; \ x' = x + y\times n) &&\text{Substitution Law twice}\\
=&\quad \textbf{if } y=0 \textbf{ then } ok \textbf{ else } x' = x +n + (y-1)\times n &&\text{now simplify}\\
=&\quad \textbf{if } y=0 \textbf{ then } ok \textbf{ else } x' = x \ + y\times n &&\text{expand } ok \text{ and rewrite } \textbf{if}\\
=&\quad y=0 \wedge x'=x \wedge y'=y \ \vee \ y\neq 0 \wedge x'=x+y\times n &&\text{In the left disjunct, } y=0 \text{ allows us to}\\
&&&\text{add } 0 \text{ in the form of } y\times n \text{ to } x. \text{ We drop } y'=y.\\
\Longrightarrow&\quad y=0 \wedge x'=x+y\times n \ \vee \ y\neq 0 \wedge x'=x+y\times n &&\text{boolean algebra}\\
=&\quad x'=x+y\times n
\end{aligned}
$$

This latest refinement has not raised any new, unrefined specifications, so we now have a complete program. Using identifiers P, Q, and R for the three specifications that are not programming notations, we have

$$
\begin{aligned}
P \quad &\Longleftarrow \quad x:= n; \ Q; \ Q\\
Q \quad &\Longleftarrow \quad y:= x; \ x:= 0; \ R\\
R \quad &\Longleftarrow \quad \textbf{if } y=0 \textbf{ then } ok \textbf{ else } (x:= x+n; \ y:= y-1; \ R)
\end{aligned}
$$

and we can compile it to C as follows:

```
void P (void) {x = n; Q( ); Q( );}
void Q (void) {y = x; x = 0; R( );}
void R (void) {if (y==0) ; else {x = x+n; y = y-1; R( );}}
```

or, to avoid the poor implementation of recursive call supplied by most compilers,

```
void P (void) {x = n; Q( ); Q( );}
void Q (void) {y = x; x = 0; R: if (y==0) ; else {x = x+n; y = y-1; goto R;}}
```

To account for time, we add a time variable t. We can account for real time if we know the computing platform well enough, but let's just count iterations. We augment the specifications to talk about time, and we increase the time variable each iteration.

$$
\begin{aligned}
x'=n^3 \wedge t'=t+n^2+n \quad &\Longleftarrow \quad x:= n; \ x'=x\times n \wedge t'=t+x; \ x'=x\times n \wedge t'=t+x\\
x'=x\times n \wedge t'=t+x \quad &\Longleftarrow \quad y:= x; \ x:= 0; \ x' = x + y\times n \wedge t'=t+y\\
x' = x + y\times n \wedge t'=t+y \quad &\Longleftarrow\\
&\qquad \textbf{if } y=0 \textbf{ then } ok \textbf{ else } (x:= x+n; \ y:= y-1; \ t:= t+1; \ x' = x + y\times n \wedge t'=t+y)
\end{aligned}
$$

We leave these proofs for the interested reader.

Here is a linear solution in which n is a natural variable. We can try to find n^3 in terms of $(n-1)^3$ using the identity $n^3 = (n-1)^3 + 3\times n^2 - 3\times n + 1$. The problem is the occurrence of n^2, which we can find using the identity $n^2 = (n-1)^2 + 2\times n - 1$. So we need a variable x for the cubes and a variable y for the squares. We start refining:

$$
\begin{aligned}
x'=n^3 \quad &\Longleftarrow \quad x'=n^3 \wedge y'=n^2\\
x'=n^3 \wedge y'=n^2 \quad &\Longleftarrow \quad \textbf{if } n=0 \textbf{ then } (x:= 0; \ y:= 0) \textbf{ else } (n:= n-1; \ x'=n^3 \wedge y'=n^2;
\end{aligned}
$$

We cannot complete that refinement due to a little problem: in order to get the new values of x and y, we need not only the values of x and y just produced by the recursive call, but also the original value of n, which was not saved. So we revise:

$$x'=n3 \Leftarrow x'=n3 \land y'=n2 \land n'=n$$
$$x'=n3 \land y'=n2 \land n'=n \Leftarrow$$
$$\quad \text{if } n=0 \text{ then } (x:= 0; \ y:= 0)$$
$$\quad \text{else } (\ n:= n-1; \ x'=n3 \land y'=n2 \land n'=n; \ n:= n+1;$$
$$\quad\quad\quad y:= y + n + n - 1; \ x:= x + y + y + y - n - n - n + 1)$$

After we decrease n, the recursive call promises to leave it alone, and then we increase it back to its original value (which fulfills the promise). With time,

$$x'=n3 \land t'=t+n \Leftarrow x'=n3 \land y'=n2 \land n'=n \land t'=t+n$$
$$x'=n3 \land y'=n2 \land n'=n \land t'=t+n \Leftarrow$$
$$\quad \text{if } n=0 \text{ then } (x:= 0; \ y:= 0)$$
$$\quad \text{else } (\ n:= n-1; \ t:= t+1; \ x'=n3 \land y'=n2 \land n'=n \land t'=t+n; \ n:= n+1;$$
$$\quad\quad\quad y:= y + n + n - 1; \ x:= x + y + y + y - n - n - n + 1)$$

Compiling it to C produces

```
void P (void)
{if (n==0) {x = 0; y = 0;}
  else {n = n–1; P( ); n = n+1; y = y+n+n–1; x = x+y+y+y–n–n–n+1;}}
```

Here is linear solution without general recursion. Let z be a natural variable. Let

$$Q = y = 3 \times x2/3 + 3 \times x1/3 + 1 \land z = 6 \times x1/3 + 6 \Rightarrow x' = (x1/3+n)3$$

or, more convenient for proof,

$$Q = \forall k: nat \cdot x=k3 \land y = 3 \times k2 + 3 \times k + 1 \land z = 6 \times k + 6 \Rightarrow x' = (k+n)3$$

Then

$$x'=n3 \land t'=t+n \Leftarrow x:= 0; \ y:= 1; \ z:= 6; \ Q \land t'=t+n$$
$$Q \land t'=t+n \Leftarrow$$
$$\quad \text{if } n=0 \text{ then } ok$$
$$\quad \text{else } (x:= x+y; \ y:= y+z; \ z:= z+6; \ n:= n-1; \ t:= t+1; \ Q \land t'=t+n)$$

The proofs, which are just substitutions and simplifications, are left to the reader. Compiling to C produces

```
x = 0; y = 1; z = 6;
Q: if (n==0) ; else {x = x+y; y = y+z; z = z+6; goto Q;}
```

4   Exact Precondition

We say that specification S is refined by specification P if $S \Leftarrow P$ is a theorem. That means, quantifying explicitly, that

$$\forall \sigma, \sigma' \cdot S \Leftarrow P$$

can be simplified to T. For any two specifications S and P, if we quantify over only the output variables σ', we obtain the exact precondition, or necessary and sufficient precondition (called "weakest precondition" by others) for S to be refined by P. For example, in one integer variable x,

$$\forall x' \cdot x'>5 \Leftarrow (x:= x+1)$$
$$= \quad \forall x' \cdot x'>5 \Leftarrow x'=x+1 \quad\quad\quad\quad\quad\quad\quad\quad\quad\quad\quad \text{One-Point Law}$$
$$= \quad x+1 > 5$$
$$= \quad x > 4$$

This means that a computation satisfying $x:= x+1$ will also satisfy $x'>5$ if and only if it starts with $x>4$. (If instead we quantify over the input variables σ, we obtain the exact (necessary and sufficient) postcondition.)

Now suppose P is an implementable and deterministic specification, and R' is a specification that refers only to output (primed) variables. Then the exact (necessary and sufficient) precondition for P to refine R' ("weakest precondition for P to establish postcondition R'") is

$$\forall \sigma' \cdot P \Rightarrow R' \qquad \text{by a generalized one-point law}$$
$$= \quad \exists \sigma' \cdot P \wedge R'$$
$$= \quad P; R$$

where R is the same expression as R' except with unprimed variables. For example, the exact precondition for execution of $x := x+1$ to satisfy $x'>5$ is

$$x := x+1; \quad x>5 \qquad \text{Substitution Law}$$
$$= \quad x+1 > 5$$
$$= \quad x > 4$$

5   Probability

A specification tells us whether an observation is acceptable or unacceptable. We now consider how often the various observations occur. For the sake of simplicity, this paper will treat only boolean and integer program variables, although the story is not very different for rational and real variables (summations become integrals).

A distribution is an expression whose value (for all assignments of values to its variables) is a probability, and whose sum (over all assignments of values to its variables) is 1. For example, if $n: nat+1$ (n is a positive natural), then 2^{-n} is a distribution because

$$(\forall n: nat+1 \cdot 2^{-n}: prob) \wedge (\Sigma n: nat+1 \cdot 2^{-n})=1$$

where $prob$ is the reals from 0 to 1 inclusive. A distribution is used to tell the frequency of occurrence of values of its variables. For example, 2^{-n} says that n has value 3 one-eighth of the time. If we have two variables $n, m: nat+1$, then 2^{-n-m} is a distribution because

$$(\forall n, m: nat+1 \cdot 2^{-n-m}: prob) \wedge (\Sigma n, m: nat+1 \cdot 2^{-n-m})=1$$

Distribution 2^{-n-m} says that the state in which n has value 3 and m has value 1 occurs one-sixteenth of the time.

If we have a distribution of several variables and we sum over some of them, we get a distribution describing the frequency of occurrence of the values of the other variables. If $n, m: nat+1$ are distributed as 2^{-n-m}, then $\Sigma m: nat+1 \cdot 2^{-n-m}$, which is 2^{-n}, tells us the frequency of occurrence of values of n.

If a distribution of several variables can be written as a product of distributions whose factors partition the variables, then each of the factors is a distribution describing the variables in its part, and the parts are said to be independent. For example, we can write 2^{-n-m} as $2^{-n} \times 2^{-m}$, so n and m are independent.

The average value of number expression e as variables v vary over their domains according to distribution p is

$$\Sigma v \cdot e \times p$$

For example, the average value of n^2 as n varies over $nat+1$ according to distribution 2^{-n} is $\Sigma n: nat+1 \cdot n^2 \times 2^{-n}$, which is 6. The average value of $n-m$ as n and m vary over $nat+1$ according to distribution 2^{-n-m} is $\Sigma n, m: nat+1 \cdot (n-m) \times 2^{-n-m}$, which is 0.

6 Probabilistic Specifications

To facilitate the combination of specifications and probabilities, add axioms

$$\top = 1$$
$$\bot = 0$$

equating booleans with numbers.

Let S be an implementable deterministic specification. Let p be the distribution describing the initial state σ . Then the distribution describing the final state σ' is

$$\Sigma\sigma\cdot S \times p$$

which is a generalization of the formula for average. Here is an example in two integer variables x and y . Suppose x starts with value 7 one-third of the time, and starts with value 8 two-thirds of the time. Then the distribution of x is

$$(x{=}7) \times 1/3 \; + \; (x{=}8) \times 2/3$$

The probability that x has value 7 is therefore

$$(7{=}7) \times 1/3 \; + \; (7{=}8) \times 2/3$$
$$= \qquad \top \times 1/3 \; + \; \bot \times 2/3$$
$$= \qquad 1 \times 1/3 \; + \; 0 \times 2/3$$
$$= \qquad 1/3$$

Similarly, the probability that x has value 8 is 2/3 , and the probability that x has value 9 is 0. Let X be the preceding distribution of x . Suppose that y also starts with value 7 one-third of the time, and starts with value 8 two-thirds of the time, independently of x . Then its distribution Y is given by

$$Y \; = \; (y{=}7)\,/\,3 \; + \; (y{=}8) \times 2/3$$

and the distribution of initial states is $X \times Y$. Let S be

if $x{=}y$ **then** $(x{:=}\ 0;\ \ y{:=}\ 0)$ **else** $(x{:=}\ abs(x{-}y);\ \ y{:=}\ 1)$

Then the distribution of final states is

$$\Sigma x, y\cdot\ S \times X \times Y$$
$$= \qquad \Sigma x, y\cdot\quad (x{=}y \wedge x'{=}y'{=}0 \;\vee\; x{\neq}y \wedge x'{=}abs(x{-}y) \wedge y'{=}1)$$
$$\times\ ((x{=}7)\,/\,3 \;+\; (x{=}8) \times 2/3)$$
$$\times\ ((y{=}7)\,/\,3 \;+\; (y{=}8) \times 2/3)$$
$$= \qquad (x'{=}y'{=}0) \times 5/9 \;+\; (x'{=}y'{=}1) \times 4/9$$

We should see $x'{=}y'{=}0$ five-ninths of the time, and $x'{=}y'{=}1$ four-ninths of the time.

A probability distribution such as $(x'{=}y'{=}0) \times 5/9 \;+\; (x'{=}y'{=}1) \times 4/9$ describes what we expect to see. It can equally well be used as a probabilistic specification of what we want to see. A boolean specification is just a special case of probabilistic specification. We now generalize conditional composition and sequential composition to apply to probabilistic specifications as follows. If b is a probability, and P and Q are distributions of final states, then

if b **then** P **else** Q $\;=\;$ $b \times P \;+\; (1{-}b) \times Q$

$P;Q$ $\;=\;$ $\Sigma\sigma''\cdot$ (substitute σ'' for σ' in P) $\times$ (substitute σ'' for σ in Q)

are distributions of final states. For example, in one integer variable x , suppose we start by assigning 0 with probability 1/3 or 1 with probability 2/3 ; that's

if $1/3$ **then** $x{:=}\ 0$ **else** $x{:=}\ 1$

Subsequently, if $x{=}0$ then we add 2 with probability 1/2 or 3 with probability 1/2 , otherwise we add 4 with probability 1/4 or 5 with probability 3/4 ; that's

if $x{=}0$ **then if** $1/2$ **then** $x{:=}\ x{+}2$ **else** $x{:=}\ x{+}3$

else if $1/4$ **then** $x{:=}\ x{+}4$ **else** $x{:=}\ x{+}5$

Notice that the programmer's **if** gives us conditional probability. Our calculation

> **if** $1/3$ **then** $x:= 0$ **else** $x:= 1$;
> **if** $x=0$ **then if** $1/2$ **then** $x:= x+2$ **else** $x:= x+3$
> **else if** $1/4$ **then** $x:= x+4$ **else** $x:= x+5$

$=$ $\quad \Sigma x''\cdot \quad ((x''{=}0)/3 + (x''{=}1){\times}2/3)$
$\quad\quad\quad \times \ (\ (x''{=}0) \times ((x'{=}x''{+}2)/2 + (x'{=}x''{+}3)/2)$
$\quad\quad\quad\quad\quad + (x''{\neq}0) \times ((x'{=}x''{+}4)/4 + (x'{=}x''{+}5){\times}3/4))$

$=$ $\quad (x'{=}2)/6 + (x'{=}3)/6 + (x'{=}5)/6 + (x'{=}6)/2$

says that the result is 2 with probability $1/6$, 3 with probability $1/6$, 5 with probability $1/6$, and 6 with probability $1/2$.

We earlier used the formula $\Sigma\sigma\cdot S \times p$ to calculate the distribution of final states from the distribution p of initial states and an operation specified by S. We can now restate this formula as $(p'; S)$ where p' is the same as p but with primes on the variables. And the formula $(S; p)$ giving the exact precondition for implementable deterministic S to refine p' also works when S is a distribution.

Various distribution laws are provable from probabilistic sequential composition. Let n be a number, and let P, Q, and R be probabilistic specifications. Then

$$n{\times}P; Q \ = \ n{\times}(P; Q) \ = \ P; n{\times}Q$$
$$P{+}Q; R \ = \ (P; R) + (Q; R)$$
$$P; Q{+}R \ = \ (P; Q) + (P; R)$$

Best of all, the Substitution Law still works. (We postpone disjunction to Section 10.)

7   Random Number Generators

Many programming languages provide a random number generator (sometimes called a "pseudo-random number generator"). The usual notation is functional, and the usual result is a value whose distribution is uniform (constant) over a nonempty finite range. If $n: nat{+}1$, we use the notation $rand\ n$ for a generator that produces natural numbers uniformly distributed over the range $0,..n$ (from (including) 0 to (excluding) n). So $rand\ n$ has value r with probability $(r: 0,..n) / n$. (Recall: $r: 0,..n$ is $\top$ or 1 if r is one of 0, 1, 2, ..., $n{-}1$, and $\bot$ or 0 otherwise.)

Functional notation for a random number generator is inconsistent. Since $x{=}x$ is a law, we should be able to simplify $rand\ n = rand\ n$ to $\top$, but we cannot because the two occurrences of $rand\ n$ might generate different numbers. Since $x{+}x = 2{\times}x$ is a law, we should be able to simplify $rand\ n + rand\ n$ to $2 \times rand\ n$, but we cannot. To restore consistency, we replace each use of $rand\ n$ with a fresh integer variable r whose value has probability $(r: 0,..n) / n$ before we do anything else. Or, if you prefer, we replace each use of $rand\ n$ with a fresh variable $r: 0,..n$ whose value has probability $1/n$. (This is a mathematical variable, not a state variable; in other words, there is no r'.) For example, in one state variable x,

$\quad\quad x:= rand\ 2; \ x:= x + rand\ 3$ $\quad\quad\quad\quad\quad$ replace the two $rand$s with r and s
$=$ $\quad \Sigma r: 0,..2\cdot \Sigma s: 0,..3\cdot (x:= r; \ x:= x + s) \times 1/2 \times 1/3$ $\quad\quad$ Substitution Law
$=$ $\quad \Sigma r: 0,..2\cdot \Sigma s: 0,..3\cdot (x' = r{+}s) / 6$ $\quad\quad\quad\quad\quad\quad\quad\quad\quad\quad$ sum
$=$ $\quad ((x' = 0{+}0) + (x' = 0{+}1) + (x' = 0{+}2) + (x' = 1{+}0) + (x' = 1{+}1) + (x' = 1{+}2)) / 6$
$=$ $\quad (x'{=}0) / 6 + (x'{=}1) / 3 + (x'{=}2) / 3 + (x'{=}3) / 6$

which says that x' is 0 one-sixth of the time, 1 one-third of the time, 2 one-third of the time, and 3 one-sixth of the time.

Whenever $rand$ occurs in the context of a simple equation, such as $r = rand\ n$, we don't need to introduce a variable for it, since one is supplied. We just replace the deceptive equation with $(r: 0,..n) / n$. For example, in one variable x,

$$x:= rand\ 2;\ \ x:= x + rand\ 3 \qquad\qquad\qquad \text{replace assignments}$$
$$=\quad (x':\ 0,..2)/2;\ \ (x':\ x,..x+3)/3 \qquad\qquad \text{sequential composition}$$
$$=\quad \Sigma x''\cdot\ (x'':\ 0,..2)/2 \times (x':\ x'',..x''+3)/3 \qquad\qquad\qquad \text{sum}$$
$$=\quad 1/2 \times (x':\ 0,..3)/3\ \ +\ \ 1/2 \times (x':\ 1,..4)/3$$
$$=\quad (x'{=}0)\ /\ 6\ +\ (x'{=}1)\ /\ 3 + (x'{=}2)\ /\ 3\ +\ (x'{=}3)\ /\ 6$$

as before.

Although *rand* produces uniformly distributed natural numbers, it can be transformed into many different distributions. We just saw that $rand\ 2 + rand\ 3$ has value n with distribution $(n{=}0 \vee n{=}3)\ /\ 6\ +\ (n{=}1 \vee n{=}2)\ /\ 3$. As another example, $rand\ 8 < 3$ has boolean value b with distribution

$$\Sigma r:\ 0,..8\cdot\ (b = (r{<}3))\ /\ 8$$
$$=\quad (b{=}\mathsf{T}) \times 3/8\ +\ (b{=}\!\perp) \times 5/8$$
$$=\quad 5/8 - b/4$$

which says that b is T three-eighths of the time, and $\perp$ five-eighths of the time.

8 Blackjack

This example is a simplified version of the card game known as blackjack. You are dealt a card from a deck; its value is in the range 1 through 13 inclusive. You may stop with just one card, or have a second card if you want. Your object is to get a total as near as possible to 14 , but not over 14 . Your strategy is to take a second card if the first is under 7 . Assuming each card value has equal probability (actually, the second card drawn has a diminished probability of having the same value as the first card drawn, but let's ignore that complication), we represent a card as $(rand\ 13) + 1$. In one variable x , the game is

$$x:= (rand\ 13) + 1;\ \ \textbf{if}\ x{<}7\ \textbf{then}\ x:= x + (rand\ 13) + 1\ \textbf{else}\ ok$$

First we introduce variables c, d : 0,..13 for the two uses of *rand* , each with probability 1/13 . The program becomes

$$x:= c+1;\ \ \textbf{if}\ x{<}7\ \textbf{then}\ x:= x+d+1\ \textbf{else}\ ok \qquad\qquad \text{Substitution Law}$$
$$=\quad \textbf{if}\ c+1 < 7\ \textbf{then}\ x' = c+d+2\ \textbf{else}\ x' = c+1$$

Then x' has distribution

$$\Sigma c, d:\ 0,..13\cdot\ (\textbf{if}\ c+1 < 7\ \textbf{then}\ x' = c+d+2\ \textbf{else}\ x' = c+1) \times 1/13 \times 1/13$$
$$\qquad\qquad\qquad\qquad\qquad\qquad\qquad \text{by several omitted steps}$$
$$=\quad ((2{\le}x'{<}7){\times}(x'{-}1) + (7{\le}x'{<}14){\times}19 + (14{\le}x'{<}20){\times}(20{-}x'))\ /\ 169$$

Alternatively, we can use the variable provided rather than introduce new ones, as follows.

$$x:= (rand\ 13) + 1;\ \ \textbf{if}\ x{<}7\ \textbf{then}\ x:= x + (rand\ 13) + 1\ \textbf{else}\ ok$$
$$\qquad\qquad\qquad\qquad\qquad\qquad\qquad \text{replace assignments and}\ ok$$
$$=\quad (x':\ 1,..14)/13;\ \ \textbf{if}\ x{<}7\ \textbf{then}\ (x':\ x+1,..x+14)/13\ \textbf{else}\ x'{=}x \qquad \text{replace ; and } \textbf{if}$$
$$=\quad \Sigma x''\cdot\ (x'':\ 1,..14)/13 \times ((x''{<}7){\times}(x':\ x''+1,..x''+14)/13 + (x''{\ge}7){\times}(x'{=}x''))$$
$$\qquad\qquad\qquad\qquad\qquad\qquad\qquad \text{by several omitted steps}$$
$$=\quad ((2{\le}x'{<}7){\times}(x'{-}1) + (7{\le}x'{<}14){\times}19 + (14{\le}x'{<}20){\times}(20{-}x'))\ /\ 169$$

That is the distribution of x' if we use the "under 7 " strategy. We can similarly find the distribution of x' if we use the "under 8 " strategy, or any other strategy. But which strategy is best? To compare two strategies, we play both of them at once. Player x will play "under n " and player y will play "under $n+1$ " using exactly the same cards (the result would be no different if they used different cards, but it would require more variables). Here is the new game:

if $c+1 < n$ **then** $x:= c+d+2$ **else** $x:= c+1$;
if $c+1 < n+1$ **then** $y:= c+d+2$ **else** $y:= c+1$;
$y<x\leq14 \lor x\leq14<y$ This line is the condition that x wins. We want to know
                the probability that it is true. Factor out $x:=$ and $y:=$.

$=$ $x:=$ **if** $c+1 < n$ **then** $c+d+2$ **else** $c+1$;
       $y:=$ **if** $c+1 < n+1$ **then** $c+d+2$ **else** $c+1$;
       $y<x\leq14 \lor x\leq14<y$ Use the substitution law twice.

$=$ (**if** $c+1<n+1$ **then** $c+d+2$ **else** $c+1$) < (**if** $c+1<n$ **then** $c+d+2$ **else** $c+1$) $\leq$ 14
      $\lor$ (**if** $c+1<n$ **then** $c+d+2$ **else** $c+1$) $\leq$ 14 < (**if** $c+1<n+1$ **then** $c+d+2$ **else** $c+1$)

$=$ $c = n-1 \land d > 13-n$

Now the probability that x wins is

    $\Sigma c, d: 0,..13\cdot (c = n-1 \land d > 13-n) \times 1/13 \times 1/13$

$=$ $(n-1) / 169$

By similar calculations we can find that the probability that y wins is $(14-n) / 169$, and the probability of a tie is $12/13$. For $n<8$, "under $n+1$ " beats "under n ". For $n\geq 8$, "under n " beats "under $n+1$ ". So "under 8 " beats both "under 7 " and "under 9 ".

9   Dice

If you repeatedly throw a pair of six-sided dice until they are equal, how long does it take? The program is

    $R \ \Longleftarrow \ u:= (rand\ 6) + 1$; $v:= (rand\ 6) + 1$; **if** $u=v$ **then** ok **else** $(t:= t+1;\ R)$

for an appropriate definition of R . First, introduce variables $r, s: 0,..6$, each having probability $1/6$, for the two uses of $rand$, and simplify by eliminating variables u and v .

    $R \ \Longleftarrow \ $ **if** $r=s$ **then** $t'=t$ **else** $(t:= t+1;\ R)$

But there's a problem. As it stands, we could define $R \ = \ $ **if** $r=s$ **then** $t'=t$ **else** $t'=\infty$, which says that the execution time is either 0 or ∞ . The problem is that variable r stands for a single use of $rand$, and similarly for s . In the previous example, we had no loops, so a single appearance of $rand$ was a single use of $rand$. Now we have a loop, and r has the same value each iteration, and so has s . The solution to this problem is to parameterize r and s by iteration or by time. We introduce $r, s: time\rightarrow(0,..6)$, with $r\ t$ and $s\ t$ each having probability $1/6$. The program is

    $R \ \Longleftarrow \ $ **if** $r\ t = s\ t$ **then** $t'=t$ **else** $(t:= t+1;\ R)$

Now we can define R to tell us the execution time.

    $(\forall i: t,..t'\cdot r\ i \neq s\ i) \land r\ t' = s\ t'$

says that t' is the first time (from t onward) that the two dice are equal. The refinement is proved as follows:

    if $rt=st$ **then** $t'=t$ **else** $(t:= t+1;\ (\forall i: t,..t'\cdot ri\neq si) \land rt'=st')$ case and substitution

$=$ $rt=st \land t'=t \lor rt\neq st \land (\forall i: t+1,..t'\cdot ri\neq si) \land rt'=st'$ axioms of $\forall$

$=$ $(\forall i: t,..t'\cdot ri\neq si) \land rt'=st'$

    Treating ri and si as though they were simple variables, $ri\neq si$ with probability

    $\Sigma ri, si: 0,..6\cdot (ri\neq si) \times 1/6 \times 1/6 \ = \ 5/6$

and $ri=si$ with probability

    $\Sigma ri, si: 0,..6\cdot (ri=si) \times 1/6 \times 1/6 \ = \ 1/6$

So we offer the hypothesis that the final time t' has the distribution

    $(t'\geq t) \times (5/6)^{t'-t} \times 1/6$

We can verify this distribution as follows. The distribution of the implementation (right side) is

$$\Sigma rt, st\cdot (\text{if } rt{=}st \text{ then } t'{=}t \text{ else } (t:=t{+}1; \ (t'{\geq}t) \times (5/6)^{t'-t} \times 1/6)) \times 1/6 \times 1/6 \qquad \text{sum}$$

$$= \quad (6 \times (t'{=}t) \ + \ 30 \times (t:=t{+}1; \ (t'{\geq}t) \times (5/6)^{t'-t} \times 1/6)) \times 1/6 \times 1/6 \qquad \text{substitution}$$

$$= \quad (6 \times (t'{=}t) \ + \ 30 \times (t'{\geq}t{+}1) \times (5/6)^{t'-t-1} \times 1/6) \times 1/6 \times 1/6 \qquad \text{arithmetic}$$

$$= \quad (t'{=}t) \times 1/6 \ + \ (t'{\geq}t{+}1) \times (5/6)^{t'-t} \times 1/6$$

$$= \quad (t'{\geq}t) \times (5/6)^{t'-t} \times 1/6$$

The last line is the distribution of the specification, which concludes the proof.

The alternative to introducing new variables r and s is as follows. Starting with the implementation,

$$u:= (rand\ 6) + 1; \quad v:= (rand\ 6) + 1; \qquad\qquad \text{replace } rand \text{ and}$$

$$\text{if } u{=}v \text{ then } t'{=}t \text{ else } (t:=t{+}1; \ (t'{\geq}t) \times (5/6)^{t'-t} \times 1/6) \qquad \text{Substitution Law}$$

$$= \quad ((u'{:}\ 1,..7) \wedge v'{=}v \wedge t'{=}t)/6; \ (u'{=}u \wedge (v'{:}\ 1,..7) \wedge t'{=}t)/6; \qquad \text{replace first ;}$$

$$\text{if } u{=}v \text{ then } t'{=}t \text{ else } (t'{\geq}t{+}1) \times (5/6)^{t'-t-1} / 6 \qquad \text{and simplify}$$

$$= \quad ((u'{:}\ 1,..7) \wedge (v'{:}\ 1,..7) \wedge t'{=}t)/36; \qquad\qquad \text{replace remaining ;}$$

$$\text{if } u{=}v \text{ then } t'{=}t \text{ else } (t'{\geq}t{+}1) \times (5/6)^{t'-t-1} / 6 \qquad \text{and replace } \textbf{if}$$

$$= \quad \Sigma u'', v''{:}\ 1,..7\cdot \Sigma t''\cdot \quad (t''{=}t)/36 \times ((u''{=}v'') \times (t'{=}t''))$$

$$\qquad\qquad\qquad + \ (u''{\neq}v'') \times (t'{\geq}t''{+}1) \times (5/6)^{t'-t''-1} / 6) \qquad \text{sum}$$

$$= \quad 1/36 \times (6 \times (t'{=}t) \ + \ 30 \times (t'{\geq}t{+}1) \times (5/6)^{t'-t-1} / 6) \qquad \text{combine}$$

$$= \quad (t'{\geq}t) \times (5/6)^{t'-t} \times 1/6$$

which is the probabilistic specification.

The average value of t' is

$$\Sigma t'\cdot t' \times (t'{\geq}t) \times (5/6)^{t'-t} \times 1/6 \quad = \quad t{+}5$$

so on average it takes 5 additional throws of the dice to get an equal pair.

10   Nondeterminism

According to some authors, nondeterminism comes in several varieties: angelic, demonic, oblivious, and prescient. To illustrate the differences, consider

$$x:= rand\ 2; \quad y:= 0 \text{ or } y:= 1$$

and we want the result $x'{=}y'$. If **or** is angelic nondeterminism, it chooses between its operands $y:= 0$ and $y:= 1$ in such a way that the desired result $x'{=}y'$ is always achieved. If **or** is demonic nondeterminism, it chooses between its operands in such a way that the desired result is never achieved. Both angelic and demonic nondeterminism require knowledge of the value of variable x when choosing between assignments to y . Oblivious nondeterminism is restricted to making a choice without looking at the current (or past) state. It achieves $x'{=}y'$ half the time. Now consider

$$x:= 0 \text{ or } x:= 1; \quad y:= rand\ 2$$

and we want $x'{=}y'$. If **or** is angelically prescient, x will be chosen to match the future value of y , always achieving $x'{=}y'$. If **or** is demonically prescient, x will be chosen to avoid the future value of y , never achieving $x'{=}y'$. If **or** is not prescient, then $x'{=}y'$ is achieved half the time.

In predicative programming, nondeterminism is disjunction. Angelic, demonic, oblivious, and prescient are not kinds of nondeterminism, but ways of refining nondeterminism. In the example

$$x:= rand\ 2; \quad (y:= 0) \vee (y:= 1)$$

with desired result $x'{=}y'$, we can refine the nondeterminism angelically as $y:= x$, or demonically as $y:= 1{-}x$, or obliviously as either $y:= 0$ or $y:= 1$. In the example

$$(x:= 0) \vee (x:= 1); \quad y:= rand\ 2$$

with desired result $x'{=}y'$, we first have to replace $rand\ 2$ by boolean variable r having probability $1/2$. Then we can refine the nondeterminism with angelic prescience as $x:= r$, or with demonic prescience as $x:= 1{-}r$, or without prescience as either $x:= 0$ or $x:= 1$.

Suppose we have one natural variable n whose initial value is 5. After executing the nondeterministic specification $ok \lor (n:= n+1)$, we can say that the final value of n is either 5 or 6. Now suppose this specification is executed many times, and the distribution of initial states is $n=5$ (n always starts with value 5). What is the distribution of final states? Nondeterminism is a freedom for the implementer, who may refine the specification as ok, which always gives the answer $n'=5$, or as $n:= n+1$, which always gives the answer $n'=6$, or as

> **if** *even* t **then** ok **else** $n:= n+1$

which gives $n'=5$ or $n'=6$ unpredictably. In general, we cannot say the distribution of final states after a nondeterministic specification. If we apply the formula $\Sigma\sigma\cdot S{\times}p$ to a specification S that is nondeterministic, the result may not be a distribution. For example,

> $\Sigma n\cdot (ok \lor (n:= n+1)) \times (n=5) \;=\; n'=5 \lor n'=6$

which is not a distribution because

> $\Sigma n'\cdot n'=5 \lor n'=6 \;=\; 2$

Although $n'=5 \lor n'=6$ is not a distribution, it does accurately describe the final state.

Suppose the initial value of n is described by the distribution $(n=5)/2 + (n=6)/2$. Application of the formula $\Sigma\sigma\cdot S \times p$ to our nondeterministic specification yields

> $\Sigma n\cdot (ok \lor (n:= n+1)) \times ((n=5)/2 + (n=6)/2)$
> $=\quad (n'=5 \lor n'=6)/2 + (n'=6 \lor n'=7)/2$

Again, this is not a distribution, summing to 2 (the degree of nondeterminism). Interpretation of nondistributions is problematic, but this might be interpreted as saying that half of the time we will see either $n'=5$ or $n'=6$, and the other half of the time we will see either $n'=6$ or $n'=7$.

Nondeterministic choice $(P \lor Q)$, probabilistic choice (**if** *rand* 2 **then** P **else** Q), and deterministic choice (**if** b **then** P **else** Q) are not three different, competing ways of forming a choice. Rather, they are three different degrees of information about a choice. In fact, nondeterministic choice is equivalent to an unnormalized random choice. In one variable x,

> $(x:= 0) \lor (x:= 1)$
> $=\quad x'\colon 0,..2$
> $=\quad 2 \times (x'\colon 0,..2)/2$ introduce *rand* the same way we eliminate it
> $=\quad 2 \times (x' = rand\ 2)$
> $=\quad 2 \times (x:= rand\ 2)$
> $\geq\quad x:= rand\ 2$

Thus we prove

> $(x:= 0) \lor (x:= 1) \;\geq\; x:= rand\ 2$

which is the generalization of refinement to probabilistic specifications. Nondeterministic choice can be refined by probabilistic choice. More generally,

> $P \lor Q \;=\; 2 \times$ **if** *rand* 2 **then** P **else** Q

It is a well known boolean law that nondeterministic choice can be refined by deterministic choice.

> $P \lor Q \;\Longleftarrow\;$ **if** b **then** P **else** Q

In fact, nondeterministic choice is equivalent to deterministic choice in which the determining expression is a variable of unknown value.

> $P \lor Q \;=\; \exists b\colon bool\cdot$ **if** b **then** P **else** Q

(The variable introduced is a mathematical variable, not a state variable; there is no b'.)

This is what we will do: we replace each nondeterministic choice with an equivalent existentially quantified deterministic choice, choosing a fresh variable each time. Then we move the quantifier outward as far as possible. If we move it outside a loop, we must then index the variable by iteration or by time, exactly as we did with the variable that replaces occurrences of *rand* . All programming notations distribute over disjunction, so in any programming context, existential quantifiers (over a boolean domain) can be moved to the front. Before we prove that specification R is refined by a program containing a nondeterministic choice, we make the following sequence of transformations. (The dots are the context, or uninteresting parts, which remain unchanged from line to line.)

$$R \quad \Longleftarrow \quad \cdots\cdots\cdots(P \vee Q)\cdots\cdots\cdots\cdots$$
$$R \quad \Longleftarrow \quad \cdots\cdots\cdots(\exists b\cdot \textbf{ if } b \textbf{ then } P \textbf{ else } Q)\cdots\cdots\cdots\cdots$$
$$R \quad \Longleftarrow \quad (\exists b\cdot \cdots\cdots\cdots(\textbf{if } b \textbf{ then } P \textbf{ else } Q)\cdots\cdots\cdots\cdots)$$
$$\forall b\cdot \quad (R \quad \Longleftarrow \quad \cdots\cdots\cdots(\textbf{if } b \textbf{ then } P \textbf{ else } Q)\cdots\cdots\cdots\cdots)$$

A refinement is proved for all values of all variables anyway, even without explicit universal quantification, so effectively the quantifier disappears.

With this transformation, let us look again at the example $ok \vee (n:= n+1)$. With input distribution $n=5$ we get

$$\Sigma n\cdot \textbf{ (if } b \textbf{ then } ok \textbf{ else } n:= n+1) \times (n=5)$$
$$= \quad \textbf{if } b \textbf{ then } n'=5 \textbf{ else } n'=6$$

which is a distribution of n' because

$$\Sigma n'\cdot \textbf{ if } b \textbf{ then } n'=5 \textbf{ else } n'=6$$
$$= \quad \textbf{if } b \textbf{ then } (\Sigma n'\cdot n'=5) \textbf{ else } (\Sigma n'\cdot n'=6)$$
$$= \quad \textbf{if } b \textbf{ then } 1 \textbf{ else } 1$$
$$= \quad 1$$

With input distribution $(n=5)/2 + (n=6)/2$ we get

$$\Sigma n\cdot \textbf{ (if } b \textbf{ then } ok \textbf{ else } n:= n+1) \times ((n=5)/2 + (n=6)/2)$$
$$= \quad \textbf{if } b \textbf{ then } (n'=5)/2 + (n'=6)/2 \textbf{ else } (n'=6)/2 + (n'=7)/2$$

which is again a distribution of n' . These answers retain the nondeterminism in the form of variable b , which was not part of the question, and whose value is unknown.

11 Monty Hall's Problem

To illustrate the combination of nondeterminism and probability, we look at Monty Hall's problem, which was the subject of an internet discussion group; various probabilities were hypothesized and argued. We will not engage in any argument; we just calculate. The problem is also treated in [4].

Monty Hall is a game show host, and in this game there are three doors. A prize is hidden behind one of the doors. The contestant chooses a door. Monty then opens one of the doors, but not the door with the prize behind it, and not the door the contestant has chosen. Monty asks the contestant whether they (the contestant) would like to change their choice of door, or stay with their original choice. What should the contestant do?

Let p be the door where the prize is. Let c be the contestant's choice. Let m be the door Monty opens. If the contestant does not change their choice of door, the program is

$$(p:= 0) \vee (p:= 1) \vee (p:= 2);$$
$$c:= rand\, 3;$$
$$\textbf{if } c=p \textbf{ then } (m:= c\oplus1) \vee (m:= c\oplus2) \textbf{ else } m:= 3-c-p;$$
$$ok$$

The first line $(p:= 0) \vee (p:= 1) \vee (p:= 2)$ says that the prize is placed behind one of the doors; the contestant knows nothing about the criteria used for placement of the prize, so from their point of view it is a nondeterministic choice. The second line $c:= rand\, 3$ is the contestant's random choice of door. In the next line, $\oplus$ is addition modulo 3 ; if the contestant happened to choose the door with the prize, then Monty can choose either of the other two (nondeterministically); otherwise Monty must choose the one door that differs from both c and p . This line can be written more briefly and more clearly as $c'=c \neq m' \neq p=p'$. The final line ok is the contestant's decision not to change door.

We replace $rand\,3$ with variable r . We introduce variable P of type $0, 1, 2$ in order to replace the nondeterministic assignment to p with

if $P=0$ **then** $p:=0$ **else if** $P=1$ **then** $p:=1$ **else** $p:=2$

or more simply $p:=P$. And since we never reassign p , we really don't need it as a variable at all. We introduce variable M to express the nondeterminism in Monty's choice. Our program is now deterministic (in terms of unknown P and M) and so we can append to it the condition for winning, which is $c=P$. We have

$\qquad c:=r;$
$\qquad m:=$ **if** $c=P$ **then if** M **then** $c \oplus 1$ **else** $c \oplus 2$ **else** $3-c-P;$
$\qquad c=P$ $\hfill$ substitution law twice
$=\qquad r=P$

Not surprisingly, the condition for winning is that the random choice made by the contestant is the door where the prize is. Also not surprisingly, its probability is

$\qquad \Sigma r \cdot (r=P) \times 1/3$
$=\qquad 1/3$

If the contestant takes the opportunity offered by Monty of switching their choice of door, then the program, followed by the condition for winning, becomes

$\qquad c:=r;$
$\qquad m:=$ **if** $c=P$ **then if** M **then** $c \oplus 1$ **else** $c \oplus 2$ **else** $3-c-P;$
$\qquad c:=3-c-m;$
$\qquad c=P$

In the first line, the contestant chooses door c at random. In the second line, Monty opens door m , which differs from both c and P . In the next line, the contestant changes the value of c but not to m ; thanks to the second line, this is deterministic; this could be written more briefly and more clearly as $c \neq c' \neq m=m'$. The final line is the condition for winning. After a small calculation (c starts at r and then changes; the rest is irrelevant), the above four lines simplify to

$\qquad r \neq P$

which says that the contestant wins if the random choice they made originally was not the door where the prize is. Its probability is

$\qquad \Sigma r \cdot (r \neq P) \times 1/3$
$=\qquad 2/3$

Perhaps surprisingly, the probability of winning is now $2/3$, so the contestant should switch.

12 Mr.Bean's Socks

Our next example originates in [4]; unlike Monty Hall's problem, it includes a loop. Mr.Bean is trying to get a matching pair of socks from a drawer containing an inexhaustible supply of red and blue socks (in the original problem the supply of socks is finite). He begins by withdrawing two socks from the drawer. If they match, he is done. Otherwise, he throws away one of them at random, withdraws another sock, and repeats. The choice of sock to throw away is probabilistic, with probability $1/2$ for each color. As for the choice of sock to withdraw from the drawer, we are not told anything about how this choice is made, so it is nondeterministic. How long will it take him to get a matching pair?

Here is Mr.Bean's program (omitting the initialization). Variables L and R represent the color of socks held in Mr.Bean's left and right hands.

$L'=R'$ ⇐
    if $L=R$ **then** ok
    else (**if** $rand\ 2$ **then** $(L:= red) \vee (L:= blue)$ **else** $(R:= blue) \vee (R:= red)$;
        $t:= t+1$; $L'=R'$)

As always, we begin by replacing the use of $rand$ by a variable h (for hand), and we introduce variable d to express the nondeterministic choices. Due to the loop we index these variables with time. The refinement

$L'=R'$ ⇐   **if** $L=R$ **then** ok
    else (**if** $h\ t$ **then if** $d\ t$ **then** $L:= red$ **else** $L:= blue$
        else if $d\ t$ **then** $R:= blue$ **else** $R:= red$;
        $t:= t+1$; $L'=R'$)

is easily proven. Now we need a hypothesis concerning the probability of execution times.

Suppose the nondeterministic choices are made such that Mr.Bean always gets from the drawer a sock of the same color as he throws away. This means that the nondeterministic choices become

if $d\ t$ **then** $L:= red$ **else** $L:= blue$ $=$ ok
if $d\ t$ **then** $R:= blue$ **else** $R:= red$ $=$ ok

(which means that $d\ t$ just happens to have the same value as $L=red \wedge R=blue$ each time). If I were watching Mr.Bean repeatedly retrieving the same color sock that he has just thrown away, I would soon suspect him of doing so on purpose, or perhaps a malicious mechanism that puts the wrong sock in his hand. But the mathematics says nothing about purpose or mechanism; it may be just a fantastic coincidence. In any case, we can prove that execution takes either no time or forever

if $L=R$ **then** $t'=t$ **else** $t'=\infty$ ⇐
    if $L=R$ **then** ok **else** $(t:= t+1$; **if** $L=R$ **then** $t'=t$ **else** $t'=\infty)$

but we cannot prove anything about the probability of those two possibilities.

At the other extreme, suppose Mr.Bean gets from the drawer a sock of the opposite color as he throws away. Then the nondeterministic choices become

if $d\ t$ **then** $L:= red$ **else** $L:= blue$ $=$ $L:= R$
if $d\ t$ **then** $R:= blue$ **else** $R:= red$ $=$ $R:= L$

(which means that $d\ t$ just happens to have the same value as $L=blue \wedge R=red$ each time). Again, if I observed Mr.Bean doing that each time the experiment is rerun, I would suspect a mechanism or purpose, but the mathematics is silent about that. Now we can prove

if $L=R$ **then** $t'=t$ **else** $t'=t+1$ ⇐
    if $L=R$ **then** ok
    else (**if** $h\ t$ **then** $L:= R$ **else** $R:= L$;
        $t:= t+1$; **if** $L=R$ **then** $t'=t$ **else** $t'=t+1$)

which says that execution takes time 0 or 1, but we cannot attach probabilities to those two possibilities. If we make no assumption at all about dt, leaving the nondeterministic choices unrefined, then the most we can prove about the execution time is

if $L=R$ **then** $t'=t$ **else** $t'>t$

Another way to refine the nondeterministic choice is with a probabilistic choice. If we attach probability $1/2$ to each of the values of dt, then the distribution of execution times is **if** $L=R$ **then** $t'=t$ **else** $(t'>t) \times 2t-t'$. To prove it, we start with the right side of the refinement, weakening ok to $t'=t$.

$\Sigma ht, dt \cdot$ (**if** $L=R$ **then** $t'=t$

   else (**if** ht **then if** dt **then** $L:= red$ **else** $L:= blue$

   else if dt **then** $R:= blue$ **else** $R:= red$;

   $t:= t+1$; **if** $L=R$ **then** $t'=t$ **else** $(t'>t) \times 2_{t-t'}$))

$\times 1/2 \times 1/2$ factor and sum

$=$ **if** $L=R$ **then** $t'=t$

else($(L:= red; \; t:= t+1; \; $ **if** $L=R$ **then** $t'=t$ **else** $(t'>t) \times 2_{t-t'})$

   $+ (L:= blue; \; t:= t+1; \; $ **if** $L=R$ **then** $t'=t$ **else** $(t'>t) \times 2_{t-t'})$

   $+ (R:= blue; \; t:= t+1; \; $ **if** $L=R$ **then** $t'=t$ **else** $(t'>t) \times 2_{t-t'})$

   $+ (R:= red; \; t:= t+1; \; $ **if** $L=R$ **then** $t'=t$ **else** $(t'>t) \times 2_{t-t'})$) $/ 4$

                                                                       Substitution Law

$=$ **if** $L=R$ **then** $t'=t$

else((**if** $red=R$ **then** $t'=t+1$ **else** $(t'>t+1) \times 2_{t+1-t'})$

   $+$ (**if** $blue=R$ **then** $t'=t+1$ **else** $(t'>t+1) \times 2_{t+1-t'})$

   $+$ (**if** $L=blue$ **then** $t'=t+1$ **else** $(t'>t+1) \times 2_{t+1-t'})$

   $+$ (**if** $L=red$ **then** $t'=t+1$ **else** $(t'>t+1) \times 2_{t+1-t'})$) $/ 4$

                                       R is either *red* or *blue* , and similarly L

$=$ **if** $L=R$ **then** $t'=t$ **else** $(t'=t+1) / 2 \; + \; (t'>t+1) \times 2_{t+1-t'} / 2$

$=$ **if** $L=R$ **then** $t'=t$ **else** $(t'>t) \times 2_{t-t'}$

which is the probability specification. That concludes the proof. The average value of t' is

   $\Sigma t' \cdot t' \times$ **if** $L=R$ **then** $t'=t$ **else** $(t'>t) \times 2_{t-t'}$

$=$ **if** $L=R$ **then** t **else** $\Sigma t' \cdot t' \times (t'>t) \times 2_{t-t'}$

$=$ $t +$ **if** $L=R$ **then** 0 **else** $\Sigma n: nat+1 \cdot n / 2^n$

$=$ $t +$ **if** $L=R$ **then** 0 **else** 2

so, if the initial socks don't match, Mr.Bean draws an average of two more socks from the drawer.

   In the previous paragraph, we chose to leave the initial drawing nondeterministic, and to assign probabilities to the drawing of subsequent socks. Clearly we could attach probabilities to the initial state too. Or we could attach probabilities to the initial state and leave the subsequent drawings nondeterministic. The theory is quite general. But in this problem, if we leave both the initial and subsequent drawings nondeterministic, attaching probabilities only to the choice of hand, we can say nothing about the probability of execution times or average execution time.

13   Partial Probabilistic Specifications

Suppose we want x to be 0 one-third of the time. We don't care how often x is 1 or 2 or anything else, as long as x is 0 one-third of the time. To express the distribution of x would be overspecification. The first two lines below specify just what we want, and the last two lines are one way to refine the specification as a distribution.

   if $1/3$ **then** $x=0$ **else** $x \neq 0$

$=$ $(x=0)/3 + (x \neq 0) \times 2/3$

$\geq$ $(x=0)/3 + (x=1) \times 2/3$

$=$ **if** $1/3$ **then** $x=0$ **else** $x=1$

In general, a superdistribution is a partial probabilistic specification, which can be refined to a distribution. In general, a subdistribution is unimplementable.

   Now suppose we want x to be 0 or 1 one-third of the time, and to be 1 or 2 one-third of the time. Two distributions that satisfy this informally stated specification are

$$(x=0)/3 + (x=2)/3 + (x=3)/3$$
$$(x=1)/3 + (x=3)\times2/3$$

The smallest expression that is greater than or equal to both these expressions (the most refined expression that is refined by both these expressions) is

$$(x=0)/3 + (x=1)/3 + (x=2)/3 + (x=3)\times2/3$$

Unfortunately, this new expression is also refined by

$$(x=2)/3 + (x=3)\times2/3$$

which does not satisfy the informally stated specification. The problem is known as convex closure, and it prevents us from formalizing the specification as a superdistribution. We must return to the standard form of specification, a boolean expression, this time about the partially known distribution. Let $p\,x$ be the probability distribution of x. Then what we want to say is

$$(\forall x\cdot\ 0{\le}px{\le}1)\ \wedge\ (\Sigma x\cdot\ px){=}1\ \wedge\ p0{+}p1 = p1{+}p2 = 1/3$$

This specification can be refined in the normal way: by reverse implication. For example,

$$(\forall x\cdot\ 0{\le}px{\le}1)\ \wedge\ (\Sigma x\cdot\ px){=}1\ \wedge\ p0{+}p1 = p1{+}p2 = 1/3$$
$$\Longleftarrow\quad p0 = p2 = p3 = 1/3\ \wedge\ \forall x{:}\ x{\ne}0 \wedge x{\ne}2 \wedge x{\ne}3\cdot\ px{=}0$$
$$=\quad \forall x\cdot\ px = ((x{=}0)/3 + (x{=}2)/3 + (x{=}3)/3)$$

14 Conclusion

Our first approach to probabilistic programming was to reinterpret the types of variables as probability distributions expressed as functions. In that approach, if x was a variable of type T, it becomes a variable of type $T{\to}prob$ such that $\Sigma x = \Sigma x' = 1$. All operators then need to be extended to distributions expressed as functions. Although this approach works, it was too low-level; a distribution expressed as a function tells us about the probability of its variables by their positions in an argument list, rather than by their names. So we opened the probability expressions, leaving free the variables whose probabilities are being described.

By considering specifications and programs to be boolean expressions, and by considering boolean to be a subtype of numbers, we can make probabilistic calculations directly on programs and specifications. Without any new mechanism, we include probabilistic timing. From the distribution of execution times we can calculate the average execution time; this is often of more interest than the worst case execution time, which is the usual concern in computational complexity.

We include an **if then else** notation (as is standard), and we have generalized booleans to probabilities (as in [4]), so we already have a probabilistic choice notation (for example, **if** $1/3$ **then** P **else** Q); there is no need to invent another. We have used the *rand* "function", not because we advocate it (we don't), but because it is found in many programming languages; we cope with it by replacing it with something that obeys the usual laws of mathematical calculation.

Informal reasoning to arrive at a probability distribution, as is standard in studies of probability, is essential to forming a reasonable hypothesis. But probability problems are notorious for misleading even professional mathematicians; hypotheses are sometimes wrong. Sometimes the misunderstanding can be traced to a different understanding of the problem. Our first step, formalization as a program, makes one's understanding clear. After that step, we offer a way to prove a hypothesis about probability distributions.

Nondeterministic choice is handled by introducing a variable to represent the nondeterminacy. In [4], instead of calculating probabilities, they calculate a lower bound on probabilities: they find the precondition that ensures that the probability of outcome σ' is at least p . In contrast to that, from the distribution of prestates we calculate the entire range of possible distributions of poststates. With less mechanism we obtain more information. We did not treat nondeterministic choice and probabilistic choice as different kinds of choice; nondeterminism can be refined, and one way to refine it, is probabilistically; the "at least" inequality is the generalization of refinement.

The convex closure problem, which prevents partial probabilistic specification, is a serious disappointment. It limits not only the work described in this paper, but any attempt to generalize specifications to probabilities, such as [4] where it is discussed at length. The only way around it seems to be to abandon probabilistic specification, and to write boolean specifications about distribution-valued variables.

Probabilistic specifications can also be interpreted as "fuzzy" specifications. For example, $(x'{=}0)/3 + (x'{=}1){\times}2/3$ could mean that we will be one-third satisfied if the result x' is 0 , two-thirds satisfied if it is 1 , and completely unsatisfied if it is anything else.

Acknowledgements

I thank Carroll Morgan for getting me interested in probabilistic programming, and for consultation concerning nondeterminism. I thank Yannis Kassios for a suggestion concerning the sequential composition of probabilistic specifications.

References

[0]   E.C.R.Hehner: "Predicative Programming", *Communications ACM*, volume 27, number 2, pages 134-151, 1984 February

[1]   E.C.R.Hehner: *a Practical Theory of Programming*, Springer, New York, 1993; second edition 2004 available free at www.cs.utoronto.ca/~hehner/aPToP

[2]   C.A.R.Hoare: "Programs are Predicates", in C.A.R.Hoare, J.C.Shepherdson (editors): *Mathematical Logic and Programming Languages*, Prentice-Hall Intenational, pages 141-154, 1985

[3]   D.Kozen: Semantics of Probabilistic Programs, *Journal of Computer and System Sciences*, volume 22, pages 328-350, 1981

[4]   C.C.Morgan, A.K.McIver, K.Seidel, J.W.Sanders: "Probabilistic Predicate Transformers", *ACM Transactions on Programming Languages and Systems*, volume 18, number 3, pages 325-353, 1996 May

An Algebra of Scans

Ralf Hinze

Institut für Informatik III, Universität Bonn
Römerstraße 164, 53117 Bonn, Germany
ralf@informatik.uni-bonn.de
http://www.informatik.uni-bonn.de/~ralf/

Abstract. A parallel prefix circuit takes n inputs x_1, x_2, ..., x_n and produces the n outputs x_1, $x_1 \circ x_2$, ..., $x_1 \circ x_2 \circ \cdots \circ x_n$, where '$\circ$' is an arbitrary associative binary operation. Parallel prefix circuits and their counterparts in software, parallel prefix computations or scans, have numerous applications ranging from fast integer addition over parallel sorting to convex hull problems. A parallel prefix circuit can be implemented in a variety of ways taking into account constraints on size, depth, or fanout. Traditionally, implementations are either defined graphically or by enumerating the underlying graph. Both approaches have their pros and cons. A figure if well drawn conveys the possibly recursive structure of the scan but it is not amenable to formal manipulation. A description in form of a graph while rigorous obscures the structure of a scan and is equally hard to manipulate. In this paper we show that parallel prefix circuits enjoy a very pleasant algebra. Using only two basic building blocks and four combinators all standard designs can be described succinctly and rigorously. The rules of the algebra allow us to prove the circuits correct and to derive circuit designs in a systematic manner.

> LORD DARLINGTON. ... [*Sees a fan lying on the table.*] *And what a wonderful fan! May I look at it?*
> LADY WINDERMERE. *Do. Pretty, isn't it! It's got my name on it, and everything. I have only just seen it myself. It's my husband's birthday present to me. You know to-day is my birthday?*
> – Oscar Wilde, *Lady Windermere's Fan*

1 Introduction

A *parallel prefix computation* determines the sums of all prefixes of a given sequence of elements. The term sum has to be understood in a broad sense: parallel prefix computations are not confined to addition, any associative operation can be used. Functional programmers know parallel prefix computations as *scans*, a term which originates from the language APL [1]. We will use both terms synonymously.

Parallel prefix computations have numerous applications; the most well-known is probably the carry-lookahead adder [2], a *parallel prefix circuit*. Other

D. Kozen (Ed.): MPC 2004, LNCS 3125, pp. 186–210, 2004.
© Springer-Verlag Berlin Heidelberg 2004

applications include the maximum segment sum problem, parallel sorting, solving recurrences, and convex hull problems, see [3].

A parallel prefix computation seems to be inherently sequential. However, it can be made to run in logarithmic time on a parallel architecture or in hardware. In fact, scans can be implemented in a variety of ways taking into account constraints on measures such as size, depth, or fan-out.

A particular implementation can be modelled as a directed acyclic oriented graph and this is what most papers on the subject actually do. The structure is a graph as opposed to a tree because subcomputations can be shared. Actually, it is an ordered graph, that is, the inputs of a node are ordered, because the underlying binary operation is not necessarily commutative. Here is an example graph.

The edges are directed downwards; a node of in-degree two, an *operation node*, represents the sum of its two inputs; a node of in-degree one and out-degree greater than one, a *duplication node*, distributes its input to its outputs.

Different implementations can be compared with respect to several different measures: the *size* is the number of operation nodes, the *depth* is the maximum number of operation nodes on any path, and the *fan-out* is the maximal out-degree of an operation node. In the example above the size is 74, the depth is 5, and the fan-out is 17. If implemented in hardware, the size and the fan-out determine the required chip area, the depth influences the speed. Other factors include regularity of layout and interconnection.

It is not too hard – but perhaps slightly boring – to convince oneself that the above circuit is correct: given $n = 32$ inputs $x_1, x_2, \ldots, x_n$ it produces the n outputs $x_1, x_1 \circ x_2, \ldots, x_1 \circ x_2 \circ \cdots \circ x_n$, where '$\circ$' is the underlying binary operation. The 'picture as proof' technique works reasonably well for a parallel prefix circuit of a small fixed width. However, an implementation usually defines a family of circuits, one for each number of inputs. In this case, the graphical approach is not an option, especially, when it comes to proving correctness. Some papers define a family of graphs by numbering the nodes and enumerating the edges, see, for instance, [4]. While this certainly counts as a rigorous definition it is way too concrete: an explicit graph representation obscures the structure of the design and is hard to manipulate formally.

In this paper we show that parallel prefix circuits enjoy a pleasant algebra. Using only two basic building blocks and four combinators all standard designs can be described succinctly and rigorously. The rules of the algebra allow us to prove the circuits correct and to derive new designs in a systematic manner.

The rest of the paper is structured as follows. Section 2 motivates the basic combinators and their associated laws. Section 3 introduces two scan combinators: horizontal and vertical composition of scans. Using these combinators various recursive constructions can be defined and proven correct, see Section 4. Section 5 discusses more sophisticated designs: minimum depth circuits that have the minimal number of operation nodes. Section 6 then considers size-optimal circuits with bounded fan-out. Finally, Section 7 reviews related work and Section 8 concludes.

2   Basic Combinators

This section defines the algebra of scans. Throughout the paper we employ the programming language Haskell [5] as the meta language. In particular, Haskell's class system is put to good use: classes allow us to define algebras and instances allow us to define associated models.

2.1   Monoids

The binary operation underlying a scan must be associative. Without loss of generality we assume that it also has a neutral element so that we have a monoidal structure.

```
class Monoid α where
  ε    ::  α
  (∘)  ::  α → α → α
```

Each instance of $Monoid$ must satisfy the following laws.

$$
\begin{aligned}
\varepsilon \circ x &= x \\
x \circ \varepsilon &= x \\
x \circ (y \circ z) &= (x \circ y) \circ z
\end{aligned}
$$

For example, the parallel prefix circuit that computes carries in a carry-lookahead adder is based on the following monoid.

```
data KPG  =  K | P | G
instance Monoid KPG where
  ε        =  P
  K ∘ f    =  K
  P ∘ f    =  f
  G ∘ f    =  G
```

The elements of the type KPG represent *carry propagation functions*: K kills a carry ($\lambda c \to 0$), P propagates a carry ($\lambda c \to c$), and G generates a carry ($\lambda c \to 1$). The operation '∘' implements function composition, which is associative and has the identity, P, as its neutral element.

2.2   The Algebra of Fans and Scans

Reconsidering the example graph of the introduction we note that a parallel prefix circuit can be seen as a composition of *fans*. Here are fans of different widths in isolation.

A fan adds its first input – counting from left to right – to each of its remaining inputs. It consists of a duplication node and $n - 1$ operation nodes. A scan is constructed by arranging fans horizontally and vertically. As an example, the following scan consists of three fans: a 3-fan placed below two 2-fans.

Placing two circuits side by side is called *parallel* or *horizontal composition*, denoted '×'.

Placing two circuits on top of each other is called *serial* or *vertical composition*, denoted '⸴'. We require that the two circuits have the same width.

Horizontal and vertical composition, however, are not sufficient as combining forms as the following circuit demonstrates (which occurs as a subcircuit in the introductory example).

At first sight, it seems that a more general fan combinator is needed. The fans in the middle part are not contiguous: the first input is only propagated to each second remaining input, the other inputs are wired through. However, a moment's reflection reveals that the middle part is really the previous circuit stretched by a factor of two. This observation motivates the introduction of a stretch combinator: generalizing from a single stretch factor, the combinator '≻—' takes a list of widths and stretches a given circuit accordingly.

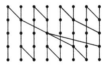

The inputs of the resulting circuit are grouped according to the given widths. In the example above, we have four groups, each of width 2. The *last* input of each group is connected to the argument circuit; the other inputs are wired through.

To summarize, the example parallel prefix circuit is denoted by the following algebraic expression (fan_i represents a fan of width i and id_i represents the identity circuit of width i).

$$fan_2 \times fan_2 \times fan_2 \times fan_2 \; \mathbin{\raise1pt\hbox{$\circ$}\kern-2pt\lower2pt\hbox{$\circ$}}$$
$$[2,2,2,2] \mathbin{\succ\!\!-} (fan_2 \times fan_2 \; \mathbin{\raise1pt\hbox{$\circ$}\kern-2pt\lower2pt\hbox{$\circ$}} \; id_1 \times fan_3) \; \mathbin{\raise1pt\hbox{$\circ$}\kern-2pt\lower2pt\hbox{$\circ$}}$$
$$id_1 \times fan_2 \times fan_2 \times fan_2 \times id_1$$

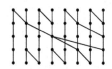

The following class declaration defines the algebra of fans and scans. Note that the class *Circuit* abstracts over a *type constructor* γ which in turn is parameterized by the underlying monoid. The type variable γ serves as a placeholder for the carrier of the algebra.

type *Width* $=$ *Nat*
type *Width*$^+$ $=$ *Nat*$^+$
class *Circuit* γ **where**

fan	::	$(Monoid\ \alpha) \Rightarrow Width \to \gamma\,\alpha$
id	::	$Width \to \gamma\,\alpha$
$(\mathbin{\raise1pt\hbox{$\circ$}\kern-2pt\lower2pt\hbox{$\circ$}})$	::	$\gamma\,\alpha \to \gamma\,\alpha \to \gamma\,\alpha$
$(\times)$	::	$\gamma\,\alpha \to \gamma\,\alpha \to \gamma\,\alpha$
$(\succ\!\!-)$	::	$[\,Width^+\,] \to \gamma\,\alpha \to \gamma\,\alpha$
$(-\!\!\prec)$	::	$\gamma\,\alpha \to [\,Width^+\,] \to \gamma\,\alpha$
$\lvert\cdot\rvert$	::	$\gamma\,\alpha \to Width$

The above class declaration makes explicit that only fans rely on the underlying monoidal structure; the remaining combinators can be seen as glue. The class additionally introduces a second stretch combinator '$-\!\!\prec$' which is similar to '$\succ\!\!-$' except that it connects the *first* input of each group to its argument circuit. The following pictures illustrate the difference between the two combinators.

$$[2,3,1] \; \succ\!\!- \; fan_3 \; = \; \text{[circuit diagram]} \qquad fan_3 \; -\!\!\prec \; [2,3,1] \; = \; \text{[circuit diagram]}$$

We shall see that '$\succ\!\!-$' is useful for combining scans, while '$-\!\!\prec$' is a natural choice for combining fans. The list argument of the stretch combinators must contain positive widths (Nat^+ is the type of naturals excluding zero).

The width of a circuit, say f, is denoted $\lvert f \rvert$. Being able to query the width of a circuit is important as some combinators are subject to width constraints: $f \mathbin{\raise1pt\hbox{$\circ$}\kern-2pt\lower2pt\hbox{$\circ$}} g$ is only defined if $\lvert f \rvert = \lvert g \rvert$, $f -\!\!\prec x$ and $x \succ\!\!- f$ require that $\lvert f \rvert = \#x$ where $\#x$ denotes the length of the list x. In particular, $f -\!\!\prec [\,]$ is only valid if $\lvert f \rvert = 0$. We lift the width combinator to lists of circuits abbreviating $[\,\lvert f \rvert \mid f \leftarrow fs\,]$ by $\lvert fs \rvert$.

To save parentheses we agree that '$-\!\!\prec$' and '$\succ\!\!-$' bind more tightly than '$\times$', which in turn takes precedence over '$\mathbin{\raise1pt\hbox{$\circ$}\kern-2pt\lower2pt\hbox{$\circ$}}$'.

infixr 1 $\mathbin{\raise1pt\hbox{$\circ$}\kern-2pt\lower2pt\hbox{$\circ$}}$
infixr 2 $\times$
infix 4 $\succ\!\!-, -\!\!\prec$

The fixity declarations furthermore ensure that the combinators bind less tightly than Haskell's list concatenation '$+\!\!+$'. As an example, $f \times g \prec x +\!\!+ y \,\mathbin{;}\, h$ abbreviates $(f \times (g \prec (x +\!\!+ y))) \,\mathbin{;}\, h$.

The following derived combinators will prove useful in the sequel.

$$
\begin{array}{lll}
par & :: & (\mathit{Circuit}\ \gamma) \Rightarrow [\gamma\,\alpha] \to \gamma\,\alpha \\
par & = & \mathit{foldr}\ (\times)\ \mathit{id}_0 \\[4pt]
seq & :: & (\mathit{Circuit}\ \gamma) \Rightarrow \mathit{Width} \to [\gamma\,\alpha] \to \gamma\,\alpha \\
seq_n & = & \mathit{foldr}\ (\mathbin{;})\ \mathit{id}_n
\end{array}
$$

The combinator par generalizes '$\times$' and places a list of circuits side by side. Likewise, seq generalizes '$\mathbin{;}$' and places a list of circuits above each other.

infix 4 $\succ, \prec$

$$
\begin{array}{lll}
(\succ) & :: & (\mathit{Circuit}\ \gamma) \Rightarrow [\gamma\,\alpha] \to \gamma\,\alpha \to \gamma\,\alpha \\
\mathit{fs} \succ f & = & par\ \mathit{fs} \,\mathbin{;}\, |\mathit{fs}| \succ\!\!\!- f \\[4pt]
(\prec) & :: & (\mathit{Circuit}\ \gamma) \Rightarrow \gamma\,\alpha \to [\gamma\,\alpha] \to \gamma\,\alpha \\
f \prec \mathit{fs} & = & f \prec\!\!\!- |\mathit{fs}| \,\mathbin{;}\, par\ \mathit{fs}
\end{array}
$$

The combinators '$\succ$' and '$\prec$' are convenient variants of '$\succ\!\!\!-$' and '$\prec\!\!\!-$': the expression $f \prec [f_1, \ldots, f_n]$ connects the i-th output of f to the first input of f_i while $[f_1, \ldots, f_n] \succ f$ connects the last output of f_i to the i-th input of f. Thus, '$\succ$' is similar to the composition of an n-ary function with n argument functions.

In Haskell, we can model circuits as list processing functions of type $[\alpha] \to [\alpha]$ where α is the underlying monoid. Serial composition is then simply forward function composition; parallel composition satisfies $(f \times g)\,(x +\!\!+ y) = f\,x +\!\!+ g\,y$ where '$+\!\!+$' denotes list concatenation and $|f| = \#x$, $|g| = \#y$. Figure 1 displays the complete instance declaration, which can be seen as *the standard model of Circuit*. Put differently, the intended semantics of the combinators is given by the list processing functions in Figure 1. Some remarks are in order. The expression Σx denotes the sum of the elements of the list x. The function *group* that is used in the definition of '$\prec\!\!\!-$' and '$\succ\!\!\!-$' takes a list of lengths and partitions its second argument accordingly. The expression $[e \mid a \leftarrow x \mid b \leftarrow y]$ is a *parallel list comprehension* and abbreviates $[e \mid (a, b) \leftarrow \mathit{zip}\ x\ y]$.

The algebraic laws each instance of the class *Circuit* has to satisfy are listed in Figure 2. The reader is invited to convince themself that the instance of Figure 1 is indeed a model in that sense. The list is not complete though: Figure 2 includes only the *structural laws*, rules that do not involve fans. The properties of fans will be discussed in separate paragraph below. Most of the laws except, perhaps, those concerned with '$\prec\!\!\!-$' and '$\succ\!\!\!-$' are straightforward: '$\mathbin{;}$' is associative with id_n as its neutral element; '$\times$' is associative with id_0 as its neutral element; '$\times$' preserves identity and vertical composition. Most of the laws are subject to width constraints: $(f \times g) \,\mathbin{;}\, (f' \times g') = (f \,\mathbin{;}\, f') \times (g \,\mathbin{;}\, g')$, for instance, is only valid if $|f| = |f'|$ and $|g| = |g'|$. Use of these laws in subsequent proofs will be signalled by the hint *composition*.

Figure 2 only lists the laws for '$\prec\!\!\!-$'; its companion combinator '$\succ\!\!\!-$' satisfies analogous properties. The equations show that '$\prec\!\!\!-$' preserves identity and com-

data $Trans\ \alpha\ =\ Trans\{width :: Width,\ apply :: [\alpha] \rightarrow [\alpha]\}$

instance $Circuit\ Trans$ **where**

$$
\begin{aligned}
fan_n\quad &=\quad Trans\ n\ (\lambda u \rightarrow \textbf{case}\ u\ \textbf{of}\\
&\qquad\qquad\qquad [\,] \rightarrow [\,]\\
&\qquad\qquad\qquad a : as \rightarrow a : [a \circ b \mid b \leftarrow as])\\[4pt]
id_n\quad &=\quad Trans\ n\ (\lambda u \rightarrow u)\\[4pt]
f \mathbin{\fatsemi} g\quad &=\quad Trans\ |f|\ (\lambda u \rightarrow apply\ g\ (apply\ f\ u))\\[4pt]
f \times g\quad &=\quad Trans\ (|f| + |g|)\ (\lambda u \rightarrow \textbf{let}\ (y, z) = splitAt\ |f|\ u\\
&\qquad\qquad\qquad\qquad\qquad\qquad \textbf{in}\ apply\ f\ y \mathbin{+\!\!+} apply\ g\ z)\\[4pt]
x \succ f\quad &=\quad Trans\ (\Sigma x)\ (\lambda u \rightarrow \textbf{let}\ ys = group\ x\ u\\
&\qquad\qquad\qquad\qquad\qquad\quad as = apply\ f\ [last\ y \mid y \leftarrow ys]\\
&\qquad\qquad\qquad\qquad \textbf{in}\ concat\ [init\ y \mathbin{+\!\!+} [a] \mid y \leftarrow ys \mid a \leftarrow as])\\[4pt]
f \prec x\quad &=\quad Trans\ (\Sigma x)\ (\lambda u \rightarrow \textbf{let}\ ys = group\ x\ u\\
&\qquad\qquad\qquad\qquad\qquad\quad as = apply\ f\ [head\ y \mid y \leftarrow ys]\\
&\qquad\qquad\qquad\qquad \textbf{in}\ concat\ [[a] \mathbin{+\!\!+} tail\ y \mid y \leftarrow ys \mid a \leftarrow as])\\[4pt]
|f|\quad &=\quad width\ f
\end{aligned}
$$

$$
\begin{aligned}
group\quad &::\quad [Int] \rightarrow [\alpha] \rightarrow [[\alpha]]\\
group\ [\,]\ as\quad &=\quad [\,]\\
group\ (i : x)\ as\quad &=\quad bs : group\ x\ cs\\
\textbf{where}\ (bs, cs)\quad &=\quad splitAt\ i\ as
\end{aligned}
$$

Fig. 1. The standard model of the scan algebra

$$
\begin{array}{rcl}
id_{|f|} \mathbin{\fatsemi} f &=& f\\
f \mathbin{\fatsemi} id_{|f|} &=& f\\
f \mathbin{\fatsemi} (g \mathbin{\fatsemi} h) &=& (f \mathbin{\fatsemi} g) \mathbin{\fatsemi} h
\end{array}
\qquad
\begin{array}{rcl}
id_0 \times f &=& f\\
f \times id_0 &=& f\\
f \times (g \times h) &=& (f \times g) \times h\\
id_m \times id_n &=& id_{m+n}\\
(f \times g) \mathbin{\fatsemi} (f' \times g') &=& (f \mathbin{\fatsemi} f') \times (g \mathbin{\fatsemi} g')
\end{array}
$$

$$
\begin{array}{rcl}
|id_n| &=& n\\
|f \mathbin{\fatsemi} g| &=& |f| = |g|\\
|f \times g| &=& |f| + |g|\\
|fan_n| &=& n\\
|f \prec x| &=& \Sigma x\\
|x \succ f| &=& \Sigma x
\end{array}
\qquad
\begin{array}{rcl}
id_{\#x} \prec x &=& id_{\Sigma x}\\
f \prec replicate\ |f|\ 1 &=& f\\
(f \mathbin{\fatsemi} g) \prec x &=& (f \prec x) \mathbin{\fatsemi} (g \prec x)\\
(f \times g) \prec (x \mathbin{+\!\!+} y) &=& (f \prec x) \times (g \prec y)\\
(f \prec x) \prec y &=& f \prec [\Sigma z \mid z \leftarrow group\ x\ y]\\
id_{i-1} \times (f \prec y \mathbin{+\!\!+} [k]) &=& ([i] \mathbin{+\!\!+} y \succ f) \times id_{k-1}
\end{array}
$$

Fig. 2. The structural laws of the scan algebra

position (*replicate n a* constructs a list containing exactly n copies of a). The second but last law in the right column demonstrates that nested occurrences of stretch combinators can be flattened. The last equation, termed *flip law*, shows that '$\prec$' can be defined in terms of '$\succ$' and vice versa. Recall that '$\succ$' connects last inputs and '$\prec$' connects first inputs. So strictly, only one stretch combinator is necessary. It is, however, convenient to have both at our disposal. Use of these laws will be signalled by the hint *stretching*.

As a warm-up in scan calculations, let us derive two simple consequences, which we need later on.

$$f \prec x \mathbin{+\!\!\!+} [j + k] \quad = \quad (f \prec x \mathbin{+\!\!\!+} [j]) \times id_k \tag{1}$$

$$(f \times id_{\#y-1}) \prec x \mathbin{+\!\!\!+} y \quad = \quad f \prec x \mathbin{+\!\!\!+} [\Sigma y] \tag{2}$$

The rules allow us to push the identity, id_n, in and out of a stretch. To prove (1) we argue

$$f \prec x \mathbin{+\!\!\!+} [j + k]$$
$$= \quad \{ \text{flip law} \}$$
$$([1] \mathbin{+\!\!\!+} x \succ f) \times id_{j+k-1}$$
$$= \quad \{ \text{composition} \}$$
$$([1] \mathbin{+\!\!\!+} x \succ f) \times id_{j-1} \times id_k$$
$$= \quad \{ \text{flip law} \}$$
$$(f \prec x \mathbin{+\!\!\!+} [j]) \times id_k$$

Property (2) is equally easy to show.

$$(f \times id_{\#y-1}) \prec x \mathbin{+\!\!\!+} y$$
$$= \quad \{ \text{stretching} \}$$
$$(f \prec x \mathbin{+\!\!\!+} [head\ y]) \times (id_{\#y-1} \prec tail\ y)$$
$$= \quad \{ \text{stretching} \}$$
$$(f \prec x \mathbin{+\!\!\!+} [head\ y]) \times id_{\Sigma(tail\ y)}$$
$$= \quad \{ \text{derived stretch law (1)} \}$$
$$f \prec x \mathbin{+\!\!\!+} [\Sigma y]$$

Let us now turn to the axioms involving fans. Fans of width less than two are equal to the identities.

$$fan_0 \quad = \quad id_0$$
$$fan_1 \quad = \quad id_1$$

As an aside, this implies that the identity combinator, id_n, can be defined as a horizontal composition of fans.

$$id_n \quad = \quad \underbrace{fan_1 \times \cdots \times fan_1}_{n \text{ times}}$$

The first non-trivial fan law, equation (3) below, allows the designer of scans to trade depth for fan-out. Here is an instance of the law.

The circuit on the left has a depth of 2 and a fan-out of 5 while the circuit on the right has depth 1 and fan-out 8. The *first fan law* generalizes from the example.

$$fan_{1+n} \prec [fan_m \prec fs] +\!\!+ gs \;=\; fan_{m+n} \prec fs +\!\!+ gs \qquad (3)$$

Interestingly, this rule is still structural as it does not rely on any properties of the underlying operator. Only the very last law, equation (4) below, employs the associativity of '$\circ$'. Before we discuss the rule let us first take a look at some examples.

Both circuits have the same depth but the circuit on the right has fewer operation nodes. The left circuit consists of a big fan below a layer of smaller fans. The big fan adds its first input to each of the intermediate values; the same effect is achieved on the right by broadcasting the first input to each of the smaller fans. Here is the smallest instance of this optimization.

The left circuit, $id_1 \times fan_2 \,\fatsemi\, fan_3 = id_2 \prec [id_1, fan_2] \,\fatsemi\, fan_3$, maps the inputs x_1, x_2, x_3 to the outputs x_1, $x_1 \circ x_2$, $x_1 \circ (x_2 \circ x_3)$, while the right circuit, $fan_2 \times id_1 \,\fatsemi\, id_1 \times fan_2 = fan_2 \prec [fan_1, fan_2]$, maps x_1, x_2, x_3 to x_1, $x_1 \circ x_2$, $(x_1 \circ x_2) \circ x_3$. Clearly, the outputs are equal if and only if '$\circ$' is associative. However, the first circuit consists of three operation nodes while the second requires only two. The *second fan law* captures this optimization.

$$
\begin{aligned}
&id_{1+\#x} \prec [id_i] +\!\!+ [fan_j \mid j \leftarrow y] \,\fatsemi\, fan_{i+\Sigma x} \\
={}& fan_{1+\#x} \prec [fan_i] +\!\!+ [fan_j \mid j \leftarrow y]
\end{aligned}
\qquad (4)
$$

The size of the circuit of the right-hand side is always at most the size of the circuit on the left-hand side. Unless all the 'small' circuits are trivial, the depth of both circuits is the same. Thus, the second fan law is *the* central rule when it comes to optimizing scans.

In the sequel we will also need the following derived law, which is essentially a binary version of the second fan law.

$$id_m \times fan_{n+1} \,\fatsemi\, fan_{m+n+1} \;=\; fan_{1+m} \times id_n \,\fatsemi\, id_m \times fan_{n+1} \qquad (5)$$

We argue as follows.

$$
\begin{aligned}
& id_m \times fan_{n+1} \,\fatsemi\, fan_{m+n+1} \\
={}& \quad \{ \text{ second fan law } \}
\end{aligned}
$$

$$fan_2 \prec [fan_m, fan_{n+1}]$$
$=$ { stretching }
$$fan_2 \prec [fan_m \prec replicate\ m\ id_1, fan_{n+1}]$$
$=$ { first fan law }
$$fan_{1+m} \prec replicate\ m\ id_1 \mathbin{+\!\!\!+} [fan_{n+1}]$$
$=$ { definition of '$\prec$' }
$$fan_{1+m} \dashleftarrow replicate\ m\ 1 \mathbin{+\!\!\!+} [n+1] \mathbin{\mathring{,}} par\ (replicate\ m\ id_1 \mathbin{+\!\!\!+} [fan_{n+1}])$$
$=$ { derived stretch law (1) }
$$(fan_{1+m} \dashleftarrow replicate\ m\ 1 \mathbin{+\!\!\!+} [1])$$
$$\times id_n \mathbin{\mathring{,}} par\ (replicate\ m\ id_1 \mathbin{+\!\!\!+} [fan_{n+1}])$$
$=$ { stretching }
$$fan_{1+m} \times id_n \mathbin{\mathring{,}} par\ (replicate\ m\ id_1 \mathbin{+\!\!\!+} [fan_{n+1}])$$
$=$ { composition }
$$fan_{1+m} \times id_n \mathbin{\mathring{,}} id_m \times fan_{n+1}$$

3 Serial and Parallel Scan Combinators

The combinators we have seen so far are the basic building blocks of scans. The blocks can be composed in a multitude of ways, the resulting circuits not necessarily implementing parallel prefix circuits. By contrast, the combining forms introduced in this section take scans to scans, they are *scan combinators*.

Before we proceed, we should first make precise what we mean by 'scan' in our framework. Scans are, like fans, parameterized by the width of the circuit. We specify

$$scan_0 \quad = \quad id_0$$
$$scan_{n+1} \quad = \quad succ\ scan_n$$

where *succ* is given by

$$succ \quad :: \quad (Circuit\ \gamma, Monoid\ \alpha) \Rightarrow \gamma\ \alpha \to \gamma\ \alpha$$
$$succ\ f \quad = \quad id_1 \times f \mathbin{\mathring{,}} fan_{|f|+1}$$

Whenever we introduce a new implementation of scans in the sequel, we will show using the laws of the algebra that the family of circuits is equal to $scan_n$.

The first scan combinator implements the *serial or vertical composition of scans*: the last output of the first circuit is fed into the first input of the second circuit.

infixr 3 $\backslash\!\backslash$
$$(\backslash\!\backslash) \quad :: \quad (Circuit\ \gamma) \Rightarrow \gamma\ \alpha \to \gamma\ \alpha \to \gamma\ \alpha$$
$$f \backslash\!\backslash g \quad = \quad f \times id_{|g|-1} \mathbin{\mathring{,}} id_{|f|-1} \times g$$

Because of the overlap the width of the resulting circuit is one less than the sum of the widths of the two arguments: $|f \backslash\!\backslash g| = |f| + |g| - 1$. The depth does not necessarily increase, as the following example illustrates.

The rightmost operation node of the first circuit is placed upon the uppermost leftmost duplication node of the second circuit.

Serial composition of scans is associative with id_1 as its neutral element.

$$
\begin{aligned}
id_1 \setminus f &= f \\
f \setminus id_1 &= f \\
f \setminus (g \setminus h) &= (f \setminus g) \setminus h
\end{aligned}
$$

The first two laws are straightforward to show; the proof of associativity is quite instructive: it reveals that $f \setminus (g \setminus h)$ and $(f \setminus g) \setminus h$ are even structurally equivalent, that is, they can be rewritten into each other using only structural rules.

$$
\begin{aligned}
& f \setminus (g \setminus h) \\
= \quad & \{ \text{ definition of `} \setminus \text{' } \} \\
& f \times id_{|g|+|h|-1} \, \mathbin{\mathring{\,}} \, id_{|f|-1} \times (g \setminus h) \\
= \quad & \{ \text{ definition of `} \setminus \text{' } \} \\
& f \times id_{|g|+|h|-1} \, \mathbin{\mathring{\,}} \, id_{|f|-1} \times (g \times id_{|h|-1} \, \mathbin{\mathring{\,}} \, id_{|g|-1} \times h) \\
= \quad & \{ \text{ composition } \} \\
& f \times id_{|g|+|h|-1} \, \mathbin{\mathring{\,}} \, id_{|f|-1} \times g \times id_{|h|-1} \, \mathbin{\mathring{\,}} \, id_{|f|+|g|-2} \times h \\
= \quad & \{ \text{ composition } \} \\
& (f \times id_{|g|-1} \, \mathbin{\mathring{\,}} \, id_{|f|-1} \times g) \times id_{|h|-1} \, \mathbin{\mathring{\,}} \, id_{|f|+|g|-2} \times h \\
= \quad & \{ \text{ definition of `} \setminus \text{' } \} \\
& (f \setminus g) \times id_{|h|-1} \, \mathbin{\mathring{\,}} \, id_{|f|+|g|-2} \times h \\
= \quad & \{ \text{ definition of `} \setminus \text{' } \} \\
& (f \setminus g) \setminus h
\end{aligned}
$$

Serial composition interacts nicely with stretching. Let $\#x = |f| - 1$ and $\#y = |g|$, then

$$
(f \setminus g) \prec x \mathbin{+\!\!+} y = (f \prec x \mathbin{+\!\!+} [1]) \setminus (g \prec y) \tag{6}
$$

The proof builds upon the derived stretch laws.

$$
\begin{aligned}
& (f \setminus g) \prec x \mathbin{+\!\!+} y \\
= \quad & \{ \text{ definition of `} \setminus \text{' } \} \\
& (f \times id_{|g|-1} \, \mathbin{\mathring{\,}} \, id_{|f|-1} \times g) \prec x \mathbin{+\!\!+} y \\
= \quad & \{ \text{ stretching } \} \\
& (f \times id_{|g|-1}) \prec x \mathbin{+\!\!+} y \, \mathbin{\mathring{\,}} \, (id_{|f|-1} \times g) \prec x \mathbin{+\!\!+} y \\
= \quad & \{ \text{ derived stretch laws (1) and (2) } \}
\end{aligned}
$$

$$(f \prec x + [1]) \times id_{\Sigma y - 1} \,\mathbin{\raise0.3ex\hbox{$\scriptstyle\circ$}}\, (id_{|f|-1} \times g) \prec x + y$$

$=$ { stretching }

$$(f \prec x + [1]) \times id_{\Sigma y - 1} \,\mathbin{\raise0.3ex\hbox{$\scriptstyle\circ$}}\, id_{\Sigma x} \times (g \prec y)$$

$=$ { definition of '$\backslash\!\backslash$' }

$$(f \prec x + [1]) \,\backslash\!\backslash\, (g \prec y)$$

The second scan combinator is the *parallel or horizontal composition of scans*: both circuits are placed side by side, an additional fan adds the last output of the left circuit to each output of the right circuit.

infixl 3 $[\!]$
$([\!])$ $::$ $(Circuit\ \gamma, Monoid\ \alpha) \Rightarrow \gamma\ \alpha \to \gamma\ \alpha \to \gamma\ \alpha$
$f\ [\!]\ g$ $=$ $f \times g \,\mathbin{\raise0.3ex\hbox{$\scriptstyle\circ$}}\, id_{|f|-1} \times fan_{|g|+1}$

The widths sum up: $|f\ [\!]\ g| = |f| + |g|$. Because of the additional fan the depth increases by one. Here is an example application of '$[\!]$'.

Before we turn to the algebraic properties of '$[\!]$', let us first note that the parallel composition of scans is really a serial composition in disguise.

$$f\ [\!]\ g\ =\ f \,\backslash\!\backslash\, succ\ g$$

The proof is straightforward.

$f\ [\!]\ g$

$=$ { definition of '$[\!]$' }

$f \times g \,\mathbin{\raise0.3ex\hbox{$\scriptstyle\circ$}}\, id_{|f|-1} \times fan_{|g|+1}$

$=$ { composition }

$f \times id_{|g|} \,\mathbin{\raise0.3ex\hbox{$\scriptstyle\circ$}}\, id_{|f|} \times g \,\mathbin{\raise0.3ex\hbox{$\scriptstyle\circ$}}\, id_{|f|-1} \times fan_{|g|+1}$

$=$ { composition }

$f \times id_{|g|} \,\mathbin{\raise0.3ex\hbox{$\scriptstyle\circ$}}\, id_{|f|-1} \times (id_1 \times g \,\mathbin{\raise0.3ex\hbox{$\scriptstyle\circ$}}\, fan_{|g|+1})$

$=$ { definition of '$\backslash\!\backslash$' }

$f \,\backslash\!\backslash\, (id_1 \times g \,\mathbin{\raise0.3ex\hbox{$\scriptstyle\circ$}}\, fan_{|g|+1})$

$=$ { definition of $succ$ }

$f \,\backslash\!\backslash\, succ\ g$

Parallel composition is associative, as well, and has id_0 as its right unit. It does not possess a left unit though as $id_0\ [\!]\ f$ is undefined (the first argument must have a positive width).

$f\ [\!]\ id_0$ $=\ f$
$f\ [\!]\ (g\ [\!]\ h)$ $=\ (f\ [\!]\ g)\ [\!]\ h$

As opposed to serial composition, the circuits $f \mathbin{[\!]} (g \mathbin{[\!]} h)$ and $(f \mathbin{[\!]} g) \mathbin{[\!]} h$ are *not* structurally equivalent: the latter circuit has fewer operation nodes. The proof rests upon the above characterization of parallel composition.

$$f \mathbin{[\!]} (g \mathbin{[\!]} h)$$
$$= \quad \{ \text{ characterization of `}\mathbin{[\!]}\text{' } \}$$
$$f \mathbin{\backslash\!\backslash} succ\ (g \mathbin{\backslash\!\backslash} succ\ h)$$
$$= \quad \{ \text{ see below } \}$$
$$f \mathbin{\backslash\!\backslash} succ\ g \mathbin{\backslash\!\backslash} succ\ h$$
$$= \quad \{ \text{ characterization of `}\mathbin{[\!]}\text{' } \}$$
$$(f \mathbin{[\!]} g) \mathbin{[\!]} h$$

The second step is justified by the following calculations.

$$succ\ (f \mathbin{\backslash\!\backslash} succ\ g)$$
$$= \quad \{ \text{ definition of } succ \text{ and `}\mathbin{\backslash\!\backslash}\text{' } \}$$
$$id_1 \times f \times id_{|g|} \mathbin{\mathring{,}} id_{|f|+1} \times g \mathbin{\mathring{,}} id_{|f|} \times fan_{|g|+1} \mathbin{\mathring{,}} fan_{|f|+|g|+1}$$
$$= \quad \{ \text{ derived fan law (5) } \}$$
$$id_1 \times f \times id_{|g|} \mathbin{\mathring{,}} id_{|f|+1} \times g \mathbin{\mathring{,}} fan_{|f|+1} \times id_{|g|} \mathbin{\mathring{,}} id_{|f|} \times fan_{|g|+1}$$
$$= \quad \{ \text{ composition } \}$$
$$id_1 \times f \times id_{|g|} \mathbin{\mathring{,}} fan_{|f|+1} \times id_{|g|} \mathbin{\mathring{,}} id_{|f|+1} \times g \mathbin{\mathring{,}} id_{|f|} \times fan_{|g|+1}$$
$$= \quad \{ \text{ definition of } succ \text{ and `}\mathbin{\backslash\!\backslash}\text{' } \}$$
$$succ\ f \mathbin{\backslash\!\backslash} succ\ g$$

Since the proof relies on the second fan law, $succ\ f \mathbin{\backslash\!\backslash} succ\ g$ has fewer nodes than $succ\ (f \mathbin{\backslash\!\backslash} succ\ g)$.

Let us finally record the fact that $succ$, `$\mathbin{\backslash\!\backslash}$' and `$\mathbin{[\!]}$' are *scan combinators*.

$$
\begin{aligned}
succ\ scan_n &= scan_{n+1} \\
scan_{m+1} \mathbin{\backslash\!\backslash} scan_n &= scan_{m+n} \\
scan_m \mathbin{[\!]} scan_n &= scan_{m+n}
\end{aligned}
$$

The first law holds by definition. The third equation implies the second and the third equation can be shown by a straightforward induction over m.

4 Simple Scans

It is high time to look at some implementations of parallel prefix circuits. We have already encountered one of the most straightforward implementations, a simple nest of fans, which serves as the specification.

$$
\begin{aligned}
scan_0 &= id_0 \\
scan_{n+1} &= succ\ scan_n
\end{aligned}
$$

Here is an example circuit of width 8.

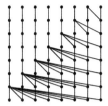

The circuit $scan_n$ is, in fact, the worst possible implementation as it has maximum depth and the maximal number of operation nodes, namely, $n * (n - 1) / 2$ among all scans of the same width. Since $succ\ f = id_1 \backslash\backslash\ succ\ f = id_1 \parallel f$, we can alternatively define $scan_n$ as a parallel composition of trivial circuits.

$$scan_{n+1}\ \ =\ \ id_1 \parallel scan_n$$

Now, if we bracket the parallel composition differently, we obtain the *serial scan*, whose correctness is immediate.

$$
\begin{aligned}
ser_0 \ \ &=\ \ id_0 \\
ser_1 \ \ &=\ \ id_1 \\
ser_{n+1} \ \ &=\ \ ser_n \parallel id_1
\end{aligned}
$$

The graphical representation illustrates why ser_n is called serial scan.

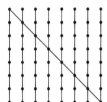

The serial scan has maximum depth, but the least number of operation nodes, namely, $n - 1$ among all scans of the same width. In a sequential language ser_n is the implementation of choice; it corresponds, for instance, to Haskell's *scanl* operation. Using $f \parallel id_1 = f \backslash\backslash\ succ\ id_1 = f \backslash\backslash\ fan_2$ we can rewrite the definition of ser_n to emphasize its serial nature.

$$ser_{n+1}\ \ =\ \ ser_n \backslash\backslash\ fan_2$$

Now, if we balance the parallel composition more evenly, we obtain parallel prefix circuits of minimum depth.

$$
\begin{aligned}
rec_n \\
\mid n \leqslant 1 \ \ \ \ \ &=\ \ id_n \\
\mid otherwise \ \ &=\ \ rec_{\lceil n/2 \rceil} \parallel rec_{\lfloor n/2 \rfloor}
\end{aligned}
$$

Here is a minimum-depth circuit of width 32.

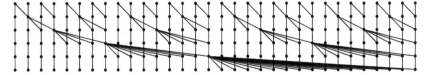

Note that the tree of operation nodes that computes the last output is fully balanced, which explains why the depth is minimal. If the width is not a power of two, then rec_n constructs a slightly skewed tree, known as a Braun tree [6]. Since '$[]$' is associative, we can, of course, realize arbitrary tree shapes; other choices include *left-complete trees* or *quasi left-complete trees* [7]. For your amusement, here is a Fibonacci-tree of width 34

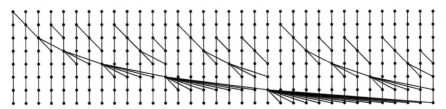

defined in the obvious way.

$$
\begin{array}{rcl}
fib_0 & = & id_0 \\
fib_1 & = & id_1 \\
fib_{n+2} & = & fib_{n+1} \; [] \; fib_n
\end{array}
$$

5   Depth-Optimal Scans

5.1   Brent-Kung Circuits

The rec_n family of circuits implements a simple divide-and-conquer scheme. A different recursive decomposition was devised by Brent and Kung [8]. As an example, here is a Brent-Kung circuit of width 32.

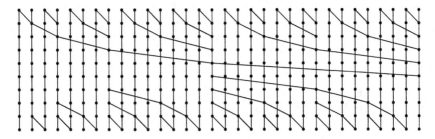

The inputs are 'paired' using a layer of 2-fans. Every second output is then fed into a Brent-Kung circuit of half the width; the other inputs are wired through. A final layer of 2-fans, shifted by one position, distributes the results of the nested Brent-Kung circuit to the wired-through signals. Every recursive step halves the number of inputs and increases the depth by *two*. Consequently, Brent-Kung circuits have logarithmic but not minimum depth. On the other hand, they use fewer operation nodes than the rec_n circuits and furthermore they have only a fan-out of 2!

Turning to the algebraic description, we note that the first layer of 2-fans can be generalized to a layer of *scans* of arbitrary, not necessarily equal widths.

$$
\begin{aligned}
(\rhd) \qquad &:: \; (\text{Circuit } \gamma, \text{Monoid } \alpha) \Rightarrow [\gamma\,\alpha] \to \gamma\,\alpha \to \gamma\,\alpha \\
[\,]\rhd g \qquad &= \; g \\
(f:\mathit{fs})\rhd g \qquad &= \; (f:\mathit{fs}) \succ g \,\fatsemi\, \mathit{id}_{|f|-1} \times \mathit{par}\ \mathit{gs} \\
\textbf{where } \mathit{gs} \qquad &= \; [\mathit{fan}_{|f|} \mid f \leftarrow \mathit{fs}] + [\mathit{id}_1]
\end{aligned}
$$

Each scan, except the first one, is complemented by a *fan* in the final layer, shifted one position to the left. The operator '$\rhd$' is also a *scan combinator*; it takes a list of scans and a scan to a resulting scan.

$$
[\mathit{scan}_i \mid i \leftarrow x] \rhd \mathit{scan}_{\#x} \;=\; \mathit{scan}_{\Sigma x} \tag{7}
$$

The Brent-Kung circuit is given by the following definition.

$$
\begin{aligned}
\mathit{bk}_n & \\
\mid n \leqslant 1 \quad &= \; \mathit{id}_n \\
\mid \textit{otherwise} \quad &= \; (\text{replicate } \lfloor n/2 \rfloor\ \mathit{fan}_2 + [\mathit{id}_1 \mid \textit{odd } n]) \rhd \mathit{bk}_{\lceil n/2 \rceil}
\end{aligned}
$$

The nested scan has width $\lceil n/2 \rceil$: if the number of inputs is odd, then the nested scan additionally takes the last input. As an aside to non-Haskell experts, the idiom $[e \mid b]$ is a trivial list comprehension that evaluates to $[\,]$ if b is *False* and to $[e]$ if b is *True*. Furthermore note, that bk_n is a so-called *restricted* parallel prefix circuit, whose last output has minimum depth.

The Brent-Kung decomposition is based on the binary number system. Since the operator '$\rhd$' works for arbitrary scans, it is not hard to generalize the decomposition to an arbitrary base.

$$
\begin{aligned}
\mathit{gbk}\ b\ n & \\
\mid n \leqslant b \quad &= \; \mathit{ser}_n \\
\mid r == 0 \quad &= \; (\text{replicate } d\ \mathit{ser}_b) \rhd \mathit{gbk}\ b\ d \\
\mid \textit{otherwise} \quad &= \; (\text{replicate } d\ \mathit{ser}_b + [\mathit{ser}_r]) \rhd \mathit{gbk}\ b\ (d+1) \\
\textbf{where } (d, r) \quad &= \; \mathit{divMod}\ n\ b
\end{aligned}
$$

The definition of *gbk* uses serial scans as 'base' circuits. This is, of course, an arbitrary choice; any scan will do. Here is a base-3 circuit of width 27.

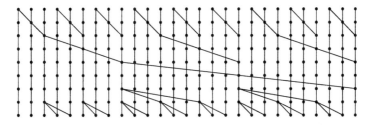

This circuit has size 46 and depth 8, while its binary cousin has size 47 and depth 10.

Let us turn to the proof that '$\triangleright$' is a scan combinator. Property (7) can be proven by induction over the length of x. We confine ourselves to showing the induction step. Let $k = \#ss = \#fs$, $i = |s|$, $j = |head\ ss|$, $n = j + \Sigma|fs|$ and finally $fs = [fan_{|s|} \mid s \leftarrow tail\ ss] \mathbin{+\!\!+} [fan_1]$, then

$$s : ss \triangleright scan_{k+1}$$
$=$ \quad { definition of '$\triangleright$' }
$$s : ss \succ scan_{k+1} \mathbin{\mathring{,}} id_{i-1} \times par\ (fan_j : fs)$$
$=$ \quad { property of scan }
$$s : ss \succ (id_1 \mathbin{[\!]} scan_k) \mathbin{\mathring{,}} id_{i-1} \times par\ (fan_j : fs)$$
$=$ \quad { definition of '$[\!]$' }
$$s : ss \succ (id_1 \times scan_k \mathbin{\mathring{,}} fan_{k+1}) \mathbin{\mathring{,}} id_{i-1} \times par\ (fan_j : fs)$$
$=$ \quad { stretching }
$$s : ss \succ (id_1 \times scan_k \mathbin{\mathring{,}} fan_{k+1}) \mathbin{\mathring{,}} id_{i-1} \times (id_{k+1} \prec fan_j : fs)$$
$=$ \quad { shift law (8), see below }
$$s : ss \succ (id_1 \times scan_k) \mathbin{\mathring{,}} id_{i-1} \times (fan_{k+1} \prec fan_j : fs)$$
$=$ \quad { fan law }
$$s : ss \succ (id_1 \times scan_k) \mathbin{\mathring{,}} id_{i-1} \times (id_{k+1} \prec id_j : fs \mathbin{\mathring{,}} fan_n)$$
$=$ \quad { stretching }
$$s : ss \succ (id_1 \times scan_k) \mathbin{\mathring{,}} id_{i-1} \times (par\ (id_j : fs) \mathbin{\mathring{,}} fan_n)$$
$=$ \quad { composition }
$$s \times (ss \succ scan_k) \mathbin{\mathring{,}} id_{i-1} \times (par\ (id_j : fs) \mathbin{\mathring{,}} fan_n)$$
$=$ \quad { composition }
$$s \times (ss \succ scan_k) \mathbin{\mathring{,}} id_{i-1} \times par\ (id_j : fs) \mathbin{\mathring{,}} id_{i-1} \times fan_n$$
$=$ \quad { composition }
$$s \times (ss \succ scan_k \mathbin{\mathring{,}} par\ (id_{j-1} : fs)) \mathbin{\mathring{,}} id_{i-1} \times fan_n$$
$=$ \quad { definition of '$[\!]$' }
$$s \mathbin{[\!]} (ss \succ scan_k \mathbin{\mathring{,}} par\ (id_{j-1} : fs))$$
$=$ \quad { definition of par }
$$s \mathbin{[\!]} (ss \succ scan_k \mathbin{\mathring{,}} id_{j-1} \times par\ fs)$$
$=$ \quad { definition of '$\triangleright$' }
$$s \mathbin{[\!]} (ss \triangleright scan_k)$$

The *shift law*, used in the fourth step, is a combination of the flip law and the laws for stretching.

$$(fs \succ (l \mathbin{\mathring{,}} m)) \times f \mathbin{\mathring{,}} g \times (r \prec gs) \;=\; (fs \succ l) \times f \mathbin{\mathring{,}} g \times ((m \mathbin{\mathring{,}} r) \prec gs) \quad (8)$$

We reason as follows.

$$(fs \succ (l \mathbin{\,\raise.1ex\hbox{$\scriptstyle\circ$}\kern-.2ex\raise-.4ex\hbox{$\scriptstyle\circ$}\,} m)) \times f \mathbin{\,\raise.1ex\hbox{$\scriptstyle\circ$}\kern-.2ex\raise-.4ex\hbox{$\scriptstyle\circ$}\,} g \times (r \prec gs)$$

$= \quad \{ \text{ composition } \}$

$$par\ fs \times f \mathbin{\,\raise.1ex\hbox{$\scriptstyle\circ$}\kern-.2ex\raise-.4ex\hbox{$\scriptstyle\circ$}\,} (|fs| \succ (l \mathbin{\,\raise.1ex\hbox{$\scriptstyle\circ$}\kern-.2ex\raise-.4ex\hbox{$\scriptstyle\circ$}\,} m)) \times id_{|f|} \mathbin{\,\raise.1ex\hbox{$\scriptstyle\circ$}\kern-.2ex\raise-.4ex\hbox{$\scriptstyle\circ$}\,} id_{|g|} \times (r \prec |gs|) \mathbin{\,\raise.1ex\hbox{$\scriptstyle\circ$}\kern-.2ex\raise-.4ex\hbox{$\scriptstyle\circ$}\,} g \times par\ gs$$

$= \quad \{ \text{ flip law } \}$

$$par\ fs \times f \mathbin{\,\raise.1ex\hbox{$\scriptstyle\circ$}\kern-.2ex\raise-.4ex\hbox{$\scriptstyle\circ$}\,} id_{|g|} \times ((l \mathbin{\,\raise.1ex\hbox{$\scriptstyle\circ$}\kern-.2ex\raise-.4ex\hbox{$\scriptstyle\circ$}\,} m) \prec\!\!\!\!- |gs|) \mathbin{\,\raise.1ex\hbox{$\scriptstyle\circ$}\kern-.2ex\raise-.4ex\hbox{$\scriptstyle\circ$}\,} id_{|g|} \times (r \prec |gs|) \mathbin{\,\raise.1ex\hbox{$\scriptstyle\circ$}\kern-.2ex\raise-.4ex\hbox{$\scriptstyle\circ$}\,} g \times par\ gs$$

$= \quad \{ \text{ stretching } \}$

$$par\ fs \times f \mathbin{\,\raise.1ex\hbox{$\scriptstyle\circ$}\kern-.2ex\raise-.4ex\hbox{$\scriptstyle\circ$}\,} id_{|g|} \times (l \prec\!\!\!\!- |gs|) \mathbin{\,\raise.1ex\hbox{$\scriptstyle\circ$}\kern-.2ex\raise-.4ex\hbox{$\scriptstyle\circ$}\,} id_{|g|} \times ((m \mathbin{\,\raise.1ex\hbox{$\scriptstyle\circ$}\kern-.2ex\raise-.4ex\hbox{$\scriptstyle\circ$}\,} r) \prec\!\!\!\!- |gs|) \mathbin{\,\raise.1ex\hbox{$\scriptstyle\circ$}\kern-.2ex\raise-.4ex\hbox{$\scriptstyle\circ$}\,} g \times par\ gs$$

$= \quad \{ \text{ flip law } \}$

$$par\ fs \times f \mathbin{\,\raise.1ex\hbox{$\scriptstyle\circ$}\kern-.2ex\raise-.4ex\hbox{$\scriptstyle\circ$}\,} (|fs| \succ l) \times id_{|f|} \mathbin{\,\raise.1ex\hbox{$\scriptstyle\circ$}\kern-.2ex\raise-.4ex\hbox{$\scriptstyle\circ$}\,} id_{|g|} \times ((m \mathbin{\,\raise.1ex\hbox{$\scriptstyle\circ$}\kern-.2ex\raise-.4ex\hbox{$\scriptstyle\circ$}\,} r) \prec\!\!\!\!- |gs|) \mathbin{\,\raise.1ex\hbox{$\scriptstyle\circ$}\kern-.2ex\raise-.4ex\hbox{$\scriptstyle\circ$}\,} g \times par\ gs$$

$= \quad \{ \text{ composition } \}$

$$(fs \succ l) \times f \mathbin{\,\raise.1ex\hbox{$\scriptstyle\circ$}\kern-.2ex\raise-.4ex\hbox{$\scriptstyle\circ$}\,} g \times ((m \mathbin{\,\raise.1ex\hbox{$\scriptstyle\circ$}\kern-.2ex\raise-.4ex\hbox{$\scriptstyle\circ$}\,} r) \prec gs)$$

5.2   Ladner-Fischer Circuits

Can we combine the good properties of *rec* and *bk* – *rec* has minimum depth, while *bk* gets away with fewer operation nodes? Yes, we can! Reconsider the circuit rec_{32} in Section 4 and note that the left part does not occupy the bottom level. The idea, which is due to Ladner and Fischer [9], is to use the Brent-Kung decomposition for the left part – recall that it increases the depth by two – and the 'usual' decomposition for the right part. The following combinator captures one step of the Brent-Kung scheme.

$$double \quad :: \quad (Circuit\ \gamma, Monoid\ \alpha) \Rightarrow (Width \to \gamma\ \alpha) \to (Width \to \gamma\ \alpha)$$
$$double\ s\ n \ = \ (replicate\ \lfloor n/2 \rfloor\ fan_2 + [id_1 \mid odd\ n]) \rhd s\ \lceil n/2 \rceil$$

Using *double* we can define a *depth-optimal* parallel prefix circuit that has the minimal number of operation nodes among all minimum-depth circuits [10].

$$opt\ n$$
$$\mid n \leqslant 1 \qquad = \quad id_n$$
$$\mid otherwise \quad = \quad double\ opt\ \lceil n/2 \rceil\ \|\ opt\ \lfloor n/2 \rfloor$$

The following example circuit of width 32 illustrates that all layers are nicely exploited.

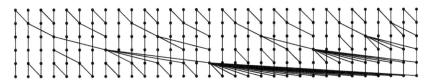

The size of the circuit is 74. By contrast, rec_{32} consists of 80 operation nodes.

The *double* combinator allows the scan designer to trade depth for size. The *Ladner-Fischer circuit*, defined below, generalizes *opt* introducing the notion of *extra depth*: the first argument of *lf* specifies the extra depth that the designer is willing to accept in return for a smaller size.

$$
\begin{aligned}
lf\ k\ 0 &= id_0 \\
lf\ k\ 1 &= id_1 \\
lf\ 0\ n &= lf\ 1\ \lceil n/2 \rceil\ [\!]\ lf\ 0\ \lfloor n/2 \rfloor \\
lf\ (k+1)\ n &= double\ (lf\ k)\ n
\end{aligned}
$$

It is not hard to see that *lf* 0 specializes to *opt* and *lf* ∞ specializes to *bk*. In a sense, Ladner-Fischer mediates between the two recursive decompositions.

6   Size-Optimal Scans

6.1   Lin-Hsiao Circuits

The '$\triangleright$' combinator constructs a slightly asymmetric circuit: not every scan has a corresponding fan. Circuits with a more symmetric design were recently introduced by Lin and Hsiao [4]. As an example, here is one of their circuits of width 25, called wl_6.

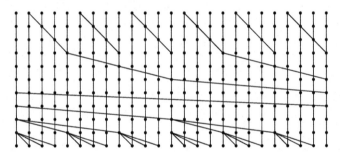

Every scan in the upper part is complemented by a corresponding fan in the lower part. The two parts are joined by a '⌐'-like shape (turned 90° degrees clockwise) that connects the first input to the last output. The '⌐' combinator is easy to derive.

$$
\begin{aligned}
& scan_{n+1} \\
=\quad & \{ \text{ property of } scan \} \\
& id_1\ [\!]\ scan_n \\
=\quad & \{ \text{ definition of '}[\!]\text{' } \} \\
& id_1 \times scan_n\ \fatsemi\ fan_{n+1} \\
=\quad & \{ \text{ stretching } \} \\
& [id_1, scan_n] \succ id_2\ \fatsemi\ fan_{n+1} \\
=\quad & \{ \text{ fan laws } \} \\
& [id_1, scan_n] \succ id_2\ \fatsemi\ fan_2 \prec [fan_n, id_1]
\end{aligned}
$$

Thus, we define

$$(\smallfrown) \quad :: \quad (Circuit\ \gamma, Monoid\ \alpha) \Rightarrow \gamma\ \alpha \to \gamma\ \alpha \to \gamma\ \alpha$$
$$f \smallfrown g \quad = \quad [id_1, f] \succ id_2 \fatsemi fan_2 \prec [g, id_1]$$

We have $|f \smallfrown g| = |f| + 1 = |g| + 1$. The derivation above implies that $scan_n \smallfrown fan_n = scan_{n+1}$. The '$\smallfrown$' combinator constructs a so-called *zig-zag* circuit whose height difference is one. The *height difference* is the length of the path from the first input to the last output. The low height difference of one renders zig-zag circuits attractive for serial composition. This is utilized in [4] to construct size-optimal circuits. A *size-optimal circuit* has the minimal number of operation nodes among all circuits of a *fixed* given depth.

Perhaps surprisingly, a serial composition of two zig-zag circuits can again be written as a zig-zag circuit.

$$(l_1 \smallfrown u_1) \backslash\!\backslash (l_2 \smallfrown u_2) \quad = \quad ([l_1, l_2] \succ scan_2) \smallfrown (fan_2 \prec [u_1, u_2]) \tag{9}$$

To justify this we argue ($i_1 = |l_1| = |u_1|$ and $i_2 = |l_2| = |u_2|$)

$(l_1 \smallfrown u_1) \backslash\!\backslash (l_2 \smallfrown u_2)$

$= \{$ definition of '$\backslash\!\backslash$' $\}$

$(l_1 \smallfrown u_1) \times id_{i_2} \fatsemi id_{i_1} \times (l_2 \smallfrown u_2)$

$= \{$ definition of '$\smallfrown$' $\}$

$(id_1 \times l_1 \fatsemi fan_2 \prec [u_1, id_1]) \times id_{i_2} \fatsemi id_{i_1} \times (id_1 \times l_2 \fatsemi fan_2 \prec [u_2, id_1])$

$= \{$ composition $\}$

$id_1 \times l_1 \times l_2 \fatsemi (fan_2 \prec [i_1, 1]) \times id_{i_2} \fatsemi id_{i_1} \times (fan_2 \prec [i_2, 1]) \fatsemi u_1 \times u_2 \times id_1$

$= \{$ derived stretch law (6) $\}$

$id_1 \times l_1 \times l_2 \fatsemi (fan_2 \backslash\!\backslash fan_2) \prec [i_1, i_2, 1] \fatsemi u_1 \times u_2 \times id_1$

$= \{$ $fan_2 \backslash\!\backslash fan_2 = scan_3 = id_1 \parallel scan_2 = id_1 \times scan_2 \fatsemi fan_3$ $\}$

$id_1 \times l_1 \times l_2 \fatsemi (id_1 \times scan_2 \fatsemi fan_3) \prec [i_1, i_2, 1] \fatsemi u_1 \times u_2 \times id_1$

$= \{$ stretching $\}$

$id_1 \times l_1 \times l_2 \fatsemi [1, i_1, i_2] \succ (id_1 \times scan_2) \fatsemi fan_3 \prec [i_1, i_2, 1] \fatsemi u_1 \times u_2 \times id_1$

$= \{$ composition $\}$

$[id_1, l_1, l_2] \succ (id_1 \times scan_2) \fatsemi fan_3 \prec [u_1, u_2, id_1]$

$= \{$ composition and fan law $\}$

$id_1 \times ([l_1, l_2] \succ scan_2) \fatsemi fan_2 \prec [fan_2 \prec [u_1, u_2], id_1]$

$= \{$ definition of '$\smallfrown$' $\}$

$([l_1, l_2] \succ scan_2) \smallfrown (fan_2 \prec [u_1, u_2])$

The property can even be generalized to an n-fold composition.

$$(l_1 \smallfrown u_1) \backslash\!\backslash \cdots \backslash\!\backslash (l_n \smallfrown u_n) \quad = \quad ([l_1, \ldots, l_n] \succ scan_n) \smallfrown (fan_n \prec [u_1, \ldots, u_n])$$

The proof of this property proceeds by a simple induction. We only show the induction step.

$$(l_1 \curvearrowright u_1) \setminus\!\!\setminus \cdots \setminus\!\!\setminus (l_n \curvearrowright u_n) \setminus\!\!\setminus (l_{n+1} \curvearrowright u_{n+1})$$
$$= \{ \text{ ex hypothesi } \}$$
$$(([l_1, \ldots, l_n] \succ scan_n) \curvearrowright (fan_n \prec [u_1, \ldots, u_n])) \setminus\!\!\setminus (l_{n+1} \curvearrowright u_{n+1})$$
$$= \{ \text{ see above } \}$$
$$([[l_1, \ldots, l_n] \succ scan_n, l_{n+1}] \succ scan_2) \curvearrowright (fan_2 \prec [fan_n \prec [u_1, \ldots, u_n], u_{n+1}])$$
$$= \{ \text{ scan law (10), see below } \}$$
$$([l_1, \ldots, l_n, l_{n+1}] \succ scan_{n+1}) \curvearrowright (fan_2 \prec [fan_n \prec [u_1, \ldots, u_n], u_{n+1}])$$
$$= \{ \text{ fan law } \}$$
$$([l_1, \ldots, l_n, l_{n+1}] \succ scan_{n+1}) \curvearrowright (fan_{n+1} \prec [u_1, \ldots, u_n, u_{n+1}])$$

The scan law used in the third step is analogous to the first fan law.

$$[fs \succ scan_m] \mathbin{+\!\!+} gs \succ scan_{1+n} \;=\; fs \mathbin{+\!\!+} gs \succ scan_{m+n} \tag{10}$$

The proof is left as an exercise to the reader.

To summarize, '$\curvearrowright$' combines a tree of scans with a corresponding tree of fans to a scan. The combinator allows us to shape a scan after an arbitrary tree structure. This makes it easy, for instance, to take constraints on the fan-out into account – the fan-out corresponds directly to the degree of a tree. As an example, let us define the Lin-Hsiao circuit wl shown above. The following Haskell data declaration introduces a suitable tree type and its associated fold operation.

$$
\begin{array}{lll}
\textbf{data } \textit{Tree } \alpha & = & \textit{Leaf } \alpha \mid \textit{Node } [\textit{Tree } \alpha] \\
\textit{fold} & :: & (\alpha \to \beta) \to ([\beta] \to \beta) \to (\textit{Tree } \alpha \to \beta) \\
\textit{fold leaf node } (\textit{Leaf a}) & = & \textit{leaf a} \\
\textit{fold leaf node } (\textit{Node ts}) & = & \textit{node } [\textit{fold leaf node } t \mid t \leftarrow ts]
\end{array}
$$

The scan tree and the fan tree of a zig-zag circuit can be implemented as two simple folds.

$$
\begin{array}{lll}
\textit{zig-zag} & :: & (\textit{Circuit } \gamma, \textit{Monoid } \alpha) \Rightarrow \textit{Tree Width} \to \gamma\,\alpha \\
\textit{zig-zag t} & = & \textit{fold ser s-node t} \curvearrowright \textit{fold fan f-node t} \\[4pt]
\textit{s-node ts} & = & \textit{ts} \succ \textit{ser}_{\#ts} \\
\textit{f-node ts} & = & \textit{fan}_{\#ts} \prec \textit{ts}
\end{array}
$$

The 'base' circuit of the s-node can be any scan. The same is true of the f-node – recall that the first fan law allows us to rewrite a single fan as a nest of fans.

Now, the tree underlying the wl circuit is given by the following definition (note that the argument does *not* correspond to the width).

$$
\begin{array}{lll}
\textit{wl-tree}_5 & = & \textit{Node } [\textit{Leaf 4, Leaf 4, Leaf 4}] \\
\textit{wl-tree}_{n+1} & = & \textit{Node } [\textit{wl-tree}_n, \textit{wl-tree}_n]
\end{array}
$$

The circuit is then simply defined as the composition of *zig-zag* and *wl-tree*.

$$wl_n \;\; = \;\; zig\text{-}zag\ wl\text{-}tree_n$$

Lin and Hsiao show that a slightly optimized version of wl_n – using the first fan law the two 2-fans in the center are merged into a 3-fan – is size-optimal [4].

6.2   Brent-Kung, Revisited

Interestingly, the Brent-Kung circuit can be seen as a zig-zag circuit in disguise, or rather, as a serial composition of zig-zag circuits. Reconsider the example graph given in Section 5.1 and note that the right part has the characteristic shape of a zig-zag circuit: the tree in the upper part is mirrored in the lower part, in fact, they can be mapped onto each other through a 180° rotation (this is because binary fans and binary scans are equal).

The tree shape underlying a Brent-Kung circuit is that of a Braun tree.

$$
\begin{aligned}
braun_n & \\
\mid n \leqslant 2 \quad &= \quad Leaf\ n \\
\mid otherwise \quad &= \quad Node\ [\,braun_{\lceil n/2 \rceil}, braun_{\lfloor n/2 \rfloor}\,]
\end{aligned}
$$

Here is the alternative definition of Brent-Kung as a serial composition of zig-zag circuits.

$$
\begin{aligned}
bk'_n & \\
\mid n \leqslant 2 \quad &= \quad ser_n \\
\mid otherwise \quad &= \quad bk'_{d+r} \;\backslash\!\backslash\; zig\text{-}zag\ braun_d \\
\mathbf{where}\ (d, r) \quad &= \quad divMod\ n\ 2
\end{aligned}
$$

The graphical representation reveals that this variant is more condensed: every fan is placed at the topmost possible position.

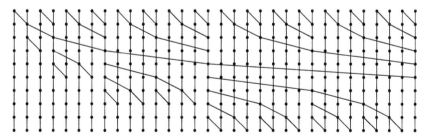

7   Related Work

Parallel prefix computations are nearly as old as the history of computers. One of the first implementations of fast integer addition using carry-lookahead was described by Weinberger and Smith [11]. However, the operation of the circuit seemed to rely on the particularities of carry propagation. It was only 20 years later that Ladner and Fischer formulated the abstract problem of prefix computation and showed that carry computation is an instance of this class [9]. In fact, they showed the more general result that any finite-state transducer can be simulated in logarithmic time using a parallel prefix circuit.

As an aside, the idea underlying this proof is particularly appealing to functional programmers as it relies on currying. Let $\phi :: (X, A) \to A$ be an arbitrary binary operation not necessarily associative. To compute the value of

$$\phi \left(x_1, \phi \left(x_2, \ldots \phi \left(x_n, a \right) \ldots \right) \right)$$

and all of the intermediate results we rewrite the expression into a form suitable for a prefix computation

$$\left(curry \ \phi \ x_1 \cdot curry \ \phi \ x_2 \cdot \cdots \cdot curry \ \phi \ x_n \right) a$$

The underlying binary operation is then simply function composition. An implementation in hardware additionally requires that the elements of $A \to A$ can be finitely represented (see Section 2.1).

Fich later proved that the Ladner-Fischer family of scans is depth-optimal [10]. Furthermore, he improved the design for an extra depth of one. Since then various other families have been proposed taking into account restrictions on depth and, in particular, on fan-out. Lin and Hsiao, for instance, describe a family of size-optimal scans with a fan-out of 4 and a small depth. One main ingredient is the circuit wl introduced in Section 6.1. The construction is given as an algorithm that transforms an explicit graph representing wl_n into a graph representing wl_{n+1}. The transformation essentially implements the rule

$$\left(l_1 \ \lrcorner\ u_1 \right) \setminus\!\!\setminus \left(l_2 \ \lrcorner\ u_2 \right) \ = \ \left([l_1, l_2] \succ scan_2 \right) \ \lrcorner\ \left(fan_2 \prec [u_1, u_2] \right)$$

However, since the graph representation is too concrete, the algorithm is hard to understand and even harder to prove correct.

There are a few papers that deal with the derivation of parallel prefix circuits. Misra [12] calculates the Brent-Kung circuit via the data structure of *powerlists*[1]. Since powerlists capture the recursive decomposition of Brent-Kung, the approach while elegant is not easily applicable to other implementations of scans. In a recent pearl, O'Donnell and Rünger [13] derive the recursive implementation using the digital circuit description language Hydra. The resulting specification contains all the necessary information to simulate or fabricate a circuit.

The parallel prefix computation also serves as a building block of parallel programming. We have already noted in the introduction that many algorithms can be conveniently expressed in terms of scans [3]. Besides encouraging well-structured programming this coarse-grained approach to parallelism allows for various program optimizations. Gorlach and Lengauer [14], for instance, show that a composition of two scans can be transformed into a single scan. The scan function itself is an instance of a so-called *list homomorphism*. For this class of

---

[1] Misra actually claims to derive the Ladner-Fischer scheme. However, the function presented in the paper implements Brent-Kung – recall in this respect that $lf \ \infty$ specializes to bk.

functions, parallel programs can be derived in a systematic manner [15]. Applying the approach of [15] to scan yields the optimal hypercube algorithm. This algorithm can be seen as a *clocked circuit*. Consequently, there is no direct correspondence to any of the algorithms given here, which are purely combinatorial.

8 Conclusion

This paper shows that parallel prefix circuits enjoy a surprisingly rich algebra. The algebraic approach has several benefits: it allows us to specify scans in a readable and concise way, to prove them correct, and to derive new designs. In the process of preparing the paper the algebra of scans has undergone several redesigns. We hope that the final version presented here will stand the test of time.

Acknowledgements

I am grateful to the five anonymous referees for valuable suggestions regarding presentation and for pointing out related work.

References

1. Iverson, K.E.: APL: A Programming Language. John Wiley & Sons (1962)
2. Cormen, T.H., Leiserson, C.E., Rivest, R.L.: Introduction to Algorithms. First edn. The MIT Press, Cambridge, Massachusetts (1990)
3. Blelloch, G.: Prefix sums and their applications. Technical Report CMU-CS-90-190, School of Computer Science, Carnegie Mellon University, Pittsburgh, PA (1990) Also appears in *Synthesis of Parallel Algorithms*, ed. John E. Reif, Morgan Kaufmann Publishers Inc., San Francisco, CA, USA, 1993.
4. Lin, Y.C., Hsiao, J.W.: A new approach to constructing optimal prefix circuits with small depth. In: Proceedings of the International Symposium on Parallel Architectures, Algorithms and Networks (ISPAN'02). (2002)
5. Peyton Jones, S.: Haskell 98 Language and Libraries. Cambridge University Press (2003)
6. Braun, W., Rem, M.: A logarithmic implementation of flexible arrays. Memorandum MR83/4, Eindhoven University of Technology (1983)
7. Hinze, R.: Constructing red-black trees. In Okasaki, C., ed.: Proceedings of the Workshop on Algorithmic Aspects of Advanced Programming Languages, WAAAPL'99, Paris, France. (1999) 89–99 The proceedings appeared as a technical report of Columbia University, CUCS-023-99, also available from http://www.cs.columbia.edu/~cdo/waaapl.html.
8. Brent, R., Kung, H.: The chip complexity of binary arithmetic. In: Twelfth Annual ACM Symposium on Theory of Computing (STOC '80), New York, ACM Press (1980) 190–200
9. Ladner, R.E., Fischer, M.J.: Parallel prefix computation. Journal of the ACM **27** (1980) 831–838

10. Fich, F.E.: New bounds for parallel prefix circuits. In ACM, ed.: Proceedings of the fifteenth annual ACM Symposium on Theory of Computing, Boston, Massachusetts, April 25–27, 1983, New York, NY, USA, ACM Press (1983) 100–109

11. Weinberger, A., Smith, J.: A one-microsecond adder using one-megacycle circuitry. IRE Transactions on Electronic Computers **EC-5** (1956)

12. Misra, J.: Powerlist: A structure for parallel recursion. ACM Transactions on Programming Languages and Systems **16** (1994) 1737–1767

13. O'Donnell, J.T., Rünger, G.: Derivation of a logarithmic time carry lookahead addition circuit. Journal of Functional Programming, Special Issue on Functional Pearls (2004) to appear.

14. Gorlatch, S., Lengauer, C.: (De)Composition rules for parallel scan and reduction. In: Proc. 3rd Int. Working Conf. on Massively Parallel Programming Models (MPPM'97), IEEE Computer Society Press, pages 23–32 (1998)

15. Gorlatch, S.: Extracting and implementing list homomorphisms in parallel program development. Science of Computer Programming **33** (1999) 1–27

Compiling Exceptions Correctly

Graham Hutton and Joel Wright

School of Computer Science and IT
University of Nottingham, United Kingdom

Abstract. Exceptions are an important feature of modern programming languages, but their compilation has traditionally been viewed as an advanced topic. In this article we show that the basic method of compiling exceptions using stack unwinding can be explained and verified both simply and precisely, using elementary functional programming techniques. In particular, we develop a compiler for a small language with exceptions, together with a proof of its correctness.

1 Introduction

Most modern programming languages support some form of programming with *exceptions*, typically based upon a primitive that abandons the current computation and *throws* an exception, together with a primitive that *catches* an exception and continues with another computation [3, 16, 11, 8]. In this article we consider the problem of compiling such exception primitives.

Exceptions have traditionally been viewed as an advanced topic in compilation, usually being discussed only briefly in courses, textbooks, and research articles, and in many cases not at all. In this article, we show that the basic method of compiling exceptions using *stack unwinding* can in fact be explained and verified both simply and precisely, using elementary functional programming techniques. In particular, we develop a compiler for a small language with exceptions, together with a proof of its correctness with respect to a formal semantics for this language. Surprisingly, this appears to be the first time that a compiler for exceptions has been proved to be correct.

In order to focus on the essence of the problem and avoid getting bogged down in other details, we adopt a particularly simple language comprising just four components, namely integer values, an addition operator, a single exceptional value called throw, and a catch operator for this value. This language does not provide features that are necessary for actual programming, but it *does* provide just what we need for our expository purposes in this article. In particular, integers and addition constitute a minimal language in which to consider computation using a stack, and throw and catch constitute a minimal extension in which such computations can involve exceptions.

Our development proceeds in three steps, starting with the language of integer values and addition, then adding throw and catch to this language, and finally adding explicit jumps to the virtual machine. Starting with a simpler language allows us to introduce our approach to compilation and its correctness

D. Kozen (Ed.): MPC 2004, LNCS 3125, pp. 211–227, 2004.

without the extra complexity of exceptions. In turn, deferring the introduction of jumps allows us to introduce our approach to the compilation of exceptions without the extra complexity of dealing with jump addresses.

All the programs in the article are written in Haskell [11], but we only use the basic concepts of recursive types, recursive functions, and inductive proofs, what might be termed the "holy trinity" of functional programming. An extended version of the article that includes the proofs omitted in this conference version for reasons of space is available from the authors' home pages.

2   Arithmetic Expressions

Let us begin by considering a simple language of arithmetic expressions, built up from integers using an addition operator. In Haskell, the language of such expressions can be represented by the following type:

$$\textbf{data } Expr \quad = \quad Val\ Int\ |\ Add\ Expr\ Expr$$

The semantics of such expressions is most naturally given denotationally [14], by defining a function that evaluates an expression to its integer value:

$$
\begin{aligned}
eval & \quad :: \quad Expr \rightarrow Int \\
eval\ (Val\ n) & \quad = \quad n \\
eval\ (Add\ x\ y) & \quad = \quad eval\ x + eval\ y
\end{aligned}
$$

Now let us consider compiling arithmetic expressions into code for execution using a stack machine, in which the stack is represented as a list of integers, and code comprises a list of push and add operations on the stack:

$$
\begin{aligned}
\textbf{type } Stack & \quad = \quad [Int] \\
\textbf{type } Code & \quad = \quad [Op] \\
\textbf{data } Op & \quad = \quad PUSH\ Int\ |\ ADD
\end{aligned}
$$

For ease of identification, we always use upper-case names for machine operations. Functions that compile an expression into code, and execute code using an initial stack to give a final stack, can now be defined as follows:

$$
\begin{aligned}
comp & \quad :: \quad Expr \rightarrow Code \\
comp\ (Val\ n) & \quad = \quad [PUSH\ n] \\
comp\ (Add\ x\ y) & \quad = \quad comp\ x \mathbin{+\!\!+} comp\ y \mathbin{+\!\!+} [ADD] \\
\\
exec & \quad :: \quad Stack \rightarrow Code \rightarrow Stack \\
exec\ s\ [\,] & \quad = \quad s \\
exec\ s\ (PUSH\ n : ops) & \quad = \quad exec\ (n : s)\ ops \\
exec\ (m : n : s)\ (ADD : ops) & \quad = \quad exec\ (n + m : s)\ ops
\end{aligned}
$$

For simplicity, the function *exec* does not consider the case of *stack underflow*, which arises if the stack contains less than two integers when executing an add operation. We will return to this issue in the next section.

3   Compiler Correctness

The correctness of our compiler for expressions with respect to our semantics can be expressed as the commutativity of the following diagram:

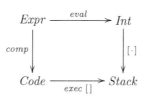

That is, compiling an expression and then executing the resulting code using an empty initial stack gives the same final stack as evaluating the expression and then converting the resulting integer into a singleton stack:

$$exec\ []\ (comp\ e)\ =\ [eval\ e]$$

In order to prove this result, however, it is necessary to generalise from the empty initial stack to an arbitrary initial stack.

Theorem 1 (compiler correctness).

$$exec\ s\ (comp\ e)\ =\ eval\ e : s$$

Proof. By induction on $e :: Expr$.

Case: $e = Val\ n$

$$exec\ s\ (comp\ (Val\ n))$$
$$=\quad \{\text{ definition of } comp \}$$
$$exec\ s\ [PUSH\ n]$$
$$=\quad \{\text{ definition of } exec \}$$
$$n : s$$
$$=\quad \{\text{ definition of } eval \}$$
$$eval\ (Val\ n) : s$$

Case: $e = Add\ x\ y$

$$exec\ s\ (comp\ (Add\ x\ y))$$
$$=\quad \{\text{ definition of } comp \}$$
$$exec\ s\ (comp\ x \mathbin{+\!\!+} comp\ y \mathbin{+\!\!+} [ADD])$$
$$=\quad \{\text{ execution distributivity (lemma 1) }\}$$
$$exec\ (exec\ s\ (comp\ x))\ (comp\ y \mathbin{+\!\!+} [ADD])$$
$$=\quad \{\text{ induction hypothesis }\}$$
$$exec\ (eval\ x : s)\ (comp\ y \mathbin{+\!\!+} [ADD])$$
$$=\quad \{\text{ execution distributivity }\}$$
$$exec\ (exec\ (eval\ x : s)\ (comp\ y))\ [ADD]$$
$$=\quad \{\text{ induction hypothesis }\}$$

$$exec\ (eval\ y\ :\ eval\ x\ :\ s)\ [ADD]$$
$=$ { definition of $exec$ }
$$eval\ x + eval\ y\ :\ s$$
$=$ { definition of $eval$ }
$$eval\ (Add\ x\ y)\ :\ s$$

$\square$

Note that without first generalising the result, the second induction hypothesis step above would be invalid. The distribution lemma is as follows.

Lemma 1 (execution distributivity).

$$exec\ s\ (xs \mathbin{+\!\!+} ys)\ =\ exec\ (exec\ s\ xs)\ ys$$

That is, executing two pieces of code appended together gives the same result as executing the two pieces of code separately in sequence.

Proof. By induction on $xs :: Code$.

When performing an addition in this proof, the stack not containing at least two integers corresponds to a stack underflow error. In this case, the equation to be proved is trivially true, because the result of both sides is undefined ($\bot$), provided that we assume that $exec$ is strict in its stack argument ($exec\ \bot\ ops\ =\ \bot$.) This extra strictness assumption could be avoided by representing and managing stack underflow explicitly, rather than implicitly using $\bot$. In fact, however, both lemma 1 and its consequent underflow issue can be avoided altogether by further generalising our correctness theorem to also consider additional code.

Theorem 2 (generalised compiler correctness).

$$exec\ s\ (comp\ e \mathbin{+\!\!+} ops)\ =\ exec\ (eval\ e\ :\ s)\ ops$$

That is, compiling an expression and then executing the resulting code appended together with arbitrary additional code gives the same result as pushing the value of the expression to give a new stack, which is then used to execute the additional code. Note that with $s = ops = []$, theorem 2 simplifies to $exec\ []\ (comp\ e) = [eval\ e]$, our original statement of compiler correctness.

Proof. By induction on $e :: Expr$.

Case: $e = Val\ n$

$$exec\ s\ (comp\ (Val\ n) \mathbin{+\!\!+} ops)$$
$=$ { definition of $comp$ }
$$exec\ s\ ([PUSH\ n] \mathbin{+\!\!+} ops)$$
$=$ { definition of $exec$ }
$$exec\ (n\ :\ s)\ ops$$
$=$ { definition of $eval$ }
$$exec\ (eval\ (Val\ n)\ :\ s)\ ops$$

Case: $e = Add\ x\ y$

$$exec\ s\ (comp\ (Add\ x\ y) +\!\!+ ops)$$
$=$ { definition of $comp$ }
$$exec\ s\ (comp\ x +\!\!+ comp\ y +\!\!+ [ADD] +\!\!+ ops)$$
$=$ { induction hypothesis }
$$exec\ (eval\ x\ :\ s)\ (comp\ y +\!\!+ [ADD] +\!\!+ ops)$$
$=$ { induction hypothesis }
$$exec\ (eval\ y\ :\ eval\ x\ :\ s)\ ([ADD] +\!\!+ ops)$$
$=$ { definition of $exec$ }
$$exec\ (eval\ x + eval\ y\ :\ s)\ ops$$
$=$ { definition of $eval$ }
$$exec\ (eval\ (Add\ x\ y)\ :\ s)\ ops$$

$\square$

In addition to avoiding the problem of stack underflow, the above proof also has the important benefit of being approximately one third of the combined length of our previous two proofs. As is often the case in mathematics, generalising a theorem in the appropriate manner can considerably simplify its proof.

4   Adding Exceptions

Now let us extend our language of arithmetic expressions with simple primitives for throwing and catching an exception:

$$\textbf{data}\ Expr\ =\ \ldots \mid Throw \mid Catch\ Expr\ Expr$$

Informally, *Throw* abandons the current computation and throws an exception, while *Catch x h* behaves as the expression x unless it throws an exception, in which case the catch behaves as the *handler* expression h. To formalise the meaning of these new primitives, we first recall the *Maybe* type:

$$\textbf{data}\ Maybe\ a\ =\ Nothing \mid Just\ a$$

That is, a value of type *Maybe a* is either *Nothing*, which we think of as an exceptional value, or has the form *Just x* for some x of type a, which we think of as normal value [15]. Using this type, our denotational semantics for expressions can now be rewritten to take account of exceptions as follows:

$$
\begin{array}{lll}
eval & :: & Expr \to Maybe\ Int \\
eval\ (Val\ n) & = & Just\ n \\
eval\ (Add\ x\ y) & = & \textbf{case}\ eval\ x\ \textbf{of} \\
& & \quad Nothing \to Nothing \\
& & \quad Just\ n \to \textbf{case}\ eval\ y\ \textbf{of} \\
& & \quad\quad Nothing \to Nothing \\
& & \quad\quad Just\ m \to Just\ (n + m) \\
eval\ (Throw) & = & Nothing \\
eval\ (Catch\ x\ h) & = & \textbf{case}\ eval\ x\ \textbf{of} \\
& & \quad Nothing \to eval\ h \\
& & \quad Just\ n \to Just\ n
\end{array}
$$

Note that addition propagates an exception thrown in either argument. By exploiting the fact that *Maybe* forms a *monad* [17], the above definition can be expressed more abstractly and concisely using monadic syntax [12]:

$$
\begin{array}{lll}
eval & :: & Expr \rightarrow Maybe \; Int \\
eval \; (Val \; n) & = & return \; n \\
eval \; (Add \; x \; y) & = & \textbf{do} \; n \leftarrow eval \; x \\
& & \quad\quad m \leftarrow eval \; y \\
& & \quad\quad return \; (n + m) \\
eval \; (Throw) & = & mzero \\
eval \; (Catch \; x \; h) & = & eval \; x \; `mplus` \; eval \; h
\end{array}
$$

For the purposes of proofs, however, we use our non-monadic definition for *eval*. To illustrate our new semantics, here are a few simple examples:

$$
\begin{array}{lll}
eval \; (Add \; (Val \; 2) \; (Val \; 3)) & = Just \; 5 & \text{– no exceptions} \\
eval \; (Add \; Throw \; (Val \; 3)) & = Nothing & \text{– uncaught exception} \\
eval \; (Catch \; (Val \; 2) \; (Val \; 3)) & = Just \; 2 & \text{– unused handler} \\
eval \; (Catch \; Throw \; (Val \; 3)) & = Just \; 3 & \text{– caught exception}
\end{array}
$$

Now let us consider how the exception primitives can be compiled. First of all, we introduce three new machine operations:

$$\textbf{data} \; Op \; = \; \ldots \mid THROW \mid MARK \; Code \mid UNMARK$$

Informally, *THROW* throws an exception, *MARK* pushes a piece of code onto the stack, while *UNMARK* pops such code from the stack. Using these operations, our compiler for expressions can now be extended as follows:

$$
\begin{array}{lll}
comp \; (Throw) & = & [\, THROW \,] \\
comp \; (Catch \; x \; h) & = & [\, MARK \; (comp \; h) \,] \; \mathbin{+\!\!+} \; comp \; x \; \mathbin{+\!\!+} \; [\, UNMARK \,]
\end{array}
$$

That is, *Throw* is compiled directly to the corresponding machine operation, while *Catch x h* is compiled by first *marking the stack* with the compiled code for the handler *h*, then compiling the expression to be evaluated *x*, and finally *unmarking the stack* by removing the handler. In this way, the mark and unmark operations delimit the scope of the handler *h* to the expression *x*, in the sense that the handler is only present on the stack during execution of the expression. Note that the stack is marked with the actual compiled code for the handler, rather than some form of *pointer* to the code as would be used in a real implementation. We will return to this issue later on in the article.

Because the stack can now contain handler code as well as integer values, the type for stacks must itself be rewritten:

$$
\begin{array}{lll}
\textbf{type} \; Stack & = & [\, Item \,] \\
\textbf{data} \; Item & = & VAL \; Int \mid HAN \; Code
\end{array}
$$

In turn, our function that executes code is now rewritten as follows:

$$
\begin{array}{lll}
exec & :: & Stack \rightarrow Code \rightarrow Stack \\
exec\ s\ [] & = & s \\
exec\ s\ (PUSH\ n\ :\ ops) & = & exec\ (VAL\ n\ :\ s)\ ops \\
exec\ s\ (ADD\ :\ ops) & = & \textbf{case}\ s\ \textbf{of} \\
\quad (VAL\ m\ :\ VAL\ n\ :\ s') & \rightarrow & exec\ (VAL\ (n+m)\ :\ s')\ ops \\
exec\ s\ (THROW\ :\ ops) & = & unwind\ s\ (skip\ ops) \\
exec\ s\ (MARK\ ops'\ :\ ops) & = & exec\ (HAN\ ops'\ :\ s)\ ops \\
exec\ s\ (UNMARK\ :\ ops) & = & \textbf{case}\ s\ \textbf{of} \\
\quad (x\ :\ HAN\ \_\ :\ s') & \rightarrow & exec\ (x\ :\ s')\ ops
\end{array}
$$

That is, push and add are executed as previously, except that we must now take account of the fact that values on the stack are tagged. For execution of a throw, there are a number of issues to consider. First of all, the current computation needs to be abandoned, which means removing any intermediate values that have been pushed onto the stack by this computation, as well as skipping any remaining code for this computation. And secondly, the current handler code needs to be executed, if there is any, followed by any code that remains after the abandoned computation. The function *exec* implements these ideas using an auxiliary function *unwind* that pops items from the stack until a handler is found, at which point the handler is executed followed by the remaining code, which is itself produced using a function *skip* that skips to the next unmark:

$$
\begin{array}{lll}
unwind & :: & Stack \rightarrow Code \rightarrow Stack \\
unwind\ []\ \_ & = & [] \\
unwind\ (VAL\ \_\ :\ s)\ ops & = & unwind\ s\ ops \\
unwind\ (HAN\ ops'\ :\ s)\ ops & = & exec\ s\ (ops' +\!\!+ ops) \\
\\
skip & :: & Code \rightarrow Code \\
skip\ [] & = & [] \\
skip\ (UNMARK\ :\ ops) & = & ops \\
skip\ (MARK\ \_\ :\ ops) & = & skip\ (skip\ ops) \\
skip\ (\_\ :\ ops) & = & skip\ ops
\end{array}
$$

Note that *unwind* has the same type as *exec*, and can be viewed as an alternative mode of this function for the case when the virtual machine is in the process of handling an exception. For simplicity, *unwind* returns the empty stack in the case of an uncaught exception. For a language in which the empty stack was a valid result, a separate representation for an uncaught exception would be required. Note also the double recursion when skipping a mark, which reflects the fact that there may be nested mark/unmark pairs in the remaining code.

Returning to the remaining cases in the definition of *exec* above, a mark is executed simply by pushing the given handler code onto the stack, and dually, an unmark by popping this code from the stack. Between executing a mark and its corresponding unmark, however, the code delimited by these two operations will have pushed its result value onto the stack, and hence when the handler code is popped it will actually be the second-top item.

To illustrate our new compiler and virtual machine, their behaviour on the four example expressions from earlier in this section is shown below, in which the symbol $$ denotes the result of the last compilation:

$$comp \ (Add \ (Val \ 2) \ (Val \ 3)) \quad = \quad [PUSH \ 2, PUSH \ 3, ADD]$$
$$exec \ [] \ \$\$ \qquad\qquad\qquad = \quad [VAL \ 5]$$

$$comp \ (Add \ Throw \ (Val \ 3)) \quad = \quad [THROW, PUSH \ 3, ADD]$$
$$exec \ [] \ \$\$ \qquad\qquad\qquad = \quad []$$

$$comp \ (Catch \ (Val \ 2) \ (Val \ 3)) \ = \quad [MARK \ [PUSH \ 3], PUSH \ 2, UNMARK]$$
$$exec \ [] \ \$\$ \qquad\qquad\qquad = \quad [VAL \ 2]$$

$$comp \ (Catch \ Throw \ (Val \ 3)) \ = \quad [MARK \ [PUSH \ 3], THROW, UNMARK]$$
$$exec \ [] \ \$\$ \qquad\qquad\qquad = \quad [VAL \ 3]$$

5   Compiler Correctness

Generalising from the examples in the previous section, the correctness of our new compiler is expressed by the commutativity of the following diagram:

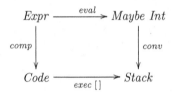

That is, compiling an expression and then executing the resulting code using an empty initial stack gives the same final stack as evaluating the expression and then converting the resulting semantic value into the corresponding stack, using an auxiliary function *conv* that is defined as follows:

$$conv \qquad\qquad :: \quad Maybe \ Int \rightarrow Stack$$
$$conv \ Nothing \quad = \quad []$$
$$conv \ (Just \ n) \quad = \quad [VAL \ n]$$

As previously, however, in order to prove this result we generalise to an arbitrary initial stack and also consider additional code, and in turn rewrite the function *conv* to take account of these two extra arguments.

Theorem 3 (compiler correctness).

$$exec \ s \ (comp \ e +\!\!\!+ ops) \quad = \quad conv \ s \ (eval \ e) \ ops$$

where

$$conv \qquad\qquad\qquad\quad :: \quad Stack \rightarrow Maybe \ Int \rightarrow Code \rightarrow Stack$$
$$conv \ s \ Nothing \ ops \quad = \quad unwind \ s \ (skip \ ops)$$
$$conv \ s \ (Just \ n) \ ops \quad = \quad exec \ (VAL \ n : s) \ ops$$

Note that with $s = ops = [\,]$, this theorem simplifies to our original statement of correctness above. The right-hand side of theorem 3 could also be written as *exec s* (*conv* (*eval e*) : *ops*) using a simpler version of *conv* with type *Maybe Int* → *Op*, but the above formulation leads to simpler proofs.

Proof. By induction on $e :: Expr$.

Case: $e = Val\ n$

$\quad$ *exec s* (*comp* (*Val n*) ⧺ *ops*)
= $\quad$ { definition of *comp* }
$\quad$ *exec s* ([*PUSH n*] ⧺ *ops*)
= $\quad$ { definition of *exec* }
$\quad$ *exec* (*VAL n* : *s*) *ops*
= $\quad$ { definition of *conv* }
$\quad$ *conv s* (*Just n*) *ops*
= $\quad$ { definition of *eval* }
$\quad$ *conv s* (*eval* (*Val n*)) *ops*

Case: $e = Throw$

$\quad$ *exec s* (*comp Throw* ⧺ *ops*)
= $\quad$ { definition of *comp* }
$\quad$ *exec s* ([*THROW*] ⧺ *ops*)
= $\quad$ { definition of *exec* }
$\quad$ *unwind s* (*skip ops*)
= $\quad$ { definition of *conv* }
$\quad$ *conv s Nothing ops*
= $\quad$ { definition of *eval* }
$\quad$ *conv s* (*eval Throw*) *ops*

Case: $e = Add\ x\ y$

$\quad$ *exec s* (*comp* (*Add x y*) ⧺ *ops*)
= $\quad$ { definition of *comp* }
$\quad$ *exec s* (*comp x* ⧺ *comp y* ⧺ [*ADD*] ⧺ *ops*)
= $\quad$ { induction hypothesis }
$\quad$ *conv s* (*eval x*) (*comp y* ⧺ [*ADD*] ⧺ *ops*)
= $\quad$ { definition of *conv* }
$\quad$ **case** *eval x* **of**
$\quad\quad$ *Nothing* → *unwind s* (*skip* (*comp y* ⧺ [*ADD*] ⧺ *ops*))
$\quad\quad$ *Just n* → *exec* (*VAL n* : *s*) (*comp y* ⧺ [*ADD*] ⧺ *ops*)

The two possible results from this expression are simplified below.

1:

$\qquad$ *unwind s* (*skip* (*comp y* ++ [*ADD*] ++ *ops*))
= $\qquad$ { skipping compiled code (lemma 2) }
$\qquad$ *unwind s* (*skip* ([*ADD*] ++ *ops*))
= $\qquad$ { definition of *skip* }
$\qquad$ *unwind s* (*skip ops*)

2:

$\qquad$ *exec* (*VAL n* : *s*) (*comp y* ++ [*ADD*] ++ *ops*)
= $\qquad$ { induction hypothesis }
$\qquad$ *conv* (*VAL n* : *s*) (*eval y*) ([*ADD*] ++ *ops*)
= $\qquad$ { definition of *conv* }
$\qquad$ **case** *eval y* **of**
$\qquad\qquad$ *Nothing* → *unwind* (*VAL n* : *s*) (*skip* ([*ADD*] ++ *ops*))
$\qquad\qquad$ *Just m* → *exec* (*VAL m* : *VAL n* : *s*) ([*ADD*] ++ *ops*)
= $\qquad$ { definition of *unwind*, *skip* and *exec* }
$\qquad$ **case** *eval y* **of**
$\qquad\qquad$ *Nothing* → *unwind s* (*skip ops*)
$\qquad\qquad$ *Just m* → *exec* (*VAL* (*n* + *m*) : *s*) *ops*

We now continue the calculation using the two simplified results.

$\qquad$ **case** *eval x* **of**
$\qquad\qquad$ *Nothing* → *unwind s* (*skip ops*)
$\qquad\qquad$ *Just n* → **case** *eval y* **of**
$\qquad\qquad\qquad$ *Nothing* → *unwind s* (*skip ops*)
$\qquad\qquad\qquad$ *Just m* → *exec* (*VAL* (*n* + *m*) : *s*) *ops*
= $\qquad$ { definition of *conv* }
$\qquad$ **case** *eval x* **of**
$\qquad\qquad$ *Nothing* → *conv s Nothing ops*
$\qquad\qquad$ *Just n* → **case** *eval y* **of**
$\qquad\qquad\qquad$ *Nothing* → *conv s Nothing ops*
$\qquad\qquad\qquad$ *Just m* → *conv s* (*Just* (*n* + *m*)) *ops*
= $\qquad$ { distribution over **case** }
$\qquad$ *conv s* (**case** *eval x* **of**
$\qquad\qquad$ *Nothing* → *Nothing*
$\qquad\qquad$ *Just n* → **case** *eval y* **of**
$\qquad\qquad\qquad$ *Nothing* → *Nothing*
$\qquad\qquad\qquad$ *Just m* → *Just* (*n* + *m*)) *ops*
= $\qquad$ { definition of *eval* }
$\qquad$ *conv s* (*eval* (*Add x y*)) *ops*

Case: $e = Catch\ x\ h$

$\qquad exec\ s\ (comp\ (Catch\ x\ h) + ops)$
$=\qquad \{\ \text{definition of } comp\ \}$
$\qquad exec\ s\ ([MARK\ (comp\ h)] + comp\ x + [UNMARK] + ops)$
$=\qquad \{\ \text{definition of } exec\ \}$
$\qquad exec\ (HAN\ (comp\ h)\ :\ s)\ (comp\ x + [UNMARK] + ops)$
$=\qquad \{\ \text{induction hypothesis}\ \}$
$\qquad conv\ (HAN\ (comp\ h)\ :\ s)\ (eval\ x)\ ([UNMARK] + ops)$
$=\qquad \{\ \text{definition of } conv\ \}$
$\qquad$ **case** $eval\ x$ **of**
$\qquad\quad Nothing \rightarrow unwind\ (HAN\ (comp\ h)\ :\ s)\ (skip\ ([UNMARK] + ops))$
$\qquad\quad Just\ n \rightarrow exec\ (VAL\ n\ :\ HAN\ (comp\ h)\ :\ s)\ ([UNMARK] + ops)$
$=\qquad \{\ \text{definition of } unwind,\ skip\ \text{and}\ exec\ \}$
$\qquad$ **case** $eval\ x$ **of**
$\qquad\quad Nothing \rightarrow exec\ s\ (comp\ h + ops)$
$\qquad\quad Just\ n \rightarrow exec\ (VAL\ n\ :\ s)\ ops$
$=\qquad \{\ \text{induction hypothesis}\ \}$
$\qquad$ **case** $eval\ x$ **of**
$\qquad\quad Nothing \rightarrow conv\ s\ (eval\ h)\ ops$
$\qquad\quad Just\ n \rightarrow exec\ (VAL\ n\ :\ s)\ ops$
$=\qquad \{\ \text{definition of } conv\ \}$
$\qquad$ **case** $eval\ x$ **of**
$\qquad\quad Nothing \rightarrow conv\ s\ (eval\ h)\ ops$
$\qquad\quad Just\ n \rightarrow conv\ s\ (Just\ n)\ ops$
$=\qquad \{\ \text{distribution over}\ \textbf{case}\ \}$
$\qquad conv\ s\ (\textbf{case}\ eval\ x\ \textbf{of}$
$\qquad\quad Nothing \rightarrow eval\ h$
$\qquad\quad Just\ n \rightarrow Just\ n)\ ops$
$=\qquad \{\ \text{definition of } eval\ \}$
$\qquad conv\ s\ (eval\ (Catch\ x\ h))\ ops$

$\square$

The two distribution over **case** steps in the above proof rely on the fact that *conv* is strict in its semantic value argument ($conv\ s\ \bot\ ops\ =\ \bot$), which is indeed the case because *conv* is defined by pattern matching on this argument. The skipping lemma used in the above proof is as follows.

Lemma 2 (skipping compiled code).

$$skip\ (comp\ e + ops)\quad =\quad skip\ ops$$

That is, skipping to the next unmark in compiled code followed by arbitrary additional code gives the same result as simply skipping the additional code. Intuitively, this is the case because the compiler ensures that all unmarks in compiled code are matched by preceding marks.

Proof. By induction on $e :: Expr$.

6   Adding Jumps

Now let us extend our virtual machine with primitives that allow exceptions to be compiled using explicit jumps, rather than by pushing handler code onto the stack. First of all, we introduce three new machine operations:

$$\textbf{data } Op \;=\; \dots \mid MARK\ Addr \mid LABEL\ Addr \mid JUMP\ Addr$$

Informally, $MARK$ pushes the address of a piece of code onto the stack (replacing our previous mark operator that pushed code itself), $LABEL$ declares an address, and $JUMP$ transfers control to an address. Addresses themselves are represented simply as integers, and we ensure that each address is declared at most once by generating addresses in sequential order using a function $fresh$:

$$
\begin{aligned}
\textbf{type } Addr \;&=\; Int \\
fresh \quad &::\quad Addr \rightarrow Addr \\
fresh\ a \;&=\; a + 1
\end{aligned}
$$

Our compiler for expressions is now extended to take the next fresh address as an additional argument, and is rewritten in terms of another function $compile$ that also returns the next fresh address as an additional result:

$$
\begin{aligned}
comp \quad &::\quad Addr \rightarrow Expr \rightarrow Code \\
comp\ a\ e \;&=\; fst\ (compile\ a\ e)
\end{aligned}
$$

$$
\begin{aligned}
compile \quad &::\quad Addr \rightarrow Expr \rightarrow (Code, Addr) \\
compile\ a\ (Val\ n) \;&=\; ([PUSH\ n], a) \\
compile\ a\ (Add\ x\ y) \;&=\; (xs \mathbin{+\!\!+} ys \mathbin{+\!\!+} [ADD], c) \\
&\quad \textbf{where} \\
&\qquad (xs, b) = compile\ a\ x \\
&\qquad (ys, c) = compile\ b\ y \\
compile\ a\ (Throw) \;&=\; ([THROW], a) \\
compile\ a\ (Catch\ x\ h) \;&=\; ([MARK\ a] \mathbin{+\!\!+} xs \mathbin{+\!\!+} [UNMARK, JUMP\ b, \\
&\qquad LABEL\ a] \mathbin{+\!\!+} hs \mathbin{+\!\!+} [LABEL\ b], e) \\
&\quad \textbf{where} \\
&\qquad b = fresh\ a \\
&\qquad c = fresh\ b \\
&\qquad (xs, d) = compile\ c\ x \\
&\qquad (hs, e) = compile\ d\ h
\end{aligned}
$$

Note that integer values, addition, and throw are compiled as previously, except that the next fresh address is threaded through, while $Catch\ x\ h$ is now compiled to the following sequence, in which a: abbreviates $LABEL\ a$:

$$
\begin{aligned}
&MARK\ a \\
&compiled\ code\ for\ x \\
&UNMARK \\
&JUMP\ b \\
a{:}\ &compiled\ code\ for\ h \\
b{:}\ &rest\ of\ the\ code
\end{aligned}
$$

That is, *Catch x h* is now compiled by first marking the stack with the address of the compiled code for the handler *h*, compiling the expression to be evaluated *x*, then unmarking the stack by removing the address of the handler, and finally jumping over the handler code to the rest of the code.

By exploiting the fact that the type for *compile* can be expressed using a *state monad* [17], the above definition can also be expressed more abstractly and concisely using monadic syntax. As with the function *eval*, however, for the purposes of proofs we use our non-monadic definition for *compile*.

Because the stack can now contain handler addresses rather than handler code, the type for stack items must be rewritten:

$$\textbf{data } Item \quad = \quad VAL \ Int \mid HAN \ Addr$$

In turn, our function that executes code requires four modifications:

$$
\begin{aligned}
exec \ s \ (THROW \ : \ ops) \ &= \ unwind \ s \ ops \\
exec \ s \ (MARK \ a \ : \ ops) \ &= \ exec \ (HAN \ a \ : \ s) \ ops \\
exec \ s \ (LABEL \ \_ \ : \ ops) \ &= \ exec \ s \ ops \\
exec \ s \ (JUMP \ a \ : \ ops) \ &= \ exec \ s \ (jump \ a \ ops)
\end{aligned}
$$

For execution of a throw, the use of explicit jumps means that the function *skip* is no longer required, and there are now only two issues to consider. First of all, the current computation needs to be abandoned, by removing any intermediate values that have been pushed onto the stack by this computation. And secondly, the current handler needs to be executed, if there is any. Implementing these ideas requires modifying one line in the definition of *unwind*:

$$unwind \ (HAN \ a \ : \ s) \ ops \quad = \quad exec \ s \ (jump \ a \ ops)$$

That is, once the address of a handler is found, the handler is executed using a function *jump* that transfers control to a given address:

$$
\begin{aligned}
jump \quad &:: \quad Addr \rightarrow Code \rightarrow Code \\
jump \ \_ \ [] \quad &= \quad [] \\
jump \ a \ (LABEL \ b \ : \ ops) \quad &= \quad \textbf{if } a == b \textbf{ then } ops \textbf{ else } jump \ a \ ops \\
jump \ a \ (\_ \ : \ ops) \quad &= \quad jump \ a \ ops
\end{aligned}
$$

Note that our language only requires forward jumps. If backward jumps were also possible, a slightly generalised virtual machine would be required.

Returning to the remaining modified cases in the definition of *exec* above, a mark is executed simply by pushing the given address onto the stack, a label is executed by skipping the label, and a jump is executed by transferring control to the given address using the function *jump* defined above.

The behaviour of our new compiler and virtual machine on the four example expressions from earlier in the article is shown below:

$$comp\ 0\ (Add\ (Val\ 2)\ (Val\ 3))\quad =\quad [PUSH\ 2, PUSH\ 3, ADD]$$
$$exec\ []\ \$\$\quad\quad\quad\quad\quad\quad\quad =\quad [VAL\ 5]$$

$$comp\ 0\ (Add\ Throw\ (Val\ 3))\quad =\quad [THROW, PUSH\ 3, ADD]$$
$$exec\ []\ \$\$\quad\quad\quad\quad\quad\quad\quad =\quad []$$

$$comp\ 0\ (Catch\ (Val\ 2)\ (Val\ 3))\ =\ [MARK\ 0, PUSH\ 2, UNMARK, JUMP\ 1,$$
$$\qquad\qquad\qquad\qquad\qquad\qquad\qquad\qquad LABEL\ 0, PUSH\ 3, LABEL\ 1]$$
$$exec\ []\ \$\$\quad\quad\quad\quad\quad\quad\quad =\quad [VAL\ 2]$$

$$comp\ 0\ (Catch\ Throw\ (Val\ 3))\ =\ [MARK\ 0, THROW, UNMARK, JUMP\ 1,$$
$$\qquad\qquad\qquad\qquad\qquad\qquad\qquad\qquad LABEL\ 0, PUSH\ 3, LABEL\ 1]$$
$$exec\ []\ \$\$\quad\quad\quad\quad\quad\quad\quad =\quad [VAL\ 3]$$

Note that our compiler now once again produces "flat" code, in contrast to our previous version, which produced tree-structured code.

7   Compiler Correctness

The correctness of our new compiler is expressed by the same diagram as the previous version, except that new compiler takes the next fresh address as an additional argument, for which we supply zero as the initial value:

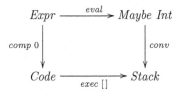

For the purposes of proofs we once again generalise this result to an arbitrary initial stack and additional code, and extend the function *conv* accordingly. In turn, we also generalise to an arbitrary initial address that is fresh with respect to the initial stack, using a predicate *isFresh* that decides if a given address is greater than every address that occurs in a stack.

Theorem 4 (compiler correctness).

> If *isFresh a s* then *exec s* (*comp a e* ++ *ops*) = *conv s* (*eval e*) *ops*
>
> *where*

$$
\begin{array}{lll}
isFresh & :: & Addr \rightarrow Stack \rightarrow Bool \\
isFresh\ \_\,[] & = & True \\
isFresh\ a\ (VAL\ \_ : s) & = & isFresh\ a\ s \\
isFresh\ a\ (HAN\ b : s) & = & a > b\ \wedge\ isFresh\ a\ s \\[4pt]
conv & :: & Stack \rightarrow Maybe\ Int \rightarrow Code \rightarrow Stack \\
conv\ s\ Nothing\ ops & = & unwind\ s\ ops \\
conv\ s\ (Just\ n)\ ops & = & exec\ (VAL\ n : s)\ ops
\end{array}
$$

Proof. By induction on $e :: Expr$ in a similar manner to theorem 3, except that five lemmas concerning fresh addresses are required:

Lemma 3 (unwinding operators).

$$\text{If } op = LABEL\ a \;\Rightarrow\; isFresh\ a\ s \;\; then$$

$$unwind\ s\ (op : ops) \;=\; unwind\ s\ ops$$

That is, when unwinding the stack the first operator in the code can be discarded, provided that it is not an address that may occur in the stack.

Proof. By induction on $s :: Stack$.

Lemma 4 (unwinding compiled code).

$$\text{If } isFresh\ a\ s \;\; then \;\; unwind\ s\ (comp\ a\ e \mathbin{+\!\!+} ops) \;=\; unwind\ s\ ops$$

That is, unwinding the stack on compiled code followed by arbitrary additional code gives the same result as simply unwinding the stack on the additional code, provided that the initial address for the compiler is fresh for the stack.

Proof. By induction on $e :: Expr$, using lemma 3 above.

Lemma 5 ($isFresh$ is monotonic).

$$\text{If } a \leqslant b \wedge isFresh\ a\ s \;\; then \;\; isFresh\ b\ s$$

That is, if one address is at most another, and the first is fresh with respect to a stack, then the second is also fresh with respect to this stack.

Proof. By induction on $s :: Stack$.

Lemma 6 ($compile$ is non-decreasing).

$$snd\ (compile\ a\ e) \;\geqslant\; a$$

That is, the next address returned by the compiler will always be greater than or equal to the address supplied as an argument.

Proof. By induction on $e :: Expr$.

Lemma 7 (jumping compiled code).

$$\text{If } a < b \;\; then \;\; jump\ a\ (comp\ b\ e \mathbin{+\!\!+} ops) \;=\; jump\ a\ ops$$

That is, jumping to an address in compiled code followed by arbitrary additional code gives the same result as simply jumping in the additional code, provided that the jump address is less than the initial address for the compiler.

Proof. By induction on $e :: Expr$, using lemma 6 above.

8   Further Work

We have shown how the compilation of exceptions using stack unwinding can be explained and verified in a simple manner. In this final section we briefly describe a number of possible directions for further work.

- *Mechanical verification.* The correctness of our two compilers for exceptions has also been verified mechanically. In particular, theorem 3 was verified in Lego by McBride [6], and theorem 4 in Isabelle by Nipkow [10]. A novel aspect of the Lego verification that merits further investigation is the use of dependent types to precisely capture the stack demands of the virtual machine operations (e.g. add requires a stack with two integers on the top), which leads to a further simplification of our correctness proof, at the expense of requiring a more powerful type system.
- *Modular compilers.* Inspired by the success of using monads to define the denotational semantics of languages in terms of the semantics of individual features [9], similar techniques are now being applied to build compilers in a modular manner [4]. To date, however, this work has not considered the compilation of exceptions, so there is scope for trying to incorporate the present work into this modular framework.
- *Calculating the compiler.* Rather than first defining the compiler and virtual machine and then proving their correctness with respect to the semantics, another approach would be to try and calculate the definition of these functions starting from the compiler correctness theorem itself [7,1], with the aim of giving a systematic *discovery* of the idea of compiling exceptions using stack unwinding, as opposed to a post-hoc verification.
- *Generalising the language.* Arithmetic expressions with exceptions served as a suitable language for the purposes of this article, but it is important to explore how our approach can be scaled to more expressive languages, such as a simple functional or imperative language, to languages with more than one kind of exception and user-defined exceptions, and to other notions of exception, such as imprecise [13] and asynchronous [5] exceptions.
- *Compiler optimisations.* The basic compilation method presented in this article can be optimised in a number of ways. For example, we might rearrange the compiled code to avoid the need to jump over handlers in the case of no exceptions being thrown, use a separate stack of handler addresses to make the process of stack unwinding more efficient, or use a separate table of handler scopes to avoid an execution-time cost for installing a handler. It would be interesting to consider how such optimisations can be incorporated into our compiler and its correctness proof.

Acknowledgements

This work was jointly funded by the University of Nottingham and Microsoft Research Ltd in Cambridge. Thanks to Simon Peyton Jones and Simon Marlow at Microsoft for answering many questions about exceptions and their semantics, to Thorsten Altenkirch, Olivier Danvy, Conor McBride, Simon Peyton Jones and the anonymous referees for useful comments and suggestions, and to Ralf Hinze for the lhs2TeX system for typesetting Haskell code.

QuickCheck [2] was used extensively in the production of this article, and proved invaluable as an aid to getting the definitions and results correct before proceeding to formal proofs. A number of (often subtle) mistakes in our definitions and results were discovered in this way.

References

1. R. Backhouse. *Program Construction: Calculating Implementations from Specifications.* John Wiley, 2003.
2. K. Claessen and J. Hughes. QuickCheck: A Lightweight Tool for Random Testing of Haskell Programs. In *Proceedings of the Fifth ACM SIGPLAN International Conference on Functional Programming,* Montreal, Canada, Sept. 2000.
3. J. Gosling, B. Joy, G. Steele, and G. Bracha. *The Java Language Specification, Second Edition.* Addison-Wesley, 2000.
4. W. Harrison. *Modular Compilers and Their Correctness Proofs.* PhD thesis, University of Illinois, 2001.
5. S. Marlow, S. Peyton Jones, A. Moran, and J. Reppy. Asynchronous Exceptions In Haskell. In *Proceedings of the ACM SIGPLAN Conference on Programming Language Design and Implementation,* Snowbird, Utah, June 2001.
6. C. McBride. Personal communication, 2003.
7. E. Meijer. *Calculating Compilers.* PhD thesis, Nijmegen University, 1992.
8. R. Milner, M. Tofte, R. Harper, and D. MacQueen. *The Definition of Standard ML (Revised).* MIT Press, 1997.
9. E. Moggi. An Abstract View of Programming Languages. Technical Report ECS-LFCS-90-113, Laboratory for Foundations of Computer Science, University of Edinburgh, 1990.
10. T. Nipkow. Personal communication, 2004.
11. S. Peyton Jones. *Haskell 98 Language and Libraries: The Revised Report.* Cambridge University Press, 2003.
12. S. Peyton Jones and J. Launchbury. State in Haskell. University of Glasgow, 1994.
13. S. Peyton Jones, A. Reid, T. Hoare, S. Marlow, and F. Henderson. A Semantics For Imprecise Exceptions. In *Proceedings of the ACM SIGPLAN Conference on Programming Language Design and Implementation,* Atlanta, Georgia, May 1999.
14. D. A. Schmidt. *Denotational Semantics: A Methodology for Language Development.* Allyn and Bacon, Inc., 1986.
15. M. Spivey. A Functional Theory of Exceptions. *Science of Computer Programming,* 14(1):25–43, 1990.
16. B. Stroustrup. *The C++ Programming Language, Third Edition.* Addison-Wesley, 1997.
17. P. Wadler. The Essence of Functional Programming. In *Proc. Principles of Programming Languages,* 1992.

Modelling Nondeterminism

Clare E. Martin[1], Sharon A. Curtis[1], and Ingrid Rewitzky[2]

[1] Department of Computing, Oxford Brookes University, UK
[2] Department of Mathematics and Applied Mathematics,
University of Cape Town, South Africa

1 Introduction

For many years the realm of total functions was considered to be the natural domain in which to reason about functional programs [B90]. The limitation of this domain is that it can only be used to describe deterministic programs: those that deliver only one output for each input. More recently, the development of the relational calculus for program derivation [BdM97] has allowed programmers to reason about programs together with their specifications, which may be nondeterministic: they may offer a choice of outputs for each input. Specifications expressed in this calculus can be manipulated and refined into functions that can be translated into an appropriate functional programming language. We now propose to go one step further, since the domain of relations can be used to describe only angelic or demonic nondeterminism, but not both.

Angelic nondeterminism occurs when the choice is made by an 'angel': it is assumed that the angel will choose the best possible outcome. Demonic nondeterminism occurs when the choice is made by a 'demon': no assumption can be made about the choice made by the demon, so we must be prepared for the worst possible outcome. It is well known that both these kinds of behaviour can be described in the domain of monotonic predicate transformers [BvW98,Mor98], but this is usually associated with the derivation of imperative, rather than functional programs.

An equivalent relational model that has recently been proposed consists of up-closed multirelations [R03].

Relational equivalents of predicate transformers have been introduced in the past (see [LyV92] for example), but Rewitzky has extended this equivalence to show that any monotonic function over a boolean algebra has an alternative representation as a multirelation.

We will show how specifications involving both angelic and demonic nondeterminism can be expressed and manipulated as multirelations. Such specifications can be refined until they contain only one kind of nondeterministic choice. Then they can be translated into programs in which those remaining choices are made interactively by an external agent at run time.

This is not the first attempt to introduce angelic and demonic nondeterminism into a calculus for the derivation of functional programs. Ward [W94] developed a refinement calculus for this purpose, in a similar style to that of [BvW98,Mor98], and with a corresponding predicate transformer semantics.

D. Kozen (Ed.): MPC 2004, LNCS 3125, pp. 228–251, 2004.

However, we argue that multirelations will provide a better model for several reasons. First, one of the beauties of the relational calculus (for examples of its use see [BaH93], [BdM97], [ScS88]) is that specifications are simply relations: there is no separate command language. As such, they can be manipulated by all the familiar operations on relations, such as composition and inverse, as well as those developed specifically for the derivation of functional programs. In contrast, in the refinement calculus of both [BvW98,Mor98] and [W94] the command language is distinct from its predicate transformer semantics. So specifications can only be manipulated using laws that were previously derived from the semantics. This places a burden on the developer to memorise all the laws, and can complicate the reasoning about operations as fundamental as composition, which can be expressed simply for predicate transformers, but much less so for specifications in the command language. One solution to this problem could be to represent specifications directly as predicate transformers, but this might be counter-intuitive because they model programs in reverse, mapping postconditions to preconditions. In contrast, multirelations can be used to relate inputs, or initial states, to outputs, or final states, so we propose to blur the distinction between multirelations and the specifications they represent.

As an illustration of our theory, we will give examples demonstrating how multirelations can be used to specify and manipulate some games and resource-sharing protocols. For example, in a two-player game the choices of our player could be modelled by angelic nondeterminism, and those of our opponent by demonic nondeterminism. The resulting specification would allow us to reason about the game as a whole, and then derive an implementation that achieves some goal, such as an optimal strategy for the player. The implementation would then consist of a computerised player, who would play according to the strategy against a human opponent who could make demonic choices in an attempt to defeat the machine.

2   Nondeterministic Specifications

2.1   Agents

We are primarily interested in specifying systems that contain both angelic and demonic choice. One way to think of such specifications is as a contract [BvW98] between two agents, both of whom are free to make various choices. One of the agents represents our interests, but the other may not. In this context, the angelic choices are interpreted as those made by our agent, since we assume that he will always make the choice that results in the best outcome for us. Conversely, the demonic choices are those made by the other agent, and since we have no control over them we must be prepared for all possibilities, including the worst.

For example, the specification of a simple vending machine from a customer's viewpoint might contain an angelic choice of coin insertion and chocolate bar selection, followed by a demonic choice of coins returned by the machine as change. This can be viewed as a contract where our agent is the customer and the other agent is the machine designer who can choose how the machine gives out change.

Specifications like this, featuring both angelic and demonic nondeterminism, have been modelled previously using monotonic predicate transformers [BvW98,Mor98], but until now there has been no equivalent relational model. The problem with the ordinary relational calculus is that only one kind of nondeterminism can be described at a time, but fortunately this is not the case for the multirelational calculus as we shall now see.

2.2   Multirelations

Multirelations were introduced in [R03] as an alternative to predicate transformers for reasoning about programs. As the name suggests, they are to relations what multifunctions (relations) are to functions: that is to say, they are relations whose target type is a powerset type.

Definition 1 (multirelation) A *multirelation* with source A and target B is a subset of the cartesian product $A \times \mathbb{P}\, B$. As such, it is a set of ordered pairs (x, X) where $x \in A$ and $X \subseteq B$.

We will interpret values of the source type as input values to a program, and subsets of the target type as predicates on that type (a given value satisfies a predicate if and only if it lies within the set).

Multirelations model programs in a very different way from ordinary relations: a relation R relates two values x and y, written $x\ R\ y$, if and only if the corresponding program can terminate with output y given input x. In contrast, a multirelation M relates two values x and *post*, written $x\ M\ post$, if and only if the corresponding program can terminate with an output value that satisfies the predicate *post* given input x. Expressed in terms of a contract between two agents, this means that our agent can make choices to ensure that the output value satisfies *post*, no matter what choices are made by the other agent. The other agent's goals may not be directly opposed to ours, but since we have no influence over the choices he makes we must be prepared for the worst possible outcome. Therefore we can only say that a specification can achieve a given postcondition from some initial state if our agent can ensure this under all circumstances.

For example, suppose that, given an input value of x, our agent has the choice of two predicates $\{x - 2, x + 2\}$ and $\{x - 1\}$. If he chooses the former, then the choice of output value is $x - 2$ or $x + 2$ and determined by the other agent. In the latter case the other agent has no choice and $x - 1$ is the output value.

Not every multirelation is suitable for the specification of a contract. Suppose that *post*, *post'* $\subseteq B$ are two postconditions such that *post* $\subseteq$ *post'*. Clearly, if our agent can make choices to ensure that an output value satisfies *post*, it must also satisfy *post'*. Consequently, a multirelation can only represent a contract between two agents if it is up-closed in the following sense:

Definition 2 (up-closure) A multirelation M with source A and target B is *up-closed* if for all $x \in A$ and $X, Y \subseteq B$,

$$x \ M \ X \wedge X \subseteq Y \Rightarrow x \ M \ Y$$

We will denote the type of all up-closed multirelations with source A and target B by $A \rightrightarrows B$.

We will use the standard lattice theoretic notation [DaP02] to denote the *upward closure* ($\uparrow$) of a set of sets $Z \in \mathbb{P}\mathbb{P}\,B$, or a single set $X \in \mathbb{P}\,B$:

$$\uparrow Z = \{\, Y \mid (\exists\, X : X \in Z : X \subseteq Y)\}$$
$$\uparrow X = \{\, Y \mid X \subseteq Y\}$$

Before moving on to some examples, we describe how the nondeterminism in an up-closed multirelation corresponds to angelic and demonic nondeterminism. The key to understanding the choices offered comes from considering strongest postconditions [DiS90], since the set of all strongest postconditions of a specification represents the set of all choices offered to our agent.

Definition 3 (strongest postcondition) Let $M : A \rightrightarrows B$, $x \in A$ and $post \subseteq B$. Then $post$ is a *strongest postcondition* of M with respect to x if and only if

1. $x \ M \ post$
2. $(\forall\, post' : post' \subseteq B : x \ M \ post' \Rightarrow (post' \not\subseteq post))$

So, for example, let Int denote the type of all integers, $M : Int \rightrightarrows Int$, and suppose that for all $x : Int$ and $X : \mathbb{P}\,Int$

$$x \ M \ X \Leftrightarrow (\{x - 1\} \subseteq X \vee \{x - 2, x + 2\} \subseteq X)$$

then our agent can choose between the two strongest postconditions $\{x - 1\}$ and $\{x - 2, x + 2\}$. In general, we shall refer to the set of all strongest postconditions of a multirelation M with respect to an initial state x by $sp(x, M)$.

To show how up-closed multirelations can be used to model specifications, we will now look at a few simple examples, some deterministic and some nondeterministic. In the former case, our agent is not offered any choice, and neither is the other agent, and thus the deterministic specifications are guaranteed to satisfy any postcondition which holds for an output value corresponding to the given input value.

Examples 4

1. Each type A has identity specification $\in_A : A \rightrightarrows A$, where $\in_A$ (also denoted by id_A) represents the set membership relation on subsets of A. So, given an input value $x \in A$, the (sole) strongest postcondition it can achieve is $\{x\}$, which means that the value x is output. This specification is guaranteed to establish all postconditions that are satisfied by x itself.

2. For each pair of types A, B, and each value $b \in B$, the constant specification *const* $b : A \rightrightarrows B$ is defined by

$$const \; b = A \times \uparrow \{b\}$$

Here, the strongest postcondition that is satisfied for any input value is $\{b\}$, ensuring that the value b is output.

3. Let *Bool* denote the type of booleans, and let *guard* $: A \rightarrow Bool$. We define the specification $\langle\!\mid guard \mid\!\rangle : A \rightrightarrows A$, which asserts that a given input value satisfies *guard* for all $x : A$, $X : \mathbb{P}\,A$ by

$$x \; \langle\!\mid guard \mid\!\rangle \; X \quad \Leftrightarrow \quad guard \; x \;\wedge\; x \in X$$

So, if x satisfies the guard, this specification will output x, but it will not output anything otherwise.

4. Consider the multirelation $A \times \uparrow \{1, 2\}$, for some source type A. Here the strongest postcondition for any input value is $\{1, 2\}$, so our agent has no choice and must select the postcondition $\{1, 2\}$, giving the other agent the choice between output values 1 and 2. This is an example of demonic non-determinism.

5. In contrast, now consider the multirelation $A \times (\uparrow \{1\} \cup \uparrow \{2\})$, for some source type A. Here the strongest postconditions for any input value are $\{1\}$ and $\{2\}$, so our agent can always choose between output values 1 and 2, with no choice available for the other agent. This is an example of angelic nondeterminism.

The last two of these examples illustrate the following more general characterisation of multirelations that contain purely demonic or angelic nondeterminism respectively:

Definition 5 Let $M : A \rightrightarrows B$, then

1. M is *demonic* if, for all $x : A$, and $Z : \mathbb{P}\mathbb{P}\,B$,

$$x \; M \; (\textstyle\bigcap Z) \quad \Leftrightarrow \quad (\forall\, X : X \in Z : x \; M \; X)$$

2. M is *angelic* if, for all $x : A$, and $Z : \mathbb{P}\mathbb{P}\,B$,

$$x \; M \; (\textstyle\bigcup Z) \quad \Leftrightarrow \quad (\exists\, X : X \in Z : x \; M \; X)$$

Notice that a demonic multirelation has only one strongest postcondition for any initial state, which is to be expected since it contains no angelic choice. In contrast, an angelic one may have many strongest postconditions, but each non-empty one must be a singleton set since it contains no demonic choice.

We will now introduce some operations on multirelations so that we can show how they can be used to model more interesting specifications.

2.3   Operations on Multirelations

All of the definitions that follow are taken directly from [R03].

Definition 6 (angelic choice) The *angelic choice* of two programs M, N : $A \rightrightarrows B$ is the union $M \cup N : A \rightrightarrows B$.

Given any input value, our agent can ensure that $M \cup N$ establishes any postcondition that could be achieved by either M or N alone, given the same input value.

Example 7 For each pair of types A, B and values $a, b : B$, we have

$$const\ a \cup const\ b = A \times \uparrow \{a\} \ \cup \ A \times \uparrow \{b\}$$

Here, our agent can choose between the two strongest postconditions $\{a\}$ and $\{b\}$. So he can ensure that this specification establishes any postcondition that is satisfied by either of the values a or b, depending on what outcome we aim to achieve.

The dual of angelic choice is demonic choice:

Definition 8 (demonic choice) The *demonic choice* of two programs M, N : $A \rightrightarrows B$ is the intersection $M \cap N : A \rightrightarrows B$.

Given any input value, our agent can ensure that $M \cap N$ establishes any postcondition that could be satisfied by both M and N, given the same input value.

Example 9 For each pair of types A, B and values $a, b : B$, we have

$$const\ a \cap const\ b = A \times \uparrow \{a\} \ \cap \ A \times \uparrow \{b\}$$
$$= A \times \uparrow \{a, b\}$$

Our agent has no choice here: this specification will establish any postcondition that is satisfied by both a and b. The strongest postcondition it satisfies is $\{a, b\}$, showing that it will output one of the values a or b, but we cannot say which.

Multirelations cannot be composed using ordinary relational composition for obvious type reasons. Instead, composition is defined as follows:

Definition 10 (composition) The *composition* of two multirelations $M : A \rightrightarrows B$, $N : B \rightrightarrows C$ is denoted by $M \mathbin{\overset{\circ}{,}} N : A \rightrightarrows C$ where for all $x : A$, $X : \mathbb{P}\,C$

$$x\ (M \mathbin{\overset{\circ}{,}} N)\ X \ \Leftrightarrow \ (\exists\ Y :: x\ M\ Y \wedge (\forall\ y : y \in Y : y\ N\ X))$$

So, given input value x, our agent can only guarantee that $M \mathbin{\overset{\circ}{,}} N$ will output a value that satisfies X if he can ensure that M will establish some intermediate postcondition Y and if he can also guarantee that N will establish X given any value in Y.

It is routine to check that the composition operator is associative, with identity id_A for each A, and preserves up-closure. An equivalent formulation of its definition that can be useful in calculations is given below.

Lemma 11 Let $M : A \rightrightarrows B$ and $N : B \rightrightarrows C$, then for all $x : A$, $X : \mathbb{P} C$

$$x \; (M \, \mathbin{\substack{\circ \\ 9}} \, N) \; X \;\; \Leftrightarrow \;\; (\exists Z : Z \in sp(x, M) : (\forall z : z \in Z : z \; N \; X))$$

The proof of this lemma is in the Appendix. We are now in a position to give some more interesting examples of specifications.

Examples 12

In these examples, we will show how multirelations can be used to model part of a simplified version of the game of Nim [BvW98]. For details of the proper game, see [BCG01] for example. The simplified game involves two players and a pile of matches. The players take it in turns to remove either one or two matches from the pile. The loser is the player who removes the last match. So suppose that for all $n : Int$, $sub\ n : Int \rightrightarrows Int$ represents the program that subtracts the value n from its argument: for all $x : Int$, $X : \mathbb{P} Int$

$$x \; (sub\ n) \; X \Leftrightarrow (x - n) \in X$$

We will model the choices of our player by angelic nondeterminism and our opponent by demonic nondeterminism, so we have

$$
\begin{aligned}
player \;&:\; Int \rightrightarrows Int \\
player \;&=\; sub\ 1 \cup sub\ 2 \\
opponent \;&:\; Int \rightrightarrows Int \\
opponent \;&=\; sub\ 1 \cap sub\ 2
\end{aligned}
$$

More explicitly, for all $x : Int$, $X : \mathbb{P} Int$

$$
\begin{aligned}
x\ player\ X \;\;&\Leftrightarrow\;\; \{x - 1\} \subseteq X \;\vee\; \{x - 2\} \subseteq X \\
x\ opponent\ X \;\;&\Leftrightarrow\;\; \{x - 1, x - 2\} \subseteq X
\end{aligned}
$$

In each case the input value x is an integer which represents the number of matches in the pile at the start of that player's move. For simplicity, we do not check that this integer is positive, unlike [BvW98].

Although Nim is a symmetric game, the following examples illustrate that the guarantees for our player are very different depending on whether he moves first or second.

1. First suppose that our player has the first move, then a round of the game is defined by

$$
\begin{aligned}
round \;&:\; Int \rightrightarrows Int \\
round \;&=\; player \, \mathbin{\substack{\circ \\ 9}} \, opponent
\end{aligned}
$$

and we can calculate that for all $x : Int$, $X : \mathbb{P} Int$

$$x\ round\ X$$
$$\Leftrightarrow \quad \{\text{Definition of } round\}$$

$x \ (player \mathbin{\substack{\circ \\ 9}} opponent) \ X$

$\Leftrightarrow$ {Lemma 11}

$(\exists\, Z : Z \in sp(x, player) : (\forall\, z : z \in Z : z \ opponent \ X))$

$\Leftrightarrow$ {Definition of $player$}

$(\exists\, Z : Z \in \{\{x - 1\}, \{x - 2\}\} : (\forall\, z : z \in Z : z \ opponent \ X))$

$\Leftrightarrow$ {$\exists$, range}

$((x - 1) \ opponent \ X) \vee ((x - 2) \ opponent \ X)$

$\Leftrightarrow$ {Definition of $opponent$}

$\{x - 2, x - 3\} \subseteq X \vee \{x - 3, x - 4\} \subseteq X$

We will use this program to reason about the game of Nim as a whole in Section 4.

2. Now suppose that the opponent has the first move, and so a round of the game is now defined by

$newround \ : \ Int \rightrightarrows Int$

$newround = opponent \mathbin{\substack{\circ \\ 9}} player$

By a similar calculation to that for $round$ we can deduce that for all $x : Int$, $X : \mathbb{P}\, Int$

$$x \ newround \ X \Leftrightarrow \{x - 2, x - 4\} \subseteq X \vee \{x - 3\} \subseteq X$$

This is exactly what we would expect from our intuition about angelic and demonic nondeterminism, since the value input to $player$ is either $x - 1$ or $x - 2$, and so our player can always choose to output $x - 3$, or alternatively one of $x - 2$ or $x - 4$.

The notation M^n will be used to denote the composition of a homogeneous multirelation $M : A \rightrightarrows A$ with itself n times. This operator satisfies the following fusion law:

Lemma 13 Suppose $M, N, K : A \rightrightarrows A$, and let $n : \mathbb{N}^+$, then

$$M \mathbin{\substack{\circ \\ 9}} K = K \mathbin{\substack{\circ \\ 9}} N \ \wedge \ N = K \mathbin{\substack{\circ \\ 9}} N \ \Rightarrow \ M^n \mathbin{\substack{\circ \\ 9}} K = N^n$$

The proof of this lemma is in the Appendix.

Two more operators that are frequently useful for defining repetition in program specifications are transitive closure and reflexive transitive closure:

Definition 14 Let $M : A \rightrightarrows A$.

1. The *transitive closure* of M is denoted by $M^+ : A \rightrightarrows A$, where

$$M^+ = \bigcup \{M^n \mid n > 0\}$$

2. The *reflexive transitive closure* of M is denoted by $M^* : A \rightrightarrows A$, where

$$M^* = \bigcup \{M^n \mid n \geq 0\}$$

These operators satisfy many laws, including the following:

Lemma 15 Suppose $M : A \rightrightarrows A$, then

$$M \subseteq M^+$$
$$M^+ \subseteq M \mathbin{\substack{\circ \\ \circ}} M^*$$

Another pair of operators that are useful in program specifications are the following well-known functions for lifting relations to multirelations [BvW98]:

Definitions 16 (lifting) Let $R : A \to B$, then

1. the *angelic lifting* $\langle R \rangle : A \rightrightarrows B$ is defined for all $x : A$, $X : \mathbb{P} B$ by

$$x \langle R \rangle X \iff (\exists y : x \ R \ y : y \in X)$$

2. the *demonic lifting* $[R] : A \rightrightarrows B$ is defined for all $x : A$, $X : \mathbb{P} B$ by

$$x [R] X \iff (\forall y : x \ R \ y : y \in X)$$

Note that if R is a total function, then the angelic and demonic liftings coincide. These operators are so-called because they map relations to angelic and demonic multirelations respectively. Both operators distribute through relational composition, which will be denoted by $;$. The difference between these operators can be illustrated by the game of Nim of Examples 12:

Example 17 Let $x, y : Int$ and define

$$move \ : \ Int \to Int$$
$$x \ move \ y \quad \iff \quad y = x - 1 \ \lor \ y = x - 2$$

then an alternative definition of the moves is given by

$$player = \langle move \rangle \quad \text{and} \quad opponent = [move]$$

We have now seen that the set of up-closed multirelations is closed under angelic choice, demonic choice and composition, the latter of which can be used to define the familiar transitive closure operations. They are not closed under negation or set difference, and the converse operator cannot be defined, but union and intersection can be lifted to multirelations from the target set in an obvious way. Although negation cannot be lifted directly from relations to multirelations, it does have an analogue in the *dual* operator, which can be thought of as performing an allegiance swap, so that our (angelic) agent becomes demonic, and the other (demonic) agent becomes the angel:

Definition 18 (dual) The *dual* of a specification $M : A \rightrightarrows B$ is denoted by $M^\circ : A \rightrightarrows B$ where for all $x \in A$, $X \in \mathbb{P} B$,

$$x \ M^\circ \ X \iff \neg (x \ M \ \bar{X})$$

where $\bar{X}$ denotes the complement of X in B.

The dual of a multirelation corresponds to the conjugate operator on predicate transformers [DiS90]. The significance of this operator will become more apparent after the discussion of correctness in the following section.

3   Correctness, Refinement and Feasibility

There are many different notions of refinement for ordinary relations. For example, two opposing definitions are given in [BvW98], depending on whether the relations are being used to model angelic or demonic nondeterminism. In the former case, it is defined by subset inclusion, and in the latter by its inverse. Since the predicate transformer model of specifications is capable of expressing both kinds of nondeterminism within a single framework, it has not previously been thought necessary to endow it with more than one refinement ordering. Likewise, it has only one notion of correctness and feasibility. However, we argue that any specification containing both angelic and demonic nondeterminism must offer certain guarantees of behaviour to both the angel and the demon. These guarantees can be formalised as two contrasting correctness conditions, each of which has an associated refinement ordering and feasibility condition. The choice of which one to use depends on whether we see the specification from the viewpoint of the angel or the demon. Either way, this choice must be made at the start of program development and stay fixed throughout the design process.

3.1   Correctness

To demonstrate the need for a second correctness criterion, we consider again the following simple example of a multirelation. For $x : Int$ and $X : \mathbb{P}\, Int$, define $M : Int \rightrightarrows Int$ by

$$x \; M \; X \Leftrightarrow (\{x - 1\} \subseteq X \vee \{x - 2, x + 2\} \subseteq X)$$

Clearly, as the angel can choose between the two strongest postconditions $\{x-1\}$ and $\{x-2, x+2\}$, the angel has some guarantees on the output value. In addition, the demon also has some guarantees. For example, he is never obliged to output the value $x - 2$ if he chooses not to.

Both these kinds of guarantee are instances of the two more general correctness conditions defined below. One requirement of such conditions is that they should be monotonic in the following sense: suppose that a specification $M : A \rightrightarrows B$ is correct with respect to an initial state $x \in A$ and postcondition $post \subseteq B$, and suppose that $post' \subseteq B$ is another postcondition with the property that $post \subseteq post'$. Then M must also be correct with respect to x and $post'$.

Angelic Correctness. Correctness for the angel is easily defined in the multirelational model. By definition, $x \; M \; post$ if and only if the angel can make choices to ensure that the output value satisfies $post$. So we can simply say that a specification $M : A \rightrightarrows B$ is *angelically correct* with respect to an initial state $x \in A$ and postcondition $post \subseteq B$ if

$$x \; M \; post \tag{1}$$

The upward closure of M ensures that this condition is monotonic. It is equivalent to the traditional notion of correctness for predicate transformers in the refinement calculus [BvW98,Mor98].

Demonic Correctness. Correctness for the demon is more difficult to express because of the asymmetry of the multirelational model. Conditions that a demon can guarantee to satisfy are given by the following definition of correctness: a specification $M : A \rightrightarrows B$ is *demonically correct* with respect to an initial state $x \in A$ and postcondition $post \subseteq B$ if

$$x \; M^{\circ} \; post \tag{2}$$

This means that the angel can never establish the complement of $post$, thereby ensuring that the demon can establish $post$. It is easy to check that this definition of correctness satisfies the monotonicity condition imposed above.

The following example gives an illustration of both the foregoing correctness criteria.

Example 19 (Cake Cutting Protocol)

We will look at a well-known two-participant protocol which can be described as "I cut; you choose".

A cake can be modelled as the unit interval $I = [0, 1]$, and slices of cake as sub-intervals of the form $[x, y]$, where $0 \leq x \leq y \leq 1$. A single cut dividing the cake into two pieces can be modelled by the relation $cut : 1 \rightarrow I$, defined to be

$$cut = 1 \times I$$

Thus, given the (null) input, cut may output any cutting position from 0 to 1. The selection of one of the two resulting pieces of cake can be modelled by the relation $choose : I \rightarrow I \times I$, where if $p : I$ and $i : I \times I$

$$p \; choose \; i \quad \Leftrightarrow \quad i = [0, p] \; \vee \; i = [p, 1]$$

where square brackets have been used instead of the more familiar braces to indicate that this pair of values represents an interval. The following cake cutting protocol describes our agent cutting the cake first, followed by the other agent selecting one of the resulting pieces:

$$\langle cut \rangle \; {}^{\circ}_{9} \; [choose] \tag{3}$$

The two agents may have different preferences for cake slices (for example, one may prefer chocolate sprinkles and another may like hazelnuts but not sprinkles). So two different functions are used for measuring the value of cake slices. The value function for our agent will be denoted by $value_a$, and that for the opposing agent by $value_d$. Both functions have type $I \times I \rightarrow I$, and they must be continuous and additive. This means that if the cake is divided into slices, the sum of the values of the slices is the value of the whole cake (defined to be 1). In particular, we have for each b:

$$(\forall p : p \in I : value_b \; [0, p] + value_b \; [p, 1] = 1) \tag{4}$$

The set of strongest postconditions offered to our agent by the protocol can be calculated as

$$\{\{[0, p], \; [p, 1]\} \mid p \in I\} \tag{5}$$

(these describe predicates on the other agent's cake slice).

A common aim of a cake cutting protocol is to achieve fair division: for n participants, this means that each participant receives a slice that they consider to be worth at least $1/n$ of the whole. So for two participants this means that each agent b should be able to achieve the postcondition $fair_b$ (on the slice chosen by the demon agent), where

$$fair_d = \{i \mid \exists\, p : p \in I : (i = [0, p] \vee i = [p, 1]) \wedge value_d\, i \geq 0.5\}$$
$$fair_a = \{i \mid \exists\, p : p \in I : (i = [0, p] \vee i = [p, 1]) \wedge value_a\, i \leq 0.5\}$$

Thus $fair_d$ expresses that the demon agent wants his own slice of cake to be at least half the whole, and $fair_a$ expresses that the angelic agent wants the demon's slice of cake to be no more than half the whole. More precisely, to achieve fair division of the cake, the multirelation $\langle cut \rangle \,\stackrel{\circ}{,}\, [choose]$ must be angelically correct with respect to $fair_a$, and demonically correct with respect to $fair_d$. We will now show that this is indeed the case.

First, consider our agent. As $value_a$ is continuous, our agent can choose a value x such that

$$value_a\, [0, x] \;=\; value_a\, [x, 1] \;=\; 0.5$$

and thus our agent can achieve the postcondition $\{[0, x], [x, 1]\}$ (5). By upward closure and (1) the protocol is therefore angelically correct with respect to $fair_a$.

Now consider the other agent. By (2), the protocol is demonically correct with respect to $fair_d$ if and only if our agent cannot establish the postcondition $\overline{fair_d}$. By (4), one of the slices of cake must be worth at least 0.5 to the other agent, that is to say,

$$(\forall\, p : p \in I : value_d\, [0, p] \geq 0.5 \vee value_d\, [p, 1] \geq 0.5)$$

Hence by (5), every postcondition that our agent can establish contains a value in $fair_d$, and thus we cannot establish $\overline{fair_d}$. So the other agent is also able to ensure receiving what he considers to be a fair slice of cake.

3.2   Refinement

One requirement of a refinement relation is that it should preserve correctness, but there are now two possible interpretations of this requirement, corresponding to the two notions of correctness defined above. Both are valid in different circumstances.

As motivation of this idea, consider an arbitrary specification involving two agents. Usually, one of the agents represents an external decision maker of some kind, such as a human user of the system; we will refer to this as the *external* agent. The choices offered to this agent could include menu options, passwords, or moves in a game. The second agent in a typical specification usually represents the system designer; we will refer to this as the *internal* agent. The choices offered to this agent represent deferred design decisions. As such, the designer is free to implement them however he chooses. If the system is to be implemented in a deterministic language, then ultimately all such choices must be removed completely, or at least hidden so that they depend on information that is not visible to the external agent. A refinement of a specification represents a move towards such an implementation, so it must consist of a decrease in internal choice, but not of external choice, which may even be increased. Either way, a refinement must preserve any guarantee of system behaviour that has been offered to the external agent by the original specification. So if the external agent is angelic, refinement must preserve angelic correctness, and dually if it is demonic. We will refer to these two separate concepts as *angelic* and *demonic* refinement respectively.

Angelic Refinement. The situation where the external agent is angelic is shared by many specifications. For example, consider a customer who is contracting a programmer to deliver a piece of software to accomplish some task. If such a specification includes choices, then it is assumed that the software user will make the best (angelic) choice to achieve the desired goal, regardless of any (demonic) design choices made by the programmer. This is the interpretation of nondeterminism used in the refinement calculus : our agent is external, and the other one is internal. So a refinement consists of a possible decrease in demonic choice and a possible increase in angelic choice, and can be defined for all $M, M' : A \rightrightarrows B$ by

$$M \sqsubseteq_A M' \equiv M \subseteq M' \qquad (angelic\ refinement)$$

Clearly, this preserves the corresponding notion of angelic correctness (1). Intuitively, this definition means that a refinement can only increase the set of postconditions that our agent can choose to satisfy and hence makes it easier to satisfy the specification.

Demonic Refinement. A less common situation is that where we are concerned with developing a program that is as uncooperative as possible with the user, who is potentially hostile and might be capable of preventing our program from achieving its goal. For example, consider the game of Nim (Examples 12), where the external agent is the human opponent and the internal agent is the programmer of the computerised player. Here, the goal of the programmer is to implement a winning strategy to defeat the human adversary who is free to experiment with different strategies each time he plays. Any such implementation of the player must still offer some guarantee of behaviour to the user. For instance, the player must not remove more than two matches.

Another kind of specification that must guard against harmful users might be a security application such as a password protection mechanism. Here, the programmer will make the best choices to achieve a secure system that minimises the probability of a successful breach by an attacker.

In both these examples we assume that if the programmer wishes to achieve some outcome then he will implement the angelic choice that does so regardless of the choice made by the user. So a refinement must consist of a possible decrease in angelic choice and a possible increase in demonic choice: for all $M, M' : A \rightrightarrows B$

$$M \sqsubseteq_D M' \equiv M \supseteq M' \qquad (demonic\ refinement)$$

Once again, this preserves the corresponding notion of correctness (2). Here, a refinement narrows down the selection of achievable postconditions to exclude those that our agent definitely does not want to satisfy. So, for example, one refinement of the player's move in the specification of Nim would be to always remove one match if there are only two left in the pile:

$$rplayer \ = \ (\langle\!| \, (=2) \,|\!\rangle \,\mathbin{\S}\, sub \ 1) \ \cup \ (\langle\!| \, (\neq 2) \,|\!\rangle \,\mathbin{\S}\, player)$$

where the notation $\langle\!| \ \ |\!\rangle$ was introduced in Examples 4. A better refinement of the player's move will be considered in Section 4.

It is interesting to note that the definitions of angelic and demonic refinement given above are identical to those given for ordinary relations in [BvW98], even though they are used here for an entirely different purpose.

3.3 Feasibility

A specification is *feasible* if it can be translated into an equivalent implementation in the target programming language. So if the language is deterministic, a feasible program must be free of all internal choice. It may still contain some external choice however, since this can be resolved through user interaction at run-time. Therefore, if the external agent is our agent, a specification is feasible if and only if it contains only angelic choice, which is to say that it is *angelic* in the sense of Definition 5. Dually, if the external agent is not our agent, a specification is feasible if and only if it contains only demonic choice, which is to say that it is *demonic* in the sense of Definition 5. Hence either of the refinement rules of Section 3.2 can be used to transform any specification into one that is feasible.

4 Applications

4.1 Nim

The version of the Nim considered here was introduced in Examples 12. It involves two players and a pile of matches. The players take it in turns to remove either one or two matches from the pile and the loser is the player who removes the last match. The model that follows differs from that in [BvW98] in that the number of matches in the pile is allowed to become negative. So a game can be modelled as an indefinite number of rounds:

$$nim \ : \ Int \Rightarrow Int$$
$$nim \ = \ round^*$$

where *round* was defined previously in Examples 12 (1). At each round, our player can guarantee to establish one of two postconditions:

Lemma 20 For all $x : Int$, $n : \mathbb{N}^+$ and $X : \mathbb{P}\, Int$,

$$x \ round^n \ X \ \Leftrightarrow \ \{y, y+1\} \subseteq X \vee \{y-1, y\} \subseteq X$$

where $y = x - 3n$.

The proof of this lemma is in the Appendix.

Our player can choose to win the game if and only if he can establish the postcondition $\{0, -1\}$, since then the opponent is forced to remove the last match. By Lemma 20, this postcondition can be guaranteed if and only if there exists a natural number n for which y is equal to 0 or -1, which is equivalent to saying that x must be positive and satisfy $x \bmod 3 \neq 1$. In either case our player can win after p rounds, where

$$p = (x - 1) \ div \ 3 \ + 1 \tag{6}$$

Having established the existence of conditions under which our player can achieve a win, we must now refine the specification towards a feasible implementation of a winning strategy, assuming that the role of our player will be taken by a computer. So, suppose $win : Int \rightrightarrows Int$ is a refinement of nim:

$$nim \sqsubseteq_D win$$

where the demonic refinement ordering is used here because our agent is the internal agent. Starting with x matches, our player is guaranteed to win in the refined game win iff for all $X : \mathbb{P} \ Int$

$$x \ win \ X \ \Leftrightarrow \ \{0, -1\} \subseteq X$$

since this condition asserts that win has a single strongest postcondition, namely $\{0, -1\}$. We will begin to specify a refinement as follows:

$$win = round^p \ _9^o \ choosewin$$

where p was defined in (6) to be the round on which the last match will be removed, and $choosewin$ is a specification that selects the winning output from that round, so $choosewin \subseteq id$. To see that $nim \sqsubseteq_D win$ we calculate

$$nim$$
$$= \quad \{\text{definition of } nim\}$$
$$round^*$$
$$\supseteq \quad \{\text{definition of } ^*\}$$
$$round^p$$
$$\supseteq \quad \{choosewin \subseteq id \text{ and monotonicity}\}$$
$$round^p \ _9^o \ choosewin$$

The most obvious way to define $choosewin$ is to use the notation for converting guards to multirelations of Examples 4 to define:

$$winner \ : \ Int \rightarrow Bool$$
$$winner \ x \ = \ x \in \{0, -1\}$$
$$choosewin_0 \ = \ \langle\!| \ winner \ |\!\rangle$$

It is not difficult to check that this does indeed implement a winning strategy in the sense of (7), but as a practical method it is useless, as it gives no insight into the choice of move that our player must make at each round. Instead we need to generalise the definition of *choosewin*:

$$nearwin \; : \; Int \rightarrow Bool$$
$$nearwin \; x \; = \; x \; mod \; 3 \neq 1$$
$$choosewin \; = \; \langle\!| \; nearwin \; |\!\rangle$$

This implementation still has the effect of filtering out unwanted postconditions, but it also has the advantage that it can be fused into the definition of *win* to provide a practical winning strategy for our player. Using Lemma 13, we have

$$win \; = \; round^p \; \S \; choosewin \; = \; (round \; \S \; choosewin)^p$$

since $round \; \S \; choosewin = choosewin \; \S \; round \; \S \; choosewin$. If we also observe that *nearwin* satisfies the following property

$$\neg \; (nearwin \; x) \Leftrightarrow (nearwin(x - 1) \wedge nearwin(x - 2)) \tag{7}$$

for all $x \in \mathbb{N}$, we may calculate further that

$$round \; \S \; choosewin$$
$$= \quad \{\text{definition of } round\}$$
$$player \; \S \; opponent \; \S \; choosewin$$
$$= \quad \{\text{definition of } choosewin\}$$
$$player \; \S \; opponent \; \S \; \langle\!| \; nearwin \; |\!\rangle$$
$$= \quad \{\text{composition and (7)}\}$$
$$player \; \S \; \langle\!| \; \neg \; nearwin \; |\!\rangle \; \S \; opponent$$

So we can replace the player's move by the new, winning move $playerwin_0 = player \; \S \; \langle\!| \; \neg \; nearwin \; |\!\rangle$, and hence compute that for all $x : Int, X : \mathbb{P} \; Int$,

$$x \; playerwin_0 \; X$$
$$\Leftrightarrow$$
$$(x \; mod \; 3 = 0 \wedge x - 2 \in X) \vee (x \; mod \; 3 = 2 \wedge x - 1 \in X)$$

which is the well known strategy of making the number of matches always satisfy the invariant $x \; mod \; 3 = 1$.

This strategy still has a problem, which is that $playerwin_0$ is not demonic, and hence not feasible in the sense of Section 3.3. The reason it is not demonic is that our player fails to make a move in the case that $x \; mod \; 3 = 1$, since he cannot guarantee to win in this case. For the refinement to be feasible, player must still remove either one or two matches in this case. Suppose for simplicity that player chooses a strategy *playerwin* always to remove one match if $x \; mod \; 3 = 1$:

$$x \; playerwin \; X \Leftrightarrow x \; playerwin_0 \; X \vee (x \; mod \; 3 = 1 \wedge x - 1 \in X)$$

and define

$$strategy = (playerwin \; \S \; opponent)^p$$

This is still a valid refinement of *nim*, since *player* $\sqsubseteq_D$ *playerwin*, and it still implements a winning strategy in the sense of (7) if $x \bmod 3 \neq 1$ because *win* $\subseteq$ *strategy* and so by monotonicity

$$x \; win \; \{0, -1\} \Rightarrow x \; strategy \; \{0, -1\}$$

Since *strategy* is demonic it has a single strongest postcondition, which must be $\{0, -1\}$.

4.2   Team Selection

The following resource sharing protocol concerns the selection of two sports teams from a list of available players. Each team is to have n players, and there are more than $2n$ available players for the team managers to choose from.

For this team selection problem, fair division is not always possible. For example, if one player was so talented that both team managers would value any team containing that player more highly than any team without, then one of the managers will end up disappointed. We will consider Dawson's team selection protocol from [Daw97], which does however satisfy correctness conditions that are close to fair, as we shall see. The following is a slightly simplified version of Dawson's protocol:

Step 1 The manager for the first team (Manager 1) selects two (disjoint) teams of n players.

Step 2 Manager 2 selects one of the two teams, giving the other team to Manager 1.

Step 3 Beginning with Manager 2, the managers take turns to swap some (possibly none) of the players on their own team with some from the pool of leftover players. The protocol ends when neither manager wishes to make any further swaps.

Given a type *Player*, a relation describing the first step of the protocol is *partition* : $\mathbb{P} \; Player \to \mathbb{P} \, \mathbb{P} \; Player \times \mathbb{P} \; Player$, where

$$ps \; partition \; (\{t, t'\}, pool) \Leftrightarrow ps \; = \; t \uplus t' \uplus p$$
$$\wedge \; \#t = \#t' = n$$

where *ps* represents the input list of players, and $\uplus$ is disjoint set union.

The second step of the team selection protocol can be described by the relation *select* : $\mathbb{P} \, \mathbb{P} \; Player \times Player \to \mathbb{P} \; Player \times \mathbb{P} \; Player \times \mathbb{P} \; Player$, where

$$(\{t_1, t_2\}, p) \; select \; (t_1, t_2, p)$$

Thus t_1 is the team for Manager 1, t_2 is the team for Manager 2, and p is the pool of unselected players.

The swapping described in the third step of the protocol can be defined with the two relations

$$(t_1 \uplus q, t_2, p \uplus q') \; swap_1 \; (t_1 \uplus q', t_2, p \uplus q), \quad \text{if } \#q \; = \; \#q'$$
$$(t_1, t_2 \uplus q, p \uplus q') \; swap_2 \; (t_1, t_2 \uplus q', p \uplus q), \quad \text{if } \#q \; = \; \#q'$$

If we now deem Manager 1 (say) to be the angel, and Manager 2 to be the demon, then the description of the protocol can be translated into the multirelation P, where

$$P = \langle partition \rangle \, \mathring{9} \, [select] \, \mathring{9} \, ([swap_2] \, \mathring{9} \, \langle swap_1 \rangle)^+$$

Instead of starting from a specification of some kind and refining it to produce the above protocol, here we have simply modelled an existing protocol by expressing it in the calculus of multirelations. As discussed above, this protocol cannot possibly guarantee a fair division for all input sets of players, but we would still like to be able to prove that certain other correctness conditions do hold.

We will use a simplistic model, assuming that each Manager i has a value function $value_i : Player \to \mathbb{R}$ and values a whole team by the sum of its players' values. It could then be said that the protocol achieves fair division if each manager can select a team containing half of his $2n$ most highly valued players. It turns out that this is achievable for Manager 2, and nearly achievable for Manager 1. Defining N_2 to be half the sum of the values of the best $2n$ players (with respect to $value_2$), this is the (demonic) correctness condition C_2 we shall prove that Manager 2 can satisfy:

$$C_2 \, (t_1, t_2, p) \equiv (\sum_{q \in t_2} value_2 \; q) \geq N_2$$

Turning to the interests of Manager 1, it would be ill-advised to let high value players lie unchosen in the pool at the first step of the protocol, because they can be swapped into the team of Manager 2 at the first swap. The best Manager 1 can hope for is to partition the teams from the $2n$ players he considers best, making the teams as even as possible. Thus, we define N_1 to be the largest possible sum of a team composed of n of the $2n$ best players (with respect to $value_1$), such that the other n players have a total value at least as high. Thus this is the (angelic) correctness condition that we will use for Manager 1:

$$C_1 \, (t_1, t_2, p) \equiv (\sum_{q \in t_1} value_1 \; q) \geq N_1$$

In order to show that the protocol P is correct with respect to C_1 it is sufficient to show, for some other multirelation P_1 such that $P_1 \sqsubseteq_A P$, that P_1 is correct with respect to C_1, because correctness is preserved by refinement. We can calculate

P

$=$ {Definition}

$\langle partition \rangle \, \mathring{9} \, [select] \, \mathring{9} \, ([swap_2] \, \mathring{9} \, \langle swap_1 \rangle)^+$

$\sqsupseteq$ {Transitive closure, Lemma 15}

$\langle partition \rangle \, \mathring{9} \, [select] \, \mathring{9} \, [swap_2] \, \mathring{9} \, \langle swap_1 \rangle$

Denoting the resulting multirelation by P_1, it is straightforward to see that P_1 satisfies C_1: if Manager 1 partitions the input set of players ps to produce two teams containing his $2n$ best players that are as evenly matched as possible, then by definition each team will have total value (with respect to $value_1$) at least N_1, so that $ps(\langle partition\rangle \mathbin{\overset{\circ}{\circ}} [select])\,C_1$. Subsequently, $[swap_2]$ cannot change t_1, and $\langle swap_1\rangle$ has the option of leaving t_1 unchanged, so Manager 1 can guarantee to be able to satisfy condition C_1.

For Manager 2, we must look at demonic correctness, and we now perform a similar calculation, this time with respect to demonic refinement:

$$P$$

$=$ {Definition}

$\quad \langle partition\rangle \mathbin{\overset{\circ}{\circ}} [select] \mathbin{\overset{\circ}{\circ}} ([swap_2] \mathbin{\overset{\circ}{\circ}} \langle swap_1\rangle)^+$

$\sqsubseteq$ {Closure, Lemma 15}

$\quad \langle partition\rangle \mathbin{\overset{\circ}{\circ}} [select] \mathbin{\overset{\circ}{\circ}} [swap_2] \mathbin{\overset{\circ}{\circ}} \langle swap_1\rangle \mathbin{\overset{\circ}{\circ}} ([swap_2] \mathbin{\overset{\circ}{\circ}} \langle swap_1\rangle)^*$

$=$ {Lifting distributes through composition}

$\quad \langle partition\rangle \mathbin{\overset{\circ}{\circ}} [select \,;\, swap_2] \mathbin{\overset{\circ}{\circ}} \langle swap_1\rangle \mathbin{\overset{\circ}{\circ}} ([swap_2] \mathbin{\overset{\circ}{\circ}} \langle swap_1\rangle)^*$

Denoting the result by P_2, we thus have that $P_2 \sqsubseteq_D P$, and so if we can prove that Manager 2 can guarantee P_2 to satisfy C_2, then that must also be the case for P. The correctness of P_2 is now easier to demonstrate, by considering demonic guarantees for $[select \,;\, swap_2]$.

At the first step, Manager 1 (the angel) has complete control over the partitioning. To complete the subsequent step, $select \,;\, swap_2$, Manager 2 should first note where, within the suggested teams and pool, his $2n$ most highly valued players are. Suppose that this set of players is represented by the disjoint union

$$b_1 \uplus bp_1 \uplus b_2 \uplus bp_2$$

for player sets satisfying

$$b_1 \subseteq t \quad \wedge \quad b_2 \subseteq t' \quad \wedge \quad bp_1 \uplus bp_2 \subseteq p$$
$$\wedge \quad \#b_1 + \#bp_1 = \#b_2 + \#bp_2 = n$$

for teams and pool $(\{t, t'\}, p)$.

Manager 2 should then choose the most valuable of $b_1 \uplus bp_1$ and $b_2 \uplus bp_2$ for his team (t_2) during his execution of $[select;\, swap_2]$. As the value of the players in $b_1 \uplus bp_1 \uplus b_2 \uplus bp_2$ is $2N_2$, this offers Manager 2 a guarantee of being able to satisfy C_2, and therefore $\langle partition\rangle\mathbin{\overset{\circ}{\circ}}[select;\, swap_2]$ satisfies the demonic correctness condition C_2. Subsequently, for $\langle swap_1\rangle \mathbin{\overset{\circ}{\circ}} ([swap_2] \mathbin{\overset{\circ}{\circ}} \langle swap_1\rangle)^*$, a similar argument to that for Manager 1 can be used, as Manager 1 cannot guarantee to change t_2 subsequently and Manager 2 always has the option to keep t_2 unchanged. Thus Manager 2 can guarantee to satisfy C_2, and the protocol is demonically correct for C_2.

5   Conclusion

This paper consists of some preliminary steps towards the construction of a new calculus for modelling nondeterministic specifications as multirelations. The model is appealing because it combines some of the merits of the existing models of relations and predicate transformers. Like relations, multirelations model specifications from initial to final state, and like predicate transformers, they can model two kinds of nondeterminism within a single framework. This is achieved by mapping input values to postconditions rather than output values. So the multirelational model is more expressive than that of relations, but not quite as transparent. Therefore we recommend its use only for the description of systems that cannot be expressed more simply using ordinary relations.

The two forms of nondeterminism in a multirelational specification represent two potentially conflicting interests that can be viewed in a number of different ways. Typically, we think of one of these interests as representing an angel and the other as a demon, where the angel is on our side but the demon is not. Not all systems can be uniquely categorised in this way however. For example, in the case of a game or resource sharing protocol involving two participants with opposing interests, either participant could be modelled as the angel, depending on the circumstances. Consequently, it is sometimes useful to associate the different interests in a specification with different agents, without necessarily labelling them as angelic or demonic. The number of agents involved in such a specification is not limited to two, but it can only be modelled as a multirelation if the allegiance of each agent is known, with the choices made by our allies treated as angelic, and those of our enemies as demonic. This observation is made in [BvW98], where the choices of multiple agents are first represented by indexed operators, but later categorised as simply angelic or demonic.

The concept of agents is also useful for distinguishing between the internal and external choices in a specification. We use this idea to motivate the need for a new notion of refinement: we claim that a refinement is equivalent to a reduction in internal choice or an increase in external choice. This leads to two opposing definitions of angelic and demonic refinement that are identical to those that have been suggested for relations [BvW98]. The choice of which one to use must be made at the start of program development and stay fixed throughout the design process. We have provided corresponding new notions of correctness and feasibility, and demonstrated that refinement is a correctness preserving operation. Feasibility is interpreted to mean the absence of internal choice, since external choices can remain in the program to be executed interactively at runtime.

Although none of the calculus presented so far is tied exclusively to the derivation of functional programs, this is one of the areas we plan to develop in the future. The central result that we wish to exploit concerns the extension of initial algebras from relations to multirelations [Moo92]. This result was originally expressed in the context of predicate transformers, but was difficult to apply in practice, because predicate transformers, unlike multirelations, model programs in reverse. The reason that we feel that this is an important result is that its counterpart for total functions and relations is one of the primary building blocks of the relational calculus of [BdM97]: it provides the key to the extension of the fold operator on regular datatypes of functional programming to relations. The corresponding extension of fold to multirelations has a very familiar form, unlike its predicate transformer equivalent. Associated with this definition is a universal property and fusion law that can be used in the calculation of programs.

Some of the areas that we are currently exploring as applications of this theory are security protocols, resource-sharing protocols and game theoretic mechanisms such as voting procedures. We hope to use multirelations to reason about such systems and derive implementations that meet various requirements. In the case of a game, this could be interpreted as the implementation of a winning strategy, and in the case of resource-sharing protocol, it could be a protocol that achieves fair division. In practice, few games actually have a winning strategy, but there are weaker game theoretic concepts that are desirable in an implementation. For example, Pauly [P03] proposes the existence of a subgame equilibrium as an alternative notion of correctness. Similarly, there are a number of different criteria that are desirable in a resource-sharing protocol.

References

[BvW98] Back, R. J. R. and von Wright, J. (1998) *Refinement Calculus: A Systematic Introduction.* Graduate Texts in Computer Science. New York: Springer-Verlag.

[BaH93] Roland Backhouse and Paul Hoogendijk (1993). Elements of a relational theory of datatypes. In Helmut Partsch Bernhard Möller and Steve Schumann, editors, *[FIP TC2/WG2.1 State-of-the-Art Report on Formal Program Development]*, LNCS 755, pages 7–42. Springer-Verlag, 1993.

[BCG01] Berlekamp, E.R., Conway, J. H. and Guy, R.K. (2001) *Winning Ways For Your Mathematical Plays* Second Edition. A. K. Peters Ltd.

[B90] Bird, R. S.(1990) A calculus of functions for program derivation. In Turner, D. A., editor, *Research Topics in Functional Programming*, University of Texas at Austin Year of Programming series, p 287-308, Addison-Wesley.

[BdM97] Bird, R. S. and de Moor, O. (1997)*Algebra of Programming.* Prentice Hall.

[DaP02] Davey, B. A. and Priestley, H. A. (2002) *Introduction to Lattices and Order (Second Edition).* Cambridge University Press.

[Daw97] C. Bryan Dawson. A better draft: Fair division of the talent pool. *College Mathematics Journal*, 28(2):82–88, March 1997.

[DiS90] Dijkstra, E. W. and Scholten, C. S. (1990) *Predicate Calculus and Program Semantics.* Springer Verlag.

[LyV92] Lynch, N and Vaandrager, F (1992) Forward and Backward Simulations for Timing-Based Systems. In J. W. de Bakker, W. P. de Roever, C. Huizing and G. Rozenberg, editors, Proceedings of real-Time: Theory in Practice (REX Workshop, Mook, The Netherlands, June 1991). *Lecture Notes in Computer Science* Vol 600, p 397-446. Springer-Verlag.

[Moo92] de Moor, O. (1992) Inductive Data Types for Predicate Transformers. *Information Processing Letters* 43(3): 113-117.

[Mor98] Morgan, C. C. (1998) *Programming from Specifications.* Prentice Hall.

[P03] Pauly, M. (2002) Programming and verifying Subgame Perfect Mechanisms. http://www.csc.liv.ac.uk/ pauly/

[R03]   Rewitzky, I. (2003) Binary Multirelations. In: Theory and Application of Relational Structures as Knowledge Instruments. (H de Swart, E Orlowska, G Schmidt, M Roubens (eds)).*Lecture Notes in Computer Science* 2929 : 259-274
[ScS88]   G. Schmidt and T. Ströhlein. (1988) *Relationen und Grafen.* Springer Verlag.
[W94]   Ward, N. T. E. (1994) *A Refinement Calculus for Nondeterministic Expressions.* www.dstc.monash.edu.au/staff/nigel-ward/nwthesis.pdf

Appendix

Proof of Lemma 11

$$x \; (M \mathbin{\mathring{,}} N) \; X$$
$\Rightarrow$ {Definition 10}
$$(\exists \, Y :: x \; M \; Y \wedge (\forall y : y \in Y : y \; N \; X))$$
$\Rightarrow$ {Definition 3}
$$(\exists \, Y :: (\exists \, Z : Z \in sp(x, M) : Z \subseteq Y \wedge (\forall y : y \in Y : y \; N \; X)))$$
$\Rightarrow$ {Logic}
$$(\exists \, Z : Z \in sp(x, M) : (\forall z : z \in Z : z \; N \; X))$$

Conversely,

$$(\exists \, Z : Z \in sp(x, M) : (\forall z : z \in Z : z \; N \; X))$$
$\Rightarrow$ {Definition 3}
$$(\exists \, Y :: x \; M \; Y \wedge (\forall y : y \in Y : y \; N \; X))$$
$\Rightarrow$ {Definition 10}
$$x \; (M \mathbin{\mathring{,}} N) \; X$$

$\square$

Proof of Lemma 13 The proof is by induction on n. For ease of reference, we will number the two assumptions in this lemma as follows

1. $M \mathbin{\mathring{,}} K = K \mathbin{\mathring{,}} N$
2. $N = K \mathbin{\mathring{,}} N$

Base case. Suppose $n = 1$, then

$$M \mathbin{\mathring{,}} K$$
$=$ {(1)}
$$K \mathbin{\mathring{,}} N$$
$=$ {(2)}
$$N$$

Inductive step. Suppose that $M^n \mathbin{\overset{\circ}{,}} K = N^n$, then

$$M^{n+1} \mathbin{\overset{\circ}{,}} K$$

$=$ {Definition of M^{n+1}}

$$M^n \mathbin{\overset{\circ}{,}} M \mathbin{\overset{\circ}{,}} K$$

$=$ {(1)}

$$M^n \mathbin{\overset{\circ}{,}} K \mathbin{\overset{\circ}{,}} N$$

$=$ {Inductive hypothesis}

$$N^n \mathbin{\overset{\circ}{,}} N$$

$=$ {Definition of N^{n+1}}

$$N^{n+1}$$

□

Proof of Lemma 15 That $M \subseteq M^+$ follows directly from the definition of M^+. For $M^+ \subseteq M \mathbin{\overset{\circ}{,}} M^*$, we have

$$x \; M^+ X$$

$\equiv$ {Definition 14}

$$(x, X) \in \bigcup \{M^m \mid m > 0\}$$

$\equiv$ {Logic}

$$(\exists m : m > 0 : x \; M^m \; X)$$

$\equiv$ {Taking $n = m - 1$; composition}

$$(\exists n : n \geq 0 : x(M \mathbin{\overset{\circ}{,}} M^n)X)$$

$\equiv$ {Definition 10}

$$(\exists n : n \geq 0 : (\exists Y :: x \; M \; Y \wedge (\forall y : y \in Y : y \; M^n \; X)))$$

$\equiv$ {Logic}

$$(\exists Y :: x \; M \; Y \wedge (\exists n : n \geq 0 : (\forall y : y \in Y : y \; M^n \; X)))$$

$\Rightarrow$ {Logic}

$$(\exists Y :: x \; M \; Y \wedge (\forall y : y \in Y : (\exists n : n \geq 0 : y \; M^n \; X)))$$

$\equiv$ {Logic; Definition 14}

$$(\exists Y :: x \; M \; Y \wedge (\forall y : y \in Y : y \; M^* \; X))$$

$\equiv$ {Definition 10}

$$x \; (M \mathbin{\overset{\circ}{,}} M^*) \; X$$

□

Proof of Lemma 20 The proof is by induction on n.

Base case. By the definition of *round*, the result holds if $n = 1$.

Inductive step. Suppose that

$$x \; round^n \; X \quad \Leftrightarrow \quad \{y, y + 1\} \subseteq X \vee \{y - 1, y\} \subseteq X$$

where $y = x - 3n$.

$\qquad x \; round^{n+1} \; X$

$\Leftrightarrow \quad$ {Definition of $round^{n+1}$}

$\qquad x \; (round^n \mathbin{\overset{\circ}{\scriptstyle 9}} round) \; X$

$\Leftrightarrow \quad$ {Lemma 11}

$\qquad (\exists\, Z : Z \in sp(x, round^n) : (\forall\, z : z \in Z : z \; round \; X))$

$\Leftrightarrow \quad$ {Inductive hypothesis}

$\qquad (\exists\, Z : Z \in \{\{y, y+1\}, \{y-1, y\}\} : (\forall\, z : z \in Z : z \; round \; X))$

$\Leftrightarrow \quad$ {logic}

$\qquad ((y-1) \; round \; X \wedge y \; round \; X) \vee (y \; round \; X \wedge (y+1) \; round \; X)$

$\Leftrightarrow \quad$ {Distributive law, commutativity}

$\qquad y \; round \; X \wedge ((y-1) \; round \; X \vee (y+1) \; round \; X)$

$\Leftrightarrow \quad$ {Definition of $round$}

$\qquad (\; \{y-2, y-3\} \subseteq X \vee \{y-3, y-4\} \subseteq X \;) \wedge$
$\qquad (\; \{y-1, y-2\} \subseteq X \vee \{y-2, y-3\} \subseteq X \quad \vee$
$\qquad \;\;\; \{y-3, y-4\} \subseteq X \vee \{y-4, y-5\} \subseteq X \;)$

$\Leftrightarrow \quad$ {Absorption}

$\qquad (\{y-2, y-3\} \subseteq X \vee \{y-3, y-4\} \subseteq X)$

$\Leftrightarrow \quad$ {Let $w = x - 3(n+1)$}

$\qquad (\{w, w+1\} \subseteq X \vee \{w-1, w\} \subseteq X)$

$\qquad\qquad\qquad\qquad\qquad\qquad\qquad\qquad\qquad\qquad\qquad\quad \square$

Lazy Kleene Algebra

Bernhard Möller

Institut für Informatik, Universität Augsburg
Universitätsstr. 14, D-86135 Augsburg, Germany
moeller@informatik.uni-augsburg.de

Abstract. We propose a relaxation of Kleene algebra by giving up strictness and right-distributivity of composition. This allows the subsumption of Dijkstra's computation calculus, Cohen's omega algebra and von Wright's demonic refinement algebra. Moreover, by adding domain and codomain operators we can also incorporate modal operators. Finally, it is shown that predicate transformers form lazy Kleene algebras again, the disjunctive and conjunctive ones even lazy Kleene algebras with an omega operation.

1 Introduction

Kleene algebra (KA) provides a convenient and powerful algebraic axiomatization of the basic control constructs composition, choice and iteration. In its standard version, composition is required to distribute over choice in both arguments; also, 0 is required to be both a left and right annihilator. Algebraically this is captured by the notion of an idempotent semiring or briefly *I-semiring*.

Models include formal languages under concatenation, relations under standard composition and sets of graph paths under path concatenation.

The idempotent semiring addition induces a partial order that can be thought of as the approximation order or as (angelic) refinement. Addition then coincides with the binary supremum operator, i.e., every semiring is also an upper semilattice. Moreover, 0 is the least element and thus plays the rôle of $\perp$ in denotational semantics.

If the semilattice is even a complete lattice, the least and greatest fixpoint operators allow definitions of the finite and infinite iteration operators $*$ and $^\omega$, resp. However, to be less restrictive, we do *not* assume completeness and rather add, as is customary, $*$ and $^\omega$ as operators of their own with particular axioms.

The requirement that 0 be an annihilator on both sides of composition makes the algebra *strict*. This prohibits a natural treatment of lazy computation systems in which e.g. infinite sequences of states may occur. Therefore we study a "one-sided" variant of KAs in which composition is strict in one argument only. This treatment fits well with systems such as the calculus of finite and infinite streams which is also used in J. Lukkien's operational semantics for the guarded command language [15, 16] or R. Dijkstra's computation calculus [8, 9]. Inspired by the latter papers, we obtain a very handy algebraic characterization of finite and infinite elements that also appears already in early work

D. Kozen (Ed.): MPC 2004, LNCS 3125, pp. 252–273, 2004.

on so-called quemirings by Elgot [10]. In addition, we integrate the theory with Cohen's ω-algebra [4] and von Wright's demonic refinement algebra [21, 22].

There is some choice in what to postulate for the right argument of composition. Whereas the above-mentioned authors stipulate binary or even general positive disjunctivity, we investigate how far one gets if only isotonicity is required. This allows general isotone predicate transformers as models.

Fortunately, our lazy KAs are still powerful enough to admit the incorporation of domain and codomain operators and hence an algebraic treatment of modal logic. Of course, the possibility of nontrivial infinite computations leads to additional terms in the corresponding assertion logic; these terms disappear when only finite elements are considered.

Altogether, we obtain a quite lean framework that unites assertion logic with algebraic reasoning while admitting infinite computations. The axiomatization is simpler and more general than that of von Karger's sequential calculus [11].

2   Left Semirings

Definition 2.1 A *left (or lazy) semiring*, briefly an *L-semiring*, is a quintuple $(K, +, 0, \cdot, 1)$ with the following properties:

1. $(K, +, 0)$ is a commutative monoid.
2. $(K, \cdot, 1)$ is a monoid.
3. The $\cdot$ operation distributes over $+$ in its left argument and is *left-strict*:

$$(a + b) \cdot c = a \cdot c + b \cdot c , \qquad 0 \cdot a = 0 .$$

Definition 2.2 An *idempotent* left semiring, or briefly *IL-semiring* is an L-semiring $(K, +, 0, \cdot, 1)$ with idempotent addition in which $\cdot$ is right-isotone:

$$a + a = a \ \wedge \ (b \le c \Rightarrow a \cdot b \le a \cdot c) ,$$

where the *natural order* $\le$ on K is given by $a \le b \overset{\text{def}}{\Leftrightarrow} a + b = b$.

Note that left-isotonicity of $\cdot$ follows from its left-distributivity. Moreover, 0 is the least element w.r.t. the natural order. The left semiring structure without the requirement of right-isotonicity is also at the core of process algebra frameworks (see e.g. [3]) where δ (inaction) plays the rôle of 0. Since, however, we will make essential use of right-isotonicity, only few of our results will carry over to that setting.

By isotonicity, $\cdot$ is universally superdisjunctive and universally subconjunctive in both arguments; we state these properties for the right argument:

$$a \cdot (\sqcup L) \ge \sqcup \{a \cdot l : l \in L\} \qquad a \cdot (\sqcap L) \le \sqcap \{a \cdot l : l \in L\} .$$

Analogous properties hold for the left argument.

From this we can conclude a weak form of right distributivity for the left hand side of inequations:

Lemma 2.3 *For $a, b, c, d \in K$ we have*

$$b + c \leq d \;\Rightarrow\; a \cdot b + a \cdot c \leq a \cdot d \;. \tag{1}$$

Proof. By isotonicity and superdisjunctivity we get

$$b + c \leq d \;\Rightarrow\; a \cdot (b + c) \leq a \cdot d \;\Rightarrow\; a \cdot b + a \cdot c \leq a \cdot d \;. \qquad \square$$

Definition 2.4   1. A function between partial orders is called *universally disjunctive* if it preserves all existing suprema. A binary operation is called *universally left-(right-)disjunctive* if it is universally disjunctive in its left (right) argument.
  2. An IL-semiring $(K, +, 0, \cdot, 1)$ is *bounded* if K has a greatest element $\top$ w.r.t. the natural order. It is *complete* if the semilattice $(K, \leq)$ is a complete lattice and $\cdot$ is universally left-disjunctive.
  3. Finally, K is *Boolean* if $(K, \leq)$ is a *Boolean algebra*, i.e., a complemented distributive lattice. Every Boolean IL-semiring is bounded.

Now we look at the composition from the other end.

Definition 2.5 For a binary operation $\cdot : K \times K \to K$ we define its *mirror operation* $\breve{\cdot} : K \times K \to K$ by $x \,\breve{\cdot}\, y = y \cdot x$. We call $(K, +, 0, \cdot, 1)$ an *(idempotent) right semiring* (briefly *(I)R-semiring*) if $(K, +, 0, \breve{\cdot}, 1)$ is an (I)L-semiring. The notions of a *complete* and *Boolean* (I)R-semiring are defined analogously. If K is both an (I)L-semiring and an (I)R-semiring it is called an *(I-)semiring*. The notions of a *complete* and *Boolean* (I-)semiring are defined analogously. A complete I-semiring is also called a *standard Kleene algebra* [5] or a *quantale* [19].

Note, however, that in (I-)semirings composition is also right-strict; hence these structures are not very interesting if one wants to model lazy computation systems. Prominent I-semirings are the algebra of binary relations under relational composition and the algebra of formal languages under concatenation or join (fusion product).

3   Particular IL-Semirings

We now introduce our two main models of the notion of IL-semiring. Both of them are based on finite and infinite strings over an alphabet A. Next to their classical interpretation as characters, the elements of A may e.g. be thought of as states in a computation system, or, in connection with graph algorithms, as graph nodes. Then, as usual, A^* is the set of all finite words over A; the empty word is denoted by ε. Moreover, A^ω is the set of all infinite words over A. We set $A^\infty \stackrel{\text{def}}{=} A^* \cup A^\omega$. The length of word s is denoted by $|s|$. By $\bullet$ we denote concatenation, where $s \bullet t \stackrel{\text{def}}{=} s$ if $|s| = \infty$. A *language* over A is a subset of A^∞. As usual, we identify a singleton language with its only element. For language $S \subseteq A^\infty$ we define its infinite and finite parts by

$$\inf S \stackrel{\text{def}}{=} \{s \in S : |s| = \infty\} \;,$$
$$\operatorname{fin} S \stackrel{\text{def}}{=} S - \inf S \;.$$

Definition 3.1 The algebra WOR $= (\mathcal{P}(A^\infty), \cup, \emptyset, \bullet, \varepsilon)$ is obtained by extending $\bullet$ to languages in the following way:

$$S \bullet T \stackrel{\text{def}}{=} \inf S \cup \{s \bullet t : s \in \mathsf{fin}\, S \wedge t \in T\} \ .$$

Note that in general $S \bullet T \neq \{s \bullet t : s \in S \wedge t \in T\}$; using the set on the right hand side as the definition of $S \bullet T$ one would obtain a right-strict operation. With the definition given, we have $S \bullet \emptyset = \inf S$ and hence $S \bullet \emptyset = \emptyset$ iff $\inf S = \emptyset$. It is straightforward to show that WOR is an IL-semiring. The algebra is well-known from the classical theory of ω-languages (see e.g. [20] for a recent survey).

Next to this model we will use a second one that has a more refined view of composition and hence allows more interesting modal operators.

Definition 3.2 For words $s, t \in A^\infty$ we define their *join* or *fusion product* $s \bowtie t$ as a language-valued operation:

$$s \bowtie t \stackrel{\text{def}}{=} \begin{cases} s & \text{if } |s| = \infty \ , \\ init(s) \bullet (last(s) \cap head(t)) \bullet tail(t) & \text{otherwise} \ , \end{cases}$$

where $head(\varepsilon) \stackrel{\text{def}}{=} tail(\varepsilon) \stackrel{\text{def}}{=} init(\varepsilon) \stackrel{\text{def}}{=} last(\varepsilon) \stackrel{\text{def}}{=} \varepsilon$, viewed as a singleton language.

The definition entails $\varepsilon \bowtie \varepsilon = \varepsilon$ and $s \bowtie t = \emptyset$ when $last(s) \neq head(t)$, i.e., a non-empty finite word s can be joined with a non-empty word t iff the last letter of s coincides with the first one of t; only one copy of that letter is kept in the joined word. Since we view the infinite words as streams of computations, we call the model based on this composition operation STR.

Definition 3.3 The algebra STR $\stackrel{\text{def}}{=} (\mathcal{P}(A^\infty), \cup, \emptyset, \bowtie, A \cup \varepsilon)$ is given by extending $\bowtie$ to languages in the following way:

$$S \bowtie T \stackrel{\text{def}}{=} \inf S \cup \{s \bowtie t : s \in \mathsf{fin}\, S \wedge t \in T\} \ .$$

Analogously to above, we have $S \bowtie \emptyset = \inf S$ and hence $S \bowtie \emptyset = \emptyset$ iff $\inf S = \emptyset$. It is straightforward to show that STR is an IL-semiring. Its subalgebra $(\mathcal{P}(A^\infty - \varepsilon), \cup, \emptyset, \bowtie, A)$ of nonempty words is at the heart of the papers by Lukkien [15, 16] and Dijkstra [8, 9].

Both WOR and STR are even Boolean IL-semirings. Further IL-semirings are provided by predicate transformer algebras (see below).

4 Terminating and Non-terminating Elements

As stated, we want to model computation systems in such a way that the operator $\cdot$ represents sequential composition and 0 stands for the totally useless system **abort** which does not make any progress and hence may also be viewed as never terminating.

As we are interested in treating finite and infinite computations uniformly, we need to characterize these notions algebraically. This will be achieved using the above properties of the finite and infinite parts of a language.

Operationally, an infinite, non-terminating computation a cannot be followed by any further computation. Algebraically this means that composing a with any other element on the "infinite side" has no effect, i.e., just a again results. We write temporal succession from left to right, i.e., $a \cdot b$ means "first perform computation a and then b". Therefore we give the following

Definition 4.1 Consider an IL-semiring $(K, +, 0, \cdot, 1)$. An element $a \in K$ is called *non-terminating* or *infinite* if it is a left zero w.r.t. composition, i.e., if

$$\forall\, b \in K : a \cdot b = a \,.$$

The set of all non-terminating elements is denoted by N.

From the left-strictness of $\cdot$ we immediately get $0 \in \mathsf{N}$. Moreover, we have the following characterization of non-terminating elements:

Lemma 4.2 $a \in \mathsf{N} \Leftrightarrow a \cdot 0 = a$.

Proof. ($\Rightarrow$) Choose $b = 0$ in the definition of N.
($\Leftarrow$) Using the assumption, associativity, left strictness and the assumption again, we calculate $a \cdot b = a \cdot 0 \cdot b = a \cdot 0 = a$. $\square$

By this characterization N coincides with the set of fixpoints of the isotone function $\lambda z \,.\, z \cdot 0$. Hence, if K is even a complete lattice, by Tarski's fixpoint theorem N is a complete lattice again.

Next we state two closure properties of N.

Lemma 4.3 *Denote by $\cdot$ also the pointwise extension of $\cdot$ to subsets of K.*

1. *An arbitrary computation followed by a non-terminating one is non-terminating, i.e., $K \cdot \mathsf{N} \subseteq \mathsf{N}$ (and hence $K \cdot \mathsf{N} = \mathsf{N}$).*
2. *If $\cdot$ is universally left-disjunctive then N is closed under $\bigsqcup$.*

Proof. 1. Consider $a \in K$ and $b \in \mathsf{N}$. Then $(a \cdot b) \cdot 0 = a \cdot (b \cdot 0) = a \cdot b$. The inclusion $\mathsf{N} \subseteq K \cdot \mathsf{N}$ follows by $1 \in K$.
2. Consider $L \subseteq \mathsf{N}$ such that $\bigsqcup L$ exists. Then, by the assumptions, $(\bigsqcup L) \cdot 0 = \bigsqcup (L \cdot 0) = \bigsqcup L$. $\square$

So the supremum in N coincides with the one in the overall algebra K. Now we relate the notions of right-strictness and termination.

Lemma 4.4 *The following properties are equivalent:*

1. *The $\cdot$ operation is right-strict.*
2. *$|\mathsf{N}| = 1$.*
3. *$\top \cdot 0 = 0$ (provided K is bounded).*

Proof. $(1 \Rightarrow 2)$ It follows that $\mathsf{N} = \{0\}$.
$(2 \Rightarrow 3)$ Since $0 \in \mathsf{N}$ and $\top \cdot 0 \in \mathsf{N}$ we get $\top \cdot 0 = 0$.
$(3 \Rightarrow 1)$ For arbitrary $a \in K$ we have, by isotonicity, $a \cdot 0 \leq \top \cdot 0 = 0$.   □

Next we show

Lemma 4.5 *1.* $\mathsf{N} = \{a \cdot 0 : a \in K\}$.
2. $b \cdot 0$ *is the greatest element of* $\mathsf{N}(b) \stackrel{\text{def}}{=} \{a \in \mathsf{N} : a \leq b\}$.
3. *If* K *is bounded then* $\top \cdot 0$ *is the greatest element of* N. *In particular,* $\top \cdot 0 = \sqcup \mathsf{N}$.
4. *If* N *is downward closed and* $\top \in \mathsf{N}$ *then* $1 = 0$ *and hence* $|K| = 1$.

Proof. 1. $(\subseteq)$ Immediate from the definition of N.
  $(\supseteq)$ Assume $z = a \cdot 0$. Then $z \cdot 0 = a \cdot 0 \cdot 0 = a \cdot 0 = z$.
2. First, assume $a \in \mathsf{N} \wedge a \leq b$. Then by right-isotonicity of $\cdot$ we have $a = a \cdot 0 \leq b \cdot 0$. So $b \cdot 0$ is an upper bound of $\mathsf{N}(b)$.
   Second, by 1. we have $b \cdot 0 \in \mathsf{N}$. By right-neutrality of 1 and isotonicity we get $b \cdot 0 \leq b \cdot 1 = b$, i.e., $b \cdot 0 \in \mathsf{N}(b)$, which shows the claim.
3. Immediate from 2.
4. By downward closure, $1 \in \mathsf{N}$, hence $1 = 1 \cdot 0 = 0$ by neutrality of 1.   □

Property 3 of this lemma says that $\top \cdot 0$ is an adequate algebraic representation of the collection of all non-terminating elements of a bounded IL-semiring. This is used extensively in [8,9], where $\top \cdot 0$ is called the eternal part of K. However, we want to manage without the assumption of completeness or boundedness and therefore prefer to work with the set N rather than with its greatest element.

By Property 3 we may call $b \cdot 0$ the *non-terminating* or *infinite part* of b. This leads to the following

Definition 4.6 We call an element a *finite* if its infinite part is trivial, i.e., if $a \cdot 0 = 0$. The set of all finite elements is denoted by F. By this definition $0 \in \mathsf{F}$. To mirror our operational understanding we call an element a *terminating* if a is finite and $a \neq 0$. We set $\mathsf{T} \stackrel{\text{def}}{=} \mathsf{F} - \{0\}$.

A number of properties of F and T are collected in

Lemma 4.7 *1.* F *is downward closed.*
2. $1 \in \mathsf{F}$. *If* $1 \neq 0$ *then* $1 \in \mathsf{T}$ (skip *is terminating*).
3. *For non-empty* $S \subseteq K$ *we have* $S \subseteq \mathsf{F} \Leftrightarrow S \cdot \{0\} = \{0\}$.
4. $K \cdot \mathsf{F} = K = \mathsf{F} \cdot K$.
5. $\mathsf{F} + \mathsf{F} \subseteq \mathsf{F}$ *and* $\mathsf{T} + \mathsf{T} \subseteq \mathsf{T}$ (*finite and terminating computations are closed under choice*). *Since* $+$ *is idempotent we have even equality in both cases. If* $\cdot$ *is universally left-disjunctive then* F *is closed under arbitrary joins and* T *under non-empty ones.*
6. $\mathsf{F} \cdot \mathsf{F} \subseteq \mathsf{F}$ (*finite computations are closed under composition*). *By neutrality of 1 we have even equality.* T *need not be closed under composition.*

Proof. 1. Immediate from isotonicity.
2. Immediate from left-neutrality of 1.
3. Immediate from the definition of F.
4. By left-neutrality of 1 we get $K = 1 \cdot K \subseteq F \cdot K$. Similarly, by right-neutrality $K \subseteq K \cdot F$. The reverse inclusions are trivial.
5. Immediate from distributivity/disjunctivity.
6. By 2. we have $F \cdot F \cdot \{0\} = F \cdot \{0\} = \{0\}$, and 2. again shows the claim. $\square$

Notation. Although we do not assume a general meet operation $\sqcap$, we will sometimes use the formula $y \sqcap z = 0$; it is an abbreviation for $\forall\, u\,.\, u \leq y \wedge u \leq z \Rightarrow u = 0$.

With the help of this, we can describe the interaction between F and N.

Lemma 4.8 *1.* $N \cap F = \{0\}$.
2. If N is downward closed, then for $x \in N$ and $y \in F$ we have $x \sqcap y = 0$.
3. Assume $x \in N \wedge y \in F$. Then $x + y \in N \Leftrightarrow y \leq x$. Hence if N is downward closed, $x + y \in N \Leftrightarrow y = 0$.

Proof. 1. If $x \in N \cap F$ then $x = x \cdot 0 = 0$.
2. Suppose $z \leq x \wedge z \leq y$ for some $z \in K$. Then the assumption and Lemma 4.7.1 imply $z \in N \cap F$, hence $z = 0$ by 1.
3. First we note that, by the assumption,

$$(x + y) \cdot 0 = x \cdot 0 + y \cdot 0 = x + 0 = x \,. \quad (*)$$

($\Rightarrow$) If $(x + y) \cdot 0 = x + y$ then by $(*)$ $x = x + y$, i.e., $y \leq x$.
($\Leftarrow$) If $y \leq x$ then $x = x + y$ and hence $x + y = x = (x + y) \cdot 0$ by $(*)$. $\square$

5   Separated IL-Semirings

5.1   Motivation

Although our definitions of finite and nonterminating elements have led to quite a number of useful properties, we are not fully satisfied, since the axiomatization does not lead to full symmetry of the two notions, whereas in actual computation systems they behave much more symmetrically. Moreover, a number of other desirable properties do not follow from the current axiomatization either. We list the desiderata:

– While $\inf a \stackrel{\text{def}}{=} a \cdot 0$ gives us the nonterminating part of a, we have no corresponding operator fin that yields the finite part of a. Next, inf is disjunctive; by symmetry we would expect that for fin as well.
– The set F of finite elements is downward closed, whereas we cannot guarantee that for the set N of nonterminating elements. However, since $a \leq b$ means that a has at most as many choices as b, one would expect a to be nonterminating if b is: removing choices between infinite computations should not produce finite computations. Then, except for 0, the finite and nonterminating elements would lie completely separately.
– Every element should be decomposable into its finite and nonterminating part.

The task is now to achieve this without using a too strong restriction on the semiring (such as requiring it to be a distributive or even a Boolean lattice).

5.2   Kernel Operations

To prepare the treatment, we first state a few properties of kernel operations that will be useful both for partitioning functions and in connection with tests in the next section.

Definition 5.1 A *kernel* operation is an isotone, contractive and idempotent function $f : K \to K$ from some partial order $(K, \leq)$ into itself. The latter two properties spell out to $f(x) \leq x$ and $f(f(x)) = f(x)$ for all $x \in K$.

Example 5.2 It is straightforward to see that multiplication by an idempotent element and hence, in particular, inf, is a kernel operation.   □

It is well-known that the image $f(K)$ of a kernel operation f consists exactly of the fixpoints of f.

Lemma 5.3 *Let* $f : K \to K$ *be a kernel operation.*

1. $f(x) = \sqcup \{y \in f(K) : y \leq x\}$.
2. *If* K *has a least element* 0 *then* $f(0) = 0$.
3. *If* K *is an upper semilattice with join operation* $+$ *then* $f(f(x) + f(y)) = f(x) + f(y)$, *i.e.,* $f(K)$ *is closed under* $+$.

Proof. 1. By isotonicity and the above fixpoint property, $f(x)$ is an upper bound of $S \stackrel{\text{def}}{=} \{y \in f(K) : y \leq x\}$. But $f(x) \in S$, since $f(x) \leq x$, and so $f(x)$ is the supremum of S.

2. Immediate from contractivity of f.

3. ($\leq$) follows by contractivity of f.
   ($\geq$) By isotonicity and idempotence of f,

$$f(f(x) + f(y)) \geq f(f(x)) + f(f(y)) = f(x) + f(y) .$$

□

Lemma 5.4 *For a kernel operation* $f : K \to K$ *the following two statements are equivalent:*

1. $f(K)$ *is downward closed.*
2. *For all* $a, b \in K$ *such that* $a \sqcap b$ *exists, also* $f(a) \sqcap b$ *and* $f(a) \sqcap f(b)$ *exist and* $f(a \sqcap b) = f(a) \sqcap b = f(a) \sqcap f(b)$.

Proof. First we show that the first equation in 2. implies the second one. Assume $f(a \sqcap b) = f(a) \sqcap b$ for all a, b such that $a \sqcap b$ exists. Then by idempotence of f we get, using this assumption twice,

$$f(a \sqcap b) = f(f(a \sqcap b)) = f(f(a) \sqcap b) = f(a) \sqcap f(b) .$$

(1. ⇒ 2.) By isotonicity and contractivity of f we have $f(a \sqcap b) \leq f(b) \leq b$ and $f(a \sqcap b) \leq f(a)$. Consider now an arbitrary lower bound c for $f(a)$ and b. Then by downward closure of $f(K)$ also $c \in f(K)$, i.e., $c = f(c)$. Moreover, $c \leq f(a) \leq a$ by contractivity of f. Therefore $c \leq a \sqcap b$ and hence $c = f(c) \leq f(a \sqcap b)$ by isotonicity of f.

(2. ⇒ 1.) Consider an $a \in f(K)$ and $b \leq a$, i.e., $b = a \sqcap b$. Then by assumption $f(b) = f(a \sqcap b) = f(a) \sqcap b = a \sqcap b = b$ and hence $b \in f(K)$ as well.   □

Corollary 5.5 *Suppose that* $f : K \to K$ *is a kernel operation and* $f(K)$ *is downward closed.*

1. *If* $a, b \in K$ *with* $b \leq a$ *then* $f(b) = f(a) \sqcap b$.
2. *If* K *is bounded then* $f(a) = a \sqcap f(\top)$ *for all* $a \in K$.

5.3   Partitions

We now study the decomposition of elements into well-separated parts. For this, we assume a partial order $(K, \leq)$ that is an upper semilattice with join operation $+$ and a least element 0.

Definition 5.6 Consider a pair of isotone functions $f_1, f_2 : K \to K$. Let f range over f_1, f_2 and set $\tilde{f}_1 \overset{\text{def}}{=} f_2, \tilde{f}_2 \overset{\text{def}}{=} f_1$. Note that $\tilde{\tilde{f}} = f$. The pair is said to *weakly partition* K if for all $a \in K$ we have

$$f(a) + \tilde{f}(a) = a \, , \qquad \text{(WP1)} \qquad \tilde{f}(f(a)) = 0 \, . \qquad \text{(WP2)}$$

Of course, the concept could easily be generalized to systems consisting of more than two functions. Let us prove a few useful consequences of this definition. Note that by our notational convention also $f(\tilde{f}(a)) = 0$.

Lemma 5.7 *Let* f *and* $\tilde{f}$ *weakly partition* K.

1. f *is a kernel operation.*
2. $x \in f(K) \Leftrightarrow x = f(x) \Leftrightarrow \tilde{f}(x) = 0$.
3. *The image set* $f(K)$ *is downward closed.*
4. $f(K) \cap \tilde{f}(K) = \{0\}$.
5. *For* $y \in f(K)$ *and* $z \in \tilde{f}(K)$ *we have* $y \sqcap z = 0$. *In particular,* $f(x) \sqcap \tilde{f}(x) = 0$ *for all* $x \in K$.

Proof.   1. By assumption f is isotone. Moreover, by (WP1) we have $f(x) \leq x$. Idempotence is shown, using (WP1) and (WP2), by

$$f(x) = f(f(x)) + \tilde{f}(f(x)) = f(f(x)) + 0 = f(f(x)) \, .$$

2. The first equivalence holds, since by 1. f is a kernel operation. For the second one we calculate, using (WP1) and (WP2),

$$x = f(x) \Rightarrow \tilde{f}(x) = \tilde{f}(f(x)) = 0 \Rightarrow x = f(x) + \tilde{f}(x) = f(x) \, .$$

3. Assume $z \leq f(y)$ for some $y \in K$. By isotonicity of $\tilde{f}$ then $\tilde{f}(z) \leq \tilde{f}(f(y)) = 0$ and hence, again by 2., also $z \in f(K)$.
4. Assume $x \in f(K) \cap \tilde{f}(K)$. By 2. then $x = f(x)$ and $f(x) = 0$ which shows the claim.
5. For a lower bound z of $x \in f(K)$ and $y \in \tilde{f}(K)$ we get by 3. and 4. that $z \in f(K) \cap \tilde{f}(K) = \{0\}$.   □

The last property means that the f_i decompose every element into two parts that have only a trivial overlap; in other words $f_1(a)$ and $f_2(a)$ have to be relative pseudocomplements of each other.

Although weak partitions already enjoy quite a number of useful properties, they do not guarantee uniqueness of the decomposition. Hence we need the following stronger notion.

Definition 5.8 A pair of functions $f_1, f_2 : K \to K$ is said to *strongly partition* K if they weakly partition K and are additive, i.e., satisfy $f_i(a+b) = f_i(a)+f_i(b)$.

Lemma 5.9 *Let $f_1, f_2 : K \to K$ strongly partition K.*

1. $f(\tilde{f}(a) + b) = f(b)$, *i.e., $\tilde{f}$-parts of elements are ignored by f.*
2. *f is uniquely determined by $\tilde{f}$, i.e.*

$$a = x + \tilde{f}(a) \wedge x \in f(K) \Rightarrow x = f(a) .$$

Proof. 1. By additivity and (WP2),
$$f(\tilde{f}(a) + b) = f(\tilde{f}(a)) + f(b) = 0 + f(b) = f(b).$$
2. By the assumption and 1. we get $f(a) = f(x + \tilde{f}(a)) = f(x) = x$.   □

Property 2. is equivalent to additivity in this context: applying (WP1) twice, then 1. twice and then Lemma 5.3.3, we obtain

$$f(a + b) = f(f(a) + \tilde{f}(a) + f(b) + \tilde{f}(b)) =$$
$$f(f(a) + f(b)) = f(a) + f(b) .$$

5.4   Separating Finite and Infinite Elements

Definition 5.10 An IL-semiring K is called *separated* if, in addition to the function inf $: K \to K$ defined by inf $x \stackrel{\text{def}}{=} x \cdot 0$, there is a function fin $: K \to K$ that together with inf strongly partitions K and satisfies fin $K = \mathsf{F}$.

Example 5.11 In [10] the related notion of *quemiring* is studied, although no motivation in terms of finite and infinite elements is given. A quemiring is axiomatized as a left semiring in which each element a has a unique decomposition $a = a\P + a \cdot 0$ such that $\P$ distributes over $+$ and multiplication by an image under $\P$ is also right-distributive. So $\P$ corresponds to our fin-operator. However, the calculation

$$a \cdot (b + c) = (a\P + a \cdot 0) \cdot (b + c) = a\P \cdot (b + c) + a \cdot 0 \cdot (b + c) =$$
$$a\P \cdot b + a\P \cdot c + a \cdot 0 = a\P \cdot b + a\P \cdot c + a \cdot 0 \cdot b + a \cdot 0 \cdot c =$$
$$(a\P + a \cdot 0) \cdot b + (a\P + a \cdot 0) \cdot c = a \cdot b + a \cdot c$$

shows that a quemiring actually is a semiring and hence not too interesting from the perspective of the present paper. □

Example 5.12 Every Boolean IL-semiring K (and hence, in particular, WOR and STR) is separated. To see this, we first observe that for arbitrary $b \in K$ the functions

$$f_1(x) \stackrel{\text{def}}{=} x \sqcap b , \qquad f_2(x) \stackrel{\text{def}}{=} x \sqcap \bar{b} ,$$

strongly partition K, as is easily checked. In particular, by Lemma 5.7 they are kernel operations and hence satisfy $f_i(x) = x \sqcap f_i(\top)$ by Corollary 5.5.2.

Choosing now $b = \top \cdot 0$ we obtain $\inf x = x \sqcap \top \cdot 0$. Therefore we define $\operatorname{fin} x \stackrel{\text{def}}{=} x \sqcap \overline{\top \cdot 0}$. Then $\operatorname{fin} K = \mathsf{F}$ follows from Lemma 5.7 and $x \in \mathsf{F} \Leftrightarrow \inf x = 0$.

It follows that for Boolean K we have

$$x \in \mathsf{N} \Leftrightarrow x \le \top \cdot 0 , \qquad x \in \mathsf{F} \Leftrightarrow x \le \overline{\top \cdot 0} .$$

This was used extensively in [8, 9].

For Boolean K we have also

$$\inf \top = \inf (1 + \bar{1}) = \inf 1 + \inf \bar{1} = \inf \bar{1} .$$

□

Example 5.13 Now we give an example of an IL-semiring that is *not* separable. The carrier set is $K = \{0, 1, 2\}$ with natural ordering $0 \le 1 \le 2$. Composition is given by the equations

$$0 \cdot x = 0 , \qquad 1 \cdot x = x , \qquad 2 \cdot x = 2 .$$

Then $\mathsf{N} = \{0, 2\}$ and $\mathsf{F} = \{0, 1\}$, so that N is not downward closed as it would need to be by Lemma 5.7 if K were (weakly) separable. □

In the presence of a left residual we can give a closed definition of fin.

Lemma 5.14 *Assume an IL-semiring K with a left residuation operation $/$ satisfying the Galois connection*

$$y \le x/z \Leftrightarrow y \cdot z \le x .$$

If K is separated then $\operatorname{fin} x = x \sqcap 0/0$.

Proof. By separation and Lemma 5.3.1, $\operatorname{fin} x = \bigsqcup \{y \in \mathsf{F} : y \le x\}$. Therefore, by downward closure of F

$$y \le \operatorname{fin} x \Leftrightarrow y \in \mathsf{F} \wedge y \le x \Leftrightarrow y \cdot 0 \le 0 \wedge y \le x \Leftrightarrow y \le 0/0 \wedge y \le x .$$

Now the claim follows by the universal characterization of meet. □

We conclude this section by listing a few properties concerning the behaviour of inf and fin w.r.t. composition.

Lemma 5.15 *Assume a separated IL-semiring K.*

1. $a \cdot b = \inf a + \operatorname{fin} a \cdot b$.
2. $\inf (a \cdot b) = \inf a + \operatorname{fin} a \cdot \inf b$.
3. $\operatorname{fin} (a \cdot b) = \operatorname{fin} (\operatorname{fin} a \cdot b) \geq \operatorname{fin} a \cdot \operatorname{fin} b$. *If K is right-distributive, the latter inequation can be strengthened to an equality.*

Proof. 1. $a \cdot b = (\inf a + \operatorname{fin} a) \cdot b = \inf a \cdot b + \operatorname{fin} a \cdot b = \inf a + \operatorname{fin} a \cdot b$.
2. $\inf (a \cdot b) = a \cdot b \cdot 0 = a \cdot \inf b = (\inf a + \operatorname{fin} a) \cdot \inf b = \inf a \cdot \inf b + \operatorname{fin} a \cdot \inf b = \inf a + \operatorname{fin} a \cdot \inf b$.
3. By 1. and isotonicity,

$$\operatorname{fin} (a \cdot b) = \operatorname{fin} (\inf a + \operatorname{fin} a \cdot b) = \operatorname{fin} (\operatorname{fin} a \cdot b) = \operatorname{fin} (\operatorname{fin} a \cdot (\inf b + \operatorname{fin} b)) \geq$$
$$\operatorname{fin} (\operatorname{fin} a \cdot \inf b) + \operatorname{fin} (\operatorname{fin} a \cdot \operatorname{fin} b) = \operatorname{fin} a \cdot \operatorname{fin} b .$$

If K is right-distributive, the fourth step and hence the whole calculation can be strengthened to equalities. □

6 Iteration – Lazy Kleene Algebras

The central operation that moves a semiring to a Kleene algebra (KA) [5] is the star that models arbitrary but finite iteration. Fortunately, we can re-use the conventional definition [12] for our setting of IL-semirings. In connection with laziness, the second essential operation is the infinite iteration of an element. This has been studied intensively in the theory of ω-languages [20]. A recent algebraic account is provided by Cohen's ω-algebras [4] and von Wright's demonic refinement algebra [21, 22]. However, both assume right-distributivity, Cohen even right-strictness of composition. While safety analysis of infinite computations is also possible using star only [14], omega iteration serves to describe liveness aspects (see e.g. [17]).

Definition 6.1 A *left* or *lazy Kleene algebra (LKA)* is a structure $(K,^*)$ such that K is an IL-semiring and the *star* * satisfies, for $a, b, c \in K$, the *unfold* and *induction laws*

$$1 + a \cdot a^* \leq a^* , \qquad (2) \qquad b + a \cdot c \leq c \Rightarrow a^* \cdot b \leq c . \qquad (3)$$

An LKA is *strong* if it also satisfies the symmetrical star induction law

$$b + c \cdot a \leq c \Rightarrow b \cdot a^* \leq c . \qquad (4)$$

Therefore, a^* is the least pre-fixpoint and the least fixpoint of the function $\lambda x . a \cdot x + b$. Star is isotone with respect to the natural ordering. Even the weak star axioms suffice to prove the following laws:

$$a^* \cdot a^* = a^* , \qquad \text{(idempotence)}$$
$$(a + b)^* = a^* \cdot (a \cdot b^*)^* , \qquad \text{(decomposition)}$$
$$a \cdot c \leq c \cdot b \Rightarrow a^* \cdot c \leq c \cdot b^* . \qquad \text{(semicommutation)}$$

In a strong LKA the star also satisfies the symmetrical star unfold axiom

$$1 + a^* \cdot a \le a^* \tag{5}$$

and hence is the least pre-fixpoint and least fixpoint of the function $\lambda x \,.\, x \cdot a + b$.

Next we note the behaviour of finite elements under the star:

Lemma 6.2 $a \in \mathsf{F} \Rightarrow a^* \in \mathsf{F}$.

Proof. By neutrality of 0 we get $a \cdot 0 \le 0 \Leftrightarrow a \cdot 0 + 0 \le 0$, so that star induction (3) shows $a^* \cdot 0 \le 0$. □

We now turn to infinite iteration.

Definition 6.3 An ω-*LKA* is a structure $(K, {}^\omega)$ consisting of an LKA K and a unary *omega* operation ${}^\omega$ that satisfies, for $a, b, c \in K$, the *unfold* and *coinduction* laws

$$a^\omega = a \cdot a^\omega \,, \tag{6}$$

$$c \le a \cdot c + b \Rightarrow c \le a^\omega + a^* \cdot b \,. \tag{7}$$

One may wonder why we did not formulate omega unfold as $a^\omega \le a \cdot a^\omega$. The reason is that in absence of right-strictness we cannot show the reverse inequation. By the coinduction law, the greatest (post-)fixpoint of $\lambda x \,.\, a \cdot x$ is $a^\omega + a^* \cdot 0$ and $a^* \cdot 0$ need not vanish in the non-strict setting. This may seem paradoxical now. But by star induction we can easily show $a^* \cdot 0 \le a^\omega$ using $a \cdot a^\omega \le a^\omega$, so that indeed a^ω coincides with the greatest (post-)fixpoint of $\lambda x \,.\, a \cdot x$. The inequation $a^* \cdot 0 \le a^\omega$ seems natural, since by an easy induction one can show $a^i \cdot 0 \le a^\omega$ for all $i \in \mathbb{N}$ anyway.

For ease of comparison we note that von Wright's a^ω corresponds to $a^* + a^\omega$ in our setting.

Some consequences of the axioms are the following.

Lemma 6.4 *Consider an ω-LKA K and an element $a \in K$.*

1. *K has a greatest element $\top \stackrel{\text{def}}{=} 1^\omega$.*
2. *Omega is isotone with respect to the natural ordering.*
3. *$a^* \cdot a^\omega = a^\omega$.*
4. *a^ω is a right ideal, i.e., $a^\omega \cdot \top = \top$.*

Proof. 1. This follows from neutrality of 1 and omega coinduction (7).

2. Immediate from isotonicity of the fixed point operators.

3. The inequation $a^* \cdot a^\omega \le a^\omega$ is immediate from the star induction law (3). The reverse inequation follows from $1 \le a^*$ and isotonicity.

4. First, by the fixpoint property of a^ω we get $a^\omega \cdot \top = a \cdot a^\omega \cdot \top$. Hence $a^\omega \cdot \top \le a^\omega$. The reverse inequation is immediate from neutrality of 1 and isotonicity. □

We note that in a separated ω-LKA the set F has the greatest element $\mathsf{fin}\,\top$; this element is sometimes termed "havoc", since it represents the most nondeterministic but always terminating program.

Further laws together with applications to termination analysis can be found in [7]. We conclude this section with some decomposition properties for star and omega.

Lemma 6.5 *Assume a separated ω-LKA K.*

1. $a^* = (\mathsf{fin}\,a)^* \cdot (1 + \mathsf{inf}\,a)$.
2. $\mathsf{inf}\,a^* = (\mathsf{fin}\,a)^* \cdot \mathsf{inf}\,a$.
3. $a \cdot (\mathsf{fin}\,a)^* \cdot \mathsf{inf}\,a = (\mathsf{fin}\,a)^* \cdot \mathsf{inf}\,a$.
4. $a^\omega = (\mathsf{fin}\,a)^* \cdot \mathsf{inf}\,a + (\mathsf{fin}\,a)^\omega$.

Proof.
1. $a^* = (\mathsf{fin}\,a + \mathsf{inf}\,a)^* = (\mathsf{fin}\,a)^* \cdot (\mathsf{inf}\,a \cdot (\mathsf{fin}\,a)^*)^* =$
   $(\mathsf{fin}\,a)^* \cdot (\mathsf{inf}\,a)^* = (\mathsf{fin}\,a)^* \cdot (1 + \mathsf{inf}\,a \cdot (\mathsf{inf}\,a)^*) = (\mathsf{fin}\,a)^* \cdot (1 + \mathsf{inf}\,a)$.
2. Using 1. we get
   $$a^* \cdot 0 = (\mathsf{fin}\,a)^* \cdot (1 + \mathsf{inf}\,a) \cdot 0 =$$
   $(\mathsf{fin}\,a)^* \cdot (1 \cdot 0 + \mathsf{inf}\,a \cdot 0) = (\mathsf{fin}\,a)^* \cdot \mathsf{inf}\,a$.
3. $a \cdot (\mathsf{fin}\,a)^* \cdot \mathsf{inf}\,a = (\mathsf{fin}\,a + \mathsf{inf}\,a) \cdot (\mathsf{fin}\,a)^* \cdot \mathsf{inf}\,a =$
   $\mathsf{fin}\,a \cdot (\mathsf{fin}\,a)^* \cdot \mathsf{inf}\,a + \mathsf{inf}\,a \cdot (\mathsf{fin}\,a)^* \cdot \mathsf{inf}\,a = \mathsf{fin}\,a \cdot (\mathsf{fin}\,a)^* \cdot \mathsf{inf}\,a + \mathsf{inf}\,a =$
   $(\mathsf{fin}\,a \cdot (\mathsf{fin}\,a)^* + 1) \cdot \mathsf{inf}\,a = (\mathsf{fin}\,a)^* \cdot \mathsf{inf}\,a$.
4. The inequation $\geq$ holds by isotonicity of omega, by 3 and omega coinduction. The reverse inequation reduces by omega unfold to
   $$a^\omega \leq (\mathsf{fin}\,a) \cdot a^\omega + \mathsf{inf}\,a \Leftrightarrow a^\omega \leq (\mathsf{fin}\,a) \cdot a^\omega + (\mathsf{inf}\,a) \cdot a^\omega \Leftrightarrow$$
   $$a^\omega \leq (\mathsf{fin}\,a + \mathsf{inf}\,a) \cdot a^\omega \Leftrightarrow a^\omega \leq a \cdot a^\omega \Leftrightarrow \text{TRUE} \ . \qquad \square$$

7 Tests, Domain and Codomain

Definition 7.1 1. A *left test semiring* is a two-sorted structure $(K, \mathsf{test}(K))$, where K is an IL-semiring and $\mathsf{test}(K) \subseteq K$ is a Boolean algebra embedded into K, such that the join and meet operations of $\mathsf{test}(K)$ coincide with the restrictions of $+$ and $\cdot$ of K to $\mathsf{test}(K)$, respectively, and such that 0 and 1 are the least and greatest elements of $\mathsf{test}(K)$. In particular, $p \leq 1$ for all $p \in \mathsf{test}(K)$. But in general, $\mathsf{test}(K)$ is only a subalgebra of the subalgebra of all elements below 1 in K. The symbol $\neg$ denotes complementation in $\mathsf{test}(K)$.
2. A *lazy Kleene algebra with tests* is a left test semiring (K, B) such that K is a lazy KA.

This definition generalizes the one in [13]. We will consistently use the letters $a, b, c \ldots$ for semiring elements and $p, q, r, \ldots$ for Boolean elements. We will also use relative complement $p - q = p \cdot \neg q$ and implication $p \to q = \neg p + q$ with their standard laws. For all $p \in \mathsf{test}(K)$ we have that $p^* = 1$ and $p^\omega = p \cdot \top$.

If the overall IL-semiring K is Boolean, one can always choose $\mathsf{test}(K) = \{p \mid p \leq 1\}$ as the set of tests and define $\neg p \stackrel{\text{def}}{=} \overline{p} \sqcap 1$, where $\overline{a}$ is the complement of element a in the overall algebra. Note that by Lemma 4.7.1 all tests are finite.

Lemma 7.2 *Assume a left test semiring K. Then the following hold for all $a, b, c \in K$ and all $p, q \in \text{test}(K)$.*

1. *If $a \sqcap b$ exists then $p \cdot (a \sqcap b) = p \cdot a \sqcap b = p \cdot a \sqcap p \cdot b$.*
2. *$(p \sqcap q) \cdot a = p \cdot a \sqcap q \cdot a$.*
3. *$p \sqcap q = 0 \Rightarrow p \cdot a \sqcap q \cdot a = 0$.*
4. *If $b \leq a$ then $p \cdot b = b \sqcap p \cdot a$.*
   In particular, if K is bounded then $p \cdot b = b \sqcap p \cdot \top$.

Proof. We first note that for any test $p \in \text{test}(K)$ the function $f_p(a) \overset{\text{def}}{=} p \cdot a$ is a kernel operation by $p \leq 1$, isotonicity of $\cdot$ in both arguments and multiplicative idempotence of tests. Next we want to show that $f_p(K)$ is downward closed. Suppose $b \leq p \cdot a$. Then by isotonicity, $\neg p \cdot b \leq \neg p \cdot p \cdot a = 0$ and hence

$$b = 1 \cdot b = (p + \neg p) \cdot b = p \cdot b + \neg p \cdot b = p \cdot b ,$$

i.e., $b = f_p(b) \in f_p(K)$, too.

Now the claims other than 2. follow immediately from Lemma 5.4 and Corollary 5.5. For 2. set $b = a$ and use 1 twice together with $p \sqcap q = p \cdot q$. $\square$

Let now semiring element a describe an action or abstract program and a test p a proposition or assertion on its states. Then $p \cdot a$ describes a restricted program that acts like a when the initial state satisfies p and aborts otherwise. Symmetrically, $a \cdot p$ describes a restriction of a in its possible final states.

To show the interplay of tests with infinite iteration we prove a simple invariance property:

Lemma 7.3 *$p \cdot a = p \cdot a \cdot p \Rightarrow p \cdot a^\omega = (p \cdot a)^\omega$. This means that an invariant of a will hold throughout the infinite iteration of a.*

Proof. ($\geq$) We do not even need the assumption:
$(p \cdot a)^\omega = p \cdot a \cdot (p \cdot a)^\omega = p \cdot p \cdot a \cdot (p \cdot a)^\omega =$
$p \cdot (p \cdot a)^\omega \leq p \cdot a^\omega$.
($\leq$) By the fixpoint property of omega and the assumption,

$$p \cdot a^\omega = p \cdot a \cdot a^\omega = p \cdot a \cdot p \cdot a^\omega ,$$

which means that $p \cdot a^\omega$ is a fixpoint of $\lambda x . p \cdot a \cdot x$ and hence below its greatest fixpoint $(p \cdot a)^\omega$. $\square$

We now introduce an abstract domain operator $\ulcorner$ that assigns to a the test that describes precisely its starting states.

Definition 7.4 A *semiring with domain* [6] (a $\ulcorner$-semiring) is a structure $(K, \ulcorner)$, where K is an idempotent semiring and the *domain operation* $\ulcorner : K \to \text{test}(K)$ satisfies for all $a, b \in K$ and $p \in \text{test}(K)$

$$a \leq \ulcorner a \cdot a , \quad \text{(d1)} \qquad \ulcorner(p \cdot a) \leq p , \quad \text{(d2)} \qquad \ulcorner(a \cdot \ulcorner b) \leq \ulcorner(a \cdot b) . \quad \text{(d3)}$$

If K is an LKA, we speak of an *LKA with domain*, briefly $\ulcorner$-*LKA*.

These axioms can be understood as follows. (d1), which by isotonicity can be strengthened to an equality, means that restriction to all *all* starting states is no actual restriction, whereas (d2) means that after restriction the remaining starting states should satisfy the restricting test. (d3) states that the domain of $a \cdot b$ is not determined by the inner structure or the final states of b; information about $\ulcorner b$ in interaction with a suffices.

To further explain (d1) and (d2) we note that their conjunction is equivalent to each of

$$\ulcorner a \leq p \Leftrightarrow a \leq p \cdot a , \qquad \text{(llp)} \qquad \ulcorner a \leq p \Leftrightarrow \neg p \cdot a \leq 0 . \qquad \text{(gla)}$$

(llp) says that $\ulcorner a$ is the least left preserver of a. (gla) says that $\neg \ulcorner a$ is the greatest left annihilator of a. By Boolean algebra (gla) is equivalent to

$$p \cdot \ulcorner a \leq 0 \Leftrightarrow p \cdot a \leq 0 .$$

Because of (llp), domain is uniquely characterized by the axioms. Moreover, if $\mathsf{test}(K)$ is complete then domain always exists. If $\mathsf{test}(K)$ is not complete, this need not be the case.

Although the axioms are the same as in [6], one has to check whether their consequences in KA can still be proved in LKA. Fortunately, this is the case. Right-distributivity was used in [6] only for the proofs of additivity and the import/export law $\ulcorner(pa) = p\ulcorner a$. But the latter follows from (d3) and stability $\ulcorner p = p$ (which, in turn, follows from (llp) and idempotence of tests). Additivity is a special case of

Lemma 7.5 *Domain is universally disjunctive. In particular, $\ulcorner 0 = 0$.*

The proof has been given in [18]; it only uses (llp) and isotonicity of domain. But the latter follows easily from (gla).

From (d1) and left strictness of composition we also get

$$\ulcorner a = 0 \Rightarrow a = 0 . \tag{8}$$

Two other useful properties are

Lemma 7.6 *1. $\ulcorner(a \cdot b) \leq \ulcorner a$.*
2. If K is bounded then $\ulcorner(a \cdot \top) = \ulcorner a$.

Proof. 1. Using (llp) we get

$$\ulcorner a \leq p \Leftrightarrow a \leq p \cdot a \Rightarrow a \cdot b \leq p \cdot a \cdot b \Leftrightarrow \ulcorner(a \cdot b) \leq p ,$$

and the claim follows by indirect inequality, i.e., by

$$x \leq y \Leftrightarrow \forall z . y \leq z \Rightarrow x \leq z .$$

2. The inequation $\leq$ follows from 1., whereas $\geq$ follows from $1 \leq \top$ and isotonicity. $\qquad \square$

Finally, the induction law $\ulcorner(ap)\urcorner \leq p \Rightarrow \ulcorner(a^*p)\urcorner \leq p$ can be proved as in [6] (the LKA does not even need to be strong).

We now turn to the dual case of the codomain operation. In the KA case where we have also right-distributivity, a codomain operation $\urcorner$ can easily be defined as a domain operation in the opposite semiring where, as usual in algebra, opposition just swaps the order of composition. But by lack of right distributivity this does not work in the LKA setting; we additionally have to postulate isotonicity of codomain (in the form of superdisjunctivity to have a purely equational axiom).

Definition 7.7 A *left semiring with codomain* (a $\urcorner$-semiring) is a structure $(K, \urcorner)$, where K is a left test semiring and the *codomain operation* $\urcorner : K \to \text{test}(K)$ satisfies, for all $a, b \in K$ and $p \in \text{test}(K)$,

$$a \leq a \cdot a^\urcorner, \qquad \text{(cd1)} \qquad\qquad (a \cdot p)^\urcorner \leq p, \qquad \text{(cd2)}$$

$$(a^\urcorner \cdot b)^\urcorner \leq (ab)^\urcorner, \qquad \text{(cd3)} \qquad\qquad (a+b)^\urcorner \geq a^\urcorner + b^\urcorner. \qquad \text{(cd4)}$$

If K is an LKA, we speak of an *LKA with codomain*, briefly $\urcorner$-*LKA*.

As for domain, the conjunction of (cd1) and (cd2) is equivalent to

$$a^\urcorner \leq p \Leftrightarrow a \leq ap, \qquad \text{(lrp)}$$

i.e., $a^\urcorner$ is the least right preserver of a. However, by lack of right-strictness, $\neg p^\urcorner$ is *not* the greatest right annihilator of a; (lrp) only *implies*

$$a^\urcorner \leq p \Leftrightarrow a \cdot \neg p \leq a \cdot 0. \qquad \text{(wgra)}$$

The reverse implication (wgra) $\Rightarrow$ (lrp) holds in presence of *weak right-distributivity*

$$a = a \cdot p + a \cdot \neg p \qquad \text{(wrd)}$$

and provided a is finite. Note that (wrd) holds automatically for all $a \in \mathsf{N}$. Moreover, (wrd) is equivalent to full right-distributivity over sums of tests: assuming (wrd), we calculate

$$\begin{aligned} a \cdot (p+q) &= a \cdot (p+q) \cdot p + a \cdot (p+q) \cdot \neg p = \\ a \cdot (p \cdot p + q \cdot p) &+ a \cdot (p \cdot \neg p + q \cdot \neg p) = \\ a \cdot p + a \cdot q \cdot \neg p &\leq a \cdot p + a \cdot q. \end{aligned}$$

The reverse inequation follows from monotonicity and superdisjunctivity. We will not assume (wrd) in the sequel, though.

In an LKA, the symmetry between domain and codomain is broken also in other respects. The analogue of (8) does not hold; rather we have

Lemma 7.8 $a^\urcorner = 0 \Leftrightarrow a \in \mathsf{N}$.

Proof. Recall that $a \in \mathsf{N} \Leftrightarrow a = a \cdot 0$. Now, by (cd1), $a^\urcorner = 0$ implies $a = a \cdot 0$, whereas the reverse implication is shown by (cd2). $\qquad\qquad \square$

However, since for domain the proof of preservation of suprema only involves isotonicity and (llp), we can carry it over to codomain and obtain

Lemma 7.9 *Codomain is universally disjunctive and hence, in particular, additive and strict.*

Also, the proof of stability of domain uses only (llp) and hence is also valid for the codomain case, so that $p^\ulcorner = p$ for all $p \in \mathsf{test}(K)$. The import/export law $(a \cdot p)^\ulcorner = a^\ulcorner \cdot p$ follows from (cd3) and stability. Finally,

Lemma 7.10 *In a domain/codomain LKA, $a^\ulcorner \cdot {}^\ulcorner b = 0 \ \Rightarrow \ a \cdot b = a \cdot 0$.*

Further properties of domain and codomain can be found in [6].

8   Modal LKAs

Definition 8.1 A *modal left semiring* is a left test semiring K with domain and codomain. If K in addition is an LKA, we call it a *modal LKA*.

Let K be a modal left semiring. We introduce forward and backward diamond operators via abstract preimage and image.

$$|a\rangle p = {}^\ulcorner (a \cdot p) , \qquad (9) \qquad\qquad \langle a|p = (p \cdot a)^\ulcorner , \qquad (10)$$

for all $a \in K$ and $p \in \mathsf{test}(K)$. The box operators are, as usual, the de Morgan duals of the diamonds:

$$|a]p = \neg |a\rangle \neg p , \qquad (11) \qquad\qquad [a|p = \neg \langle a| \neg p . \qquad (12)$$

If $a \in \mathsf{N}$ then these definitions specialize to

$$|a\rangle p = {}^\ulcorner a , \qquad (13) \qquad\qquad \langle a|p = 0 , \qquad (14)$$

$$|a]p = \neg {}^\ulcorner a , \qquad (15) \qquad\qquad [a|p = 1 , \qquad (16)$$

since then also $p \cdot a \in \mathsf{N}$ by Lemma 4.3.1.

In the KA case, diamonds and boxes satisfy an *exchange law*. Let us work out the meaning of the two formulas involved in that law. Using the definitions, Boolean algebra and (gla)/(wgra), we obtain

$$p \leq |a]q \Leftrightarrow p \leq \neg {}^\ulcorner (a \cdot \neg q) \Leftrightarrow {}^\ulcorner (a \cdot \neg q) \leq \neg p \Leftrightarrow p \cdot a \cdot \neg q \leq 0$$

and

$$\langle a|p \leq q \Leftrightarrow (p \cdot a)^\ulcorner \leq q \Leftrightarrow p \cdot a \cdot \neg q \leq a \cdot 0 .$$

So for finite a we regain the Galois connection

$$p \leq |a]q \Leftrightarrow \langle a|p \leq q ,$$

which, however, does not hold for $a \in \mathsf{N}$. By an analogous argument one can show that also

$$p \leq [a|q \Leftrightarrow |a\rangle p \leq q$$

holds when $a \in \mathsf{F}$.

The Galois connections have interesting consequences. In particular diamonds (boxes) of finite elements commute with all existing suprema (infima) of the test algebra.

In the sequel, when the direction of diamonds and boxes does not matter, we will use the notation $\langle a \rangle$ and $[a]$. For a test p the modal operators satisfy $\langle p \rangle q = p \cdot q$ and $[p]q = p \to q$. Hence, $\langle 1 \rangle = [1]$ is the identity function on tests. Moreover, $\langle 0 \rangle p = 0$ and $[0]p = 1$. Finally, in an LKA with converse $\breve{}$ we have $|a^\breve{}\rangle = \langle a|$ and $|a^\breve{}] = [a|$.

By left-distributivity, the forward modalities distribute over $+$ in the following way:

$$|a + b\rangle p = |a\rangle p + |b\rangle p \, , \qquad |a + b]p = (|a]p) \cdot (|b]p) \, .$$

Hence, in a separated test semiring we obtain

$$|a\rangle p = |\text{fin } a\rangle p + \ulcorner(\text{inf } a) \, , \qquad |a]p = |\text{fin } a]p - \ulcorner(\text{inf } a) \, .$$

Using the forward box we can give another characterization of finite elements:

Lemma 8.2 $a \in \mathsf{F} \Leftrightarrow |a]1 = 1$.

Proof. By the definitions, $|a]1 = \neg\ulcorner(a \cdot 0)$. Now
$$a \in \mathsf{F} \Leftrightarrow a \cdot 0 = 0 \Leftrightarrow \ulcorner(a \cdot 0) = 0 \Leftrightarrow \neg\ulcorner(a \cdot 0) = 1 \Leftrightarrow |a]1 = 1. \qquad \square$$

Further applications of modal operators, notably for expressing Noethericity and performing termination analysis, can be found in [7].

9   Predicate Transformer Algebras

Assume a left test semiring $(K, +, \cdot, 0, 1)$. By a *predicate transformer* we mean a function $f : \text{test}(K) \to \text{test}(K)$. It is *disjunctive* if $f(p + q) = f(p) + f(q)$ and *conjunctive* if $f(p \cdot q) = f(p) \cdot f(q)$. It is *strict* if $f(0) = 0$. Finally, *id* is the identity transformer and $\circ$ denotes function composition.

Let P be the set of *all* predicate transformers, M the set of isotone and D the set of strict and disjunctive ones. Under the pointwise ordering $f \leq g \overset{\text{def}}{\Leftrightarrow} \forall p. f(p) \leq g(p)$, P forms a lattice where the supremum $f + g$ and infimum $f \sqcap g$ of f and g are the pointwise liftings of $+$ and $\cdot$, resp.:

$$(f + g)(p) \overset{\text{def}}{=} f(p) + g(p) \, , \qquad (f \sqcap g)(p) \overset{\text{def}}{=} f(p) \cdot g(p) \, .$$

The least element of P (and M and D) is the constant 0-valued function $\mathbf{0}$. The substructure $(M, +, \mathbf{0}, \circ, id)$ is an IL-semiring. In fact, $\circ$ is even universally left-disjunctive and preserves all existing infima, as the following calculation and a dual one for infima show:

$$((\sqcup F) \circ g)(x) = (\sqcup F)(g(x)) = \sqcup F(g(x)) = \sqcup (F \circ g)(x) \, .$$

The modal operator $|\_\rangle$ provides a left semiring homomorphism from K into M. The substructure $(D, +, \mathbf{0}, \circ, id)$ is even an idempotent semiring.

If $\mathsf{test}(K)$ is a complete Boolean algebra then P is a complete lattice with M and D as complete sublattices. Hence we can extend M and D by a star operation via a least fixpoint definition:

$$f^* \stackrel{\mathrm{def}}{=} \mu g \,.\, id + f \circ g \,,$$

where μ is the least-fixpoint operator.

Using μ-subfusion (see below) one sees that by this definition M becomes an LKA which, however, is not strong. Only the subalgebra of universally disjunctive predicate transformers is strong.

Similarly, if $\mathsf{test}(K)$ is complete we can define the infinite iteration $f^\omega \stackrel{\mathrm{def}}{=} \nu g \,.\, f \circ g$, where ν is the greatest-fixpoint operator. Whereas in M this does not imply the omega coinduction law, it does so in D.

Combining these two observations, we conclude that only the subalgebra of universally disjunctive predicate transformers can be made into an ω-LKA (which is even strong).

By passing to the mirror ordering, we see that also the subalgebra of universally conjunctive predicate transformers can be made into a strong ω-LKA; this is essentially the approach taken in [21, 22].

As a sample proof we show that the omega coinduction law holds for disjunctive predicate transformers. First we briefly repeat the fixpoint fusion laws (see e.g. [2] for further fixpoint properties). Let $F, G, H : L \to L$ be isotone functions on a complete lattice $(L, \leq)$ with least element $\perp$ and greatest element $\top$. Suppose that G is continuous, i.e., preserves suprema of nonempty chains, and assume $G(\perp) \leq \mu H$. Then

$$G \circ H \leq F \circ G \Rightarrow G(\mu h) \leq \mu F \,. \qquad (\mu\text{-subfusion})$$

Suppose now dually that G is cocontinuous, i.e., preserves infima of nonempty chains, and assume $G(\top) \geq \mu H$. Then

$$G \circ H \geq F \circ G \Rightarrow G(\nu h) \geq \nu F \,. \qquad (\nu\text{-superfusion})$$

For the proof of omega coinduction we define $F(x) \stackrel{\mathrm{def}}{=} f \circ x + g$ and $G(x) \stackrel{\mathrm{def}}{=} x + f^* \circ g = x + \mu F$ and $H(x) \stackrel{\mathrm{def}}{=} f \circ x$, where x ranges over D. Since we have assumed $\mathsf{test}(K)$ to be complete, $+$ is universally disjunctive in both arguments, so that G is continuous. The coinduction law is implied by $\nu F \leq G(\nu H)$, which by ν-superfusion reduces to $G \circ H \geq F \circ G$. This is shown by

$$G(H(x)) = f \circ x + \mu F = f \circ x + F(\mu F) = f \circ x + f \circ \mu F + g =$$
$$f \circ (x + \mu F) + g = f \circ G(x) + g = F(G(x)) \,.$$

Note that this calculation uses finite, but not universal, disjunctivity of f in an essential way. For the subclass of universally disjunctive predicate transformers over a power set lattice the result is well-known, since they are isomorphic to relations [1].

It should also be mentioned that the treatment, of course, generalizes to functions $f : L \to L$ over an arbitrary complete lattice L.

10   Conclusion and Outlook

We have seen that it is possible to integrate non-strictness with finite and infinite iteration as well as with modal operators. This framework allows, for instance, an abstract and more concise reworking of the stream applications treated in [17]; this will be the subject of further papers. But hopefully the framework will have many more applications.

Acknowledgements

I am grateful to J. Desharnais, T. Ehm, D. Kozen, D, Naumann and G. Struth for valuable discussions and support, and to Z. Esik for pointing out reference [10].

References

1. R. Back, J. von Wright: Refinement calculus – a systematic introduction. Springer 1998
2. R. C. Backhouse et al.: Fixed point calculus. *Inform. Proc. Letters*, 53:131–136, 1995.
3. J.A. Bergstra, I. Bethke, A. Ponse: Process algebra with iteration and nesting. The Computer Journal 37(4), 243–258, 1994
4. E. Cohen: Separation and reduction. In R. Backhouse and J.N. Oliveira (eds.): Mathematics of Program Construction. Lecture Notes in Computer Science **1837**. Berlin: Springer 2000, 45–59
5. J.H. Conway: Regular algebra and finite machines. London: Chapman and Hall 1971
6. J. Desharnais, B. Möller, G. Struth: Kleene algebra with domain. Technical Report 2003-07, Universität Augsburg, Institut für Informatik, June 2003
7. J. Desharnais, B. Möller, G. Struth: Termination in modal Kleene algebra. Technical Report 2004-04, Universität Augsburg, Institut für Informatik, January 2004. Revised version: Proc. IFIP World Computer Congress 2004, Toulouse, August 22–27, 2004, Subconference TCS-Logic (to appear)
8. R.M. Dijkstra: Computation calculus – bridging a formalization gap. In: J. Jeuring (ed.): Proc. MPC 1998. LNCS 1422, 151–174
9. R.M. Dijkstra: Computation calculus bridging a formalization gap. Science of Computer Programming **37**, 3-36 (2000)
10. C.C. Elgot: Matricial theories. Journal of Algebra **42**, 391–422 (1976)
11. B. von Karger, C.A.R. Hoare: *Sequential calculus*. Information Processing Letters **53**, 1995, 123–130
12. D. Kozen: A completeness theorem for Kleene algebras and the algebra of regular events. Information and Computation **110:2**, 366–390 (1994)
13. D. Kozen: Kleene algebras with tests. *ACM TOPLAS* 19:427–443, 1997.
14. D. Kozen: Kleene Algebra with Tests and the Static Analysis of Programs. Cornell University, Department of Computer Science, Technical Report TR2003-1915, 2003
15. J.J. Lukkien: An operational semantics for the guarded command language. In: R.S. Bird, C.C. Morgan, J.C.P. Woodcock (eds.): Mathematics of Program Construction. Lecture Notes in Computer Science **669**. Berlin: Springer 1993, 233–249

16. J.J. Lukkien: Operational semantics and generalized weakest preconditions. Science of Computer Programming **22**, 137–155 (1994)
17. B. Möller: Ideal stream algebra. In: B. Möller, J.V. Tucker (eds.): Prospects for hardware foundations. Lecture Notes in Computer Science **1546**. Berlin: Springer 1998, 69–116
18. B. Möller, G. Struth: Modal Kleene algebra and partial correctness. Technical Report 2003-08, Universität Augsburg, Institut für Informatik, May 2003. Revised version: Proc. AMAST 2004, Stirling, July 12–16, 2004 (to appear)
19. K.I. Rosenthal: *Quantales and their applications*. Pitman Research Notes in Mathematics Series, Vol. 234. Longman Scientific&Technical 1990.
20. L. Staiger: Omega languages. In G. Rozenberg, A. Salomaa (eds.): Handbook of formal languages, Vol. 3. Springer 1997, 339–387
21. J. von Wright: From Kleene algebra to refinement algebra. In E. Boiten, B. Möller (eds.): Mathematics of Program Construction. Lecture Notes in Computer Science **2386**. Berlin: Springer 2002, 233–262
22. J. von Wright: Towards a refinement algebra. Science of Computer Programming **51**, 23–45 (2004)

Augmenting Types with Unbounded Demonic and Angelic Nondeterminacy

Joseph M. Morris

School of Computing
Dublin City University
Ireland
Joseph.Morris@computing.dcu.ie

Abstract. We show how to introduce demonic and angelic nondeterminacy into the term language of each type in typical programming or specification language. For each type we introduce (binary infix) operators $\sqcap$ and $\sqcup$ on terms of the type, corresponding to demonic and angelic nondeterminacy, respectively. We generalise these operators to accommodate unbounded nondeterminacy. We axiomatise the operators and derive their important properties. We show that a suitable model for nondeterminacy is the free completely distributive complete lattice over a poset, and we use this to show that our axiomatisation is sound. In the process, we exhibit a strong relationship between nondeterminacy and free lattices that has not hitherto been evident. Although nondeterminacy arises naturally in specification and programming languages, we speculate that it combines fruitfully with function theory to the extent that it can play an important role in facilitating proofs of programs that have no apparent connection with nondeterminacy.

Keywords: angelic nondeterminacy, demonic nondeterminacy, free completely ditributive lattice.

1 Introduction

Specification languages typically include operators $\sqcap$ and $\sqcup$ on specifications. For specifications s_0 and s_1, $s_0 \sqcap s_1$ denotes the disjunction of s_0 and s_1, i.e. the specification which requires that either s_0 or s_1 (or both) be satisfied, and $s_0 \sqcup s_1$ denotes their conjunction, i.e. the specification which requires that both s_0 and s_1 be satisfied. They occur, for example, in the specification language **Z** [13] as so-called schema disjunction and conjunction, respectively. They have analogues in programming languages where they are operationally interpreted as *demonic* and *angelic* nondeterministic choice, respectively. In the language of guarded commands [5], for example, the statement $s_0 \sqcap s_1$ is executed by executing precisely one of the statements s_0 and s_1. The choice is made afresh each time $s_0 \sqcap s_1$ is executed, and is made by a demon who chooses vagariously. Consequently if we have a particular goal in mind for $s_0 \sqcap s_1$ then each of s_0 and s_1 must achieve it individually. $s_0 \sqcup s_1$ is also executed by executing one of s_0 or s_1, but in this case the choice is made by an angel. The angel knows what

D. Kozen (Ed.): MPC 2004, LNCS 3125, pp. 274–288, 2004.

we want to achieve and selects whichever of s_0 and s_1 will do so. In this paper, we show how $\sqcap$ and $\sqcup$ may be introduced into specification and programming languages at the term level, rather than at the statement level. In other words, we will show how $\sqcap$ and $\sqcup$ may be introduced into each type in a specification or programming language such that for t and u any terms of type T, say, $t \sqcap u$ and $t \sqcup u$ are also terms of type T which behave as we have outlined informally.

There are two reasons why we should do this: to support formal reasoning about nondeterminacy, and – more surprisingly – to support reasoning about programs and specifications in general, regardless of whether they employ nondeterminacy or not. We already know the role of demonic choice at the term level in specifying and programming, and we know how to formalise it; see [8, 12, 10, 11], for example. Angelic choice on terms has received less attention and even then has usually been given a second class status. In [11], for example, functions distribute over demonic choice but little is said with respect to angelic choice. Our first contribution is to place both kinds of nondeterminacy on an equal footing in a single satisfying theory.

Nondeterminacy can be seen as a way of populating a type with extra "imaginary" values, and as a consequence some operators classically regarded as partial can become total (or at least less partial). To take a trivial example, a function f has a right inverse f^{-1} satisfying $f \circ f^{-1} = Id$ only when f is bijective (Id denotes the identity function). If we admit nondeterminacy, however, only surjectivity is required. The fact that the inverse may now rely on nondeterminacy need not intrude on our reasoning because we typically only exploit the defining property. As another example, we know that every monotonic function on a complete lattice is rich in fixpoints, and in particular has a least and a greatest fixpoint. If we admit nondeterminacy, we no longer require a complete lattice: every monotonic function is rich in fixpoints. Our theory of nondeterminacy combines seamlessly with function theory, to the extent that we believe that nondeterministic functions can play a significant role in formalising programming techniques that have no obvious connection with nondeterminacy, such as data refinement and abstract interpretation. We will explore these issues in a later paper, but first we need a general theory of dually nondeterministic types, and that is what we set out to achieve here.

$\sqcap$ and $\sqcup$ can only give rise to bounded choice. We shall extend them in the body of the paper to accommodate unbounded choice. Nondeterminacy is always accompanied by a partial ordering relation $\sqsubseteq$, called the *refinement* relation. Informally, terms t and u satisfy $t \sqsubseteq u$ if t is at least as demonically nondeterministic as u, and u is at least as angelically nondeterministic as t. In that case we say that u is a *refinement* of t, or that t is *refined* by u. We shall also axiomatise $\sqsubseteq$.

A formal treatment of types with demonic choice has already been done, for example in [11], and angelic choice can be formalised as its dual. One would expect therefore that coalescing the two kinds of nondeterminacy would not be difficult. Surprisingly, this turns out not to be at all the case, either with respect to the proof theory or the model theory. In particular, dual nondeterminacy requires a much more sophisticated model, which turns out to be a neglected construct of lattice theory called the free completely distributive lattice over a poset. In constructing this free lattice, we exhibit a more intimate relationship between nondeterminacy and lattice theory than has hitherto been evident. Indeed we conjecture that free completely distributive lattices are the natural model for nondeterminacy.

1.1   Outline of Rest of Paper

In the next section we describe the syntax of terms when angelic and demonic choice is introduced, and describe their semantics informally. We present some small examples to help intuition. After that we present the axioms that govern nondeterminacy and derive the important algebraic properties of demonic and angelic choice. In the penultimate section we address the model theory, the greater part of which is constructing the free completely distributive lattice over a poset. We conclude with some commentary on the work.

Our primary contribution is the first axiomatisation of dually nondeterministic types, complete with a proof of soundness. A secondary contribution is revealing a more intimate relationship between nondeterminacy and lattice theory, and in particular that a certain class of free lattices are the natural model for nondeterminacy.

2   Syntax and Informal Semantics

2.1   Terms and Finite Choice

We assume a typed specification/programming language. We use T, U, ... to stand for types, and t, u, v ... to stand for terms. We write $t, u : T$ to assert that terms t and u are of type T, and similarly for other than two terms. For terms t and u of type T, say, $t \sqcap u$ and $t \sqcup u$ are also terms of type T with the informal meanings described in the introduction. It should be intuitively clear that both operators are associative, commutative, and idempotent; we will use associativity to omit some bracketing from the start. We intend that $\sqcap$ and $\sqcup$ should distribute over one another in all possible ways.

A consequence of our semantics is that operators distribute over $\sqcap$ and $\sqcup$. For example, in $(2 \sqcap 3) - (2 \sqcap 3)$ the first occurrence of $(2 \sqcap 3)$ may have outcome 2, while the second may have outcome 3, or vice versa, and hence $(2 \sqcap 3) - (2 \sqcap 3) = -1 \sqcap 0 \sqcap 1$ which is consistent with subtraction distributing over $\sqcap$.

Operators have the following relative precedence, higher precedence first (the list anticipates some operators we have yet to introduce):

function application

$\sqcap$	$\sqcup$	$\wedge$	$\vee$
$\sqcap$	$\sqcup$		
$=$	$\neq$	$\leq$	$\sqsubseteq$
$\neg$			
$\wedge$	$\vee$		
$\Rightarrow$			
$\Longleftrightarrow$			

For example, the brackets in the following are superfluous:

$$((t \sqcap u) \sqsubseteq \bigsqcup X) \iff ((t \sqsubseteq \bigsqcup X) \vee (u \sqsubseteq \bigsqcup X))$$

2.2 Ordering on Terms

We assume each type T in the language comes equipped with a partial ordering $\leq_T$ (we omit the type subscript when it can be inferred from context or is not significant). In the case of base types such as the integers or booleans, the partial ordering will nearly always be the discrete ordering, i.e. $x \leq y$ iff $x = y$. If the reader has in mind a type with no obvious partial ordering, then it can be trivially ordered by the discrete ordering. For every type T we introduce a refinement relation $\sqsubseteq_T$ on terms of type T (again, we usually omit the type subscript). We intend that $\sqsubseteq_T$ agrees with $\leq_T$ on terms that employ no nondeterminacy, and otherwise $t \sqsubseteq_T u$ holds iff t is at least as demonically nondeterministic as u, and u is at least as angelically nondeterministic as t, where $t, u : T$. For example, all of the following hold: $2 \sqsubseteq 2$, $2 \sqcap 3 \sqcap 4 \sqsubseteq 2 \sqcap 4$, $2 \sqcup 4 \sqsubseteq 2 \sqcup 3 \sqcup 4$, and $(2 \sqcap 3) \sqcup 4 \sqsubseteq 2 \sqcup 4 \sqcup 5$. We might expect from lattice theory that refinement and choice are related via $t \sqsubseteq u \Leftrightarrow t \sqcap u = t \Leftrightarrow t \sqcup u = u$, and that will turn out to be the case.

2.3 Unbounded Choice

To accommodate unbounded demonic choice we introduce the term $(\sqcap x{:}T|P{\cdot}t)$. Here variable x is bound by $\sqcap$ and may occur free in predicate P and term t (playing the role of a term of type T). $(\sqcap x{:}T|P \cdot t)$ is equivalent to the demonic choice over terms $t[x \backslash i]$ for each $i \in T$ satisfying $P[x \backslash i]$. Above and elsewhere, $t[x \backslash u]$ denotes term t in which term u is substituted for x, with the usual caveats about avoiding variable capture, and similarly for substitution in predicates. $(\sqcap x{:}T|P \cdot t)$ has the same type as t. For example, $(\sqcap x{:}\mathbf{Z}|0 \leq x < 3 \cdot x \sqcup 5)$ has type $\mathbf{Z}$ and is equivalent to $(0 \sqcup 5) \sqcap (1 \sqcup 5) \sqcap (2 \sqcup 5)$. Simple abbreviations include $(\sqcap x{:}T|P)$ for $(\sqcap x{:}T|P \cdot x)$, and $(\sqcap x{:}T \cdot t)$ for $(\sqcap x{:}T|true \cdot t)$ where $true$ stands for some theorem. $(\sqcup x{:}T|P{\cdot}t)$ and its obvious abbreviations are defined analogously. Observe that where precisely two values of type T satisfy P – call them j and k – then $(\sqcap x{:}T|P)$ is equivalent to $j \sqcap k$, and analogously for $(\sqcup x{:}T|P)$. When just a single value k of type T satisfies P, then both $(\sqcap x{:}T|P)$ and $(\sqcup x{:}T|P)$ are equivalent to k.

Let $false$ stand for $\neg true$. $(\sqcup x{:}T|false)$ is given the special name $\perp_T$ (pronounced $bottom$), and $(\sqcap x{:}T|false)$ is given the name $\top_T$ (pronounced top). $(\sqcup x{:}T|true)$ is given the special name $some_T$, and $(\sqcap x{:}T|true)$ is given the name all_T. Again, we commonly omit the type subscripts. As suggested by their names, $\perp$ and $\top$ satisfy $\perp \sqsubseteq t \sqsubseteq \top$ for every term t. It follows that $\perp$ is the unit of $\sqcup$ and the zero of $\sqcap$, and $\top$ is the unit of $\sqcap$ and the zero of $\sqcup$.

2.4 Examples

We exercise the notation on a few small examples. To begin, the function $\lambda z{:}\mathbf{Z} \cdot (\sqcap x{:}\mathbf{Z} \times \mathbf{Z}|add\, x = z)$ is a right inverse of add, the addition function on $\mathbf{Z} \times \mathbf{Z}$. So also is $\lambda z{:}\mathbf{Z} \cdot (\sqcup x{:}\mathbf{Z} \times \mathbf{Z}|add\, x = z)$.

Suppose the type *PhoneBook* is comprised of all relations from type *Name* to type *PhoneNumber*. Then the following function looks up a person's phone number in a phone book:

$$lookUp \mathrel{\hat{=}} \lambda n{:}Name \cdot \lambda b{:}PhoneBook \cdot (\sqcap x{:}PhoneNumber | (n, x) \in b).$$

For a more interesting example, consider the function

$$leastWRT_T : (T \to \mathbf{Z}) \to \mathbb{P}T \to T$$

which takes as arguments a function f and a set s, and selects some element a of s such that $f\ a$ is minimized. We omit the type subscript in what follows. Formally, for any type T:

$$leastWRT \mathrel{\hat{=}} \lambda f{:}T \to \mathbf{Z} \cdot \lambda s{:}\mathbb{P}T \cdot (\sqcap x{:}T | x \in s \land (\forall y{:}s \cdot f\ x \leq f\ y)).$$

To illustrate its use, we make a function which yields a place to which two people should travel if they wish to meet as soon as possible. We assume a type *Place* whose elements represent all places of interest, and a function *time:Place* $\times$ *Place* $\to \mathbf{N}$ which yields the travelling time (in minutes, say) between any two places. The function we want is:

$$\lambda me, you{:}Place \cdot leastWRT\ (\lambda c{:}Place \cdot time(me, c)\ \max\ time(you, c))\ Place.$$

(We have taken the liberty of overloading *Place* so that it also denotes the set of values in type *Place*.)

Many games can be expressed using a combination of angelic and demonic nondeterminacy [1]. Consider the classical game *Nim*, for example, in which two players alternately remove from 1 to 3 matches, say, from a pile until none remain. The player who removes the last match loses. Let us refer to the players as the *home* and *away* player, respectively, where the home player goes first. A single move made by each player is represented by the functions *moveH* and *moveA*, respectively:

$$moveH, moveA : \mathbf{N} \to \mathbf{N}$$

moveH n (*moveA n*) yields the number of matches remaining after the home (away) player has made one move when offered n matches. We introduce the two-value type *Player* with elements *Home* and *Away*. The complete game played by each player is represented by functions *playH* and *playA*, respectively:

$$playH, playA : \mathbf{N} \to Player$$

playH n (*playA n*) yields the winner of a game in which the home (away) player is initially offered n matches. Formally:

$$
\begin{aligned}
playH \mathrel{\hat{=}} \lambda n{:}\mathbf{N}\cdot\ &\textbf{if } n = 0 \textbf{ then } Home \\
&\textbf{else } (playA \circ moveH)\,n
\end{aligned}
$$

$$playA \ \hat{=} \ \lambda n{:}\mathbf{N}{\cdot} \ \mathbf{if} \ n = 0 \ \mathbf{then} \ Away$$
$$\mathbf{else} \ (playH \circ moveA) \, n$$

It only remains to code *moveH* and *moveA* in whatever way we choose. We choose to make the home player play the best possible game. No knowledge of *Nim* strategy is needed, as it suffices to offer all possible moves to the angel who will choose the best one:

$$moveH \ \hat{=} \ \lambda n{:}\mathbf{N} \cdot (\sqcup m{:}\mathbf{N}|0 < n - m \le 3)$$

The away player sets out to thwart the home player's ambition, by offering him the demon's choice among all possible moves (and so obliging him to counter all of them):

$$moveA \ \hat{=} \ \lambda n{:}\mathbf{N} \cdot (\sqcap m{:}\mathbf{N}|0 < n - m \le 3)$$

There is a winning strategy for the opening player in *Nim* with n matches initially ($n > 0$), iff the home player as we have coded it always wins, i.e. iff the following holds

$$Home \sqsubseteq playH \, n$$

We write $Home \sqsubseteq playH \, n$ rather than $Home = playH \, n$ because $playH$ yields an angelic choice of possibilities of which only one need be $Home$. This example is interesting because it employs both kinds of nondeterminacy to express a property ("there is a winning strategy for the opening player in *Nim*") that has no evident connection with nondeterminacy.

2.5   Quantifications and Nondeterminacy

In introducing nondeterminacy, we have to make clear whether instantiation extends to terms that rely essentially on nondeterminacy. It is analogous to the situation in partial function theory in which we explicitly accommodate "undefined" terms such as $3/0$. We expect that from $(\forall n{:}\mathbf{Z} \cdot x - x = 0)$ we can infer $3 - 3 = 0$, but probably not $3/0 - 3/0 = 0$. We adopt a similar convention here: from $(\forall n{:}\mathbf{Z} \cdot x - x = 0)$ we may infer $3 - 3 = 0$, but not $\bot_{\mathbf{Z}} - \bot_{\mathbf{Z}} = 0$ or $(2 \sqcap 3) - (2 \sqcap 3) = 0$. In other words, we adopt the convention that the range of the bound variable does not extend to nondeterministic terms. We extend this convention to all quantifications. For example, $(\sqcup x{:}\mathbf{Z}|x = 1 \sqcap 2)$ is equivalent to $\bot_{\mathbf{Z}}$, not $1 \sqcap 2$.

3   Proof Theory

In presenting the axioms, we employ more syntactically abstract forms of demonic and angelic nondeterminacy, viz. $\sqcap S$ and $\sqcup S$ for S any set of terms. These denote the demonic and angelic choice, respectively, over the constituent terms of S. $t \sqcap u$ is equivalently $\sqcap\{t, u\}$ and $(\sqcap x{:}T|P{\cdot}t)$ is equivalently $\sqcap\{x{:}T|P{\cdot}t\}$ (and similarly for angelic choice). Above and elsewhere we write $\{x{:}T|P \cdot t\}$ to denote the set of $t[x\backslash i]$ for each $i \in T$ satisfying $P[x\backslash i]$; $\{x{:}T|P\}$ is short for $\{x{:}T|P \cdot x\}$, and $\{x{:}T \cdot t\}$ is short for $\{x{:}T|true \cdot t\}$. We write $(\forall X{\subseteq}T \ \cdots)$ as an abbreviation for $(\forall X{:}\mathbb{P}T \ \cdots)$, and similarly for other quantifications. We write $\{x{\in}X \cdot t\}$ as an abbreviation for $\{x{:}T|x{\in}X \cdot t\}$ where $X{:}\mathbb{P}T$. We denote the set of terms of type T by $term_T$ (which includes terms that employ nondeterminacy).

The axioms have to define not just demonic and angelic nondeterminacy, but refinement as well. Firstly, $\sqsubseteq$ agrees with $\leq$ on the deterministic values in each type T.

$\sqsubseteq$-ext: $(\forall x, y{:}T \cdot x \sqsubseteq y \iff x \leq y)$

Refinement is antisymmetric.

$\sqsubseteq$-asym: $t \sqsubseteq u \wedge u \sqsubseteq t \Rightarrow t = u$

The following relate refinement to demonic and angelic choice, respectively, where $t, u : T$.

$\sqsubseteq$-$\sqcap$: $t \sqsubseteq u \iff (\forall X{\subseteq}T \cdot \bigsqcap X \sqsubseteq t \Rightarrow \bigsqcap X \sqsubseteq u)$
$\sqsubseteq$-$\sqcup$: $t \sqsubseteq u \iff (\forall X{\subseteq}T \cdot u \sqsubseteq \bigsqcup X \Rightarrow t \sqsubseteq \bigsqcup X)$

The axioms for demonic and angelic choice follow, where $X \subseteq T$, $S \subseteq term_T$.

$\sqcap$-defn: $\bigsqcap S \sqsubseteq \bigsqcup X \iff (\exists t{\in}S \cdot t \sqsubseteq \bigsqcup X)$
$\sqcup$-defn: $\bigsqcap X \sqsubseteq \bigsqcup S \iff (\exists t{\in}S \cdot \bigsqcap X \sqsubseteq t)$

The remaining axioms are just definitions. The following define $\sqcap$ and $\sqcup$.

$\sqcap$-defn: $t \sqcap u = \bigsqcap\{t, u\}$
$\sqcup$-defn: $t \sqcup u = \bigsqcup\{t, u\}$

Finally we define the constants.

$\bot$-defn: $\bot_T = \bigsqcup \emptyset$
$\top$-defn: $\top_T = \bigsqcap \emptyset$
all-defn: $all_T = \bigsqcap T$
$some$-defn: $some_T = \bigsqcup T$

This completes the list of axioms. Just to reassure that we have catered for $(\sqcap x{:}T|P \cdot t)$ and $(\sqcup x{:}T|P \cdot t)$, below is $\bigsqcup$-defn with S instantiated as $\{x{:}T|P \cdot t\}$:

$$\bigsqcap X \sqsubseteq (\sqcup x{:}T|P \cdot t) \iff (\exists x{:}T \cdot P \wedge (\bigsqcap X \sqsubseteq t))$$

All the properties we would expect of $\sqcap$, $\sqcup$, and $\sqsubseteq$ follow from the axioms; see Figure 1 (in which $t, u, v : T$, $X \subseteq T$, and $S \subseteq term_T$).

It is clerical routine to prove the theorems in the order presented. We prove $all \sqsubseteq t \iff t \neq \bot$ as an example.

$$all \sqsubseteq t$$
$$\Longleftrightarrow \qquad all\text{-defn, } \sqsubseteq\text{-}\sqcup$$
$$(\forall X \subseteq T \cdot t \sqsubseteq \bigsqcup X \Rightarrow \bigsqcap T \sqsubseteq \bigsqcup X)$$
$$\Longleftrightarrow \qquad \bigsqcap\text{-defn}$$
$$(\forall X \subseteq T \cdot t \sqsubseteq \bigsqcup X \Rightarrow (\exists y{:}T \cdot y \sqsubseteq \bigsqcup X))$$
$$\Longleftrightarrow \qquad \bigsqcap\{y\} = y$$
$$(\forall X \subseteq T \cdot t \sqsubseteq \bigsqcup X \Rightarrow (\exists y{:}T \cdot \bigsqcap\{y\} \sqsubseteq \bigsqcup X))$$
$$\Longleftrightarrow \qquad \bigsqcup\text{-defn, } \bigsqcap\{y\} = y$$
$$(\forall X \subseteq T \cdot t \sqsubseteq \bigsqcup X \Rightarrow (\exists y{:}T \cdot (\exists x{\in}X \cdot y \sqsubseteq x)))$$
$$\Longleftrightarrow \qquad \sqsubseteq \text{ reflexive, logic}$$
$$(\forall X \subseteq T \cdot t \sqsubseteq \bigsqcup X \Rightarrow X \neq \emptyset)$$
$$\Longleftrightarrow \qquad \text{logic}$$
$$(\forall X \subseteq T \cdot X = \emptyset \Rightarrow \neg(t \sqsubseteq \bigsqcup X))$$
$$\Longleftrightarrow \qquad \text{logic}$$
$$\neg(t \sqsubseteq \bigsqcup \emptyset)$$
$$\Longleftrightarrow \qquad \bot\text{-defn, } \bot \sqsubseteq t$$
$$t \neq \bot$$

4   Model Theory

4.1   Lattice Fundamentals

In this section and the two following we give a short dense summary of lattice theory to the extent that we need it to construct a model for our axioms. Everything is standard and is available in more detail in any standard text (such as [4, 3]).

A *lattice* L is a partially ordered set (we'll use $\leq$ to represent the partial ordering) such every finite subset of L has a greatest lower bound in L with respect to $\leq$, and similarly has a least upper bound in L with respect to $\leq$. L is a *complete lattice* if greatest lower and least upper bounds are not restricted to finite subsets of L. For $S \subseteq L$, the greatest lower bound of S is denoted by $\bigwedge S$, and the least upper bound is denoted by $\bigvee S$. Greatest lower bounds are also called *meets*, and least upper bounds are also called *joins*. A complete lattice is *completely distributive* iff meets distribute over joins, and vice versa. When we say that a lattice is completely distributive, we mean to imply that it is also complete.

A function f from poset $(C, \leq_C)$ to poset$(D, \leq_D)$ is *monotonic* iff $x \leq_C y \Rightarrow fx \leq_D fy$ for all $x, y \in C$, and an *order embedding* iff $x \leq_C y \Longleftrightarrow fx \leq_D fy$ for all $x, y \in C$. An order embedding from $(C, \leq_C)$ to a complete lattice is said to be a *completion* of $(C, \leq_C)$.

Let f be a function from complete lattice L to complete lattice M. f is $\bigwedge$-*distributive* iff $f(\bigwedge S) = \bigwedge(f S)$ for all $S \subseteq L$; $\bigvee$-*distributive* is defined dually. By $f S$ above and in what follows, we mean the image of S through f, i.e. $\{x \in S \cdot f x\}$. f is a *complete homomorphism* if f is $\bigwedge$- and $\bigvee$-distributive. Now let f be a function from poset C to lattice M; C may well be a lattice, but in any event subsets of C may have greatest lower bounds and least upper bounds

Fundamental theorems

$$t = u \iff (\forall X {\subseteq} T \cdot \bigsqcap X \sqsubseteq t \iff \bigsqcap X \sqsubseteq u)$$
$$t = u \iff (\forall X {\subseteq} T \cdot t \sqsubseteq \bigsqcup X \iff u \sqsubseteq \bigsqcup X)$$

$$\bigsqcap \{t\} = t$$
$$\bigsqcup \{t\} = t$$

$\sqcap, \sqcup$ are symmetric, associative, and idempotent
$\sqsubseteq$ is a partial order

$$t \sqcap u \sqsubseteq \bigsqcup X \iff t \sqsubseteq \bigsqcup X \vee u \sqsubseteq \bigsqcup X$$
$$\bigsqcap X \sqsubseteq t \sqcup u \iff \bigsqcap X \sqsubseteq t \vee \bigsqcap X \sqsubseteq u$$

$$t \sqsubseteq u \sqcap v \iff t \sqsubseteq u \wedge t \sqsubseteq v$$
$$u \sqcup v \sqsubseteq t \iff u \sqsubseteq t \wedge v \sqsubseteq t$$

$$t \sqsubseteq \bigsqcap S \iff (\forall u {\in} S \cdot t \sqsubseteq u)$$
$$\bigsqcup S \sqsubseteq t \iff (\forall u {\in} S \cdot u \sqsubseteq t)$$

$$t \sqsubseteq u \iff t \sqcap u = t$$
$$t \sqsubseteq u \iff t \sqcup u = u$$

$\sqcap, \sqcup$ distribute over one another, as do $\bigsqcap, \bigsqcup$

$$\bot \sqsubseteq t \sqsubseteq \top$$
$$all \sqsubseteq t \iff t \neq \bot$$
$$t \sqsubseteq some \iff t \neq \top$$

$$t \sqcap \bot = \bot, t \sqcap \top = t, t \sqcup \bot = t, t \sqcup \top = \top$$

$$t = (\sqcap X {\subseteq} T | t \sqsubseteq \bigsqcup X \cdot \bigsqcup X)$$
$$t = (\sqcup X {\subseteq} T | \bigsqcap X \sqsubseteq t \cdot \bigsqcap X)$$

Fig. 1. Fundamental theorems $(t,u,v : T, \; X \subseteq T, \; S \subseteq term_T)$

in C. We say that f is *existentially $\bigwedge$-distributive* iff $f(\bigwedge S) = \bigwedge(f \, S)$ for all $S \subseteq C$ such that $\bigwedge S$ exists in C; *existentially $\bigvee$-distributive* is defined dually.

4.2   Upsets and Downsets

Let $(C, \leq)$ be a poset. A set $S \subseteq C$ is said to be *downclosed* (with respect to $\leq$) iff $(\forall x, y {\in} C | x \leq y \cdot y \in S \Rightarrow x \in S)$, and *upclosed* (with respect to $\leq$) iff $(\forall x, y {\in} C | x \leq y \cdot x \in S \Rightarrow y \in S)$. We denote by $\mathcal{D} C$ the set of downclosed subsets (or *downsets*) of C, and by $\mathcal{U} C$ the set of upclosed subsets (or *upsets*). $\mathcal{D} C$ is a completely distributive lattice partially ordered by $\subseteq$ and with joins and meets given by unions and intersections, respectively. $\mathcal{U} C$ is a completely distributive lattice partially ordered by $\supseteq$ and with joins and meets given by intersections and unions, respectively. For $S \subseteq C$, we denote by $S\downarrow$ the *downclosure* of S, i.e. the smallest downset containing S (this is well defined because downsets are closed under intersection). We denote by $S\uparrow$ the *upclosure* of S, i.e. the smallest upset containing S. The function $\mathsf{down}{:}C \rightarrow \mathcal{D}C$ which maps c to $\{c\}\downarrow$ is a completion of C, as is $\mathsf{up}{:}C \rightarrow \mathcal{U}C$ which maps c to $\{c\}\uparrow$, where the ordering on $\mathcal{D}C$ and $\mathcal{U}C$ is as given above.

4.3 Denseness and Primeness

The definitions in this section are needed primarily in proofs, and can be lightly passed over if it is not intended to follow the proofs.

A completion $f{:}C \rightarrow L$ is said to be *join dense* iff $x = \bigvee\{c{\in}C | f\,c \leq x{\cdot}f\,c\}$ for all $x \in L$. f is *meet dense* iff $x = \bigwedge\{c{\in}C | x \leq f\,c \cdot f\,c\}$ for all $x \in L$. Join dense completions are existentially $\bigwedge$-distributive, and meet dense completions are existentially $\bigvee$-distributive. An element x of a complete lattice L is *completely join prime* iff $x \leq \bigvee S \iff (\exists y{\in}S \cdot x \leq y)$ for all $S \subseteq L$. x is *completely meet prime* iff $\bigwedge S \leq x \iff (\exists y{\in}S \cdot y \leq x)$ for all $S \subseteq L$. A completion $f : C \rightarrow L$ is said to be completely join prime (completely meet prime) if every $x \in f\,C$ is completely join prime (completely meet prime, respectively). up is meet dense and completely meet prime, and down is join dense and completely join prime.

4.4 Free Completely Distributive Lattice over a Poset

A completely distributive lattice L is called the *free completely distributive lattice over a poset* C iff there is a completion $\phi{:}C \rightarrow L$ such that for every completely distributive lattice M and monotonic function $f{:}C \rightarrow M$ there is a unique complete homomorphism $f_\phi^*{:}L \rightarrow M$ satisfying $f = f_\phi^* \circ \phi$. In this context we say that ϕ is a *free completely distributive completion* with *simulator* $-_\phi^*$.

Definition 1. *Let $\phi{:}C \rightarrow L$ be a completion of poset C into complete lattice L. For any monotonic $f{:}C \rightarrow M$, where M is a complete lattice, we define $f_\phi^\vee$, $f_\phi^\wedge{:}L \rightarrow M$ by*
(i) $f_\phi^\vee = \lambda x{:}L \cdot \bigvee\{c{\in}C | \phi\,c \leq x \cdot f\,c\}$
(ii) $f_\phi^\wedge = \lambda x{:}L \cdot \bigwedge\{c{\in}C | x \leq \phi\,c \cdot f\,c\}$.   □

It is easy to see that both $f_\phi^\vee$ and $f_\phi^\wedge$ are monotonic. The central theorem that allows us to construct the free completely distributive lattice over a poset is the following.

Theorem 1. *Let $\phi{:}C \rightarrow L$ be a completion of poset C into complete lattice L, and $\theta{:}L \rightarrow M$ be a completion of L into completely distributive lattice M.*
(i) If θ is join dense and completely join prime, and ϕ is meet dense and completely meet prime, then $\theta \circ \phi$ is a free completely distributive completion of C with simulator $(-_\phi^\wedge)_\theta^\vee$
(ii) If θ is meet dense and completely meet prime, and ϕ is join dense and completely join prime, then $\theta \circ \phi$ is a free completely distributive completion of C with simulator $(-_\phi^\vee)_\theta^\wedge$ □

We shall prove Theorem 1 shortly. We need only exhibit a θ and ϕ as described in the theorem to have a free completely distributive lattice. By a standard argument on free objects, all free completely distributive lattices on a given poset are isomorphic. We denote by $\mathbf{FCD}(C, \leq)$ the free completely distributive lattice on poset $(C, \leq)$.

Theorem 2. $\mathbf{FCD}(C, \leq)$ *exists for every poset* $(C, \leq)$.

Proof. Apply Theorem 1 (i) with θ instantiated as **down** and ϕ instantiated as **up**, or Theorem 1 (ii) with θ instantiated as **up** and ϕ instantiated as **down**.   □

The rest of this section is devoted to proving Theorem 1, via a series of lemmas (Lemma 5 will play a second role in showing soundness).

Lemma 1. *Let* $\phi{:}C \to L$ *be a completion of poset* C *into complete lattice* L, *and let* $f{:}C \to M$ *be monotonic. Then* $f = f_\phi^\vee \circ \phi$ *and* $f = f_\phi^\wedge \circ \phi$.

Proof. Easy exercise, needing only that f is monotonic and ϕ is an order embedding.   □

Lemma 2. *Let* $\phi{:}C \to L$ *be a completion of poset* C *into complete lattice* L, *and let* $f{:}C \to M$ *be monotonic.*
(i) If ϕ *is completely join prime then* $f_\phi^\vee$ *is* $\bigvee$*-distributive.*
(ii) If ϕ *is completely meet prime then* $f_\phi^\wedge$ *is* $\bigwedge$*-distributive.*

Proof. We prove (i). Let $S \subseteq L$.
$$f_\phi^\vee(\bigvee S)$$
$$\Longleftrightarrow \quad \text{defn } f_\phi^\vee$$
$$\bigvee\{c \in C | \phi c \leq \bigvee S \cdot f\, c\}$$
$$\Longleftrightarrow \quad \phi \text{ completely join prime}$$
$$\bigvee\{c \in C | (\exists y \in S \cdot \phi c \leq y) \cdot f\, c\}$$
$$\Longleftrightarrow \quad \text{set theory}$$
$$\bigvee(\bigcup\{y \in S \cdot \{c \in C | \phi c \leq y \cdot f\, c\}\})$$
$$\Longleftrightarrow \quad \bigvee \text{ distributes over } \bigcup$$
$$\bigvee\{y \in S \cdot \bigvee\{c \in C | \phi c \leq y \cdot f\, c\}\})$$
$$\Longleftrightarrow \quad \text{defn } f_\phi^\vee$$
$$\bigvee(\{y \in S \cdot f_\phi^\vee y\}$$
$$\Longleftrightarrow \quad \text{defn of image function}$$
$$\bigvee(f_\phi^\vee S)$$
   □

Lemma 3. *Let* $\theta{:}C \to L$ *be a completion of poset* C *into complete lattice* L, *and let* $f{:}C \to M$ *be monotonic with* M *a complete lattice.*
(i) If θ *is join dense then* $f_\theta^\vee$ *inherits the* $\bigwedge$*-distributivity of* f, *i.e. whenever* f *distributes over* $\bigwedge S$, $f_\theta^\vee$ *distributes over* $\bigwedge(\theta S)$ *for all* $S \subseteq C$ *such that* $\bigwedge S$ *exists.*
(ii) If θ *is meet dense then* $f_\theta^\wedge$ *inherits the* $\bigvee$*-distributivity of* f

Proof. The proof of (i) is an easy inference from Lemma 1 and that fact that ϕ is $\bigwedge$-distributive (because it is join dense). The proof of (ii) is dual. □

We need notation to capture arbitrary distributions of meets over joins. Let I denote a set and let J_i denote a set for each $i \in I$. We denote by $[i{:}I{\rightarrow}J_i]$ the set of functions f from I to $\bigcup\{i \in I \cdot J_i\}$ satisfying $f\,i \in J_i$ for each $i \in I$. That complete lattice L is completely distributive is expressed as follows:

$$\bigwedge\{i{\in}I \cdot \bigvee\{j{\in}J_i \cdot x_{i,j}\}\} = \bigvee\{f{\in}[i{:}I{\rightarrow}J_i] \cdot \bigwedge\{i{\in}I \cdot x_{i,f\,i}\}\}$$

where $x_{i,j} \in L$ for each $i \in I$ and $j \in J_i$. We use the notation in the following lemma which is the crux of proving Theorem 1.

Lemma 4. *Let $\theta{:}L \rightarrow M$ be a completion where L is a complete lattice and M is a completely distributive lattice, and let $f{:}L \rightarrow N$ where N is a complete lattice.*
(i) If θ is join dense and f is $\bigwedge$-distributive, then so also is $f_\theta^\vee$ $\bigwedge$-distributive.
(ii) If θ is meet dense and f is $\bigvee$-distributive, then so also is $f_\theta^\wedge$ $\bigvee$-distributive.

Proof. We prove (i). Let $S \subseteq M$.

$\qquad f_\theta^\vee(\bigwedge S)$
$\Longleftrightarrow \qquad$ set notation
$\qquad f_\theta^\vee(\bigwedge\{s{\in}S \cdot s\})$
$\Longleftrightarrow \qquad$ θ join dense
$\qquad f_\theta^\vee(\bigwedge\{s{\in}S \cdot \bigvee\{k{\in}L|\theta\,k \leq s \cdot \theta\,k\}\})$
$\Longleftrightarrow \qquad$ define $L_s = \{k{\in}L|\theta\,k \leq s\}$
$\qquad f_\theta^\vee(\bigwedge\{s{\in}S \cdot \bigvee\{k{\in}L_s \cdot \theta\,k\}\})$
$\Longleftrightarrow \qquad$ M is completely distributive
$\qquad f_\theta^\vee(\bigvee\{h{\in}[s{:}S{\rightarrow}L_s] \cdot \bigwedge\{s{\in}S \cdot \theta(h\,s)\}\})$
$\Longleftrightarrow \qquad$ $f_\theta^\vee$ is $\bigvee$-distributive as θ join dense
$\qquad \bigvee\{h{\in}[s{:}S{\rightarrow}L_s] \cdot f_\theta^\vee(\bigwedge\{s{\in}S \cdot \theta(h\,s)\})\}$
$\Longleftrightarrow \qquad$ Lemma 3 (f is $\bigwedge$-distributive, θ join dense,
$\qquad\qquad$ M completely distributive)
$\qquad \bigvee\{h{\in}[s{:}S{\rightarrow}L_s] \cdot \bigwedge\{s{\in}S \cdot f_\theta^\vee(\theta(h\,s))\}\}$
$\Longleftrightarrow \qquad$ M is completely distributive
$\qquad \bigwedge\{s{\in}S \cdot \bigvee\{k{\in}L_s \cdot f_\theta^\vee(\theta\,k)\}\}$
$\Longleftrightarrow \qquad$ $f_\theta^\vee$ is $\bigvee$-distributive
$\qquad \bigwedge\{s{\in}S \cdot f_\theta^\vee(\bigvee\{k{\in}L_s \cdot \theta\,k\})\}$
$\Longleftrightarrow \qquad$ repeating the operations in steps 2–4 above, in reverse order
$\qquad \bigwedge\{s{\in}S \cdot f_\theta^\vee\,s\}$
$\Longleftrightarrow \qquad$ function image notation
$\qquad \bigwedge(f_\theta^\vee\,S)$

$\hfill \square$

Lemma 5. *Let $\phi{:}C \rightarrow L$ be a completion of poset C into complete lattice L, and $\theta{:}L \rightarrow M$ be a completion of L into complete lattice M. Then for all $p \in M$*
(i) $p = \bigvee\{S{:}\mathbb{P}C| \bigwedge(\theta(\phi\,S)) \leq p \cdot \bigwedge(\theta(\phi\,S))\}$ if θ is join dense and ϕ is meet dense

(ii) $p = \bigwedge\{S:\mathbb{P}C|p \le \bigvee(\theta(\phi\,S)) \cdot \bigvee(\theta(\phi\,S))\}$ *if θ is meet dense and ϕ is join dense.*

Proof of (i). As θ is join dense, $p = \bigvee\{q:L|\theta\,q \le p\cdot\theta\,q\}$. As ϕ is meet dense, every $q \in L$ is equivalent to $\bigwedge(\phi\,S)$ for some $S \subseteq C$, and hence $L = \{S:\mathbb{P}C\cdot\bigwedge(\phi\,S)\}$. Therefore $p = \bigvee\{S:\mathbb{P}C|\theta(\bigwedge(\phi\,S)) \le p\cdot\theta(\bigwedge(\phi\,S))\}$. As θ is a join dense function on a complete lattice it is $\bigwedge$-distributive, and hence $p = \bigvee\{S:\mathbb{P}C|\bigwedge(\theta(\phi\,S)) \le p\cdot\bigwedge(\theta(\phi\,S))\}$. □

We now have all we need to prove Theorem 1.

Proof of Theorem 1: We prove part (i). It is a simple exercise to show that $\theta\circ\phi$ is an order embedding from C to M and hence a completion. Let $f:C \to N$ be monotonic with N a completely distributive lattice. From two simple applications of Lemma 1 we have $(f_\phi^\wedge)_\theta^\vee \circ (\theta \circ \phi) = f$. As θ is completely join prime, it follows from Lemma 2 that $(f_\phi^\wedge)_\theta^\vee$ is $\bigvee$-distributive. As ϕ is completely meet prime it follows from Lemma 2 that $f_\phi^\wedge$ is $\bigwedge$-distributive, and hence from Lemma 4 that $(f_\phi^\wedge)_\theta^\vee$ is $\bigwedge$-distributive. Therefore $(f_\phi^\wedge)_\theta^\vee$ is a complete homomorphism. By Lemma 5 (i) C generates M, i.e. every element in M is obtained by taking meets and joins of elements in $(\theta \circ \phi)\,C$. As all candidate complete homomorphisms by definition agree on $(\theta \circ \phi)\,C$ and are distributive in all possible ways, it follows that $(f_\phi^\wedge)_\theta^\vee$ is unique. □

4.5   Soundness

We show that the free completely distributive lattice is a model for our axioms. We presume that in the absence of nondeterminacy, each type T is represented by a partially ordered set $([T], \le_{[T]})$ whose ordering agrees with $\le_T$, i.e. $[t] \le_{[T]} [u]$ iff $t \le_T u$ where $[t]$ is the denotation of $t : T$ in $[T]$, and similarly for $u : T$. To accommodate nondeterminacy, we elevate the representation of T from $([T], \le_{[T]})$ to $\mathbf{FCD}([T], \le_{[T]})$ represented by the *up-down* lattice $\mathcal{D}\,(\mathcal{U}\,[T])$, and we elevate the representation of each term t from $[t]$ to $(\mathsf{down} \circ \mathsf{up})[t]$. The refinement relation, demonic nondeterminacy, and angelic nondeterminacy in T are represented by the ordering relation, the meet operation, and the join operation in $\mathcal{D}\,(\mathcal{U}\,[T])$, respectively.

Our six axioms translate to the model as follows, where $t, u \in \mathcal{D}(\mathcal{U}[T])$, $X \subseteq [T]$ and $S \subseteq \mathcal{D}(\mathcal{U}[T])$:

$\sqsubseteq$-ext-M: $(\forall x, y:[T] \cdot (\mathsf{down} \circ \mathsf{up})\,x \le (\mathsf{down} \circ \mathsf{up})\,y \iff x \le_{[T]} y)$

$\sqsubseteq$-asym-M: $t \le u \wedge u \le t \Rightarrow t = u$

$\sqsubseteq$-$\sqcap$-M: $t \le u \iff (\forall X \subseteq [T] \cdot \bigwedge((\mathsf{down} \circ \mathsf{up})X) \le t \Rightarrow \bigwedge((\mathsf{down} \circ \mathsf{up})X) \le u)$

$\sqsubseteq$-$\sqcup$-M: $t \le u \iff (\forall X \subseteq [T] \cdot t \le \bigvee((\mathsf{down} \circ \mathsf{up})X) \Rightarrow u \le \bigvee((\mathsf{down} \circ \mathsf{up})X))$

$\sqcap$-defn-M: $\bigwedge S \le \bigvee((\mathsf{down} \circ \mathsf{up})X) \iff (\exists s \in S \cdot s \le \bigvee((\mathsf{down} \circ \mathsf{up})X))$

$\sqcup$-defn-M: $\bigwedge((\mathsf{down} \circ \mathsf{up})X) \le \bigvee S \iff (\exists s \in S \cdot \bigwedge((\mathsf{down} \circ \mathsf{up})X) \le s)$

$\sqsubseteq$-ext-M and $\sqsubseteq$-asym-M obviously hold: the former says that $\mathsf{down} \circ \mathsf{up}$ is an order embedding, and the latter that $\le$ in $\mathcal{D}(\mathcal{U}[T])$ is antisymmetric.

$\sqsubseteq$-$\sqcap$-M follows easily from Lemma 5 (i) in which ϕ is replaced by down and θ by up. $\sqsubseteq$-$\sqcup$-M follows similarly from Lemma 5 (ii).

We prove $\bigsqcup$-defn-M as follows.

$$\bigwedge((\mathsf{down} \circ \mathsf{up})X) \leq \bigvee S$$
$\Longleftrightarrow$ down is $\bigwedge$-distributive
$$\mathsf{down}(\bigwedge(\mathsf{up}X)) \leq \bigvee \!\cdot S$$
$\Longleftrightarrow$ down is completely join prime
$$(\exists s \in S \cdot \mathsf{down}(\bigwedge(\mathsf{up}X)) \leq s)$$
$\Longleftrightarrow$ down is $\bigwedge$-distributive
$$(\exists s \in S \cdot \bigwedge((\mathsf{down} \circ \mathsf{up})X) \leq s)$$

Dually, $\bigsqcap$-defn-M holds in the *down-up* model, i.e. $\mathcal{U}(\mathcal{D}[T])$ which is isomorphic to the up-down model. The property transfers trivially from the down-up model to the up-down model using the isomorphism that maps $(\mathsf{up} \circ \mathsf{down})\,X$ to $(\mathsf{down} \circ \mathsf{up})\,X$ for any $X \subseteq [T]$.

5   Conclusion

We have presented axioms governing angelic and demonic nondeterminacy in terms at the type level, and constructed a model to show their soundness. $\mathbf{FCD}(C, \leq)$ seems to capture unbounded nondeterminacy so closely that we are tempted to say that the theory of nondeterminacy is more or less the theory of free completely distributive lattices over a poset. Indeed, once $\mathbf{FCD}(C, \leq)$ is constructed, proving soundness of the axioms is almost trivial.

The free completely distributive lattice over a poset seems to be a neglected part of free lattice theory. At least, it does not merit a mention in the encyclopaedic [6]. Markowsky [9] described it, without proof, for the special case that the poset is discretely ordered, and Bartenschlager [2] constructed a representation of $\mathbf{FCD}(C, \leq)$ in a very different setting as a certain "concept lattice" [7]. The construction above is original as far as we know. It has been guided by our need to facilitate a proof of soundness of the axioms. Indeed, the model and axioms were constructed together because a satisfactory axiomatisation proved elusive initially.

Our interest in giving a satisfactory mathematical account of nondeterminacy was motivated originally by the role of nondeterminacy in specifications and programs. However, we believe the theory will combine elegantly with function theory to yield a richer theory of functions in which some operations become less partial. This will impact favourably on various programming techniques that have no obvious connection with nondeterminacy, such as data refinement and abstract interpretation. We are currently exploring these possibilities .

Acknowledgements

I am grateful to Malcolm Tyrrell, Eric Hehner, and anonymous referees for criticisms that have led to many improvements in the presentation.

References

1. Ralph-Johan Back and Joakim von Wright. *Refinement Calculus : a Systematic Introduction.* Springer-Verlag, 1998.
2. G. Bartenschlager. Free bounded distributive lattices over finite ordered sets and their skeletons. *Acta Mathematica Universitatis Comenianae,* 64:1–23, 1995.
3. Garrett Birkhoff. *Lattice Theory,* volume 25 of *Colloquium Publications.* American Mathematical Society, 1995.
4. B.A. Davey and H.A. Priestley. *Introduction to Lattices and Order.* Cambridge University Press, 2nd edition, 2002.
5. E. W. Dijkstra. *A Discipline of Programming.* Prentice Hall, 1976.
6. Ralph Freese, Jaroslav Jezek, and J.B. Nation. *Free Lattices,* volume 42 of *Mathematical Surveys and Monographs.* American Mathematical Society, 1995.
7. B. Ganter and R. Wille. *Formal Concept Analysis.* Springer-Verlag, 1999.
8. E. C. R. Hehner. *A Practical Theory of Programming.* Springer Verlag, New York, London, ISBN 0387941061 1993.
9. George Markowsky. Free completely distributive lattices. *Proceedings of the American Mathematical Society,* 74:227–228, 1979.
10. J. M. Morris and A. Bunkenburg. Specificational functions. *ACM Transactions on Programming Languages and Systems,* 21:677 – 701, 1999.
11. J. M. Morris and A. Bunkenburg. A Theory of Bunches. *Acta Informatica,* 37:541–561, 2001.
12. T. S. Norvell and E. C. R. Hehner. Logical specifications for functional programs. In *Proceedings of the Second International Conference on Mathematics of Program Construction, Oxford, 29 June - 3 July 1992,* volume 669 of *Lecture Notes in Computer Science,* pages 269–290. Springer Verlag, 1993.
13. J.M. Spivey. *Understanding Z : A Specification Language and its Formal Semantics.* Cambridge University Press, 1988.

An Injective Language
for Reversible Computation

Shin-Cheng Mu, Zhenjiang Hu, and Masato Takeichi

Department of Information Engineering
University of Tokyo
7-3-1 Hongo, Bunkyo-ku, Tokyo 113, Japan
{scm,hu,takeichi}@ipl.t.u-tokyo.ac.jp

Abstract. Erasure of information incurs an increase in entropy and dissipates heat. Therefore, information-preserving computation is essential for constructing computers that use energy more effectively. A more recent motivation to understand reversible transformations also comes from the design of editors where editing actions on a view need to be reflected back to the source data. In this paper we present a point-free functional language, with a relational semantics, in which the programmer is allowed to define injective functions only. Non-injective functions can be transformed into a program returning a history. The language is presented with many examples, and its relationship with Bennett's reversible Turing machine is explained. The language serves as a good model for program construction and reasoning for reversible computers, and hopefully for modelling bi-directional updating in an editor.

1 Introduction

The interest in reversible computation arose from the wish to build computers dissipating less heat. In his paper in 1961, Landauer [17] noted that it is not the computation, but the erasure of information, that generates an increase in entropy and thus dissipates heat. Since then, various models of computation that do not erase information, thus capable of reversely construct the input from the output, have been proposed. Lecerf [18] and Bennett [4] independently developed their reversible Turing machines. Toffoli [26] proposed an information preserving logic, in which traditional logic can be embedded. Fredkin and Toffoli [11] then presented their "ballistic computer", which dramatically diverts from typical computers and instead resembles movement of particles, yet computationally equivalently to reversible Turing machines. Recent research actually attempts to build VLSI chips that do not erase information [27]. Due to the interest in quantum computing, reversible computation has recently attracted a wide range of researchers [24].

As was pointed out by Baker [3], were it only a problem in the hardware, we could compile ordinary programs for reversible computers and hide the reality from the programmers. Yet it is actually the highest level of computation where the loss of information is the most difficult to deal with. It is thus desirable to

D. Kozen (Ed.): MPC 2004, LNCS 3125, pp. 289–313, 2004.
© Springer-Verlag Berlin Heidelberg 2004

have programming languages that have more structure – a language designed
for reversible computation.

Our interest in reversible computation came from yet another area. In our
Programmable Structured Documents project [25], we are developing a structural editor/viewer for XML documents with embedded computations. The
source document is transformed into a *view* in ways defined by the document designer. When a user edits the view, the changes need to be reflected back to the
original source. It is thus preferable that the transformation be programmed in
a language where only reversible transformation is allowed. When non-reversible
computation is needed, it should be made explicit what extra information needs
to be remembered to perform the view-to-source transformation. Dependency
among different parts of the view shall also be made explicit so the system
knows how to maintain consistency when parts of the view are edited.

In this paper we will present a point-free functional language in which all
functions definable are injective. Previous research was devoted to the design of
models and languages for reversible computation [26, 4, 5, 19, 3, 10, 28]. Several
features distinguish our work from previous results. Since it is a language in
which we want to specify XML transformations, we prefer a high-level, possibly
functional, programming language. It has a relational semantics, thus all programs have a relational interpretation. While some previous works focus more
on the computational aspect, our language serves as a good model for program
construction, derivation and reasoning of reversible programs. We have another
target application in mind: to extend the language to model the bi-directional
updating problem in an editor, studied by [21, 14]. We hope that the relational
semantics can shed new light on some of the difficulties in this field.

In the next three sections to follow, we introduce the basic concepts of relations, a point-free functional language, and finally our injective language Inv,
each of which is a refinement of the previous one. Some examples of useful injective functions defined in Inv are given in Section 5. We describe how non-injective
functions can be "compiled" into Inv functions in Section 6, where we also discuss
the relationship with Bennett's reversible Turing machine. Some implementation
issues are discussed in Section 7.

2   Relations

Since around the 80's, the program derivation community started to realise that
there are certain advantages for a theory of functional programming to base on
relations [2, 6]. More recent research also argued that the relation is a suitable
model to talk about program inversion because it is more symmetric [22]. In this
section we will give a minimal introduction to relations.

A relation of type $A \to B$ is a set of pairs whose first component has type A
and second component type B. When a pair (a, b) is a member of a relation R, we
say that a is mapped to b by R. A (partial) function[1], under this interpretation,

---

[1] For convenience, we refer to possibly partial functions when we say "functions".
Other papers may adopt different conventions.

is a special case of a relation that is *simple* – a value in A is mapped to at most one value in B. That is, if $(a, b) \in R$ and $(a, b') \in R$, then $b = b'$. For example, the function $fst :: (A \times B) \to A$ extracting the first component of a pair, usually denoted pointwisely as $fst\,(a, b) = a$, is defined by the following set:

$$fst = \{((a, b), a) \mid a \in A \wedge b \in B\}$$

where (a, b) indeed uniquely determines a. The function $snd :: (A \times B) \to B$ is defined similarly.

The *domain* of a relation $R :: A \to B$ is the set $\{a \in A \mid \exists b \in B :: (a, b) \in R\}$. The *range* of R is defined symmetrically. The *converse* of a relation R, written R°, is obtained by swapping the pairs in R. That is,

$$(b, a) \in R^\circ \equiv (a, b) \in R$$

An injective function is one whose converse is also a function. In such cases a value in the domain uniquely defines its image in the range, and vice versa. The term *inverse of a function* is usually reserved to denote the converse of an injective function. Given relations $R :: A \to B$ and $S :: B \to C$, their composition $R; S$ is defined by:

$$R; S = \{(a, c) \mid \exists b :: (a, b) \in R \wedge (b, c) \in S\}$$

The converse operator $^\circ$ distributes into composition contravariantly:

$$(R; S)^\circ = S^\circ; R^\circ$$

Given two relations R and S of the same type, one can take their union $R \cup S$ and intersection $R \cap S$. The union, when R and S have disjoint domains, usually corresponds to conditional branches in a programming language. The intersection is a very powerful mechanism for defining useful relations. For example, the function $dup\,a = (a, a)$, which duplicates its argument, can be defined by:

$$dup = fst^\circ \cap snd^\circ$$

Here the relation fst°, due to type constraints, has to have type $A \to (A \times A)$. It can therefore be written as the set $\{(a, (a, a')) \mid a \in A \wedge a' \in A\}$ – that is, given a, fst° maps it to (a, a') where a' is an arbitrary value in A. Similarly, snd° maps a to (a', a) for an arbitrary a'. The only point where they coincide is (a, a). That is, taking their intersection we get

$$dup = \{(a, (a, a)) \mid a \in A\}$$

which is what we expect.

The converse operator $^\circ$ distributes into union and intersection. If we take the converse of dup, we get:

$$dup^\circ = fst \cap snd$$

Given a pair, fst extracts its first component, while snd extracts the second. The intersection means that the results have to be equal. That is, dup° takes a pair and lets it go through only if the two components are equal. That explains the observation in [12] that to "undo" a duplication, we have to perform an equality test.

3   The Point-Free Functional Language Fun

The intersection is a very powerful construct for specification – with it one can
define undecidable specifications. In this section we will refine the relational constructs to a point-free functional language which is computationally equivalent
to conventional programming languages we are familiar with. The syntax of Fun
is defined by[2]:

$$F ::= C \mid C^\circ$$
$$\mid F; F \mid id$$
$$\mid \langle F, F \rangle \mid fst \mid snd$$
$$\mid F \cup F$$
$$\mid \mu(X \colon F_X)$$
$$C ::= nil \mid cons \mid zero \mid succ$$

The base types of Fun are natural numbers, polymorphic lists, and $Unit$, the
type containing only one element (). The function $nil :: B \rightarrow [A]$ is a constant
function always returning the empty list, while $cons :: (A \times [A]) \rightarrow [A]$ extends a
list by the given element. Converses are applied to base constructors (denoted by
the non-terminal C) only. We abuse the notation a bit by denoting the converse
of all elements in C by C°, and by F_X we denote the union of F and the set of
variable names X. The converse of $cons$, for example, decomposes a non-empty
list into the head and the tail. The converse of nil matches only the empty
list and maps it to anything. The result is usually thrown away. To avoid nondeterminism in the language, we let the range type of nil° be $Unit$. Functions
$zero$ and $succ$ are defined similarly. Presently we do not yet need a constructor
for the type $Unit$.

The function id is the identity function, the unit of composition. Functions
fst and snd extract the first and second components of a pair respectively. Those
who are familiar with the "squiggle" style of program derivation would feel at
home with the "split" construct, defined by:

$$\langle f, g \rangle\, a = (f\, a, g\, a)$$

The angle brackets on the left-hand side denote the split construct, while the
parentheses on the right-hand side denote pairs. This definition, however, assumes that f and g be functional. Less well-known is its relational definition in
terms of intersection:

$$\langle f, g \rangle = f; fst^\circ \,\cap\, g; snd^\circ$$

For example, the dup function in the previous section is defined by $\langle id, id \rangle$.

With fst, snd and the split we can define plenty of "piping functions" useful
for point-free programming. For example, the function $swap :: (A \times B) \rightarrow (B \times A)$,

---

[2] In Fun there are no primitive operators for equality or inequality check. They can be
defined recursively on natural numbers, so we omitted it from the language to make
it simpler. In Inv, however, we do include those checks as primitives since they are
important for inversion.

swapping the components in a pair, and the function $assocr :: ((A \times B) \times C) \to (A \times (B \times C))$, are defined by:

$$swap = \langle snd, fst \rangle$$
$$assocr = \langle fst; fst, \langle fst; snd, snd \rangle \rangle$$

The function $assocl :: (A \times (B \times C)) \to ((A \times B) \times C)$ can be defined similarly. The "product" functor $(f \times g)$, on the other hand, is defined by

$$(f \times g)(a, b) = (f\, a, g\, b)$$

Squigglists are more familiar with its point-free definition:

$$(f \times g) = \langle fst; f, snd; g \rangle$$

Union of functions is still defined as set union. To avoid non-determinism, however, we require in $f \cup g$ that f and g have disjoint domains. Arbitrary use of intersection, on the other hand, is restricted to its implicit occurrence in splits.

Finally, μF denotes the unique fixed-point of the Fun-valued function F, with which we can define recursive functions. The important issue whether a relation-valued function has an unique fixed-point shall not be overlooked. It was shown in [9] that the uniqueness of the fixed-point has close relationship with well-foundness and termination. All recursive definitions in this paper do have unique fixed-points, although it is out of the scope of this paper to verify them.

As an example, the concatenation of two cons-lists is usually defined recursively as below:

$$[]\mathbin{+\!\!+} y = y$$
$$(a : x) \mathbin{+\!\!+} y = a : (x \mathbin{+\!\!+} y)$$

Its curried variation, usually called $cat :: ([A] \times [A]) \to [A]$, can be written in point-free style in Fun as:

$$cat = \mu(X: (nil^\circ \times id); snd \;\cup\; (cons^\circ \times id); assocr; (id \times X); cons)$$

The two branches of $\cup$ correspond to the two clauses of $\mathbin{+\!\!+}$, while $(nil^\circ \times id)$ and $(cons^\circ \times id)$ act as patterns. The term $(cons^\circ \times id)$ decomposes the first component of a pair into its head and tail, while $(nil^\circ \times id)$ checks whether that component is the empty list. The piping function $assocr$ distributes the values to the right places before the recursive call.

We decided to make the language point-free because it is suitable for inversion – composition is simply run backward, and the need to use piping functions makes the control flow explicit. It is true, however, point-free programs are sometimes difficult to read. To aid understanding we will supply pointwise definition of complicated functions. The conversion between the point-free and pointwise style, however, will be dealt with loosely.

The language Fun is not closed under converse – we can define non-injective functions in Fun, such as fst and snd, whose converses are not functional. In other words, Fun is powerful enough that it allows the programmer to define functions "unhealthy" under converse. In the next section we will further refine Fun into an injective language.

4   The Injective Language Inv

In the previous section we defined a functional language Fun with a relational semantics. All constructs of Fun have relational interpretations and can thus be embedded in relations. In this section, we define a functional language Inv that allows only injective functions. All its constructs can be embedded in, and therefore Inv is strictly a subset of, Fun.

The problematic constructs in Fun include constant functions, *fst*, *snd*, and the split. Constant functions and projections lose information. The split duplicates information and, as a result, in inversion we need to take care of consistency of previously copied data. We wish to enforce constrained use of these problematic constructs by introducing more structured constructs in Inv, in pretty much the same spirit how we enforced constrained use of intersection by introducing the split in Fun. The language Inv is defined by:

$$
\begin{aligned}
I \ ::=&\ I^\circ \mid C \\
&\mid eq\ P \mid dup\ P \mid neq\ S\ S \\
&\mid I; I \mid id \\
&\mid (I \times I) \mid assocr \mid swap \\
&\mid (I \cup I) \\
&\mid \mu(X\colon I_X) \\
C \ ::=&\ succ \mid cons \\
P \ ::=&\ nil \mid zero \mid S \\
S \ ::=&\ C^\circ \mid fst \mid snd \mid id \mid S; S
\end{aligned}
$$

Each construct in Inv has its inverse in Inv. Constructors *cons* and *succ* have inverses *cons*° and *succ*°. The function *swap*, now a primitive, is its own inverse. That is, $swap^\circ = swap$. The function *assocr* has inverse *assocl*, whose definition will be given later. The inverse operator promotes into composition, product, union and fixed-point operator by the following rules:

$$
\begin{aligned}
(f; g)^\circ &= g^\circ; f^\circ \\
(f \times g)^\circ &= (f^\circ \times g^\circ) \\
(f \cup g)^\circ &= f^\circ \cup g^\circ \\
(\mu F)^\circ &= \mu(^\circ; F; ^\circ)
\end{aligned}
$$

In the last equation F is a function from Inv expressions to Inv expressions, and the composition ; is lifted. One might instead write $\mu(\lambda X \cdot (F\ X^\circ)^\circ)$ as the right-hand side. An extra restriction needs to be imposed on union. To preserve reversibility, in $f \cup g$ we require not only the domains, but the ranges of f and g, to be disjoint. The disjointness may be checked by a type system, but we have not explored this possibility.

The most interesting is the *dup/eq* pair of operators. Each of them takes an extra functional argument which is either *id*, a constant function, or a sequence of composition of *fst*s, *snd*s or constructors. They have types:

$$
\begin{aligned}
dup &:: (\mathsf{F}\,a \to a) \to \mathsf{F}\,a \to (\mathsf{F}\,a \times a) \\
eq &:: (\mathsf{F}\,a \to a) \to (\mathsf{F}\,a \times a) \to \mathsf{F}\,a
\end{aligned}
$$

where F is some type functor. A call $eq\,f\,(x, a)$ tests whether the field in x selected by f equals a. Conversely, $dup\,f\,x$ copies the selected field in x. They can be understood informally as

$$dup\,f\,x = (x, f\,x)$$
$$eq\,f\,(x, a) = x \equiv f\,x = a$$

That they are inverses of each other can be seen from their relational definition:

$$dup\,f = fst^\circ \cap f; snd^\circ$$
$$eq\,f \;\; = fst \cap snd; f^\circ$$

The definition of $dup\,f$ is similar to that in Section 2 apart from the presence of the argument f. Given the definitions it is clear that $(eq\,f)^\circ = dup\,f$ and vice versa.

According to the syntax, constant functions $zero$ and nil can appear only as arguments to dup. For example, to introduce a fresh zero one has to call $dup\,zero$, which takes an input a and returns the pair $(a, 0)$. Therefore it is guaranteed that the input is not lost. An alternative design is to restrict the domain of $zero$ and nil to the type $Unit$ (therefore they do not lose information), while introducing a variation of the dup construct that creates fresh $Unit$ values only. Considering their relational semantics, the two designs are interchangeable. For this paper we will mention only the first approach.

Some more words on the design decision of the dup/eq operators. Certainly the extra argument, if restricted to fst, snd and constructors, is only a syntactic sugar. We can always swap outside the element to be duplicated and use, for example $(id \times dup\,id)$. Nevertheless we find it quite convenient to have this argument. The natural extension to include constant functions unifies the two problematic elements for inversion, duplication and the constant function, into one language construct. For our future application about bi-directional editing, we further allow the argument to be any possibly non-injective functions (such as sum, $map\,fst$, etc), which turns out to be useful for specifying transformations from source to view. Allowing dup/eq to take two arguments, however, does not seem to be necessary, as eq is meant to be asymmetrical – after a successful equality check, one of the checked values has to go away. It is in contrast to the neq operator to be introduced below.

The $neq\,p_1\,p_2$ operator, where p_1 and p_2 are projections defined by fst and snd, is a partial function checking for inequality. It is defined by

$$neq\,p_1\,p_2\,(x, y) = (x, y) \equiv p_1\,x \neq p_2\,y$$

Otherwise (x, y) is not in its domain. The $neq\,p_1\,p_2$ operator is its own inverse. It is sometimes necessary for ensuring the disjointness of the two branches of a union.

Some more operators will be introduced in sections to come to deal with the sum type, trees, etc[3]. For now, these basic operators are enough for our purpose.

---

[3] Of course, Fun can be extended in the same way so these new operators can still be embedded in Fun.

Apparently every program in Inv is invertible, since no information is lost in any operation. Every operation has its inverse in Inv. The question, then, is can we actually define useful functions in this quite restrictive-looking language?

5   Examples of Injective Functions in Inv

In this section we give some examples of injective functions expressed in Inv.

5.1   Piping Functions

We loosely define "piping function" as functions that move around objects in pairs, copy them, or discard them, without checking their values – that is, "natural" functions on pairs. We choose not to include $assocl$ as a primitive because it can be defined in terms of other primitives – in several ways, in fact. One is as below:

$$assocl = swap; (swap \times id); assocr; (id \times swap); swap$$

Another is:

$$assocl = swap; assocr; swap; assocr; swap$$

Alternatively, one might wish to make $assocl$ a primitive, so that inverting $assocr$ does not increase the size of a program.

These piping functions will turn out to be useful:

$$
\begin{aligned}
subr\,(a, (b, c)) &= (b, (a, c)) \\
trans\,((a, b), (c, d)) &= ((a, c), (b, d)) \\
distr\,(a, (b, c)) &= ((a, b), (a, c))
\end{aligned}
$$

The function $subr$ substitutes the first component in a pair to the right, $trans$ transposes a pair of pairs, while $distr$ distributes a value into a pair. They have point-free definitions in Inv, shown below[4]:

$$
\begin{aligned}
subr &= assocl; (swap \times id); assocr \\
trans &= assocr; (id \times subr); assocl \\
distr &= (dup\ id \times id); trans
\end{aligned}
$$

From the definitions it is immediate that $subr$ and $trans$ are their own inverses. The function $distr$, on the other hand, makes use of $dup\ id$ to duplicate a before distribution. Its inverse, $trans; (eq\ id \times id)$ thus has to perform an equality check before joining the two as into one.

In Section 6.1 we will talk about automatic construction of piping functions.

---

[4] Another definition, $subr = swap; assocr; (id \times swap)$, is shorter if $assocl$ is not a primitive.

5.2   Patterns

Patterns in Fun are written in terms of products, $nil°$, and $cons°$. For example, $(cons° \times id)$ decomposes the first component of a pair, while $(nil° \times id)$ checks whether that component is the empty list. The latter is usually followed by a snd function to throw away the unit resulting from $nil°$.

The term $(cons° \times id)$ is still a legal and useful pattern in Inv. However, we do not have $nil°$ in Inv. Part of the reason is that we do not want to have to introduce snd into the language, which allows the programmer to throw arbitrary information away. Instead, to match the pattern $(x, [])$, we write $eq\ nil$, which throws $[]$ away and keeps x. It is $(id \times nil°); fst$ packaged into one function. On the other hand, its inverse $dup\ nil$ introduces a fresh empty list.

Similarly, $swap; eq\ nil$ is equivalent to $(nil° \times id); snd$. We define

$$nl = swap;\ eq\ nil$$

because we will use it later.

5.3   Snoc, or Tail-Cons

The function $wrap :: A \to [A]$, wrapping the input into a singleton list, can be defined in Fun as $wrap = \langle id, nil \rangle; cons$. It also has a definition in Inv:

$$wrap = dup\ nil;\ cons$$

Its converse is therefore $wrap° = cons°; eq\ nil$ – the input list is deconstructed and a nullity test is performed on the tail.

The function $snoc :: ([A], A) \to [A]$ appends an element to the right-end of a list. With $wrap$, we can define $snoc$ in Fun as

$$snoc = \mu(X: (nil° \times id); snd; wrap\ \cup$$
$$(cons° \times id); assocr; (id \times X); cons)$$

To define it in Inv, we notice that $(nil° \times id); snd$ is exactly nl defined above. Therefore we can rewrite $snoc$ as:

$$snoc = \mu(X: nl; wrap\ \cup$$
$$(cons° \times id); assocr; (id \times X); cons)$$

Its inverse $snoc° :: [A] \to ([A], A)$ extracts the last element from a list, if the list is non-empty. The first branch of $snoc°$, namely $wrap°; nl$, extracts the only element from a singleton list, and pairs it with an empty list. The second branch, $cons°; (id \times snoc°); assocl; (cons \times id)$, deconstructs the input list, processes the tail with $snoc°$, before assembling the result. The two branches have disjoint domains because the former takes only singleton lists while the second, due to the fact that $snoc°$ takes only non-empty lists, accepts only lists with two or more elements.

5.4   Mirroring

Consider the function *mirror* :: $[A] \rightarrow [A]$ which takes a list and returns its mirror, for example, *mirror* $[1, 2, 3] = [1, 2, 3, 3, 2, 1]$. Assume that *snoc* and its inverse exists. Its definition in Fun is given as below:

$$mirror = \mu(X: nil°; nil \cup$$
$$cons°; \langle fst, \langle snd, fst \rangle \rangle; (id \times (X \times id)); snoc); cons)$$

To rewrite *mirror* in Inv, the tricky part is to convert $\langle fst, \langle snd, fst \rangle \rangle$ into something equivalent in Inv. It turns out that $\langle fst, \langle snd, fst \rangle \rangle = dup\ fst; assocr$. Also, since $nil°$ is not available in Inv, we have to rewrite $nil°; nil$ as $dup\ id; eq\ nil$. The function *dup id* duplicates the input, before *eq nil* checks whether the input is the empty list and eliminates the duplicated copy if the check succeeds. It will be discussed in Section 6.1 how such conversion can be done automatically. As a result we get:

$$mirror = \mu(X: dup\ id; eq\ nil \cup$$
$$cons°; dup\ fst; assocr; (id \times (X \times id)); snoc); cons)$$

It is educational to look at its inverse. By distributing the converse operator inside, we get:

$$mirror° = \mu(X: dup\ nil; eq\ id \cup$$
$$cons°; (id \times snoc°; (X \times id)); assocl; eq\ fst; cons)$$

Note that *dup fst* is inverted to an equality test *eq fst*. In the second branch, $cons°; (id \times snoc°; (X \times id))$ decomposes the given list into the head, the last element, and the list in-between. A recursive call then processes the list, before *assocl; eq fst* checks that the first and the last elements are equal. The whole expression fails if the check fails, thus $mirror°$ is a partial function. It is desirable to perform the equality check *before* making the recursive call. One can show, via algebraic reasoning, that the second branch equals

$$cons°; (id \times snoc°); assocl; eq\ fst; (id \times X); cons$$

which performs the check and rejects the illegal list earlier. This is one example showing that program inversion, even in this compositional style, is more than "running it backwards". To construct a program with desirable behaviour it takes some more transformations – some are easier to be performed mechanically than others.

5.5   Labelled Concatenation and Double Concatenation

List concatenation is not injective. However, the following function *lcat* (labelled concatenation)

$$lcat\ (a, (x, y)) = (a, x \mathbin{+\!\!+} [a] \mathbin{+\!\!+} y)$$

is injective if its domain is restricted to tuples where a does not appear in x. This way a acts as a marker telling us where to split $x \mathbin{+\!\!+} y$ into two. Its point-free definition can be written as:

$$lcat = nmem\ fst; \langle fst, subr; (id \times cons); cat \rangle$$

where $nmem\ p\,(a, x) = (a, x)$ if a is not a member of the list $p\,x$. To show that it is injective, it is sufficient to show an alternative definition of $lcat$ in Inv:

$$
\begin{aligned}
lcat = \mu(X\colon\ &(dup\ id \times nl); assocr; (id \times cons)\ \cup \\
&(id \times (cons^\circ \times id)); assocr; \\
&\quad neq\ id\ fst; subr; (id \times X); subr; (id \times cons))
\end{aligned}
$$

It takes a tedious but routine inductive proof, given in the appendix, to show that the two definitions are indeed equivalent. To aid understanding, the reader can translate it to its corresponding pointwise definition:

$$
\begin{aligned}
lcat\,(a, ([\,], y)) \quad &= (a, a : y) \\
lcat\,(a, (b : x, y)) &= \mathbf{let}\ (a', xy) = lcat\,(a, (x, y)) \\
&\quad \mathbf{in}\ (a', b : xy) \qquad\qquad\qquad \text{if } a \neq b
\end{aligned}
$$

The presence of neq is necessary to guarantee the disjointness of the two branches – the first branch returns a list *starting with* a, while the second branch returns a list whose head is *not* a.

Similarly, the following function $dcat$ (for "double" concatenation)

$$dcat\,(a, ((x, y), (u, v))) = (a, (x \mathbin{+\!\!+} y, u \mathbin{+\!\!+} [a] \mathbin{+\!\!+} v))$$

is injective if its domain is restricted to tuples where a does not appear in u, and x and u are equally long. Its point-free definition can be written as:

$$dcat = pred; distr; ((id \times cat) \times subr; (id \times cons); cat)$$

where $pred$ is the predicate true of $(a, ((x, y), (u, v)))$ where a is not in u and $length\ x = length\ u$. To show that it is injective, it is sufficient to show an alternative definition of $dcat$ in Inv:

$$
\begin{aligned}
dcat = \mu(X\colon\ &(dup\ id \times (nl \times nl)); trans; (id \times cons); assocr\ \cup \\
&(id \times ((cons^\circ \times id) \times (cons^\circ \times id))); neq\ id\ (snd; fst); \\
&\quad pi; (id \times X); subr; (id \times trans; (cons \times cons)))
\end{aligned}
$$

where pi is a piping function defined by

$$pi = (id \times (assocr \times assocr)); trans); subr$$

such that $pi\,(a, (((b, x), y), ((c, u), v))) = ((b, c), (a, ((x, y), (u, v))))$. The proof is similar to the proof for $lcat$ and need not be spelt out in detail. To aid understanding, the above $dcat$ is actually equivalent to the following pointwise definition:

$$
\begin{aligned}
dcat\,(a, (([\,], y), ([\,], v))) \quad &= (a, (y, a : v)) \\
dcat\,(a, ((b : x, y), (c : u, v))) &= \mathbf{let}\ (a', (xy, uv)) = dcat\,(a, ((x, y), (u, v))) \\
&\quad \mathbf{in}\ (a', (b : xy, c : uv))
\end{aligned}
$$

5.6   Printing and Parsing XML Trees

Consider internally labelled binary trees:

data *Tree A = Null* | *Node A* (*Tree A*) (*Tree A*)

To deal with trees, we extend Inv with a new primitive *node* :: ($A \times$ (*Tree A* $\times$ *Tree A*)) $\rightarrow$ *Tree A*, the curried variation of *Node*, and extend P with a new constant function *null*. An XML tree is basically a rose tree – a tree where each node has a list of children. A *forest* of rose trees, however, can be represented as a binary tree by the child-sibling representation: the left child of the a node in the binary tree represents the leftmost child of the corresponding XML node, while the right child represents its next sibling. For example, the XML tree in Figure 1(a) can be represented as the binary tree in Figure 1(b).

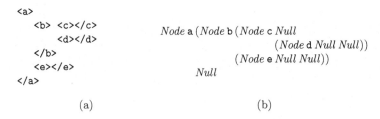

```
<a>
    <b> <c></c>
        <d></d>
    </b>
    <e></e>
</a>
```

Node a (*Node* b (*Node* c *Null*

                          (*Node* d *Null Null*))

               (*Node* e *Null Null*))

      Null

(a)   (b)

Fig. 1. Child-sibling representation of an XML tree.

To print a binary tree to its conventional serial representation, on the other hand, one has to print an opening tag (for example), its left subtree (<c></c><d></d>), a closing tag (), and then print its right subtree (<e></e>). That is similar to what *lcat* does! As a simplification, we define:

serialise :: *Tree A* $\rightarrow$ [*A*]
serialise = μ(*X*: *dup nil*; *swap*; *eq null* $\cup$
               node°; (*id* $\times$ (*X* $\times$ *X*)); *lcat*; *cons*)

The function *serialise* takes a binary tree whose values in each node do not occur in the right subtree, and flattens the tree into a list. To deal with XML trees in general, we will have to return a list of opening/closing tags and check, in *lcat*, that the tags are balanced. To perform the check, we have to maintain a stack of tags. For demonstration purpose, we deal with only the simpler case here. Its inverse, *serialise*°, parses a stream of labels back to an XML tree. By implementing printing, we get parsing for free!

However, *serialise*° is a quadratic-time parsing algorithm. The reason is that *serialise*, due to repeated calls to *lcat*, is quadratic too, and the inverted program, without further optimising transformation, always has the same efficiency as the original one. To construct a linear-time parsing algorithm, we can try to construct a linear version of *serialise*. Alternatively, we can make use of well-known program derivation techniques to construct an algorithm performing $serialise^\circ$ in linear time. We define the function $pparse$ (partial-parse) as below:

$$pparse\,(a, x) = (a, (serialise^\circ\,y, z))$$
$$\textbf{where}\ \ y + [a] + z = x$$

In point-free style it is written

$$pparse = lcat^\circ; (id \times (serialise^\circ \times id))$$

To come up with a recursive definition, we notice that the identity function id, when instantiated to take value (a, x) of type $(A \times [A])$, can be factored into $id = (id \times dup\,nil; eq\,id) \cup (id \times cons^\circ; cons)$, corresponds to the case x being empty or non-empty respectively. We start derivation with $pparse = id; pparse$ and deal with each case separately. It will turn out that we need to further split the second case into two:

$$id = (id \times dup\,nil; eq\,id)\ \cup$$
$$(id \times cons^\circ); swap; eq\,fst; dup\,fst; (cons \times id); swap\ \cup$$
$$(id \times cons^\circ; cons); neq\,id\,(cons; fst);$$

When x is non-empty, the head of x may equal a or not. We prefix $pparse$ with each of the cases, and try to simplify it using algebraic rules. It is basically a case-analysis in point-free style. Some of the branches may turn out to yield an empty relation.

We will demonstrate only the third branch. The derivation relies on the following associativity property:

$$a : ((b : (x + [b] + y)) + [a] + z) = a : (b : x + [b] + (y + [a] + z))$$

The point-free counterpart of the property, however, looks much more cumbersome. We define:

$$subrr\ \ \ = subr; (id \times subr)$$
$$subassoc = (id \times assocr; (id \times assocr)); subrr$$

The associativity property can be rewritten as:

$$(id \times (lcat; cons \times id)); lcat$$
$$= subassoc; (id \times (id \times lcat)); subrr^\circ; (id \times lcat; cons); neq\,id\,(cons^\circ; fst) \qquad (1)$$

The neq check needs to be there; otherwise only the inclusion $\subseteq$ holds. Given (1), derivation of $pparse$ is long but trivial:

$$neq\,id\,(cons^\circ; fst); pparse$$
$$=\quad \{\text{definition of } pparse\}$$
$$neq\,id\,(cons^\circ; fst); lcat^\circ; (id \times (serialise^\circ \times id))$$
$$\supseteq\quad \{\text{definition of } serialise; \text{we try its branches separately}\}$$
$$neq\,id\,(cons^\circ; fst); lcat^\circ;$$
$$(id \times (cons^\circ; lcat^\circ; (id \times (serialise^\circ \times serialise^\circ)); node \times id))$$

$=$ {products}

$neq\ id\ (cons°; fst); lcat°; (id \times (cons°; lcat° \times id));$
$(id \times ((id \times (serialise° \times serialise°)); node \times id))$

$=$ {by (1) and $neq\ f\ g; neq\ f\ g = neq\ f\ g$}

$neq\ id\ (cons°; fst); (id \times cons°; lcat°); subrr; (id \times (id \times lcat°)); subassoc°;$
$(id \times ((id \times (serialise° \times serialise°)); node \times id))$

$=$ {naturalty of $subassoc$}

$neq\ id\ (cons°; fst); (id \times cons°; lcat°); subrr; (id\times$
$(serialise° \times lcat°; (id \times (serialise° \times id)))); subassoc°; (id \times (node \times id))$

$=$ {definition of $pparse$}

$neq\ id\ (cons°; fst); (id \times cons°; lcat°); subrr;$
$(id \times (serialise° \times pparse)); subassoc°; (id \times (node \times id))$

$=$ {naturalty of $subrr$}

$neq\ id\ (cons°; fst); (id \times cons°; lcat°; (id \times (serialise° \times id))); subrr;$
$(id \times (id \times pparse)); subassoc°; (id \times (node \times id))$

$=$ {definition of $pparse$}

$neq\ id\ (cons°; fst); (id \times cons°; pparse); subrr;$
$(id \times (id \times pparse)); subassoc°; (id \times (node \times id))$

$=$ {since $neq\ f\ (cons°; g); (id \times cons°) = (id \times cons°); neq\ f\ g$}

$(id \times cons°); neq\ id\ fst; (id \times pparse); subrr;$
$(id \times (id \times pparse)); subassoc°; (id \times (node \times id))$

After some derivation, and a careful check that the recursive equation does yield unique fixed-point (see [9]), one will come up with the following definition of $pparse$:

$pparse = \mu(X\colon (id \times cons°);$
$\qquad\qquad\qquad (swap; eq\ fst; (id \times dup\ null; swap)\ \cup$
$\qquad\qquad\qquad neq\ id\ fst; (id \times X); subrr; (id \times (id \times X)); subassoc°;$
$\qquad\qquad\qquad (id \times (node \times id))))$

Now that we have $pparse$, we need to express $serialise°$ in terms of $pparse$. Some derivation would show that:

$serialise° = \mu(X\colon dup\ null; swap; eq\ nil\ \cup$
$\qquad\qquad\qquad\qquad cons°; pparse; (id \times (id \times X)); node)$

The point-free definition of $pparse$ and $serialise°$ might be rather confusing to the reader. To aid understanding, their pointwise definition is given in Figure 2.

5.7   Loops

An important feature is still missing in Inv – we can not define loops. Loops come handy when we want to show that Inv is computationally as powerful as

$$pparse\,(a, a : x) = (a, (Null, x))$$
$$pparse\,(a, b : x) =$$
$$\quad \textbf{let}\;\; (b, (t, y)) = pparse\,(b, x)$$
$$\qquad\quad (a, (u, z)) = pparse\,(a, y)$$
$$\quad \textbf{in}\quad (a, (Node\, b\, t\, u, z))$$

$$serialise^{\circ}\,[] \quad\;\;\; = Null$$
$$serialise^{\circ}\,(a : x) =$$
$$\quad \textbf{let}\;\; (a, (t, y)) = pparse\,(a, x)$$
$$\qquad\quad u \qquad\;\; = serialise^{\circ}\, y$$
$$\quad \textbf{in}\quad Node\, a\, t\, u$$

Fig. 2. Pointwise definition of $pparse$ and $serialise^{\circ}$.

Bennett's reversible Turing machine [4], since the simulation of a Turing machine is best described as a loop. In Fun, one can write a loop as a tail recursive function $\mu(X: term \cup body; X)$ where $term$ and $body$ have disjoint domains. However, the range of $body; X$ contains that of $term$, which is not allowed in Inv – when we ran the loop backwards we do not know whether to terminate the loop now or execute the body again.

Tail recursion is allowed in [13], where they resolve the non-determinism in a way similar to how left-recursive grammars are dealt with in LR parsing. Alternatively, we could introduce a special construct for loops, for example, $S; B^*; T$, where the initialisation S and loop body B have disjoint ranges, while B and the terminating condition T have disjoint domains. In [8, 9], the conditions for a loop to terminate, as well as guidelines for designing terminating loops, were discussed in a similar style. One of the earliest case study of inverting loops is [7]. Construction and reasoning of invertible loops in general has been discussed in [1].

Luckily, just to show that Inv is computationally equivalent to the reversible Turing machine, we do not need loops. One can code the reversible Turing machine as a function which returns the final state of the tapes together with an integer counting the number iterations executed. The count can then be eliminated in a clever way described by Bennett. More discussions will be given in Section 6.2.

6   Translating Non-injective Functions

Still, there are lots of things we cannot do in Inv. We cannot add two numbers, we cannot concatenate two lists. In short, we cannot construct non-injective functions. However, given a non-injective function $p :: A \to B$ in Fun, we can always construct a $p_I :: A \to (B \times H)$ in Inv such that $p_I; fst = p$. In other words, $p\,a = b$ if and only if there exists some h satisfying $p_I\,a = (b, h)$.

Such a p_I may not be unique, but always exists: you can always take $H = A$ and simply copy the input to the output. However, it is not immediately obvious how to construct such a $p_I :: A \to (B \times A)$ in Inv. Note that simply calling dup will not do, since not every function can be an argument to dup. Nor is it immediately obvious how to compose two transformed functions without throwing away the intermediate result. In Section 6.2, we will discuss the construction in more detail.

As another alternative, in Section 6.1 we will introduce what we call the "logging" translation, where a history of execution is recorded in H. The H resulting from the logging translation might not be the most interesting one, however. We can actually make p_I do different things by designing different H. We will see such an example in Section 6.3.

6.1   The Logging Translation

In this section we describe the logging translation from Fun functions to Inv. It basically works by pairing the result of the computation together with a history, where each choice of branch and each disposed piece of data is recorded, so one can always trace the computation back. It is similar to a translation for procedural languages described in [28].

Logging the History. To represent the history, we introduce several new operators: *unit*, a constant function, like *zero* and *nil*, introduces the unit value (). Functions $inl :: A \to A + B$ and $inr :: B \to A + B$ wraps a value into a sum type. Finally, *in* builds recursive types.

$$
\begin{aligned}
&log && :: \mathsf{Fun} \to (\mathsf{Inv}, \mathit{Bool})\\
&log\ succ &&= (succ, \mathsf{F})\\
&\qquad\qquad :\\
&log\ (f \cup g) = (h\ (log\ f); (id \times inl) \cup\\
&\qquad\qquad\qquad h\ (log\ g); (id \times inr), \mathsf{T})\\
&\quad\textbf{where } h\ (f, \mathsf{F}) = f; dup\ unit\\
&\qquad\qquad\quad h\ (f, \mathsf{T}) = f\\
&log\ (f \times g) = \textbf{case}\ (log\ f, log\ g)\ \textbf{of}\\
&\qquad ((f', \mathsf{F}), (g', \mathsf{F})) \to ((f' \times g'), \mathsf{F})\\
&\qquad ((f', \mathsf{T}), (g', \mathsf{F})) \to ((f' \times g'); lsub, \mathsf{T})\\
&\qquad ((f', \mathsf{F}), (g', \mathsf{T})) \to ((f' \times g'); assocl, \mathsf{T})\\
&\qquad ((f', \mathsf{T}), (g', \mathsf{T})) \to ((f' \times g'); trans, \mathsf{T})\\
&\quad\textbf{where } lsub = assocr; (id \times swap); assocl
\end{aligned}
$$

$$
\begin{aligned}
&log\ \mu F && = (\mu(X: fst\ (log\ (F(S\ X))); (id \times in)), \mathsf{T})\\
&log\ (S\ f) = (f, \mathsf{T})\\
&\quad - \text{a placeholder for recursion}\\
&log\ fs \mid unsafe && =\ compose\ (pipe\ hd)\ (log\ tl)\\
&\qquad\quad \mid otherwise =\ compose\ (log\ hd)\ (log\ tl)\\
&\quad - fs \text{ may be a split or a seq. of composition}\\
&\quad\textbf{where } (hd, unsafe, tl) = factor\ fs\\
&\qquad\qquad :\\[4pt]
&compose\ (f', \mathsf{F})\ (g', \mathsf{F}) = ((f'; g'), \mathsf{F})\\
&compose\ (f', \mathsf{T})\ (g', \mathsf{F}) = (f'; (g' \times id), \mathsf{T})\\
&compose\ (f', \mathsf{F})\ (g', \mathsf{T}) = (f'; g', \mathsf{T})\\
&compose\ (f', \mathsf{T})\ (g', \mathsf{T}) = (f'; (g' \times id); assocr, \mathsf{T})
\end{aligned}
$$

Fig. 3. The logging translation.

The interesting fragments of the logging translation is summarised in Figure 3. The function log translates a Fun function into Inv, while returning a boolean value indicating whether it carries history or not. Using the associativity of composition and the following "split absorption" rule,

$$\langle f; h, g; k \rangle = \langle f, g \rangle; (h \times k)$$

we can factor a sequence of composition into a head and a tail. The head segment uses only splits, *fst*, *snd*, converses, and constant functions. The tail segment, on the other hand, does not start with any of the constructs. For example, $\langle cons, fst \rangle$ is factored into $\langle id, fst \rangle; (cons \times id)$, while $nil^\circ; nil$ into $(nil^\circ; nil); id$. The factoring is done by the function *factor*. If the head does use one of the unsafe functions, it is compiled into Inv using the method to be discussed in the next section, implemented in the function *pipe*.

An expression $f; g$, where f and g have been translated separately, is translated into $f; (g \times id); assocr$ if both f and g carry history. If f carries history but g does not, it is translated into $f; (g \times id)$. A product $(f \times g)$, where f and g both carry history, is translated into $(f \times g); trans$, where *trans* couples the histories together. If, for example, only g carries history, it is translated into $(f \times g); assocl$.

A union $f \cup g$ is translated into $f; (id \times inl) \cup g; (id \times inr)$, where *inl* and *inr* guarantee that the ranges of the two branches are disjoint. We require both f and g to carry history. The branch not carrying history is postfixed with *dup unit* to create an empty history. Finally, the fixed-point $\mu(X: F(X))$ is translated to $\mu(X: F(X); (id \times in))$. Here we enforce that recursive functions always carry history. Known injective functions can be dealt with separately as primitives.

As an example, let us recall the function *cat* concatenating two lists. It is defined very similarly to *snoc*. The difference is that the two branches no longer have disjoint ranges.

$$cat = \mu(X: (nil^\circ \times id); snd \cup$$
$$(cons^\circ \times id); assocr; (id \times X); cons)$$

The logging translation converts *cat* into

$$cat_I = \mu(X: (nl; dup\ unit; (id \times inl) \cup$$
$$(cons^\circ \times id); assocr; (id \times X); assocl; (cons \times inr));$$
$$(id \times in))$$

The function *pipe*, to be discussed in the next section, compiles expression $(nil^\circ \times id); snd$ into *swap*; *eq nil*. The first branch, however, does not carry history since no non-constant data is thrown away. We therefore make a call to *dup unit* to create an initial history. In the second branch, the recursive call is assumed to carry history. We therefore shift the history to the right position by *assocl*. The two branches are distinguished by *inl* and *inr*.

The history returned by cat_I is a sequence of *inr*s followed by *inl* – an encoding of natural numbers! It is the length of the first argument. In general, the history would be a tree reflecting the structure of the recursion.

Compiling Piping Functions. Given a "natural" function defined in Fun in terms of splits, *fst*, *snd*, and constant functions, how does one find its equivalent, if any, in Inv? For mechanical construction, simple brute-force searching turned out to be satisfactory enough.

Take, for example, the expression $\langle\langle zero, snd; fst\rangle, \langle fst, snd; snd\rangle\rangle$. By a type inference on the expression, taking zero as a type of its own, we find that it transforms input of the form $(A, (B, C))$ to output $((0, B), (A, C))$. We can then start a breadth-first search, where the root is the input type $(A, (B, C))$, the edges are all applicable Inv formed by primitive operations and products, and the goal is the target type $((0, B), (A, C))$. To reduce the search space, we keep a count of copies of data and constants to be created. In this example, we need to create a fresh zero, so *dup zero* needs to be called once (and only once). Since no input data is duplicated, other calls to *dup* are not necessary. One possible result returned by the search is *swap; assocr; (dup zero × id); (swap × swap)*.

As another example, $nil^\circ; nil$, taking empty lists to empty lists, can be compiled into either *dup nil; eq id* or *dup id; eq nil*. Some extra care is needed to distinguish input (whose domain is to be restricted) and generated constants, such that *id* and *dup id · eq id* are not legitimate answers. The search space is finite, therefore the search is bound to terminate.

When the Fun expression throws away some data, we compile it into an Inv expression that returns a pair whose first component is the output of the collects Fun expression. The forgotten bits are stored in the second component. For example, the Fun expression ⟨*fst, snd; fst*⟩ will be compiled into an Inv expression taking $(A, (B, C))$ to $((A, B), C)$, where C is the bit of data that is left out in the Fun expression. One possibility is simply *assocl*. The left components of the compiled Inv expressions constitute the "history" of the computation.

6.2   Relationship with the Reversible Turing Machine

The logging translation constructs, from a function $p :: A \to B$, a function $p_I :: A \to (B \times H)$, where H records the history of computation. The question, then, is what to do with the history? Throwing H away merely delays the loss of information and dissipation of heat. Then answer was given by Bennett in [4].

The basic configuration of Bennett's reversible Turing machine uses three tapes: one for input, one for output, and one for the history. Given a two-tape Turing machine accepting input A on the input tape and outputting B on the output tape, Bennett showed that one can always construct a three-tape reversible Turing machine which reads the input A, and terminates with A and B on the input and output tapes, while leaving the history tape *blank*. This is how it is done: in the first phase, the program is run forward, consuming the data on the input tape while writing to the output and history tapes. The output is then copied. In the third phase the program is run backwards, this time consuming the original output and history, while regenerating the input. This can be expressed in Inv by:

$$p_I; dup\, fst; (p_I^\circ \times id) :: A \to (A \times B)$$

We cannot entirely get rid of A, or some other sufficient information, if the computation is not injective. Otherwise we are losing information. When the computed function *is* injective, however, there is a way to erase both the history and input tapes empty. Bennett's method to do it can be expressed in our notation as the following. Assume that there exists a $q :: B \to A$, defined in Fun, serving as the inverse of p. The logging translation thus yields $q_I :: B \to (A, H')$ in Inv.

$$p_I; dup\, fst; (p_I^\circ \times id); swap; (q_I \times id); eq\, fst; q_I^\circ$$

The prefix $p_I; dup\ fst; (p_I^{\circ} \times id)$, given input a, computes (a, b). The pair is swapped and b is passed though q_I, yielding $((a, h'), a)$. The duplicated a is removed by $eq\ fst$, and finally q_I° takes the remaining (a, h') and produces b.

The above discussion is relevant to us for another reason: it helps to show that Inv, even without an explicit looping construct, is computationally at least as powerful as the reversible Turing machine. Let p be a Fun function, defined tail-recursively, simulating a reversible Turing machine. The types A and B both represent states of the machine and the contents of the three tapes. The function q simulates the reversed Turing machine. They can be translated, via the logging translation, into Inv as functions that returns the final state together with an extra counter. The counter can then be eliminated using the above technique.

6.3   Preorder Traversal

To see the effect of the logging translation, and its alternatives, let us look at another example. Preorder traversal for binary trees can be defined in Fun as:

$$pre = \mu(X\colon null^{\circ}; nil\ \cup$$
$$node^{\circ}; (id \times (X \times X)); cat_I); cons)$$

The logging translation delivers the following program in Inv:

$$pre_I = \mu(X\colon (dup\ nil; eq\ null; dup\ unit; (id \times inl)\ \cup$$
$$node^{\circ}; (id \times (X \times X)); trans; (cat_I \times id); assocr); (cons \times inr));$$
$$(id \times in))$$

which returns a tree as a history. In each node of the tree is a number, returned by cat_I, telling us where to split the list into two.

However, if we choose not to reply on the logging translation, we could have chosen $H = [A]$ and defined:

$$prein = \mu(X\colon dup\ nil; eq\ null; dup\ nil\ \cup$$
$$node^{\circ}; (id \times (X \times X)); trans); dcat; assocl; (cons \times id))$$

where $dcat$ is as defined in Section 5.5. We recite its definition here:

$$dcat\ (a, ((x, y), (u, v))) = (a, (x +\!\!+ y, u +\!\!+ [a] +\!\!+ v))$$

where a does not occur in x, and x and u have the same lengths. Since $(id \times cat); cons = dcat; assocl; (cons \times id); fst$, it is obvious that $prein; fst$ reduces to pre – with a restriction on its domain. The partial function $prein$ accepts only trees with no duplicated labels. What about $prein; snd$? It reduces to inorder traversal of a binary tree. It is a known fact: we can reconstruct a binary tree having no duplicated labels from its preorder and inorder traversals [23].

7   Implementation

We have a prototype implementation of the logging translation and a simple, back-tracking interpreter for Inv, both written in Haskell. The implementation of the logging translation, though tedious, poses no substantial difficulty. Producing an efficient, non-backtracking Inv interpreter, however, turned out to be more tricky than we expected.

Implementing a relational programming language has been discussed, for example, in [15] and [20]. Both considered implementing an executable subset of Ruby, a relational language for designing circuits [16]. A functional logic programming language was used for the implementation, which uses backtracking to collect all results of a relational program.

The problem we are dealing with here, however, is a different one. We *know* that legitimate programs in Inv are deterministic. But can we implement the language without the use of backtracking? Can we detect the error when the domains or ranges of the two branches of a union are not disjoint? Consider $snoc°$, with the definition of *wrap* and *nl* expanded:

$$snoc° = \mu(X : cons°; eq\ nil; dup\ nil; swap\ \cup$$
$$cons°; (id \times X); assocl; (cons \times id))$$

Both branches start with $cons°$, and we cannot immediately decide which branch we should take.

A natural direction to go is to apply some form of domain analysis. Glück and Kawabe [13] recently suggested another approach. They observed that the problem is similar to parsing. A program is like a grammar, where the traces of a program constitute its language. Determining which branch to go is like determining which production rule to use to parse the input. In [13] they adopted the techniques used in LR parsing, such as building item sets and automatons, to construct non-backtracking programs. It is interesting to see whether the handling of parsing conflicts can be adapted to detect, report and resolve the non-disjointness of branches.

8   Conclusion and Related Work

We have presented a language, Inv, in which all functions definable are injective. It is a functional language with a relational semantics. Through examples, we find that many useful functions can be defined in Inv. In fact, it is computationally equivalent to Bennett's reversible Turing machines. Non-injective functions can be simulated in Inv via the logging translation which converts it to an Inv function returning both the result and a history.

A lot of previous work has been devoted into the design of programming languages and models for reversible computation. To the best of the authors' knowledge, they include Baker's PsiLisp [3], Lutz and Derby's JANUS [19], Frank's R [10], and Zuliani's model based on probabilistic guarded-command language [28]. Our work differs from the previous ones in several aspects: we base our model on a functional language; we do not rely on "hidden" features of the machine to record the history; and we highlight the importance of program derivation as well as mechanical inversion. We believe that Inv serves as a clean yet expressive model for the construction and reasoning of reversible programs.

The motivation to study languages for reversible programs traditionally comes from the thermodynamics view of computation. We were motivated for yet another reason – to build bi-directional editors. The source data is transformed to a view. The user can then edit the view, and the system has to work out how the source shall be updated correspondingly. Meertens [21] and Greenwald and Moore, et al. [14] independently developed their combinators for describing the source-to-view transformation, yet their results are strikingly similar. Both are combinator-like, functional languages allowing relatively unrestricted use of non-injective functions. Transformations are surjective functions/relations, and view-to-source updating is modelled by a function taking both the old source and the new view as arguments. Things get complicated when duplication is involved. We are currently exploring a slightly different approach, basing on Inv, in which the transformation is injective by default, and the use of non-injective functions is restricted to the *dup* operator. We hope this would make the model clearer, so that the difficulties can be better tackled.

Our work is complementary to Glück and Kawabe's recent work on automatic program inversion. While their focus was on automatic inversion of programs and ours on theory and language design, many of their results turned out to be highly relevant to our work. The stack-based intermediate language defined in [12] is actually an injective language. They also provided sufficient, though not necessary, conditions for the range-disjointness of branches. For a more precise check of disjointness they resort to the LR parsing technique [13]. Their insight that determining the choice of branches is like LR parsing is the key to build an efficient implementation of Inv. The authors are interested to see how conflict-handling can help to resolve the disjointness of branches.

Acknowledgements

The authors would like to thank Robert Glück and Masahiko Kawabe for valuable discussions and encouragement. This research is partly supported by the e-Society Infrastructure Project of the Ministry of Education, Culture, Sports, Science and Technology, Japan.

References

1. R. J. R. Back and J. von Wright. Statement inversion and strongest postcondition. *Science of Computer Programming*, 20:223–251, 1993.
2. R. C. Backhouse, P. de Bruin, G. Malcolm, E. Voermans, and J. van der Woude. Relational catamorphisms. In B. Möller, editor, *Proceedings of the IFIP TC2/WG2.1 Working Conference on Constructing Programs*, pages 287–318. Elsevier Science Publishers, 1991.
3. H. G. Baker. NREVERSAL of fortune–the thermodynamics of garbage collection. In *Proc. Int'l Workshop on Memory Mgmt*, number 637 in Lecture Notes in Computer Science, St. Malo, France, September 1992.
4. C. H. Bennett. Logical reversibility of computation. *IBM Journal of Research and Development*, 17(6):525–532, 1973.

5. C. H. Bennett. Thermodynamics of computation–a review. *International Journal of Theoretical Physics*, 21:905–940, 12 1982.
6. R. S. Bird and O. de Moor. *Algebra of Programming*. International Series in Computer Science. Prentice Hall, 1997.
7. E. W. Dijkstra. Program inversion. Technical Report EWD671, Eindhoven University of Technology, 1978.
8. H. Doornbos and R. C. Backhouse. Induction and recursion on datatypes. In B. Möller, editor, *Mathematics of Program Construction, 3rd International Conference*, number 947 in Lecture Notes in Computer Science, pages 242–256. Springer-Verlag, July 1995.
9. H. Doornbos and R. C. Backhouse. Reductivity. *Science of Computer Programming*, 26:217–236, 1996.
10. M. P. Frank. The R programming language and compiler. MIT Reversible Computing Project Memo #M8, Massachusetts Institute of Technology, 1997. http://www.ai.mit.edu/mpf/rc/memos/M08/M08_rdoc.html.
11. E. Fredkin and T. Toffoli. Conservative logic. *International Journal of Theoretical Physics*, 21:219–253, 1982. MIT Report MIT/LCS/TM-197.
12. R. Glück and M. Kawabe. A program inverter for a functional language with equality and constructors. In A. Ohori, editor, *Programming Languages and Systems. Proceedings*, number 2895 in Lecture Notes in Computer Science, pages 246–264. Springer-Verlag, 2003.
13. R. Glück and M. Kawabe. Derivation of deterministic inverse programs based on LR parsing (extended abstract). Submitted to the Seventh International Symposium on Functional and Logic Programming, 2004.
14. M. B. Greenwald, J. T. Moore, B. C. Pierce, and A. Schmitt. A language for bidirectional tree transformations. University of Pennsylvania CIS Dept. Technical Report, MS-CIS-03-08, University of Pennsylvani, August 2003.
15. G. Hutton. The Ruby interpreter. Technical Report 72, Chalmers University of Technology, May 1993.
16. G. Jones and M. Sheeran. Circuit design in Ruby. In *Formal Methods for VLSI Design*. Elsevier Science Publishers, 1990.
17. R. Landauer. Irreversibility and heat generation in the computing process. *IBM Journal of Research and Development*, 5:183–191, 1961.
18. Y. Lecerf. Machines de Turing réversibles. Récursive insolubilité en $n \in N$ de l'équation $u = \theta^n$, où θ est un "isomorphisme de codes". In *Comptes Rendus*, volume 257, pages 2597–2600, 1963.
19. C. Lutz and H. Derby. Janus: a time-reversible language. Caltech class project, California Institute of Technology, 1982. http://www.cise.ufl.edu/~mpf/rc/janus.html.
20. R. McPhee. Implementing Ruby in a higher-order logic programming language. Technical report, Oxford University Computing Laboratory, 1995.
21. L. Meertens. Designing constraint maintainers for user interaction. ftp://ftp.kestrel.edu/ pub/papers/meertens/dcm.ps, 1998.
22. S.-C. Mu and R. S. Bird. Inverting functions as folds. In E. Boiten and B. Möller, editors, *Sixth International Conference on Mathematics of Program Construction*, number 2386 in Lecture Notes in Computer Science, pages 209–232. Springer-Verlag, July 2002.
23. S.-C. Mu and R. S. Bird. Rebuilding a tree from its traversals: a case study of program inversion. In A. Ohori, editor, *Programming Languages and Systems. Proceedings*, number 2895 in Lecture Notes in Computer Science, pages 265–282. Springer-Verlag, 2003.

24. J. W. Sanders and P. Zuliani. Quantum programming . In R. C. Backhouse and J. N. F. d. Oliveira, editors, *Mathematics of Program Construction 2000*, number 1837 in Lecture Notes in Computer Science, pages 80–99. Springer-Verlag, 2000.
25. M. Takeichi, Z. Hu, K. Kakehi, Y. Hayashi, S.-C. Mu, and K. Nakano. TreeCalc:towards programmable structured documents. In *The 20th Conference of Japan Society for Software Science and Technology*, September 2003.
26. T. Toffoli. Reversible computing. In J. W. d. Bakker, editor, *Automata, Languages and Programming*, pages 632–644. Springer-Verlag, 1980.
27. S. G. Younis and T. F. Knight. Asymptotically zero energy split-level charge recovery logic. In *1994 International Workshop on Low Power Design*, page 114, 1994.
28. P. Zuliani. Logical reversibility. *IBM Journal of Research and Development*, 46(6):807–818, 2001. Available online at http://www.research.ibm.com/journal/rd45-6.html.

A   Proof for the Labelled Concatenation

Let *lcat* be defined by

$$lcat = nmem\,fst \cdot \langle fst, id\rangle; (id \times subr; (id \times cons); cat)$$

where $nmem\,p\,(a, x) = (a, x)$ if a is not a member of the list $p\,x$, and $lcat_I$ be the fixed-point of $lcatF$, where

$$lcatF\,X = (dup\,id \times nl); assocr; (id \times cons)\ \cup$$
$$(id \times (cons^\circ \times id)); assocr);$$
$$neq\,id\,fst; subr; (id \times X); subr; (id \times cons))$$

The aim is to show that *lcat* is also a fixed-point of *lcatF*. Starting with the more complicated branch of *lcatF*, we reason

$(id \times (cons^\circ \times id)); assocr); neq\,id\,fst; subr; (id \times lcat); subr; (id \times cons)$

= {definition of *lcat*}

$(id \times (cons^\circ \times id)); assocr); neq\,id\,fst; subr;$
$(id \times nmem\,fst; \langle fst, id\rangle; (id \times subr; (id \times cons); cat)); subr; (id \times cons)$

= {since $(id \times (id \times R)); subr = subr; (id \times (id \times R))$}

$(id \times (cons^\circ \times id)); assocr); neq\,id\,fst; subr; (id \times$
$nmem\,fst; \langle fst, id\rangle; (id \times subr)); subr; (id \times (id \times (id \times cons); cat); cons)$

= {since $subr; (id \times nmem\,fst) = nmem\,(snd; fst); subr$}

$(id \times (cons^\circ \times id)); assocr); neq\,id\,fst; nmem\,(snd; fst);$
$subr; (id \times \langle fst, id\rangle; (id \times subr)); subr; (id \times (id \times (id \times cons); cat); cons)$

= {expressing the piping in terms of splits}

$(id \times (cons^\circ \times id)); assocr); neq\,id\,fst; nmem\,(snd; fst);$
$\langle fst, \langle snd; fst, \langle snd; snd; fst, \langle fst, snd; snd; snd\rangle\rangle\rangle\rangle;$
$(id \times (id \times (id \times cons); cat); cons)$

= {associativity: $(id \times cat); cat = assocl; (cons \times id); cat,$
    and naturalty: $(id \times (id \times R)); assocl = assocl; (id \times R)$}

$(id \times (cons^\circ \times id); assocr); neq\ id\ fst; nmem\ (snd; fst);$
$\langle fst, \langle snd; fst, \langle snd; snd; fst, \langle fst, snd; snd; snd \rangle\rangle\rangle\rangle;$
$(id \times assocl); (id \times (cons \times cons); cat)$

$=$ $\{$move $(id \times assocr)$ rightwards$\}$

$(id \times (cons^\circ \times id)); neq\ id\ (fst; fst); nmem\ (fst; snd); (id \times assocr)$
$\langle fst, \langle snd; fst, \langle snd; snd; fst, \langle fst, snd; snd; snd \rangle\rangle\rangle\rangle;$
$(id \times assocl); (id \times (cons \times cons); cat)$

$=$ $\{$ cancelling $assocl$ and $assocr$ with splits$\}$

$(id \times (cons^\circ \times id)); neq\ id\ (fst; fst); nmem\ (fst; snd);$
$\langle fst, \langle snd; fst, \langle fst, snd; snd \rangle\rangle\rangle; (id \times (cons \times cons); cat)$

$=$ $\{$split absorption$\}$

$(id \times (cons^\circ \times id)); neq\ id\ (fst; fst); nmem\ (fst; snd);$
$\langle fst, \langle snd; fst, cons, \langle fst, snd; snd \rangle\rangle\rangle; (id \times (id \times cons); cat)$

$=$ $\{$products$\}$

$(id \times (cons^\circ \times id)); neq\ id\ (fst; fst); nmem\ (fst; snd);$
$(id \times (cons \times id)); \langle fst, \langle snd; fst, \langle fst, snd; snd \rangle\rangle\rangle; (id \times (id \times cons); cat)$

$=$ $\{$since $neq\ id\ (fst; fst); nmem\ (fst; snd); (id \times (cons \times id))$
        $= (id \times (cons \times id)); nmem\ fst\}$

$(id \times (cons^\circ; cons \times id)); nmem\ fst;$
$\langle fst, \langle snd; fst, \langle fst, snd; snd \rangle\rangle\rangle; (id \times (id \times cons); cat)$

$=$ $\{$products$\}$

$(id \times (cons^\circ; cons \times id)); nmem\ fst; \langle fst, id \rangle; (id \times subr);$
$(id \times (id \times cons); cat)$

$=$ $\{$folding $lcat\}$

$(id \times (cons^\circ; cons \times id)); lcat$

For the other branch we reason:

$(id \times (nil^\circ; nil \times id)); lcat$

$=$ $\{$definition of $lcat$ and $(id \times (nil \times id)); nmem\ fst = (id \times (nil \times id))\}$

$(id \times (nil^\circ; nil \times id)); \langle fst, id \rangle; (id \times subr; (id \times cons); cat)$

$=$ $\{$since $h; \langle f, g \rangle = \langle h; f, h; g \rangle$ for total $h, f, g\}$

$(id \times (nil^\circ \times id)); \langle fst, (id \times (nil \times id)) \rangle; (id \times subr; (id \times cons); cat)$

$=$ $\{$split absorption$\}$

$(id \times (nil^\circ \times id)); \langle fst, (id \times (nil \times id)); subr; (id \times cons); cat \rangle$

$=$ $\{$since $(f \times (g \times h)); subr = subr; (g \times (f \times h))\}$

$(id \times (nil^\circ \times id)); \langle fst, subr; (nil \times cons); cat \rangle$

$=$ $\{$since $(nil \times id); cat = snd\}$

$(id \times (nil^\circ \times id)); \langle fst, subr; (id \times cons); snd \rangle$

$=$ $\{$since $(id \times f); snd = snd; f$ for total $f\}$

$$(id \times (nil^{\circ} \times id)); \langle fst, subr; snd; cons \rangle$$

$= \quad \{\text{split absorption, backwards}\}$

$$(id \times (nil^{\circ} \times id)); \langle fst, subr; snd \rangle; (id \times cons)$$

$= \quad \{\text{piping}\}$

$$(dup\ id \times swap; eq\ nil); assocr; (id \times cons)$$

Therefore we conclude that

$lcatF\ lcat$

$= \quad \{\text{with the reasoning above}\}$

$$(id \times (cons^{\circ}; cons \times id)); lcat \cup (id \times (nil^{\circ}; nil \times id)); lcat)$$

$= \quad \{\text{composition distributes into union}\}$

$$((id \times (cons^{\circ}; cons \times id)) \cup (id \times (nil^{\circ}; nil \times id))); lcat$$

$= \quad \{\text{since } cons^{\circ}; cons \cup nil^{\circ}; nil = id\}$

$lcat$

Prototyping Generic Programming
in Template Haskell

Ulf Norell and Patrik Jansson*

Computing Science, Chalmers University of Technology, Göteborg, Sweden

Abstract. Generic Programming deals with the construction of programs that can be applied to many different datatypes. This is achieved by parameterizing the generic programs by the structure of the datatypes on which they are to be applied. Programs that can be defined generically range from simple map functions through pretty printers to complex XML tools.

The design space of generic programming languages is largely unexplored, partly due to the time and effort required to implement such a language. In this paper we show how to write flexible prototype implementations of two existing generic programming languages, PolyP and Generic Haskell, using Template Haskell, an extension to Haskell that enables compile-time meta-programming. In doing this we also gain a better understanding of the differences and similarities between the two languages.

1   Introduction

Generic functional programming [9] aims to ease the burden of the programmer by allowing common functions to be defined once and for all, instead of once for each datatype. Classic examples are small functions like maps and folds [8], but also more complex functions, like parsers and pretty printers [11] and tools for editing and compressing XML documents [5], can be defined generically. There exist a number of languages for writing generic functional programs [1, 3, 6, 7, 10, 12, 13], each of which has its strengths and weaknesses, and researchers in generic programming are still searching for *The Right Way*. Implementing a generic programming language is no small task, which makes it cumbersome to experiment with new designs.

In this paper we show how to use Template Haskell [16] to implement two generic programming extensions to Haskell: PolyP [10, 15] and Generic Haskell [6]. With this approach, generic functions are written in Haskell (with the Template Haskell extension), so there is no need for an external tool. Furthermore the support for code generation and manipulation in Template Haskell greatly simplifies the compilation of generic functions, thus making the implementations

---

* This work is partially funded by the Swedish Foundation for Strategic Research as part of the research program "Cover - Combining Verification Methods in Software Development".

D. Kozen (Ed.): MPC 2004, LNCS 3125, pp. 314–333, 2004.

very lightweight and easy to experiment with. Disadvantages of this approach are that we do not get the nice syntax we can get with a custom made parser and because we have not implemented a type system, generic functions are only type checked at instantiation time.

The rest of this section gives a brief introduction to Template Haskell, PolyP and Generic Haskell (GH). Section 2 compares PolyP and GH. Section 3 introduces the concepts involved in implementing generic programming using Template Haskell. Sections 4 and 5 outline the implementations of PolyP and GH and Section 6 points to possible future work.

1.1   Template Haskell

Template Haskell [16] is a language extension implemented in the Glasgow Haskell Compiler that enables compile-time meta-programming. This means that we can define code generating functions that are run at compile-time. In short you can *splice* abstract syntax into your program using the $(...) notation and *lift* an expression to the abstract syntax level using the quasi-quotes [|...|]. Splices and quasi-quotes can be nested arbitrarily deep. For example, it is possible to define the printf function with the following type:

```
printf :: String -> Q Exp
```

Here printf takes the format string as an argument and produces the abstract syntax for the printf function specialized to that particular format string. To use this function we can write, for instance

```
Main> $(printf "Hello %s, number %d!") "World" 100
"Hello World, number 100!"
```

Template Haskell comes with libraries for manipulating the abstract syntax of Haskell. The result type Q Exp of the printf function models the abstract syntax of an expression. The type constructor Q is the quotation monad, that takes care of, for instance, fresh name generation and the Exp type is a normal Haskell datatype modeling Haskell expressions. Similar types exist for declarations (Dec) and types (Type). The quotation monad is built on top of the IO monad, so if we want to escape it we have to use the function unsafePerformIO :: IO a -> a.

The definition of printf might look a bit complicated with all the lifts and splices, but ignoring those we have precisely what we would have written in an untyped language.

```
printf :: String -> Q Exp
printf fmt = prAcc fmt [| "" |]
  where
    prAcc :: String -> Q Exp -> Q Exp
    prAcc fmt r = case fmt of
      '%':'d':f -> [| \n -> $(prAcc f [| $r ++ show n |]) |]
      '%':'s':f -> [| \s -> $(prAcc f [| $r ++ s        |]) |]
      c:f        -> prAcc f [| $r ++ [c] |]
      ""         -> r
```

The `prAcc` function uses an accumulating parameter `r` containing (the abstract syntax of) an expression representing the string created so far. Every time we see a `%` code we add a lambda at the top level and update the parameter with the argument.

The keen observer will note that this definition of `printf` is quadratic in the length of the format string. This is easy to fix but for the sake of brevity we chose the inefficient version, which is slightly shorter.

Template Haskell supports program reflection or reification, which means that it is possible to get hold of the type of a named function or the declaration that defines a particular entity. For example:

```
reifyType id    :: Q Type
reifyDecl Maybe :: Q Dec
```

We can use this feature to find the definitions of the datatypes that a generic function is applied to.

1.2 PolyP

PolyP [10, 15] is a language extension to Haskell for generic programming, that allows generic functions over unary regular datatypes. A regular datatype is a datatype with no function spaces, no mutual recursion and no nested recursion[1]. Examples of unary regular datatypes are `[]`, `Maybe` and `Rose`:

```
data Rose a = Fork a [Rose a]
```

Generic programming in PolyP is based on the notion of *pattern functors*. Each datatype is associated with a pattern functor that describes the structure of the datatype. The different pattern functors are shown in Figure 1. The `(:+:)` pattern functor is used to model multiple constructors, `(:*:)` and `Empty` model the list of arguments to the constructors, `Par` is a reference to the parameter type, `Rec` is a recursive call, `(:@:)` models an application of another regular datatype and `Const` is a constant type. The pattern functors of the datatypes mentioned above are (the comments show the expanded definitions applied to two type variables `p` and `r`):

```
type ListF  = Empty :+: (Par :*: Rec) -- Either () (p,r)
type MaybeF = Empty :+: Par            -- Either () p
type RoseF  = Par :*: ([] :@: Rec)     -- (p, [r])
```

PolyP provides two functions `inn` and `out` to fold and unfold the top-level structure of a datatype. Informally, for any regular datatype `D` with pattern functor `F`, `inn` and `out` have the following types:

```
inn :: F a (D a) -> D a
out :: D a -> F a (D a)
```

Note that only the top-level structure is folded/unfolded.

---

[1] The recursive calls must have the same form as the left hand side of the definition.

```
type (g :+: h) p r = Either (g p r) (h p r)
type (g :*: h) p r = (g p r, h p r)
type Empty     p r = ()
type Par       p r = p
type Rec       p r = r
type (d :@: g) p r = d (g p r)
type Const t   p r = t
```

Fig. 1. Pattern functors

A special construct, `polytypic`, is used to define generic functions over pattern functors by pattern matching on the functor structure. As an example, the definition of `fmap2`, a generic map function over pattern functors, is shown in Figure 2. Together with `inn` and `out` these polytypic functions can be used to define generic functions over regular datatypes. For instance:

```
pmap :: (a -> b) -> D a -> D b
pmap f = inn . fmap2 f (pmap f) . out
```

The same polytypic function can be used to create several different generic functions. We can, for instance, use `fmap2` to define generic cata- and anamorphisms (generalized folds and unfolds):

```
cata :: (F a b -> b) -> D a -> b
cata f = f . fmap2 id (cata f) . out

ana :: (b -> F a b) -> b -> D a
ana f = inn . fmap2 id (ana f) . f
```

1.3   Generic Haskell

Generic Haskell [2] is an extension to Haskell that allows generic functions over datatypes of arbitrary kinds. Hinze [4] observed that the type of a generic function depends on the kind of the datatype it is applied to, hence each generic function in Generic Haskell comes with a generic (kind indexed) type. The kind indexed type associated with the generic map function is defined as follows:

```
Map {[ * ]}      s t = s -> t
Map {[ k -> l ]} s t = forall a b. Map {[ k ]} a b ->
                                   Map {[ l ]} (s a) (t b)
```

Generic Haskell uses the funny brackets ({[ ]}) to enclose kind arguments. The type of the generic map function `gmap` applied to a type `t` of kind `k` can be expressed as

```
gmap {| t :: k |} :: Map {[ k ]} t t
```

```
polytypic fmap2 :: (a -> c) -> (b -> d) -> f a b -> f c d
    = \p r -> case f of
          g :+: h -> fmap2 p r -+- fmap2 p r
          g :*: h -> fmap2 p r -*- fmap2 p r
          Empty     -> const ()
          Par       -> p
          Rec       -> r
          d :@: g -> pmap (fmap2 p r)
          Const t -> id

(-+-) :: (a -> c) -> (b -> d) -> Either a b -> Either c d
(f -+- g) (Left  x) = Left  (f x)
(f -+- g) (Right y) = Right (g y)

(-*-) :: (a -> c) -> (b -> d) -> (a,b) -> (c,d)
(f -*- g) (x,y) = (f x, g y)
```

Fig. 2. The definition of fmap2 in PolyP

The second type of funny brackets ({| |}) encloses type arguments. Following are the types of gmap for some standard datatypes.

```
gmap {| Bool |}   :: Bool -> Bool
gmap {| [] |}     :: forall a b. (a -> b) -> [a] -> [b]
gmap {| Either |} :: forall a b. (a -> b) ->
                     forall c d. (c -> d) ->
                     Either a c -> Either b d
```

The kind indexed types follow the same pattern for all generic functions. A generic function applied to a type of kind $\kappa \to \nu$ is a function that takes a generic function for types of kind κ and produces a generic function for the target type of kind ν.

The generic functions in Generic Haskell are defined by pattern matching on the top-level structure of the type argument. Figure 3 shows the definition of the generic map function gmap. The structure combinators are similar to those in PolyP. Sums and products are encoded by :+: and :*: and the empty product is called Unit. A difference from PolyP is that constructors and record labels are represented by the structure combinators Con c and Label l. The arguments (c and l) contain information such as the name and fixity of the constructor or label. A generic function must also contain cases for primitive types such as Int. The type of the right hand side of each clause is the type of the generic function instantiated with the structure type on the left. The definitions of the structure types are shown in Figure 4. Note that the arguments to Con and Label containing the name and fixity information are only visible in the pattern matching and not in the actual types.

Generic Haskell contains many features that we do not cover here, such as type indexed types, generic abstraction and constructor cases.

```
gmap {| t :: k |} :: Map {[ k ]} t t
gmap {| :+: |} gmapA gmapB (Inl a)    = Inl (gmapA a)
gmap {| :+: |} gmapA gmapB (Inr b)    = Inr (gmapB b)
gmap {| :*: |} gmapA gmapB (a :*: b) = gmapA a :*: gmapB b
gmap {| Unit |}                       = id
gmap {| Con c |}   gmapA (Con a)      = Con   (gmapA a)
gmap {| Label l |} gmapA (Label a)    = Label (gmapA a)
gmap {| Int |}                        = id
```

Fig. 3. A generic map function in Generic Haskell

```
data a :+: b = Inl a | Inr b
data a :*: b = a :*: b
data Unit    = Unit
data Con a   = Con a
data Label a = Label a
```

Fig. 4. Structure types in Generic Haskell

2   Comparing PolyP and Generic Haskell

The most notable difference between PolyP and Generic Haskell is the set of
datatypes available for generic programmers. In PolyP generic functions can only
be defined over unary regular datatypes, while Generic Haskell allows generic
functions over (potentially non-regular) datatypes of arbitrary kinds. There is a
trade-off here, in that more datatypes means fewer generic functions. In PolyP it
is possible to define generic folds and unfolds such as **cata** and **ana** that cannot
be defined in Generic Haskell.

Even if PolyP and Generic Haskell may seem very different, their approaches
to generic programming are very similar. In both languages generic functions are
defined, not over the datatypes themselves, but over a structure type acquired
by unfolding the top-level structure of the datatype. The structure types in
PolyP and Generic Haskell are very similar. The differences are that in PolyP
constructors and labels are not recorded explicitly in the structure type and the
structure type is parameterized over recursive occurrences of the datatype. This
is made possible by only allowing regular datatypes. For instance, the structure
of the list datatype in the two languages is (with Generic Haskell's sums and
products translated into Either, (,) and ()):

```
type ListF a r = Either        ()        (a, r )  -- PolyP
type ListS a   = Either (Con ()) (Con (a,[a])) -- GH
```

To transform a generic function over a structure type into a generic function
over the actual datatype, conversion functions between the datatype and the
structure type are needed. In PolyP they are called **inn** and **out** (described
in Section 1.2) and they are primitives in the language. In Generic Haskell this

conversion is done by the compiler and the conversion functions are not available to the programmer.

As mentioned above, generic functions in both languages are primarily defined over the structure types. This is done by pattern matching on a type code, representing the structure of the datatype. The type codes differ between the languages, because they model different sets of datatypes, but the generic functions are defined in very much the same way. The most significant difference is that in Generic Haskell the translations of type abstraction, type application and type variables are fixed and cannot be changed by the programmer.

Given a generic function over a structure type it should be possible to construct a generic function over the corresponding datatype. In Generic Haskell this process is fully automated and hidden from the programmer. In PolyP, however, it is the programmer's responsibility to take care of this. One reason for this is that the structure types are more flexible in PolyP, since they are parameterized over the recursive occurrences of the datatype. This means that there is not a unique datatype generic function for each structure type generic function. For instance the structure type generic function `fmap2` from Figure 2 can be used not only to define the generic map function, `pmap`, but also the generic cata- and anamorphisms, `cata` and `ana`.

3   Generic Programming in Template Haskell

Generic functions in both PolyP and Generic Haskell are defined by pattern matching over the code for a datatype. Such a generic function can be viewed as an algorithm for constructing a Haskell function given a datatype code. For instance, given the type code for the list datatype a generic map function can generate the definition of a map function over lists. Program constructing algorithms like this can be implemented nicely in Template Haskell; a generic function is simply a function from a type code to the abstract syntax for the function specialized to the corresponding type. When embedding a generic programming language like PolyP or Generic Haskell in Template Haskell there are a few things to consider:

- **Datatype codes**
  The structure of a datatype has to be coded in a suitable way. How this is done depends, of course, on the set of datatypes to be represented, but we also have to take into account how the type codes affect the generic function definitions. Since we are going to pattern match on the type codes we want them to be as simple as possible.
  To avoid having to create the datatype codes by hand we can define a (partial) function from the abstract syntax of a datatype definition to a type code. The (abstract syntax of the) datatype definition can be acquired using the reification facilities in Template Haskell.
- **Structure types**
  To avoid having to manipulate datatype elements directly, generic functions are defined over a structure type, instead of over the datatype itself. The

structure type reveals the top-level structure of the datatype and allows us to manipulate datatype elements in a uniform way. Both PolyP and Generic Haskell use a binary sum type to model multiple constructors and a binary product to model the arguments to the constructors. In this paper we use `Either` as the sum type and `(,)` as the product type.

When applied to the code for a datatype a generic function produces a function specialized for the structure type of that datatype. This means that we have to know how to translate between type codes and structure types. For instance, the type code `Par` in PolyP is translated to the structure type with the same name. Note that while there is a unique structure type for each type code, it is possible for several datatypes to have the same code (and thus the same structure).

– **Generic function definitions**
  A generic function is implemented as a function from a type code to (abstract syntax for) the specialized version of the function. It might also be necessary to represent the type of a generic function in some way as we will see when implementing Generic Haskell in Section 5.

– **From structure types to datatypes**
  The generic functions defined as described above produce functions specialized for the structure types. What we are interested in, on the other hand, are specializations for the actual datatypes. As described in Section 2, PolyP and Generic Haskell take two different approaches to constructing these specializations. In PolyP it is the responsibility of the user whereas in Generic Haskell, it is done by the compiler. In any case we need to be able to convert between an element of a datatype and an element of the corresponding structure type. How difficult the conversion functions are to generate depends on the complexity of the structure types. Both PolyP and Generic Haskell have quite simple structure types, so the only information we need to generate the conversion functions is the names and arities of the datatype constructors. In the approach taken by PolyP, the conversion functions (`inn` and `out`) are all the compiler needs to define. The programmer of a generic function will then use these to lift her function from the structure type level to the datatype level. Implementing the Generic Haskell approach on the other hand requires some more machinery. For each generic function, the compiler must convert the specialization for a structure type into a function that operates on the corresponding datatype. In Section 5 we will see how to do this for Generic Haskell.

– **Instantiation**
  Both the PolyP and Generic Haskell compilers do selective specialization, that is, generic functions are only specialized to the datatypes on which they are actually used in the program. This requires traversing the entire program to look for uses of generic functions. When embedding generic programming in Template Haskell we do not want to analyze the entire program to find out which specializations to construct. What we can do instead is to in-line the body of the specialized generic function every time it is used. This makes the use of the generic functions easy, but special care has to be taken

to avoid that recursive generic functions give rise to infinite specializations. This is the approach we use when embedding PolyP in Template Haskell (Section 4). Another option is to require the user to decide which functions to specialize on which datatypes. This makes it harder on the user, but a little easier for the implementor of the generic programming language. Since our focus is on fast prototyping of generic languages, this is the method we choose when implementing Generic Haskell.

4   PolyP in Template Haskell

Following the guidelines described in Section 3 we can start to implement our first generic programming language, PolyP.

4.1   Datatype Codes

The first thing to do is to decide on a datatype encoding. In PolyP, generic functions are defined by pattern matching on a pattern functor, so to get a faithful implementation of PolyP we should choose the type code to model these pattern functors.

```
data Code = Code :+: Code | Code :*: Code | Empty
          | Par | Rec | Regular :@: Code | Const Type
```

This coding corresponds perfectly to the definition of the pattern functors in Figure 1, we just have to decide what **Type** and **Regular** mean. The Template Haskell libraries define the abstract syntax for Haskell types in a datatype called **Type** so this is a natural choice to model types. The model of a regular datatype should contain a code for the corresponding pattern functor, but it also needs to contain the constructor names of the regular datatype. This is because we need to generate the **inn** and **out** functions for a regular datatype. Consequently we choose the following representation of a regular datatype:

```
type Regular = ([ConName], Code)
```

To make it easy to get hold of the code for a datatype, we want to define a function that converts from the (abstract syntax of a) datatype definition to **Regular**. A problem with this is that one regular datatype might depend on another regular datatype, in which case we have to look at the definition of the second datatype as well. So instead of just taking the definition of the datatype in question our conversion function takes a list of all definitions that might be needed together with the name of the type to be coded.

```
regular :: [Q Dec] -> TypeName -> Regular
```

Note that if **regular** fails, which it will if a required datatype definition is missing or the datatype is not regular, we will get a compile time error, since the function is executed by the Template Haskell system at compile time.

We can use the function `regular` to get the code for the `Rose` datatype defined in Section 1.2 as follows:

```
roseD = regular [reifyDecl Rose, reifyDecl []] "Rose"
```

4.2   Structure Types

The structure type of a regular datatype is a pattern functor. See Section 1.2 and Figure 1 in particular for their definitions. The mapping between the datatype codes (`Code`) and the pattern functors is the obvious one (a type code maps to the pattern functor with the same name).

4.3   Generic Function Definitions

Generic functions over pattern functors are implemented as functions from type codes to (abstract) Haskell code. For example, the function `fmap2` from Figure 2 in Section 1.2 is implemented as shown in Figure 5. The two definitions are strikingly similar, but there are a few important differences, the most obvious one being the splices and quasi-quote brackets introduced in the Template Haskell definition. Another difference is in the type signature. PolyP has its own type system capable of expressing the types of generic functions, but in Template Haskell everything inside quasi-quotes has type `Q Exp`, and thus the type of `fmap2` is lost. The third difference is that in Template Haskell we have to pass the type codes explicitly.

```
fmap2 :: Code -> Q Exp
fmap2 f =
  [| \p r -> $(
       case f of
         g :+: h -> [| $(fmap2 g) p r -+- $(fmap2 h) p r |]
         g :*: h -> [| $(fmap2 g) p r -*- $(fmap2 h) p r |]
         Empty   -> [| const () |]
         Par     -> [| p |]
         Rec     -> [| r |]
         d :@: g -> [| $(pmap d) ($(fmap2 g) p r) |]
         Const t -> [| id |]
     )
  |]
```

Fig. 5. fmap2 in Template Haskell

The (`:@:`)-case in the definition of `fmap2` uses the datatype level function `pmap` to map over the regular datatype d. The definition of `pmap` is described in Section 4.4.

4.4   From Structure Types to Datatypes

The generic functions described in Section 4.3 are defined over pattern functors, whereas the functions we are (really) interested in operate on regular datatypes. Somehow we must bridge this gap. In PolyP these datatype level functions are defined in terms of the pattern functor functions and the functions inn and out, that fold and unfold the top-level structure of a datatype. In PolyP, inn and out are primitive but in our setting they can be treated just like any generic function, that is, they take a code for a datatype and produce Haskell code. However, the code for a pattern functor is not sufficient, we also need to know the names of the constructors of the datatype in order to construct and deconstruct values of the datatype. This gives us the following types for inn and out.

```
inn, out :: Regular -> Q Exp
```

To see what code has to be generated we can look at the definition of inn and out for lists:

```
out_List :: [a] -> Either () (a, [a])
out_List = \xs -> case xs of
    []   -> Left ()
    x:xs -> Right (x,xs)

inn_List :: Either () (a, [a]) -> [a]
inn_List = \xs -> case xs of
    Left ()      -> []
    Right (x,xs) -> x:xs
```

Basically we have to generate a case expression with one branch for each constructor. In the case of out we match on the constructor and construct a value of the pattern functor whereas inn matches on the pattern functor and creates a value of the datatype. Note that the arguments to the constructors are left untouched, in particular the tail of the list is not unfolded.

   With inn and out at our disposal we define the generic map function over a regular datatype, pmap. The definition is shown in Figure 6 together with the same definition in PolyP. In PolyP, pmap is a recursive function and we might be tempted to define it recursively in Template Haskell as well. This is not what we want, since it would make the generated code infinite, instead we want to *generate* a recursive function which we can do using a let binding.

4.5   Instantiation

The generic functions defined in this style are very easy to use. To map a function f over a rose tree tree we simply write

```
$(pmap roseD) f tree
```

where roseD is the representation of the rose tree datatype defined in Section 4.1.

```
pmap :: Regular d => (a -> b) -> d a -> d b
pmap f = inn . fmap2 f (pmap f) . out

pmap :: Regular -> Q Exp
pmap d = [| let pmap_d f = $(inn d)
                         . $(fmap2 $ functorOf d) f (pmap_d f)
                         . $(out d)
            in pmap_d
         |]
```

Fig. 6. The `pmap` function in PolyP and Template Haskell

5   Generic Haskell in Template Haskell

In Section 4 we outlined an embedding of PolyP into Template Haskell. In this
section we do the same for the core part of Generic Haskell. Features of Generic
Haskell that we do not consider include constructor cases, type indexed types
and generic abstraction. Type indexed types and generic abstraction should be
possible to add without much difficulty; constructor cases might require some
work, though.

5.1   Datatype Codes

To be consistent with how generic functions are defined in Generic Haskell we
choose the following datatype for type codes:

```
data Code = Sum | Prod | Unit
          | Con ConDescr | Label LabelDescr
          | Fun | TypeCon TypeName
          | App Code Code | Lam VarName Code | Var VarName
```

The first seven constructors should be familiar to users of Generic Haskell, although you do not see the `TypeCon` constructor when matching on a specific
datatype in Generic Haskell. The last three constructors `App`, `Lam` and `Var` you
never see in Generic Haskell. The reason why they are not visible is that the
interpretation of these type codes is hard-wired into Generic Haskell and cannot
be changed by the programmer. By making them explicit we get the opportunity
to experiment with this default interpretation.

The types `ConDescr` and `LabelDescr` describe the properties of constructors
and labels. In our implementation this is just the name, but it could also include
information such as fixity and strictness.

If we define the infix application of `App` to be left associative, we can write
the type code for the list datatype as follows:

```
listCode = Lam "a" $
  Sum 'App' (Con "[]" 'App' Unit)
      'App' (Con ":"
                'App' (Prod
                          'App' Var "a"
                          'App' (TypeCon "[]" 'App' Var "a")
                      )
            )
```

This is not something we want to write by hand for every new datatype, even though it can be made much nicer by some suitable helper functions. Instead we define a function that produces a type code given the abstract syntax of a datatype declaration.

```
typeCode :: Q Dec -> Code
```

Thus, to get the above code for the list datatype we just write

```
typeCode (reifyDecl [])
```

5.2   Structure Types

The structure type for a datatype is designed to model the structure of that datatype in a uniform way. Similarly to PolyP, Generic Haskell uses binary sums and products to model datatype structures. We diverge from Generic Haskell in this implementation in that we use the Haskell prelude types `Either` and `(,)` for sums and products instead of defining our own. Another difference between our Template Haskell implementation and standard Generic Haskell is that constructors and labels are not modeled in the structure type. Compare, for example, the structure types of the list datatype in standard Generic Haskell (first) to our implementation (second):

```
type ListS a = Sum (Con Unit) (Con (Prod a [a])) -- std GH
type ListS a = Either    ()            (a,[a])   -- prototype
```

Since we are not implementing all features of Generic Haskell, we can allow ourselves this simplification.

5.3   Generic Function Definitions

The type of a generic function in Generic Haskell depends on the kind of the datatype the function is applied to. At a glance it would seem like we could ignore the types of a generic function, since Template Haskell does not have any support for typing anyway. It turns out, however, that we need the type when generating the datatype level functions. There are no type level lambdas in the abstract syntax for types in Template Haskell and there is no datatype for kinds. We need both these things when defining kind indexed types[2], so we define a

---

[2] Type level lambdas are not strictly needed, but they make things much easier.

```
data Kind = Star | FunK Kind Kind
data Type = ForallT [VarName] Context Type
          | VarT VarName | ConT ConName
          | TupleT Int | ListT | ArrowT
          | AppT Type Type
          | LamT [VarName] Type

a --> b = ArrowT 'AppT' a 'AppT' b
```

Fig. 7. Datatypes for kinds and types

datatype for kinds and a new datatype for types, shown in Figure 7. The kind indexed type Map from Section 1.3 can be defined as

```
_Map Star = LamT ["s","t"] $ VarT "s" --> VarT "t"
_Map (FunK k l) = LamT ["s","t"] $ ForallT ["a","b"] $
                     _Map k 'AppT' a 'AppT' b -->
                     _Map l 'AppT' AppT s a 'AppT' AppT t b
  where [s,t,a,b] = map VarT ["s","t","a","b"]
```

This is much clumsier than the Generic Haskell syntax, but we can make things a lot easier by observing that all type indexed types follow the same pattern. The only thing we need to know is the number of generic and non-generic arguments and the type for kind ⋆. With this information we define the function kindIndexedType:

```
kindIndexedType :: Int         -- # generic arguments
                -> Int         -- # non-generic arguments
                -> Type        -- type for kind *
                -> Kind -> Type
```

Using this function we define the type Map as

```
_Map = kindIndexedType 2 0 $ LamT ["s","t"]
                           $ VarT "s" --> VarT "t"
```

Now, the type of a generic function depends on the kind of the datatype it is applied to as well as the datatype itself. So we define a generic type to be a function from a kind and a type to a type.

```
type GenericType = Kind -> Type -> Type
```

The type of the generic map function from Section 1.3 can be defined as

```
gmapType :: GenericType
gmapType k t = _Map k 'AppT' t 'AppT' t
```

A generic function translates a type code to abstract Haskell syntax – we capture this in the type synonym GenericFun:

```
type GenericFun = Code -> Q Exp
```

To deal with types containing variables and abstraction, we also need an environment in which to store the translation of variables.

```
type GEnv      = [(VarName, Q Exp)]
type GenericFun' = GEnv -> GenericFun
```

With these types at our disposal we define the default translation, that will be the same for most generic functions. The function `defaultTrans`, defined in Figure 8, takes the name of the generic function that is being constructed and a `GenericFun'` that handles the non-standard translation and produces a `GenericFun'`. The idea is that a generic function should call `defaultTrans` on all type codes that it does not handle (see the generic map function in Figure 9 for an example).

```
defaultTrans :: VarName -> GenericFun' -> GenericFun'
defaultTrans name gfun env t = case t of
    Con _      -> [| id |]
    Label _    -> [| id |]
    TypeCon c -> varE $ gName name c
    App s t    -> [| $(gfun env s) $(gfun env t) |]
    Lam x t    -> [| \gx -> $(gfun ((x,[|gx|]):env) t) |]
    Var x      -> fromJust $ lookup x env

varE :: String -> Q Exp
```

Fig. 8. Default generic translations

The default translation for constructors and labels is the identity function. Since the structure type corresponding to Con and Label is the type level identity function of kind $\star \to \star$, a generic function applied to Con or Label expects a generic function for a type of kind $\star$ and should return a generic function for the same type.

The default translation of a named type is to call the specialized version of the generic function for that type. The function gName takes the name of a generic function and the name of a type and returns the name of the specialization of the generic function to that type. In our implementation it is the responsibility of the user to make sure that this specialization exists.

In Generic Haskell, the first three cases in `defaultTrans` can be changed by the programmer, for instance using the name of a constructor when pretty printing or defining special cases for particular types. The last three cases, on the other hand, are hidden from Generic Haskell users. A type level application is always translated into a value application, when encountering a type abstraction a generic function takes the translation of the abstracted variable as an argument, stores it in the environment and calls itself on the body of the abstraction. The translation of a type variable is looked up in the environment.

Provided that it does not need to change the default actions a generic function only has to provide actions for Sum, Prod and Unit. The definition of the generic map function from Section 1.3 is shown in Figure 9. For Sum and Prod the generic map function returns the map functions for Either and (,), and mapping over the unit type is just the identity functions. For all other type codes we call the defaultTrans function to perform the default actions.

```
gmap :: GenericFun
gmap t = gmap' [] t
  where
    gmap' env t = case t of
      Sum  -> [| (-+-) |]
      Prod -> [| (-*-) |]
      Unit -> [| id |]
      t    -> defaultTrans "gmap" gmap' env t
```

Fig. 9. Generic map

5.4   From Structure Types to Datatypes

The generic functions defined in the style described in the previous section generate specializations for structure types, so from these structure type functions we have to construct functions for the corresponding datatypes. In our implementation of PolyP (Section 4) this was the responsibility of the programmer of the generic function. The reason for this was that in PolyP, the conversion could be done in several different ways, yielding different datatype functions. In Generic Haskell, on the other hand, we have a unique datatype function in mind for every structure type function. For instance, look at the type of the function generated by applying gmap to the code for the list datatype:

```
gmap_ListS :: (a -> b) -> Either () (a, [a])
                       -> Either () (b, [b])
gmap_ListS = $(gmap listS)
```

From this function we want to generate the map function for List with type

```
gmap_List :: (a -> b) -> [a] -> [b]
```

To be able to do this we first have to be able to convert between the List datatype and its structure type. For this purpose we define a function structEP that given the names and arities of a datatype's constructors generates the conversion functions between the datatype and its structure type.

```
structEP :: TypeName -> [(ConName, Int)] -> Q Dec
```

The structEP function generates a declaration of the conversion functions, so for the list datatype it would generate something like the following:

```
listEP :: EP [a] (Either () (a,[a]))
listEP = EP out inn
  where
    out []              = Left ()
    out (x:xs)          = Right (x,xs)
    inn (Left ())       = []
    inn (Right (x,xs))  = x:xs
```

The EP type, shown in Figure 10, models an embedding projection pair.

```
data EP a b = EP { from :: a -> b, to :: b -> a }

idEP :: EP a a
idEP = EP id id

funEP :: EP a a' -> EP b b' -> EP (a -> b) (a' -> b')
funEP epA epB = EP (\f -> from epB . f . to   epA)
                   (\g -> to   epB . g . from epA)
```

Fig. 10. Embedding projection pairs

Using `listEP` we define the map function for the list datatype as

```
gmap_List :: (a -> b) -> [a] -> [b]
gmap_List f = to (funEP listEP listEP) (gmap_ListS f)
```

The embedding projection pair is generated directly from the type of the generic function. In this case an embedding projection pair of type

```
EP ([a] -> [b]) (Either () (a,[a]) -> Either () (b,[b]))
```

should be generated. Embedding projection pairs between function types can be constructed with `funEP`, and `listEP` can convert between a list and an element of the list structure type. We define the function `typeEP` to generate the appropriate embedding projection pair.

```
typeEP :: Q Exp -> Kind -> GenericType -> Q Exp
```

The first argument to `typeEP` is the embedding projection pair converting between the datatype and its structure type, the second argument is the kind of the datatype and the third argument is the type of the generic function. So to get the embedding projection pair used in `gmap_List` we write

```
typeEP [| listEP |] (KFun Star Star) gmapType
```

5.5   Instantiation

The focus of this article is on fast prototyping of generic programming languages; this means that we do not make great efforts to facilitate the use of the generic functions. In particular what we do not do is figuring out which specializations to generate. Instead we provide a function `instantiate` that generates the definition of the specialization of a generic function to a particular datatype, as well as a function `structure`, that generates the embedding projection pair definition converting between a datatype and its structure type using the function `structEP` from Section 5.4.

```
type Generic  = (VarName, GenericType, GenericFun)
type Datatype = (TypeName, Kind, Code)

instantiate :: Generic -> Datatype -> Q [Dec]
structure   :: Datatype -> Q [Dec]
```

Using these functions a map function for rose trees can be generated by

```
data Rose a = Fork a [Rose a]
listD = ("[]", KFun Star Star, typeCode (reifyDecl []))
roseD = ("[]", KFun Star Star, typeCode (reifyDecl Rose))
gmapG = ("gmap", gmapType, gmap)
$(structure listD)
$(structure roseD)
$(instantiate gmapG listD)
$(instantiate gmapG roseD)
```

Since the rose trees contain lists we have to create specializations for the list datatype as well. The code generated for `gmap` specialized to rose trees will look something like the following (after some formatting and alpha renaming). Note that `gmap_RoseS` uses both `gmap_List` and `gmap_Rose`.

```
gmap_RoseS :: (a -> b) -> (a, [Rose a]) -> (b, [Rose b])
gmap_RoseS = \f -> f -*- gmap_List (gmap_Rose f)

gmap_Rose :: (a -> b) -> Rose a -> Rose b
gmap_Rose f = to (funEP roseEP roseEP) (gmap_RoseS f)
```

6   Conclusions and Future Work

Efforts to explore the design space of generic programming have been hampered by the fact that implementing a generic programming language is a daunting task. In this paper we have shown that this does not have to be the case. We have presented two prototype implementations of generic programming approximating PolyP and Generic Haskell. Thanks to the Template Haskell machinery, these prototypes could be implemented in a short period of time (each implementation consists of a few hundred lines of Haskell code). Comparing these two implementations we obtain a better understanding of the design space when it comes to implementations of generic programming languages.

There are a few different areas one might want to focus future work on:

- The idea of fast prototyping is to make it possible to experiment with different ideas in an easy way. So far, most of our work has been concentrated on how to write the prototypes and not so much on experimenting.
- One of the biggest problems with current generic programming systems is efficiency. The conversions between datatypes and structure types takes a lot of time and it would be a big win if one could remove this extra cost. We have started working on a simplifier for Haskell expressions that can do this.
- It would be interesting to see how other generic programming styles fit into this framework. In particular one could look at the Data.Generics libraries in GHC [13] and also at the generic traversals of adaptive OOP [14].
- The design of a generic programming language includes the design of a type system. In this paper we have ignored the issue of typing, leaving it up to the Haskell compiler to find type errors in the specialized code. Is there an easy way to build prototype type systems for our implementations?

References

1. A. Alimarine and R. Plasmeijer. A generic programming extension for Clean. In T. Arts and M. Mohnen, editors, *Proceedings of the 13th International Workshop on the Implementation of Functional Languages, IFL 2001*, volume 2312 of *LNCS*, pages 168–185. Springer-Verlag, 2001.
2. D. Clarke and A. Löh. Generic haskell, specifically. In J. Gibbons and J. Jeuring, editors, *Proceedings of the IFIP TC2 Working Conference on Generic Programming*, pages 21–48. Kluwer, 2003.
3. R. Cockett and T. Fukushima. About Charity. Yellow Series Report No. 92/480/18, Dep. of Computer Science, Univ. of Calgary, 1992.
4. R. Hinze. Polytypic values possess polykinded types. In *Mathematics of Program Construction*, volume 1837 of *LNCS*, pages 2–27. Springer-Verlag, 2000.
5. R. Hinze and J. Jeuring. Generic Haskell: Applications. In *Generic Programming, Advanced Lectures*, volume 2793 of *LNCS*, pages 57–97. Springer-Verlag, 2003.
6. R. Hinze and J. Jeuring. Generic Haskell: Practice and theory. In *Generic Programming, Advanced Lectures*, volume 2793 of *LNCS*, pages 1–56. Springer-Verlag, 2003.
7. R. Hinze and S. Peyton Jones. Derivable type classes. In G. Hutton, editor, *Proceedings of the 2000 ACM SIGPLAN Haskell Workshop*, volume 41.1 of Electronic Notes in Theoretical Computer Science. Elsevier Science, 2001.
8. G. Hutton. A tutorial on the universality and expressiveness of fold. *Journal of Functional Programming*, 9(4):355–372, July 1999.
9. P. Jansson. *Functional Polytypic Programming*. PhD thesis, Computing Science, Chalmers University of Technology and Göteborg University, Sweden, May 2000.
10. P. Jansson and J. Jeuring. PolyP — a polytypic programming language extension. In *POPL'97*, pages 470–482. ACM Press, 1997.
11. P. Jansson and J. Jeuring. Polytypic data conversion programs. *Science of Computer Programming*, 43(1):35–75, 2002.
12. C. Jay and P. Steckler. The functional imperative: shape! In C. Hankin, editor, *Programming languages and systems: 7th European Symposium on Programming, ESOP'98*, volume 1381 of *LNCS*, pages 139–53. Springer-Verlag, 1998.

13. R. Lämmel and S. Peyton Jones. Scrap your boilerplate: a practical design pattern for generic programming. *SIGPLAN Not.*, 38(3):26–37, 2003.
14. K. J. Lieberherr. *Adaptive Object-Oriented Software: The Demeter Method with Propagation Patterns.* PWS Publishing Company, Boston, 1996. ISBN 0-534-94602-X.
15. U. Norell and P. Jansson. Polytypic programming in Haskell. In *Implementation of Functional Languages*, LNCS, 2004. In press for LNCS. Presented at IFL'03.
16. T. Sheard and S. P. Jones. Template meta-programming for Haskell. In *Proceedings of the Haskell workshop*, pages 1–16. ACM Press, 2002.

Transposing Relations:
From *Maybe* Functions to Hash Tables

José Nuno Fonseca de Oliveira and César de Jesus Pereira Cunha Rodrigues

Dep. Informática, Universidade do Minho, Campus de Gualtar, 4700-320 Braga, Portugal
{jno,cjr}@di.uminho.pt

Abstract. Functional transposition is a technique for converting relations into functions aimed at developing the relational algebra *via* the algebra of functions. This paper attempts to develop a basis for *generic transposition*. Two instances of this construction are considered, one applicable to any relation and the other applicable to simple relations only.

Our illustration of the usefulness of the generic transpose takes advantage of the *free theorem* of a polymorphic function. We show how to derive laws of relational combinators as free theorems of their transposes. Finally, we relate the topic of functional transposition with the *hashing* technique for efficient data representation.

1 Introduction

This paper is concerned with techniques for functional transposition of binary relations. By functional transposition we mean the *faithful* representation of a relation by a (total) function. But – what is the purpose of such a representation?

Functions are well-known in mathematics and computer science because of their rich theory. For instance, they can be dualized (as happens e.g. with the projection/ injection functions), they can be Galois connected (as happens e.g. with inverse functions) and they can be parametrically polymorphic. In the latter case, they exhibit theorems "for free" [20] which can be inferred solely by inspection of their types.

However, (total) functions are not enough. In many situations, functions are *partial* in the sense that they are undefined for some of their input data. Programmers have learned to deal with this situation by enriching the codomain of such functions with a special error mark indicating that *nothing* is output. In C/C++, for instance, this leads to functions which output *pointers* to values rather than just values. In functional languages such as Haskell [13], this leads to functions which output $Maybe$-values rather than values, where $Maybe$ is datatype $Maybe\ a = Nothing\ |\ Just\ a$.

Partial functions are still not enough because one very often wants to describe *what* is required of a function rather than prescribe *how* the function should compute its result. A well-known example is *sorting*: sorting a list amounts to finding an ordered permutation of the list *independently* of the particular sorting algorithm eventually chosen to perform the task (eg. quicksort, mergesort, etc.). So one is concerned not only with *implementations* but also with *specifications*, which can be vague (eg. which square root is meant when one writes "$\sqrt{x}$"?) and non-deterministic. Functional programmers have

D. Kozen (Ed.): MPC 2004, LNCS 3125, pp. 334–356, 2004.

learned to cope with (bounded) non-determinism by structuring the codomain of such functions as *sets* or *lists* of values.

In general, such powerset valued functions are models of binary relations: for each such f one may define the binary relation R such that bRa means $b \in (f\ a)$ for all suitably typed a and b. Such R is unique for the given f. Conversely, any binary relation R is *uniquely* transposed into a set-valued function f. The existence and uniqueness of such a transformation leads to the identification of a *transpose* operator Λ [6] satisfying the following *universal property*,

$$f = \Lambda\ R \equiv (bRa \equiv b \in f\ a) \tag{1}$$

for all R from A to B and $f\ :\ A \longrightarrow \mathcal{P}B$. ($\mathcal{P}B$ denotes the set of all subsets of B.)

The power-transpose operator Λ establishes a well-known isomorphism between relations and set-valued functions which is often exploited in the algebra of relations, see for instance textbook [6]. Less popular and usually not identified as a transpose is the conversion of a partial function into a $Maybe$-valued function, for which one can identify, by analogy with (1), isomorphism Γ defined by (for all suitably typed a and b)

$$f = \Gamma\ R \equiv (bRa \equiv (f\ a = Just\ b)) \tag{2}$$

where R ranges over partial functions.

Terms *total* and *partial* are avoided in relation algebra because they clash with a different meaning in the context of *partial orders* and *total orders*, which are other special cases of relations. Instead, one writes *entire* for *total*, and *simple relation* is written instead of *partial function*. The word *function* is reserved for total, simple relations which find a central place in the taxonomy of binary relations depicted in Fig. 1 (all other entries in the taxonomy will be explained later on).

Paper objectives. This paper is built around three main topics. First, we want to show that Λ is not the only operator for transposing relations. It certainly is the most general, but we will identify other such operators as we go down the hierarchy of binary relations. Our main contribution will be to unify such operators under a single, *generic transpose construct* based on the notion of generic membership which extends "$\in$" to collective types other than the powerset [6, 10, 11]. In particular, one of these operators will be related with the technique of representing finite data collections by *hash-tables*, which are efficient data-structures well-known in computer science [21, 12].

Second, we want to stress on the usefulness of transposing relations by exploiting the calculation power of functions, namely *free theorems*. Such powerful reasoning devices can be applied to relations provided we represent relations as functions (by functional transposition), reason functionally and come back to relations where appropriate. In fact, several relational combinators studied in [6] arise from the definition of the *power-transpose* $\Lambda\ R$ of a relation R. However, some results could have been produced as free-theorems, as we will show in the sequel.

Last but not least, we want to provide evidence of the practicality of the *pointfree* relation calculus. The fact that pointfree notation abstracts from "points" or variables makes the reasoning more compact and effective, as is apparent in our final example on hash-tables, if compared with its pointwise counterpart which one of the authors did several years ago [16].

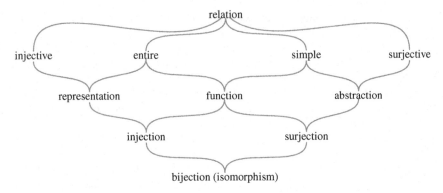

Fig. 1. Binary relation taxonomy

Related work. In the literature, equations (1) and (2) have been dealt with in disparate contexts. While (1) is adopted as "the" standard transpose in [6], for instance, (2) is studied in [9] as an example of an *adjunction* between the categories of total and partial functions. From the literature on the related topic of *generic membership* we select [6] and [11].

Paper structure. This paper is structured as follows. In the next section we present an overview of (pointfree) relation algebra. Section 3 presents our relational study of generic transpose. In section 4, the two transposes (1) and (2) are framed in the generic view. Section 5 presents an example of reasoning based on the generic transpose operator and its instances. In the remainder of the paper we relate the topic of functional transposition with the *hash table* technique for data representation and draw some conclusions which lead to plans for future work.

2   Overview of the Relational Calculus

Relations. Let $B \xleftarrow{\ R\ } A$ denote a binary relation on datatypes A (source) and B (target). We write bRa to mean that pair (b, a) is in R. The underlying partial order on relations will be written $R \subseteq S$, meaning that S is either more defined or less deterministic than R, that is, $R \subseteq S \equiv bRa \Rightarrow bSa$ for all a, b. $R \cup S$ denotes the union of two relations and $\top$ is the largest relation of its type. Its dual is $\bot$, the smallest such relation. Equality on relations can be established by $\subseteq$-antisymmetry: $R = S \equiv R \subseteq S \wedge S \subseteq R$.

Relations can be combined by three basic operators: composition $(R \cdot S)$, converse (R°) and meet $(R \cap S)$. R° is the relation such that $a(R^\circ)b$ iff bRa holds. Meet corresponds to set-theoretical intersection and composition is defined in the usual way: $b(R \cdot S)c$ holds wherever there exists some mediating $a \in A$ such that $bRa \wedge aSc$. Everywhere $T = R \cdot S$ holds, the replacement of T by $R \cdot S$ will be referred to as a "factorization" and that of $R \cdot S$ by T as "fusion". Every relation $B \xleftarrow{\ R\ } A$ admits two trivial factorizations, $R = R \cdot id_A$ and $R = id_B \cdot R$ where, for every X, id_X is the identity relation mapping every element of X onto itself.

Coreflexives. Some standard terminology arises from the id relation: a (endo)relation $A \xleftarrow{\quad R \quad} A$ (often called an *order*) will be referred to as *reflexive* iff $id_A \subseteq R$ holds and as *coreflexive* iff $R \subseteq id_A$ holds. As a rule, subscripts are dropped wherever types are implicit or easy to infer.

Coreflexive relations are fragments of the identity relation which can be used to model predicates or sets. The meaning of a *predicate* p is the coreflexive $[\![p]\!]$ such that $b[\![p]\!]a \equiv (b = a) \wedge (p\, a)$, that is, the relation that maps every a which satisfies p (and only such a) onto itself. The meaning of a *set* $S \subseteq A$ is $[\![\lambda a.a \in S]\!]$, that is, $b[\![S]\!]a \equiv (b = a) \wedge a \in S$. Wherever clear from the context, we will omit the $[\![\ ]\!]$ brackets.

Orders. Preorders are reflexive, transitive relations, where R is transitive iff $R \cdot R \subseteq R$ holds. Partial orders are anti-symmetric preorders, where R is anti-symmetric wherever $R \cap R^\circ \subseteq id$ holds. A preorder R is an *equivalence* if it is symmetric, that is, if $R = R^\circ$.

Converse is of paramount importance in establishing a wider taxonomy of binary relations. Let us first define the *kernel* of a relation, $\ker R = R^\circ \cdot R$ and its dual, $\operatorname{img} R = \ker(R^\circ)$, called the *image* of R. Alternatively, we may define $\operatorname{img} R = R \cdot R^\circ$, since converse commutes with composition, $(R \cdot S)^\circ = S^\circ \cdot R^\circ$ and is involutive, that is, $(R^\circ)^\circ = R$. Kernel and image lead to the following terminology: a relation R is said to be *entire* (or total) iff its kernel is reflexive; or *simple* (or functional) iff its image is coreflexive. Dually, R is *surjective* iff R° is entire, and R is *injective* iff R° is simple. This terminology is recorded in the following summary table:

	Reflexive	Coreflexive
$\ker R$	entire R	injective R
$\operatorname{img} R$	surjective R	simple R

$$(3)$$

Functions. A relation is a *function* iff it is both simple and entire. Functions will be denoted by lowercase letters (f, g, etc.) and are such that $b f a$ means $b = f\, a$. Function converses enjoy a number of properties of which the following is singled out because of its rôle in pointwise-pointfree conversion [3]:

$$b(f^\circ \cdot R \cdot g)a \equiv (f\, b)R(g\, a) \tag{4}$$

The overall taxonomy of binary relations is pictured in Fig. 1 where, further to the standard classification, we add *representations* and *abstractions*. These are classes of relations useful in data-refinement [15]. Because of $\subseteq$-antisymmetry, $\operatorname{img} S = id$ wherever S is an *abstraction* and $\ker R = id$ wherever R is a *representation*. This ensures that "no confusion" arises in a representation and that all abstract data are reachable by an abstraction ("no junk").

Isomorphisms (such as Λ and Γ above) are functions, abstractions and representations at the same time. A particular isomorphism is id, which also is the smallest equivalence relation on a particular data domain. So, $b\, id\, a$ means the same as $b = a$.

Functions and relations. The interplay between functions and relations is a rich part of the binary relation calculus. This arises when one relates the arguments and results of pairs of functions f and g in, essentially, two ways:

$$f \cdot S \subseteq R \cdot g \tag{5}$$

$$f^\circ \cdot S = R \cdot g \tag{6}$$

As we shall see shortly, (5) is equivalent to $S \subseteq f^\circ \cdot R \cdot g$ which, by (4), means that f and g produce R-related outputs $f\ b$ and $g\ a$ provided their inputs are S-related (bSa). This situation is so frequent that one says that, everywhere f and g are such that (5) holds, f is $(R \leftarrow S)$-*related* to g:

$$f(R \leftarrow S)g \equiv f \cdot S \subseteq R \cdot g \quad \text{cf. diagram}$$

(7)

$$
\begin{array}{ccc}
B & \xleftarrow{\ S\ } & A \\
f \downarrow & \subseteq & \downarrow g \\
C & \xleftarrow{\ R\ } & D
\end{array}
$$

For instance, for partial orders $R, S := \leq, \sqsubseteq$, fact $f(\leq \leftarrow \sqsubseteq)f$ means that f is monotone. For $R, S := \leq, id$, fact $f(\leq \leftarrow id)g$ means

$$f \stackrel{.}{\leq} g \equiv f \subseteq\ \leq \cdot g \tag{8}$$

that is, f and g are such that $f\ b \leq g\ b$ for all b. Therefore, $\stackrel{.}{\leq}$ lifts pointwise ordering $\leq$ to the functional level. In general, relation $R \leftarrow S$ will be referred to as "Reynolds arrow combinator" (see section 5), which is extensively studied in [3].

Concerning the other way to combine relations with functions, equality (6) becomes interesting wherever R and S are preorders,

$$f^\circ \cdot \sqsubseteq\ =\ \leq \cdot g \quad \text{cf. diagram:}$$

(9)

$$
\begin{array}{ccc}
\leq & & \sqsubseteq \\
\curvearrowleft & f & \curvearrowright \\
B & \underset{g}{\overset{f}{\rightleftarrows}} & C
\end{array}
$$

in which case f, g are always monotone and said to be *Galois connected*. Function f (resp. g) is referred to as the *lower* (resp. *upper*) adjoint of the connection. By introducing variables in both sides of (9) via (4) we obtain

$$(f\ b) \sqsubseteq a \equiv b \leq (g\ a) \tag{10}$$

Note that (9) boils down to $f^\circ = g$ (ie. $f = g^\circ$) wherever $\leq$ and $\sqsubseteq$ are id, in which case f and g are isomorphisms, that is, f° is also a function and $f\ b = a \equiv b = f^\circ a$ holds.

For further details on the rich theory of Galois connections and examples of application see [1, 3]. Galois connections in which the two preorders are relation inclusion $(\leq, \sqsubseteq := \subseteq, \subseteq)$ are particularly interesting because the two adjoints are relational combinators and the connection itself is their universal property. The following table lists connections which are relevant for this paper:

$(f\,X) \subseteq Y \equiv X \subseteq (g\,Y)$			
Description	f	g	**Obs.**
Converse	$(\_)^\circ$	$(\_)^\circ$	
Shunting rule	$(f\cdot)$	$(f^\circ\cdot)$	NB: f is a function
"Converse" *shunting* rule	$(\cdot f^\circ)$	$(\cdot f)$	NB: f is a function
Left-division	$(R\cdot)$	$(R \setminus\,)$	read "R under ..."
Right-division	$(\cdot R)$	$(\,/\,R)$	read "...over R"
Difference	$(\_ - R)$	$(R \cup\,)$	

$$(11)$$

From the two of these called *shunting rules* one infers the very useful fact that equating functions is the same as comparing them in either way:

$$f = g \equiv f \subseteq g \equiv g \subseteq f \qquad (12)$$

Membership. Equation (1) involves the set-theoretic membership relation $A \xleftarrow{\;\in\;} \mathcal{P}A$. Sentence $a \in x$ (meaning that "a belongs to x" or "a occurs in x") can be generalized to x's other than sets. For instance, one may check whether a particular integer occurs in one or more leaves of a binary tree, or of any other *collective* or *container* type F.

Such a generic membership relation will have type $A \xleftarrow{\;\in\;} \mathsf{F}A$, where F is a type *parametric on* A. Technically, the parametricity of F is captured by regarding it as a *relator* [5], a concept which extends *functors* to relations: F A describes a parametric type while F R is a relation from F A to F B provided R is a relation from A to B. Relators are monotone and commute with composition, converse and the identity.

The most simple relators are the *identity* relator Id, which is such that Id $A = A$ and Id $R = R$, and the *constant* relator K (for a particular concrete data type K) which is such that K $A = K$ and K $R = id_K$.

Relators can also be multi-parametric. Two well-known examples of binary relators are product and sum,

$$R \times S = \langle R \cdot \pi_1, S \cdot \pi_2 \rangle \qquad (13)$$
$$R + S = [i_1 \cdot R, i_2 \cdot S] \qquad (14)$$

where π_1, π_2 denote the projection functions of a Cartesian product, i_1, i_2 denote the injection functions of a disjoint union, and the *split/either* relational combinators are defined by

$$\langle R, S \rangle = \pi_1^\circ \cdot R \cap \pi_2^\circ \cdot S \qquad (15)$$
$$[R, S] = (R \cdot i_1^\circ) \cup (S \cdot i_2^\circ) \qquad (16)$$

By putting these four kinds of relator (product, sum, identity and constant) together with fixpoint definition one is able to specify a large class of parametric structures – called *polynomial* – such as those implementable in Haskell. For instance, the *Maybe* datatype is an implementation of polynomial relator $F = Id + 1$ (ie. $F A = A + 1$), where 1 denotes the *singleton* datatype, written () in Haskell.

There is more than one way to generalize $A \xleftarrow{\in} \mathcal{P} A$ to relators other than the powerset. (For a thorough presentation of the subject see chapter 4 of [10].) For the purpose of this paper it will be enough to say that $A \xleftarrow{\in_F} F A$, if it exists, is a *lax natural transformation* [6], that is,

$$\in_F \cdot F R \subseteq R \cdot \in_F \tag{17}$$

holds. Moreover, relators involving $+, \times, Id$ and constants have membership defined inductively as follows:

$$\in_K \overset{\text{def}}{=} \perp \tag{18}$$

$$\in_{Id} \overset{\text{def}}{=} id \tag{19}$$

$$\in_{F \times G} \overset{\text{def}}{=} (\in_F \cdot \pi_1) \cup (\in_G \cdot \pi_2) \tag{20}$$

$$\in_{F+G} \overset{\text{def}}{=} [\in_F, \in_G] \tag{21}$$

3 A Study of Generic Transposition

Thanks to rule (4), it is easy to remove variables b and a from transposition rules (1) and (2), yielding

$$f = \Lambda R \equiv (R = \in \cdot f) \tag{22}$$

$$f = \Gamma R \equiv (R = i_1^\circ \cdot f) \tag{23}$$

where, in the second equivalence, R ranges over simple relations and $Just$ is replaced by injection i_1 associated with relator $Id + 1$. In turn, f and R can also be abstracted from (22,23) using the same rule, whereby we end up with $\Lambda = (\in \cdot)^\circ$ and $\Gamma = (i_1^\circ \cdot)^\circ$.

The generalization of both equations starts from the observation that, in the same way $\in$ is the membership relation associated with the powerset, i_1° is the membership relation associated with $Id + 1$, as can be easily checked:

$$\in_{Id+1}$$

$$= \quad \{ \text{ by (21) } \}$$

$$[\in_{Id}, \in_1]$$

$$= \quad \{ \text{ by (19) and (18) } \}$$

$$[id, \perp] \tag{24}$$

$$= \quad \{ \text{ by (16) and properties of } \perp \}$$

$$id \cdot i_1^\circ$$

$$= \quad \{ \text{ identity } \}$$

$$i_1^\circ$$

This suggests the definitions and results which follow.

Definition. Given a relator F with membership relation $\in_\mathsf{F}$, a particular class of binary relations $A \xleftarrow{\quad R \quad} B$ is said to be F-*transposable* iff, for each such R, there exists a unique function $f : B \longrightarrow \mathsf{F}A$ such that $\in_\mathsf{F} \cdot f = R$ holds. This is equivalent (by skolemisation) to saying that there exists a function Γ_F (called the F-*transpose*) such that, for all such R and f,

$$f = \Gamma_\mathsf{F} R \equiv \in_\mathsf{F} \cdot f = R \quad \text{cf. diagram} \qquad A \xleftarrow{\quad R \quad} B \qquad (25)$$

$$\begin{array}{c} \in_\mathsf{F} \uparrow \quad \swarrow f \\ \mathsf{F}\,A \end{array}$$

In other words, such a generic F-transpose operator is the converse of membership post-composition:

$$\Gamma_\mathsf{F} = (\in_\mathsf{F}\cdot)^\circ \qquad (26)$$

The two instances we have seen of (25) are the power-transpose ($\mathsf{F}\,A = \mathcal{P}A$) and the $Maybe$-transpose ($\mathsf{F}\,A = A + 1$). While the former is known to be applicable to every relation [6], the latter is only applicable to simple relations, a result to be justified after we review the main properties of generic transposition. These extend those presented in [6] for the power-transpose.

Properties. Cancellation and reflection

$$\in_\mathsf{F} \cdot \Gamma_\mathsf{F} R = R \qquad (27)$$

$$\Gamma_\mathsf{F} \in_\mathsf{F} = id \qquad (28)$$

arise from (25) by substitutions $f := \Gamma_\mathsf{F} R$ and $f := id$, respectively. Fusion

$$\Gamma_\mathsf{F}(T \cdot S) = (\Gamma_\mathsf{F} T) \cdot S \Leftarrow (\Gamma_\mathsf{F} T) \cdot S \text{ is a function} \qquad (29)$$

arises in the same way – this time for substitution $f := (\Gamma_\mathsf{F} T) \cdot S$ – as follows (assuming the side condition ensuring that $(\Gamma_\mathsf{F} T) \cdot S$ is a function):

$$(\Gamma_\mathsf{F} T) \cdot S = \Gamma_\mathsf{F} R \equiv \in_\mathsf{F} \cdot ((\Gamma_\mathsf{F} T) \cdot S) = R$$

$$\equiv \qquad \{ \text{ associativity } \}$$

$$(\in_\mathsf{F} \cdot \Gamma_\mathsf{F} T) \cdot S = R$$

$$\equiv \qquad \{ \text{ cancellation (27) } \}$$

$$T \cdot S = R$$

The side condition of (29) requires S to be entire but not necessarily simple. In fact, it suffices that $img\, S \subseteq ker\,(\Gamma_\mathsf{F} T)$ since, in general, the simplicity of $f \cdot S$ equivales $img\, S \subseteq ker\, f$:

$$img\ S \subseteq ker\ f$$

$\equiv$ $\quad$ { definitions }

$$(S \cdot S^\circ) \subseteq f^\circ \cdot f$$

$\equiv$ $\quad$ { id is the unit of composition }

$$(S \cdot S^\circ) \subseteq f^\circ \cdot id \cdot f$$

$\equiv$ $\quad$ { shunting rules (11) }

$$f \cdot (S \cdot S^\circ) \cdot f^\circ \subseteq id$$

$\equiv$ $\quad$ { composition is associative ; converse of composition }

$$(f \cdot S) \cdot (f \cdot S)^\circ \subseteq id$$

$\equiv$ $\quad$ { definition of img }

$$img\ (f \cdot S) \subseteq id$$

$\equiv$ $\quad$ { simplicity }

$$(f \cdot S)\ \text{is simple}$$

In summary, the simplicity of (entire) S is a sufficient (but not necessary) condition for the fusion law (29) to hold. In particular, S can be a function, and it is under this condition that the law is presented in [6][1].

Substitution $f := \Gamma_F S$ in (25) and cancellation (27) lead to the *injectivity law*,

$$\Gamma_F S = \Gamma_F R \equiv S = R \qquad (30)$$

Finally, the generic version of the *absorption property*,

$$F\,R \cdot \Gamma_F S = \Gamma_F (R \cdot S) \Leftarrow R \cdot \in_F \subseteq \in_F \cdot F\,R \qquad (31)$$

is justified as follows:

$$F\,R \cdot \Gamma_F S = \Gamma_F (R \cdot S)$$

$\equiv$ $\quad$ { universal property (25) }

$$\in_F \cdot F\,R \cdot \Gamma_F S = R \cdot S$$

$\equiv$ $\quad$ { assume $\in_F \cdot F\,R = R \cdot \in_F$) }

$$R \cdot \in_F \cdot \Gamma_F S = R \cdot S$$

$\equiv$ $\quad$ { cancellation (27) }

$$R \cdot S = R \cdot S$$

The side condition of (31) arises from the property assumed in the second step of the proof. Together with (17), it establishes the required equality by anti-symmetry, which is equivalent to writing $F\,R = \Gamma_F (R \cdot \in_F)$ in such situations.

---

[1] Cf. exercise 5.9 in [6]. See also exercise 4.48 for a result which is of help in further reasoning about the side condition of (29).

Unit and inclusion. Two concepts of set-theory can be made generic in the context above. The first one has to do with *singletons*, that is, data structures which contain a single datum. The function τ_F mapping every A to its singleton of type F is obtainable by transposing id, $\tau_F = \Gamma_F id$, and is such that (by the fusion law) $\tau_F \cdot f = \Gamma_F f$. Another concept relevant in the sequel is *generic inclusion*, defined by

$$F\,A \xleftarrow{\;\in_F \backslash \in_F\;} F\,A \tag{32}$$

and involving *left division* (11), the relational operator which is defined by the fact that $(R \backslash\ )$ is the upper-adjoint of $(R \cdot\ )$ for every R.

4   Instances of Generic Transposition

In this section we discuss the power-transpose ($F = \mathcal{P}$) and the *Maybe*-transpose ($F = \mathsf{Id} + 1$) as instances of the generic transpose (25). Unlike the former, the latter is not applicable to every relation. To conclude that only simple relations are *Maybe*-transposable, we first show that, for every F-transposable R, its image is at most the image of $\in_F$:

$$img\ R \subseteq img\ \in_F \tag{33}$$

The proof is easy to follow:

$$img\ R$$
$$=\qquad \{\ \text{definition}\ \}$$
$$R \cdot R^\circ$$
$$=\qquad \{\ R\ \text{is}\ F\text{-transposable ; cancellation (27)}\ \}$$
$$(\in_F \cdot \Gamma_F R) \cdot (\in_F \cdot \Gamma_F R)^\circ$$
$$=\qquad \{\ \text{converses}\ \}$$
$$\in_F \cdot \Gamma_F R \cdot (\Gamma_F R)^\circ \cdot \in_F{}^\circ$$
$$\subseteq\qquad \{\ \Gamma_F R\ \text{is simple ; monotonicity}\ \}$$
$$\in_F \cdot \in_F{}^\circ$$
$$=\qquad \{\ \text{definition}\ \}$$
$$img\ \in_F$$

So, $\in_F$ restricts the class of relations R which are *F-transposable*. Concerning the power-transpose, it is easy to see that $img\ \in_F = \top$ since, for every a, a', there exists at least the set $\{a, a'\}$ which both a and a' belong to. Therefore, no restriction is imposed on $img\ R$ and transposition witnesses the well-known isomorphism $(2^A)^B \cong 2^{B \times A}$ (writing 2^A for $\mathcal{P}A$ and identifying every relation with its *graph*, a set of pairs).

By contrast, simple memberships can only be associated to the transposition of simple relations. This is what happens with $\in_{\mathsf{Id}+1} = i_1^\circ$ which, as the converse of an injection, is simple (3).

Conversely, appendix A shows that all simple relations are $(\mathsf{Id} + 1)$-transposable. Therefore, $(\mathsf{Id} + 1)$-transposability *defines* the class of simple relations and witnesses isomorphism $(B + 1)^A \cong A \rightharpoonup B$, where $A \rightharpoonup B$ denotes the set of all simple relations from A to B [2].

Another difference between the two instances of generic transposition considered so far can be found in the application of the absorption property (31). That its side condition holds for the $Maybe$-transpose is easy to show:

$$R \cdot i_1^\circ \subseteq i_1^\circ \cdot (R + id)$$

$$\equiv \qquad \{ \text{ shunting } \}$$

$$i_1 \cdot R \subseteq (R + id) \cdot i_1$$

$$\Leftarrow \qquad \{ \text{ anti-symmetry } \}$$

$$i_1 \cdot R = (R + id) \cdot i_1$$

$$\equiv \qquad \{ \ R + S \ (14) \text{ is a coproduct [6] } \}$$

$$i_1 \cdot R = i_1 \cdot R$$

Concerning the power-transpose, [6] define the absorption property for the *existential image* functor, $\mathsf{E}R = \Lambda(R \cdot \in)$, which coincides with the powerset relator for functions. However, E is not a relator[3]. So, the absorption property of the power-transpose can only be used where R is a function: $\mathcal{P}f \cdot \Lambda S = \Lambda(f \cdot S)$.

Finally, inclusion (32) for the power-transpose is the set-theoretic *subset ordering* [6], while its $Maybe$ instance corresponds to the expected "*flat-cpo* ordering":

$$x(\in_{\mathsf{Id}+1} \setminus \in_{\mathsf{Id}+1})y \equiv \forall a . \, x = (i_1 \, a) \Rightarrow y = (i_1 \, a)$$

So $Nothing$ will be included in anything and every "non-$Nothing$" x will be included only in itself[4].

5   Applications of Generic Transpose

The main purpose of representing relations by functions is to take advantage of the (sub)calculus of functions when applied to the transposed relations. In particular, transposition can be used to infer properties of relational combinators. Suppose that $f \oplus g$ is a functional combinator whose properties are known, for instance, $f \oplus g = [f, g]$ for which we know universal property

$$k = [f, g] \equiv \begin{cases} k \cdot i_1 = f \\ k \cdot i_2 = g \end{cases} \tag{34}$$

---

[2] This isomorphism is central to the data refinement calculus presented in [15].
[3] See [10] and exercise 5.15 in [6].
[4] This is, in fact, the ordering <= which is derived for $Maybe$ as instance of the Ord class in the Haskell Prelude [13].

We may inquire about the corresponding property of another, this time *relational*, combinator $R \otimes S$ induced by transposition:

$$\Gamma_F(R \otimes S) = (\Gamma_F R) \oplus (\Gamma_F S) \tag{35}$$

$$\equiv \quad \{ (25) \}$$

$$R \otimes S = \in_F \cdot ((\Gamma_F R) \oplus (\Gamma_F S)) \tag{36}$$

This can happen in essentially two ways, which are described next.

Proof of universality by transposition. It may happen that the universal property of functional combinator $\oplus$ is carried intact along the move from functions to relations. A good example of this is relational coproduct, whose existence is shown in [6] to stem from functional coproducts (34) by transposition[5]. One only has to instantiate (34) for $k, f, g := \Gamma_F T, \Gamma_F R, \Gamma_F S$ and reason:

$$\Gamma_F T = [\Gamma_F R, \Gamma_F S] \equiv (\Gamma_F T) \cdot i_1 = \Gamma_F R \wedge (\Gamma_F T) \cdot i_2 = \Gamma_F S$$

$$\equiv \quad \{ (25) \text{ and fusion } (29) \text{ twice, for } S := i_1, i_2 \}$$

$$T = \in \cdot [\Gamma_F R, \Gamma_F S] \equiv \Gamma_F(T \cdot i_1) = \Gamma_F R \wedge \Gamma_F(T \cdot i_2) = \Gamma_F S$$

$$\equiv \quad \{ \text{ injectivity } (30) \}$$

$$T = \in \cdot [\Gamma_F R, \Gamma_F S] \equiv T \cdot i_1 = R \wedge T \cdot i_2 = S$$

$$\equiv \quad \{ \text{ define } [R, S] = \in \cdot [\Gamma_F R, \Gamma_F S] \}$$

$$T = [R, S] \equiv T \cdot i_1 = R \wedge T \cdot i_2 = S$$

$$\equiv \quad \{ \text{ coproduct definition } \}$$

$$[R, S] \text{ is a coproduct}$$

Defined in this way, relational coproducts enjoy all properties of functional coproducts, eg. fusion, absorption etc.

This calculation, however, cannot be dualized to the generalization of the *split*-combinator $\langle f, g \rangle$ to relational $\langle R, S \rangle$. In fact, relational product is not a categorical product, which means that some properties will not hold, namely the fusion law,

$$\langle g, h \rangle \cdot f = \langle g \cdot f, h \cdot f \rangle \tag{37}$$

when g, h, f are replaced by relations. According to [6], what we have is

$$\langle R, S \rangle \cdot f = \langle R \cdot f, S \cdot f \rangle \tag{38}$$

whose proof can be carried out by resorting to the explicit definition of the *split* combinator (15) and some properties of simple relations grounded on the so-called *modular law*[6].

---

[5] For the same outcome *without* resorting to transposition see §2.5.2 of [10].
[6] See Exercise 5.9 in [6].

In the following we present an alternative proof of (38) as an example of the calcula-tion power of transposes *combined* with *Reynolds abstraction theorem* in the pointfree style [3]. The proof is more general and leads to other versions of the law, depending upon which transposition is adopted, that is, which class of relations is considered.

From the type of functional *split*,

$$\langle \_, \_ \rangle : ((A \times B) \leftarrow C) \leftarrow ((A \leftarrow C) \times (B \leftarrow C)) \tag{39}$$

we want to define the relational version of this combinator – denote it by $(\_ \otimes \_)$ for the time being – via the adaptation of $\langle \_, \_ \rangle$ (39) to transposed relations, to be denoted by $(\_ \oplus \_)$. This will be of type

$$t = (\mathsf{F}\,(A \times B) \leftarrow C) \leftarrow ((\mathsf{F}\,A \leftarrow C) \times (\mathsf{F}\,B \leftarrow C))) \tag{40}$$

Reynolds abstraction theorem. Instead of defining $(\_ \oplus \_)$ explicitly, we will reason about its properties by applying the *abstraction theorem* due to J. Reynolds [19] and advertised by P. Wadler [20] under the *"theorem for free"* heading. We follow the point-free styled presentation of this theorem in [3], which is remarkably elegant: let f be a polymorphic *function* $f : t$, whose type t can be written according to the following "grammar" of types:

$$t ::= t' \leftarrow t''$$
$$t ::= \mathsf{F}(t_1, \ldots, t_n) \qquad \text{for } n\text{-ary relator } \mathsf{F}$$
$$t ::= v \qquad \text{for } v \text{ a type variable (= polymorphism "dimension")}$$

Let V be the set of type variables involved in type t; $\{R_v\}_{v \in V}$ be a V-indexed family of relations (f_v in case all such R_v are functions); and R_t be a relation defined inductively as follows:

$$R_{t:=\mathsf{F}(t_1,\ldots,t_n)} = \mathsf{F}(R_{t_1}, \ldots, R_{t_n})$$
$$R_{t:=v} = R_v$$
$$R_{t:=t' \leftarrow t''} = R_{t'} \leftarrow R_{t''}$$

where $R_{t'} \leftarrow R_{t''}$ is defined by (7). The *free theorem of type* t reads as follows: *given any function $f : t$ and V as above, $f\,R_t\,f$ holds for any relational instantiation of type variables in V*. Note that this theorem is a result about t and holds for *any* polymorphic function of type t *independently* of its actual definition[7].

In the remainder of this section we deduce the *free theorem* of type t (40) and draw conclusions about the fusion and absorption properties of relational split based on such a theorem. First we calculate R_t:

$$R_t$$

$\equiv$ \qquad { induction on the structure of t (40) }

[7] See [3] for comprehensive evidence on the the power of this theorem when combined with Galois connections, which stems basically from the interplay between equations (5) and (6).

$$(F (R_A \times R_B) \leftarrow R_C) \leftarrow ((F R_A \leftarrow R_C) \times (F R_B \leftarrow R_C)))$$

$\equiv$ { substitution $R_A, R_B, R_C := R, S, Q$ in order to remove subscripts }

$$(F (R \times S) \leftarrow Q) \leftarrow ((F R \leftarrow Q) \times (F S \leftarrow Q)))$$

Next we calculate the free theorem of $(\_ \oplus \_) : t$:

$$(\_ \oplus \_)(R_t)(\_ \oplus \_)$$

$=$ { expansion of R_t }

$$(\_ \oplus \_)(F (R \times S) \leftarrow Q) \leftarrow ((F R \leftarrow Q) \times (F S \leftarrow Q)))(\_ \oplus \_)$$

$=$ { meaning of Reynolds arrow combinator (7) }

$$(\_ \oplus \_) \cdot ((F R \leftarrow Q) \times (F S \leftarrow Q)) \subseteq F (R \times S) \leftarrow Q) \cdot (\_ \oplus \_)$$

$=$ { *shunting* (11) }

$$(F R \leftarrow Q) \times (F S \leftarrow Q) \subseteq (\_ \oplus \_)^\circ \cdot (F (R \times S) \leftarrow Q) \cdot (\_ \oplus \_)$$

$=$ { going pointwise and (4) }

$$(f, g)((F R \leftarrow Q) \times (F S \leftarrow Q))(h, k) \Rightarrow (f \oplus g)(F (R \times S) \leftarrow Q)(h \oplus k)$$

$=$ { product relator and (7) }

$$f(F R \leftarrow Q)h \wedge g(F S \leftarrow Q)k \Rightarrow (f \oplus g) \cdot Q \subseteq F (R \times S) \cdot (h \oplus k)$$

$=$ { Reynolds arrow combinator (7) three times }

$$f \cdot Q \subseteq F R \cdot h \wedge g \cdot Q \subseteq F S \cdot k \Rightarrow (f \oplus g) \cdot Q \subseteq F (R \times S) \cdot (h \oplus k)$$

Should we replace functions f, h, g, k by transposed relations $\Gamma_F U, \Gamma_F V, \Gamma_F X, \Gamma_F Z$, respectively, we obtain

$$((\Gamma_F U) \oplus (\Gamma_F X)) \cdot Q \subseteq F (R \times S) \cdot ((\Gamma_F V) \oplus (\Gamma_F Z)) \tag{41}$$

provided conjunction

$$(\Gamma_F U) \cdot Q \subseteq F R \cdot (\Gamma_F V) \wedge (\Gamma_F X) \cdot Q \subseteq F S \cdot (\Gamma_F Z) \tag{42}$$

holds. Assuming (35), (41) can be re-written as

$$\Gamma_F(U \otimes X) \cdot Q \subseteq F (R \times S) \cdot \Gamma_F(V \otimes Z) \tag{43}$$

At this point we restrict Q to a function q and apply the fusion law (29) without extra side conditions:

$$\Gamma_F((U \otimes X) \cdot q) \subseteq F (R \times S) \cdot \Gamma_F(V \otimes Z) \tag{44}$$

For $R, S := id, id$ we will obtain –"for free" – the standard fusion law

$$(U \otimes X) \cdot q = (U \cdot q \otimes X \cdot q)$$

presented in [6] for the *split* combinator (38), ie. for $(R \otimes S) = \langle R, S \rangle$. In the reasoning, all factors involving R and S disappear and fusion takes place in both conjuncts of (42). Moreover, inclusion $(\subseteq)$ becomes equality of transposed relations – thanks to (12) – and injectivity (30) is used to remove all occurrences of Γ_{F}.

Wherever R and S are not identities, one has different results depending on the behaviour of the chosen transposition concerning the absorption property (31).

Maybe transpose. In case of *simple* relations under the $Maybe$-transpose, absorption has no side condition, and so (44) rewrites to

$$(U \otimes X) \cdot q = (R \times S) \cdot (V \otimes Z) \tag{45}$$

by further use of (12) – recall that transposed relations are functions – and injectivity (30), provided (42) holds, which boils down to $U \cdot q = R \cdot V$ and $X \cdot q = S \cdot Z$ under a similar reasoning. For $q := id$ and $(\_ \otimes \_)$ instantiated to relational split, this becomes absorption law

$$\langle R \cdot V, S \cdot Z \rangle = (R \times S) \cdot \langle V, Z \rangle \quad \text{if } R, S, V, Z \text{ are simple} \tag{46}$$

In summary, our reasoning has shown that the *absorption* law for *simple* relations is a free theorem.

Power transpose. In case of arbitrary relations under the power-transpose, absorption requires R and S in (44) to be functions (say r, s), whereby the equation re-writes to

$$\Gamma_{\mathsf{F}}((U \otimes X) \cdot q) \subseteq \Gamma_{\mathsf{F}}((r \times s) \cdot (V \otimes Z)) \tag{47}$$

provided $\Gamma_{\mathsf{F}}(U \cdot q) \subseteq \Gamma_{\mathsf{F}}(r \cdot V)$ and $\Gamma_{\mathsf{F}}(X \cdot q) \subseteq \Gamma_{\mathsf{F}}(s \cdot Z)$ hold. Again by combined use of (12) and injectivity (30) one gets

$$(U \otimes X) \cdot q = \mathsf{F}(r \times s) \cdot (V \otimes Z) \tag{48}$$

provided $U \cdot q = r \cdot V$ and $X \cdot q = s \cdot Z$ hold. Again instantiating $q := id$ and $(\_ \otimes \_) = \langle \_, \_ \rangle$, this becomes absorption law

$$\langle r \cdot V, s \cdot Z \rangle = (r \times s) \cdot \langle V, Z \rangle \tag{49}$$

Bird and Moor [6] show, in (admittedly) a rather tricky way, that product absorption holds for *arbitrary* relations. Our calculations have identified two restricted versions of such a law – (46) and (49) – as "free" theorems, which could be deduced in a more elegant, *parametric* way.

6   Other Transposes

So far we have considered two instances of transposition, one applicable to *any* relation and the other restricted to *simple* relations. That *entire* relations will have their own instance of transposition is easy to guess: it will be a variant of the power-transpose imposing *non-empty* power objects (see exercise 4.45 in [6]). Dually, by (3) we will obtain a method for reasoning about *surjective* and *injective* relations.

We conclude our study of relational transposition by relating it with a data representation technique known in computer science as *hashing*. This will require further restricting the class of the transposable relations to *coreflexive* relations. On the other hand, the transpose combinator will be enriched with an extra parameter called the "hash function".

7   The Hash Transpose

Hashing. Hash tables are well known data structures [21, 12] whose purpose is to efficiently combine the advantages of both static and dynamic storage of data. Static structures such as *arrays* provide random access to data but have the disadvantage of filling too much primary storage. Dynamic, *pointer*-based structures (*eg.* search lists, search trees etc.) are more versatile with respect to storage requirements but access to data is not as immediate.

The idea of *hashing* is suggested by the informal meaning of the term itself: a large database file is "hashed" into as many "pieces" as possible, each of which is randomly accessed. Since each sub-database is smaller than the original, the time spent on accessing data is shortened by some order of magnitude. Random access is normally achieved by a so-called *hash function*, say $B \xleftarrow{\ h\ } A$, which computes, for each data item a (of type A), its *location* $h\ a$ (of type B) in the *hash table*. Standard terminology regards as *synonyms* all data competing for the same location. A set of synonyms is called a *bucket*.

Data collision can be handled either by *eg. linear probing* [21] or *overflow handling* [12]. The former is not a totally correct representation of a data collection. Overflow handling consists in partitioning a given data collection $S \subseteq A$ into n-many, disjoint buckets, each one addressed by the relevant hash index computed by h [8].

This partition can be modelled by a function t of type $\mathcal{P}A \xleftarrow{\ t\ } B$ and the so-called "hashing effect" is the following: the membership test $a \in S$ (which requires an inspection of the whole dataset S) can be replaced by $a \in t(h\ a)$ (which only inspects the bucket addressed by location $h\ a$). That is, equivalence

$$a \in S \equiv a \in t(h\ a) \tag{50}$$

must hold for t to be regarded as a *hash table*.

Hashing as a transpose. First of all, we reason about equation (50):

$$a \in S \equiv a \in t(h\ a)$$

$$=\qquad \{\text{ introduce } b = h\ a\ \}$$

$$a \in S \wedge b = h\ a \equiv a \in (t\ b)$$

---

[8] In fact, such buckets ("collision segments") are but the *equivalence* classes of *ker h* restricted to S (note that the kernel of a function is always an equivalence relation).

$$= \quad \{ \text{ introduce } a = a' \}$$

$$a \in S \wedge a = a' \wedge b = h\, a' \equiv a \in (t\, b)$$

$$= \quad \{ \text{ introduce } S \text{ as a coreflexive ; converse of hash function } \}$$

$$aSa' \wedge a'h^\circ b \equiv a \in (t\, b)$$

$$= \quad \{ \text{ relational composition and rule (4) } \}$$

$$a(S \cdot h^\circ)b \equiv a(\in \cdot t)b$$

$$= \quad \{ \text{ going pointfree } \}$$

$$S \cdot h^\circ = \in \cdot t$$

$$= \quad \{ \text{ power transpose } \}$$

$$t = \Lambda(S \cdot h^\circ)$$

So, for an arbitrary coreflexive relation $A \xleftarrow{\;S\;} A$, its hash-transpose (for a fixed hash function $B \xleftarrow{\;h\;} A$) is a function $\mathcal{P}A \xleftarrow{\;t\;} B$, satisfying

$$\in \cdot t = S \cdot h^\circ$$

$$
\begin{array}{ccc}
A & \xleftarrow{\;S\;} & A \\
{\scriptstyle \in} \uparrow & & \uparrow {\scriptstyle h^\circ} \\
\mathcal{P}A & \xleftarrow{\;t\;} & B
\end{array}
$$

By defining

$$\Theta_h\, S = \Lambda(S \cdot h^\circ) \tag{51}$$

we obtain a h-indexed family of *hash transpose* operators and associated universal properties

$$t = \Theta_h\, S \quad \equiv \quad \in \cdot t = S \cdot h^\circ \tag{52}$$

and thus the cancellation law

$$\in \cdot (\Theta_h\, S) = S \cdot h^\circ \tag{53}$$

etc.

In summary, the hash-transpose extends the power-transpose of coreflexive relations in the sense that $\Lambda = (\Theta_{id})$. That is, the power-transpose is the hash-transpose using id as hash function. In practice, this is an extreme case, since some "lack of injectivity" is required of h for the hash effect to take place. Note, in passing, that the other extreme case is $h = !_A$, where $1 \xleftarrow{\;!_A\;} A$ denotes the unique function of its type: there is a maximum loss of injectivity and all data become synonyms!

Hashing as a Galois connection. As powerset-valued functions, hash tables are ordered by the lifting of the subset ordering $\mathcal{P}A \xleftarrow{\leq} \mathcal{P}A$ defined by $\leq = \in \setminus \in$, recall (32).

That the construction of hash tables is monotonic can be shown using the relational calculus. First we expand $\dot{\leq}$:

$$t \,\dot{\leq}\, t'$$

$\equiv$ { pointwise ordering lifted to functions (8) }

$$t \subseteq \,\leq\, \cdot\, t'$$

$\equiv$ { definition of the subset ordering (32) }

$$t \subseteq (\in \setminus \in) \cdot t'$$

$\equiv$ { law $(R \setminus S) \cdot f = R \setminus (S \cdot f)$ [6], since t' is a function }

$$t \subseteq \in \setminus (\in \cdot t')$$

$\equiv$ { $(\in\cdot)$ is lower adjoint of $(\in\setminus)$, recall (11) }

$$\in \cdot\, t \subseteq \in \cdot\, t' \tag{54}$$

Then we reason:

$$(\Theta_h)S \,\dot{\leq}\, (\Theta_h)R$$

$\equiv$ { by (54) }

$$\in \cdot (\Theta_h)S \subseteq \in \cdot (\Theta_h)R$$

$\equiv$ { cancellation (53) }

$$S \cdot h^\circ \subseteq R \cdot h^\circ$$

$\Leftarrow$ { $(\cdot h^\circ)$ is monotone, cf. lower-adjoints in (11) }

$$S \subseteq R$$

So, the smallest hash-table is that associated with the empty relation $\bot$, that is $\Lambda\bot$, which is constant function $t = \emptyset$, and the largest one is $t = \Lambda h^\circ$, the hash-transpose of id_A. In set-theoretic terms, this is A itself, the "largest" set of data of type A.

That the hash-transpose is not an isomorphism is intuitive: not every function t mapping B to $\mathcal{P}A$ will be a hash-table, because it may fail to place data in the correct bucket. Anyway, it is always possible to "filter" the wrongly placed synonyms from t yielding the "largest" (correct) hash table t' it contains,

$$t' = t \,\dot{\cap}\, \Lambda(h^\circ)$$

where, using *vector notation* [4], $f \,\dot{\cap}\, g$ is the lifting of $\cap$ to powerset-valued functions, $(f \,\dot{\cap}\, g)b = (f\, b) \cap (g\, b)$ for all b. In order to recover all data from such filtered t' we evaluate

$$\mathit{rng}\,(\in \cdot t')$$

where *rng R* (read "range of R") means *img* $R \cap id$. Altogether, we may define a function on powerset valued functions $\Xi_h t = rng \, (\in \cdot (t \cap \Lambda(h^\circ)))$ which extracts the coreflexive relation associated with all data correctly placed in t. By reconverting $\Xi_h t$ into a hash-table again one will get a table smaller than t:

$$\Theta_h(\Xi_h t) \stackrel{\cdot}{\leq} t \qquad (55)$$

(See proof in [18].) Another fact we can prove is a "perfect" cancellation on the other side:

$$\Xi_h(\Theta_h S) = S \qquad (56)$$

(See proof in [18].) These two cancellations, together with the monotonicity of the hash transpose Θ_h and that of Ξ_h (this is monotone because it only involves monotonic combinators) are enough, by Theorem 5.24 in [1], to establish *perfect* Galois connection

$$\Theta_h S \stackrel{\cdot}{\leq} t \; \equiv \; S \subseteq rng \, (\in \cdot (t \stackrel{\cdot}{\cap} \Lambda(h^\circ)))$$

cf. diagram $\{S \mid S \subseteq id_A\} \underset{\Xi_h}{\overset{\Theta_h}{\rightleftarrows}} (\mathcal{P}A)^B$. Being a lower adjoint, the hash-transpose will distribute over union, $\Theta_h(R \cup S) = (\Theta_h R) \,\dot{\cup}\, (\Theta_h S)$ (so hash-table construction is compositional) and enjoy other properties known of Galois connections.

From (56) we infer that Θ_h (resp. Ξ_h) is injective (resp. surjective) and so can be regarded as a data *representation* (resp. *abstraction*) in the terminology of Fig. 1, whereby typical "database" operations such as *insert*, *find*, and *remove* (specified on top of the powerset algebra) can be implemented by calculation [16, 18].

8   Conclusions and Future Work

Functional transposition is a technique for converting relations into functions aimed at developing the algebra of binary relations indirectly *via* the algebra of functions. A functional transpose of a binary relation of a particular class is an "F-resultric" function where F is a parametric datatype with membership. This paper attempts to develop a basis for a theory of *generic transposition* under the following slogan: *generic transpose is the converse of membership post-composition*.

Instances of *generic transpose* provide universal properties which all relations of particular *classes* of relations satisfy. Two such instances are considered in this paper, one applicable to any relation and the other applicable only to simple relations. In either cases, *genericity* consists of reasoning about the transposed relations without using the explicit definition of the transpose operator itself.

Our illustration of the purpose of transposition takes advantage of the *free theorem* of a polymorphic function. We show how to derive laws of relational combinators as free theorems involving their transposes. Finally, we relate the topic of functional transposition with *hashing* as a foretaste of a generic treatment of this well-known data representation technique [18].

Concerning future work, there are several directions for improving the contents of this paper. We list some of our concerns below.

Generic membership. Our use of this device, which has received some attention in the literature [6, 10, 11], is still superficial. We would like to organize the taxonomy of binary relations in terms of morphisms among the membership relations of their "characteristic" transposes. We would also like to assess the rôle of transposition in the context of coalgebraic process refinement [14], where structural membership and inclusion seem to play a prominent rôle.

The monadic flavour. Transposed relations are "F-resultric" functions and can so be framed in a monadic structure wherever F is a monad. This is suggested in the study of the power-transpose in [6] but we haven't yet checked the genericity of the proposed constructs. This concern is related to exploiting the adjoint situations studied in [9, 8] and, in general, those involving the Kleisli category of a monad [2].

Generic hashing. Our approach to *hashing* in this paper stems from [16]. "Fractal" types [17] were later introduced as an attempt to generalize the process of hash table construction, based on characterizing datatype invariants by *sub-objects* and *pullbacks*. In the current paper we could dispense with such machinery by using *coreflexive* relations instead. The extension of this technique to other transposes based on Galois connections is currently under research [18].

Acknowledgments

The work reported in this paper has been carried out in the context of the PURE Project *(Program Understanding and Re-engineering: Calculi and Applications)* funded by FCT (the Portuguese Science and Technology Foundation) under contract POSI/ICHS/44304/2002.

The authors wish to thank Roland Backhouse for useful feedback on an earlier version of this work. The anonymous referees also provided a number of helpful suggestions.

References

1. Chritiene Aarts, Roland Backhouse, Paul Hoogendijk, Ed Voermans, and Jaap van der Woude. A relational theory of datatypes, December 1992.
2. J. Adámek, H. Herrlich, and G.E. Strecker. *Abstract and Concrete Categories.* John Wiley & Sons, Inc., 1990.
3. K. Backhouse and R.C. Backhouse. Safety of abstract interpretations for free, via logical relations and Galois connections. *Science of Computer Programming*, 2003. Accepted for publication.

4. R.C. Backhouse. Regular algebra applied to language problems. Available from http://www.cs.nott.ac.uk/~rcb/papers/ (Extended version of *Fusion on Languages* published in ESOP 2001. Springer LNCS 2028, pp. 107–121.).

5. R.C. Backhouse, P. de Bruin, P. Hoogendijk, G. Malcolm, T.S. Voermans, , and J. van der Woude. Polynomial relators. In *2nd Int. Conf. Algebraic Methodology and Software Technology (AMAST'91)*, pages 303–362. Springer LNCS, 1992.

6. R. Bird and O. de Moor. *Algebra of Programming*. Series in Computer Science. Prentice-Hall International, 1997. C. A. R. Hoare, series editor.

7. J. Fitzgerald and P.G. Larsen. *Modelling Systems: Practical Tools and Techniques for Software Development*. Cambridge University Press, 1st edition, 1998.

8. M.M. Fokkinga. Monadic maps and folds for arbitrary datatypes. Memoranda Informatica 94-28, University of Twente, June 1994.

9. M.M. Fokkinga and L. Meertens. Adjunctions. Memoranda Informatica 94-31, University of Twente, June 1994.

10. Paul Hoogendijk. *A Generic Theory of Data Types*. PhD thesis, University of Eindhoven, The Netherlands, 1997.

11. Paul F. Hoogendijk and Oege de Moor. Container types categorically. *Journal of Functional Programming*, 10(2):191–225, 2000.

12. E. Horowitz and S. Sahni. *Fundamentals of Data Structures*. Computer Software Engineering Series. Pitman, 1978. E. Horowitz (Ed.).

13. S.L. Peyton Jones. *Haskell 98 Language and Libraries*. Cambridge University Press, Cambridge, UK, 2003. Also published as a Special Issue of the Journal of Functional Programming, 13(1) Jan. 2003.

14. Sun Meng and L.S. Barbosa. On refinement of generic state-based software components. In C. Rettray, S. Maharaj, and C. Shankland, editors, *10th Int. Conf. Algebraic Methods and Software Technology (AMAST)*, Stirling, July 2004. Springer Lect. Notes Comp. Sci. (to appear).

15. J. N. Oliveira. *Software Reification using the SETS Calculus*. In Tim Denvir, Cliff B. Jones, and Roger C. Shaw, editors, *Proc. of the BCS FACS 5th Refinement Workshop, Theory and Practice of Formal Software Development, London, UK*, pages 140–171. ISBN 0387197524, Springer-Verlag, 8–10 January 1992. (Invited paper).

16. J. N. Oliveira. *Hash Tables — A Case Study in ≤-calculation*. Technical Report DI/INESC 94-12-1, INESC Group 2361, Braga, December 1994.

17. J. N. Oliveira. *'Fractal' Types: an Attempt to Generalize Hash Table Calculation*. In *Workshop on Generic Programming (WGP'98), Marstrand, Sweden*, June 1998.

18. J. N. Oliveira. Hash tables as transposed data structures, 2004. PURe Project technical report (in preparation).

19. J. C. Reynolds. Types, abstraction and parametric polymorphism. *Information Processing 83*, pages 513–523, 1983.

20. P. Wadler. Theorems for free! In *4th International Symposium on Functional Programming Languages and Computer Architecture*, London, Sep. 1989. ACM.

21. N. Wirth. *Algorithms + Data Structures = Programs*. Prentice-Hall, 1976.

A   Proof That All Simple Relations Are $Maybe$-Transposable

We want to prove the existence of function $\Gamma_{\mathsf{Id}+1}$ which converts *simple* relations into $(\mathsf{Id} + 1)$-resultric functions and is such that $\Gamma_{\mathsf{Id}+1} = (\in_{\mathsf{Id}+1}\cdot)^{\circ}$, that is,

$$\in \cdot f = R \equiv f = \Gamma\, R$$

omitting the $\mathsf{Id} + 1$ subscripts for improved readability. Our proof is inspired by [9]:

$$f = \Gamma\, R$$

$\equiv$ { introduce id }

$$id \cdot f = \Gamma\, R$$

$\equiv$ { coproduct reflexion }

$$[i_1, i_2] \cdot f = \Gamma\, R$$

$\equiv$ { uniqueness of $1 \xleftarrow{\ !\ } 1\, = id$ }

$$[i_1, i_2 \cdot !] \cdot f = \Gamma\, R$$

$\equiv$ { require "obvious" properties (57,58) below}

$$[\Gamma\, id, \Gamma \perp] \cdot f = \Gamma\, R$$

$\equiv$ { see (63) below }

$$(\Gamma[id, \perp]) \cdot f = \Gamma\, R$$

$\equiv$ { the required fusion law stems from (62) below }

$$(\Gamma[id, \perp]) \cdot f = \Gamma\, R$$

$\equiv$ { Γ is injective, see (60) below }

$$[id, \perp] \cdot f = R$$

$\equiv$ { recall (24) }

$$\in \cdot f = R$$

A number of facts were assumed above whose proof is on demand. Heading the list are

$$\Gamma\perp = i_2 \cdot ! \tag{57}$$
$$\Gamma f = i_1 \cdot f \tag{58}$$

which match our intuition about the introduction of "error" outputs: totally undefined relation $\perp$ should be mapped to the "everywhere-$Nothing$" function $i_2 \cdot !$, while any other simple relation R should "override" $i_2 \cdot !$ with the (non-$Nothing$) entries in $i_1 \cdot R$. Clearly, entirety of R will maximize the overriding – thus property (58).

Arrow $B + 1 \xleftarrow{\ \Gamma\, R\ } A$ suggests its converse $B + 1 \xrightarrow{\ (\Gamma R)^{\circ}\ } A$ expressed by

$$(\Gamma R)^{\circ} = [R^{\circ}, \cdots] \tag{59}$$

which is consistent with (57) and (58) – it is easy to infer $(\Gamma \perp)^\circ = [\perp^\circ, !^\circ]$ and $(\Gamma f)^\circ = [f^\circ, \perp]$ from (16) – and is enough to prove that Γ has $\in = i_1^\circ$ as left-inverse,

$$\in \cdot \Gamma = id \tag{60}$$

that is, that Γ is injective. We reason, for all R:

$$i_1^\circ \cdot \Gamma R = R$$
$$\equiv \qquad \{ \text{ take converses } \}$$
$$(\Gamma R)^\circ \cdot i_1 = R^\circ$$
$$\equiv \qquad \{ \text{ assumption (59) } \}$$
$$[R^\circ, \cdots] \cdot i_1 = R^\circ$$
$$\equiv \qquad \{ \text{ coproduct cancellation } \}$$
$$R^\circ = R^\circ$$

The remaining assumptions in the proof require us to complete the construction of the transpose operator. Inspired by (57) and (58), we define

$$\Gamma_{\mathsf{Id}+1} R \stackrel{\text{def}}{=} (i_2 \cdot !) \dagger (i_1 \cdot R) \tag{61}$$

where $R \dagger S$, the "relation override" operator[9], is defined by $(R \cdot (id - \ker S)) \cup S$, or simply by $R \dagger S = S \triangleleft S \triangleright R$ if we resort to relational *conditionals* [1]. This version of the override operator is useful in proving the particular instance of fusion (29) required in the proof: this stems from

$$(R \dagger S) \cdot f = (R \cdot f) \dagger (S \cdot f) \tag{62}$$

itself a consequence of a fusion property of the relational conditional [1].

It can be checked that (61) validates all other previous assumptions, namely (57,58) and (59). Because $R \dagger S$ preserves entirety on any argument and simplicity on both (simultaneously), ΓR will be a function provided R is simple.

The remaining assumption in the proof stems from equalities

$$[\Gamma id, \Gamma \perp] = \Gamma[id, \perp] = \Gamma(i_1^\circ) = img\ i_1 \cup img\ i_2 = id \tag{63}$$

which arise from (61) and the fact that i_1 and i_2 are (dis)jointly surjective injections.

---

[9] This extends the *map override* operator of VDM [7].

Pointer Theory and Weakest Preconditions without Addresses and Heap

Birgit Schieder

Bodenschneidstr. 3, 81549 München, Germany
`birgit.schieder@t-online.de`

Abstract. Theories of programming languages formalize pointers by formalizing the addresses, the heap and the stack of a computer storage. These are implementation concepts. The aim of this paper is a theory that formalizes pointers in terms of concepts from high-level programming languages. We begin with a graph theory, which formalizes the implementation concepts but avoids some common distinctions. From it, we calculate the theory of trace equivalences, which formalizes concepts of high-level programming languages. From that theory, we calculate definitions in terms of weakest (liberal) preconditions. We consider the assignment and the copy operation, which is introduced in the paper; the object creation (i.e. the *new*-statement) is a sequential composition of them. Those *wlp*/*wp*-definitions and the concept of trace equivalence are the result of the paper. They are intended as a foundation for program design; in particular, for an object-oriented one.

0   Introduction

By pointer theory, I mean a mathematical theory that formalizes pointers. Diverse pointer theories can be found in the literature (e.g. $[1, 2, 11–13, 15–18]$). In spite of their diversity, they have two characteristics in common.

First, these pointer theories formalize the addresses, the heap and the stack of a computer storage. Apart from differences in the mathematical concepts, the formalization is as follows. The stack holds the directly accessible program variables: it maps them into values. Among the values are integers, booleans, etc. and addresses. The heap holds the program variables that can be accessed only through a sequence of pointers: it maps pairs of an address and such a program variable into values. As an example, consider singly-linked lists. For any list element, let program variable *data* contain its integer value, and let program variable *next* point to the next list element. Let x be a directly accessible program variable that points to a singly-linked list with at least two elements. The access to the integer value of the second list element is described as follows:

> The stack maps x to an address m. At address m of the heap begins the first list element. The heap maps m and *next* to an address n. At address n of the heap begins the second list element. The heap maps n and *data* to an integer. $\qquad(0)$

In this way, pointers are formalized by addresses of the heap.

D. Kozen (Ed.): MPC 2004, LNCS 3125, pp. 357–380, 2004.

But addresses, the heap and the stack are not concepts of a high-level programming language. They belong to its implementation. Instead of (0), we write in the programming language (for example, in an object-oriented one)

$$x.next.data \ . \tag{1}$$

Description (1) is much simpler than (0). But when we use a pointer theory, we must think as in (0).

In contrast, consider control structures, for example the while-loop. When we design a while-loop, we do not think about the labels and jumps by which it is implemented. Thanks to Dijkstra's predicate-transformer semantics and to Hoare's rule for the while-loop, we can think about it much more abstractly.

Second, pointer theories make several distinctions. They distinguish pointer *nil* from the other pointers. Since it points to no object, they do not formalize *nil* by an address. This distinguishes it from all other pointers.

Pointer *nil* must not be followed. When it is followed in an expression, pointer theories assign an undefined value to that expression. The undefined value is yet another value of pointers: it is not an address, nor is it equal to *nil*.

Another distinction concerns values such as integers, booleans etc. Pointer theories distinguish them from pointers so that they must be dealt with separately. These three distinctions complicate our thinking about pointers.

Pointer theories are a foundation for program design. In particular, they are a foundation for object-oriented programming. (Throughout this paper, 'address' can be read as 'object identifier' and 'heap' as 'object environment'.) Simplicity of pointer theories is therefore a major concern.

In this paper, the task is to devise a pointer theory that is free of the two characteristics discussed above: it must not formalize addresses, the heap and the stack, and it must avoid the three distinctions. It is intended as a foundation for program design. In contrast to the pointer theories in the literature, it still lacks predicates and theorems that are tailored to program design.

We must ensure that the pointer theory for which we are heading formalizes the usual idea of pointers and pointer operations. To ensure this, we begin with a pointer theory that formalizes addresses, the heap and the stack. That theory specializes Hoare's and He's graph theory [9, 10]. The specialization eliminates the above three distinctions. In our graph theory, we define assignment, object creation and an operation called copy operation. We introduce the copy operation because it is simpler than the object creation, and the object creation can readily be expressed by it and the assignment. Therefore we can concentrate on the copy operation instead of the object creation.

Then we eliminate addresses, the heap and the stack from the graph theory. A theory results that we call the theory of trace equivalences. The assignment and the copy operation are redefined in the new theory. These new definitions are calculated from the graph-theoretic ones.

From the new definitions of the assignment and the copy operation, we calculate definitions in terms of weakest liberal preconditions and weakest preconditions. They conclude the derivation of our pointer theory.

The result of the paper is the concept of trace equivalence and the definition of the assignment and the copy operation in terms of weakest (liberal) preconditions. Thus, we have a pointer theory that uses only concepts of high-level programming languages. We intend this result as a foundation for program design; in particular, for the design of object-oriented programs.

The following notions and notations are used in the paper. Function application is denoted by an infix point '.'. All functions are total. Classical substitution is denoted by $\leftarrow$ so that the simultaneous substitution of a list E of expressions for a list x of variables is denoted by $x \leftarrow E$. When applied to an expression, substitution is written in prefix position. The operators have the following relative binding powers that decrease from line to line:

$$.$$
$$\neg$$
$$= \neq$$
$$\vee \wedge$$
$$\Rightarrow \Leftarrow$$
$$\equiv \not\equiv$$
$$\leftarrow$$

Equality of pairs is defined as follows: for all $a0$, $a1$, $b0$, $b1$

$$(a0, a1) = (b0, b1) \quad \equiv \quad a0 = b0 \wedge a1 = b1 .$$

Crossed symbols, for example $\neq$, are defined as follows: for all a, b

$$a \neq b \quad \equiv \quad \neg (a = b) .$$

Set operations have the following binding powers: $*$ binds tighter than $\times$, which binds tighter than $\rightarrow$, which binds tighter than $\in$.

We often introduce names with 'let'. Unless stated otherwise, the scope ends with the surrounding section whose number contains one dot (e.g. 1.0).

1   Graphs

We begin with a pointer theory that formalizes addresses, the heap and the stack.

1.0   Modelling Pointers

Let a program state be given in terms of addresses, the heap and the stack. At some addresses, let objects be allocated, which consist of program variables. The program state is modelled by a graph in the following way.

The addresses at which objects are allocated in the heap are nodes of the graph. Integers, booleans etc. are nodes, too. (We assume that the set of addresses and the set of integers, booleans etc. are disjoint.) Let an object be allocated at address m; let that object have a program variable x whose value is n, and let n be an integer, boolean etc. or an address. That program variable is modelled by a directed edge from node m to node n with label x on the edge. This part of the graph can be depicted as follows:

To model pointers that point to no object, we introduce a node *null*; it models 'no object'. Let the object that is allocated at address m have a program variable y; let y's value be a pointer that points to no object. That program variable is modelled by a directed edge from node m to node *null* with label y on the edge. This part of the graph can be depicted as follows:

In this way, we treat a pointer that points to no object like any other pointer.

In a program, some program variables are directly accessible whereas others can be accessed only through a sequence of pointers. To indicate direct accessibility, we introduce a node *root*. Any directly accessible program variable z is modelled by a directed edge from node *root* with label z on the edge:

Thus, node *root* suffices to distinguish the stack from the heap. In high-level programming languages, no pointer points to a directly accessible program variable. In terms of graphs, we can say: node *root* has no ingoing edges. In the definition of graph, this requirement will be formalized by healthiness condition (2).

Node *root* serves a second purpose. There is a directed edge from node *root* to each node that models an integer, boolean, etc.; the label of such an edge is the respective integer, boolean, etc. For example, there is an edge from node *root* to the node that models the integer 3 with label 3 on the edge:

$$\underset{root}{\bigcirc} \overset{3}{\longrightarrow} \underset{3}{\bigcirc}$$

In this way, we treat addresses, 'no object' and values such as integers, booleans, etc. alike. Therefore, we can leave types out of consideration.

Similarly, there is a directed edge from node *root* to node *null* with label *nil* on the edge:

$$\underset{root}{\bigcirc} \overset{nil}{\longrightarrow} \underset{null}{\bigcirc}$$

Thus, name *nil* models a pointer that points to no object. This requirement will be formalized by healthiness condition (3).

Since we deal with program variables (e.g. x, z) and integers, booleans, etc. and *nil* in this uniform way, one set of labels will suffice. We will call it the alphabet.

In any program state, any program variable has at most one value. This means, for example, that node m from above cannot have a second outgoing edge with label x. The edges of a graph can therefore be defined by a function e: there exists an edge from a node m to a node n with a label x iff $e.(m, x) = n$. Thus, we avoid relations.

Function e is total. This means that for all labels, any node has an outgoing edge with that label. In particular, node *null* has outgoing edges. When a pointer that points to no object is followed further, no object is reached. We therefore define the outgoing edges of *null* to lead back to *null*. This requirement will be formalized by healthiness condition (4).

By defining e to be a total function, we avoid undefinedness. Node *null* plays a double rôle: it models 'no object', and it stands in for an undefined value.

1.1 Definition of Graph

Now we define our notion of graph.

In the rest of this paper, let A be a set that contains the element *nil*, i.e.,

$$nil \in A .$$

We call A the *alphabet*. We call the elements of A *labels*. In the rest of this paper, x, y and z stand for labels.

Let N be a set that contains the elements *root* and *null*, i.e.,

$$root \in N \text{ and } null \in N .$$

Let e be a function with

$$e \in N \times A \to N .$$

Let for all $n \in N$ and for all x

$$e.(n, x) \neq root . \tag{2}$$

Let for all $n \in N$

$$e.(n, nil) = null . \tag{3}$$

Let for all x

$$e.(null, x) = null . \tag{4}$$

We call the pair (N, e) a *graph*. We call the elements of N the *nodes* of the graph. We call (2), (3) and (4) *healthiness conditions* of the graph. From the definition, it follows immediately that $root \neq null$. In the rest of this paper, l, m and n stand for nodes.

1.2   Assignment

Let (N, f) be a graph. Let $l : l \neq null$ and $m : m \neq root$ be nodes of the graph. Let $y : y \neq nil$ be a label. We call

$$l \xrightarrow{y} := m$$

an *assignment*. We define it to have the following effect on graph (N, f). It directs the edge from node l with label y to node m. All other edges and the node-set remain unchanged. The restriction to l that differs from *null* reflects the rule of programming languages that *nil*-pointers must not be followed. The restriction to m that differs from *root* reflects the rule of programming languages that no pointer points to the directly accessible program variables.

Formally, we define

$$(l \xrightarrow{y} := m).(N, f)$$

to be the pair (N, g) where g:

$$g \in N \times A \to N$$

is the following function: for all $n \in N$ and for all x

$$g.(l, y) = m \tag{5}$$
$$(n, x) \neq (l, y) \Rightarrow g.(n, x) = f.(n, x) \ . \tag{6}$$

It follows immediately that (N, g) is a graph.

1.3   Object Creation

Let (N, f) be a graph. Let $l : l \neq null$ be a node of the graph. Let $y : y \neq nil$ be a label. We call

$$new(l \xrightarrow{y})$$

an *object creation*. We define it to have the following effect on graph (N, f). It adds a new node and directs the edge from node l with label y to the new node. All edges from the new node are directed to node *null*.

Formally, we define the effect as follows. Let nn be a new node, i.e., let nn be such that $nn \notin N$, and let nn be uniquely determined by graph (N, f). We define

$$(new(l \xrightarrow{y})).(N, f)$$

to be the pair $(N \cup \{nn\}, g)$ where g:

$$g \in (N \cup \{nn\}) \times A \to (N \cup \{nn\})$$

is the following function: for all $n \in N$ and for all x

$$g.(l, y) = nn \tag{7}$$
$$g.(nn, x) = null \tag{8}$$
$$(n, x) \neq (l, y) \Rightarrow g.(n, x) = f.(n, x) \ . \tag{9}$$

It follows immediately that $(N \cup \{nn\}, g)$ is a graph.

1.4   Copy Operation

In Sect. 1.3, we defined an object creation. It directs all edges from the new node to node *null*. This part of its effect can be expressed by assignments. For example, the edge from the new node and with label x can be directed to node *null* by the assignment

$$nn \overset{x}{\to} := null \; .$$

We split the object creation into a new operation, which we call copy operation, and assignments. It is simpler to study the copy operation in isolation because we study the assignment anyway.

Let (N, f) be a graph. Let $l : l \neq null$ be a node of the graph. Let $y : y \neq nil$ be a label. We call

$$copy(l \overset{y}{\to})$$

a *copy operation*. We define it to have the following effect on graph (N, f). It adds a new node and directs the edge from node l with label y to the new node. For all labels x, an edge from the new node is added to the graph; this edge is directed to the same node as the edge from node $f.(l, y)$ with label x. In this sense, the new node is a copy of node $f.(l, y)$.

Formally, we define the copy operation as follows. Let nn be a new node, i.e., let nn be such that $nn \notin N$, and let nn be uniquely determined by graph (N, f). We define

$$(copy(l \overset{y}{\to})).(N, f)$$

to be the pair $(N \cup \{nn\}, g)$ where g:

$$g \in (N \cup \{nn\}) \times A \to (N \cup \{nn\})$$

is the following function: for all $n \in N$ and for all x

$$g.(l, y) = nn \tag{10}$$
$$g.(nn, x) = f.(f.(l, y), x) \tag{11}$$
$$(n, x) \neq (l, y) \Rightarrow g.(n, x) = f.(n, x) \; . \tag{12}$$

It follows immediately that $(N \cup \{nn\}, g)$ is a graph.

2   Trace Equivalences

Addresses and object identifiers are not concepts of a high-level programming language. Programs do not refer to objects by addresses or object identifiers but by sequences of labels (cf. (1)). Therefore we will eliminate nodes from our graph theory and bring in sequences of labels.

The nodes of a graph serve a single purpose. They tell us that two sequences of labels lead from *root* to the same node or to different nodes. This is the only information about nodes that we will keep.

2.0   Traces

A *trace* is a finite sequence of labels, i.e., an element of set A^*. In the rest of this paper, p, r, s, t, u and v stand for traces.

The empty trace is denoted by ε. For all x, the singleton trace consisting of x is denoted by $<x>$. The append operation is denoted by the infix symbol $\triangleright$. It has a higher binding power than $=$ but a lower binding power than the infix dot. Catenation of traces is denoted by the infix symbol $+\!\!+$. It has the same binding power as symbol $\triangleright$.

2.1   From Graphs to Trace Equivalences

Let (N, e) be a graph. We introduce the raised star * as a postfix operator. It has a higher binding power than the infix dot. We define a function e^* from a trace to a node, i.e.,

$$e^* \in A^* \to N \ ,$$

as follows:

$$e^*.\varepsilon = root \tag{13}$$

and for all t, x

$$e^*.(t \triangleright x) = e.(e^*.t, x) \ . \tag{14}$$

Thus, in graph (N, e), any trace t leads from node $root$ to node $e^*.t$. We say that a node n is *accessible* in graph (N, e) iff there exists t such that $e^*.t = n$. Since a program refers to nodes by traces, it can refer to accessible nodes only.

We define a binary relation $\sim$ on the set of traces, i.e., on A^*. Symbol $\sim$ has the same binding power as symbol $=$. We define for all t, u

$$t \sim u \ \equiv \ e^*.t = e^*.u \ . \tag{15}$$

Theorem 0. $\sim$ *is an equivalence relation.*

Proof. Follows immediately from the definition of $\sim$ (15).   □

Lemma 1. *We have for all t, u, x*

$$t \sim u \ \Rightarrow \ t \triangleright x \sim u \triangleright x \ .$$

Proof. Follows from the definition of $\sim$ (15) and the definition of e^* (14).   □

Lemma 2. *We have*

$$e^*.<nil> = null \ .$$

Proof. Follows from the definition of e^* (14) and healthiness condition (3).   □

Lemma 3. *We have for all t*

$$t \triangleright nil \sim <nil> \ .$$

Proof. Follows from the definitions of $\sim$ (15) and e^* (14) and from healthiness condition (3) and Lemma 2. $\qquad\square$

Lemma 4. *We have for all x*

$$<nil> \triangleright x \sim <nil> .$$

Proof. Follows from the definitions of $\sim$ (15) and e^* (14) and from Lemma 2 and healthiness condition (4). $\qquad\square$

The distinction between the stack and the heap boils down to the following theorem.

Theorem 5. *We have for all t*

$$t \sim \varepsilon \;\equiv\; t = \varepsilon . \tag{16}$$

Proof. When $t = \varepsilon$, (16) follows immediately. When $t \neq \varepsilon$, it follows from definition (13) and healthiness condition (2). $\qquad\square$

Theorem 6. *We have for all t, u, v*

$$t \sim u \;\Rightarrow\; t + v \sim u + v . \tag{17}$$

Proof. Follows by structural induction on v and Lemma 1. $\qquad\square$

Theorem 7. *We have for all t, u*

$$t + <nil> + u \;\sim\; <nil> . \tag{18}$$

Proof. The proof is by structural induction on u. The base case, i.e., (18) with $u \leftarrow \varepsilon$, follows immediately from Lemma 3. The inductive case follows from Lemma 1 and Lemma 4. $\qquad\square$

We call a binary relation on A^* a *trace equivalence* iff it is an equivalence relation and satisfies (16), (17) and (18). We call (16), (17) and (18) *healthiness conditions* of trace equivalences.

Theorem. $\sim$ *is a trace equivalence.*

Proof. Follows immediately from Theorems 0, 5, 6 and 7. $\qquad\square$

We say that graph (N, e) *induces* trace equivalence $\sim$. In the pointer theory we are deriving now, program states are trace equivalences.

The following two lemmata will be used later.

Lemma 8. *We have for all t*

$$e^*.t = root \;\equiv\; t = \varepsilon .$$

Proof. Follows immediately from the definition of $\_^*$ (13) and Theorem 5. $\qquad\square$

Lemma 9. *We have for all t*

$$e^*.t = null \;\equiv\; t \sim <nil> .$$

Proof. Follows immediately from Lemma 2. $\qquad\square$

2.2   From Trace Equivalences to Graphs

Let $\sim$ be a trace equivalence. For all t, let $[t]$ denote t's equivalence class with regard to $\sim$. Our task is to define a graph (N, e) that induces $\sim$, i.e., such that for all t, u

$$[t] = [u] \quad \equiv \quad e^*.t = e^*.u \ .$$

To ensure this requirement, we define the graph such that for all t

$$e^*.t = [t] \ .$$

Since e^* is a function from a trace to a node, we define node-set N to be the set of equivalence classes. To ensure (13), we define *root* to be $[\varepsilon]$. To ensure (14), we define function e as follows: for all t, x

$$e.([t], x) = [t \triangleright x] \ .$$

The right-hand side is independent of which element is chosen from $[t]$ because of healthiness condition (17) of trace equivalences. We must define *null* so that healthiness condition (3) of graphs holds. Because of healthiness condition (18) of trace equivalences, we define *null* to be $[<nil>]$. Healthiness condition (2) of graphs follows from healthiness condition (16) of trace equivalences. Healthiness condition (4) of graphs follows from healthiness condition (18) of trace equivalences.

We have defined a graph (N, e), which induces $\sim$. Thus, we have proved that every trace equivalence is induced by a graph.

2.3   Assignment

Now we define the assignment in terms of trace equivalences. We calculate the definition from the graph-theoretic one.

Let (N, f) be a graph. Let $l : l \neq null$ and $m : m \neq root$ be nodes of the graph. Let l and m be accessible: let r and p be traces with

$$f^*.r = l \tag{19}$$

and

$$f^*.p = m \ . \tag{20}$$

Let $y : y \neq nil$ be a label. We consider the assignment

$$l \xrightarrow{y} := m \ .$$

Let (N, g) be the graph $(l \xrightarrow{y} := m).(N, f)$.

Our task is to define the assignment in terms of trace equivalences. Let graph (N, f) induce the trace equivalence $\sim_f$, i.e., for all t, u

$$t \sim_f u \quad \equiv \quad f^*.t = f^*.u \ . \tag{21}$$

Let graph (N, g) induce the trace equivalence $\sim_g$, i.e., for all t, u

$$t \sim_g u \equiv g^*.t = g^*.u . \tag{22}$$

Our task is to define $\sim_g$ in terms of $\sim_f$. Hence, we have to eliminate g^* from the definition of $\sim_g$ (22) and to bring in f^*. For that purpose, we need a relation between g^* and f^*. We seek for a function α (from a trace to a trace) such that for all t

$$g^*.t = f^*.(\alpha.t) \tag{23}$$

because this is a simple relation between g^* and f^*. From specification (23), we calculate α. Our calculation is by induction because the definition of g^* is by induction. In the base case, i.e., for $t \leftarrow \varepsilon$, we observe

$g^*.\varepsilon$
$=$ {definition of $\_^*$ (13)}
$\quad root$
$=$ {definition of $\_^*$ (13)}
$\quad f^*.\varepsilon$
$=$ {definition of α (24), see below}
$\quad f^*.(\alpha.\varepsilon) .$

We define

$$\alpha.\varepsilon = \varepsilon . \tag{24}$$

In the inductive case, i.e., for (23) with $t \leftarrow t \triangleright x$, we observe

$g^*.(t \triangleright x)$
$=$ {definition of $\_^*$ (14)}
$\quad g.(g^*.t, x)$
$=$ {inductive hypothesis (23)}
$\quad g.(f^*.(\alpha.t), x) . \tag{25}$

For g's arguments in (25), we distinguish the two cases of g's definition (cf. (5) and (6)). In the first case, i.e., when $(f^*.(\alpha.t), x) = (l, y)$, we observe

(25)
$=$ {definition of g (5)}
$\quad m$
$=$ {specification of p (20)}
$\quad f^*.p$
$=$ {definition of α (26), see below}
$\quad f^*.(\alpha.(t \triangleright x)) .$

For the premise of the case in question, we observe

$(f^*.(\alpha.t), x) = (l, y)$
$\equiv$ {equality of pairs; specification of r (19)}
$\quad f^*.(\alpha.t) = f^*.r \wedge x = y$
$\equiv$ {definition of $\sim_f$ (21)}
$\quad \alpha.t \sim_f r \wedge x = y .$

We define
$$\alpha.t \sim_f r \,\wedge\, x = y \;\Rightarrow\; \alpha.(t \triangleright x) = p \;. \tag{26}$$

In the second case, i.e., when $(f^*.(\alpha.t), x) \neq (l, y)$, we observe

$\qquad$ (25)
$=\qquad$ {definition of g (6) with $n \leftarrow f^*.(\alpha.t)$}
$\qquad f.(f^*.(\alpha.t), x)$
$=\qquad$ {definition of $\_^*$ (14)}
$\qquad f^*.(\alpha.t \triangleright x)$
$=\qquad$ {definition of α (27), see below}
$\qquad f^*.(\alpha.(t \triangleright x))$.

We define
$$\neg(\alpha.t \sim_f r \,\wedge\, x = y) \;\Rightarrow\; \alpha.(t \triangleright x) = \alpha.t \triangleright x \;. \tag{27}$$

Thus, we have defined α so that (23) holds. In particular, α is total.

$\qquad$ Now we return to our main task. We eliminate g^* from the definition of $\sim_g$ (22) and bring in f^*. We observe for any t, u

$\qquad t \sim_g u$
$\equiv\qquad$ {definition of $\sim_g$ (22)}
$\qquad g^*.t = g^*.u$
$\equiv\qquad$ {(23) and (23) with $t \leftarrow u$}
$\qquad f^*.(\alpha.t) = f^*.(\alpha.u)$
$\equiv\qquad$ {definition of $\sim_f$ (21) with $t, u \leftarrow \alpha.t, \alpha.u$}
$\qquad \alpha.t \sim_f \alpha.u$.

$\qquad$ It remains to express the premises $l \neq null$ and $m \neq root$ in terms of traces and $\sim_f$. We observe

$\qquad m \neq root$
$\equiv\qquad$ {specification of p (20)}
$\qquad f^*.p \neq root$
$\equiv\qquad$ {Lemma 8 with $e, t \leftarrow f, p$}
$\qquad p \neq \varepsilon$

and

$\qquad l \neq null$
$\equiv\qquad$ {specification of r (19)}
$\qquad f^*.r \neq null$
$\equiv\qquad$ {Lemma 9 with $e, t, \sim \;\leftarrow f, r, \sim_f$}
$\qquad r \not\sim_f <nil>$. $\hfill (28)$

Since a trace r that violates (28) cannot be excluded syntactically, we define the assignment for any r. We define it to terminate iff it is started in a program state $\sim_f$ that satisfies (28).

$\qquad$ In the syntax of the assignment, i.e., in $l \overset{y}{\to} := m$, we replace nodes by traces. Because of (19) and (20), we replace l by r and m by p; we write

$$r \triangleright y := p \;.$$

We restrict this assignment so that no *nil*-pointers are followed. For the left-hand side, this is ensured by (28). Since the right-hand side is non-empty, there exist s, z such that

$$p = s \triangleright z \ ;$$

we require $s \not\rightarrow_f <nil>$. (For the given assignment on graphs, this requirement is satisfiable: the p in (20) can be chosen so that the requirement holds.)

We summarize the definition of the assignment in isolation from graphs. We introduce all names afresh. Let r and s be traces, and let $y : y \neq nil$ and z be labels. We call

$$r \triangleright y := s \triangleright z$$

an *assignment*. It is defined to terminate iff it is started in a program state $\sim$ such that

$$r \not\rightarrow <nil> \ \wedge \ s \not\rightarrow <nil> \ .$$

If the assignment terminates it does so in the program state $\sim_g$ that is defined as follows: for all t, u

$$t \sim_g u \ \equiv \ \alpha.t \sim \alpha.u \tag{29}$$

where function α is defined as follows:

$$\alpha.\varepsilon = \varepsilon \tag{30}$$

and for all t, x

$$\alpha.t \sim r \ \wedge \ x = y \ \Rightarrow \ \alpha.(t \triangleright x) = s \triangleright z \tag{31}$$

and

$$\neg (\alpha.t \sim r \ \wedge \ x = y) \ \Rightarrow \ \alpha.(t \triangleright x) = \alpha.t \triangleright x \ . \tag{32}$$

In the case of termination, it remains to prove that the relation $\sim_g$ defined in terms of $\sim$ and α is a trace equivalence. We know that every trace equivalence is induced by a graph. Hence, $\sim$ is induced by a graph, say, (N, f). As every graph does, $(f^*.r \xrightarrow{y} := f^*.(s \triangleright z)).(N, f)$ induces a trace equivalence. This trace equivalence is relation $\sim_g$ as our calculations have proved.

We give an example of this definition of the assignment.

Example 0. Let $x0$ and $x1$ be two program variables. Let $r, s \leftarrow <x0>, \varepsilon$, i.e., we consider the assignment

$$<x0> \triangleright y := <z> \ .$$

Let $<x0> \not\rightarrow <nil>$. When $<x0> \sim <x1>$, we observe for program state $\sim_g$, in which the assignment terminates,

$$\begin{aligned}
&<x0> \triangleright y \sim_g <x1> \triangleright y \\
\equiv \quad &\{(29)\} \\
&\alpha.(<x0> \triangleright y) \sim \alpha.(<x1> \triangleright y) \\
\equiv \quad &\{(33), \text{ see below}\} \\
&true \ .
\end{aligned}$$

From (32) with $t, x \leftarrow \varepsilon, x1$, it follows that

$$\alpha.<x1> = <x1> \ .$$

When $<x0> \sim <x1>$, it follows from (31) with $t, x \leftarrow <x1>, y$ that

$$\alpha.(<x1> \triangleright y) = <z> \ .$$

Similarly, it follows that

$$\alpha.(<x0> \triangleright y) = <z> \ .$$

When $<x0> \sim <x1>$, we therefore have

$$\alpha.(<x0> \triangleright y) \sim \alpha.(<x1> \triangleright y) \ . \tag{33}$$

When $<x0> \not\sim <x1>$, it follows from (32) with $t, x \leftarrow <x1>, y$ that

$$\alpha.(<x1> \triangleright y) = <x1> \triangleright y \ .$$

When $<x0> \not\sim <x1>$, we therefore have

$$\alpha.(<x0> \triangleright y) \sim \alpha.(<x1> \triangleright y) \quad \equiv \quad <z> \sim <x1> \triangleright y \ , \tag{34}$$

which we will use in a later example.

2.4   Copy Operation

Now we define the copy operation in terms of trace equivalences. As we did for the assignment, we calculate the definition from the graph-theoretic one.

Let (N, f) be a graph. Let $l : l \neq null$ be a node of the graph. Let l be accessible: let r be a trace with

$$f^*.r = l \ . \tag{35}$$

Let $y : y \neq nil$ be a label. We consider the copy operation

$$copy(l \xrightarrow{y}) \ .$$

Let $(N \cup \{nn\}, g)$ be the graph $(copy(l \xrightarrow{y})).(N, f)$.

We begin with a simple lemma that will not direct our calculations. It only saves us the repetition of some lines of proof.

Lemma 10. *We have*

$$g^*.\varepsilon \neq nn \tag{36}$$

and for all t, x

$$g^*.(t \triangleright x) = nn \quad \equiv \quad (g^*.t, x) = (l, y) \ . \tag{37}$$

Proof. To prove (36), we observe

$$g^*.\varepsilon$$
$=$ {definition of $\_^*$ (13)}
 $root$
$\neq$ {$root \in N$; $nn \notin N$}
 nn .

To prove (37), we observe for any t, x

$$g^*.(t \triangleright x) = nn$$
$\equiv$ {definition of $\_^*$ (14)}
 $g.(g^*.t, x) = nn$
$\equiv$ {definition of g (10), (11), (12)}
 $(g^*.t, x) = (l, y)$.

$\hfill \square$

Our task is to define the copy operation in terms of trace equivalences. Let graph (N, f) induce trace equivalence $\sim_f$, i.e., for all t, u

$$t \sim_f u \;\equiv\; f^*.t = f^*.u \; . \tag{38}$$

Let graph $(N \cup \{nn\}, g)$ induce trace equivalence $\sim_g$, i.e., for all t, u

$$t \sim_g u \;\equiv\; g^*.t = g^*.u \; . \tag{39}$$

Our task is to define $\sim_g$ in terms of $\sim_f$. Hence, we have to eliminate g^* from the definition of $\sim_g$ (39) and to bring in f^*. For that purpose, we need a relation between g^* and f^*. The simplest relation would be equality for all arguments, i.e., for all t

$$g^*.t = f^*.t \; .$$

But this equality does not hold for all t: $g^*.t$ may equal nn, but $f^*.t$ may not because nn is not a node of graph (N, f). Therefore we try the following weaker formula: for all t

$$g^*.t \neq nn \;\Rightarrow\; g^*.t = f^*.t \; . \tag{40}$$

The proof of (40) is by structural induction on t because the definition of g^* is by induction. In the base case, i.e., for $t \leftarrow \varepsilon$, we observe for (40)'s consequent

$$g^*.\varepsilon$$
$=$ {definition of $\_^*$ (13)}
 $root$
$=$ {definition of $\_^*$ (13)}
 $f^*.\varepsilon$.

In the inductive case of (40), i.e., for $t \leftarrow t \triangleright x$, we observe

$$g^*.(t \triangleright x) \neq nn \;\Rightarrow\; g^*.(t \triangleright x) = f^*.(t \triangleright x)$$
$\equiv$ {Lemma 10 (37); definition of $\_^*$ (14), twice}
 $(g^*.t, x) \neq (l, y) \;\Rightarrow\; g.(g^*.t, x) = f.(f^*.t, x)$. $\tag{41}$

In (41), g has the arguments $g^*.t$ and x. For them, we distinguish the three cases of g's definition (cf. (10), (11) and (12)). In case (10), i.e., when $(g^*.t, x) = (l, y)$, (41) holds trivially because its antecedent is equivalent to $false$. In case (11), i.e., when $g^*.t = nn$, we observe for (41)'s consequent

$$
\begin{aligned}
& g.(g^*.t, x) = f.(f^*.t, x) \\
\equiv\ & \{\text{definition of } g \ (11)\} \\
& f.(f.(l, y), x) = f.(f^*.t, x) \\
\Leftarrow\ & \{\text{Leibniz's Rule}\} \\
& f.(l, y) = f^*.t \ .
\end{aligned}
\tag{42}
$$

Since we cannot simplify (42), we exploit the premise $g^*.t = nn$. From Lemma 10, it follows immediately that there exists u such that

$$
t = u \triangleright y \ \wedge \ g^*.u = l \ .
\tag{43}
$$

To prove (42), we observe

$$
\begin{aligned}
& f.(l, y) \\
=\ & \{\text{second conjunct of } (43)\} \\
& f.(g^*.u, y) \\
=\ & \{\text{by } (43)\text{'s second conjunct, } g^*.u \neq nn; \text{ by } (43)\text{'s first conjunct, } u \text{ is a prefix} \\
& \quad \text{of } t; \text{ inductive hypothesis } (40) \text{ with } t \leftarrow u\} \\
& f.(f^*.u, y) \\
=\ & \{\text{definition of } \_^* \ (14)\} \\
& f^*.(u \triangleright y) \\
=\ & \{\text{first conjunct of } (43)\} \\
& f^*.t \ .
\end{aligned}
$$

In case (12), i.e., when $g^*.t \in N \wedge (g^*.t, x) \neq (l, y)$, we observe for (41)'s consequent

$$
\begin{aligned}
& g.(g^*.t, x) \\
=\ & \{\text{definition of } g \ (12) \text{ with } n \leftarrow g^*.t\} \\
& f.(g^*.t, x) \\
=\ & \{\text{premise } g^*.t \in N; \text{ inductive hypothesis } (40)\} \\
& f.(f^*.t, x) \ .
\end{aligned}
$$

Hence, we have proved (40). The calculation following formula (43) proves an additional result: we have for all t

$$
g^*.t = nn \ \Rightarrow \ f.(l, y) = f^*.t \ .
$$

From this result, it follows immediately that for all t, u

$$
g^*.t = nn \ \wedge \ g^*.u = nn \ \Rightarrow \ f^*.t = f^*.u \ .
\tag{44}
$$

In (40) and (44), we have found a relation between g^* and f^*.

Now we return to our main task. We eliminate g^* from the definition of $\sim_g$ (39) and bring in f^*. We observe for any t, u

$t \sim_g u$

$\equiv$ {definition of $\sim_g$ (39)}

    $g^*.t = g^*.u$

$\equiv$ {Law of the Excluded Middle}

    $g^*.t = g^*.u \wedge (g^*.t = nn \vee g^*.t \neq nn)$

$\equiv$ {$\wedge$ distributes over $\vee$}

    $(g^*.t = g^*.u \wedge g^*.t = nn) \vee (g^*.t = g^*.u \wedge g^*.t \neq nn)$

$\equiv$ {$=$ is transitive, twice}

    $(g^*.t = g^*.u \wedge g^*.t = nn \wedge g^*.u = nn) \vee (g^*.t = g^*.u \wedge g^*.t \neq nn \wedge g^*.u \neq nn)$

$\equiv$ {$=$ is transitive}

    $(g^*.t = nn \wedge g^*.u = nn) \vee (g^*.t = g^*.u \wedge g^*.t \neq nn \wedge g^*.u \neq nn)$

$\equiv$ {(40) and (40) with $t \leftarrow u$}

    $(g^*.t = nn \wedge g^*.u = nn) \vee (f^*.t = f^*.u \wedge g^*.t \neq nn \wedge g^*.u \neq nn)$

$\equiv$ {(44)}

    $(f^*.t = f^*.u \wedge g^*.t = nn \wedge g^*.u = nn) \vee$
    $(f^*.t = f^*.u \wedge g^*.t \neq nn \wedge g^*.u \neq nn)$

$\equiv$ {$\wedge$ distributes over $\vee$}

    $f^*.t = f^*.u \wedge ((g^*.t = nn \wedge g^*.u = nn) \vee (g^*.t \neq nn \wedge g^*.u \neq nn))$

$\equiv$ {definition of $\sim_f$ (38); predicate calculus}

    $t \sim_f u \wedge (g^*.t = nn \equiv g^*.u = nn)$.

It remains to eliminate g^* and nn from the last line. We seek for a predicate β such that for all t

$$\beta.t \equiv g^*.t = nn . \tag{45}$$

We calculate β from specification (45). Our calculation is by structural induction on t because the definition of g^* is by induction. In the base case, i.e., for (45) with $t \leftarrow \varepsilon$, we observe

$g^*.\varepsilon = nn$

$\equiv$ {Lemma 10 (36)}

    $false$

$\equiv$ {definition of β (46), see below}

    $\beta.\varepsilon$.

We define

$$\neg\beta.\varepsilon . \tag{46}$$

In the inductive case, i.e., for (45) with $t \leftarrow t \triangleright x$, we observe

$g^*.(t \triangleright x) = nn$

$\equiv$ {Lemma 10 (37)}

    $g^*.t = l \wedge x = y$

$\equiv$ {$l \neq nn$}

    $g^*.t = l \wedge g^*.t \neq nn \wedge x = y$

$\equiv$ {(40)}

    $f^*.t = l \wedge g^*.t \neq nn \wedge x = y$

$\equiv$ {specification of r (35)}

$f^*.t = f^*.r \wedge g^*.t \neq nn \wedge x = y$
$\equiv$ {definition of $\sim_f$ (38) with $u \leftarrow r$; inductive hypothesis (45)}
$t \sim_f r \wedge \neg \beta.t \wedge x = y$
$\equiv$ {definition of β (47), see below}
$\beta.(t \triangleright x)$.

We define for all t, x

$$\beta.(t \triangleright x) \;\equiv\; t \sim_f r \wedge x = y \wedge \neg \beta.t . \qquad (47)$$

This definition of β concludes our redefinition of $\sim_g$. In particular, β is total.

It remains to express the premise $l \neq null$ in terms of traces and $\sim_f$. We observe

$l \neq null$
$\equiv$ {specification of r (35)}
$f^*.r \neq null$
$\equiv$ {Lemma 9 with $e, t, \sim \;\leftarrow f, r, \sim_f$}
$r \not\sim_f <nil>$. $\qquad (48)$

Since a trace r that violates (48) cannot be excluded syntactically, we define the copy operation for any r. We define it to terminate iff it is started in a program state $\sim_f$ that satisfies (48).

We summarize the definition of the copy operation in isolation from graphs. We introduce all names afresh. Let r be a trace, and let $y : y \neq nil$ be a label. We call

$$copy(r \triangleright y)$$

a *copy operation*. It is defined to terminate iff it is started in a program state $\sim$ such that

$$r \not\sim <nil> .$$

If the copy operation terminates it does so in the program state $\sim_g$ that is defined as follows: for all t, u

$$t \sim_g u \;\equiv\; t \sim u \wedge \beta.t = \beta.u \qquad (49)$$

where predicate β is defined as follows:

$$\neg \beta.\varepsilon \qquad (50)$$

and for all t, x

$$\beta.(t \triangleright x) \;\equiv\; t \sim r \wedge x = y \wedge \neg \beta.t . \qquad (51)$$

In the case of termination, it remains to prove that the relation $\sim_g$ defined in terms of $\sim$ and β is a trace equivalence. We know that every trace equivalence is induced by a graph. Hence, $\sim$ is induced by a graph, say, (N, f). As every graph does, $(copy(f^*.r \xrightarrow{y}))\,.(N, f)$ induces a trace equivalence. This trace equivalence is relation $\sim_g$ as our calculations have proved.

We give an example of this definition of the copy operation.

Example 1. Let x be an additional program variable. Let $r \leftarrow \varepsilon$, i.e., we consider the copy operation

$$copy(<y>) \ .$$

For program state $\sim_g$, in which the copy operation terminates, we observe

$\quad <x> \sim_g <y>$
$\equiv \quad \{(49)\}$
$\quad <x> \sim <y> \wedge \beta.<x> = \beta.<y>$
$\equiv \quad \{(52), \text{ see below}\}$
$\quad false \ .$

We observe

$\quad \beta.<x>$
$\equiv \quad \{(51) \text{ with } t \leftarrow \varepsilon\}$
$\quad \varepsilon \sim \varepsilon \wedge x = y \wedge \neg\beta.\varepsilon$
$\equiv \quad \{x \neq y\}$
$\quad false \ ;$

similarly, it follows that $\beta.<y>$. Hence, we have

$$\beta.<x> \neq \beta.<y> \ , \tag{52}$$

which concludes the example.

3 Weakest (Liberal) Preconditions

The theory of trace equivalences contains only concepts of high-level programming languages: traces and trace equivalences. But the assignment and the copy operation are still defined in a style that has proved unwieldy for program design: they are defined as functions that map the program state in which an operation is started to the program state in which it terminates (if it terminates).

Now we define the assignment and the copy operation in terms of weakest liberal preconditions and weakest preconditions [7, 8]. We derive the definitions from those given in terms of trace equivalences.

In the rest of Sect. 3, let $\sim$ be a variable that stands for the program state. We denote the 'everywhere'-operator by a pair of square brackets. It quantifies universally over $\sim$, i.e., over all program states.

3.0 Deterministic Statements

In the following, we write "_" to indicate a syntactic argument. Let "S" be a deterministic statement, i.e.: started in any program state, "S" has exactly one computation. By definition of wp, the computation terminates iff "S" is started in a program state in which

$$wp.\text{"}S\text{"}.true \tag{53}$$

holds. We define a function S (without the "_") as follows: it maps a program state that satisfies (53) and in which "S" is started to the program state in which the computation of "S" terminates.

Let P be a predicate that depends on variable $\sim$. When $\sim$ follows an opening bracket immediately or precedes a closing bracket immediately, then it is treated like an alphanumeric name. Since $(\sim) \leftarrow S.(\sim)$ substitutes $S.(\sim)$ for variable $\sim$, we have

$$[\,wlp.\text{``}S\text{''}.P \;\equiv\; wp.\text{``}S\text{''}.true \;\Rightarrow\; (\sim\leftarrow S.\sim).P\,] \tag{54}$$

and

$$[\,wp.\text{``}S\text{''}.P \;\equiv\; wp.\text{``}S\text{''}.true \;\wedge\; (\sim\leftarrow S.\sim).P\,] \;. \tag{55}$$

For the sake of simplicity, we abbreviate $(\sim \leftarrow S.\sim)$ by S. Precisely, we specify a predicate transformer S by

$$[\,wp.\text{``}S\text{''}.true \;\Rightarrow\; (S.P \;\equiv\; (\sim\leftarrow S.\sim).P)\,] \;. \tag{56}$$

From (56) it follows immediately that in all program states with (53), predicate transformer S distributes over the boolean operators ($\vee$, $\wedge$, $\equiv$, $\not\equiv$, $\Rightarrow$, $\Leftarrow$, $\neg$) and over the logical quantifiers ($\forall$ and $\exists$). Values such as integers, booleans, labels, traces, etc. are independent of the program state $\sim$. It therefore follows immediately from (56) with $P \leftarrow E = F$ that for all values E, F

$$[\,wp.\text{``}S\text{''}.true \;\Rightarrow\; (S.(E = F) \;\equiv\; E = F)\,] \;.$$

Traces are independent of the program state $\sim$. It therefore follows immediately from (56) with $P \leftarrow t \sim u$ that for all t, u

$$[\,wp.\text{``}S\text{''}.true \;\Rightarrow\; (S.(t \sim u) \;\equiv\; (t, u) \in S.\sim)\,] \;. \tag{57}$$

In (57), we can simplify the right-hand side of the equivalence when "S" is an assignment or a copy operation. In the simplification, we will now exploit their definitions that were given in terms of trace equivalences.

3.1   Assignment

Let

$$r \triangleright y := s \triangleright z$$

be an assignment. From the definition of its termination in Sect. 2.3, it follows immediately that

$$[\,wp.\text{``}r \triangleright y := s \triangleright z\text{''}.true \;\equiv\; r \not\sim <\!nil\!> \;\wedge\; s \not\sim <\!nil\!>\,] \;. \tag{58}$$

Let function α be defined by (30), (31) and (32). When $r \not\sim <\!nil\!> \;\wedge\; s \not\sim <\!nil\!>$, we observe for any t, u

$(r \triangleright y := s \triangleright z).(t \sim u)$
$\equiv$ $\{(57)$ with $S \leftarrow (r \triangleright y := s \triangleright z)\}$
$(t, u) \in (r \triangleright y := s \triangleright z).(\sim)$
$\equiv$ $\{(29)$ with $\sim_g \leftarrow (r \triangleright y := s \triangleright z).(\sim)\}$
$\alpha.t \sim \alpha.u$.

Hence, we have for all t, u

$$[r \not\sim <nil> \ \wedge \ s \not\sim <nil> \ \Rightarrow$$
$$((r \triangleright y := s \triangleright z).(t \sim u) \ \equiv \ \alpha.t \sim \alpha.u)] \ . \tag{59}$$

This formula concludes the definition of wlp and wp for the assignment.

Example. We continue Example 0. We consider the assignment

$$<x0> \triangleright y := <z> \ .$$

We calculate the weakest liberal precondition of predicate $<x0> \triangleright y \sim <x1> \triangleright y$. We observe

$$wlp.\text{``}<x0> \triangleright y := <z>\text{''}.(<x0> \triangleright y \sim <x1> \triangleright y)$$
$\equiv \quad \{(54)\}$
$$wp.\text{``}<x0> \triangleright y := <z>\text{''}.true \ \Rightarrow \ (<x0> \triangleright y := <z>).(<x0> \triangleright y \sim <x1> \triangleright y)$$
$\equiv \quad \{(58) \text{ and } (59), \text{ both with } r, s \leftarrow <x0>, \varepsilon\}$
$$<x0> \not\sim <nil> \ \wedge \ \varepsilon \not\sim <nil> \ \Rightarrow \ \alpha.(<x0> \triangleright y) \sim \alpha.(<x1> \triangleright y)$$
$\equiv \quad \{\text{healthiness condition } (16); \text{ Example 0: } (33)\}$
$$<x0> \not\sim <nil> \ \Rightarrow \ (<x0> \not\sim <x1> \ \Rightarrow \ \alpha.(<x0> \triangleright y) \sim \alpha.(<x1> \triangleright y))$$
$\equiv \quad \{\text{Example 0: } (34)\}$
$$<x0> \not\sim <nil> \ \Rightarrow \ (<x0> \not\sim <x1> \ \Rightarrow \ <z> \sim <x1> \triangleright y)$$
$\equiv \quad \{\text{predicate calculus}\}$
$$<x0> \sim <nil> \ \vee \ <x0> \sim <x1> \ \vee \ <z> \sim <x1> \triangleright y \ .$$

This concludes the example.

3.2   Copy Operation

Let

$$copy(r \triangleright y)$$

be a copy operation. From the definition of its termination in Sect. 2.4, it follows immediately that

$$[wp.\text{``}copy(r \triangleright y)\text{''}.true \ \equiv \ r \not\sim <nil>] \ . \tag{60}$$

Let predicate β be defined by (50) and (51). When $r \not\sim <nil>$, we observe for any t, u

$$(copy(r \triangleright y)).(t \sim u)$$
$\equiv \quad \{(57) \text{ with } S \leftarrow copy(r \triangleright y)\}$
$$(t, u) \in (copy(r \triangleright y)).(\sim)$$
$\equiv \quad \{(49) \text{ with } \sim_g \leftarrow (copy(r \triangleright y)).(\sim)\}$
$$t \sim u \ \wedge \ \beta.t = \beta.u \ .$$

Hence, we have for all t, u

$$[r \not\sim <nil> \ \Rightarrow \ ((copy(r \triangleright y)).(t \sim u) \ \equiv \ t \sim u \ \wedge \ \beta.t = \beta.u)] \ . \tag{61}$$

This formula concludes the definition of wlp and wp for the copy operation.

Example. We continue Example 1. We consider the copy operation

$$copy(<y>) \ .$$

We calculate the weakest precondition of predicate $<x> \not\sim <y>$. We observe

$$
\begin{aligned}
&wp.\text{``}copy(<y>)\text{''}.(<x> \not\sim <y>) \\
\equiv \quad &\{(55)\} \\
&wp.\text{``}copy(<y>)\text{''}.true \ \wedge \ (copy(<y>)).(<x> \not\sim <y>) \\
\equiv \quad &\{(60) \text{ with } r \leftarrow \varepsilon; \ copy(<y>) \text{ distributes over } \neg\} \\
&\varepsilon \not\sim <nil> \ \wedge \ \neg \, (copy(<y>)).(<x> \sim <y>) \\
\equiv \quad &\{\text{healthiness condition (16); (61) with } r \leftarrow \varepsilon\} \\
&\neg \, (<x> \sim <y> \ \wedge \ \beta.<x> = \beta.<y>) \\
\equiv \quad &\{\text{Example 1: (52)}\} \\
&true \ .
\end{aligned}
$$

Hence, we have

$$[\, wp.\text{``}copy(<y>)\text{''}.(<x> \not\sim <y>)\,] \ ,$$

which concludes the example.

4   Conclusion

The result of this paper is the concept of trace equivalence and the definition of the assignment and the copy operation in terms of weakest (liberal) preconditions. Instead of implementation concepts, this result uses concepts of high-level programming languages.

We intend the result as a foundation for program design. One hope is that program specification may become simpler and clearer when we do not have to think in terms of addresses and the heap. As an example, consider the specification of singly-linked lists. We define a predicate SL on a trace of integers and a trace. The infix symbol $\triangleleft$ denotes the prepend operation and has the same binding power as $\triangleright$. For example, we want

$$SL.(0 \triangleleft 1 \triangleleft <2>).t$$

to denote that $0\triangleleft1\triangleleft<2>$ is represented by singly-linked list t. As in the introduction (Sect. 0), program variable *data* contains the integer value of a list element, and program variable *next* points to the next list element. The definition of SL is by structural induction on the trace of integers. We define for all t

$$[\, SL.\varepsilon.t \ \equiv \ t \sim <nil>\,] \ ;$$

we define for all integers d, traces σ of integers and t

$$[\, SL.(d \triangleleft \sigma).t \ \equiv \ t \triangleright data \sim <d> \ \wedge \ SL.\sigma.(t \triangleright next)\,] \ .$$

Another hope is that program derivation may be free of operational arguments. The classical explanation of object creation is quite operational. It says that object creation allocates space on the heap, perhaps assigns values to program variables, returns the initial address of the space and assigns the address to a program variable, and it says that distinct executions of an object creation allocate distinct spaces and return different addresses. Many programming theories formalize this explanation directly. It is reflected even in Hoare-rules, as e.g. in [1]: 'The rule for object construction has a complicated transition relation, but this transition relation directly reflects the operational semantics.' Although other rules are less operational (e.g. [2–4, 6]), they are still rather complicated.

To be useful in program design, the presented pointer theory needs to be extended. Useful predicates on traces have to be defined. Hoare-rules that are tailored to practical needs have to be derived. In particular, Hoare-rules are needed for the object creation, which so far has been expressed as a sequential composition of the copy operation and assignments.

The pointer theory is intended especially as a foundation for object-oriented programming. When object-oriented concepts are added, their formalizations can be adopted from existing theories. Of particular interest are theories that leave pointers out of consideration [5]. Especially in object-oriented programming, implementation concepts still determine our thinking. The notations of object-oriented programming, however, allow it to be more abstract.

Acknowledgements

I am deeply grateful to Prof. Dr. Edsger W. Dijkstra. Both for reading a previous version of this paper and for his teaching, I remain grateful to him.

I thank Ria Dijkstra very much for encouraging me while I was writing this paper. For reading a previous version of the paper, for comments and discussions, I very much thank Manfred Broy, Wim Feijen and the ETAC, Tony Hoare, Bernhard Möller, David Naumann, and the members of SOOP. I thank the anonymous referees very much for their comments.

References

1. Martín Abadi and K. Rustan M. Leino. A logic of object-oriented programs. Research Report 161, Digital Systems Research Center, 130 Lytton Avenue, Palo Alto, California 94301, September 1998.
2. Pierre America and Frank de Boer. Reasoning about dynamically evolving process structures. *Formal Aspects of Computing*, 6:269–316, 1994.
3. Richard Bornat. Proving pointer programs in Hoare logic. In Roland Backhouse and José Nuno Oliveira, editors, *MPC*, volume 1837 of *Lecture Notes in Computer Science*, pages 102–126. Springer, 2000.
4. Cristiano Calcagno, Samin Ishtiaq, and Peter W. O'Hearn. Semantic analysis of pointer aliasing, allocation and disposal in Hoare logic. In Maurizio Gabbrielli and Frank Pfenning, editors, *Principles and Practice of Declarative Programming*, Lecture Notes in Computer Science. Springer, 2000. http://www.dcs.qmw.ac.uk/~ccris/ftp/ppdp00.ps.

5. Ana Cavalcanti and David A. Naumann. A weakest precondition semantics for an object-oriented language of refinement. In J. Wing, J. Woodcock, and J. Davies, editors, *Formal Methods*, volume 1709 of *Lecture Notes in Computer Science*, pages 1439–1459. Springer, 1999.

6. Frank S. de Boer. A WP-calculus for OO. In Wolfgang Thomas, editor, *Foundations of Software Science and Computation Structures*, volume 1578 of *Lecture Notes in Computer Science*, pages 135–149. Springer, 1999.

7. Edsger W. Dijkstra. *A Discipline of Programming*. Prentice Hall, Englewood Cliffs, 1976.

8. Edsger W. Dijkstra and Carel S. Scholten. *Predicate Calculus and Program Semantics*. Springer, 1990.

9. C.A.R. Hoare and He Jifeng. A trace model for pointers and objects. In Manfred Broy and Ralf Steinbrüggen, editors, *Calculational System Design*, volume 173 of *NATO Science Series F: Computer and Systems Sciences*, pages 3–23, Amsterdam, 1999. IOS Press.

10. C.A.R. Hoare and He Jifeng. A trace model for pointers and objects. In Rachid Guerraoui, editor, *ECOOP'99—Object-Oriented Programming*, volume 1628 of *Lecture Notes in Computer Science*, pages 1–17. Springer, 1999.

11. Bernhard Möller. Calculating with pointer structures. In Richard Bird and L. Meertens, editors, *Algorithmic Languages and Calculi*, pages 24–48. Chapman & Hall, 1997.

12. Bernhard Möller. Linked lists calculated. Technical Report 1997-07, Universität Augsburg, Institut für Informatik, D-86135 Augsburg, Germany, December 1997.

13. Peter W. O'Hearn, John C. Reynolds, and Hongseok Yang. Local reasoning about programs that alter data structures. In Laurent Fribourg, editor, *CSL*, volume 2142 of *Lecture Notes in Computer Science*, pages 1–19. Springer, 2001.

14. Manfred Paul and Ulrich Güntzer. On a uniform formal description of data structures. In E.K. Blum, M. Paul, and S. Takasu, editors, *Mathematical Studies of Information Processing*, volume 75 of *Lecture Notes in Computer Science*, pages 322–405. Springer, 1979.

15. Arnd Poetzsch-Heffter. *Specification and Verification of Object-Oriented Programs*. Habilitationsschrift, Fakultät für Informatik, Technische Universität München, January 1997. http://softech.informatik.uni-kl.de/en/publications/habil.html.

16. John C. Reynolds. Intuitionistic reasoning about shared mutable data structure. In Jim Davies, Bill Roscoe, and Jim Woodcock, editors, *Millennial Perspectives in Computer Science*, pages 303–321. Palgrave, 2000.

17. John C. Reynolds. Separation logic: A logic for shared mutable data structures. In *Logic in Computer Science*, pages 55–74. IEEE, 2002. http://www-2.cs.cmu.edu/afs/cs.cmu.edu/% hspace0ptuser/jcr/www/.

18. John C. Reynolds. Separation logic: Course CS 819A4. http://www-2.cs.cmu.edu/afs/cs.cmu.edu/project/fox-19/member/jcr/www15819A4s2003/cs819A4-03.html, March 2003.

Travelling Processes

Xinbei Tang and Jim Woodcock

Computing Laboratory, University of Kent
Canterbury, Kent, CT2 7NF, UK
{xt2,J.C.P.Woodcock}@kent.ac.uk

Abstract. This paper describes a refinement-based development method for mobile processes. Process mobility is interpreted as the assignment or communication of higher-order variables, whose values are process constants or parameterised processes, in which target variables update their values and source variables lose their values. The mathematical basis for the work is Hoare and He's *Unifying Theories of Programming (UTP)*. In this paper, we present a set of algebraic laws to be used for the development of mobile systems. The correctness of these laws is ensured by the UTP semantics of mobile processes. We illustrate our theory through a simple example that can be implemented in both a centralised and a distributed way. First, we present the π-calculus specification for both systems and demonstrate that they are observationally equivalent. Next, we show how the centralised system may be step-wisely developed into the distributed one using our proposed laws.

Keywords: Mobile processes, refinement, UTP, higher-order programming.

1 Introduction

Mobile processes are becoming increasingly popular in software applications; they can roam from host to host in a network, carrying their own state and program code. A common example is a Java applet that is downloaded from a server across the Internet, and then executed in a client. Such processes bring new programming problems, and so require their own theoretical foundations for the correct and rigorous development of applications.

The most well-known formal theory for mobile processes is the π-calculus [7, 8, 13], where processes may exchange channel names, and thus change their interconnections dynamically. The higher-order π-calculus (HOπ in short) [12] treats mobility by exchanging processes themselves. The π-calculus and the HOπ are usually given an operational semantics, and then provided with an equivalence relation for comparing processes using bisimulation. Our interest lies in combining programming theories; *Circus* [15] combines theories of sequential and concurrent programming. Unfortunately, it is not easy to combine theories that are based on operational semantics, because of the fragility of results based on induction [5]. We are interested in refinement calculi, which arise more naturally from denotational semantics. Finally, we are interested in the phenomenon of divergence, which is ignored in the π-calculus and its variants.

D. Kozen (Ed.): MPC 2004, LNCS 3125, pp. 381–399, 2004.
© Springer-Verlag Berlin Heidelberg 2004

We propose a theory of mobile processes that is suitable for refinement, so that it can support step-wise development of mobile systems. Especially, starting with an abstract specification, we develop a distributed system by using mobile processes, in which each step of the derivation is provable in the theory.

In this paper, we present our initial results, a set of algebraic laws. The mathematical basis for the work is Hoare and He's *Unifying Theories of Programming (UTP)* [5], which uses a simple alphabetised form of Tarski's relational calculus. The correctness of these laws is proved using the UTP semantics for mobile processes. We study a simple example in both π-calculus and our theory. The results show the suitability of our laws for the step-wise development of a mobile system from a centralised specification.

Process mobility is exhibited in the higher-order variable assignment or communication, in which both the source and the target are variables, and have process behaviours as their values. When a higher-order mobile-variable assignment or communication takes place, the target variable is updated, more or less as one would expect; but at the same time, the source variable becomes undefined. In this way, processes are moved around in the system.

The presence of process-valued variables has an impact on monotonicity with respect to refinement, and we require that process assignment should be monotonic in the assigned value. This follows the treatment of higher-order programming in [5].

The remainder of this paper is organised as follows. The next section gives a simple example implemented in both a centralised and a distributed way, and shows that they are observationally equivalent in the π-calculus. Section 3 presents the syntax of mobile processes and an brief overview of its UTP semantics. In Section 4, we illustrate our development method for distributed systems through a set of laws; thereafter, we apply the laws in the example in Section 5. We conclude the presented work in Section 6 and outline some future work.

2   A Simple Example in the π-Calculus

Suppose that there is a data centre that needs to analyse data based on information residing in different hosts on a network. For simplicity, we assume that this analysis amounts to getting the sum of the data in each host. This small application can be implemented in two ways. In the first implementation (Figure 1), the data center directly communicates with each host, one by one, getting the local information and then updating its running total; all calculations are carried out in the data centre. This implementation is very simple, and so is obviously correct.

In the second implementation (Figure 2), similar pieces of specification are abstracted and encapsulated in a parameterised process variable, which travels from the data centre and roams the network to each host, taking its own state and operations. After its arrival at a host, it is plugged into a local channel c_i and activated, getting the local information and updating its running total. After visiting all hosts, it comes back to the data centre with the final result.

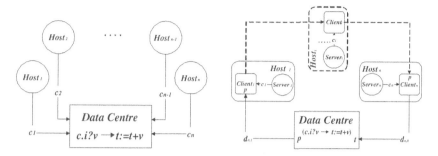

Fig. 1. Centralised Implementation   **Fig. 2.** Distributed Implementation

Both implementations can complete the simple task, but the latter one has a richer structure that might make it more useful. For example, if the nature of the analysis changes, then only the mobile process needs to be changed. Consider an international bank: it may change both data (exchange rates) and function (services offered to customers) frequently. If this is programmed as a mobile process, then the very latest upgrade arrives automatically in local branches. It may also be more efficient to move the process from the centre to each host, as local communication would replace remote communication.

Both systems can be specified in the π-calculus. As the π-calculus syntax does not have assignment, we use a suitable translation to convert assignment into π-terms as the composition of an input and an output action over a restricted (or bound) name. The π-calculus syntax that we adopt is from [8].

Definition 1 (π-calculus assignment).

$$[\![(t := e).P]\!] \;\;\widehat{=}\;\; \text{new } h \; (\overline{h}\langle e\rangle.0 \mid h(t).[\![P]\!]) \qquad\qquad [t \in \text{fn}(P), h \notin \text{fn}(P)]$$

where the part enclosed in [ ] is the side condition that the definition should satisfy, and $\text{fn}(P)$ denotes the free names of P. □

Observationally, the effect of the assignment of a value to variable t followed by executing P immediately is the same as substituting this value for all the free occurrences of the variable t in P. This is shown by the following simple theorem that states the bisimilarity between the two.

Theorem 1 (Assignment bisimulation).

$$(t := e).P \;\approx\; \{e/t\}P \qquad\qquad [t \in \text{fn}(P)]$$

where $\{e/t\}P$ denotes the systematic substitution of e for t in P.

Proof.

LHS	[definition of assignment]
$= \mathsf{new}\ h\ (\overline{h}\langle e\rangle.0 \mid h(t).P)$	[strong bisimilarity]
$\sim \tau.(0 \mid \{e/t\}P)$	[weak bisimilarity]
$\approx 0 \mid \{e/t\}P$	[structural congruence]
$\equiv RHS$	

$\square$

The centralised system is the composition of a *Centre* process and n *Hosts* over restricted channel names.

$$System \ \widehat{=}\ (\mathsf{new}\ c_1, c_2, \cdots, c_n)(Centre \mid Host_1 \mid Host_2 \mid \cdots \mid Host_n)$$

where the *Centre* is defined as:

$$Centre \ \widehat{=}\ (t := 0).c_1(v).(t := t + v).\cdots.c_n(v).(t := t + v).result\langle t\rangle.0$$

where $c_i(v)$ is the input of the data that needs to be retrieved from the ith host.

In the assignment $t := t+v$ of *Centre*, the t in the left hand side is a restricted name while the t in the right is a free name. We can better comprehend the scope of each t and v using renaming. The effect of *Centre* is the same as

$$Centre\ =$$
$$(t_0 := 0).c_1(v_1).(t_1 := t_0 + v_1).\cdots.c_n(v_n).(t_n = t_{n-1} + v_n).result\langle t_n\rangle.0$$

In the HOπ [12] and polyadic π-calculus [8], abstractions (parameterised processes) or multiple names can be transmitted directly along channel names. In the distributed implementation, an abstraction $(z, in, out, done).P$ and the value of t are transmitted at the same time, where $(z, in, out, done).P$ and its execution $((z, in, out, done).P)\langle c_i, t_{i-1}, tmp, tg\rangle$ are defined as follows:

$$(z, in, out, done).P \ \widehat{=}\ z(v).(out := in + v).\overline{done}\langle out\rangle.0$$
$$((z, in, out, done).P)\langle c_i, t_{i-1}, tmp, tg\rangle \ \widehat{=}\ c_i(v).(tmp := t_{i-1} + v).\overline{tg}\langle tmp\rangle.0$$

Let $d_{0,1}$ be the name of the channel connecting *Centre* and $Host_1$, $d_{n,0}$ be the name of the channel connecting $Host_n$ and *Centre*, and $d_{i,i+1}(1 \le i \le n-1)$ be the name of the channel connecting $Host_i$ and $Host_{i+1}$. The specification for the distributed system is

$$MSystem\ \widehat{=}$$
$$(\mathsf{new}\ d_{0,1}, d_{1,2}, \cdots, d_{n,0})(MCentre \mid MHost_1 \mid MHost_2 \mid \cdots \mid MHost_n)$$

The *Centre* now has the task of initialising its total, sending the mobile process and total on its way, and then waiting for the total to return home[1], before outputting the result.

$$MCentre \ \widehat{=}\ (t := 0).\overline{d_{0,1}}\langle(z, in, out, done).P, t\rangle.d_{n,0}(final).result\langle final\rangle.0$$

---

[1] The mobile process is discarded in the last-visited host after its mission in order to save network cost, but extra cost arises for specifying the last host separately.

Each host now has an extra component: one that receives the mobile process, executes it, and then passes it on to the next host. This component is merely added to the previous behaviour of the host.

$MHost_i \; \widehat{=} \; (\mathsf{new} \; c_i)(HostC_i \mid Host_i)$

$HostC_i \; \widehat{=}$

$$
\begin{cases}
d_{i-1,i}(p, t_{i-1}).(\mathsf{new} \; tg)(p\langle c_i, t_{i-1}, tmp, tg\rangle \mid tg(t_i).\overline{d_{i,i+1}}\langle p, t_i\rangle.0) \\
\hspace{8cm} \text{for } i = 1 \,.. \, n - 1 \\
d_{n-1,n}(p, t_{n-1}).(\mathsf{new} \; tg)(p\langle c_n, t_{n-1}, tmp, tg\rangle \mid tg(t_n).\overline{d_{n,0}}\langle t_n\rangle.0) \\
\hspace{8cm} \text{for } i = n
\end{cases}
$$

In $HostC_i$, we use a restricted name tg to make the output via $d_{i,i+1}$ possible after p's execution. If we discard $\overline{done}\langle out\rangle$ in the transmitted abstraction, then the value of the updated t would not be passed on to the next host, and $p\langle c_i, t_{i-1}, tmp\rangle.\overline{d_{i,i+1}}\langle p, t_i\rangle.0$ would be syntactically wrong, because $p\langle c_i, t_{i-1}, tmp\rangle$ is a process rather than a prefix.

The centralised and distributed systems are observationally equivalent, and the π-calculus can be used to verify this. So, if we are convinced that the centralised system calculates the right answer, then we have an argument that the distributed system does so too.

We are interested in a step-wise development process in the spirit of Morgan's refinement calculus for sequential programs [9]. We would like to start from an abstract, centralised specification, and develop a concrete, distributed implementation, proceeding in small steps that are easy to justify and that explain design decisions. It is not easy to follow this discipline in the π-calculus. Instead, we would like to base our language of mobile processes firmly on the notion of refinement, and develop sets of laws that encourage piece-wise development. In later sections, after we present the denotational semantics and laws for mobile processes, we show this step-wise development in our proposed approach.

3   Syntax and Semantics

The syntax of our language is a subset of occam [6] and CSP [4, 10], but enriched with primitives for process variables, mobile and clone assignment and communication, and (parameterised) process variable activation. These mobility constructs are inspired by occam$_M$ [1].

In discussing the semantics, we make use of the following conventions for meta-variables. p and q range over all program variables; t ranges over data variables; e ranges over data; h ranges over process variables; E ranges over data or process values; x, y and z range over formal name, value, and result parameters; ne, ve, and re range over actual name, value, and result parameters; b ranges over boolean values; X ranges over sets of events.

The basic elements in our model are processes, which are constructed from the following rules:

$$P \quad ::= SKIP \mid STOP \mid CHAOS \mid \textbf{vid} \; p : T \mid \textbf{end} \; p$$
$$\mid \; h := \{\!\{P\}\!\} \mid h := \{\!\{\lambda \, x : var(T_1), y : val(T_2), z : res(T_3) \bullet P\}\!\}$$
$$\mid \; t := e \mid p :=_m q \mid p := q \mid <h> \mid h(ne, ve, re)$$
$$\mid \; Comm \to P \mid P \lhd b \rhd Q \mid P \; ; \; Q \mid b * P$$
$$\mid \; P \parallel Q \mid P \,\square\, Q \mid P \sqcap Q \mid P \setminus X$$

$$\textbf{vid} \quad ::= \textbf{var} \mid \textbf{proc}$$
$$Comm ::= ch?p \mid ch!q \mid ch!!q \mid ch.E$$

SKIP terminates immediately; *STOP* represents deadlock; *CHAOS* is the worst process and the bottom element of the complete lattice of mobile processes: its behaviour is arbitrary.

The variable declaration **vid** $p : T$ introduces a new variable p of type T; correspondingly **end** p terminates the scope of p. When it is clear from the context that p is a data variable or a process variable, we use **var** or **proc** for its declaration. The type T determines the range of values that p can have. When p is a process variable, its type determines the alphabet and interface[2] of the process that may be assigned to p. For convenience, we often omit types when they are irrelevant.

Higher-order programming treats program as data, and higher-order assignment or communication assigns process constants to higher-order variables. Process constants are enclosed in brackets, which have no semantic importance and are ignored when the process is activated. We distinguish simple process constants from parameterised ones. The higher-order constant assignment $h := \{\!\{P\}\!\}$ assigns a simple process constant P to h, and $h := \{\!\{\lambda \, x : var(T_1), y : val(T_2), z : res(T_3) \bullet P\}\!\}$ assigns h a parameterised process constant, which has a body P and a formal name parameter x, value parameter y, and result parameter z.

The first-order constant assignment $t := e$ assigns a value e to the data variable t. The clone variable assignment $p := q$ is similar to constant assignment, except that the term in its right hand side is a variable rather than a value. After this clone assignment, the value of p is updated according to q's value, and q gets a value that is better than its original one (in section 3.1, we explain what a better value is and why the value should be better). The notation $p :=_m q$ denotes mobile variable assignment. On its termination, the value of the target variable p is updated and the source variable q is undefined, thus the result of any attempt of using q is unpredictable.

The notation $ch.E$ stands for a communication that takes place as soon as both participants are ready. The input prefix $ch?p \to P$ accepts a message from the channel, assigns it to p, and then behaves like P. The mobile output prefix $ch!!q \to P$ transfers the value of variable q through channel ch and then executes P. As in mobile assignment, any attempt to use q after output is unpredictable. The clone output prefix $ch!q \to P$ outputs the value of q, but retains q's value.

Once initialised, a process variable h may be activated by executing it, denoted by $<h>$. A parameterised process variable can be activated by providing

---

[2] The interface is defined as parameters and input/output channels through which the process can interact with its environment.

parameters. If a process variable h has the value of $(\lambda x : var(T_1), y : val(T_2), z : res(T_2) \bullet P)$, then the effect of the activation $h(ne, ve, re)$ is calculated by

$$h(ne, ve, re) = \mathbf{var}\ x := ne, y := ve, z;\ P;\ ne := x, re := z;\ \mathbf{end}\ x, y, z$$

It initially assigns the values of actual parameters ne and ve to the formal name and value parameters of P, and executes P. On the termination of P, the values of the name and result parameters are passed back to the actual parameters ne and re.

A conditional $(P \lhd b \rhd Q)$ behaves as P if b is *true*, otherwise as Q. The sequential composition of two processes $(P\ ;\ Q)$ results in a process that behaves as P, and, on termination of P, behaves as Q. An iteration $(b * P)$ repeatedly executes P until b is *false*. A parallel composition $(P \parallel Q)$ executes P and Q concurrently, such that events in the alphabet of both parties require their simultaneous participation, whereas the remaining events occur independently. An external choice $(P \,\square\, Q)$ allows the environment to choose between P and Q, whereas the internal choice $(P \sqcap Q)$ selects one of the two processes nondeterministically. $P \setminus X$ hides the events in the set X, so that they happen invisibly, without the participation of the environment.

3.1   Semantics

The denotational semantics of the model is given in the style of Hoare & He's unifying theories [5]. In the UTP, the semantics of a process P is given in terms of an implicit description of its entire behaviour using the following observational and program variables (denoted by αP), in which the undecorated variables record the initial state before P is started, and the dashed ones record the intermediate or final state at the time of observation.

- $\mathcal{A}$, the set of events in which P can engage
- ok, ok': $\mathbb{B}$, indicating freedom from divergence
- $wait, wait'$: $\mathbb{B}$, indicating waiting for interaction with the environment
- tr, tr': $\text{seq}\,\mathcal{A}$, recording traces of events
- ref, ref': $\mathbb{P}\mathcal{A}$, indicating events currently refused
- v, v', program variables (including higher-order variables)

We use $\mathbf{obs}$ to represent all observable variables $ok, wait, tr, ref$ in short. P's behaviour is described by a relation between undashed and dashed variables. By using this model, the failure can be indicated by a pair $\langle tr, ref \rangle$, and the divergence is captured by the ok variable. Therefore, we are able to reason about the failure and divergence of processes.

Healthiness conditions distinguish feasible specifications or designs from infeasible ones. There are five healthiness conditions for mobile processes as follows.

M1 $P = P \wedge (tr \leq tr')$

M2 $P = \sqcap \{P[s, s^\frown(tr' - tr)/tr, tr'] \mid s \in \text{seq } \mathcal{A}\}$

M3 $P = II \lhd wait \rhd P$

where

$II \;\hat{=}\; I \lhd ok \rhd (tr \leq tr')$

$I \;\hat{=}\; (ok' = ok) \wedge (tr' = tr) \wedge (wait' = wait) \wedge (ref' = ref) \wedge (v' \sqsupseteq v)$

M4 $P = P \lhd ok \rhd (tr \leq tr')$

M5 $P = P \,;\, J$

where

$J \;\hat{=}\; (ok \Rightarrow ok') \wedge (tr' = tr) \wedge (wait' = wait) \wedge (ref' = ref) \wedge (v' \sqsupseteq v)$

M1 says that a process can never undo its execution. **M2** indicates that the initial value of trace tr has no influence on a process. **M3** describes the fact that if a process starts in the waiting state of its predecessor, then it will leave the state unchanged. **M4** states that if a process starts in a non-stable state, then we cannot predict its behaviour except trace expansion. **M5** shows the fact that divergence is something that is never wanted, which is characterised by the monotonicity of ok'. All processes in our language are healthy processes. More details can be found in [5] and [14].

There are two differences between our approach and first-order programming: the refinement ordering between variables; and the semantics of higher-order assignment and communication. In first-order programming, we say a process P is refined by Q, denoted by $P \sqsubseteq Q$, if for all variables in the alphabet, the behaviour of Q is more predictable and controllable than that of P.

Definition 2 (Process refinement).

$$P \sqsubseteq Q \;\hat{=}\; \forall \, \boldsymbol{obs}, \boldsymbol{obs'}, v, v' \bullet Q \Rightarrow P$$

The universal closure over the alphabet is written more concisely: $[\, Q \Rightarrow P \,]$. □

As higher-order variables hold processes as their values, the ordering between program variables can be defined in the light of the refinement ordering between their values. Two process variables can be compared only when they have the same types. We say a process variable h is a refinement of g, if the activation behaviour of h is more controllable and predictable than that of g. For first-order data variables, two variables are comparable only when they are equal. More specifically, we define the refinement ordering between variables as follows.

Definition 3 (Variable refinement). *Let p and q be two program variables of the same type*

$p \sqsubseteq q \;\hat{=}\;$

$$\begin{cases} p = q & \textit{if } p, q \textit{ are data variables} \\ [\, q(ne, ve, re) \Rightarrow p(ne, ve, re) \,] & \textit{if } p, q \textit{ are parameterised process variables} \\ [\, <q> \Rightarrow <p> \,] & \textit{otherwise} \end{cases}$$

where ne, ve, and re are the actual name parameter, value parameter and result parameter for the activations of p and q.   □

First-order assignment $t := e$ has no interaction with the environment. It always terminates and never diverges. On termination, it equates the final value of t with value e, but does not change the other variables.

Definition 4 (First-order assignment).

$$[\![t := e]\!] \ \widehat{=} \ \textbf{\textit{M34}}(ok' \wedge \neg \ wait' \wedge tr' = tr \wedge t' = e \wedge v' = v)$$

where v contains all program variables except t, $\textbf{\textit{M3}}(P) = \textit{II} \lhd wait \rhd P$, $\textbf{\textit{M4}}(P) = P \lhd ok \rhd (tr \leq tr')$, $\textbf{\textit{M34}}$ is $\textbf{\textit{M3}} \circ \textbf{\textit{M4}}$. The healthiness conditions are required to make sure that the assignment does not take place unless the preceding process terminated properly. The satisfaction of the other healthiness conditions can be derived from the definition [14]. □

As discussed above, we must give a semantics to assignment that makes it monotonic with respect to refinement.

Definition 5 (Higher-order constant assignment).

$$[\![h := \{\!|P|\!\}]\!] \ \widehat{=} \ \textbf{\textit{M34}} \ (ok' \wedge \neg \ wait' \wedge tr' = tr \wedge h' \sqsupseteq P \wedge v' \sqsupseteq v)$$

$$[h, h' \notin \alpha P]$$

where v contains all program variables except h. □

Theorem 2 (Monotonicity). *Suppose that h is a higher-order variable.*

$$P \sqsubseteq Q \ \Rightarrow \ h := \{\!|P|\!\} \sqsubseteq h := \{\!|Q|\!\}$$ □

It may be instructive to see what would happen if we had used equalities in Definition 5.

$$
\begin{aligned}
&h := \{\!|P|\!\} \sqsubseteq h := \{\!|Q|\!\} && \text{[refinement (definition 2)]}\\
&= [\, h := \{\!|Q|\!\} \Rightarrow h := \{\!|P|\!\}\,] && \text{[assumption (definition of assignment)]}\\
&= [\, \textbf{\textit{M34}} \, (ok' \wedge \neg \ wait' \wedge tr' = tr \wedge h' = \{\!|Q|\!\} \wedge v' = v) \Rightarrow\\
&\qquad \textbf{\textit{M34}} \, (ok' \wedge \neg \ wait' \wedge tr' = tr \wedge h' = \{\!|P|\!\} \wedge v' = v)\,]\\
&&& \text{[definition of } \textbf{\textit{M3}} \text{ and } \textbf{\textit{M4}}]\\
&= [\, ok' \wedge \neg \ wait' \wedge tr' = tr \wedge h' = \{\!|Q|\!\} \wedge v' = v \Rightarrow\\
&\qquad ok' \wedge \neg \ wait' \wedge tr' = tr \wedge h' = \{\!|P|\!\} \wedge v' = v\,]\\
&&& \text{[one-point rule, three times]}\\
&= [\, ok' \wedge \neg \ wait' \Rightarrow ok' \wedge \neg \ wait' \wedge \{\!|Q|\!\} = \{\!|P|\!\}\,] && \text{[propositional calculus]}\\
&= [\, ok' \wedge \neg \ wait' \Rightarrow \{\!|Q|\!\} = \{\!|P|\!\}\,] && \text{[universal closure, case analysis]}\\
&= (P = Q)
\end{aligned}
$$

So, monotonicity would hold only in a trivial sense.

For the same reason, we also adopt the inequation in the definitions of higher-order communication and I, $\textit{II}$ and *SKIP*. For first-order data, two values are comparable if and only if they are equal. Therefore higher-order assignment or communication and *SKIP* are consistent with their counterpart in first-order programming. We extend the language, but we are interested in a conservative extension in which the new semantics is not only suitable for the extension part, but also for the original part. Interested readers may refer to [14] for more details about the semantics of mobile processes.

4   Development Method for Distributed Systems

Our development procedure involves two main steps. In the first step we abstract predicates and assign them to parameterised process variables (see Section 4.1). In the second step, by converting assignment into communication, we make the variable mobile: consequently, the activations of the variable can be completed in different hosts over a network (see Section 4.2).

We present the development procedure through a set of algebraic properties and laws for mobile processes. The proofs of these laws are largely straightforward, therefore we omit them in this paper. Some of the proofs have been given in [14].

We use two syntactic abbreviations: we write $(\textbf{proc } h := \{\!\{Q\}\!\})$ instead of $(\textbf{proc } h; \ h := \{\!\{Q\}\!\})$; and we abbreviate $(\textbf{proc } h; \ Q; \ \textbf{end } h)$ by $(\textbf{proc } h \bullet Q)$ to represent that the scope of h is valid in Q.

The mobility of processes is expressed in the following law.

Law 1 (Undefined activation) *For distinct higher-order variables g and h.*

$$(g :=_m h \ ; \ <h>) \ = \ CHAOS \qquad\qquad\qquad [\text{Law 1.A}]$$
$$(ch!!h \rightarrow <h>) \ = \ ch.h \ ; \ CHAOS \qquad\qquad [\text{Law 1.B}]$$

where ch is a channel name.   □

Law 1 captures the fact that a mobile process has moved after assignment or communication, since its value has been passed to a new location (g, or the other end of the channel ch), and none of its behaviours is available at its old location (the higher-order variable h). In Law 1.A, as there is no communication with the environment, the update of g cannot be observed, therefore the whole effect is the same as *CHAOS*; however, in Law 1.B, the execution of h still leads to *CHAOS*, but this does not undo the communication that has already happened.

4.1   Abstracting Process Variables

Law 2 (Process constant) *A process constant is not subject to substitutions for the variables it contains.*

$$(P(x)_{+h} \ ; \ h := \{\!\{Q(x)\}\!\}) \ = \ (h := \{\!\{Q(x)\}\!\} \ ; \ P(x)_{+h})$$
$$[h, h' \notin \alpha P, \ h, h' \notin \alpha Q]$$

where $P(x)$ and $Q(x)$ are processes in which x occurs as a variable. Note the use of alphabet extension: P_{+h} is the relation $P \wedge h' \sqsupseteq h$, with alphabet $\alpha P \cup \{h, h'\}$. This is needed in order to balance alphabets.   □

Law 3 (Variable introduction) *We can always include a process in the scope of a new variable, assuming this variable is not in the alphabet of the process.*

$$Q \ = \ (\textbf{\textit{vid}} \ p \ ; \ Q_{+p} \ ; \ \textbf{\textit{end}} \ p) \hspace{3cm} [p, p' \notin \alpha Q]$$

□

Law 4 (Vacuous constant assignment) *The assignment of a constant to a process variable at the end of its scope is vacuous.*

$$(h := \{\!|Q|\!\} \ ; \ \textbf{\textit{end}} \ h) \ = \ (\textbf{\textit{end}} \ h) \hspace{3cm} [h, h' \notin \alpha Q]$$

*The assignment $h :=_m g$; **end** h would not have been vacuous, since the effect on g (making its value undefined) would persist beyond the end of h's scope.* □

Law 5 (Vacuous mobile variable assignment) *The corresponding law for mobile variable assignment is stronger in that it requires both variable scopes to end.*

$$(p :=_m q \ ; \ \textbf{\textit{end}} \ p \ ; \ \textbf{\textit{end}} \ q) \ = \ (\textbf{\textit{end}} \ p \ ; \ \textbf{\textit{end}} \ q)$$

Of course, it does not matter in which order the scopes are ended. □

Law 6 (Vacuous identity assignment) *The effect of the assignment of a variable to itself is the same as SKIP.*

$$(p := p) \ = \ (p :=_m p) \ = \ SKIP$$

When the mobile assignment terminates, on the right hand side, p's value becomes arbitrary; however, on the left hand side p gets a value that refines the original value of right-hand-side p. Therefore, the whole conjunctive effect is that p refines its original value, which is the same as SKIP. □

Law 7 (Scope-extension/shrinkage) *The scope of a variable may be extended by moving its declaration in front of a process that contains no free occurrences of it, or moving its variable undeclaration after this process.*

$$(P \ ; \ \textbf{\textit{vid}} \ p) \ = \ (\textbf{\textit{vid}} \ p \ ; \ P_{+p})$$
$$(\textbf{\textit{end}} \ p \ ; \ P) \ = \ (P_{+p} \ ; \ \textbf{\textit{end}} \ p) \hspace{3cm} [p, p' \notin \alpha P]$$

□

Law 8 (Copy-rule-1) *Following the meaning of process variable activation, a process can be replaced by the activation of a variable which has been assigned by this process constant before.*

$$(h := \{\!|Q|\!\} \ ; \ Q) \ = \ (h := \{\!|Q|\!\} \ ; \ <\!h\!>) \hspace{3cm} [h, h' \notin \alpha Q]$$

Even though we have adopted inequality in higher-order assignment, this rule is an equality rather than a refinement. It is because h is assigned nondeterministically by a process that refines Q, consequently, activating h is the same as executing $\bigsqcap_R \{R \mid R \sqsupseteq Q\}$, and the result of this non-deterministic choice equals to the weakest process Q. □

Law 9 (Copy-rule-2) *Any process can be replaced by assigning this process constant to a newly-declared process variable and following by its activation.*

$$Q \; = \; (\textbf{proc } h := \{\!| Q |\!\} \bullet <h>) \hspace{3cm} [h, h' \notin \alpha Q]$$

□

Law 10 (Parameterised copy-rule) *The law for parameterised processes differs in that we activate them by providing actual parameters.*

$$Q(i, j, k) \; = \\ \textbf{proc } h := \{\!| \lambda \, x : var(T_1), y : val(T_2), z : res(T_3) \bullet Q(x, y, z) |\!\} \bullet \\ h(i, j, k)$$

$$[h, h' \notin \alpha Q]$$

where $Q(i, j, k)$ is a parameterised process with actual name, value and result parameters i, j and k of type T_1, T_2 and T_3 respectively. □

Law 9 and Law 10 are the key rules to abstract the same or similar segments by a higher-order process variable.

We introduce two notations to represent a series of sequential compositions.

Definition 6 (Indexed sequential composition). *An indexed sequential composition is the sequential composition of a series of processes in order.*

$$(\S i : 1 \mathbin{..} n \bullet P_i) \; \widehat{=} \; \begin{cases} SKIP & n = 0 \\ (\S i : 1 \mathbin{..} n - 1 \bullet P_i);\; P_n & n \geq 1 \end{cases}$$

□

Definition 7 (Iterated sequential composition). *Sequential composition may be iterated over any sequence s.*

$$(\S i : s \bullet P(i)) \; \widehat{=} \; \begin{cases} SKIP & s = \langle\rangle \\ P(head(s));\; (\S i : tail(s) \bullet P(i)) & s \neq \langle\rangle \end{cases}$$

where i is one of the elements in the sequence of parameters, and P is a parameterised process, $head(s)$ is the first element of s, $tail(s)$ is a subsequence of s after removing its first element. □

For example, we denote the program $(t := t + 2;\; t := t + 7;\; t := t + 5)$ as

$$\S i : \langle 2, 7, 5 \rangle \bullet \{\!| \lambda j : val(\mathbb{N}) \bullet t := t + j |\!\}(i)$$

For a series of similar pieces of program, we may be able to assign the parameterised process to a newly-introduced process variable, and activate it in series with proper arguments.

Law 11 (Iterated parameterised copy-rule) *Suppose Q is a parameterised process with a value parameter of type I, then, for any sequence s,*

$$(\, _9^i : s \bullet \{\!|\lambda j : val(I) \bullet Q(j)|\!\}(i) \,) \ = \ \left(\begin{array}{c} \textbf{proc } h := \{\!|\lambda j : val(I) \bullet Q(j)|\!\} \bullet \\ (\, _9^i : s \bullet h(i)) \end{array} \right)$$

$$[h, h' \notin \alpha Q]$$

$\square$

For instance, by using this law, we have the following derivation

$$(t := t + 2; \ t := t + 7; \ t := t + 5) \ = \\ \left(\begin{array}{c} \textbf{proc } h := \{\!|\lambda j : val(\mathbb{N}) \bullet t := t + j|\!\} \\ \frac{1}{1} \bullet (h(2); \ h(7); \ h(5)) \end{array} \right)$$

As a special case of the above law, when $s = \langle 1, 2, \ldots, n \rangle$,

$$(\, _9^i : 1 \ldots n \bullet P(i) \,) \ = \ \left(\begin{array}{c} \textbf{proc } h := \{\!|\lambda j : val(\mathbb{N}) \bullet P(j)|\!\} \bullet \\ (\, _9^i : 1 \ldots n \bullet h(i)) \end{array} \right)$$

In the same way, we have similar laws for an iterated parameterised process that has name or result parameters.

4.2   Moving Process Variables

Even though we group similar pieces of specification as the value of a newly introduced parameterised process variable and activate it at necessary occurrences (Law 11), the whole specification is still centralised. In order to achieve a distributed system, we may consider putting many activations of this variable in different distributed components. To make sure that the variables activated in different components have the same process values or similar structures, we initialise the variable at one component but make it mobile, transmitted from one distributed component to another one. It is necessary to introduce communication in this step. Actually, the assignment and the communication are semantically equivalent.

Law 12 (Assignment-communication equivalence)

$$(p := q) \ = \ ((ch?p \rightarrow SKIP) \parallel (ch!q \rightarrow SKIP)) \setminus \{ch\}$$
$$(p :=_m q) \ = \ ((ch?p \rightarrow SKIP) \parallel (ch!!q \rightarrow SKIP)) \setminus \{ch\}$$

$\square$

We borrow the concepts of pipes and chaining in CSP [4, 10]. Pipes are special processes which have only two channels, namely an input channel *left* and an output channel *right*. For example, a pipe that recursively accepts a number from *left*, and outputs its double to *right* can be represented by:

$$\mu X \bullet left?p \rightarrow right!(p + p) \rightarrow X$$

Definition 8 (Chaining). *Chaining links two pipes together as a new pipe.*

$$P \gg Q \;\hat{=}\; (P[mid/right] \parallel Q[mid/left]) \setminus \{mid\}$$

□

An indexed chaining connects a series of processes in order as a long pipe.

Definition 9 (Indexed-chaining).

$$(\gg i : 1..n \bullet P_i) \;\hat{=}\; \begin{cases} P_1 & n = 1 \\ (\gg i : 1..n-1 \bullet P_i) \gg P_n & n > 1 \end{cases}$$

□

Definition 10 (Double-chaining). *Double chaining links two pipes as a ring.*

$$P \lll\ggg Q \;\hat{=}\;$$
$$(P[mid_1, mid_2/right, left] \parallel Q[mid_1, mid_2/left, right]) \setminus \{mid_1, mid_2\}$$

All the communications between pipes are hidden from the environment.   □

The double chaining operator is commutative.

Law 13 (Double-chaining commutative)

$$P \lll\ggg Q \;=\; Q \lll\ggg P$$

□

A ring of processes can be viewed as a long chain with the two chain ends connected. The order of processes in the ring is important, but the connecting point of the chain can be arbitrary. In other words, the chain can be started from any process and ended at one of its backwards adjacent process. This feature is captured by the following law.

Law 14 (Exchange)

$$\begin{aligned} & P_1 \lll\ggg (\gg i : 2..n \bullet P_i) \\ =\; & P_k \lll\ggg ((\gg i : k+1..n \bullet P_i) \gg (\gg i : 1..k-1 \bullet P_i)) \quad 1 < k < n \\ =\; & P_n \lll\ggg (\gg i : 1..n-1 \bullet P_i) \end{aligned}$$

□

The update of a variable p by an expression of p can be implemented by double chaining two pipes, where the first pipe mobile outputs p, while the second pipe inputs the value of p to r and then outputs the value of the updated variable immediately to the first pipe.

Law 15 (Delegation with double-chaining)

$$(p := f(p)) \;=\; \begin{pmatrix} (right!!p \to left?p \to SKIP) \\ \lll\ggg (\textbf{vid}\, r;\; left?r \to right!f(r) \to \textbf{end}\, r) \end{pmatrix}$$

where $f(p)$ is an expression of p.   □

As the update is executed in the second pipe, the value of p in the first pipe is irrelevant after the second pipe receives it. At the same time, the value of the intermediate variable q is of no use after p gets its value by assignment. Therefore, we adopt mobile output for p and mobile assignment for q in the first pipe. In the second pipe, $f(r)$ is not a variable but a value based on variable r, so that we use normal output for $f(r)$.

Similarly, the serial update of a variable can also be implemented by a ring of pipes, in which different updates are executed in different pipes.

Law 16 (Serial delegation with chaining)

$$(w := g(f(w))) \;=\; \left(\begin{array}{l} right!!w \to left?w \to SKIP \\ \mbox{\Large$\ll\!\!\gg$} \left(\begin{array}{l} \boldsymbol{vid}\, p; \; left?p \to right!f(p) \to \boldsymbol{end}\; p \\ \gg \\ \boldsymbol{vid}\, q; \; left?q \to right!g(q) \to \boldsymbol{end}\; q \end{array} \right) \end{array} \right)$$

Proof. *Similar to the proof of Law 15.* □

In a more general rule, a series of updating p through different processes $F_i(p, p')$ can be replaced by a loop pipelining, in which the series of update task are allocated in different pipes.

Law 17 (Loop pipelining)

$$(\S i : 1 \mathinner{\ldotp\ldotp} n \bullet F_i(p, p'); \; w := p) \;=\; \left(\begin{array}{l} (right!!p \to left?p \to w := p) \\ \mbox{\Large$\ll\!\!\gg$} \\ \gg i : 1 \mathinner{\ldotp\ldotp} n \bullet (\boldsymbol{vid}\, r; \; left?r \to F_i(r, r'); \; right!!r \to \boldsymbol{end}\; r) \end{array} \right)$$

□

In the right hand side of the above law, the value of p travels from the first pipe to the series of pipes. Its final value, which is stored in w, is retrieved after p's travelling back from the series of pipes.

When updating is performed by a series of activations of the same process variable, we can move this process variable around the loop pipelining and distribute the activations in different pipes.

Lemma 1 (Loop pipelining). *Suppose that h is a parameterised process variable with a value parameter i and a name parameter t, then*

$$(\S i : 1 \mathinner{\ldotp\ldotp} n \bullet h(i, t); \; w := t) \;=\; \left(\begin{array}{l} (right!!h!!t \to left?h?t \to w := t) \\ \mbox{\Large$\ll\!\!\gg$} \\ \gg i : 1 \mathinner{\ldotp\ldotp} n \bullet (\boldsymbol{vid}\, g, r; \; left?g?r \to g(i, r); \; right!!g!!r \to \boldsymbol{end}\; g, r) \end{array} \right)$$

□

In practice, t is the local state of mobile process variable h. When the mobile process variable moves, it takes not only its process value but also its local state; however, in our current work, we have not formalised the local state of a mobile process, therefore we simply send the local state together with the process variable in multiple data transfer [10], which also says that the two variables h and t are output at the same time.

5   Decentralising the Data Centre

Using the laws in Section 4, we are able to show the derivation of the distributed system from the centralised one in Section 2. As the behaviour of the hosts to send out the information is not our main concern, we simply ignore this part in our specification.

In the centralised system, initially, the variable t is initialised to 0. The data centre then repeats the task of communicating with each host, obtaining the information and updating t until all the hosts have been processed. Finally the data centre outputs the data through channel $result$. This specification can be written as

$$\textbf{var } t := 0 \bullet$$
$$\S i : 1 .. n \bullet (c.i?v \rightarrow t := t + v); \; result!t \rightarrow SKIP$$

where $c.i$ is the channel connecting the data centre and the ith host. We notice that similar pieces of specification involving input and update occurs iteratively, therefore we can assign a parameterised process to a process variable, and then activate it repeatedly with proper arguments. In the parameterised process, the initial value of t needs to be known at the beginning of every communication with the host, and certainly we need to store the result of t after its update, therefore we select t as a name parameter. By applying the iterated parameterised copy rule (Law 10), we reach the step:

$$= \{\text{iterated-parameterised-copy-rule}\}$$
$$\textbf{var } t := 0 \bullet$$
$$\left(\begin{array}{l} \textbf{proc } p := \{\!\lambda j : val(1 .. n); \; u : var(\mathbb{N}) \bullet c.j?v \rightarrow u := u + v\!\} \bullet \\ (\S i : 1 .. n \bullet p(i, t)) \end{array} \right);$$
$$result!t \rightarrow SKIP$$

The channel index j is only of relevance at the beginning of the variable activation, therefore it is a value parameter.

As the output $result!t$ does not contain variable p, it can be moved inside the scope of p. By an application of Law 7, we calculate the following:

$$= \{\text{variable-}p\text{-scope-extension}\}$$
$$\textbf{var } t := 0 \bullet$$
$$\left(\begin{array}{l} \textbf{proc } p := \{\!\lambda j : val(1 .. n); \; u : var(\mathbb{N}) \bullet c.j?v \rightarrow u := u + v\!\} \bullet \\ \S i : 1 .. n \bullet p(i, t); \; result!t \rightarrow SKIP \end{array} \right)$$

The task of updating t by activating p can be completed using a series of pipes. The whole specification can be replaced by double chaining this series of pipes with another pipe, in which the value of process variable p and the initial value of t are sent out, and the final value of t is retrieved. As the intermediate values of t and process variable p are of no concern, we use mobile output for t and p. When the activations have been completed in every host, the process variable is of no use to us, therefore we discard it in the last-visited host n and only the variable w that stores the data is retrieved by the first pipe. By applying the loop-pipelining law (Lemma 1), we get the following specification.

$$= \{\text{loop-pipelining}\}$$
$$\boldsymbol{var}\ t := 0\ \bullet$$
$$\left(\begin{array}{l} \boldsymbol{proc}\ p := \{\!\!\{\lambda j : val(1\mathbin{..}n);\ u : var(\mathbb{N}) \bullet c.j?v \to u := u + v\}\!\!\}\ \bullet \\ \quad right!!p!!t \to left?t \to result!t \to SKIP \\ \lll\!\gg\!\ggg \\ \left(\begin{array}{l} \left(\begin{array}{l} \gg i : 1\mathbin{..}(n-1)\ \bullet \\ \left(\begin{array}{l} \boldsymbol{proc}\ q;\ \boldsymbol{var}\ w;\ left?q?w \to q(i, w); \\ right!!q!!w \to \boldsymbol{end}\ q, w \end{array} \right) \\ \gg \left(\begin{array}{l} \boldsymbol{proc}\ q;\ \boldsymbol{var}\ w;\ left?q?w \to q(n, w); \\ right!!w \to \boldsymbol{end}\ q, w \end{array} \right) \end{array} \right) \end{array} \right) \end{array} \right)$$

This specification is still centralised, as the scopes of p and t are valid for all the pipes. We notice, however, these two variables do not occur in the pipes involved in updating, therefore we can take these pipes out of the scope of p and t. Applying the variable scope shrinkage (Law 7), we reach a distributed system.

$$= \{\text{variable-}t\text{-and-}p\text{-scope-shrinkage}\}$$
$$\left(\begin{array}{l} \boldsymbol{var}\ t := 0\ \bullet \\ \quad \boldsymbol{proc}\ p := \{\!\!\{\lambda j : val(1\mathbin{..}n);\ u : var(\mathbb{N}) \bullet c.j?v \to u := u + v\}\!\!\}\ \bullet \\ \qquad right!!p!!t \to left?t \to result!t \to SKIP \end{array} \right)$$
$$\lll\!\gg\!\ggg$$
$$\left(\left(\begin{array}{l} \gg i : 1\mathbin{..}(n-1)\ \bullet \\ \quad \boldsymbol{proc}\ q;\ \boldsymbol{var}\ w;\ left?q?w \to q(i, w);\ right!!q!!w \to \boldsymbol{end}\,q, w \\ \gg (\boldsymbol{proc}\ q;\ \boldsymbol{var}\ w;\ left?q?w \to q(n, w);\ right!!w \to \boldsymbol{end}\ q, w) \end{array} \right) \right)$$

In the distributed system, the data centre and the hosts are arranged as a ring. The first component of the double chaining is the data centre, in which the variables t and p are mobile sent out, along channel $right$, after initialisation. The hosts are specified as a series of pipes, in which the process variable and the data are received from channel $left$, and then output to channel $right$ after activation of the process variable.

6   Conclusions and Future Work

We have presented a set of laws for the development of mobile distributed systems. All the laws can be proven [14] within Hoare and He's unifying theories.

Through a simple example that can be implemented in both a centralised and a distributed fashion, we have shown these laws are suitable for a step-wise development, starting with a centralised specification and ending up with a distributed implementation, while we cannot achieve this using the π-calculus.

Our current work on the semantics of mobile processes mainly focuses on their mobility, and our development method applies to an initial specification without any mobile process; however, we simply ignore the process type and rich data structure within a mobile process. In occam$_M$ [1], a process type determines an interface, a mobile process can implement multiple process types, and the value of a process variable is an instance of a mobile process that implements the type of this variable. Therefore, the activation of a process variable is determined by its type, and the process from which it is initialised. We formalise these issues, and then study the refinement of a mobile process itself.

In occam$_M$ [1], channels have mobility. Channel variables reference only one of the ends of a channel bundle and those ends are mobile, and can be passed through channels. Moving one of the channel-bundle ends around a network enables processes to exchange communication capabilities, making the communication highly flexible. We intend to formalise this channel-ends mobility in the UTP and study its refinement calculus.

In the example in this paper, the derivation from the centralised system to the distributed one centres around the introduction of a higher-order variable. Actually, moving processes can decrease network cost by replacing remote communication with local communication. Furthermore, after a mobile assignment or a mobile communication, the source variable is undefined and its allocated memory space is released to the environment. Clearly, consuming less network cost and occupying less memory space can be a performance enhancement, and in this sense, we have not demonstrated a performance improvement in our mobile system. We intend to investigate techniques for reasoning about this.

Our main objective is to include the semantics of mobile processes and its associated refinement calculus in *Circus* [15], a unified language for describing state-based reactive systems. The semantics [16] of *Circus* is based on UTP and a development method for *Circus* based on refinement [11, 2, 3] has been proposed. This inclusion will enhance the *Circus* model and allow *Circus* specification to reason about mobility.

Acknowledgements

We thank the anonymous referees for the helpful comments. We are grateful to Zhu Huibiao and Alistair A. McEwan for the discussions and suggestions, and to Damien Karkinsky for correcting an error in earlier versions of this paper. The first author is partially supported by QinetiQ and an EBS scholarship from the Computing Laboratory of the University of Kent.

References

1. F. R. M. Barnes and P. H. Welch. Prioritised dynamic communicating and mobile processes. *IEE Proceedings Software*, 150(2):121–136, April 2003.
2. A. L. C. Cavalcanti, A. C. A. Sampaio, and J. C. P. Woodcock. Refinement of actions in *Circus*. In *REFINE'2002, Electronic notes in Theoretical Computer Science*, 2002.
3. A. L. C. Cavalcanti, A. C. A. Sampaio, and J. C. P. Woodcock. A refinement strategy for *Circus*. *Formal Aspects of Computing*, 2003(15):146–181, 2003.
4. C. A. R. Hoare. *Communicating Sequential Process*. Prentice Hall, 1985.
5. C. A. R. Hoare and He Jifeng. *Unifying Theories of Programming*. Prentice Hall, 1998.
6. INMOS Limited. occam2.1 reference manual. Technical report, May 1995.
7. R. Milner, J. Parrow, and D. Walker. *A calculus of mobile processes, parts I and II*. Technical Report ECS-LFCS-89-85 and -86, University of Edinburgh, 1989.
8. Robin Milner. *Communicating and Mobile Systems: the π-calculus*. Cambridge University Press, 1999.
9. Carrol Morgan. *Programming from Specifications*. Prentice Hall, second edition, 1998.
10. A. W. Roscoe. *The Theory and Practice of Concurrency*. Prentice Hall, 1998.
11. A. C. A. Sampaio, J. C. P. Woodcock, and A. L. C. Cavalcanti. Refinement in *Circus*. In L. Eriksson and P. A. Lindsay, editors, *FME 2002: Formal Methods – Getting IT Right*, volume 2391 of *Lecture Notes in Computer Science*, pages 451–470. Springer-Verlag, 2002.
12. D. Sangiorgi. *Expressing Mobility in Process Algebras: First-order and Higher-order Paradigms*. PhD thesis, Department of Computer Science, University of Edinburgh, 1992.
13. Davide Sangiorgi and David Walker. *The π-calculus: A Theory of Mobile Processes*. Cambridge University Press, 2001.
14. Xinbei Tang. Mobile processes in unifying theories. Technical report 1-04, Computing Laboratory, University of Kent, Canterbury, Kent CT2 7NF, UK, January 2004.
15. J. C. P. Woodcock and A. L. C. Cavalcanti. A concurrent language for refinement. In A. Butterfield and C. Paul, editors, *IWFM'01: 5th Irish Workshop in Formal Methods*, Dublin, Ireland, July 2001.
16. J. C. P. Woodcock and A. L. C. Cavalcanti. The semantics of *Circus*. In J. P. Bowen, M. C. Henson, and K. Robinson, editors, *ZB2002: Formal Specification and Development in Z and B*, volume 2272 of *Lecture Notes in Computer Science*, pages 184–203. Springer-Verlag, 2002.

Author Index

Lecture Notes in Computer Science

For information about Vols. 1–3012

please contact your bookseller or Springer-Verlag